The Humanities
VOLUME II

Mary Ann Frese Witt
North Carolina State University at Raleigh

Charlotte Vestal Brown
North Carolina State University at Raleigh

Roberta Ann Dunbar
University of North Carolina at Chapel Hill

Frank Tirro
Yale University

Ronald G. Witt
Duke University

With the collaboration of
Ernest D. Mason
North Carolina Central University

John R. Kelly
North Carolina State University at Raleigh

THE Humanities

Cultural Roots and Continuities

Volume II—The Humanities and the Modern World

Third Edition

D. C. Heath and Company • Lexington, Massachusetts • Toronto

Acquisitions Editor: Paul Smith
Developmental Editor: Holt Johnson
Production Editor: Bryan Woodhouse
Designer: Mark Fowler
Production Coordinators: Kim Wallin and Lisa Arcese
Photo Researcher: Mary Stuart Lang
Text Permissions Editor: Margaret Roll

COVER: Albert Marquet, *Le Cheval à Marseille* (Musée des Beaux-Arts de Bordeaux)

Published simultaneously in Canada.

Printed in the United States of America.

International Standard Book Number: 0-669-15426-1

Library of Congress Catalog Card Number: 88-82179

10 9 8 7 6 5 4 3 2 1

Credits

Preface

Changes in this Edition

This third edition of *The Humanities: Cultural Roots and Continuities* has benefited from the suggestions of readers, professors, and teachers from a wide variety of geographical locations and teaching situations, as well as from our own thinking about the problems of presenting the humanities in an integrated, interdisciplinary framework. Although the format and the spirit of the book remain basically the same, we have made some important changes. We have rewritten the introduction to reflect recent developments in thinking about the role of the humanities in education. In the Greco-Roman section of Volume I, we have added larger portions of *The Iliad* and *The Aeneid*; a discussion of and a passage from Aristotle's *Poetics*; and a more extensive treatment of Roman civilization. The Judeo-Christian section includes more chapters from the Old Testament (Psalms, Book of Amos) and more exploration of Jewish history, as well as more se-

lections from the New Testament (letters of the apostle Paul). We have adopted a verse translation of Chaucer's *The Miller's Tale* and we have included Erasmus's *The Shipwreck*. The chapter on the early Renaissance has been entirely reworked.

Readers of Volume II will note a more extended treatment of the scientific revolution, including excerpts from Bacon's *The New Organon* and from Hobbes's *Leviathan*, as well as a more in-depth study of seventeenth-century art. Although we continue to explore the Don Juan theme in various manifestations, we have eliminated Byron's *Don Juan* from the romantic section, and have added Tirso de Molina's *The Trickster of Seville* in the baroque section. In response to popular demand, we have eliminated Voltaire's *Micromegas* and substituted a somewhat abridged version of *Candide*. The romantic section now includes Wordsworth's "Tintern Abbey" and a section of Walt Whitman's "Song of Myself."

As in the second edition, we have retained the coverage of the contributions of women and the development of feminism in Western culture, but this time we have also included a chapter from a crucial, previously neglected text, Mary Wollstonecraft's *A Vindication of the Rights of Woman.* The influence of feminism in the visual arts also receives more attention, particularly with Judy Chicago's *The Dinner Party.* We have enlarged the treatment of the development of political theory with selections from Hobbes, Locke, and Rousseau, and we have written a section on the Great Awakening in the United States, with an extract from Jonathan Edwards. Our approach to the question of modernism is now more unified because of a focus on the theme of the city, illustrated by selections from Engels, Baudelaire, and T.S. Eliot. The arts of photography and cinema receive more attention here than in previous editions.

Our commitment to emphasizing the important contributions of Afro-Americans to our cultural heritage continues, but in this edition we have also given more recognition to the contributions of Hispanic cultures. Chapter 35, now entitled "New Americans on the World Cultural Scene: The Rise of Afro-American and Latin American Cultures" points out certain parallels in two "minority" cultures that began to assume worldwide importance around the same time, while subsequent chapters include literary and artistic works illustrating the impact of both cultures on modernism and postmodernism in the arts. New items include stories by Borges and Cabrera-Infante, poetry by Pablo Neruda and Ernesto Cardenal, examples of Latin American mural painting and architecture, poems by Sonia Sanchez and Gwendolyn Brooks, jazz of Ornette Coleman, and a story by Alice Walker.

Our new chapter on postmodernism reflects some of the latest thinking on the subject in what we believe is a lucid but not oversimplified approach to this complex issue. In addition to the new selections mentioned above, our treatment of postmodernism includes more poems and different prose by Adrienne Rich and a new short story by John Barth. The bibliography and information on audio-visual material in the Instructor's Guide has been updated and expanded.

Despite the several changes in and expanded coverage of this new edition, our overall view of the purpose of an interdisciplinary humanities text remains basically the same. We feel that in an introductory humanities course the student's personal growth should take place on three levels—historical, aesthetic, and philosophical. The overall purpose of the two volumes can best be described by breaking it down into these three categories.

The Historical Level

We stress the concept of "cultural roots" because one cannot understand the culture in which one lives without some notion of what went into its making. Therefore, we have made every effort here to link the "roots" discussed to aspects of the contemporary American cultural environment. This can be a knotty problem because such links can sometimes be too facile, and we would also like students to discover that cultures remote in time or space can be worth studying simply for themselves. Volume I treats three cultural roots: Greco-Roman, Judeo-Christian, and West African. This choice needs some justification, because many Americans have other cultural roots as well: oriental, Middle Eastern, North European, Hispanic, and Native American, to name a few. Still, the Greco-Roman and the Judeo-Christian traditions undoubtedly constitute the bases of the Western humanities. African culture, a long-neglected field of study, has contributed significantly to modern Afro-American art and thought and in many ways to Western culture in general. In addition, African culture offers the opportunity to study some fundamental aspects of the humanities in a truly interdisciplinary context.

In our examination of each of these "roots," we adopted the policy of focusing on one period and/or place. The focus for the Greco-Roman root is on fifth-century-B.C. Athens, that for the Judeo-Christian on medieval Europe, that for Africa on the Yoruba people. This means, for example, that some significant monuments of classical Greek drama, sculpture, and architecture can be examined rather extensively, while early Greece and Rome receive a briefer treatment. In our exploration of the Renaissance and Reformation periods we emphasize the fusion of the Greco-Roman and Judeo-Christian roots and focus on the development of humanism in fifteenth-century Italy and its diffusion in the north.

If we pursued the same metaphor, Volume II might

be called "stems, leaves, and flowers." Here, too, an attempt is made to focus and spread out, more than to survey and spread thin. The court of Louis XIV in the seventeenth century, the Enlightenment in France and America, the romantic movement, the Industrial Revolution, the modernist movement, and the controversial notion of postmodernism all provide centers around which the many interrelated facets of the humanities can be discussed.

The Aesthetic Level

On the whole, we follow the same "focal" principle in the aesthetic domain. In presenting music, we operate on the assumption that a student will retain more from listening to and analyzing an entire work than from reading music history and theory and hearing snippets. In dealing with art and literature, it is sometimes possible to make an important point with a photograph and a caption or with a close analysis of a brief literary passage. Likewise, in the presentation of major works in the focal periods, we assume that it is more useful for a student to look at the whole of Chartres cathedral than to skim the history of medieval art, and to read all of *Oedipus Rex* rather than bits and summaries from several Greek tragedies. With lengthy works, such as epics and novels, this is, of course, not possible. We have thus chosen portions of *The Iliad, The Aeneid*, and *The Divine Comedy* that are significant in themselves and representative of the whole.

Dance, an often-neglected art form, is given more extensive treatment here than in other humanities texts. Entire dance compositions can, of course, be appreciated only in live performance or film, and we suggest that instructors exploit those resources as much as possible. Although some art forms may seem unfamiliar to students at the beginning, it has been our experience that a long introductory chapter on how to look, listen, and read is largely wasted; therefore, we cover such matters in the introductions to individual works. Questions on the nature of genre are considered in the cultural context in which they originate, notably in ancient Greece. We place much importance on study questions that require the student to read, look, and listen carefully.

Although we try to avoid jargon, we feel that some knowledge of the technical vocabulary of criticism in the arts is essential for literate discussion. Difficult or unfamiliar terms appear in italics the first time they are used in any given chapter, indicating that they are defined in the Glossary.

The Philosophical Level

It may well be objected that we compromise the focal method in our presentation of philosophy, because no entire philosophical works appear in the book. This is largely due to considerations of space; but it is also true that, when dealing with a work in terms of certain fundamental ideas rather than in terms of aesthetic wholeness, the "snippet" method is not so objectionable. Beginning humanities students are probably not ready to read Aristotle's *Ethics* in its entirety, but they should be able to see how Aristotle's ideas are essential to the cultural roots of the modern world.

The student's personal growth in the philosophical area means, however, something much broader than his or her contact with formal philosophy. The (ideal) student—whose historical awareness is increased by an understanding of cultural roots and whose aesthetic sensitivity is heightened by personal confrontation with a variety of works of art—should also be able to grow intellectually through contact with diverse ideas. A humanities course should enable students to refine their thinking on the basic questions that affect all human beings, to formulate more clearly their personal values, and to discuss these with intellectual rigor rather than in vaporous "bull" sessions. Instructors should welcome debates that might arise from comparing Genesis and African mythology, the "woman" question in *Lysistrata* and in John Stuart Mill, or the relative merits of realistic and abstract art or tonal and atonal music. They and their students will find many more such issues for debate.

Individual instructors will decide which aspects of the humanities and which cultural roots they wish to emphasize. We believe that this book offers enough flexibility to be useful for a variety of approaches.

Mary Ann Frese Witt
Charlotte Vestal Brown
Roberta Ann Dunbar
Frank Tirro
Ronald G. Witt

Acknowledgments

Many people have contributed time, work, ideas, and encouragement to the creation of this book. Gratitude is due, first of all, to those who provided their own research and writing: In Volume II, Professor Ernest Mason of North Carolina Central University wrote the introduction to Freud as well as the material on Afro-American culture, and Professor John Kelly of North Carolina State University wrote the sections on Latin American culture. Professor Emeritus Alan Gonzalez, of North Carolina State University, wrote the material on the Spanish baroque. In Volume I, Professor Edmund Reiss wrote the sections on courtly love and on medieval English poetry.

The plan for the First (1980) Edition of *The Humanities* grew out of the four years I spent initiating and directing an interdisciplinary humanities program at North Carolina Central University in Durham. It would not have been possible without the stimulation and aid of my students and colleagues there. The late Professor Charles Ray and Dean Cecil Patterson provided me with the time, encouragement, and wherewithal to create the program. The professors who worked closely with me—Elizabeth Lee, Phyllis Lotchin, Ernest Mason, Norman Pendergraft, Earl Sanders, Winifred Stoelting, and Randolph Umberger—have all left their mark on this book. The generous support of the Kenan Foundation, which provided the humanities program with a four-year grant, enabled me to research and compile much of the material. The Kenan Foundation also provided me with the opportunity to attend numerous conferences on the humanities. The workshops given at North Carolina Central University by Clifford Johnson, of the Institute for Services to Education, also provided inspiration.

The authors wish to thank Bruce McNair for his painstaking assistance in updating the *Instructor's Guide*, as well as Roger Manley and Margaret S. Smith, who read portions of the third-edition manuscript and offered helpful advice and comments. We have all benefited greatly from the guidance, the wisdom, and the patience of Holt Johnson of D. C. Heath over the years of collaborative effort. Thanks are due as well to Bryan Woodhouse of D. C. Heath for his scrupulous attention to the details of the publishing process. We are also grateful to Betty Cowan and Dorothy Sapp of Duke University for assistance in preparing the manuscript.

I would like to express my continuing gratitude to, and friendship for, my collaborating authors.

Mary Ann Frese Witt

Contents

PART SEVEN INDUSTRIALISM AND THE
HUMANITIES:
THE MIDDLE AND LATE NINETEENTH
CENTURY

PART NINE   CULTURAL PLURALITY:
THE MIDDLE AND LATE TWENTIETH
CENTURY

COLOR ILLUSTRATIONS

MAPS

Chronicle of Events

	AFRICA	MESOPOTAMIA-SYRIA-PALESTINE	GREECE
3000 B.C.			
	Lower and Upper Egypt unite First to Second Dynasty (3110–2615)	Sumerian city-states Successive waves of Semites occupy Palestine	
2900			
2800			
2700			
	Age of Pyramids (c. 2650–2150)		
2600			
2500			
2400			
2300			
2200			
2100			Minoan palace construction begins on island of Crete
2000		Phoenician (Canaanite) city culture	
1900			
1800		Babylonian Dynasty established	
1700			
	Hyksos invasions (1678–1570)		
1600			High point of Minoan civilization (1600–1400)
1500			
	Eighteenth Dynasty and Imperial Age (1525–1075)		
1400		Phoenicians develop alphabet	
	Akhenaten introduces monotheism (1370–1353)		Destruction of Minoan palace Mycenaean expansion
1300			
1200		Hebrews enter Palestine Phoenicians flourish (1200–900)	Traditional date for sack of Troy (c. 1184)
1100			
		Early Assyrian Empire Early Biblical books written Saul made King of Hebrews (c. 1025)	Greek cities on Aegean coast and Greek colonies in Asia Minor established

	AFRICA	MESOPOTAMIA-SYRIA-PALESTINE	ROME	GREEK POLITICAL EVENTS	GREEK CULTURAL EVENTS	
1000 B.C.		David King of Hebrews (1000–961)				
		Solomon (961–922)				
		Hebrew kingdom divides into Israel and Judah (922)				
900		Assyria conquers Phoenicians and Israel (876–605)				
800	Phoenicians found Carthage (814)				Homer?	
			Traditional date for founding of Rome (783)	Beginning of *polis*		
700	Iron age begins at Meroe	Nineveh falls (612) Neo-Babylonian Empire of Nebuchadnezzar			Sappho (c. 600)	
600		Jews taken captive to Babylon (586)			Beginning of Drama and Panathenian Festivals	*Archaic Age (750–480)*
	Persia conquers Egypt (525)	Persians take Babylon (539) Jews return home (538) Darius of Persia (521–486)	Kings expelled and Republic created (509)		Aeschylus (525–456)	
500				Persian Wars (499–479) Pericles (498–427)	Euripides (480–406) Thucydides (470–400) Socrates (470–399) Building of Parthenon (447–432)	*Classical Age (480–350)*
				Peloponnesian War (431–404)	Plato (427–347) Aristophanes' *Lysistrata* (411) Sophocles' *Oedipus* (406)	
400				Philip of Macedon (382–336) Alexander of Macedon (the Great) (356–323)	Aristotle (384–322) Epicurus (342–270) Zeno (336–264) and founding of Stoic school	
	Alexander conquers Egypt (332) Greek dynasty rules (331–304)		Vigorous program of Roman conquest of Italy begins (343)			*Hellenistic Age (350–150)*
300			I Punic War (264–241)			
			Sardinia and Corsica annexed (238)			
200			II Punic War (218–201)			

	AFRICA	MESOPOTAMIA-SYRIA-PALESTINE	ROME	GREEK POLITICAL EVENTS	GREEK CULTURAL EVENTS
200	Nok civilization at its height (200 B.C.–200 A.D.)		Terence (195–159)	Rome begins conquest of Greece	
	Carthage sacked (146) Rome conquers North Africa		III Punic War (149–146)		
100			Cicero (106–43) Caesar (100–44) Lucretius (99–55)		
		Occupation of Israel by Romans (63)			
		Reign of Herod the Great in Palestine (37 B.C.–4 A.D.)	Horace's *Satires* (35–29) Virgil's *Aeneid* (29–19) Augustus begins reign (27)		

	AFRICA	ROME AND EUROPE	PAGAN AND CHRISTIAN CULTURE
A.D.			Birth of Jesus Christ
		Death of Augustus (14) Conquest of Britain (43–51) Sack of Jerusalem (70)	Death of Paul (c. 62–64) Persecution of Christians by Nero (64)
100			Juvenal's *Satires* (c. 100) Roman Pantheon built (118–125)
200			
		Period of disorder (235–284)	Plotinus (205–270) and Neo-Platonism
300		Reforms of Diocletian (285–305)	
			Edict of Toleration by Constantine (313) Building of Old St. Peter's (330–340)
400			
		Alaric sacks Rome (410)	
		Vandals sack Rome (455) Traditional date for end of Western Roman Empire (476)	
500			Justinian (483–565) extends Roman Empire in East and temporarily conquers parts of Italy, Africa, and Spain—Codifies Roman Law
600	Moslem conquest of Africa		
700	Empire of Ghana (700–1230)		
		Moslem conquest of Spain (711) Defeat of Moslems at Poitiers (732)	
		Charlemagne (768–814)	
800			

AFRICA	ROME AND EUROPE	PAGAN AND CHRISTIAN CULTURE
800	Second period of invasions (c. 800–950): Northmen, Hungarians, and Saracens	
900		
Beginnings of Benin	Northmen establish Normandy (911) Otto I founds German Empire (962) Hugh Capet King of France (987)	First systematic teaching of Aristotle's Logic (975)

AFRICA	EUROPE	EUROPEAN CULTURE	
1000		Building of St. Sernin—Romanesque (11th and 12th centuries)	
1050			*Romanesque Style (11th and 12th centuries)*
1100	Norman invasion of England (1066) First Crusade (1095)	St. Bernard (1090–1153)	
1150		*Play of Daniel* (12th century) Rebuilding of St. Denis on new lines—early Gothic	
		Bernart de Ventadorn (late 12th century) Marie de France (late 12th century) Chartres Cathedral begun (1194)	
1200 Revolt of Mande peoples against Ghana (c. 1200) and rise of Mali Empire	Mongol invasion of Russia European embassy sent to China St. Louis (1214–1270)	Aquinas (1225–1274) Giotto (1276–1337)	
1300		Dante's *Divine Comedy* (1300–1321) Petrarch (1304–1374) Boccaccio (1310–1375)	
Mansa Musa pilgrimage to Mecca (1324) Exploration of Canaries (1330s and 1340s)	Hundred Years War begins (1337) First appearance of Black Death (1348–1350)		*Gothic Style (12th–15th centuries)*
1350		Bruni (1370–1444) Brunelleschi (1377–1446) Chaucer's *Canterbury Tales* (1390–1400)	
1400		Masaccio (1401–1428) Henry the Navigator founds navigation school at Sagres (1419) Piero della Francesca (1420–1492) Medici dominate Florence (1434) Alberti's *On Painting* (1435) Leonardo da Vinci (1442–1519) Botticelli (1444–1510) Lorenzo il Magnifico (1449–1492)	*Renaissance Style (15th and 16th centuries)*
	Jeanne d'Arc burned (1431)		
1450			
John Affonso d'Aveiro visits Benin (1485–1486)	Spanish Inquisition established (1478) Columbus discovers America (1492) DaGama sails for India (1497)	Pico della Mirandola (1463–1494) Isaac's *On the Death of Lorenzo* Erasmus (1466?–1536)	

	AFRICA	EUROPE	EUROPEAN CULTURE		NEW WORLD
1500	Duarte Pacheco Pereira's *Esmeraldo de situ orbis* (1507) Benin at the height of its power (16th and 17th centuries)		Michelangelo's *David* (1504) Raphael's *School of Athens* (1510–1511) Machiavelli's *Prince* (1513) First edition of Erasmus's *Colloquies* (1516) Luther publishes German *New Testament* (1521)		First black slaves in New World (1505) Magellan circumnavigates the globe (1519) Cortez in Mexico (1519–1521) Verrazano establishes French claims in North America (1524)
1525		Peasants' Revolt in Germany (1525) Henry VIII declares himself head of Church of England (1534) Jesuit Order founded (1540) Council of Trent (1545–1563)	First edition of Calvin's *Institutes* (1536) Copernicus's *Revolution of Heavenly Bodies* (1543)		
1550		Peace of Augsburg legalizes Lutheranism in Germany (1555) Reign of Queen Elizabeth I of England (1558–1603) Wars of Religion begin in France (1561) Massacre of French Protestants (1572)	Titian (1477–1576) Bruegel (1520–1569)		Building of St. Augustine in Florida (1565)
1575		Defeat of Spanish Armada (1588) Edict of Nantes (1598)	First edition of Montaigne's *Essays* (1580–1588) Shakespeare (1564–1616) Kepler (1571–1630) Caravaggio's *Calling of St. Matthew* (1599–1600)		
1600		Thirty Years War begins (1618)	Rubens's *Raising of the Cross* (1609–1610) Giambattista Marino (1569–1625) John Donne (1572–1631) Descartes (1596–1650) Corneille (1606–1684) Bacon's *Novum Organum* (1620)		Settlement at Jamestown (1607) Founding of Quebec (1608) First slaves in Virginia (1619) Plymouth colony established (1620)
1625		Civil War in England begins (1643) Peace of Westphalia in Germany (1648)	Harvey demonstrates circulation of blood (1628) French Academy founded (1635) Tirsa de Molina's *The Trickster of Seville* 1635) Galileo's *Discourse on Two New Sciences* (1638) Richard Crashaw (1612–1649)		
1650					

Renaissance Style (15th and 16th centuries)

	AFRICA	EUROPE	EUROPEAN CULTURE	NEW WORLD
1650		Restoration of English Monarchy (1660) Louis XIV (1638–1715) Louis revokes Edict of Nantes (1685)	Hobbes' *Leviathan* (1651) Rome's Cornaro Chapel (1645–1652) Rembrandt (1606–1669) Milton (1609–1674) Lully (1632–1687) Royal Society of London created (1662) Construction of Versailles begins (1669) Molière's *Le Bourgeois Gentilhomme* (1670) Robert Boyle (1627–1691) Newton publishes *Mathematical Principles* (1687) Locke's *An Essay Concerning Human Understanding* (1690)	New York City taken by English from Dutch (1664) Salem Witch Trials (1692)
1700	Foundation of Ashanti Confederacy (1701)	Union of Scotland and England (1707) War of Spanish Succession (1701–1713) Hanover (Windsor) dynasty begins in England (1714)	Darby cokes coal (1709) Johann Sebastian Bach (1685–1750)	
1725		War of Austrian Succession (1740–1748)	Building of Hôtel Soubise (1732) Kay's Flying Shuttle (1733) English repeal laws against witchcraft (1736) Great Awakening (1730s) Handel's *Messiah* (1742) Montesquieu's *Spirit of the Laws* (1748)	Georgia, last of original thirteen colonies, founded (1733)
1750		Death of George II (1760) Accession of Louis XVI (1774)	Volume I of the *Encyclopédie* (1751) Mozart (1756–1791) Rousseau's *On the Origins of Inequality* (1755) Voltaire's *Candide* (1759) First blast furnace (1761) Rousseau's *Social Contract* (1762) Watt patents steam engine (1769) Schiller (1759–1805)	French and Indian War (1754–1763) English take Quebec (1759) English acquire Canada by Treaty of Paris (1763) Boston Massacre (1770) Revolutionary War begins (1775)
1775		Meeting of Estates General (May, 1789) Taking of Bastille (July, 1789) Fall of Robespierre (1794) Napoleon's coup d'état (1799)	Goethe's *Werther* (1787) Wollstonecraft's *Vindication of Rights of Women* (1792)	Treaty of Paris ends war (1783) Constitution goes into effect (1789) Washington dies (1799)
1800	Rise of Fulani Empire (19th century) Britain abolishes slave trade (1807)	Napoleon Consul for life (1802) Napoleon crowned Emperor (1804) End of Holy Roman Empire (1806)	David (1748–1825) Madame de Staël (1766–1817) Wordsworth (1770–1850) Constable (1776–1837)	Jefferson elected President (1801)
1810	France abolishes slave trade (1815)	Defeat of Napoleon and Congress of Vienna (1815) Industrialization of England (1815–1850)	Stephenson's locomotive (1814) Byron (1788–1824) Goya *Executions of the 3rd of May* (1814) Blake (1757–1827)	War of 1812 (1812–1814) Founding of *North American Review* (1815)
1820				

	AFRICA	EUROPE	EUROPEAN CULTURE	NEW WORLD
1820				
	Liberia established (1832)	Greek War of Independence (1821–1829)	Beethoven's *Ninth Symphony* (1824)	
1830	France annexes Algeria (1830)	Revolutions in France, Germany, Italy, Belgium, and Poland (1830)	Heine (1797–1856)	
1840		Industrialization of France and Belgium (1830–1860) Industrialization of Germany (1840–1870)	Delacroix (1799–1863) Dickens' *Old Curiosity Shop* (1840) *Giselle* (1841) Chopin (1810–1849) Turner's *Rain, Steam, and Speed* (1845) Marx-Engels' *Communist Manifesto* (1848)	Emerson (1803–1882) Poe (1809–1849)
1850		Revolutions in France, Italy, Germany, and Austria (1848)		Mexican War (1846–1848) Gold discovered in California (1848)
	Livingstone at Victoria Falls (1853–1856)	Second Empire founded in France (1852) Crimean War (1855)	Crystal Palace (1851) Millet (1814–1875) Courbet's *Manifesto* (1855) Baudelaire (1821–1867) Darwin's *Origin of Species* (1859)	Walt Whitman (1819–1892)
1860		Foundation of Kingdom of Italy (1860) Emancipation of serfs in Russia (1861)	Mill's *On Subjection of Women* (1861) Ford Maddox Brown's *Work* (1862–1863) van Gogh (1853–1890)	Civil War (1861–1865) Emily Dickinson (1830–1886) Period of Reconstruction (1867–1877)
1870	Opening of Suez Canal (1869)	Creation of Dual Monarchy Austria-Hungary (1867)		
		Franco-Prussian War (1870–1871) German Empire and Third French Republic created (1871)	Nietzsche (1844–1900) Monet's *Impressions: Sunrise* (1873) Gauguin (1848–1903)	Stephen Crane (1871–1900)
	Brazza explores Lower Congo (1875)			
1880		Dual Alliance: Germany and Austria-Hungary (1879)	Dostoevsky's *Brothers Karamazov* (1880)	
	France occupies Tunisia (1881) Britain occupies Egypt (1882) Germans in Togo and Cameroon (1886) Gold found in South Africa (1886) Rhodes establishes Rhodesia (1889–1891)	Triple Alliance: Germany, Austria-Hungary, and Italy (1882) German-Russian Reinsurance Treaty (1887)	Mallarmé (1842–1898) Verlaine (1844–1896) Rimbaud (1854–1891)	William Dean Howells (1837–1920) Henry James (1843–1916)
1890				

	AFRICA	INTERNATIONAL POLITICS	EUROPEAN CULTURE	AMERICAN CULTURE
1890				
	French annex Guinea and Ivory Coast (1893)	Industrialization of Russia (1890–1914)	Cézanne (1839–1906)	Reliance Building (1891)
		Franco-Russian Alliance (1894)	Matisse (1869–1954)	Spanish-American War (1898) Chesnutt's *The Conjure Woman* (1899)
1900	British conquest of N. Nigeria (1900–1903)	Entente Cordiale: France and Great Britain (1902)	Apollinaire (1880–1918)	Louis H. Sullivan (1856–1924)
		First Russian Revolution (1905)	Picasso's *Les demoiselles d'Avignon* (1907)	
1910				
	Morocco becomes French protectorate (1912)	Balkan Wars (1912–1913)	Duchamp's *Nude Descending a Staircase* (1912) Mondrian (1872–1944)	Armory Show (1913)
	Conquest of German colonies (1914–1915)	First World War (1914–1918) Russian Revolution (1917) Treaty of Versailles (1919) German Weimar Republic created (1919)	Kandinsky's *On the Spiritual in Art* (1912) Stravinsky's *Rite of Spring* (1913) Kirchner's *Street* (1914) Bauhaus founded (1919)	U.S. declares war on Germany and Austria-Hungary (1917) Harlem Renaissance (1919–1932)
1920				
		Irish Free State (1922) Mussolini establishes Fascism in Italy (1922) Great Depression begins (1929)	Kafka (1883–1924) Nijinsky (1890–1950) Hitler's *Mein Kampf* (1925–1926) Spengler's *Decline of the West* (1926–1928) Lipchitz' *Figure* (1926–1928) Brancusi's *Bird in Space* (1928)	W.E.B. Dubois (1868–1963) Mariano Azuela (1873–1952) Davis' *Egg Beater No. 1* (1927) Stock Market Crash (1929)
1930	Nigerian youth movement begins (early 1930s)		Freud's *Civilization and Its Discontents* (1930)	Shahn's *Passion of Sacco and Vanzetti* (1930)
	Italy conquers Ethiopia (1936)	Hitler rises to power (1933) Official rearmament of Germany (1935) Spanish Civil War (1936–1939) Second World War begins (1939)	Le Corbusier's *Villa Savoye* (1929–1930) Malraux's *la Condition humaine* (1933)	New Deal begins (1933) Louis Armstrong (1900–1971) Claude McKay (1890–1948) Jean Toomer (1894–1967) Georgia O'Keeffe (1887–1986)
			James Joyce (1882–1941) Virginia Woolf (1882–1941) Picasso's *Guernica* (1937)	
1940				
	Ethiopia liberated (1941)	Formation of United Nations (1945) Fourth French Republic established (1945)	Giacometti (1901–1966)	Welles' *Citizen Kane* (1941) Japanese attack Pearl Harbor (1941)
	Léopold Sédar Senghor (1903–) Léon Damas (1912–1987) Aimé Césaire (1913–)	Communist takeover in E. Europe (1946–1948) China becomes communist (1949)	Sartre (1905–1980) Simone de Beauvoir (1908–1986)	Albert Einstein (1879–1955) T.S. Eliot (1888–1965) E.E. Cummings (1894–1962) Richard Wright (1908–1960) Jackson Pollock (1912–1956) Charley Parker (1920–1955)
1950		Korean War (1950–1953)		
	Algerian War begins (1954) Morocco and Tunisia freed (1955) Ghana first colony to gain independence (1957) Guinea independent (1958) François Fanon (1925–1961) David Diop (1927–1960)	Russian Sputnik (1957) Common Market (1957) de Gaulle's Fifth Republic (1958)	Camus (1913–1960) Charlie Chaplin (1889–1977) Arrabal's *Picnic on the Battlefield* (1952) Beckett's *Endgame* (1957) Levi's *If This Is a Man* (1958)	Frank Lloyd Wright (1869–1959) Ezra Pound (1885–1972) Langston Hughes (1902–1967) Duke Ellington (1899–1974) Martha Graham (1895–) Jorge Luis Borges (1899–1986)
1960				

	AFRICA	INTERNATIONAL POLITICS	EUROPEAN CULTURE	AMERICAN CULTURE
1960	Nigeria and most French colonies independent (1960) Algeria and Tanganyika freed (1962) Dennis Brutus (1924–)	Berlin Wall (1961) Beginning of Russia-China split (1962) Great Cultural Revolution in China (1966)	Jean Genet (1910–1985) Roland Barthes (1915–1980)	Ralph Ellison (1914–) Katherine Dunham (1919–) Kurt Vonnegut, Jr. (1922–) James Baldwin (1924–1987) Miles Davis (1926–) Ornette Coleman (1930–)
1970	Amin gains power in Uganda (1971) Breakdown of Portuguese African Empire (1974) Wathiong'O Ngugi (1938–) Soweto Uprising (1976)	Withdrawal of U.S. from Vietnam (1972) Oil price rise (1973) Shah leaves Iran and Khomeini takes power (1979) Russian troops sent to Afghanistan (1979)	Michel Foucault (1926–1984)	Adrienne Rich (1929–) Andy Warhol (1931–1987) Alvin Ailey (1931–) LeRoi Jones (1934–) Nikki Giovanni (1943–) Judy Chicago's *The Dinner Party* (1979)
1980	Rhodesia becomes Zimbabue (1980) Liberation struggles continue in Africa (1988)	Polish solidarity movement repressed (1981) Marcos ousted in Philippines (1986) Chernobyl nuclear explosion (1986) USA-USSR agreement on medium-range strategic force (1988)		Ernesto Cardenal (1925–) Guillermo Cabrera Infante (1929–) John Barth (1930–) Alice Walker (1944–)
1990				

The Humanities
VOLUME II

PART FIVE

Science and Splendor: the Seventeenth Century

19

The Beginnings of Modernity

There are a number of reasons for designating the seventeenth century as the beginning of a new era for the Western world. By 1650 religious issues had ceased to be matters of life and death, religion had become detached from politics, and life was secular six days a week. Literature, painting, and sculpture increasingly depicted secular subjects by this time; the palace and the theater exerted immense influence on the architectural, artistic, and ceremonial forms of the churches.

The centralized state resting on a bureaucracy, a standing army, and a system of taxation developed into the dominant form of European government in the seventeenth century. These relatively stronger governments (which had their roots in the Middle Ages) endeavored to control and expand the economic life of their respective countries, fostering in the process the conception of a national economy in competition with other national economies for the world's riches. While importation of gold and spices from other continents had been important for European commerce before 1600, the development of the plantation system in the Americas (tied to the African slave trade and the establishment of elaborate networks of trading posts on the coasts of Africa and Asia) reflects the existence of a worldwide market by the late seventeenth century. To meet the demands of such expanded economic horizons, Europeans devised such financial and business institutions as the joint-stock company and the national bank that characterize modern commercial life. At the same time that Europe set out to dominate the rest of the world through its stronger political and economic structures, its scientists turned their attention as never before to mastering nature for man's use. This attitude, born in the so-called Scientific Revolution, has eventually made possible immense material improvements in the human condition and has become the dominant goal—for good or ill—not only of Europeans but of the rest of the world as well.

Reform and Counter Reform

By 1550 an objective observer of the European scene would perhaps have predicted the ultimate triumph of Protestantism over the old religion. England, which had broken with the Roman church in 1534 primarily for political motives, was by this time a Protestant power. The Lutherans had gained half of Germany and were advancing; theirs had become the dominant religion in the Scandinavian peninsula. Calvinism was spreading rapidly in areas like France, the Low Countries, and Poland.

Such a prophet, however, would have misjudged the determination of the most powerful country in Europe—Spain—and the continued vitality of the Catholic Church. After centuries of campaigning to drive the Moslems from the Iberian peninsula, the Spanish, after their final victory at Grenada in 1492, could at last play a role on the European scene. By the mid-sixteenth century, through a series of wars and accidents of birth and death, the king of Spain ruled an empire much greater in area than that of Rome at its height. Charles I of Spain was, at the time of his abdication in 1553, not

only king of the combined monarchies of Castile and Aragon, inherited from his grandparents Ferdinand and Isabella, but also Emperor of Germany, lord of more than half of Italy, direct lord of the Low Countries, Austria, and Bohemia, and heir to the vast lands claimed by Castile in South, Central, and North America. The wealth of the silver mines of the New World allowed him to maintain the largest, most powerful army in Europe. Whereas Spain's nearest competitor, France, was riven by religious dissension, Charles and his immediate successors presided over a people whose Catholic faith had been successfully tested by centuries of crusading against the Spanish Muslims. The Spanish monarchs throughout the sixteenth and early seventeenth centuries were unquestionably the major champions of the faith throughout Western Europe.

The success of the Catholic counteroffensive was not, however, simply built on the power of the Spanish infantry. The Council of Trent, the church council that met at Trent in northern Italy at various times between 1545 and 1563, laid the groundwork for a great church reform. The basic results of the Council of Trent were to define clearly what Catholics should believe, to make some crucial administrative reforms, and to provide for the creation of seminaries for the education of the clergy. Henceforth Catholics could no longer fall into heresy because they were not aware of the orthodox doctrines. The administrative reforms made the Church less vulnerable to criticism, and the steps to raise the educational level of the clergy resulted after decades in a new respect by laymen for their priests. Therefore, while establishing a platform on which to base an attack on the Protestants, Trent also provided a program of reforms that would attract individual Christians back to the faith.

The new agencies of the Church (the Jesuit order founded in 1540 and the Holy Office of the Roman Inquisition established in 1542) played an extremely important part in seconding these efforts. Heresy or false belief had always been regarded as a disease that not only destroyed the soul of the heretic but also, if diffused, could corrupt the immortal souls of others. Once identified by a commission of experts, the *inquisition*, the heretic was expected to abjure the errors for the good of the immortal soul. If he or she did not, or first abjured and then returned to the errors, the duty of the

Inquisition was to have the person executed to prevent further infecting the community of believers.

The Inquisition   There had been various forms of inquisitions established over the centuries, mostly at the level of the bishopric or archbishopric. The most famous of all, however, was the Spanish Inquisition. It was set up in 1478 by Ferdinand and Isabella of Spain as a department of their government to ferret out Moors who, while professing Christianity, remained faithful to Islam. Independent of the papacy, this inquisition was introduced into North America along with the Spanish conquistadors. By contrast, the Holy Office of the Roman Inquisition represented an effort of the papacy to concentrate investigation of heresy throughout the Catholic world at Rome. From that vantage point heresy could be pursued even among the princes of Europe and the Church. In the decades after its foundation more than one cardinal, for example, was forced to renounce a heretical or dangerous belief under threat of death or imprisonment. The efficiency of the new organization had the desired effect of preventing the diffusion of Protestantism as well as of more exotic beliefs among Catholic populations.

The Jesuits   Recognized as an order by the papacy in 1540, the Jesuits, founded by the Spanish knight Ignatius Loyola, were to become the right arm of the pope in the Counter Reformation. Like previous religious orders the Jesuits took a vow of poverty, chastity, and obedience, but in their case the last vow included a promise of complete obedience to the papacy at all times. As Loyola wrote: "If we wish to proceed securely in all things, we must hold fast to the following principle: What seems to be white, I will believe black if the hierarchical Church so defines."

The Jesuits formed an elitist body, composed of men admitted because of their intelligence, finesse, physical stamina, and deep commitment. Given a superb university education, they were capable of holding their own in any situation or discussion. They actively promoted papal policies on the international level as diplomats. More humbly, but perhaps more importantly in the long run, they became the prime educators of the middle and upper classes of Catholic Europe through the hundreds of schools that they established over the next century. Everywhere they diffused the brand of spirituality developed by their founder. In his effort to bring the believer to a higher state of religious awareness, Loyola focused on training and disciplining the will. All sorts of appeals were made, at least in the initial stages of development, to the senses, emotions, and imagination. As we will see, this type of spirituality was intimately related to the evolution of the artistic styles called *baroque* in Catholic countries.

Having, in a sense, experienced a revival of heart and conviction through the Council of Trent, resting on two powerful instruments for orthodoxy, the Inquisition and the Jesuits, backed by the military power of the greatest European monarchy, the Church in the last forty years of the sixteenth century set off on its campaign to drive the Protestant menace back and eventually to destroy its heresies. By 1600 Poland had all but completely returned to the Catholic camp; in France the French Calvinists, the Huguenots, had already reached their maximum membership and their power was on the wane. In Germany as well, the Protestant advance was by this date turning into a retreat. The Catholic reform, relying there on two powerful German states, Austria and Bavaria, was meeting success in converting one city after another back to the old faith. Everywhere the Jesuits were leaders in the campaign.

Religious Wars   This German Catholic campaign, however, was to precipitate one of the bloodiest wars in modern times. We have already discussed in the Reformation section of Volume I the thirty-year period of French religious wars that ended in 1594. In terms of the extent of destruction and the numbers of people killed, the German Thirty Years' War between 1618 and 1648 dwarfed its earlier French counterpart. This war began directly as a response of Bohemian Protestants to the efforts of their Catholic king (who was also the ruler of Austria) to suppress the Protestant faith in their country. After the Bohemians revolted, the war gradually spread to the whole empire; no one could safely remain neutral. The war was fought on both sides by large mercenary armies over which the German princes had little control. These armies had no interest in peace; wherever they went they brought death and devastation. Moreover, after the first few years the war in Germany became the focus for international ri-

EUROPE in 1648

- Austrian Habsburgs
- Spanish Monarchy
- Swedish Dominions
- Brandenburg-Prussia
- Church Lands
- —— Boundary of the Holy Roman Empire

valries, and the provinces of the empire served as a battlefield for invading armies of Denmark, Sweden, Spain, and France.

By 1648, when peace was finally signed at Westphalia, Germany was ruined from one end to the other. In effect the peace treaty reestablished the religious policy that had dominated Germany in the seventy years prior to the war: each German prince had the right to

determine the religion of his state. The advance of the Counter Reformation was, for all practical purposes, stopped. Spain, the bulwark of the Catholic offensive, was financially exhausted and in the grip of a serious demographic decline, and from 1648 on, ceased to play a central role in European politics.

The Thirty Years' War, at least in the beginning a religious struggle, constitutes the last major European war fought for motives of religion. Europe had had its orgy of religious passion; now both sides sensibly recognized the sphere of influence held by the other. The lines separating Catholics in southern Europe from Protestants in the northern areas have remained fairly stable from that time to this. While religious persecution of minorities might continue within individual countries, even at this level a new sense of toleration was developing. King Louis XIV's revocation of the Protestant rights to worship in 1685 and his expulsion of Protestants from France were perhaps the last grand gestures of the Counter Reformation.

By the end of the Thirty Years' War Europeans generally realized the senselessness of such struggles and the misery that they produced. But beneath the apparent tolerance of religious dissent also lay a growing religious indifference. Europeans on the whole no longer felt the need to judge their experience and to set their goals within a Christian frame of reference. Well might the student of European culture after 1650 ask: "What happened to God?"

The Scientific Revolution

So enormous and dazzling was the progress made in the course of the seventeenth century toward the understanding of the human body, the earth, and the heavens, that it is not too much to say that by 1700 a radical change was taking place in the attitude of Europeans toward the interrelationship between man, God, and nature. At least in its initial stages this progress consisted in a rejection of the "commonsense" approach of ancient and medieval science. The European view of the universe in 1500 was substantially the same as that of Dante in 1300. The earth was at rest in the center, just as it appears, and the heavens rotated around it. These heavens—beginning with the moon, the sun, the planets out to the fixed stars—were either nine or ten in number. Beyond the outermost heaven, or the "first mover" that gave motion to everything in the universe, lay the region of God and the blessed. This universe was finite. God made the earth of heavy inferior substance, placing the finer heavenly bodies above the earth in ascending order of perfection. Since ancient times, however, astronomers had recognized a good deal of irregularity in the movement of the heav-

ens. In order to make this conception fit the appearances, the astronomers had to add a whole series of special movements for individual bodies.

While medieval and early Renaissance scholars were often very dedicated to the investigation of nature, they worked within the shadow of the ancients. The diffusion of knowledge of Greek in the fifteenth century, moreover, made available to Europeans a great number of ancient scientific writings not hitherto known, and this new scientific literature had to be absorbed. By the beginning of the sixteenth century, however, that process was completed. The translated works of Plato and his followers provided Europeans with the idea that all physical objects could be reduced to numbers and that mathematics was the key to understanding nature. This approach differed considerably from the medieval conception of science that investigated nature in terms of qualities: heavy or light, colored or transparent, voluntary or natural in movement, and the like. The increased cooperation during the Renaissance between workmen skilled with their hands and scholars laid the basis for a joint effort in making new instruments for observing and calculating nature's operations. While the methodology of ancient philosophers could be useful, their authority now had to be tested against experience.

Copernicus and Kepler The first fruit of the new concern with mathematics and experimentation was the work of the Polish priest and astronomer Nicholas Copernicus (1473–1543), who in fact had no intention of making an aggressive attack on received ideas of his day. In his *On the Revolution of the Heavenly Bodies*, published in 1543 and dedicated to the pope, Copernicus generally accepted the traditional conception of a finite universe characterized by a series of heavens, the moon, the planets, and the fixed stars. Copernicus' innovation was to substitute the sun for the earth at the center of the universe. For him the earth became one of the planets and, like other bodies, circulated around the center.

Copernicus' primary reason for switching the position of the sun and earth was that this conception furnished a better explanation of the observed motions of the heavens, reducing the need to ascribe exceptional movements to individual bodies as in the earth-centered theory. According to the deeply religious Copernicus, the ability of his sun-centered theory to explain the appearances and to show heavenly motion to be simple and regular magnified the perfection of the divine creator.

Copernicus presented his ideas as an hypothesis; but, over succeeding decades as new observations were recorded and found to support it, some thinkers came to insist that the theory was proved. The ancient picture of the universe gradually disintegrated. Although embracing the finitude of the universe, Copernicus' theory laid the foundation for the idea of the infinite nature of God's creation. Whereas the earth-centered view of the universe maintained an absolute up and down, potentially Copernicus' theory suggested that space was relative. Even though the Copernican earth circulated around the sun, heavy bodies still fell to the earth. If the sun, which all agreed was a nobler body than the earth, was at the center of the universe, then the old view (that, beginning with the earth, other heavenly bodies increased in perfection as they came nearer to the outermost sphere) made no sense at all. Finally, the fact that mathematics played such a primary role in Copernicus' original analysis and in subsequent efforts to test it made mathematics appear as a key to scientific truth.

It fell to the mathematician-astronomer Johann Kepler (1571–1630) to discover that the orbit of the planets around the sun, including that of the earth, took the form of an ellipse. Kepler worked out a single set of mathematical formulas that could be applied to every planet. While he could not say why the planets moved in this way, he was finally able to make sense of the appearance of planetary motion with his simple equations.

Galileo   An aggressive publicist of the Scientific Revolution and one of its greatest contributors was a Florentine, Galileo Galilei (1564–1642). Both Copernicus and Kepler had worked with the naked eye. Galileo, informed of a new optical instrument developed in the Netherlands, the telescope, constructed one for himself and turned it on the heavens. Through the lens of the fantastic instrument he was the first human being to see that Jupiter had moons like the earth and that the earth's own moon was made of material similar to that found on earth. The momentous conclusion was that heavenly bodies were not made of more perfect material. Rather they resembled the earth and were governed by the same laws.

Galileo's conclusions were equally revolutionary when he turned to consider the behavior of bodies in motion. Traditional theories of dynamics, geared to the assumption that the natural state of a body was at rest, attempted to explain what caused motion to occur. For Galileo there was no "natural" motion of the body; rather, if a body was in motion, it would continue in a straight line at the same speed forever unless deflected, quickened, or retarded by another force—the principle of inertia. Thus, what concerned Galileo was not why things move but why changes in motion occur and how one describes these changes mathematically. His formula for the acceleration of a freely falling body in terms of time and space represents the kind of solutions he had in mind.

A magnificent stylist, courageous to the point of rashness, Galileo trumpeted his discoveries in a series of eloquent works that brought him to the attention of the Inquisition. The Inquisition found his teachings dangerous in that they not only reduced the eternal heavens to the level of the earth but specifically contradicted passages of Scripture. After a period of imprisonment Galileo was forced to live under house arrest in Florence until his death. Although he was forbidden to work on astronomy, he was allowed to continue his researches on motion. In 1638 his *Discourse on Two New Sciences*, which provided the foundation for modern physics, was published in the Dutch republic.

Bacon   Like his contemporary Galileo, the Englishman Francis Bacon (1561–1626) was a gifted writer. Recognized as an outstanding essayist, Bacon has also been curiously designated by some scholars as the true author of the plays attributed to William Shakespeare. An ambitious and unscrupulous politician, he was lord chancellor of England between 1618 and 1621, under James I of England. Convicted of accepting bribes, he was dismissed and died in disgrace. Bacon is perhaps best remembered, however, as an early propagandist for the Scientific Revolution. His *New Organon* (1620), designed to replace Aristotle's logical works collectively called the *Organon*, called for a new approach to the study of nature. Science for Bacon was the means by which men could gain power over nature and use it for their own purposes. To do this, they needed a new instrument, a new method of approach. This new method was *empiricism.*

As far back as Aristotle, scholars had discussed the inductive method, but Bacon gave it a systematic presentation and is generally credited with being the founder of empiricism. The empirical method, which has profoundly influenced English and American thought ever since, relies on observation and experience as the roads to truth. Bacon held that we must begin by closer observation of nature, because every generalization has to be controlled by reference to specific instances. The following passages are taken from the opening sections of the *New Organon.*

FRANCIS BACON

From New Organon

APHORISMS

[BOOK ONE]

I

Man, being the servant and interpreter of Nature, can do and understand so much and so much only as he has observed in fact or in thought of the course of nature. Beyond this he neither knows anything nor can do anything.

II

Neither the naked hand nor the understanding left to itself can effect much. It is by instruments and helps that the work is done, which are as much wanted for the understanding as for the hand. And as the instruments of the hand either give motion or guide it, so the instruments of the mind supply either suggestions for the understanding or cautions.

III

Human knowledge and human power meet in one; for where the cause is not known the effect cannot be produced. Nature to be commanded must be obeyed.

IV

Toward the effecting of works, all that man can do is to put together or put asunder natural bodies. The rest is done by nature working within.

V

The study of nature with a view to works is engaged in by the mechanic, the mathematician, the physician, the alchemist, and the magician; but by all (as things now are) with slight endeavor and scanty success.

VI

It would be an unsound fancy and self-contradictory to expect that things which have never yet been done can be done except by means which have never yet been tried.

VIII

Moreover, the works already known are due to chance and experiment rather than to sciences; for the sciences we now possess are merely systems for the nice ordering and setting forth of things already invented, not methods of invention or directions for new works.

XI

As the sciences which we now have do not help us in finding out new works, so neither does the logic which we now have help us in finding out new sciences.

XII

The logic now in use serves rather to fix and give stability to the errors which have their foundation in commonly received notions than to help the search after truth. So it does more harm than good.

XVIII

The discoveries which have hitherto been made in the sciences are such as lie close to vulgar notions, scarcely beneath the surface. In order to penetrate into the inner and further recesses of nature, it is necessary that both notions and axioms be derived from things by a more sure and guarded way, and that a method of intellectual operation be introduced altogether better and more certain.

XIX

There are and can be only two ways of searching into and discovering truth. The one flies from the senses and particulars to the most general axioms, and from these principles, the truth of which it takes for settled and immovable, proceeds to judgment and to the discovery of middle axioms. And this way is now in fashion. The other derives axioms from the senses and particulars, rising by a gradual and unbroken ascent, so that it arrives at the most general axioms last of all. This is the true way, but as yet untried.

XXIV

It cannot be that axioms established by argumentation should avail for the discovery of new works, since the subtlety of nature is greater many times over than the subtlety of argument. But axioms duly and orderly formed from particulars easily discover the way to new particulars, and thus render sciences active.

XXXVI

One method of delivery alone remains to us which is simply this: we must lead men to the particulars themselves, and their series and order; while men on their side must force themselves for a while to lay their notions by and begin to familiarize themselves with facts.

XXXVII

The doctrine of those who have denied that certainty could be attained at all has some agreement with my way of proceeding at the first setting out; but they end in being infinitely separated and opposed. For the holders of that doctrine assert simply that nothing can be known. I also assert that not much can be known in nature by the way which is now in use. But then they go on to destroy the authority of the senses and understanding; whereas I proceed to devise and supply helps for the same.

XXXVIII

The idols and false notions which are now in possession of the human understanding, and have taken deep root therein, not only so beset men's minds that truth can hardly find entrance, but even after entrance is obtained, they will again in the very instauration of the sciences meet and trouble us, unless men being fore-warned of the danger fortify themselves as far as may be against their assaults.

XXXIX

There are four classes of Idols which beset men's minds. To these for distinction's sake I have assigned names, calling the first class *Idols of the Tribe*; the second, *Idols of the Cave*; the third, *Idols of the Market Place*; the fourth, *Idols of the Theater*.

XLI

The Idols of the Tribe have their foundation in human nature itself, and in the tribe or race of men. For it is a false assertion that the sense of man is the measure of things. On the contrary, all perceptions as well of the sense as of the mind are according to the measure of the individual and not according to the measure of the universe. And the human understanding is like a false mirror, which, receiving rays irregularly, distorts and discolors the nature of things by mingling its own nature with it.

XLII

The Idols of the Cave are the idols of the individual man. For everyone (besides the errors common to human nature in general) has a cave or den of his own, which refracts and discolors the light of nature, owing either to his own proper and peculiar nature; or to his education and conversation with others; or to the reading of books, and the authority of those whom he esteems and admires; or to the differences of impressions, accordingly as they take place in a mind preoccupied and predisposed or in a mind indifferent and settled; or the like. So that the spirit of man (according as it is meted out to different individuals) is in fact a thing variable and full of perturbation, and governed as it were by chance. Whence it was well observed by Heraclitus that men look for sciences in their own lesser worlds, and not in the greater or common world.

XLIII

There are also Idols formed by the . . . association of men with each other, which I call Idols of the Market Place, on account of the commerce and consort of men there. For it is by discourse that men associate, and words are imposed according to the apprehension of the vulgar. And therefore the ill and unfit choice of words wonderfully obstructs the understanding. Nor do the definitions or explanations wherewith in some things learned men are wont to guard and defend themselves, by any means set the matter right. But words plainly force and overrule the understanding, and throw all into confusion, and lead men away into numberless empty controversies and idle fancies.

XLIV

Lastly, there are Idols which have immigrated into men's minds from the various dogmas of philosophies, and also from wrong laws of demonstration. These I call Idols of the Theater, because in my judgment all the received systems are but so many stage plays, representing worlds of their own creation after an unreal and scenic fashion. Nor is it only of the systems now in vogue, or only of the ancient sects and philosophies, that I speak; for many more plays of the same kind may yet be composed and in like artificial manner set forth; seeing that errors the most widely different have nevertheless causes for the most part alike. Neither again do I mean this only of entire systems, but also of many principles and axioms in science, which by tradition, credulity, and negligence have come to be received.

LXXXI

Again there is another great and powerful cause why the sciences have made but little progress, which is this. It is not possible to run a course aright when the goal itself has not been rightly placed. Now the true and lawful goal of the sciences is none other than this: that human life be endowed with new discoveries and powers. But of this the great majority have no feeling, but are merely hireling and professorial; except when it occasionally happens that some workman of acuter wit and covetous of honor applies himself to a new invention, which he mostly does at the expense of his fortunes. But in general, so far are men from proposing to themselves to augment the mass of arts and sciences, that from the mass already at hand they neither take nor look for anything more than what they may turn to use in their lectures, or to gain, or to reputation, or to some similar advantage. And if any one out of all the multitude court science with honest affection and for

her own sake, yet even with him the object will be found to be rather the variety of contemplations and doctrines than the severe and rigid search after truth. And if by chance there be one who seeks after truth in earnest, yet even he will propose to himself such a kind of truth as shall yield satisfaction to the mind and understanding in rendering causes for things long since discovered, and not the truth which shall lead to new assurance of works and new light of axioms. If then the end of the sciences has not as yet been well placed, it is not strange that men have erred as to the means.

COMMENTS AND QUESTIONS

1. What does Bacon mean by "instruments of the mind"? What is their purpose?
2. Explain: "Nature to be commanded must be obeyed."
3. Why had there been so few scientific discoveries up to Bacon's time?
4. Why does Bacon define the four classes of idols?
5. Why does he feel it necessary to declare the goal of science? What is its objective?

The great shortcomings of Bacon's conception of science were his failure to appreciate the need to establish hypotheses in research and the value of mathematics. Although his methodology would ultimately prove effective in areas like biology and chemistry, it was of little use in the fields of physics and astronomy, in which the most spectacular advances were made in the seventeenth century. Closer observation furnished data in these fields, but the scientist employed mathematics for their interpretation of the data, thus essentially working by deduction. Nevertheless, Bacon's far-reaching criticism of contemporary natural science, his reliance on the independent judgment of the scientist based on personal observation, and his vision of the enormous benefits accruing to humanity from the scientific enterprise proved fundamental in the formation of a new attitude toward the study of nature.

Newton Bacon himself made no significant scientific discoveries, but another Englishman, Isaac Newton (1642–1727), accomplished the most dazzling scientific feat of the eighteenth century. This was to bring together Galileo's laws of inertia and falling bodies,

Kepler's laws of celestial mechanics, and his own theory of gravitational force into a monumental system of physical principles and mathematical formulas by which every physical movement in the universe could potentially be described. Newton came to see that every body in the universe attracted every other body with a force proportional to the product of the two masses and inversely proportional to the square of the distance between them. Galileo's law that a moving body would fly off in a straight line unless affected by an external force held true for the heavens as for the earth. A planet moved in an elliptical motion around the sun and the moon in similar fashion around the earth because the mutual attraction of the two bodies drew the smaller in toward the larger and deflected the motion of the smaller into an orbit. The shape of the orbit and its velocity could be described by Galileo's formula for falling bodies.

Other Scientific Discoveries and Their Effects   Newton's findings, published in his *Mathematical Principles of Natural Philosophy* in 1687, marked the high point of the scientific revolution of the seventeenth century. But, if less spectacular, the discoveries in other areas of science were nonetheless important. In 1628 William Harvey (1578–1657) demonstrated the circulation of the blood, and at mid-century Anton Leeuwenhoek (1632–1723) had developed the microscope, thus revealing a whole world hidden from the naked eye. Scientists like Robert Boyle (1627–1691) were in subsequent decades involved in investigation of the action of gases.

No longer working in isolation, the scientists of this "revolution" developed communities. Societies like the Royal Society of London, founded in 1662, not only helped the diffusion of information among scientists but also brought their work to the attention of an educated public. For many, there were great expectations of a new era when, through the use of reason and new instruments, the human race would gradually eliminate the area of the unknown. But if the new discoveries brought confidence to some, others felt uncertain and confused. The Inquisition had justifiably regarded Galileo's doctrines as dangerous: men had now to deal with an order of truth appearing to contradict the Bible at several points. More than this, whereas the God of

the Christians had been a God intimately connected with man's life and world, scientists like Galileo and Newton approached the universe as if, after creating it, God had stepped aside and let nature run itself. The French philosopher Blaise Pascal phrased it: "The eternal silence of infinite spaces terrifies me."

Economic Life

Historians tend to date the birth of modern capitalism in the late sixteenth and early seventeenth centuries, but to understand what actually occurred an important distinction must be made. There are basically two types of capitalism: commercial and industrial. In commercial capitalism the capitalist is usually a merchant who invests his money both in buying the raw material and in marketing the finished product once produced. In the case of wool cloth, for example, the merchant buys the raw wool; then either he or an agent carries the wool to artisans who spin, weave, and dye it in their shops or homes. They usually work by the piece and own or rent their equipment. When the cloth is finished, the merchant then sells the product; his profit lies in the difference between what the cloth cost him to produce and market and the purchase price of the finished goods.

This form of capitalism, with the merchant as the capitalist, began in the Middle Ages and remained the dominant form for the production of industrial goods down to the eighteenth century. The economic boom of the sixteenth century did not significantly affect the way that goods were produced; what did change was the number of people engaged in producing. The production of industrial goods significantly increased in the sixteenth century because the merchant had so many more independent producers working for him.

Industrial capitalism, on the other hand, refers to investment in the modes or means of production. In this case the capitalist is not the merchant but the factory or mine owner. Investment in machines means more productivity per worker and more variety in products. In order to print books at all, for example, a significant investment must be made in a printing press. In the sixteenth century a rapid surge in the amount of investment in machinery occurred in areas like metal, glass, paper, coal mining, and firearms. While the output of goods provided by industrial capitalism climbed significantly after 1550, still down to the end of the eighteenth century commercial capitalism was responsible for most of the industrial production of Europe.

By 1550, European observers demonstrate an awareness of a long-term rise in prices that had begun by the end of the fifteenth century. Initially, the price rise came mainly in food products, testifying to the beginnings of a population increase after a century of demographic stagnation. But clearly the price rise was reinforced by the tremendous quantities of bullion pouring into Europe from the Spanish silver mines in the New World. In the long-term price rise, so favorable for investment, is to be found the major cause of the tremendous economic development that took place in most of Europe by the mid-sixteenth century.

In Spain, however, the prime source for the bullion, an expensive policy of conquest and an oppressive taxation policy falling on all but the upper classes combined to strangle commercial and economic development. In an increasingly stratified society, the military, government service, and religion became the only valued professions. Spanish silver became diffused throughout Europe in the sixteenth century, partly through Spain's military expenditures abroad but also through its exportation to pay for imported goods its own investment-starved economy could not provide and to settle its ever-growing debts to foreign bankers.

In contrast with Spain's experience, the sixteenth century had proven highly profitable for Italy, the other major southern European country and the traditional economic center of Europe. The seventeenth century, however, witnessed a definitive movement of that center to the North Atlantic countries: France, England, and Holland. The two latter countries, both dominated by Protestants, were the leading seapowers of Europe. Both were also advanced in developing organizational forms of business capable of collecting large amounts of capital. While the rest of Europe was characterized by family businesses until the nineteenth century, these two countries utilized the means of the joint-stock company in order to attract money into business ventures. Amsterdam was the center of a thriving stock exchange. In England and especially in Holland, banking arrangements so developed that businesses and private individuals were able to borrow large sums of money on credit.

These relatively enormous financial assets available for commercial investment meant that the Dutch and English would play a preponderant role in business ventures overseas. The plantation economy of the New World was in large part a product of this flow of capital that brought the slaves from Africa, purchased the sugar, rice, coffee, tobacco, and other commodities that the slaves produced, and marketed the goods in Europe. Even French, Spanish, and Portuguese planters depended for their survival on Dutch willingness to extend credit on purchases from harvest to harvest, a convenience that their own countrymen could not provide.

The Age of Absolutism

The last half of the seventeenth century and most of the eighteenth has come to be recognized as the age of "absolute" monarchs. While the king or queen had all sorts of practical limitations on what could be done without provoking a rebellion, he or she was absolute in the sense that there were no legal restraints or alternative constitutional institutions that could block the monarch's will. Of course, even in France, the ideal absolute monarchy, there were law courts and some provincial assemblies that could lawfully impede the royal decrees for a time; but eventually, if the king was willing to pay the price for publicizing the opposition, he could have his way.

By 1650 such investment of power in the royal office appeared to most observers the only way that the centralized state could advance against forces of decentralization such as the great nobility, the provincial government, and the autonomous cities. The two notable exceptions to this situation were the Dutch and the English. The fact that the Dutch had a small country, densely populated, with good communications and a weak nobility made its republican government feasible. The development of constitutional monarchy in England must be explained in the light of its small size and its early centralization and development of Parliament.

Whereas the English Parliament had established a tradition of consultation with the monarch, assemblies in France, Spain, Germany, and elsewhere brought together forces of localism opposed to concentration of power. Since the Middle Ages these were the elements that, in moments when the monarchy was weak, seized the opportunity to destroy the carefully accumulated powers of the state over its territories. The religious wars of the sixteenth and early seventeenth centuries had created an ideal situation for subjects of one religion to revolt against their king who had another. For instance, the revolt of some of the highest French nobility in the sixteenth century, while done in the name of the Protestant faith, was unquestionably also motivated by political ambitions. Consequently, monarchs and their advisers came to believe that only by taking legal authority out of the hands of cities, provinces, and the nobility—instead centering it in the monarch's hands—could their countries ever experience domestic peace. In large part this policy was also supported by intellectuals and by the common people who had to choose between this or institutionalized anarchy.

Yet the monarch could not make a frontal attack on political privileges without provoking massive revolt. Basically the European social structure was divided into three general classes: the nobility, the peasants (both in the countryside), and the bourgeois in the towns and cities. The latter class included groups as far apart as humble shoemakers and wealthy bankers. Consequently, we must distinguish the upper bourgeoisie, who controlled the cities, from the lower bourgeoisie, who often were economically not superior to the peasants.

From the sixteenth century in Spain and France and a century later in other parts of the continent, the monarchy developed a policy of compromise with the privileged middle classes in the cities and with the nobility. In return for sanctioning the political domination of the monarch and accepting the extension of his authority, the powerful interest groups were promised exemption from many of the burdens entailed. The king guaranteed the nobility and the upper bourgeoisie that they would not have to pay many of the new taxes and that the heaviest impositions would fall on the poor. Besides, the king acknowledged the monopoly of the nobility over the officer corps in the army and over the great ceremonial posts at court. By dazzling the bourgeoisie with the prospect of offices in his expanded central bureaucracy, the absolute monarch of the seventeenth century had the means to incorporate families of new wealth into the establishment and thus to ren-

der them supporters of the system; otherwise they would have constituted a disgruntled and potentially subversive bourgeois leadership.

Farther to the east, in countries like Brandenburg-Prussia and Austria, the monarchies had emerged from the Middle Ages much weaker and more unstable than those in the west; as a result, eastern rulers were forced to go even further in order to obtain absolute political power. They granted the nobility (the middle class was really insignificant in numbers) the right to reduce the local rural populations to the status of serfs. In Brandenburg-Prussia, moreover, the *Junkers*, or nobility, were made the only class legally allowed to own land.

As a result of these different compromises across Europe, the class structure in the various countries became more clearly defined: each had a legal relationship with the central government. At the same time the king became the sole judge of who would be admitted to the privileged classes, especially to the nobility. This right proved a great financial asset to the royal treasury, as most offices in the government were sold at a fixed price. The buyer earned only a small yearly salary from the government but was expected to make his profits from those who needed his services in that position. Some of the higher government offices—and naturally the most expensive—carried with them a patent of nobility, ennobling forever the buyer and his descendants. This system permitted humble men who had money to put their families into the upper class. If an unlikely way to staff a bureaucracy, the method proved a good means of permitting social mobility.

But the concentration of power in the hands of kings, while affording domestic peace, had a different effect on international relations. More powerful monarchs with money to spend presided over larger armies and more far-ranging wars. In the Middle Ages and Renaissance, war was fought with troops raised for short periods of time; even a war like the Hundred Years' War between France and England primarily consisted of a long series of summer campaigns spread out over more than a century. With the greater taxing power of seventeenth-century monarchies, however, kings could afford to keep an army in the field for years at a time and to do so at a distance from the sources of supply. Consequently, there was a danger that one country might try to take over the whole of Europe, and kings felt it vital to their interests to know what their colleagues were about. This led to the increasing importance of diplomacy and to wars fought on the basis of international alliances.

Furthermore, as Europe became a political system based on a balance-of-power concept, in this century Europeans spread their rivalries to the rest of the world: to the Americas, Africa, and Asia. An important consequence of the increase in royal power was that the central government assumed the responsibility of regulating the economic life of the country and a commitment to fostering its development. Thus, more than ever before, hostilities between European powers appeared to be dictated by economic concerns: having influence in other areas of the world was regarded as significant for prosperity at home.

Hobbes   The *Leviathan* of Thomas Hobbes (1588–1679) was the first attempt to develop a political theory that examined the dominant tendencies of the Scientific Revolution. Despite what contemporary scientists said, Hobbes saw that they approached nature as if it were a purely mechanical system in which all could be explained by applying mathematics to the movements of bodies relative to one another. Taking geometry as his mathematical model, he started by examining the simplest elements and, by using self-evident principles, moved forward to the analysis of problems of greater complexity. He believed that each human being, like the rest of the universe, consisted of a series of motions. The center of each series was the heart, the source of vital motion in the body. Increases and decreases in this vital motion were transmitted through the sense organs, giving rise to two basic emotions, desire and aversion—movement toward that which heightened vitality and retreat from that which threatened it. The movement of other bodies stimulated one emotion or the other, depending on whether they favored or menaced the life force. Thus Hobbes's analysis rises from the study of the movement of bodies (physics) to that of the psychology and physiology of human beings.

The basic instinct of all people is the maintenance and, if possible, the heightening of the vital force. The desire for self-preservation leads to the pursuit of power, because one can never be secure enough:

I put a general inclination of all mankind, a perpetual and restless desire of power after power, that ceases only in death . . . because he [man] cannot assure the power and means to live well, which he hath present, without the acquisition of more.

Mankind existing in the state of nature, before the existence of government, experienced almost constant war. In a phrase that was to become classic, Hobbes described the human condition in this state as "solitary, poor, nasty, brutish, and short." It is improbable that Hobbes believed that there ever had been such a time, but consistant with his geometrical model, he (and subsequent philosophers) used his conception of a state of nature to get a clear focus on what *human* nature was like. As we shall see in the passages from the *Leviathan* that follow, Hobbes viewed people as essentially isolated, selfish beings. Given the misery of their circumstances, they could live in peace only after surrendering their freedom to an artificially created unitary will (Leviathan) with absolute power to rule. With the creation of Leviathan, both government and civil society came into existence.

THOMAS HOBBES

From *Leviathan*

OF THE DIFFERENCE OF MANNERS

In the first place, I put for a general inclination of all mankind a perpetual and restless desire of power after power that ceases only in death. And the cause of this is not always that a man hopes for a more intensive delight than he has already attained to, or that he cannot be content with a moderate power, but because he cannot assure the power and means to live well which he has present without the acquisition of more.

OF THE NATURAL CONDITION OF MANKIND AS CONCERNING THEIR FELICITY AND MISERY

Nature has made men so equal in the faculties of the body and mind as that, though there be found one man sometimes manifestly stronger in body or of quicker mind than another, yet, when all is reckoned together, the difference between man and man is not so considerable as that one man can thereupon claim to himself any benefit to which another may not pretend as well as he. For as to the strength of body, the weakest has strength enough to kill the strongest, either by secret machination[1] or by confederacy with others that are in the same danger with himself.

Hereby it is manifest that, during the time men live without a common power to keep them all in awe, they are in that condition which is called war, and such a war as is of every man against every man. For WAR consists not in battle only, or the act of fighting, but in a tract of time wherein the will to contend by battle is sufficiently known; and therefore the notion of *time* is to be considered in the nature of war as it is in the nature of weather. For as the nature of foul weather lies not in a shower or two of rain but in an inclination thereto of many days together, so the nature of war consists not in actual fighting but in the known disposition thereto during all the time there is no assurance to the contrary. All other time is PEACE.

Whatsoever, therefore, is consequent[2] to a time of war where every man is enemy to every man, the same is consequent to the time wherein men live without other security than what their own strength and their own invention shall furnish them withal. In such condition there is no place for industry, because the fruit thereof is uncertain: and consequently no culture of the earth; no navigation nor use of the commodities that may be imported by sea; no commodious building; no instruments of moving and removing such things as require much force; no knowledge of the face of the earth; no account of time; no arts; no letters; no society; and, which is worst of all, continual fear and danger of violent death; and the life of man solitary, poor, nasty, brutish, and short.

It may seem strange to some man that has not well weighed these things that nature should thus dissociate [men] and render men apt to invade and destroy one another . . . Let him therefore consider with himself— when taking a journey he arms himself and seeks to go well accompanied, when going to sleep he locks his doors, when even in his house he locks his chests, and this when he knows there be laws and public officers, armed, to revenge all injuries shall be done him—what opinion he has of his fellow subjects when he rides armed, of his fellow citizens when he locks his doors, and of his children and servants when he locks his chests. Does he not there as much accuse mankind by his actions as I do by my words? But neither of us accuse man's nature in it. The desires and other passions of man are in themselves no sin. No more are the actions that proceed from those passions till they know a law that forbids them, which, till laws be made, they cannot know, nor can any law be made till they have agreed upon the person that shall make it. . . .

To this war of every man against every man, this also is consequent: that nothing can be unjust. The notions of right and wrong, justice and injustice, have there no place. Where there is no common power, there is no law; where no law, no injustice. Force and fraud are in war the two cardinal virtues. Justice and injustice are none of the faculties neither of the body nor mind. If they were, they might be in a man that were alone in the world, as well as his senses and passions. They are qualities that relate to men in society, not in solitude. It is consequent also to the same condition that there be no propriety, no dominion, no *mine* and *thine* distinct; but only that to be every man's that he can get, and for so long as he can keep it. And thus much for the ill condition which man by mere nature is actually placed in, though with a possiblity to come out of it consisting partly in the passions, partly in his reason.

It may peradventure[3] be thought there was never such a time nor condition of war as this, and I believe it was never generally so over all the world; but there are many places where they live so now. For the savage people in many places of America, except the government of small families, the concord whereof depends on natural lust, have no government at all and live at this day in that brutish manner as I said before. Howsoever, it may be perceived what manner of life there would be where there were no common power to fear by the manner of life which men that have formerly lived under a peaceful government use to degenerate into a civil war.[4]

The passions that incline men to peace are fear of death, desire of such things as are necessary to commo-

---

[1] Plotting.
[2] Attributed.

[3] Perhaps.
[4] Hobbes is referring to the English Civil War (1642–1651).

dious living, and a hope by their industry to obtain them. And reason suggests convenient articles of peace, upon which men may be drawn to agreement. These articles are they which otherwise are called the Laws of Nature.

OF THE FIRST AND SECOND NATURAL LAWS, AND OF CONTRACTS

The RIGHT OF NATURE . . . is the liberty each man has to use his own power, as he will himself, for the preservation of his own nature—that is to say, of his own life—and consequently of doing anything which, in his own judgment and reason, he shall conceive to be the aptest means thereunto. . . .

A LAW OF NATURE . . . is a precept or general rule, found out by reason, by which a man is forbidden to do that which is destructive of his life or takes away the means of preserving the same. . . .

And because the condition of man, as has been declared in the precedent chapter, is a condition of war of every one against every one—in which case everyone is governed by his own reason and there is nothing he can make use of that may not be a help unto him in preserving his life against his enemies—it follows that in such a condition every man has a right to everything, even to one another's body. And therefore, as long as this natural right of every man to everything endures, there can be no security to any man, how strong or wise soever he be, of living out the time which nature ordinarily allows men to live. And consequently it is a precept or general rule of reason *that every man ought to endeavor peace, as far as he has hope of obtaining it; and when he cannot obtain it, that he may seek and use all helps and advantages of war.* The first branch of which rule contains the first and fundamental law of nature, which is *to seek peace and follow it.* The second, the sum of the right of nature, which is, *by all means we can to defend ourselves.*

From this fundamental law of nature, by which men are commanded to endeavor peace, is derived this second law: *that a man be willing, when others are so too, as far forth as for peace and defense of himself he shall think it necessary, to lay down this right to all things, and be contented with so much liberty against other men as he would allow other men against himself.* For as long as every man holds this right of doing anything

he likes, so long are all men in the condition of war. But if other men will not lay down their right as well as he, then there is no reason for anyone to divest himself of his, for that were to expose himself to prey, which no man is bound to, rather than to dispose himself to peace. This is that law of the gospel: *whatsoever you require that others should do to you, that do ye to them.*

OF THE CAUSES, GENERATION, AND DEFINITION OF A COMMONWEALTH

The final cause, end, or design of men, who naturally love liberty and dominion over others, in the introduction of that restraint upon themselves in which we see them live in commonwealths is the foresight of their own preservation, and of a more contented life thereby—that is to say, of getting themselves out from that miserable condition of war which is necessarily consequent . . . to the natural passions of men when there is no visible power to keep them in awe and tie them by fear of punishment to the performance of their covenants and observation of those laws of nature. . . .

For the laws of nature—as *justice, equity, modesty, mercy,* and, in sum, *doing to others as we would be done to*—of themselves, without the terror of some power to cause them to be observed, are contrary to our natural passions, that carry us to partiality, pride, revenge, and the like. And covenants without the sword are but words, and of no strength to secure a man at all. . . . And in all places where men have lived by small families, to rob and spoil one another has been a trade, and so far from being reputed against the law of nature that the greater spoils they gained, the greater was their honor. . . . And as small families did then, so now do cities and kingdoms, which are but greater families, for their own security enlarge their dominions upon all pretenses of danger and fear of invasion or assistance . . . and endeavor as much as they can to subdue or weaken their neighbors by open force and secret arts, for want of other caution, justly; and are remembered for it in after ages with honor. . . .

It is true that certain living creatures, as bees and ants, live sociably one with another—which are therefore by Aristotle numbered among political creatures—and yet have no other direction than their particular judgments and appetites, nor speech whereby one of them can signify to another what he thinks expedient for the common benefit; and therefore some man may perhaps desire to know why mankind cannot do the same. To which I answer:

First, that men are continually in competition for honor and dignity, which these creatures are not; and consequently among men there arises on that ground envy and hatred and finally war, but among these not so.

Secondly, that among these creatures the common good differs not from the private; and being by nature inclined to their private, they procure thereby the common benefit. But man, whose joy consists in comparing himself with other men, can relish nothing but what is eminent.

Thirdly, that these creatures—having not, as man, the use of reason—do not see nor think they see any fault in the administration of their common business; whereas among men there are very many that think themselves wiser and abler to govern the public better than the rest, and these strive to reform and innovate, one this way, another that way, and thereby bring it into distraction and civil war.

Fourthly, that these creatures, though they have some use of voice in making known to one another their desires and other affections, yet they want that art of words by which some men can represent to others that which is good in the likeness of evil, and evil in the likeness of good, and augment or diminish the apparent greatness of good and evil, discontenting men and troubling their peace at their pleasure.

Fifthly, irrational creatures cannot distinguish between *injury* and *damage*, and therefore, as long as they be at ease, they are not offended with their fellows; whereas man is then most troublesome when he is most at ease, for then it is that he loves to show his wisdom and control the actions of them that govern the commonwealth.

Lastly, the agreement of these creatures is natural, that of men is by covenant only, which is artificial; and therefore it is no wonder if there be somewhat else required besides covenant to make their agreement constant and lasting, which is a common power to keep them in awe and to direct their actions to the common benefit.

The only way to erect such a common power as may be able to defend them from the invasion of foreigners and the injuries of one another, and thereby to secure them in such sort as that by their own industry and by the fruits of the earth they may nourish themselves and live contentedly, is to confer all their power and strength upon one man, or upon one assembly of men that may reduce all their wills, by plurality of voices, unto one will; which is as much as to say, to appoint one man or assembly of men to bear their person, and everyone to own and acknowledge himself to be author of whatsoever he that so bears their person shall act or cause to be acted in those things which concern the common peace and safety, and therein to submit their wills every one to his will, and their judgments to his judgment. This is more than consent or concord; it is a real unity of them all in one and the same person, made by covenant of every man with every man, in such manner as if every man should say to every man, *I authorize and give up my right of governing myself to this man, or to this assembly of men, on this condition, that you give up your right to him and authorize all his actions in like manner.* This done, the multitude so united in one person is called a COMMONWEALTH, in Latin CIVITAS. This is the generation of that great LEVIATHAN (or rather, to speak more reverently, of that *mortal god*) to which we owe, under the *immortal God,* our peace and defense. For by this authority, given him by every particular man in the commonwealth, he has the use of so much power and strength conferred on him that, by terror thereof, he is enabled to form the wills of them all to peace at home and mutual aid against their enemies abroad. And in him consists the essence of the commonwealth, which, to define it, is *one person, of whose acts a great multitude, by mutual covenants one with another, have made themselves every one the author, to the end he may use the strength and means of them all as he shall think expedient for their peace and common defense.* And he that carries this person is called SOVEREIGN and said to have *sovereign power;* and everyone besides, his SUBJECT.

The attaining to this sovereign power is by two ways. One, by natural force, as when a man makes his children to submit themselves and their children to his government, as being able to destroy them if they refuse, or by war subdues his enemies to his will, giving them their lives on that condition. The other is when men agree among themselves to submit to some man or assembly of men voluntarily, on confidence to be protected by him against all others. This latter may be called a political commonwealth, or commonwealth by *institution,* and the former a commonwealth by *acquisition.*

OF THE OFFICE OF THE SOVEREIGN REPRESENTATIVE

The office of the sovereign, be it a monarch or an assembly, consists in the end for which he was trusted with the sovereign power, namely, the procuration of *the safety of the people;* to which he is obliged by the law of nature, and to render an account thereof to God, the author of that law, and to none but him. But by safety here is not meant a bare preservation but also all other contentments of life which every man by lawful industry, without danger or hurt to the commonwealth, shall acquire to himself. . . .

To the care of the sovereign belongs the making of good laws. But what is a good law? By a good law I mean not a just law, for no law can be unjust. The law is made by the sovereign power, and all that is done by such power is warranted and owned by every one of the people; and that which every man will have so, no man can say is unjust. It is in the laws of a commonwealth as in the laws of gaming: whatsoever the gamesters all agree on is injustice to none of them. A good law is that which is *needful* for the *good of the people,* and withal *perspicuous.*

For the use of laws, which are but rules authorized, is not to bind the people from all voluntary actions but to direct and keep them in such a motion as not to hurt themselves by their own impetuous desires, rashness, or indiscretion—as hedges are set, not to stop travelers, but to keep them in their way. And therefore a law that is not needful, having not the true end of a law, is not good. A law may be conceived to be good when it is for the benefits of the sovereign though it be not necessary for the people; but it is not so. For the good of the sovereign and people cannot be separated. It is a weak sovereign that has weak subjects, and a weak people whose sovereign wants power to rule them at his will. . . .

It belongs also to the office of the sovereign to make a right application of punishments and rewards. And seeing the end of punishing is not revenge and discharge of choler[5] but correction, either of the offender or of others by his example, the severest punishments are to be inflicted for those crimes that are of most danger to the public: such as are those which proceed from malice to the government established; those that spring from contempt of justice; those that provoke indignation in the multitude; and those which, unpunished, seem authorized, as when they are committed by sons, servants, or favorites of men in authority. For indignation carries men not only against the actors and authors of injustice, but against all power that is likely to protect them: as in the case of Tarquin,[6] when for the insolent act of one of his sons he was driven out of Rome and the monarchy itself dissolved. But crimes of infirmity—such as are those which proceed from great provocation, from great fear, great need, or from ignorance . . . —there is place many times for lenity without prejudice to the commonwealth; and lenity, when there is such place for it, is required by the law of nature. The punishment of the leaders and teachers in a commotion, not the poor seduced people, when they are punished, can profit the commonwealth by their example. To be severe to the people is to punish that ignorance which may in great part be imputed to the sovereign, whose fault it was that they were no better instructed. . . .

Concerning the offices of one sovereign to another, which are comprehended in that law which is commonly called the *law of nations,* I need not say anything in this place because the law of nations and the law of nature is the same thing. And every sovereign has the same right in procuring the safety of his people that any particular man can have in procuring the safety of his own body. And the same law that dictates to men that have no civil government what they ought to do and what to avoid in regard of one another dictates the same to commonwealths—that is,

---

[5] Anger.

[6] According to legend, Tarquin, the last Roman king, was driven from the city (510 B.C.) by a popular rising after his son had raped—and thereby occasioned the suicide of—the virtuous Lucretia (Livy I).

to the consciences of sovereign princes and sovereign assemblies, there being no court of natural justice but in the conscience only, where not man but God reigns, whose laws, such of them as oblige all mankind, in respect of God as he is the author of nature are *natural*, and in respect of the same God as he is King of kings are *laws*.

COMMENTS AND QUESTIONS

1. Why does the fact that all people are roughly equal lead in the state of nature to continuous insecurity and warfare?
2. Why does Hobbes believe there can be no sin or injustice before there is law?
3. What are the roles of passion and reason in helping people escape from the state of nature?
4. People never lose the right of nature (the right of self-defense) even when living in our organized state, but reason tells them that the best way to defend themselves is through the first law of nature (the pursuit of peace). In what way does the second law of nature follow from the first?
5. In describing how people differ from social animals like bees, how does Hobbes indicate that reason has a bad aspect?
6. For Hobbes the state and society come into existence at the same time and are really the same entity. They are the artificial creation of a covenant sworn to by each isolated individual. What does each individual swear to do?
7. Why can no law be unjust and yet some laws can be bad? Although Leviathan can do as he pleases, does Hobbes see him as a tyrant?
8. Why are sovereign powers in the state of nature in relationship to one another?

Hobbes wrote his book in the belief that his theories would bolster the cause of monarchical absolutism, but he and his ideas were shunned by those he meant to defend. Whereas seventeenth-century monarchs justified their power as based on divine right, Hobbes considered it deriving from utilitarian needs: the alternative to royal absolutism was anarchy. His materialism, atheism, and denial that there was any absolute right or wrong also shocked his generation and earned him the epithet the Monster of Malmesbury.

20

The Baroque Style in the Arts

The social, religious, intellectual, and economic upheavals that characterized the late sixteenth and early seventeenth centuries were accompanied by a new style in the arts. The High Renaissance conventions of human beauty expressed in ideal proportions seemed to lead to a dead end. Luther and Calvin took to task the whole Catholic tradition of visual art in the service of religion, and they found Italian religious painting of the sixteenth century completely pagan. In literature and in music, too, Protestant doctrine demanded an art form less tied to classical antiquity and formal standards and more suitable to individualistic piety. Some of the best poetry and music of seventeenth-century Protestant Europe took the form of hymns. Catholics, zealous to defend their faith after the Council of Trent, found High Renaissance art inadequate for other reasons. In contrast to the Protestants, they vigorously reaffirmed the importance of rich visual and auditory imagery in churches and worship rituals. The intellectual and classical qualities of Renaissance art were found wanting in emotional appeal. They wanted art that could enrapture the viewer, listener, or reader, appealing to the spirit through the senses and serving as an instrument of conversion.

Political and economic changes also had their effect on the development of new artistic forms. If the Protestant capitalists discouraged the decoration of churches, they encouraged paintings of themselves and the material objects surrounding them. Absolutist monarchy created a style of its own. Catholic monarchs liked to be shown in opulence and splendor, thus also encouraging a sensuous exploration of reality. One of the persistent characteristics of the new style in visual arts, literature, and music was a heightened sensuality combined with spirituality. Perhaps the long-lived disasters of the religious wars gave human beings zest for a life that seemed precarious and, at the same time, fervor for the life to come. Expanded trade and colonization in Africa and the New World gave artists wealth, more exotic themes, and an enlarged sense of space. The scientific and philosophical revolutions inevitably influenced artists' portrayals of reality. The shift from an authoritarian view of nature to an experimental one also encouraged the artist to portray what he actually saw.

On the other hand, the new knowledge that the earth was no longer the center of the universe led artists to seek a depiction of enlarged space in contrast to the ordered, limited space suggested by Renaissance conventions. Seventeenth-century church architects and painters loved to give illusions of infinite space; musicians enlarged their tonal space to echo an illusion of infinity; poets and playwrights became preoccupied with the idea that life on earth is transient and precarious, or as the title of Calderón de la Barca's famous play states, *La Vida es Sueño*; life is a dream, an illusion. An English poet of the new age, John Donne, captured something of the effect of the scientific revolution on men's minds and spirits in a poem called "An Anatomie of the World."

> And new Philosophy calls all in doubt,
> The element of fire is quite put out;
> The Sun is lost, and th'earth, and no man's wit
> Can well direct him where to looke for it.
> And freely men confess that this world's spent,

> When in the Planets, and the Firmament
> They seeke so many new; they see that this
> Is crumbled out againe to his Atomies.
> 'Tis all in peeces, all coherence gone;
> All just supply, and all Relation.

The sense of being on a little planet in space rather than on firm earth is accompanied by a kind of breathless vertigo that is characteristic of much of seventeenth-century art. Yet the sense of earthly life as an illusion often appears along with a realistic depiction of it. This is one of the many contradictions of the period.

Historians of Spanish, Dutch, French, and sometimes English culture call the seventeenth century the "great century" or the "golden century." The power attained by these countries was accompanied by a great cultural outpouring in all fields. Italy, though waning in prominence, took an early lead in architecture, painting, music, and poetry, while Germany, toward the end of the century, produced the period's greatest musicians. Yet this period of rich productivity in the arts shows a diversity of style that makes it hard to classify. The stylistic terms most often used now to describe all of the arts in this century are taken from the vocabulary of visual arts: *baroque* and *neoclassical*.

Some cultural historians like to divide the century into two neat parts: the first, until roughly 1680, politically and religiously chaotic, is characterized as baroque, and the late part, a period of relative stability, as neoclassical. This may be approximately true of literature and art in most Western countries, but the great period of baroque music did not end until the middle of the eighteenth century and in the Slavic countries, the baroque style in all the arts continued through that period. Even in France, where neoclassicism as a doctrine prevailed during the late-seventeenth-century reign of Louis XIV, certain elements of the baroque can still be found in the arts. We will focus on the reign of the "sun king" in Chapter 22. For now, we will attempt to define some aspects of the baroque in the late sixteenth and early seventeenth centuries in the visual arts and poetry and in the seventeenth and early eighteenth centuries in music.

Baroque in the Visual Arts

The rather strange word *baroque* (from Italian *barocco*) originally meant a logical process that was

20-1 Bruegel, *Landscape with the Fall of Icarus.* (Copyright A.C.L—Bruxelles; Institut Royal du Patrimoine Artistique)

contorted or involuted. In Portuguese, *perola barroca* was a term used by jewelers to designate a rough or irregularly shaped pearl. The French, by the eighteenth century, used the word *baroque* to mean "a painting . . . in which the rules of proportion are not observed and everything is represented according to the artist's whim." All of these meanings were, like "Gothic," originally pejorative. What these definitions share in common is the sense of divergence from an established, accepted ideal. As art history and criticism evolved and the seventeenth century was revalued, *baroque* appeared to be the opposite of *classical*, either in reference to antiquity or to the High Renaissance. In this sense the term suggested art that was naturalistic rather than ideal, and emotional rather than rational. Translated visually, this would produce an art of movement, vitality, and brilliant color. Subjects could be chosen from daily life, as well as antiquity and the Bible, and presented to achieve maximum emotional impact or intense, detached observation.

Baroque Painting

Italian artists fashioned a new vision of the world that created an artistic revolution in the fifteenth century. This new way of seeing and painting inspired art-

ists all over Europe. The artistic accomplishments of the Italians were disseminated north and west, where they married with the explorations, ideas, and traditions of other countries. Artists in the Netherlands, Spain, France, and England gave their art a particular flavor drawn from their place and its expectations. For example, many Dutch and German artists painted scenes from daily life—farmers, skaters, hunters, village celebrations—subjects absent from the work of most Italian artists of the sixteenth century. Pieter Bruegel the Elder (born in Flanders, c. 1525–1569), who painted *Hunters in the Snow* and *Haymaking* (1565) (Color Plate I), created a substantial body of work dealing with classical myths and Christian subjects. His human subjects, however, frequently appear subsumed by his sublime rendering of the natural world. In *Landscape with the Fall of Icarus* (Fig. 20-1) (1554–1555) the drowning young man seems an afterthought in this scene of spring plowing. Icarus's naked legs and his gesticulating father in the lower right midground of the painting are far less interesting than the sunlit world of coast, farm, and sky.

In contrast, the work of El Greco (born Domenikos Theotokopoulos in Crete, 1541–1614), a student in Italy and a successful artist in Spain at the end of the sixteenth century, seems both courtly and intensely mystical. *The Burial and the Count of Orgaz* (1586) (Fig. 20-2) uses a vocabulary of form and color whose sources are Italian painting but whose feeling is uniquely El Greco's. The interment of the saintly Orgaz, being laid to rest by priests and friends, fills the lower half of the large canvas; the upper half is aswirl with saints, angels, Christ, and the Virgin, who welcome his soul to heaven. The expressive faces of the noblemen who attend Orgaz, the glittering surface of objects rendered vividly, have a life and energy far different from work by Raphael and his peers. By 1600, when El Greco painted his *View of Toledo* (Color Plate II), sky, earth, and air take on unearthly tones of light and movement that seem to be the product of an intensely personal experience and artistic language. El Greco's painting speaks of an independent vision, an individual soul.

By the end of the sixteenth century, the artistic vocabulary of Europe had expanded to create masterpieces removed both visually and emotionally from the art of the preceding one hundred years. It was this legacy, a vast body of paintings, prints, sculpture, and architecture, that provided the artists of the seventeenth century with unlimited resources for their own personal development. And the general term *baroque*, which is used to characterize their work, must always be qualified by reference to time, artist, and place of its production. Painters from France, Italy, the Netherlands, and Spain created works that demonstrate both the diversity and the shared characteristics of painting in the seventeenth century.

Caravaggio (1573–1610)   Born Michelangelo Merisi, Caravaggio took the name of his home town in Lombardy. He arrived in Rome during his late teens. There he lived like a rebel, was constantly in trouble for fighting and other violence, killed a man over a tennis match, and fled the city around 1606. His intense anger spilled over into his painting. Caravaggio seems to have deliberately sought to shock people with his art. He produced pictures that seem to dwell on the harsh and brutal reality of daily life—his painting of Christ's mother's corpse (Fig. 20-3) portrays a dead, bloated, old woman. But these realities were a means of triggering the intense, internal reality of conflicting feelings that Christ and his message brought to sinful men.

20-2 El Greco, *The Burial of the Count of Orgaz*. (Art Resource)

The Calling of St. Matthew (1599–1600) (Color Plate III), one of three scenes from the apostle's life painted by Caravaggio to decorate the Contarelli Chapel in a church in Rome demonstrates the psychological reality Caravaggio could draw from a simple scene. The event takes place in a Roman tavern, filtered light falls from the oiled paper in the window onto the bare walls and floor. Another, stronger light slashes across the top third of the canvas. This light reveals the face and uplifted hand of Jesus who, with Peter, steps into the room. Matthew the publican is seated at a table with three somewhat rustic, tacky youths. An older man leans over Matthew's shoulder and Matthew himself, who looks up somewhat surprised, shows with his face and gesture the eternal "Who, me?" even as he draws away from Christ.

jects in the painting itself are rendered with hard, firm edges and substantial, varied textures, eliciting a powerful tactile response in the viewer. How could a spiritual event be portrayed with such earthy power? The contrasts reinforce the power of Christ's gesture that makes the earthly divine.

Peter Paul Rubens (1577–1640) Rubens was the son of a wealthy Antwerp Protestant who fled to Germany to avoid persecution by the Catholics seeking control of the Netherlands. After his father's death, his family returned to Antwerp, and Rubens grew up a Catholic. Amiable, handsome, and energetic, he was already a successful painter when he journeyed to Italy in 1600. He remained there until 1608, assimilating the art of the High Renaissance and ancient Rome, and the revolutionary naturalism of Caravaggio. From these sources he created his own distinctive, optimistic, and visually rich view of the world.

When Rubens returned to Flanders, he was made court painter to the Spanish regent, and commissions began to flow into his workshop. He married well and lived in a magnificent townhouse in Antwerp that housed his collections of sculptures, paintings, antique coins and gems, and his personal library. His studio was soon filled with assistants who transferred his sketches onto large canvases. Even when he was absent on diplomatic and professional visits to France, England, or Spain, work was still produced to await his final approval and finishing touches.

The Raising of the Cross (Fig. 20-4), painted in 1609–1610, is the central panel of a *triptych*, a three-part altarpiece executed for the cathedral in Antwerp. It is a splendid example of the new style that emerged from his Italian sojourn. The athletic, muscular figure of Christ on the cross is placed on a diagonal away from the front plane established by the surface of the canvas. Massive, muscular figures struggle to raise the cross. The background is a dark one, where leaves are silhouetted against a stormy sky. The light, falling from right to left, is a dramatic stage light that picks out faces and limbs. The physical stress and earthly faces of the soldiers contrast with Christ's upward-turned eyes and sagging body. The body types owe much to Michelangelo, and the essentially triangular *composition* is based on a similar Renaissance device. But the energy

20-3 Caravaggio, *The Death of the Virgin*. (Art Resource)

What has Caravaggio done to make this such a revolutionary picture? He has located this event in a specific, real setting; a tavern populated with figures who are certainly not idealized in any way. They seem to lounge casually around the table, turning away from the event and the viewer, heightening a sense of irony. Peter and Christ seem like momentary intruders who bring with them an unexpected, uncomfortable, revealing light. The viewer, who knows more than Matthew, stands very close, indeed, almost in the scene. Nothing really separates the real from the painted and the obduring the minority of her son, Louis XIII. These canvases transform an inglorious, occasionally unscrupulous, and not too beautiful woman into an object of splendor through the unity of myth, fact, history, and allegory. For example, Marie's arrival at Marseilles (Fig. 20-5 shows her greeted by helmeted France, attended by Fame and Neptune, whose court rises from the water to celebrate her safe voyage. Marie, at the center right, is only a part of the rather glorious assemblage, which is beautiful for its rich colors, textures, and vitality of light and movement. We realize that the paintings for Marie were commissioned not only for self-glorification but also for the glorification of the French monarchy and its increasing power. Baroque art could serve to glorify the absolute monarchy as well as the Church Militant.

20-4 Rubens, *The Raising of the Cross,* Antwerp Cathedral. (Copyright A.C.L. Bruxelles)

and vitality of the figures, the movement back into deep space, and the dramatic lighting contrast with the order and symmetry of Renaissance painting. There is a loving attention to the color and textures of flesh, armor, and other objects—such as the curly, soft coat of the agitated dog in the lower foreground—that heightens our awareness of this event. *Colors* themselves are strong, and the paint surface is a smooth, rich one, which enables paint to be seen as paint as well as the delineator of form and surface. Rubens has used naturalistic details, but how do they differ in effect from those of Caravaggio?

Rubens received many important commissions, but surely one of the most important was for a series of twenty-one canvases to celebrate the career of Marie de' Medici, widow of Henry IV and regent of France

20-5 Rubens, *Arrival of Marie de' Medici at Marseilles.* (Louvre, Paris/photo © ARCH. PHOT. PARIS—S.P.A.D.E.M., 1980)

Rubens was adept at this kind of commission; indeed his portraits of kings and queens, prelates and courtiers depict the brilliant world of the first half of the seventeenth century. But it is important to remember that this great master could render not only memorable scenes of both spiritual and temporal power but also those of his own life and of the world of persons and objects that he loved.

The Garden of Love, painted in 1638 and inspired by Rubens' second marriage, demonstrates the earthly love whose divine counterpart was the impetus for his great paintings of Christian subjects (Color Plate IV). Rubens and his young wife, Helene, the couple at the far left, are shown in a garden, about to join a group of obviously loving couples—husbands and wives or friends and lovers, it is hardly important. The fantastic fountain house from the artist's garden in Antwerp provides background. A statue of Venus and mischievous cupids complete this vision. The colors are soft and warm, light, gay, ripe, and sensuous. The figures—who stand, sit, lean, talk, and gaze—melt into each other in a soft, flowing rhythm. Velvet and satin, soft skin and hair, sparkling eyes, and rosy lips seduce us with a vision of the joy of life and love that is suspended in this spring garden. The courtly man in the broad-brimmed hat introduces us to a world that will be, more and more, the subject of art—a golden time without pain or anxiety.

Rembrandt van Rijn (1606–1669)   Born in Leiden, near Amsterdam, Rembrandt spent his life in the Protestant society of Holland. This society appears sober and restrained, in contrast to that of Ruben's patrons. The Calvinists did not permit the painting of images, and the churches were not great patrons of the arts. But the country of the Dutch Calvinists and Lutherans was prosperous. These industrious, democratic antiroyalists established a worldwide commercial empire that brought wealth and power to many people. The land of tulips was also a country in which, for the first time, many people actively sought to buy and own art to adorn their own homes. Travelers in Holland in the seventeenth century noted that almost every family owned at least one original work of art. And for the first time, many painters made their livelihood in a free market. Paintings and prints of the flat country of land and water, with its huge, tumultuous sky, the rich and lovely interiors of private homes, as well as sumptu-

20-6 Rembrandt, *The Three Trees.* Etching, 1643. (The Metropolitan Museum of Art, Bequest of Mrs. H. O. Havemeyer, 1929. The H. O. Havemeyer Collection)

ous, still-life pictures, were popular. *The Three Trees,* an etching made by Rembrandt about 1643 (Fig. 20-6) depicts the Dutch landscape. His great portraits, subjects from the Bible and mythology, adorned the interiors that his pictures celebrate as they also celebrate the material world, personal success, and pietistic faith of the independent Dutch.

Seated around a table covered with a magnificent red oriental rug, attended by a servant, the black-coated *Syndics of the Drapers' Guild* discuss the affairs of the guild (Color Plate V). Yet the moment is not altogether public, for they seem to have been caught in a quiet conversation. One man rises from his seat to greet someone who has come into the room, and all eyes focus on that person. The intruder is, of course, the viewer, and this is one of the qualities that gives the picture its life. The men, who seem completely unposed, become the focus of our attention through their glances, their alert faces, the direction of light, and the white collars and broad-brimmed hats. Each is an individual, each face exhibits age, experience, and reserve. The surface textures, contours of form, and the features of faces and hair are all rendered with soft, easily flowing brushstrokes. The firm clarity that is present in much of Rubens' work is absent here, but the painting exhibits a softness derived from suffused light more comparable to that in *The Garden of Love.*

Rembrandt's sympathy with his patrons and their view of life grew from his own experience. His subject is always humankind, and the face, costume, and demeanor become a means to explore the internal life, with its pain, power, and pride. Thus, in his self-portraits, his own face becomes a vehicle for exploring the changes that life leaves on the body and the soul. One can follow his transformation from a foppish, well-dressed young man in the *Self-Portrait with Saskia* (his first wife) (Fig. 20-7) painted about 1635, to a mature, introspective man (Fig. 20-8) to a balding and turbaned artist holding his palette (Color Plate VI).

Rembrandt's genius, like Rubens', lay in the unity of composition achieved by light and by the revelation of surface features, textures, and colors in light. Renaissance painting developed conventions in which light was generally clear, even, and uniformly revealing. Masaccio, Piero, Botticelli, Raphael, and Leonardo all employed a representation of light that is not intrusive. It

20-7   Rembrandt, *Self-Portrait with Saskia.* (Staatliche Kunstsammlungen, Dresden)

is a steady light that has been studied in nature but controlled in the studio. It may be slightly *warm*—that is, tending to emphasize the warm reds, yellows, and oranges of the spectrum—or it may be *cool*—emphasizing the cool blues, greens, and purples of the spectrum—but, above all, it is consistent. Along with this convention of uniform light, the Renaissance painters used another by designating *shade* or *shadow* with gray, brown, or black layers of paint. This is not the way that shades and shadows are colored in nature, but it is the way that they were conventionally depicted. Without shade and shadow there is little or no sense of volume and space. Showing shade and shadow as an absence of color gives a great sense of uniformity to a picture, particularly uniformity of light.

Just as Caravaggio used light in a new way, so, too, did Rubens and Rembrandt, who experimented with

20-8   Rembrandt, *Self-Portrait* (1658). (The Frick Collection)

and elaborated on the conventions that had defined the way light would be rendered in fifteenth- and six- teenth-century painting. Rubens, like Caravaggio, used light dramatically to reveal and focus on objects, but unlike Caravaggio, whose light usually revealed the harsh reality of things, Rubens used light to reveal color and texture and to enliven and enhance objects. Rem- brandt used light to create much sharper contrasts be- tween figures and objects in space. In deep shadows and shadowed faces we find that same mystery of life and death, pain and joy. Though these themes were present in Rubens' work, Rembrandt portrays them without explosive theatricality. The drama becomes more per- sonal and introspective; it is not something that we wit- ness; it is something that we experience. The contrast is indicative of the difference in emphasis between the theatricality of Counter Reformation Catholicism and the individual piety of the Protestant north.

The Return of the Prodigal Son (ca. 1669) (Color Plate VII) is such a shadowed, almost soundless pic- ture. The warm light falling on figures and faces rein- forces the general warmth of the picture that is derived from gesture as well as from color scheme. The faces that witness this reunion seem observed in light re- flected from the two major figures. There is no boister- ous welcome but, instead, tender, loving forgiveness. This is earthly love raised to a divine power by the sim- plicity of composition. The paint itself seems thin ex- cept in the figures of father and son, where heavy *im- pastoed* layers, creating form and shadow, allude to textures. Unlike the uniformly smooth surface of Ren- aissance pictures, these contrasting layers of paint tell, as they do in Ruben's work, of the expansion of another Renaissance convention.

Jan Vermeer (1632–1675)   The ability to make paint give the illusion of reality has almost no limits. The Dutch landscape painters of the sixteenth century created a means of capturing a feeling of space and light, of movement, air, and color that created remark- able windows onto the world. But the size of the pic- ture itself, as well as its careful, studio-produced com- position, always checks the viewer's feeling that it is the natural world observed. Vermeer of Delft, the third great northern painter of the seventeenth century, took his experiences in the natural world and refined them to create visions that seem to be nothing so much as fragmentary moments of real time captured in a paint- ing. His apparently simple subjects are very much in the tradition of painting in Holland and the Low Coun- tries. City views like *The Music Lesson* (Fig. 20-9) had been popular for many generations. But in the work of Vermeer, these transient moments are rendered perma- nent.

In *The Kitchen-Maid* (Color Plate IX) a maidservant stands before a window pouring milk from a pitcher into a basin. The light from the window is cool and subdued; the colors of her sleeves, apron, and the table- cloth are also cool. The pottery basin and bowl, the cut bread, the basket, the gold of her bodice, and the red of her skirt challenge the cool, quiet northern light that falls from the window above her head. The woman is unself-conscious and unremarkable, solid and three- dimensional; her weight and volume act as a fulcrum

20-9 Vermeer, *Woman with a Lute*. Oil on canvas. (The Metropolitan Museum of Art, Bequest of Collis P. Huntington, 1900)

for all the objects in the room. The milk falls of its own weight into the basin.

What is so remarkable about this painting? The original, more than a reproduction, emits an incredible transparency and glow. It is possible to imagine that, should the light be gone from the room, the painting itself would provide light—so natural and convincing is its revelation of every surface, fold, and wrinkle. The colors themselves vibrate; shadows and folds are not rendered in gray, brown, or black but in thin layers of color itself—deeper blue in her apron, deeper golden red on the basin.

Light, of course, is the most essential and most recalcitrant element in all painting that seeks to render an account of nature as we perceive it. Artists have captured it by conventionalizing its representation. Raphael's even harmonious light, Rubens' dramatic spotlight effects, or Rembrandt's reflected light are some examples of the different ways to render light convincingly without absolute fidelity to light as it is experienced

naturally. Vermeer, however, by confining his subjects almost exclusively to figures before windows, proclaims his interest in the transient, cool light that comes from outside and is therefore subject to immediate change. Yet change never occurs, and that is what delights: it is "real" and it is not! We know that *The School of Athens* or *Primavera* are rendered through knowledge of the behavior of light, but there is no attempt to cajole us into thinking that it is "real" or experienced light—not so with Vermeer. Moreover, a woman weighing gold, a girl reading a letter, or a geographer in his study are all intimate revelations of transience where light reveals and suggests the brevity of life and the ephemeral pleasure of things.

As we experience these pictures by Vermeer, we add another layer to our perception of the seventeenth century. Here is a vision very different from that of a Rubens or a Rembrandt. In its realism it is more like Caravaggio, but its order recalls Piero and Raphael. Above all, however, Vermeer's study of light and delineation of space is uniquely his own, as individual and personally centered as he could make it.

Diego Rodríquez de Silva y Velásquez (1599–1660)

It is perhaps curious that of all the acknowledged masters of the seventeenth century a painter at the court of Philip IV, in the period of Spain's decline, could have created a highly original and personal style based on pure sensibility and perceptual experience. During the same years that Rubens executed great religious paintings, and Ribera and Zurbarán, Spanish contemporaries of Velásquez, made deeply moving and powerful religious pictures for Spanish patrons and the Church, the court painter (he had joined the court in 1623, remained there, and was made court chamberlain in 1652) produced few religious subjects. Rather, his fame grew from his stunning portraits and scenes of classical allegory and myth. Visiting Italy twice provided inspiration but did not essentially alter his manner. Velásquez's manner is most comparable to that of Vermeer. Like Vermeer, he was fascinated by light on objects, the light that reveals and conceals the images the artist sees and reproduces. Thus the actual surfaces of Velásquez's paintings reveal an elegant and systematic brushwork that depicts objects as fragments of light and shade, of colors placed side by each. The edges of objects are slightly indeterminate; the surface is never harsh or crisp but rather seems perpetually modulated by the movement of air and light. The most telling experience is to see a painting by Velásquez, to stalk it silently, in an attempt to discover the precise moment at which the surface dissolves into the fragments, layers, and dots that constitute the source of the painted image. This is very difficult, however, for the moment of dissolution is so close to the moment of seeing the image as a complete whole.

This kind of painting seems to lend itself to speculations about kinds of reality—the reality of image, of surface, of object. Yet like Vermeer's paintings, Velásquez's works do not suggest speculation; rather, they seem truly to depict reality. His most famous work, *Las Meninas* (The Ladies-in-Waiting), painted in 1656, typifies his greatest work (Color Plate X).

In the center of the large canvas, near the front edge, stands the five-year-old princess who has come to visit the painter in his studio. To the left stands Velásquez, a very large canvas on his easel. The ladies-in-waiting attend the princess, and to the right are two dwarfs, whose plainness plays against the glitter of royalty. A dog lies quietly in the foreground, a court official enters a lighted doorway at the back of the room. It is then that the viewer sees, or is shown, the images of the king and queen, reflected by a mirror at the back of the room. They, too, have come to the studio of their painter, who must be working on a painting of the royal family.

The light in this painting seems to fall into the room from an unseen window to the left. It lights the figures, the foreground, and the king and queen, who stand where the viewer might be. As with Vermeer's painting, it is possible to imagine that one would see into the painting in the dark, because it seems to contain its own light. The surface is fairly smooth, but rich with the paints that so carefully recreate the varying surfaces of hair, skin, fabric, fur, embroidery, jewelry. It is a remarkable achievement; the painting seems to breathe with a life drawn from experienced reality, captured on canvas.

Rubens, Rembrandt, and Caravaggio, each in his own way, explore human emotions with power, drama, and sometimes the rhetoric of experience. Vermeer and Velásquez, on the other hand, seem to explore the experienced world in a direct and candid way, sacrificing

nothing to give an account of the essentials of seeing, yet creating an extraordinary series of masterpieces that are, in fact, as carefully considered, composed, and conceptualized as the work of their predecessors or their peers.

Baroque Architecture and Sculpture in Rome

It was in a Rome dominated by the papacy and the militant Counter Reformation that the baroque style in architecture began. In the late sixteenth century the popes began to transform the city. A system of wide thoroughfares and squares united the major churches and sites of the pilgrim processional. There was innovative accommodation for wheeled and pedestrian traffic. There was also a sense of order to the city, recalling that produced by the ancient Forum. The pope's cathedral, Saint Peter's, was begun in the early sixteenth century (Fig. 20-10), the dome and east end, carried forth under Michelangelo, was brought to completion and aggrandized by a succession of powerful popes. Gian Lorenzo Bernini, the greatest sculptor of the seventeenth century, was commissioned to finish the interior. He designed the great canopy that stands over the high altar; the enormous elevated throne, the Chair of Saint Peter, in the east end (Fig. 20-11); and the magnificent staircase that connects the papal apartments with the west front of the church.

All these features seem like sets for a grand spectacle but none more so than the great plaza and colonnade set before the church to provide the necessary vista for a view of the great hovering dome of Saint Peter's. The arms of the Tuscan Doric colonnade reach down from the ends of the church façade, compress slightly, and then swell into the curved arms of the oval that welcomes the pilgrim to Saint Peter's (Fig. 20-12). The architectural vocabulary is that of Rome and the Renaissance but employed on a massive, monumental scale. The colonnade, for example, is four columns deep. Decorated with fountains and an Egyptian obelisk, this piazza—and others like it, opened in Rome and decorated by Bernini and his peers—became important in the development of urban planning. Rome itself was adorned with new churches and palaces. In their interiors are still found paintings and sculptures and represent persuasive, powerful propaganda for the faith.

20-10 Above left. Saint Peter's, Rome, aerial view. (Alinari/ Editorial Photocolor Archives)

20-11 Above right. Bernini, Chair of Saint Peter. (St. Peter's, Rome—Alinari/Editorial Photocolor Archives)

20-12 Left. Groundplan. Saint Peter's Square.

20-13 Cornaro Chapel, Santa Maria della Vittoria, Rome. Anonymous 18th-century painting. (Staatliches Museum Schwerin, German Democratic Republic)

a stage for the cloud with its burden of a limp, sagging Saint Theresa and a beautiful, smiling angel who holds an arrow in his upraised hand and with the other gently raises her habit to reveal her heart. In her autobiography Saint Theresa had described this vision in which an angel with a flaming golden arrow pierced her heart. "The pain was so great that I screamed aloud, but simultaneously felt such infinite sweetness that I wished the pain to last eternally. It was the sweetest caressing of the soul by God." The saint's mouth is open, as if to cry out, but the movement of her complex drapery contrasts with her thrown-back head and arm so that she seems to move both away from and toward this awesome divine love (Fig. 20-14). There is a distinctly erotic tone to pose and gesture, which is enhanced by the realistic rendition of hands, feet, and face of the saint and the angel's soft feathered wings and curls.

20-14 Bernini, *The Ecstasy of Saint Theresa*, (S. Maria della Vittoria, Rome—Alinari/Editorial Photocolor Archives)

In contrast to the vast adornments of Saint Peter's, Bernini planned other, more intimate decorative schemes that were focused on his magnificent sculptures. Such a scheme is the Cornaro Chapel at Santa Maria della Vittoria in Rome (1645-1652) (Fig. 20-13). An anonymous eighteenth-century painting of the chapel gives us the best idea of the ensemble, whose subject is *The Ecstasy of Saint Theresa*. Theresa of Avila was a sixteenth-century Spanish nun whose writings on her ecstatic vision particularly appealed to the sensibility of the seventeenth century. The ceiling of the vaulted chapel seems to disappear as angels greet the dove of the Holy Spirit in a burst of divine, heavenly light. The architectural frame swells out to create

The bronze rays falling behind the group reinforce the real light, and the marble paneling of the wall is continuous with that in the rest of the chapel. We observe from the ground, but members of the Cornaro family are in boxes on either side—these are also part of the total ensemble of sculpted and painted decoration, for the figures are marble reliefs. It is significant that many Catholics, including Bernini, practiced exercises of prayer and self-denial that were designed to induce suffering and delight comparable to that of Christ and the saints.

It was in Rome, then, that some of the greatest monuments of the seventeenth century were produced. It was from Rome also that the baroque was carried to other artistic centers. Baroque in the visual arts thus includes a rich diversity of styles and cultural patterns from the Catholic south to the Protestant north.

Literary Baroque

Although some scholars still dispute its usage, the term *baroque* has in recent decades been applied to literature, as well as to the other arts. Late-sixteenth- and early-seventeenth-century drama and poetry, as well as some fiction, in all European languages do indeed show some characteristics similar to those we have seen in the visual arts: conflict, paradox and contrast, metaphysical concern, and a heightened spirituality, combined with a lively sensuality and ultrarealism. Like the baroque style in art, literary baroque also had Catholic and Protestant representatives. German Lutheran hymns, Spanish Catholic devotional poetry, Italian erotic verse and English "metaphysical poetry" all display aspects of this multifaceted style. Here we will limit our examples to a few poems from the country that produced the earliest and perhaps the greatest baroque writers, Spain, and to an important group of early-seventeenth-century poets in England.

The Baroque Style in Spain   The names of the novelist and playwright Miguel de Cervantes (1547–1616), the dramatists Pedro Calderón de la Barca (1600–81) and Lope de Vega (1562–1635), and the poet Luis de Góngora y Argote (1561–1627) remind us that the seventeenth century was Spain's "golden age," a time that produced writers that were to have an impact on world literature comparable to the impact of Spanish civilization on the new world. To understand the flow-

ering of the Spanish baroque, it is important to look at some late-sixteenth-century precursors.

The widespread sense of disillusionment felt in late-sixteenth-century Spain was in part a manifestation of the widening gap between the ideals of a great Catholic power and reality. Ambitious military enterprises like that of the Armada forced the monarchy to live from hand to mouth and to declare periodic bankruptcies. Religious conformity discouraged independent thinking and encouraged hypocrisy. The aristocratic values of the society tended to divide the population into masters and servants.

As early as 1554, the tale of Lazarillo de Tortmes presents a revealing picture of this world. In a short first-person narrative, the anonymous author vents a constant aggressiveness against the prevailing social values in a realistic style that contrasts sharply with the idealized approach of the then-popular sentimental novels and romances of chivalry. It is an irreverent work, antiestablishment, anticlerical, bitterly satirical, attacking religious orthodoxy, purity of blood, aristocratic "virtue."

The story of Lazarillo, whose parents are members of the very lowest social stratum, is a story of corruption in which the hero, or more accurately an antihero, rises in the social scale as the prevailing social values force him to sink progressively into personal and moral degradation. What this tale does is to pose unambiguously the aesthetic values of what will years later become the very basis of baroque literature—that is, the dialectical relation between appearance and reality, between *engaño* (illusion) and its opposite, *desengaño*, which is not disillusionment but rather the process of arriving at the acceptance of truth, which is usually bitter and at odds with conventional wisdom.

St. John of the Cross (1542–1591)   Chronologically closer to the full-fledged baroque are the mystic poets who flourished in the second half of the sixteenth century. Undoubtedly, the Spanish mystics must have been influenced by the same weariness with conflict and turmoil that had caused the satirical outbursts in *Lazarillo*. In opting for a life of seclusion, a contemplative rather than an active life, they were expressing both their disdain for wordly ambition and their condemnation of the ideological oppression and the corruption that had gripped Spanish society. Many of them, including the Carmelite nun and mystic writer St. Theresa of Avila (see pp. 33, 58–60) and the poet St. John of the Cross, fell foul of the Inquisition.

Born Juan de Yepes and canonized in 1726, St. John of the Cross provides us with some of the most exalted mystic poetry ever written. He was a friend and disciple of St. Theresa, and also a Carmelite. After being imprisoned by the Inquisition in 1577, he escaped and took refuge in a monastery, from which he soon emerged to continue an active life as a reformer of the Carmelite order. His poetic production was small but intense, as well as of great originality. Mysticism, in its strictest sense, is the experience of the union of the soul with God. It transcends human reference and cannot, therefore, be rationally explained. The uniqueness of St. John lies in recording that experience directly, without attempting any intellectual explanation or exegesis. Love being the basis of the relation between God and His creatures, St. John uses the language of love and expresses divine union in terms of human love and eroticism. The human soul is the Bride; God, the Bridegroom. The stanzas that follow are from *The Living Flame of Love: Songs of the Soul in Intimate Union with God*. The translation is by Alan Gonzalez. As with other short poems throughout this volume, we have retained the original.

Liama de Amor Viva ———————— •

*Canciones que hace el alma en
la íntima unión en Dios*

¡Oh, llama de amor viva,
que tiernamente hieres
de mi alma en el más profundo centro!

Pues ya no eres esquiva,
acaba ya, si quieres;
rompe la tela de este dulce encuentro.

¡Oh cauterio suave!
¡Oh regalada llaga!
¡Oh mano blanda! ¡Oh toque delicado!
que a vida eterna sabe,
y toda deuda paga;
matando, muerte en vida la has trocado.

¡Oh lámparas de fuego,
en cuyos resplandores
las profundas cavernas del sentido,
que estaba oscuro y ciego,
con extraños primores
calor y luz dan junto a su querido!

¡Cuán manso y amoroso
recuerdas en mi seno
donde secretamente solo moras,
y en tu aspirar sabroso
de bien y gloria lleno
cuán delicadamente me enamoras!

Living Flame of Love ———————— •

Songs of the Soul in Intimate Union with God

O living flame of love
tenderly wounding my soul
in its very deepest core!

No longer coy,
close now, if it's your wish;
rend the fabric of this sweet encounter.

O softest searing burn!
O welcome ulcer!
O tender hand! O subtle touch
of life eternal tasting
and every debt redeeming;
in slaying, all death to life you've turned.

O lanterns of fire,
in whose resplendent rays
the deepest caverns of sense,
erstwhile dark and blind,
warmth, with curious care,
and light together give to its beloved.

How gentle and how loving
you wake up on my breast,
where secretly alone you dwell,
and with your tempting breath,
goodness and glory filled,
how delicately my love you inflame!

The full flowering of Spanish baroque comes in the early seventeenth century. The term *barroco* denotes, in Spanish life, literature, and fine arts, a clearly defined attitude to the external world as well as a stage in artistic development. It is an attitude conditioned by the concept of *desengaño* (see p. 34). In a world in which all values were found to be inconstant and deceptive, the nature of life itself was subjected to constant questioning. That is the quandary of Segismundo, a sort of Everyman in Calderón's play *Life Is a Dream*. He expresses it at the end of Act II: "We are in such a singular world that to live is but to dream; I have learned, in my experience, that, in living, man but dreams what he is until he wakes." There is, of course, no knowing when the awakening will come.

This view of the deceptive nature of human experience gave rise to a preoccupation with death on the one hand and with corruptible human flesh on the other. Artists resorted to overornamentation to extract from Nature the beauty that seemed (as in the painting of Velasquez) to dissolve and disappear precisely as the artist struggled to record it. Nature has lost out, they seem to be saying, and meaning has to be sought in the painful and painstaking accumulation of artifice. The most disparate notions are brought together by violence to create a new kind of aesthetic. The paintings of El Greco (Spanish for "the Greek"), though not considered baroque by all art historians, demonstrate the expressive distortion of human anatomy and of spatial relations and the violent emotion characteristic of the period (see pp. 23–24). In literature, particularly in the style of Góngora (1561–1627), this takes the form of the use of all kinds of extravagant metaphors, violent paradoxes, and an abstruse and learned vocabulary.

Sor Juana Inés de la Cruz (1651–1695)   Góngora found many followers in the overseas Spanish possessions. The viceregal courts of Mexico and Lima, for instance, were known as sophisticated centers of learning, in which writing and the fine arts flourished. Juana de Asbaje had become known at an early age in Mexico for her unusual aptitude and thirst for learning. Society, however, frowned on learned women. It is probably correct, as historians say, that, in taking vows at the age of nineteen in the order of Saint Jerome, assuming the name of Sor (Sister) Juana Inés de la Cruz, she was led by the sincere belief that, in withdrawing from the secular world, in which she found herself "sought as a beautiful woman and unhappy in her wisdom," she would be able to pursue a life of study and contemplation. As she found out, she was only partly right. Nonetheless, she managed to leave a remarkable written record as poet, playwright, and essayist. We can appreciate her tender lyricism in some of her early love poems— her "Redondillas" (Quatrains) in defense of women is probably her best-known work—but it is to her mature poetry that we must turn to see the depth of her talent. Although inspired by the style of Góngora, she found her own voice to express her disdain for the vanity of life. The sonnet that follows, on a portrait of herself, seems to dismiss the possibility of representing truth in art. The translation is by Alan Gonzalez.

Este,[1] que ves, engaño colorido,
que del arte ostentando los primores,
con falsos silogismos de colores
es cauteloso engaño del sentido;

éste, en quien la lisonja ha pretendido
excusar de los años los horrores
y, venciendo del tiempo los rigores,
triunfar de la vejez y del olvido,

es un vano artificio del cuidado,
es una flor al viento delicada,
es un resguardo inútil para el hado;

This,[1] that you see, polycromed deception
that, vaunting exquisite artifice,
in deceptive syllogisms of color
equivocates the sensed perception;

this, where flattery has attempted
to ignore the ravages of years
and, overcoming of time the rigor,
to triumph over age and oblivion,

is but artifice vain and counterfeit,
frail bloom to the harsh wind exposed,
'tis a futile protection against fate;

---

[1] the portrait of herself.

es una necia diligencia errada,
es un afán caduco y, bien mirado,
es cadáver, es polvo, es sombra, es nada.

it is a mindless, aberrant pursuit,
failing obsession and, correctly viewed,
it is a corpse, a shadow, dust, a very nothing.

The Legend of Don Juan: Tirso de Molina
The most justly famous of all of the literary works of
Spain's golden age is Cervantes' *Don Quixote*, published in 1605. The adventures of the country gentleman who tries to impose an outmoded code of chivalry
on the modern world play with the baroque themes of
reality and illusion and have delighted millions of readers. But it is with another *don* (a Spanish form of address denoting a high social status), another type of baroque figure who has had a lasting impact on European
culture, that we will concern ourselves here.

The original Don Juan Tenorio may or may not have
been a real person but was certainly a figure in Andalusian legend and oral literature when Tirso de Molina
(1571?–1648) composed the first literary work about
him, *El burlador de Sevilla y su convidado de piedra*
(*The Trickster of Seville and His Guest of Stone*),
around 1630. Tirso's Don Juan is a spoiled child of privilege, an overweening young aristocrat who, confident
in his social status, consciously sets out to break all
rules of conduct, divine as well as human, to gratify his
insatiable desire to seduce women. It is not love, and
not even lust, that prompts him so much as the game
itself, the desire for conquest. Don Juan replaces the
courtly adoration of the lady with a cynical and mocking belief in the fallibility of woman. He shows cavalier
disregard for polity and morality, trusting to a distant
day of reckoning as well as to God's infinite and all-
encompassing grace. Catholic Spain, however, believed
not in predestination but in man's proving himself
worthy of salvation through the exercise of free will.
Don Juan fails the test. His life is cut short and he is
therefore condemned to eternal damnation. In his own
way, Don Juan thus became one of the most compelling symbols of this period of despair as well as of the
intense sensory and religious experience that was the
Spanish baroque. The following English version of Tirso's play, by Roy Campbell, has been slightly abridged.

TIRSO DE MOLINA

*The Trickster of Seville and
His Guest of Stone*

DRAMATIS PERSONAE

DON DIEGO TENORIO
DON JUAN TENORIO, *his son*
CATALINÓN, *Don Juan's lackey*
THE KING OF NAPLES
DUKE OCTAVIO
DON PEDRO TENORIO, *Don Juan's uncle and Spanish Ambassa-
    dor in Naples*
THE MARQUIS OF LA MOTA
DON GONZALO DE ULLOA, *father of Doña Ana*
THE KING OF CASTILE [Alfonso XI, 1312–1350]

DOÑA ANA	BATRICIO
DUCHESS ISABEL	GASENO
THISBE	AMINTA *farmfolk*
ANFRISO	BELISA
CORIDÓN *fisherfolk*	RIPIO
BELISA	FABIO *servants*

Servants, guards, musicians, etc.

The scene is laid in Naples, Tarragona, Seville, and Dos
Hermanas. The time is the fourteenth century but not
consistently so.

ACT I

A room in the palace of the KING OF NAPLES

[*Enter* DON JUAN, *with muffled face, and* ISABEL.]

ISABEL Here, Duke Octavio, here's a safe way
    through.
DON JUAN Once more, dear Duchess, let me swear my
    troth!
ISABEL Then may I glory in each promise, oath,
    Flattery, gift, and wish—when they come true!
DON JUAN You shall, my love.
ISABEL Wait while I fetch a light.   5
DON JUAN Why?
ISABEL To convince my soul of this delight.
DON JUAN I'll crush the lamp in pieces if you do!
ISABEL Heavens above, what man are you? For shame!

DON JUAN   Who, I? I am a man without a name.

ISABEL   You're not the duke?

DON JUAN   No.

ISABEL   Help! the palace guard!   10

DON JUAN   Come, Duchess, give your hand. Don't
   shout so hard!

ISABEL   Let go, you beast! I'll make the palace ring.
   Help, soldiers, guards, and servants of the king!

[Enter the KING OF NAPLES with a lighted candle in a
candlestick.]

KING OF NAPLES   Who's there?

ISABEL   [Aside] The king, alas!

DON JUAN   Why, can't you see—
   A man here with a woman? Her and me.   15

KING OF NAPLES   [Aside] Prudence in this would seem
   the better plan.

[He runs back so as not to recognize ISABEL.]

[Aloud] Call out the palace guard! Arrest this man!

ISABEL   [Covering her face] Oh, my lost honour!

[Enter DON PEDRO TENORIO, ambassador of Spain, and
guards.]

DON PEDRO   From the king's rooms, cries
   And shouting? Sire, from what did this arise?

KING OF NAPLES   Don Pedro, you take charge of this
   arrest.   20
   Be shrewd and yet be prudent in your quest.
   Seize and identify this muffled pair
   In secret. Harm may come of this affair.
   But if it proves as it appears to me,   24
   The scandal will be less, the less I see.   [Exit.]

DON PEDRO   Seize him at once!

DON JUAN   Come, which of you will dare?
   I'm due to lose my life and much I care!
   But I shall sell it dear and some will pay!

DON PEDRO   Kill him at once!

DON JUAN   Now, don't be led astray.
   I'm resolute to die. For not in vain   30
   Am I a noble cavalier of Spain
   And of her embassy. That being known,
   Each one of you must fight with me alone:
   Such is the law.

DON PEDRO   Go, all of you, in there;
   And take the woman. Leave him to my care.   35

[The guards take ISABEL into the next room.]

DON PEDRO   And now that we two are alone at length
   Let's test this vaunted valour and this strength.

DON JUAN   Although, dear uncle, I've enough of both,
   To use them on yourself I'm something loth.

DON PEDRO   Say who you are!

DON JUAN   [Unmasking himself] I shall. Your nephew,
   sir.   40

DON PEDRO   [Aside] My heart! I fear some treason is
   astir.
[Aloud, to DON JUAN.] What's this you've done, base
   enemy? How is it
   That in this guise you come to such a visit?
   Tell me at once, since I must kill you here.
   Quick! Out with it at once! And be sincere!   45

DON JUAN   My uncle and my lord, I'm still a lad,
   As you were once. Such youthful loves you had.
   Then don't blame me that I too feel for beauty.
   But since you bid me tell it as a duty:
   In this disguise I cheated Isabel   50
   (Who took me for another man) and, well,
   Enjoyed her—

DON PEDRO   How could you so?
   If you can lower your voice, sir, let me know.

DON JUAN   [In a lower voice] Pretending I was Duke
   Octavio.

DON PEDRO   What? Say no more! Enough!
[Aside] If the king learns   55
   The truth, I'm lost. Oh, by what twists and turns
   Can I escape so dangerous a maze?
[Aloud] Say, villain, was it not enough to raise,
   With treachery and violence, such shame,
   And with another great and noble dame   60

---

14. *King of Naples*: certainly not a historical figure. Tirso is
vague about his backgrounds and his "historical" references are
fanciful.

20. *this arrest*: another example of Tirso's vagueness about titles
and functions: it is an odd notion that a king should order the
ambassador from another country to arrest one of his own subjects. At the time the play was written, Naples was a Spanish
possession, so that a Spanish ambassador would have been a figure of considerable authority in Naples. More importantly, the
scene permits an immediate identification of Don Juan within a
social setting and a system of courtly values.

Back home in Spain but you repeat the crime,
With one that is of princely rank this time,
In the king's palace? May God punish you!
Your father from Castile had shipped you through
Safely to Naples' hospitable strand,   65
Who might have hoped for better at your hand
Than in return have such shame heaped upon her—
The greatest of her ladies to dishonour!
But here we're wasting time with this delay.
Think what to do and how to get away.   70

DON JUAN   Pardon for this offence I can't implore.
It would be insincere and, what is more,
Unmanly. My blood's yours—for you to take.
Come, let it out, and let me pay my stake!
Here at your feet, my uncle and my lord,   75
I offer you my lifeblood and my sword.

DON PEDRO   Curse you! Get up and fight! Prove you're
a man!
This meek humility has spoilt my plan.
To slaughter in cold blood I never would.
Would you dare jump that balcony? You could?   80

DON JUAN   Your favour gives me wings. I surely can.

DON PEDRO   Then down you go! Seek hiding in Milan
Or Sicily!

DON JUAN   Why, soon enough!

DON PEDRO   You swear?

DON JUAN   Oh, surely!

DON PEDRO   You'll be hearing from me there
The consequences of this sad affair.   85

DON JUAN   A pleasant one for me, you must consent.
Though I may be to blame, I'm well content.

DON PEDRO   You're led astray by youth. Quick, jump
the railing!

DON JUAN   And now for Spain how happily I'm[Exit.]
sailing!

[Enter KING OF NAPLES.]

DON PEDRO   I tried to execute your orders, sire,   90
As well as your strict justice would require.
The man . . .

KING OF NAPLES   Is dead?

DON PEDRO   No, he escaped the sword
And the fierce thrusts of it.

KING OF NAPLES   How?

DON PEDRO   Thus, my lord.
You'd hardly told your orders, when, without
More said, he gripped his sword and wheeled   95
about,
Winding his cape around his arm, and so,
Ready to deal the soldiers blow for blow
And seeing death too near for hope of pardon,
Leaped desperately down into the garden
Over this balcony. Followed by all
They found him agonizing from his fall,
Contorted like a dying snake. But, when
They shouted "Kill him!" turning on the men
With such heroic swiftness he upstarted
As left me in confusion; and departed.   105
Isabel, whom I name to your surprise,
Says it was Duke Octavio in disguise
Who by this treachery enjoyed her.

KING OF NAPLES   What?

DON PEDRO   I say what she confessed upon the spot.

KING OF NAPLES   Poor Honour! If by you our value
stands   110
Why are you always placed in women's hands
Who are all fickleness and lightness?
[Calls.] Here!

[Enter a servant, and, after, ISABEL with guards.]

Bring me the woman now! Let her appear!

DON PEDRO   The guards are bringing her already, sire.

ISABEL   [Aside] How shall I dare to face the king?

KING OF NAPLES   Retire,   115
And see the doors are guarded.

[Servant and guards retire.]

Woman, say,
What force of fate, what angry planet, pray,
Makes you defile my palace and my board
With your lascivious beauty?

ISABEL   Oh, my lord—   119

KING OF NAPLES   Be silent! For your tongue can never
cleanse
Or gild the glaring fact of your offence.
Was it the Duke Octavio?

ISABEL   My lord—

82–83 *Milan . . . Sicily*: used at random; both the Milan region
and Sicily were under Spanish rule in Tirso's time.

KING OF NAPLES   Can nothing cope with Love—guards
    within call,
  Locks, bolts, and bars, and battlemented wall—
  That he, a babe, can penetrate all these?   125
  Don Pedro, on this very instant, seize
  That woman! Place her prisoner in some tower!
  Arrest the duke as well. Once in my power
  I'll have him make amends for this disgrace.
ISABEL   My lord, but once upon me turn your   130
  face!
KING OF NAPLES   For your offences when my back was
  turned,
  By the same back you now are justly spurned.
DON PEDRO   Come, Duchess.
ISABEL   [Aside] Though I know I am to blame
  Beyond excuse, it will decrease the shame   134
  If Duke Octavio's forced to save my name.[Exeunt.]

[Don Pedro comes to Don Octavio to warn him that the
king intends to arrest him for the seduction of Isabel.
Shocked and dismayed by the certainty that Isabel has
been unfaithful to him, Octavio decides to flee to
Spain. The scene then changes to a seashore near Tarragona, in Spain, where a fishermaid named Thisbe
sings of her happiness and her freedom from love. Don
Juan and his servant Catalinón, shipwrecked, come to
her shore, and she takes care of them. The scene then
switches to Seville, where the king of Castile informs
Don Gonzalo that he wishes to marry Gonzalo's
daughter Doña Ana, to a young Sevillian named Don
Juan Tenorio. The scene then returns to Tarragona.]

Seashore near Tarragona

  [*Enter* DON JUAN *and* CATALINÓN.]

DON JUAN   Now go and get those horses ready
  Since they are stabled close at hand.   720
CATALINÓN   Although I'm only just your servant
  Catalinón, please understand,
  Of decencies I am observant.
  People don't say before my nose
  Nor even yet behind my back: 725
  "Catalinón is one of those . . . "

_____

125. *a babe:* a mythogical cupid.
721. *Catalinón*, according to some scholars, may have meant
"cowardly" in vulgar speech.

  Bad names don't fit me. That's a fact.
DON JUAN   While these gay fishermen are spending
  The hours in revel, fix the horses!
  Galloping hoofs, when danger's pending,   730
  Have always been my best recourses.
CATALINÓN   But surely, sir, you won't abuse her,
  Who saved your life?
DON JUAN   As a seducer
  You've always known me. Why, then, ask me
  And with my own true nature task me?   735
  Not only that: her hut I'll fire
  To daze their minds while we retire.
CATALINÓN   Too well I know you are the scourge
  Of womankind.
DON JUAN   I'm on the verge
  Of dying for her: she's so good.   740
CATALINÓN   How generously you repay
  Your entertainment!
DON JUAN   Understood!
  Aeneas paid in the same way
  The Queen of Carthage, you poor dolt!
CATALINÓN   The way you tempt the thunderbolt!   745
  Those who cheat women with base sham
  In the long run their crime will damn
  After they're dead. You'll find out when!
DON JUAN   Well on the credit side I am
  If you extend my debt till then   750
  You'll wait till death to punish me.
CATALINÓN   Follow your bent. I'd sooner be
  Catalinón than you in what
  Pertains to cheating women. See!
  The poor unhappy soul draws near.   755
DON JUAN   Saddle those horses, do you hear?
  And get them ready, now, for dodging.
CATALINÓN   Poor trustful creature, oh, how dear
  We've paid you for our board and lodging   [*Exit.*]

  [*Enter* THISBE.]

THISBE   When I am not with you I seem without   760
  Myself.
DON JUAN   Such a pretence I beg to doubt.
THISBE   Why so?
DON JUAN   If you loved me, you'd ease my soul.
THISBE   I'm yours.
DON JUAN   If you were truly mine heart-whole,
  How could you kill me thus and make me wait?

THISBE   It is love's punishment at last I've found   765
In you, and that's what makes me hesitate.

DON JUAN   If, my beloved, I live solely in you
And ever so to serve you will continue
And give my life for you, why do you tarry
Since I shall be your husband? Yes, we'll marry!   770

THISBE   Our birth is too unequal.

DON JUAN   Love is king
And under him he matches everything:
Silk with sackcloth, lace with corduroy.

THISBE   I almost could believe you in my joy . . .
If men were not such cheats.   775

DON JUAN   With your least wish
You trawl me in your tresses like a fish.

THISBE   And I bow down beneath the hand and word
Of husband.

DON JUAN   Here I swear, O peerless eyes!
Where he who looks within them swoons and dies,
To be your husband.

THISBE   Darling, save your breath   780
But, oh, remember God exists—and death.

DON JUAN   [Aside] Yes, on the credit side I seem to be
If it's till death you'll keep on trusting me!
[Aloud] While God gives life, I'll be a slave to you,
And here's my hand and word to prove it's true.   785

THISBE   Now to repay you I shall not be coy.

DON JUAN   I cannot rest within myself for joy.

THISBE   Come, in my cabin love has built his nest
And there forever we shall be at rest.
Come in between these reeds, my love, and   790
hide.

DON JUAN   But how on earth am I to get inside?

THISBE   I'll show you.

DON JUAN   With your glory, dearest bride,
You've lit my soul.

THISBE   May that compel you, love,
To keep your word. If not, may God above
Chastise you.

DON JUAN   [Aside] Well in credit I must be   795
If not till death my reckoning: lucky me!   [Exeunt.]

[Thisbe sees her cabin burning and cries: "My poor hut
seems another Troy / Since love, eternally at war, For
want of cities to destroy / Must fire the cabins of the
poor." In despair, she almost throws herself into the
sea but is saved by the fisherfolk. This ends Act I.]

ACT II

The Alcazar at Seville

[*Enter* KING OF CASTILE *and* DON DIEGO TENORIO.]

KING OF CASTILE   What's that you say?

DON DIEGO   My lord, I know it's true.
This letter's just arrived here from my brother,
Your own ambassador. They caught him with
A noble beauty in the king's own quarters.

KING OF CASTILE   What sort of lady?

DON DIEGO   The Duchess Isabel.   5

KING OF CASTILE   But what temerity! Where is he
now?

DON DIEGO   From you my liege I can't disguise the
truth:
He's just arrived in Seville with one servant.

KING OF CASTILE   You know, Tenorio, I esteem you
highly.
I'll get particulars from the King of Naples   10
And then we'll match the boy with Isabel
Relieving Duke Octavio of his woes,
Who suffers innocently. But, on this instant,
Exile Don Juan from the town.

DON DIEGO   My lord,
Where to?

KING OF CASTILE   He must leave Seville for Lebrija   15
Tonight, at once; and let him thank your merit
His sentence is so light. Meanwhile determine
What can be told Don Gonzalo de Ulloa.
For now the thought of marriage with his daughter
Is quite beyond the question.

DON DIEGO   Well, my liege,   20
I hope that your commands will be to honour
The lady in some other way as worthy
The child of such a father.

KING OF CASTILE   Here's a plan
That will absolve me from Gonzalo's anger:
I'll make him major-domo of the palace.   25

[*Enter a servant; afterwards,* OCTAVIO.]

_____

15. *Lebrija:* a town in the province of Seville.
18. *Don Gonzalo de Ulloa:* the commander, or Comendador
Mayor, of the military-religious Order of Calatrava (see lines
44-45).

SERVANT   A noble, sire, has just come from abroad.
   He says he is the Duke Octavio.
KING OF CASTILE   The Duke Octavio?
SERVANT   Yes, my lord.
KING OF CASTILE   Let him enter.
OCTAVIO   A miserable pilgrim and an exile
   Offers himself, great monarch, at your feet.   30
   Forgetting all the hardships of his journey
   In your great presence.
KING OF CASTILE   Duke Octavio!
OCTAVIO   I have come fleeing from the fierce pursuit
   Of a demented woman, the result
   Of the unconscious fault of some philanderer—   35
   For which I have to seek your royal feet.
KING OF CASTILE   Already, Duke, I know your inno-
      cence.
   I've written to the king my vassal, also
   Restoring your estate, and any damage
   You might have suffered owing to your absence.   40
   I'll marry you in Seville (if you like
   And she agrees) to one beside whose beauty
   Isabel's would seem ugly, even were she
   An angel. Don Gonzalo of Ulloa,
   The grand commander of Calatrava   45
   Whom pagan Moors praise highly in their terror
   (For always cowards are flatterers and praisers)
   Has a young daughter whose outstanding virtue's
   A dowry in itself (I count it second
   To beauty)—and a living marvel too!   50
   She is the sun, the star of all Castile
   And it is she I wish to be your wife.
OCTAVIO   The very undertaking of this voyage
   Was worth while, sire, for this one thing alone
   That I should know and do what gives you   55
      pleasure.
KING OF CASTILE   [To DON DIEGO]
   See that the duke is entertained and lodged
   Down to his least requirement.
OCTAVIO   O my lord,
   The man who trusts in you wins every prize.
   You're first of the Alfonsos, though eleventh!

[Exeunt KING OF CASTILE and DON DIEGO. Enter RIPIO.]

RIPIO   What's happened?
OCTAVIO   All my toil's rewarded well.   60
   I told the king my wrongs. He honoured me.
   Caesar was with the Caesar: as you see
   I came, I saw, I conquered, and as well
   He's going to marry me from his own palace
   And make the King of Naples understand   65
   And so repeal the law by which I'm banned.
RIPIO   With real good reason do they call this king
   The benefactor of Castile. And so
   He's offered you a wife?
OCTAVIO   Yes, a friend, a wife
   And one from Seville. Seville breeds strong men   70
   And bold ones and breeds strapping women too.
   A dashing style within a veiling mantle
   Which covers a pure sun of dazzling beauty
   —Where do you see such things except in Seville?
   I am so happy, it was worth my troubles.   75

[Enter DON JUAN and CATALINÓN.]

CATALINÓN   [Aside to his master]
   Wait, sir, there is the injured duke,
   Isabel's Sagittarius—
   Rather, I'd say, her Capricorn.
DON JUAN   Pretend.
CATALINÓN   You flatter those you sell.
DON JUAN   I went from Naples in such haste   80
   Upon the summons of the king
   I had no time to say good-bye,
   Octavio.
OCTAVIO   For such a thing
   I hold you blameless.
[Aside] So we two
   Today have met in Seville.
DON JUAN   Who   85
   Would think I would see you in Seville
   Where I would serve you if I may
   At your commands in every way?

62–63. *Caesar . . . I conquered:* Octavio refers to himself as a
"Caesar" and he uses Caesar's famous announcement of his victory over Pharnaces at Zela in Asia Minor in 47 B.C.: *veni, vidi,
vici.*
78. *Capricorn:* In this elaborate allusion, Isabel stands to Octavio
as Heracles to Sagittarius, who is also the ninth sign of the zodiac
and as such is followed by Capricorn. Catalinón drags the latter in
because of the connotation of horns—cuckoldom.

---

38. *my vassal:* the king of Naples.

You leave good things behind, for Naples
Is good, but only Seville's worth   90
Exchanging for so fine a city
Of all the cities on this earth.

OCTAVIO   If you had told me that in Naples
Before I ever came this way
I would have laughed the thought to scorn   95
But now I credit what you say.
In fact you would have said much more:
Why such understatement, pray?
But who's that coming over there?

DON JUAN   The Marquis of la Mota! Now   100
I'll have to be discourteous . . .

OCTAVIO   If ever you should need my sword
I'm at your service, my good lord.

CATALINÓN   [Aside] And if he wants another dame,
Too, to dishonour in your name,   105
I suppose you're at his service just the same.

OCTAVIO   I'm very pleased with meeting you.

[Exeunt OCTAVIO and RIPIO. Enter the MARQUIS OF LA MOTA with servant.]

MARQUIS   All day I've been upon your track
But couldn't find you anywhere.
How strange you should be safely back   110
And your old friend be in despair
Of finding you!

DON JUAN   For heaven's sake,
That seems a lot of fuss to make.
What news in Seville?

MARQUIS   The whole court
Has changed.

DON JUAN   What women? Any sport?   115

MARQUIS   Of course.

DON JUAN   Inés?

MARQUIS   She has retired
To Vejel.

DON JUAN   Oh, she's time-expired!
And Constance?

MARQUIS   She's in sorry plight—
Moulting—both hair and eyebrows too!
A Portuguese said she was *old*   120
And she thought he meant *pretty*.

DON JUAN   True!
Our word for "lovely to behold"
Is like the Portuguese for "old."
And Theodora?

MARQUIS   Why, this summer
She cured herself of the French ill   125
That seemed about to overcome her,
Sweating it out in streams, until
She is grown so tender and polite
She pulled a tooth for me and quite
Surrounded me with heaps of flowers.   130

DON JUAN   And what of Julia Candlelight?
Does she still sell herself for trout?

MARQUIS   For stale salt cod, I have no doubt.

DON JUAN   How's Catarranas, the old slum?

MARQUIS   Why, crawling with the same old   135
scum!

DON JUAN   Are those two sisters still on view?

MARQUIS   Yes, and that monkey of Tolú
The Celestina, their old dame,
Who read them scriptures on the game.

DON JUAN   Oh, her! Beelzebub's old sow!   140
How is the elder of them now?

MARQUIS   She's spotless, and reformed at last,
And has a saint for whom to fast.

DON JUAN   A single lover, and no share?

MARQUIS   She's firm and faithful as she's fair.   145

DON JUAN   The other?

MARQUIS   Leads a livelier dance
And never yet would miss her chance.

DON JUAN   What jokes or scandals have you played?
What harlots have you left unpaid?

MARQUIS   De Esquival and I both made   150
A cruel fraud last night. Tonight
We've got a better hoax in sight.

DON JUAN   I'll come with you. Tell me: what's
brewing

---

117. *Vejel:* the original Spanish permits a pun on *vejez,* "old age."

123. *"old":* a wordplay on the Portuguese *velha* and the Spanish *vieja.*

125. *the French ill:* syphilis.

137. *Tolú:* a town in Colombia, in a region known for its monkeys.

138. *The Celestina:* named after a procuress, a famous character in Fernando de Rojas' *Comedia de Calisto y Melibea,* popularly known as *La Celestina.*

143. *a saint . . . fast:* one lover, who does not help her.

I' the way of courting, suing, wooing?
For I already, sir, have got   155
My nest eggs hatching out a plot.
MARQUIS   Speak not of territory where
My heart is buried deep in care!
DON JUAN   How so?
MARQUIS   I love one that is not
Attainable.
DON JUAN   The girl, does she   160
Reject you?
MARQUIS   No, she favours me
And loves me.
DON JUAN   Who is it?
MARQUIS   My cousin,
Ana, who has arrived here newly.
DON JUAN   Where has she been?
MARQUIS   In Lisbon with
The embassy.
DON JUAN   Good-looking?
MARQUIS   Truly   165
She's Nature's masterpiece. In her
Nature has strained her powers.
DON JUAN   Such beauty?
By God, I'd like to see her!
MARQUIS   Yes,
You'll see in her the grestest beauty
The king has seen in all his state.   170
DON JUAN   Get married then, since it's your fate.
MARQUIS   The king's betrothed her to some other.
DON JUAN   But she accepts it that you love her?
MARQUIS   Yes, and she writes me daily too.
CATALINÓN   [Aside] Keep your mouth shut or you'll be
sorry: 175
Spain's greatest trickster marks his quarry.
DON JUAN   Who, then, more satisfied than you?
MARQUIS   I've come to see what resolution
Is taken on the lady's fate.
DON JUAN   Yes, go and see, and here I'll wait   180
For your return.
MARQUIS   I'll come back soon.
CATALINÓN   [To the servant] Mister Round or Mister
Square,
Good-bye.
SERVANT   Good-bye.   [Exeunt MARQUIS and servant.]
DON JUAN   [To CATALINÓN] Now we're alone.
Shadow the marquis, keep his track,

He went into the palace there.   185
She where he goes and then come back.

[Exit CATALINÓN. A servant woman at a barred window
speaks to DON JUAN.]

WOMAN   Who am I speaking to?
DON JUAN   Who called me?
WOMAN   Now, sir.
Seeing you are a good friend of the marquis,
Prudent and courteous, take this note, and give it
Into the marquis' hands, for it contains   190
The happiness and honour of a lady.
DON JUAN   As I'm a gentleman and his good friend
I swear to give it to him.
WOMAN   Stranger, thanks.
Good-bye.   [The servant woman disappears.]
DON JUAN   The voice has gone and I'm alone.
Does it not seem like magic, what has passed   195
This minute? That this letter should arrive
As if the wind were carrier to my thoughts
And luck my letter-box? Why, this must be
A letter to the marquis from the lady
His speeches so endeared to me. In Seville   200
I'm called the Trickster; and my greatest
pleasure
Is to trick women, leaving them dishonoured.
As soon as I have left this little square
I'll open this and read it. Idle caution!
It makes me want to laugh outright. The   205
paper's
Open already. And it's plain it's hers,
For there's her signature, and here it says:
"My unkind father secretly has forced me
To marry. I cannot resist. I doubt
If I can go on living, since it's death   210
That he has given me. If you respect
My will and my dear love of you, then show it
This once. For, just to see how I adore you,
Come to my door this evening at eleven
And you will find me waiting, and it open,   215
So to enjoy the very crown of love.
Wear for a signal (that the maids may know it
And let you in) a cape of crimson colour.
My love, I trust in you; farewell; your own
Unhappy love." Why, it's as good as done!   220
Oh, I could roar with laughter! I'll enjoy her

By the same trick that limed the other one,
Isabel, back in Naples.

[*Enter* CATALINÓN.]

CATALINÓN   Here's the marquis
Returning now.

DON JUAN   Tonight the two of us
Have lots to do.

CATALINÓN   You've some new swindle!   225

DON JUAN   This one's a wonder!

CATALINÓN   Well, I disapprove.
You claim that we'll escape being caught out
But those who live by cheating must be cheated
In the long run.

DON JUAN   You've turned a bloody preacher,
Have you, you cheeky boor?

CATALINÓN   Right makes men brave!   230

DON JUAN   Yes, and fear makes men cowards, just like
you.
You earn by serving. If you'd always earn,
Act always on the spot. He who does most
Wins most.

CATALINÓN   And those who say and do the most
Collide with things the most and come to grief. 235

DON JUAN   But now I'm warning you! So, for the last
Time, listen for I shan't warn you again!

CATALINÓN   Well, yes, from now, whatever you com-
mand
I'll do as if you were flanked on either side
By a tiger and an elephant, Don Juan!   240

DON JUAN   Hark! here's the marquis.

CATALINÓN   Must he be the victim?

[*Enter* MARQUIS OF LA MOTA.]

DON JUAN   Out of this casement, Marquis, someone
gave me
A very courteous message for yourself.
I could not see who gave it but the voice
Was of a woman, and she said at twelve   245
You are to go in secret to the door,
Which at that hour will be open to you,
And you must wear a cape of crimson colour
So that the maids will know you.

MARQUIS   What?

DON JUAN   This message
Was passed me at the window here without   250
My seeing who it was who whispered it.

MARQUIS   This message has restored my life, dear
friend:
May God reward you for it without end!

DON JUAN   I haven't got your cousin here inside
So why should your embraces be applied   255
To one so worthless?

MARQUIS   You delight me so
That I am quite outside myself, I know.
O sun, go down!

DON JUAN   It slopes toward its setting.

MARQUIS   Come, friends. Come, night. My reason I'm
forgetting
I'm mad with joy.

DON JUAN   One sees that quite all right.   260
You'll reach the peak at twelve o'clock tonight.

MARQUIS   Crown of my very soul! My heart's delight
Who are to crown my loving faith tonight!

CATALINÓN   [*Aside*] Dear Christ! I would not even bet
a dozen
Bad halfpennies on that beloved cousin.   265

[*Exit the* MARQUIS *and enter* DON DIEGO.]

DON DIEGO   Don Juan!

CATALINÓN   Your father calls you.

DON JUAN   At your orders.

DON DIEGO   I'd like to see you far better behaved,
Good-natured, with a better reputation.
Can it be possible you wish to kill me
With your behaviour?

DON JUAN   Why in such a state?   270

DON DIEGO   For your behaviour and your madness
now
The king has bade me ban you from the city,
For he is justly angered by a crime
Which, though you hid it from me, *he* has heard of
In Seville here—a crime so grave and evil   275
I scarcely dare to name it. Make a cuckold
Of your best friend and in the royal palace!
May God reward you as your sins deserve:
For though it now appear that God above
Puts up with you, consenting to your crimes,   280
The punishment is certain—and how fearful
For those who've taken His great name in vain!
His justice is tremendous after death.

DON JUAN   What, after death? How long you give me
credit!

A long, long time, before I need repentance!   285

DON DIEGO   It will seem short when you receive your
    sentence.

DON JUAN   And now what would His Highness with
    myself?
    Will it be for a long, long time as well?

DON DIEGO   Until you have repaired the august insult
    Done to the Duke Octavio, and appeased   290
    The scandals you have caused with Isabel,
    You have to live in exile in Lebrija.
    The king requires you go there instantly.
    The sentence is too slight for such a crime.

CATALINÓN   [Aside] And if he also knew about the
    case   295
    Of that poor fishergirl the good old man
    Would be far angrier.

DON DIEGO   Since no punishment,
    Nor anything I say or do, affects you,
    Your chastisement I here confide to God.   [Exit.]

CATALINÓN   The dear old man was overcome.   300

DON JUAN   Tears are well suited to old age.
    Well now, the night is coming down.
    We'll seek the marquis. Come, my page.

CATALINÓN   And now you will enjoy his bride.

DON JUAN   Which promises to be great sport.   305

CATALINÓN   Pray God that we come out of it alive!

DON JUAN   Now, now!

CATALINÓN   I think the best
    Way to describe you, sir, would be
    As a locust to whom girls are grass,
    And so by public proclamation   310
    Whenever you're about to arrive
    Towns should be warned: "Here comes the plague
    Of women in a single man
    Who is their cheater and betrayer,
    The greatest trickster in all Spain."   315

DON JUAN   You've given me a charming name.

[It is night time. Enter the MARQUIS with musicians
who move up and down the stage.]

MUSICIANS   [Singing]
    To him who waits a promised pleasure
    Delay is like despair to measure.

MARQUIS   May never break of day destroy
    The night in which I take my joy.   320

DON JUAN   What's this?

CATALINÓN   Why, music.

MARQUIS   [Aside] It appears
    The poet speaks to me.
    [Aloud] Who's there?

DON JUAN   Friend!

MARQUIS   It's Don Juan?

DON JUAN   The marquis, you?

MARQUIS   Who other would it be?

DON JUAN   I knew
    You by the coloured cape you wear.   325

MARQUIS   [To the musicians] Sing, since Don Juan's
    come here too.

MUSICIANS   [Singing]
    To him who waits a promised pleasure
    Delay is like despair to measure.

DON JUAN   Whose house is that you gaze at so?

MARQUIS   Why, Don Gonzalo's.

DON JUAN   Where shall we go?   330

MARQUIS   To Lisbon.

DON JUAN   How,
    Being in Seville?

MARQUIS   Don't you know?
    And do you wonder that the worst
    Of Portugal live on the first
    And best of Spain, right here and now?   335

DON JUAN   Where do they live?

MARQUIS   Why, in the street
    Called "Of the Serpent." There one sees
    Adam, become a Portuguese,
    Wooing a thousand Eves to eat
    And take a bite out of their pockets.   340
    And, sure, it's quite a hole they make
    With all those big doubloons and ducats.

DON JUAN   You run along there while you can.
    I have to play a scurvy joke.

MARQUIS   I'm being shadowed by a man   345
    Some pimp or bravo . . .

DON JUAN   Leave him to me.
    I shan't let him escape, you'll see.

MARQUIS   Around your arm, then, wrap this cloak
    The better so to deal your stroke.

DON JUAN   A good idea; then come and show   350
    The house to which I have to go.

_____

337. "Of the Serpent": Apparently, Portuguese courtesans in
Seville lived in a street by that name.

MARQUIS   Now, while you carry out the plan,
Alter your voice and talk as though
You were indeed some other man.
D'you see that "jealousy"?

DON JUAN   I do.   355

MARQUIS   Then go to it and whisper there:
"Beatrice." Then pass right through.

DON JUAN   What sort of woman?

MARQUIS   Soft and pink.

CATALINÓN   Some water-cooling jar, I think.

MARQUIS   I'll wait for you at Gradas Stair.   360

DON JUAN   Till then, dear Marquis! I'll be there.

CATALINÓN   Now whither bound?

DON JUAN   Shut up, you bear!
I go to where my jest is played.

CATALINÓN   Nothing escapes you unbetrayed.

DON JUAN   I adore cheating.

CATALINÓN   Now to the bull!   365
Pass me your cape.

DON JUAN   Not so, the fool
Beast has passed his cape to me.

MUSICIANS   The trick appeals to such as we.

MARQUIS   That is succeeding by mistake.

MUSICIANS   And the whole world doth errors   370
make.

MUSICIANS   [Singing]
When one awaits a promised pleasure
Delay is like despair to measure.

Room in the House of DON GONZALO

[DOÑA ANA *within, with* DON JUAN *and* CATALINÓN.]

DOÑA ANA   [*Within*] False friend, you're not the marquis! You tricked me!

DON JUAN   I tell you who I am.

DOÑA ANA   [*Within*] False foe, you lie!

[*Enter* DON GONZALO *with drawn sword.*]

DON GONZALO   I hear my daughter Doña Ana's   375
voice.

DOÑA ANA   [*Within*] Will nobody kill this false traitor
here,
The murderer of my honour?

DON GONZALO   Can such effrontery exist? She said:
"My honour murdered." Then alas for me!
Her giddy tongue is like a bell to clamour   380

Our sad disgrace to all.

DOÑA ANA   [*Within*] Kill him!

[DON JUAN *and* CATALINÓN *enter with drawn swords.*]

DON JUAN   Who's this?

DON GONZALO   The closed and fallen barbican is here
Of the strong fortress of my honour, which,
Base traitor, you have falsely undermined,
Though there my life was warden.

DON JUAN   Let me pass!   385

DON GONZALO   Pass? You shall pass the point of this
bare sword.

DON JUAN   You'll die for this.

DON GONZALO   That is no matter.

DON JUAN   Look, I'll have to kill you.

DON GONZALO   Die yourself, base traitor.

DON JUAN   [*Thrusting with sword*] This is the way I die.

CATALINÓN   [*Aside*] If I get free
Then no more feasts and scurvy tricks for me!   390

DON GONZALO   He's given me my death.

DON JUAN   You took your life
By being rash.

DON GONZALO   What use was it to me?

DON JUAN   Come, let us run.
[*Exeunt* DON JUAN *and* CATALINÓN.]

DON GONZALO   My frozen blood you've swelled
With fury. I am dead. I can expect
No better thing. My fury will pursue you.   395
You are a traitor, and a traitor is
A traitor, being first of all a coward.

[*He dies. Servants enter and carry off the corpse. Enter*
MARQUIS OF LA MOTA *and musicians.*]

MARQUIS   Now midnight will be striking soon:
Don Juan's surely very late.
How hard a thing it is—to wait.   400

[*Re-enter* DON JUAN *and* CATALINÓN.]

DON JUAN   Is that the marquis?

MARQUIS   You're Don Juan?

DON JUAN   I am. Here, take your cape.

MARQUIS   Your pranks . . .

382–385. *The closed . . . warden:* Notice the appropriately "baroque" language of Don Gonzalo in expounding matters of life,
death, honor.

DON JUAN   Have had a most funereal end
In death.
CATALINÓN   Oh, flee from the dead man!
MARQUIS   Tell me, whom did you trick, my   405
friend?
CATALINÓN   [Aside] You are the latest victim, thanks
To him.
DON JUAN   This prank has cost most dear.
MARQUIS   Don Juan, the whole debt I'll clear . . .
Because the girl will be complaining
Of me . . .
DON JUAN   The stroke of twelve draws near.   410
MARQUIS   May never break of day destroy
The night in which I take my joy!
DON JUAN   Farewell then, Marquis!
CATALINÓN   What a treat
Awaits the wretch!
DON JUAN   Let's run!
CATALINÓN   My feet
Than wings of eagles feel more fleet.   415

[Exeunt except the MARQUIS OF MOTA and servants.]

MARQUIS   Now you can all go home. I'll go
Alone.
SERVANTS   God made the night for sleeping.

[Exeunt servants.]

VOICES   [Within] Was ever such a sight of woe?
Alas! How pitiless a blow!
MARQUIS   God shield me! I hear cries and   420
weeping
Resounding from the castle square.
At such an hour what could it be?
Ice freezes all my chest. I see
What seems another Troy aflare,
For torches now come wildly gleaming   425
With giant flames like comets streaming
And reeking from their pitchy hair,
A mighty horde of tarry hanks.
Fire seems to emulate the stars
Dividing into troops and ranks.   430
I'll go and find out . . .

[Enter DON DIEGO TENORIO and guards with torches.]

DON DIEGO   Who goes there?
MARQUIS   One who would know of this affair,
And why there's such a hue and cry.
DON DIEGO   [To the guards] Bind him!
MARQUIS   [Drawing his sword] What? Me? I'd sooner
die!
DON DIEGO   Give me your sword. The greatest   435
valour
Is speech without recourse to steel.
MARQUIS   And is it thus that you would deal
With me, the Marquis of la Mota?
DON DIEGO   Your sword! Whatever you may feel,
The king has ordered your arrest!   440
MARQUIS   Ye gods!

[Enter the KING OF CASTILE and his attendants.]

KING OF CASTILE   Through Spain from east to west
See that he can't escape. As well
In Italy (for who can tell
If he should get there?) start the quest.
DON DIEGO   He is here.
MARQUIS   Then, sire, I'm apprehended,   445
Truly, by your own orders. Why?
KING OF CASTILE   Take him, and have his head sus-
pended
Upon a rampart near the sky.
—Don't linger in my presence, sir.
MARQUIS   [Aside] The ecstasies of am'rous   450
passion
Always so light as they occur
Grow heavy after in this fashion.
"There's many a slip," once said the sage.
But why the king's revengeful rage?
[Aloud] I can't make out what crime I've done.   455
DON DIEGO   You know as well as anyone.
MARQUIS   Me?
DON DIEGO   Come!
MARQUIS   What strange confusion!
KING OF CASTILE   Try him
And cut his head off before day.
For the commander, don't deny him

---

424. *Troy aflare*: Trojan imagery is not infrequent in the play, perhaps because Don Juan was known as "the Hector of Seville."

453. *"There's . . . slip"*: " . . . between the cup and the lip." (The proverb is the same in Spanish.)

Solemnity and grave display   460
Such as men grant to royal or sacred
Persons. The funeral must be grand.
Statue and tomb of bronze and stone
With Gothic letters see them planned
Proclaiming vengeance is at hand.   465
And where has Dona Ana gone?

DON DIEGO   To sanctuary swift she ran
In the convent of Our Heavenly Queen.

KING OF CASTILE   This loss is grave, for such a man
Has Calatrava seldom seen.

[*The scene is in the country near Dos Hermanas, where a young betrothed couple, Batricio and Aminta, are preparing for their wedding feast. Told that a nobleman will attend his wedding feast, Batricio feels a sense of doom.*]

[*Enter* DON JUAN.]

DON JUAN   I heard by chance there was a marriage-feast
When I was passing by this village here   545
And so I've come to revel in it too
Being so lucky as to pass just then.

GASENO   Your Lordship comes to honour and ennoble
it.

BATRICIO   [*Aside*] And I, who am the host and master,
say,
Within me, that you come in evil hour.   550

GASENO   Won't you make room there for the cavalier!

DON JUAN   With your permission, I will take this
place.

[*Sits next to the bride.*]

BATRICIO   If you sit down before me, sir, you'll seem
The bridegroom.

DON JUAN   If I were, I could choose worse!

GASENO   He *is* the bridegroom.

DON JUAN   Oh, I beg your pardon   555
For my mistake.

CATALINÓN   [*Aside*] Oh, poor unhappy bridegroom!

DON JUAN   [*Aside to* CATALINÓN] He seems annoyed.

CATALINÓN   I'm quite aware of that
But if he has to serve you for a bull
What does it matter if he seems annoyed?
I would not give one horn-toss for his wife   560

Nor for his honour. Poor unhappy man
To fall into the hands of Lucifer!

DON JUAN   Can it be possible I am so lucky?
I'm almost feeling jealous of your husband.

AMINTA   You seem to flatter me.

BATRICIO   [*Aside*] Well is it said: 565
"A great one at a wedding brings bad luck."

GASENO   Come, let us eat and drink a while
So that your Lordship, while we dine,
May rest himself!

[DON JUAN *takes* AMINTA's *hand.*]

DON JUAN   Why hide your hand?

AMINTA   It's mine.

GASENO   Let's go.

BELISA   Strike up the song again!   570

DON JUAN   What do you make of it?

CATALINÓN   I fear a vile
Death at the hands of those same sturdy peasants.

DON JUAN   What lovely eyes and spotless hands—
They're burning me with flaming torches!

CATALINÓN   It's *you* will brand *her* with your   575
mark
Then put her out to winter-grazing.
Three little lambs, and this makes four.

DON JUAN   How all of them are staring at me!

BATRICIO   It is an evil-boding thing
A noble at my wedding.

GASENO   Sing!   580

BATRICIO   God! I feel as if I'm dying.

CATALINÓN   [*Aside*] They sing now, who will soon be
crying.

ACT III

[*Act III opens in the house of Gaseno, Aminta's father, in Dos Hermanas. In a soliloquy, Batricio speaks of his jealousy and of the injustices done by nobles. Then Don Juan enters and tells him (falsely) that he has already seduced his bride. Dismayed that "she's only proved a woman, after all," Batricio tells Don Juan that he has no further claims on Aminta. Don Juan plans to seduce Aminta by promising her and her father that he will marry her.*]

DON JUAN   Night spreads across the world. Silence is
black.

The Pleiades now tread the highest pole
'Mid starry clusters. Now I set my trap.
Love guides me to my joy—none can resist him.
I've got to reach her bed. Aminta!
AMINTA   Who
Calls for Aminta? Is it Batricio?   130

[*He is at her door. She comes out, as from bed.*]

DON JUAN   I'm not Batricio. No.
AMINTA   Then, who?
DON JUAN   Look slowly,
And you'll see who I am.
AMINTA   Why, sir, I'm lost.
With you outside my bedroom at these hours!
DON JUAN   Such are the hours that I am wont to keep.
AMINTA   Return, or I shall shout. Please don't   135
exceed
The courtesy you owe to my Batricio.
You'll find, in Dos Hermanas, there are Romans—
Emilias and Lucreces who avenge!
DON JUAN   Just hear two words and hide the blushing
scarlet
Of your fair cheeks deep down within your   140
heart!
AMINTA   Go, go! My husband's coming.
DON JUAN   I'm your husband.
So what have you to marvel at?
AMINTA   Since when?
DON JUAN   From now on, and forever, I am he!
AMINTA   But who arranged the marriage?
DON JUAN   My delight.
AMINTA   And who was it that married us?
DON JUAN   Your eyes.   145
AMINTA   By what authority?
DON JUAN   Why, that of sight!
AMINTA   But does Batricio know?
DON JUAN   Yes! He forgets you.
AMINTA   Has he forgotten me?
DON JUAN   Yes. I adore you.
AMINTA   How?
DON JUAN   Thus with all my heart I swoon before you.
AMINTA   Get out!
DON JUAN   How can I when you see I'm dying   150
With love for you alone?

AMINTA   What shameless lying!
DON JUAN   Aminta, listen and you'll know the truth,
Since women are the friends of truth. I am
A noble knight, the heir of the Tenorios,
The conquerors of Seville. And my father,   155
Next to the king, is honoured and esteemed
Beyond all men in court. Upon his lips
Hang life or death according to his word.
Travelling on my road, by merest chance,
I came and saw you. Love ordains these things   160
And guides them, so that even He, Himself,
Forgets that they were anything but chance.
I saw you, I adored you, I was kindled
So that I am determined now to wed you.
Even though the king forbid it, and my father   165
In anger and with threats tries to prevent it,
I have to be your husband. What's your answer!
AMINTA   I don't know what to say. Your so-called
"truths"
Are covered with deceitful rhetoric—
Because if I am married to Batricio   170
(As is well known) the fact is not annulled
Even if he deserts me.
DON JUAN   Non-consummation,
Either by malice or deceit, is reason
For an annulment.
AMINTA   In Batricio all
Was simple truth.
DON JUAN   Tush! Come, give me your hand,   175
And let's confirm our vows.
AMINTA   You're not deceiving?
DON JUAN   I'd be the one deceived.
AMINTA   Then swear before me
To carry out your promised word.
DON JUAN   I swear
By this white hand, a winter of pure snow.
AMINTA   Swear then, to God. Pray that he curse your
soul   180
If you should fail!
DON JUAN   If in my word and faith
I fail, I pray to God that by foul treason
I be murdered by a man!
[*Aside*] I mean a dead one.
For living man, may God forbid!

---

138. *Emilias and Lucreces:* Emilia are proverbial examples of virtue in Lucretia (who was raped by Tarquinius)

183. *a dead one:* tragic irony, if we consider that Don Juan *will* be killed by a dead man.

AMINTA   This promise
Has made me your own wife.
DON JUAN   My very soul   185
I offer you between my outstretched arms.
AMINTA   My life and soul are yours.
DON JUAN   Ah, my Aminta,
Tomorrow you will walk in silver buskins
Studded with tacks of gold from heel to toe.
Your alabaster throat will be imprisoned   190
In necklaces of diamonds and rubies,
And your white fingers, in their flashing rings,
Will seem transparent pearls.
AMINTA   From now to yours
My will bows down, and I am yours alone.
DON JUAN   [*Aside*] Little you know the Trickster of
Seville!   195

[*Near Tarragona we find Isabel, who meets Thisbe.
Finding that they have been wronged by the same
man, they decide to pursue vengeance together.*]

The cloister or nave of a church in Seville. In one of the
side chapels is the tomb of the commander Don Gonzalo
with a statue of the dead man.

[*Enter* DON JUAN *and* CATALINÓN.]

CATALINÓN   I tell you things are looking bad.
DON JUAN   How so?
CATALINÓN   First, that Octavio has got to know
That hoax in Italy. The marquis, too,
Knows that the message which he got from you
And which you said his cousin gave was faked. 305
Then Isabela's on the way: she's staked
A marriage claim, and also it is spoken . . .
DON JUAN   Here, hold your tongue! [*Hitting him*]
CATALINÓN   Look, master, you have broken
A molar in my mouth.
DON JUAN   Then hold your jaw.
Who told you all this nonsense?
CATALINÓN   Nonsense?
DON JUAN   Yes.   310
CATALINÓN   It's gospel truth!
DON JUAN   I don't care if it is.
And what if Duke Octavio tries to kill me—
Have I not hands as well? Where is our lodging?
CATALINÓN   Down in the darkest, hidden street.
DON JUAN   That's good

CATALINÓN   Here in this church, it's holy ground.
DON JUAN   Just so.   315
D'you think they'll kill me here in broad daylight?
And have you seen the groom from Dos Hermanas?
CATALINÓN   I saw him, too, looking both grim and
sad.
DON JUAN   For two whole weeks Aminta has not
known
How she's been tricked.
CATALINÓN   So thoroughly she's hoaxed   320
She goes about calling herself the countess!
DON JUAN   God, what a funny hoax!
CATALINÓN   Funny enough;
And one for which that girl must weep forever.

[*They both look at the sepulchre.*]

DON JUAN   Whose sepulchre is this?
CATALINÓN   Here Don Gonzalo
Lies buried.
DON JUAN   What? the same one I killed?   325
They've done him very nobly for a tomb.
CATALINÓN   This tomb was ordered by the king. What
says
That writing there?
DON JUAN   [*Reads*] HERE, TRUSTING IN THE LORD
FOR VENGEANCE ON A TRAITOR, THE MOST LOYAL
OF ALL THE KNIGHTS LIES BURIED. What a joke!   330
So you think you'll avenge yourself on me?

[*Pulling the statue's beard*]

So now you sprout a beard of solid stone,
Good gaffer?
CATALINÓN   There are beards that can't be plucked.
You watch yourself with beards that are too strong.
DON JUAN   [*Addressing the statue*]
Tonight I will await you at my inn   335
For supper. There we can arrange a duel
Although it will be difficult to fight;
A granite rapier must be stiff to handle.
CATALINÓN   Come, sir, it's getting dark. We'd better
go!
DON JUAN   [*To the statue*]
How long this vengeance seems to be in   340
coming

_____

315. *holy ground:* where Don Juan can escape arrest.

Especially if you are going to wreak it!
You mustn't be so motionless and sleepy!
And if you're willing still to wait till death,
Why, what a lot of chances you are wasting
That for so long a time you give me credit!   345

A room in an inn

[*Two servants of* DON JUAN *are laying the table.*]

FIRST SERVANT   We must prepare the room because
   Don Juan
   Dines here tonight.
SECOND SERVANT   The tables are prepared.
   If he's so late there's nothing one can do
   But let the drinks warm and the food grow cold.
   But who could order order from Don Juan,   350
   The ace of all disorder?

[*Enter* DON JUAN *and* CATALINÓN.]

DON JUAN   You've locked the doors?
CATALINÓN   I've locked the doors exactly as you
   ordered.
DON JUAN   Then bring my supper, quick.
FIRST SERVANT   It's here already.
DON JUAN   Catalinón, sit down.
CATALINÓN   I sup more slowly.
DON JUAN   Sit down, I tell you.
CATALINÓN   Well, if you insist.   355
FIRST SERVANT   [*Aside*] He must be on a journey, now,
   as well,
   To sup with his own lackey.
DON JUAN   Come, sit down.

[*A loud knock is heard on the door.*]

CATALINÓN   Say, that's some knock!
DON JUAN   It must be someone calling.
   See who it is.
FIRST SERVANT   I fly, sir, to obey you.
CATALINÓN   What if the police have come?
DON JUAN   What if they have?   360
   No need for fear!

[FIRST SERVANT *enters, fleeing in terror.*]

CATALINÓN   He has seen something evil. One can tell
   it.
DON JUAN   Don't make me lose my temper. Speak,
   man, speak!

What have you seen? Some devil's terrified you?
Go, you, and see whatever's at the door.   365
Go on! Go, quick!
CATALINÓN   Who, *I*!
DON JUAN   Yes, you, at once.
   Yes, you, get your feet moving. Aren't you going?
CATALINÓN   Who's got the keys?
SECOND SERVANT   Only the bolt is slid.
DON JUAN   What's wrong with you then? Move! Why
   don't you go?
CATALINÓN   What if the raped and ravished have
   arrived   370
   To have their final vengeance?

[*He goes out to see.* CATALINÓN *rushes back in panic,
trips, falls over, and gets up.*]

DON JUAN   What's all this?
CATALINÓN   God help me! You can kill me if you like.
DON JUAN   Who's killing you? What is it? What have
   you seen?
CATALINÓN   Master . . . there . . . I saw . . . well,
   when I got there . . .   374
   [*Aside*] But what has seized me? What has snatched
   my mind?
   [*Aloud*] I got there to the door . . . then after, I was
   blind . . .
   But there I saw . . . I swear to God . . . I saw it . . .
   I spoke and said: "Who are you?" And he answered.
   I opened, went ahead, and bumped into—
DON JUAN   Well, who? Bumped into who?
CATALINÓN   Oh, don't ask *me*!   380
DON JUAN   How wine confuses people! Here! That
   candle!
   I'll go and see myself who it can be.

[DON JUAN *takes the candle and goes towards the door.*
DON GONZALO *walks in to meet him in the form of the
statue that was on the sepulchre.* DON JUAN *staggers
backwards in a state of perturbation, holding his sword
by the hilt. In the other hand he carries a candle.* DON
GONZALO *advances towards him with slow, short steps,
and* DON JUAN *retreats before him till they reach the
middle of the stage.*]

DON JUAN   Who's this?
DON GONZALO   It's I.
DON JUAN   But who on earth are you?
DON GONZALO   The person you invited here to dine.

DON JUAN   Why, there's enough for both of us, and   385
  more,
  If you've brought any friends along with you.
  The table's set already. Sit down here.
CATALINÓN   May God be with me now in my sore
  need
  With Saint Panuncio and Saint Antón.
  What? Do the dead eat too?
  [Aside] He nods in answer.   390
DON JUAN   Catalinón, sit down with us.
CATALINÓN   Excuse me:
  I take it that he's dined.
DON JUAN   You've lost your head.
  Are you afraid of a dead man? What then?
  If he were living, how much more you'd fear him!
  What an illiterate and rustic fear!   395
CATALINÓN   Dine with your guest, sir. I have supped
  already.
DON JUAN   You wish to make me angry?
CATALINÓN   Sir, I stink
  And that's the reason I would not offend you.
  I smell too bad.
DON JUAN   Sit down! I'm waiting for you.   399
CATALINÓN   [Aside] I'm dead with fear. My bum has
  misbehaved.

[The two servants are trembling with fear.]

DON JUAN   You others there! What about you? You're
  trembling?
CATALINÓN   I never liked to eat with foreigners
  Who come from other countries. Me, my lord—
  You'd have me feasting with a guest of stone?
DON JUAN   What stupid fear! If he is stone, what
  matter?   405
CATALINÓN   It knocks me all to pieces all the same!
DON JUAN   Speak to him courteously.
CATALINÓN   Sir, are you well?
  That "other life," is it a pleasant country?
  What is it like—all plains? Or steep sierras?
  Do they give prizes there for poetry?   410
FIRST SERVANT   To every question he has nodded: Yes.
CATALINÓN   And are there lots of taverns there? Why,
  surely,
  If Noah lives around there, there must be!
DON JUAN   Fetch wine.
CATALINÓN   Señor Dead Man, say, in your country,
  Do the drinks there have ice in?

[DON GONZALO nods.]

  Ah! with ice!   415
  What a good country!
DON JUAN   If you want a song
  I'll make them sing.

[DON GONZALO nods.]

  Then sing!
CATALINÓN   The Señor Dead man
  Has real good taste.
FIRST SERVANT   He's nobly bred, and so
  He is a friend of pleasure, naturally.

[They sing within.]

If you expect it of us men   420
That our deserts shall find adjusting
But not till after death, why then,
A long, long time you are for trusting!
CATALINÓN   Either he finds the heat is overpowering
  Or else he is a man who eats but little.   425
  I cannot keep from trembling at my dinner.
  It seems that they don't drink much over there
  And so I'll drink, for both of us a [Drinks] pledge
  Of stone. I feel less terrified already.

[They go on singing within.]

If that's the date you ladies give   430
To enjoy all for whom I'm lusting
You grant a long long time to live
And burnish up my joys from rusting.

If you expect it of us men
That our deserts shall find adjusting   435
But not till after death, why then
A long, long time you are for trusting!
CATALINÓN   Of which of all the ladies you have
  cheated
  Do they make mention?
DON JUAN   I laugh at them all,
  My friend, on this occasion. Why, in Naples   440
  With Isabel . . .
CATALINÓN   She's not so badly cheated
  Since you will have to marry her, quite rightly.
  But that poor girl who saved you from the sea,
  You treated in a pretty sorry fashion.
  You cheated Dona Ana.
DON JUAN   Hold your jaw!   445

For here is someone who has suffered for her
And waits for his revenge.
CATALINÓN   He is a man
Of mighty valour, being made of stone,
And you of flesh. It's not a pleasant problem.

[DON GONZALO *makes a sign for the table to cleared,
and for* DON JUAN *and himself to be left alone together.*]

DON JUAN   Here, clear this table, since he's making
    signs   450
The rest should go and leave us both together.
CATALINÓN   It's bad! For God's sake, master, don't
    remain!
For here's a dead man that with one sole fist-cuff
Could floor a giant.
DON JUAN   All of you, get out!
Were I Catalinón, then I might flinch.   455
But go; for he approaches.

[*The servants go out, and* DON JUAN *and* DON GONZALO
remain alone together. DON GONZALO *signs to* DON JUAN
to close the door.]

DON JUAN   The door's shut
And I am at your service. What's your will,
Shade, vision, or phantasma? If your soul
Is travailing in pain, if you await
Some satisfaction or relief, then tell me,   460
And I will give my word to do whatever
You should command me. Are you in the grace
Of God? Or was it that I killed you recklessly
In a state of mortal sin? Speak! I am anxious.
DON GONZALO   [*Speaking slowly, as if from another
    world*]   465
And as a gentleman you'll keep your word?
DON JUAN   I keep my word with men, being a knight.
DON GONZALO   Then give your hand on it. Don't be
    afraid!
DON JUAN   What! *Me* afraid? Were you both hell and
    death,
I'd dare to give my hand.   [*He gives his hand.*]   469
DON GONZALO   Now lower both your hand and voice.
    Tomorrow
At ten, *I'll* be awaiting *you* for supper.
You'll come?
DON JUAN   Why, I expected something far
More dangerous than what you ask of me.
Tomorrow I shall be your guest. But where?

DON GONZALO   In my side-chapel, by my tomb.
DON JUAN   Alone?   475
DON GONZALO   No, you can bring your servant. And
    you'll honour
Your word, as I have done the same to you?
DON JUAN   Of course. I am Tenorio born and bred.
DON GONZALO   And I a born Ulloa.
DON JUAN   I'll be there,
And without fail.
DON GONZALO   I trust your word. Good-bye.   480

[*He goes towards the door.*]

DON JUAN   Wait, let me get a torch to light your way!
DON GONZALO   My soul requires no light. I am in
    grace.

[*He retires very, very slowly, looking at* DON JUAN, *until
he disappears, leaving* DON JUAN *in a state of panic.*]

DON JUAN   God save me, all my body's bathed in
    sweat!
My very heart seems frozen here inside.
For when he took me by the hand and   485
    squeezed it
It seemed I was in hell. Such was the heat.
And yet his breath and voice were like the blizzard
Of an infernal frost. But all these things,
Begot by fear on the imagination,
Are quite unreal. To fear the dead is baseness.   490
If I am not afraid of noble bodies
With all their powers, alive with wits and reason,
To fear dead bodies is a stupid thing.
Tomorrow I will go there to the chapel
Where it invited me, that all of Seville   495
May make a living legend of my valour.

[At the Alcazar at Seville, the king of Castille and Don
Diego plan the marriages of Don Juan and Isabel and
Don Octavio and Doña Ana. Aminta and Gaseno ar-
rive, telling Octavio that Aminta is to be married to
Don Juan. Octavio does not yet tell them that they are
deceived but plans to use them in revenge "against that
traitor villain, base Don Juan, / And his foul injuries to
Isabel."]

*A street in full view of the church wherein the com-
mander is buried*

[*Enter* DON JUAN *and* CATALINÓN.]

CATALINÓN   How did the king receive you?

DON JUAN   Lovingly.
As if he were my father.

CATALINÓN   Did you see   605
The Duchess Isabel?

DON JUAN   Yes. Her also.

CATALINÓN   How did she seem?

DON JUAN   An angel.

CATALINÓN   She received you
Courteously?

DON JUAN   Her face seemed bathed in milk
And blushing with her blood like a white rose
With all its dews lit by the red aurora.   610

CATALINÓN   And so the wedding is this evening, sir?

DON JUAN   Yes, without fail.

CATALINÓN   If it had been before
Perhaps you'd not have harmed so many women.
But now you take a wife with heavy charges
And grave responsibilities.

DON JUAN   Are you being   615
Impertinent and stupid once again?

CATALINÓN   You might at least have waited till
tomorrow.
Today's unlucky!

DON JUAN   What day is it?

CATALINÓN   Tuesday.
"Never travel or get married on a
Tuesday."

DON JUAN   Oh, to hell with all that nonsense   620
Which only fools and madmen take to heart!
That day alone's unlucky, cursed, and foul
When I run out of money. Other days,
All other days, are revelry and laughter.

CATALINÓN   Come, let us go, for you must dress in
style,   625
They're waiting for you now and it grows late.

DON JUAN   We have another business first at hand.
So they'll just have to wait.

CATALINÓN   What other business?

DON JUAN   To sup with the Dead Man.

CATALINÓN   What need for that?

DON JUAN   Well, don't you know I gave my word upon
it?   630

CATALINÓN   And if you broke it, sir, what could it
matter?
A jasper figure can't expect so much
From a live man as to insist on vows.

DON JUAN   The Dead Man, then, could say I was a
coward.

CATALINÓN   But anyway you see the church is   635
shut.

DON JUAN   Knock, then.

CATALINÓN   What does it matter if I knock?
There's nobody to open it inside
And all the sacristans are sleeping.

DON JUAN   Knock!
Here at this postern.

CATALINÓN   It is open.

DON JUAN   Enter.

CATALINÓN   Let friars enter with their stoles and
hyssops!   640

DON JUAN   Then follow me and hold your tongue. Be
silent.

CATALINÓN   Silent?

DON JUAN   Yes.

CATALINÓN   I am silent. Oh, my God,
Please bring me out alive from such a feast!

[*They go out on one side and will come in on the other.*]

Interior of the church

[*Enter* DON JUAN *and* CATALINÓN.]

CATALINÓN   It's very dark for such a great big church.
Oh, sir, protect me, someone grabbed my cloak!   645

[DON GONZALO *comes in as before in the form of a*

DON JUAN   Who's that?

DON GONZALO   It is I.

CATALINÓN   I am dead with fright!

DON GONZALO   I am the Dead Man: do not be afraid.
I did not think that you would keep your word
Since you delight in breaking it so often—

DON JUAN   I suppose that you imagine me a   650
coward!

DON GONZALO   Why, yes! Because, that night, you fled
from me
When you killed me.

DON JUAN   I fled from recognition.
But here I stand before you. What's your will?

DON GONZALO   Why, only to invite you here to
supper.

CATALINÓN   Pray let us be excused. Here all the
victuals   655

They serve are cold—cold supper and cold lunches.
DON JUAN   We'll sup then.
DON GONZALO   Well, to do so, you must lift
The lid, here, off this tomb.
DON JUAN   Why, if you wish it
I'll lift these pillars too!
DON GONZALO   You're very willing.

[DON JUAN, *lifting by one end the lid of the tomb which folds back easily, leaving discovered a black table already laid and set.*]

DON JUAN   Yes, I have strength and courage in my
    body.   660
CATALINÓN   This table must have come from Guinea's coast
It is so black. Are there none here to wash it?
DON GONZALO   Be seated.
DON JUAN   Where?
CATALINÓN   See two black servants come
With stools.

[*Enter two figures in black with stools.*]

So here, too, people go in mourning
With flannel made in Flanders?
DON JUAN   You! Sit down!   665
CATALINÓN   What, me, sir? I've already fed this evening.
DON JUAN   Don't answer back!
CATALINÓN   All right, I will not answer.
    [*Aside*] O God, in safety get me out of this!
    [*Aloud*] What dish is this?
DON GONZALO   Tarantulas and vipers.
CATALINÓN   Really? How nice!
DON GONZALO   That is our diet here.   670
But you're not eating.
DON JUAN   I shall eat it
Were all the snakes in hell upon one plate.
DON GONZALO   I'd like to have them sing to you a little.
CATALINÓN   What sort of wine do they have here?
DON GONZALO   There, taste it.
CATALINÓN   Vinegar, frost, and ice. That's what this
    wine is!   675
DON GONZALO   Well, that's the sort of wine that we
press here.

[*They sing within.*]

Let all those know who judge God's ways
And treat his punishments with scorn
There is no debt but that he pays,
No date but it is bound to dawn.   680
CATALINÓN   How terrible! I've heard this tune before
And now it is addressed to me,
DON JUAN   [*Aside*] My breast
is frozen, and the ice tears me apart.

[*They sing.*]

While in the world one's flesh is lusting
It is most wrong for men to say: 685
"A long long time in me your're trusting"
For very shortly dawns the day.
CATALINÓN   What is this: fricassee?
DON GONZALO   Of fingernails.
CATALINÓN   Then they must be the fingernails of
    tailors
They are so sharp and claw-like and rapacious.   690
DON JUAN   Now I have eaten, let them clear the table.
DON GONZALO   Give me your hand. Don't be afraid!
    Your hand.
DON JUAN   Afraid, you say. *Me* frightened? Here's my
hand.

[*He gives it.*]

I'm roasting, burning! Do not burn me so
With your fierce fire!
DON GONZALO   That's nothing to the fire   695
    Which you have sought yourself! The wondrous
    ways
Of God, Don Juan, are not fathomable.
And so He wishes now for you to pay
Your forfeits straight into the hands of death.
This is God's justice. What you've done, you   700
    pay for.
DON JUAN   I'm roasting. Do not grip my hand so hard!
I'll kill you with this dagger. But the blows
Strike only empty air. Look. With your daughter
I did no harm. She saw the hoax in time.
DON GONZALO   That does not matter. It was your
    intention.   705
DON JUAN   Then let me send for a confessor quickly,
So to absolve my soul before I die.

DON GONZALO   Impossible. You've thought of it too late.

DON JUAN   Oh, I am burning! Oh, I am roasting, burning!
I'm dying! [*He falls dead.*]

CATALINÓN   There is no escape. I, too,   710
Must die for having been your companion.

DON GONZALO   Such is God's justice. What is done is paid for.

[*The tomb sinks with a rumbling thunder, taking* DON JUAN *and* DON GONZALO *with it.* CATALINÓN *creeps out of the wreckage.*]

CATALINÓN   So help me God! What's this? The chapel's burning
With wondrous light. And I'm left with the corpse
To watch with it and guard it. To his father   715
I'll creep away now and proclaim the news.
Saint George and Holy Lamb of God protect me
That I may come in safety to the street!

The Alcazar

[*Enter the* KING OF CASTILE, DON DIEGO, *courtiers, and attendants.*]

DON DIEGO   The marquis wants to kiss your   719
royal feet.

KING OF CASTILE   Then let him enter. Call the Count Don Juan
As well, that he be kept no longer waiting.

[*Enter* BATRICIO *and* GASENO.]

BATRICIO   Where are such foul monstrosities permitted
That your own servants should affront, unpunished,
The humble people?

KING OF CASTILE   What is that you say?

BATRICIO   Don Juan Tenorio, treacherous,   725
detestable,
Stole my young wife the evening of our marriage,
And here I have the witnesses.

[*Enter* THISBE *and* ISABEL.]

THISBE   Sire, if Your Highness will not do me justice
On Don Juan Tenorio, both to God and men
I will complain through all my days to come!   730

When dying he was swept ashore, I gave him
Both life and hospitality. With lust
And promises of marriage he repaid
This kindness. He abused me and then left me.

KING OF CASTILE   What do you say?

ISABEL   She's telling you the truth.   735

[*Enter* AMINTA *and the* DUKE OCTAVIO.]

AMINTA   Where is my spouse?

KING OF CASTILE   Who is he?

AMINTA   What, you don't
Know, even yet? Don Juan Tenorio,
With whom I've come this evening to be wedded,
Because he owes it to my name and honour
And, being noble, will not break his word.   740

[*Enter the* MARQUIS OF LA MOTA.]

MARQUIS   It's time to drag some truths into the light,
My Lord. Know then that of the selfsame crime
For which you sentenced me, Don Juan is guilty
(A cruel fraud to put on a best friend)
And I've the witnesses to prove it here.   745

KING OF CASTILE   Could any shamelessness compare to this?

DON DIEGO   Sire, to reward my services to you,
Let him be made to expiate his crime
So that the heavens themselves don't shoot their lightning
At me, for having bred so foul a son.   750

KING OF CASTILE   So it is thus my favourites behave!

[*Enter* CATALINÓN.]

CATALINÓN   My lords, all listen to the greatest wonder
That ever happened in this world, and kill me
If, listening, you don't believe it's true.
Don Juan, making fun of the commander,   755
Having divested him of life and honour,
And all the gems and ornaments of life,
Pulling the beard upon his granite statue,
Insulted him by asking him to dine.
Oh, that he'd never done so! Then the statue   760
Went to his house, inviting him in turn,
And then (to make it short, and not to tire you)
When they had finished supper, took his hand
And squeezed it till he squeezed his life out, saying:

"God ordered me to kill you thus, and punish   765
Your monstrous crimes. For what you've done, you
    pay."
KING OF CASTILE   What are you saying?
CATALINÓN   It's the gospel truth.
Don Juan pleaded, first, that he had not
Seduced the Lady Ana: she discovered
The fraud in time.
MARQUIS   For this delightful news   770
A thousand gifts I wish to give you.
KING OF CASTILE   Just punishment from Heaven has
    been dealt.
Now let them all be married, since the cause
Of all their harm is dead.
OCTAVIO   Since Isabela's
A widow now, I wish to marry her.   775
MARQUIS   And I to wed my cousin.
BATRICIO   And us others
With our own girls. For now the GUEST OF STONE
Is ended.
KING OF CASTILE   Take the tomb to San Francisco,
The great church in Madrid, and there install it
And so preserve this memory through all time.   780

QUESTIONS

1. Notice the typically baroque mixture of tones—
   tragic and comic—the frequent changes of scenes,
   the rather complicated plot, and the improbable
   encounters. Compare and contrast these with classical and neoclassical and with Shakespearean drama.
   Would you classify *The Trickster of Seville* as primarily comic, primarily tragic, or neither?
2. Describe the character of Don Juan. Is he entirely
   villainous, or does the reader feel drawn to him in
   any way?
3. What seems to be the nature and the role of women
   in this play?
4. How does Tirso inject social criticism into his
   drama?
5. What positive religious and moral values emerge
   from the play?
6. To what extent can Don Juan be considered a "satanic" figure?
7. How does this original Don Juan compare with the
   popular stereotype of a "Don Juan"?

English "Metaphysical" Poetry   The group of
poets in mid-seventeenth-century England, including
John Donne, George Herbert, Richard Crashaw, and
Andrew Marvell, was disparagingly dubbed "metaphysical" by the critic Dryden. Although inadequate to describe this school of poetry, the term has stuck. In recent years, however, continental critics and even some
English critics have begun to see affinities between
this school of poets and the baroque sensibility that prevailed throughout Europe. Frank Kermode, while granting that "metaphysical" may be a subdepartment of
"baroque," urges caution:

> . . . When we think of metaphysical, we do not think at
> once of St. Ignatius or Bernini or Marino, though we may
> do so a little later. We think first of a special moment in
> English poetry, a moment of plain but witty magnilo-
> quence, of a passionate poetry ballasted with learning and
> propelled by a sceptical ingenuity that may strike us as
> somehow very modern.[1]

This succinct definition does express the most salient
qualities of "metaphysical" poetry. We shall briefly
sample here two of these poets who combined the spiritual with the sensual in ways that relate them to continental baroque poets and artists.

Crashaw (1612–1649)   Perhaps the most baroque of
all the seventeenth-century English poets was Richard
Crashaw. Crashaw was raised in the Puritan tradition—his father was a preacher—but he converted to
Roman Catholicism and spent the last years of his life
in Rome. He was greatly attracted to mysticism and especially to female saints; three of his best-known
poems are on Saint Theresa of Avila. Although it is unlikely that Crashaw saw Bernini's famous statue before
writing the poems, they share its spirit. Below is the last
part of the third poem in the series, entitled "The Flaming Heart." In the first part of the poem, Crashaw criticizes conventional pictorial representations of the saint
(where she usually appears as a rather placid nun). He
then describes how she should be represented. First, he
says that she, not the seraphim beside her, should hold
the dart. He then concedes to the angel "the bravery of

---

[1] Frank Kermode, ed., *The Metaphysical Poets*, (New York: Fawcett,
1969), p. 32.

all those Bright things," including "the radiant dart," and asks that Theresa be left only "the flaming heart." (The spelling has been modernized in all of the following poems.)

RICHARD CRASHAW

from *The Flaming Heart*

Leave Her alone The Flaming Heart.
  Leave her that; and thou shalt leave her
Not one loose shaft but love's whole quiver.
For in love's field was never found
A nobler weapon than a Wound.
Love's passives are his activ'st part.
The wounded is the wounding heart.
O Heart! the equal poise of love's both parts
Big alike with wounds and darts.
Live in these conquering leaves; live all the same;
And walk through all tongues one triumphant Flame.
Live here, great Heart; and love and die and kill;
And bleed and wound; and yield and conquer still.
Let this immortal life where'er it comes
Walk in a crowd of loves and Martyrdoms.
Let mystic Deaths wait on it; and wise souls be
The love-slain witnesses of this life of thee.
O sweet incendiary! show here thy art,
Upon this carcass of a hard, cold hart,
Let all thy scatter'd shafts of light, that play
Among the leaves of thy large books of day,
Combin'd against this Breast at once break in
And take away from me my self and sin,
This gracious Robbery shall thy bounty be;
And my best fortunes such fair spoils of me.
O thou undaunted daughter of desires!
By all thy dower of Lights and Fires;
By all the eagle in thee, all the dove;
By all thy lives and deaths of love;
By thy large draughts of intellectual day,
And by thy thirsts of love more large than they;
By all thy brim-fill'd Bowls of fierce desire
By thy last Morning's draught of liquid fire;
By the full kingdom of that final kiss
That seiz'd thy parting Soul, and seal'd thee his;
By all the heav'ns thou hast in him
(Fair sister of the Seraphim!)

By all of Him we have in Thee;
Leave nothing of my Self in me.
Let me so read thy life, that I
Unto all life of mine may die.

COMMENTS AND QUESTIONS

1. Baroque poets, like baroque artists, loved extreme contrasts; they expressed these with the rhetorical figures known as *oxymoron* (the juxtaposition of words with opposing meanings) and *antithesis* (the balance of parallel word groups conveying opposing ideas). An example of oxymoron here is the phrase "sweet incendiary." An example of antithesis is: "Love's passives are his activ'st part./The wounded is the wounding heart." What other examples of these figures can you find? How do they serve the poet's purpose here?

2. Another characteristic of baroque poetry is the extended use of *metaphor*. Renaissance poets tended to make more use of the *simile*, which makes a comparison between two things on an intellectual level; but the baroque sensibility preferred the more emotional fusion and identification that the metaphor provided. In this poem the poet does not compare himself to a deer but suddenly *becomes* "this carcass of a hard, cold hart." (Plays on words like *heart/hart* were also dear to baroque poets.) What other metaphors does Crashaw use here?

3. Baroque poems often tend to have a cumulative effect, comparable to the rich profusion of matter in baroque art. One way of achieving this is through the rhetorical device of *anaphora* (the repetition of the same word to introduce two or more clauses or lines). Notice here the number of lines that begin with "By all." What is the effect of this device?

4. How would you describe Crashaw's interpretation of the mystic experience of Theresa? Compare it with Bernini's in the statue.

5. Do this style and sensibility appeal to you? What in your own personality makes you answer negatively or positively?

Donne (1572–1631)   The next three poems are by John Donne, whose lines on the new science we quoted earlier. In contrast to Crashaw, Donne was brought up as a Catholic but became an Anglican. He became, in fact, one of the most successful preachers of his age, and his sermons are still read for their force and brilliant style. At the same time, Donne was a worldly man, fond of women and involved in several passionate love affairs. He was thus suited to the baroque combination of the ardently religious and the ardently erotic; his best poems successfully combine the two. The first poem here is a kind of prayer, comparable to Bernini's and to Crashaw's Saint Theresa in its use of erotic and violent imagery to describe mystic experience. The second is frankly erotic, but in it the poet speaks of the bed as "love's hallowed temple" and of women as angels and "mystic books." The third poem is set up as an argument for seduction. Centered around a tiny, apparently insignificant object (a flea), it makes use of extreme detail to portray matters of larger significance; in this sense it is more comparable to the Dutch than to the Italian baroque style in art.

JOHN DONNE

from *Holy Sonnets*

SONNET 14

Batter my heart, three-personed God; for you
As yet but knock, breathe, shine, and seek to mend;
That I may rise, and stand, o'erthrow me, and bend
Your force, to break, blow, burn, and make me new.
I, like an usurped [1] town, to another due,
Labor to admit you, but Oh, to no end,
Reason your viceroy[2] in me, me should defend,
But is captived, and proves weak or untrue.
Yet dearly I love you, and would be loved fain,[3]
But am betrothed unto your enemy:
Divorce me, untie, or break that knot again,
Take me to you, imprison me, for I
Except you enthral me, never shall be free,
Nor ever chaste, except you ravish me.

---

[1] Captured.
[2] Representative.
[3] Gladly.

QUESTIONS

1. How do the characteristics of contrast and repetition appear in this poem?

2. Are there extreme contrasts in the rhythm of the lines as well? How is this achieved?
3. How are the war metaphor and the sexual metaphor worked in together?
4. Compare Donne's expression of union with God to that of St. John of the Cross (pp. 34–35).

Elegy XIX

TO HIS MISTRESS GOING TO BED

Come, madam, come, all rest my powers defy,
Until I labor, I in labor lie.
The foe oft-times having the foe in sight,
Is tired with standing though he never fight.
Off with that girdle,[1] like heaven's zone glistering,
But a far fairer world encompassing.
Unpin that spangled breastplate which you wear,
That th' eyes of busy fools may be stopped there.
Unlace yourself, for that harmonious chime
Tells me from you that now it is bed time.
Off with that happy busk,[2] which I envy,
That still can be, and still can stand so nigh.
Your gown, going off, such beauteous state reveals,
As when from flowry meads th' hill's shadow steals.
Off with that wiry coronet and show
The hairy diadem which on you doth grow:
Now off with those shoes, and then safely tread
In this love's hallowed temple, this soft bed.
In such white robes, heaven's angels used to be
Received by men; thou, Angel, bring'st with thee
A heaven like Mahomet's Paradise;[3] and though
Ill spirits walk in white, we easily know
By this these angels from an evil sprite:
Those set our hairs, but these our flesh upright.
    License my roving hands, and let them go
Before, behind, between, above, below.
O my America! my new-found-land,
My kingdom, safeliest when with one man manned,
My mine of precious stones, my empery,
How blest am I in this discovering thee!
To enter in these bonds is to be free;
Then where my hand is set, my seal shall be.

---

[1] Belt.
[2] Undergarment worn over the breast.
[3] The Muslim idea of paradise includes beautiful women.

Full nakedness! All joys are due to thee,
As souls unbodied, bodies unclothed must be
To taste whole joys. Gems which you women use
Are like Atalanta's balls,[4] cast in men's views,
That when a fool's eye lighteth on a gem,
His earthly soul may covet theirs, not them.
Like pictures, or like books' gay coverings made
For lay-men, are all women thus arrayed;
Themselves are mystic books, which only we
(Whom their imputed grace will dignify)
Must see revealed. Then, since that I may know,
As liberally as to a midwife, show
Thyself: cast all, yea, this white linen hence,
There is no penance due to innocence.
    To teach thee, I am naked first; why then,
What needst thou have more covering than a man?

---

[4] Atalanta agreed to marry Hippomenes if he could defeat her in a foot race. As she was about to overtake him, he cast in her path three golden apples given to him by Venus. Distracted by their beauty, Atalanta stopped to retrieve them, and Hippomenes won the race.

QUESTIONS

1. Why does Donne spend so much time describing each article of clothing that he wants the woman to take off? What is the effect of this "slow motion"?
2. Could you compare the enumeration here to the numbers of sensuously depicted objects in baroque painting?
3. What use does Donne make here of the "new world" discoveries? What is the effect of this metaphor?

THE FLEA

Mark but this flea, and mark in this,
How little that which thou deny'st me is;
It sucked me first, and now sucks thee,
And in this flea our two bloods mingled be;[1]
Thou know'st that this cannot be said
A sin, nor shame, nor loss of maidenhead;
    Yet this enjoys before it woo,
      And pampered swells with one blood made of two,
      And this, alas, is more than we would do.

---

[1] It was believed at this time that conception occurred through the mixing of the man's blood with the woman's.

O stay, three lives in one flea spare,
Where we almost, yea, more than married are.
This flea is you and I, and this
Our marriage bed and marriage temple is;
Though parents grudge, and you, we are met
And cloistered in these living walls of jet.
    Though use[2] make you apt to kill me,
      Let not to that, self-murder added be,
      And sacrilege, three sins in killing three.

Cruel and sudden, hast thou since
Purpled thy nail in blood of innocence?
Wherein could this flea guilty be,
Except in that drop which it sucked from thee?
Yet thou triumph'st and say'st that thou
Find'st not thyself nor me the weaker now;
    'Tis true, then learn how false fears be:
      Just so much honor, when thou yield'st to me,
      Will waste, as this flea's death took life from thee.

---

[2] Habit, custom.

COMMENTS AND QUESTIONS

1. Donne begins this poem almost as if he were beginning a sermon, using the flea as an object-lesson. He then begins a series of arguments on the *carpe diem* ("seize the day," or "let's make love now before it's too late") theme. What arguments does he use? Are they meant to be logical?
2. Notice that the poem is set up like a three-act drama. What is supposed to have happened after stanza 1 and after stanza 2?
3. What is the effect of externalizing the lover's desire in the flea?

Baroque Music

The baroque style in music, like that in the visual arts and in literature, had its origins in late Renaissance Italy. Humanism, the same cultural and intellectual movement that used the ideas and ideals of Greece and Rome as models for contemporary artistic creation (and to a large degree, gave rise to the Renaissance itself), was also largely responsible for creating a new or "second practice" at the height of the Renaissance period.

ORAZIO VECCHI

L'Amfiparnaso

(Trans: Oh, oh! Here is the captain. Here is my loved one and my hope.)

Chordal declamation.

JACOPO PERI

Euridice

(Trans: I do not cry, nor do I sigh. O my dear Eurydice.)

Recitative.

Well before the end of the sixteenth century, musicians in Italy tried to resurrect the affective power of Greek drama: they began to experiment with *dramma per musica*, theatrical genres that developed and were later named opera and oratorio. A whole theory of *affects* became a doctrine of the baroque, a method whereby a composer could invoke specific emotional responses in an audience by employing specific musical devices. As Plato's Dorian mode stirred manly feelings in the youth of Greece, Bach's and Handel's D-major trumpet parts evoked victorious martial responses in the listeners of the eighteenth, nineteenth, and twentieth centuries.

As in the other arts, baroque music had both a Catholic and Protestant form. The Church of Rome partook in the new musical developments during the late Renaissance, since the Reformation of Luther was evidently successful in winning converts through music that was particularly attractive and meaningful to laymen—vernacular texts, simple settings, and short, "catchy" melodies. The Catholic church's Counter Reformation thus experimented with similarly appealing music. One discovers that Saint Philip Neri's congregation of secular priests sang *laude spirituali* (spiritual songs of praise) in the oratory (a large room for public discussions) of his church in Rome. His group of followers was named after the room (*Congregazione del'Oratorio*), and the baroque musical form (oratorio) was likewise named after this place of origin. A loosely connected historical line binds together a development or metamorphosis from the *laude spirituali* to spiritual dialogues and early oratorios with biblical characters to the mature oratorio of the late baroque.

Attractive dramatic music became fairly common throughout Italy toward the end of the sixteenth century, and we see that Andrea Gabrieli composed choruses for a presentation of a revived Greek drama, *Oedipus Rex*, at Vicenza in 1585; Orazio Vecchi presented his madrigal comedy *L'Amfiparnaso* in Modena in 1594; and the Florentines Jacopo Corsi, Ottavio Rinuccini, and Jacopo Peri produced an entire dramatic pastoral in a representational style inspired by antique models, *Dafne*, in Corsi's palace in 1598.

By this time musicians were calling Renaissance music old, and this music of the "second practice" new or modern. The key stylistic feature of the best music of the High Renaissance was its marvelous *counterpoint*, the smooth and complex interweaving of several melodies into a unified, organic whole. In contrast, the most distinctive feature of the new music of the early baroque was the declamatory style, a technique that might use chordal declamation by several singers or a sung recitation by a soloist to a harmonic accompaniment, a device named recitativo or *recitative*. (See examples on page 62.)

Although a straightforward declamation of text is the most obvious feature of these works to the musical layman, most musicians identify the new baroque style by its harmonic characteristics. The counterpoint of Renaissance music was clothed by *modal* sonorities—the distinctive scales or *modes* of the melodies and the coincidental blending of the various musical parts sounding simultaneously. Baroque music was produced within a new system of tonal harmonies, music that was composed with chords and chord relationships in mind. Regardless of what individual lines in a baroque composition might do, a progression of chord changes leads the ear from beginning to end, from level to level, forming the basic framework of the piece. *Harmonic organization* forms the basis of music from this period and, in fact, of all European music from the seventeenth through the twentieth centuries. The seventeenth-century composer writing in the new dramatic style notated a melodic line and a bass line, the upper and lower limits of sound for the piece; and he filled in the middle by composing or improvising chords that he indicated with figures over the bass notes. Although this generalization oversimplifies a bit, it serves to illustrate an essential element of baroque musical style. This bass part with numbers and signs over the notes was called *continuo*, *thorough bass*, or *figured bass*. Since this musical and notational feature was pervasive in baroque music, several music historians have suggested that the period ought to be called after the musical device. Be that as it may, the important fact for our understanding of the music of this period is its shift from melodic to harmonic thinking and its new approach to text setting that signaled a change from one musical style to the next.

21

Two Masterpieces of Baroque Music: Handel's *Messiah* and Bach's *Christmas Oratorio*

The artistic skies of the seventeenth and eighteenth centuries were spangled with musical lights of great magnitude: Monteverdi, Corelli, Alessandro Scarlatti, and Vivaldi in Italy; Domenico Scarlatti in Spain; Rameau, Lully, and Couperin in France; Purcell in England; Schütz, Buxtehude, and Johann Sebastian Bach in Germany; and a figure of international fame and travels, George Frederick Handel.

The centuries have taught us that the latter two composers—Bach and Handel—rise above all the others. Each has left us a vast store of musical riches that span the compass from small to large, easy to difficult, sacred to secular, instrumental to vocal, incidental to monumental. No single work can adequately represent either of these musical geniuses, but two have retained their universal appeal over the centuries: Bach's *Christmas Oratorio* and Handel's English masterpiece, *Messiah*.

George Frederick Handel (1685–1759)   Handel began his career in Germany, traveled and worked in Italy, and eventually emigrated to London. Although this German musician first established his reputation in England as a composer of Italian operas, the masterwork from his pen that has endeared him to the hearts of all English-speaking Christians is his sacred oratorio *Messiah*, a work created in response to an invitation from the Duke of Devonshire, the Lord Lieutenant of Ireland, to present some concerts for the benefit of the Charitable Musical Society of Dublin. Composed in twenty-four days, it was first performed in Dublin in 1742 and was an immediate artistic and popular success. According to popular legend, the tradition of standing for the Hallelujah Chorus began with the first London performance in 1743 when King George II, wakened from a nap by the opening chords of the chorus rose to his feet—followed, of course, by all his subjects. *Messiah* was, and remains, popular with people from all walks of life. Although written over two hundred years ago, the *Messiah* will be available to most Americans through live performance or live broadcast at least twice a year, at Christmas and Easter. Universal recognition is not the only criterion for greatness in music, but it is clear that no other musical composition has captured the sincere affection of the English-speaking world more completely. In every aspect of its existence—concept, design, scale, quality—it is a monumental work, a superb pinnacle of artistic creation, a masterpiece that brought tears to the eyes of the composer himself and caused him to say, "I did think I did see all Heaven before me and the great God Himself." In spite of all the technical accounts of how this grand work was organized and composed with borrowed material and practical concerns for particular singers' voice ranges and abilities, nothing can detract from the fact that it was an inspired work completed in feverish haste by a musical genius of the first rank.

Messiah speaks to modern ears with the same honesty of religious expression that has stirred fervent emotions in listeners for over two hundred years. It is one of the greatest expressions of the Protestant baroque. It is not enough to deal with this *oratorio* as a musical composition only, for it is first and foremost a religious piece, a remarkable setting of biblical texts dealing with the redemption of man from sin through the intervention of the Messiah. The *libretto* is a compilation of verses from the Bible, a selection that draws from both the Old and the New Testaments. The organization and unity of the work is primarily text-centered, for, like three acts of an opera, the three large divisions of the oratorio reveal the following plan: PART I. A messianic prophecy, the coming and birth of Christ. The revelation of God's plan to save mankind by the coming of the Messiah. PART II. The suffering and death of Christ, the defeat of man who rejects God's offer, and the spread of His doctrine. PART III. The redemption of man through faith, the final overthrow of death, and a hymn of thanksgiving.

With this large framework in mind, Handel fleshed out a massive construct for soloists, chorus, and orchestra by using standard forms that were second nature to him and were a regular part of the fully developed operatic style of the baroque era. He sets the spell for the entire work by opening with an orchestral overture with the same characteristics as the French overture developed by Lully decades before: a slow, majestic first movement in jagged *rhythms*, duple *meter*, and

Messiah.   OVERTURE   *(1st Movement)*

Oboes,
Strings,
and
Continuo

Messiah.   OVERTURE   *(2nd Movement)*

chordal texture; a lively, *fugal* second movement with an impressive *contrapuntal* display.[1]

The *fugue* impresses the listener because the composer successfully takes a melody and uses it against itself, or in conjunction with itself, to create logical and beautiful harmonies. Exquisite fugues are a hallmark of the baroque masters, who displayed their melodic inventiveness through this process of imitating short and distinctive melodies in succession. We can see three successive entrances of the same tune (very slightly altered) in measures 1, 5, and 9 of the fugue, and we might compare their identity by playing them simultaneously:

The fugal process was one of the most compelling in the repertoire of the baroque composers, for although its texture is "lighter in weight" than most *chordal*, or *homophonic*, compositions, it has a forward-driving rhythm and additive-layer-of-melody effect that propels the listener to the final release of the closing chords. Handel was a master of this mature form of the late baroque, and we can see its dramatic effect in the vocal fugues that he favors for climactic moments.

The overall design of the first part of *Messiah* can be seen in the chart at the top of the following page. The regularity or symmetry and the simplicity of the design are in fact *classical*, and we must keep in mind that Handel was working at the culmination of an age, a period in which the influence of new ideas in opposition to the norms of the baroque are beginning to make themselves felt. Simplicity of design is of great advantage in the function of a work that depends heavily upon text, for unnecessary complexity detracts by drawing attention to itself. No one was more aware of this than Handel himself, for he understood better than any other composer of his time how to employ the operatic forms of recitative and *aria* to communicate the inner message of the text.

A *recitative* is a musical form that has almost no melodic interest; consequently, a great store of informa-

---

[1] Any number of excellent recordings of *Messiah* complete are available, but the reader is advised to find a recent recording that seeks to approximate Handel's original scoring for small orchestra and modest chorus. The loss in dramatic power supplied by a romantic orchestra and gigantic chorus is amply compensated for by the increased clarity of line and decreased ponderosity.

Subject	Sinfonia	God's Promise			Distance between God and Man				Message of Joy		Fulfillment through Christ's Birth		
Selection Number	1	2	3	4	5	6	7	7a	8	8a	9	10	11
Form	O	R	A	C	R	A	C	R	A	C	R	A	C

Subject	Pifa	Christmas Story					Rapture at the Lord's Coming			
Selection Number	12	12a	13	13a	14	15	16	16a	17	18
Form	O	R	A	R	R	C	A	R	AA	C

O = Orchestra; R = Recitative; A = Air; AA = Air (Duet); C = Chorus

Messiah. PART I. Overall design.

tion can be related to the listener in a short time. Those points in the narrative where several ideas await telling, where persons need adequate introduction, where details of plot need be unfolded quickly, and in general where there are a great many words to be dealt with are the proper domain of the recitative. Still, within that general plan, certain points need emphasis; there Handel uses chord change and chord selection as well as slight *melodic elaboration* to achieve these ends.

Other devices are available to him too, such as *orchestration*, but the essential concept that the recitative should be used to carry a high volume of words per unit of time is not disturbed. In the last example (c) we see a typical Handelian affective device. On the statement of the word "shake," Handel literally shakes the music. He takes the notes and rapidly wiggles them back and forth, a visual effect for the performer and an aural effect for the listener. As the chorus sings "All we like sheep have gone astray" the melodic lines diverge; with "we have turned," a quickly twisting and turning figure is introduced, and with "every one to his own way" a single note is stubbornly repeated.

The *aria* or "air" has a purpose almost diametrically opposed to that of the recitative. An aria usually contains two ideas often expressed in two sentences. It is an opportunity for the soloist (or composer) to wax eloquent, to spin out gradually a thought that grows fuller in meaning as the music progresses. It is usually some-

what introspective, personal to the character of the person portrayed by the soloist. The second idea is related to the first, but it casts a slightly different light on the subject or adds to it in some contrasting way. Most Handelian airs are cast in the mold of the *da capo aria*, the *ABA* form that returns to the beginning to reiterate the message of the first idea in the new light of the second statement. The bass aria "But who may abide" is a demonstration of this principle. The soloist asks the questions, "But who may abide the day of His coming, and who shall stand when He appeareth?" In response, the listener might ask, "Why does he ask, for would we not all stand to greet the Lord?" In the B section of the aria, the soloist states the difficulty, "For He is like a refiner's fire." God is judge and he will separate the righteous from the sinful. He is like the refiner who smelts metal from ore and separates the gold or silver from the rock. When the bass returns to his initial question of who shall stand, the listener might reconsider whether he dares be among those who rise to meet God eyeball to eyeball. And the mighty chorus, like impartial observers from another world, responds in frightening tone, "And He shall purify the sons of Levi, that they may offer unto the Lord an offering in righteousness." Thus, the plan of the specific recitative-aria-chorus combination serves as the model for all the subsections of the entire work: develop an idea rapidly (recitative), elaborate a single aspect (aria), and hammer the message home (chorus). After four exact repetitions of the

a. Straightforward recitative - simple statement

Be-hold,   a   vir-gin shall con-ceive,   and bear a   son,

b. Recitative heightened by chordal activity.

The voice of him that crieth in the wil-der-ness,   Pre-pare ye the way

c. Recitative heightened by melodic embellishment.

Yet once a lit-tle while   and I will shake_____

plan, Handel, of course, varies the scheme by omitting, inverting, or repeating the three basic elements—recitative, aria, and chorus—but the affective function of each always remains the same. Thus the listener gears his expectations to the type of music offered.

The second and third parts of the *oratorio* are naturally similar in format to that of the first. The tone of the second part is sorrowful, for it accompanies the music of the Passion and, only toward the end, Easter. The libretto tells vividly how Christ was despised: "He hid not His face from shame and spitting," "He was bruised for our iniquities," "All they that see Him laugh Him to scorn," and "He was cut off out of the land of the living." This intense, doleful atmosphere is relieved briefly with words and music promising the Resurrection: "But Thou didst not leave His soul in hell" and "Lift up your heads . . . the King of Glory shall come in"; but it quickly returns to a drama of death and fear when the people are reminded of their shortcomings: "Why do the nations so furiously rage together?" and "He that dwelleth in heaven shall laugh them to scorn." In other words, a religious drama is taking place; the listeners are no longer observers but participants. They do not have to identify with characters on stage as they would at the theater or opera house; they are being explicitly identified themselves as the words of the Bible preach to them. And when the words are completely damning and reduce the attentive listener to dust—"Thou shalt break them with a rod of iron, Thou shalt dash them in pieces like a potter's vessel"—then Handel steps in and saves the victory with one of the most exultant choruses of all time: "Hallelujah! for the Lord God Omnipotent reigneth." The Hallelujah Chorus alone would have brought fame to George Frederick Handel, for it is one of those resounding strokes of genius that is able in itself to embody the concept of a victorious Lord.

The Hallelujah Chorus creates a problem for the composer. In it he achieves an artistic peak making material that follows necessarily anticlimactic. But, the oratorio is not yet over. In this hurried world of the twentieth century, one still finds *Messiah* concerts that cut off the work at this point. Musically, one comes to a satisfactory conclusion at the end of the Hallelujah Chorus, but spiritually one has missed the message of the text if the portion dealing with individual redemption through faith is left out. The only possible, or impossible, solution, of course, was to write an even more stirring and more climactic chorus for the final portion; unbelievably, Handel was able to do this. The Amen Chorus which acts as finale to the third part and the work as a whole, is one of the most awesome choral fugues conceived by man. It grows and swells, piling layer upon layer in a surprisingly brief sprint to the finish. An alternation of slow and fast chordal passages sets the stage: "Worthy is the Lamb . . . to receive power . . . worthy is the Lamb . . . to receive power. . . ." This introduction is followed by a fugue whose vocal entrances rise successively from the low range of the men's voices to the upper register of the sopranos': "Blessing and honour, glory and pow'r be unto Him that sitteth on the throne." A fugal device called *stretto* collapses the interval of time between successive entrances so that the music, which seemed to work only at greater length and expansiveness, suddenly feels to be moving faster—to be propelling forward with less caution but no greater recklessness. The voices begin to pair and rise together; suddenly they join in a unison line that reduces the texture to a penetrating knife edge. Expanding again, the voices move into a series of high, sustained chords that virtually teeter on the brink of a musical chasm. Then, at last, the voices begin to move and gain momentum in the final *fugue* to the single word "Amen." The sense of completion is achieved; the restoration of balance is accomplished; the work is consummated.

Strangely enough, *Messiah* was not composed for a church service. Handel was a bankrupt impresario-composer who was currently out of favor as a local opera composer. He seized an opportunity to perform "some of his choicest Musick" for the benefit of Mercer's Hospital in Dublin, Ireland. On the 12th of April, 1742, he performed his new oratorio in public for the first time. With its baroque harmonies and standardized forms, it reflected ideas seen emerging out of the past with a steady linkage back to the Renaissance through the operas of Lully to the congregational sacred music of Saint Philip Neri in Rome. In its expansiveness and classical balance, in its communication with a growing middle class, and in its seeming power to attract listeners from all walks of life in the modern world, it is a searching tendril that stretches upward to the future. Many works of art seem to be understood fully only within the context of the age in which they were created. Handel's *Messiah* is an exception to this rule, for it seems to have had an immediacy and direct impact on musicians and laymen alike from its origin in 1742 to the present day. It is perhaps the most substantial monument of Western musical art of all time.

Johann Sebastian Bach (1685–1750)   The Baroque era was certainly an age of contrast, and the lives and music of Handel and Bach illustrate this principle vividly. Bach led a relatively uneventful musical career that saw him employed as one of a number of musical functionaries who served at court and church in Protestant Germany. Virtually his entire life was spent within sixty miles of his birthplace. Handel, on the other hand, developed his profession in the company of the leading musical patrons of Germany, Italy, and England. His music was composed for the contemporary international taste, and the last years of his life were filled with great public acclaim and financial success. Still, it was only a few years ago, 1968, that a painted image of Bach looked out from the cover of *Time* magazine—a cover that proclaimed, "Johann Sebastian Bach: Music from the Fifth Evangelist." Media hype or a truth worthy of investigation? Inside, the five-page feature article reported, "Today, of course, Bach is universally ranked among the transcendent creators of Western civilization."[1] A transcendent creator, not just of Western *music* but of Western *civilization!* What, then, is the magic of the composer from Eisenach?

Bach, although well known as a virtuoso organist, saw few of his works published during his lifetime, and his music found almost total neglect immediately after his death. However, great composers of subsequent generations would not allow his music to die. Haydn owned a copy of the *Mass in B Minor*, Mozart studied his motets and *The Art of Fugue*, and Mendelssohn resurrected his music for the larger public with his revival of the *St. Matthew Passion* in 1829, seventy-nine years after the composer's death. Regardless of his provincial life, and regardless of the superlative creations of other masters, including his famous contemporary Handel, Bach's surviving works are so various, inventive, intellectual, and beautiful that it is difficult to name his equal among composers of any age! Today, Bach Societies and Bach Choirs thrive throughout the world. Organists know his music as the principal repertoire for the instrument, and violinists and cellists learn his solo sonatas, partitas, and suites as the tests that separate professional from beginner, master from novice. All serious keyboard players learn with the *Inventions*, mature with *The Well-Tempered Clavier*, and strive for the *Goldberg Variations* and the *Chromatic Fantasia and Fugue*. And today's composers study and marvel at the sheer genius displayed in the contrapuntal intricacies of *The Art of Fugue* and the *Musical Offering*. But the master composer's profound religious convictions come triumphantly to light in his vocal compositions, especially those for chorus, soloists, and orchestra in combination—cantatas, passions, Masses, Magnificat settings, and oratorios.

For the last twenty-seven years of his life, Bach was a Lutheran church musician in Leipzig. For the Christmas services of 1734, he composed a mammoth work in six parts, *The Christmas Oratorio*. Written for the six feast days or Sundays of the holiday season (1734–35)—the three days of Christmas (December 25–27), New Year's Day, the Sunday after New Year, and Epiphany (the manifestation of the Savior to the gentiles, or the coming of the Magi), each part is like a complete cantata in itself and lasts about thirty minutes. An unusual feature of the first performance was the publication of the entire libretto in advance, so that members of the congregation could not only understand the words more readily but also see the totality of the work. Because only one of the six portions was performed at each of the six services, it was important for the congregation to review the significance of the day's setting within the context of the whole.

[1] "A Composer for All Seasons (But Especially for Christmas)," *Time* (December 27, 1968), p. 35.

The first three parts are built on the story of Christmas as reported in the Gospel of Luke; the fourth deals with the circumcision and naming of Jesus; the fifth tells of the flight into Egypt; and the sixth deals with the story of the Three Wise Men from the East. Unlike Handel's *Messiah*, Bach's *Christmas Oratorio* places great emphasis on reflection and downplays the dramatic element. In addition to using German prose from Luther's translation of the *Bible*, Bach combines introspective poetry from an unknown librettist, possibly Picander (Friedrich Henrici). Like Handel and most of the other composers of his day, Bach reused much musical material he had composed earlier, but he constantly strove for a unified total work that was true and complete unto itself, a work that displayed perfect craftsmanship in every element.

The oratorio is a collection of biblical texts and poetic meditations underscored by sixty-four separate musical movements. Bach's composition and orchestration are superlative, and he avails himself of a rich palette of musical resources, an orchestra of organ, strings, flutes, oboes, oboes *d'amore*, oboes and horns *da caccia*,[2] bassoon, trumpets, and timpani; a chorus; and four solo voices. A tenor assumes the role of the Evangelist and narrates the bible story. The other three—soprano, alto, and bass—sometimes sing the role of a biblical character—Herod, Angel—and sometimes merely elaborate and reflect on a text. There is ample opportunity for virtuosic display by both singer and instrumentalist, but the use of this and every other musical device is always subordinated to the primary purpose of underscoring the meaning of the text, never of seeking to impress a concert audience. The music was created to help a congregation join professional musicians in musical worship.

Fourteen times in the course of the six services a chorale is inserted into the musical tapestry, and these are the congregational hymns which Bach's Lutheran parishioners knew, loved, and felt with deep emotion. The first-used chorale tune, "Herzlich tut mich Verlangen" (My Heart Is Filled with Longing), piece #5

of the sixty-four, is also the chorale that closes the entire cycle, piece #64. In Bach's day it was known as the Passion Chorale, "O Haupt voll Blut und Wunden" (O Sacred Head Sore Wounded). Bach had used several settings of this chorale in his *St. Matthew Passion* five years earlier, and its use here, with the Christmas texts, #5 ("How Best Can I Receive Thee?") and #64 ("Now Christ Will Avenge Our Satanic Foes") can also be interpreted as Bach's way of suggesting that the birth of Christ must also be interpreted as a foreshadowing of his death on the cross, if it is to have religious significance as well as musical or other artistic significance.

The musical forms and techniques displayed in this work are as diverse as the orchestral and vocal resources already mentioned, but the size and complexity of the *Christmas Oratorio* prevents detailed analysis in a limited space. However, some important and obvious features will help interpretation and understanding. Similarities to Italian and French opera, as well as to Handel's *Messiah*, exist in the recitatives and arias. The same principles of exposition of text in recitatives and reflection on one or two thoughts in an aria hold true. The same principles of tonal organization for individual pieces, daily sections, and the complete work operate here to give formal unity and variety to each part:

THE ORATORIO COMPLETE

The six days:	I	II	III	IV	V	VI
Keys of each part:	D	G	D	F	A	D

The key of D establishes the base or tonic of the entire work. The keys of G and A are closely related to D (subdominant and dominant) and provide variety with a sense of belonging. The key of F is somewhat more distantly related, but placed in the center, after the reaffirmation of the tonic, it allows greater exploration and development, and more intense contrast, within the safe framework or confines of the surrounding parts.

At the next level, the individual service, we see the same principles at work. For example,

DAY ONE
CHRISTMAS DAY

Pieces:	1	2	3	4	5	6	7	8	9
Key of each:	D	to E	A	a	a	to D	G	D	D

---

[2] The oboe *d'amore*, or oboe of love, was a baroque oboe whose tone was considered sweeter than the regular soprano oboe. The horns *da caccia*, or hunting horns, were valveless natural horns that had, in the early eighteenth century, a more trumpetlike sound.

The tonic is D, and it is firmly established at beginning and ending. The keys of A and G are the dominant and subdominant, respectively, as mentioned above, and are the most closely related keys. A-minor (pieces #4 and #5) is the minor dominant and gives some variety. Pieces #2 and #6 are recitatives that prepare the entrance to their arias (#3 and #7) by moving to the dominant of their related piece. Because this is the first of the six major sections of the oratorio, the tonal exploration and development is not as great as it will become later in the work, but the related variety is sufficient for the composer to sustain the congregation's attention for a long duration without interruption. For the non-musician, the exposition of these keys and their relationships may seem meaningless, but to all listeners these key relationships have their effect, whether or not the listener is consciously aware of their presence or technically competent to describe their intricacies. Bach knew this, and he assumed even more. He believed that D Major had affective power on his listener, that it instilled a sense of joy and exuberance that was absolute and intrinsic to the sound itself. Therefore, to set the Christmas story with its joyful opening

Praise, joy and gladness be blended in one!
Tell what the Father Almighty has done!

in the key of D was almost a requirement of the doctrine of affections that governed baroque composition. We respond to the jubilant trumpets, the energetic voices, the rush of notes, and the instrumental colors, but Bach also believed that we would react to D Major, the key of gladness and strength.

The *Christmas Oratorio* can be listened to in one sitting, of course, but the composer's original intent was to provide music for services spanning two weeks. Therefore, let us study and listen to the music for December 25, Christmas Day, as one complete unit. The opening chorus is a massive three-part structure in *da capo* format. Using the full resources of the orchestra and chorus, it has a monumental grandeur. In contrapuntal style, the forces pile one upon the other, creating an effect of both solidity and motion. The basic melodic motive is embellished, and it appears over and over in a series of fugal entries. The orchestra leads the way,

and the voices proclaim the message, "Praise, joy, and gladness be blended in one!"

There is a middle, contrasting section. Its hushed tones reflect the awe of the singers as they say, "Worship the Highest and fall down before him."

The music gradually builds again, and the *da capo* returns us to the beginning for a repeat of the entire first section.

Pieces #2 and #3 are both recitatives, but they are quite different. The first is unaccompanied except by continuo (keyboard and a bass instrument or two), and the tenor sings the biblical prose from Luke, "And it came to pass in those days, that there went out a decree from Caesar Augustus. . . ."

2. Evangelista

The second recitative, #3, is accompanied by two oboes *d'amore*, and it has an almost arioso quality. The alto sings the words of the poet,

Behold the Bridegroom, Love Divine,
Behold the hope of David's line,

3. Accompagnato

She then sings her aria in A Minor, which, even though it is structured in the *da capo* format, is composed as a trio sonata, a contrapuntal work for three equal melodic lines, usually for two melodic instruments and continuo. The first melodic line is played by violin and *oboe d'amore* in unison; the second melodic line is sung by the alto; and the third line is performed by continuo—keyboard (organ), cello, and bassoon doubling the bass melody. It was also standard practice for the keyboard player to improvise a simple chordal ac-companiment with the right hand while the left hand or pedal played the bass melody. This aria is typical of one aspect of Bach's idiom. The structure is clear and balanced, the counterpoint is obvious and fascinating, and the music moves along relentlessly through the persistent Baroque rhythm. Even though it has these features of master craftsmanship, the work is tender and expressive. The master craftsman oversteps neither the artist nor the devout Lutheran.

4. Aria

Be - rei - te dich, Zi - on, mit zärt - li - chen Trie - ben,

Dei - ne Wan - gen müs - sen heut viel schö - ner pran - gen,

The choir and instruments respond with a simple setting of the chorale usually associated with the Crucifixion. Its tentative, inconclusive ending on the dominant (E in the key of A Minor) might be attributed to the composer's supposed attempt to express a foreshadow-ing of future tragedy, or it might simply be the result of a modal melody that begins and ends on E. Either way, the Lutheran congregation cannot help but respond sympathetically to its depth and beauty.

5. Choral

Wie soll ich dich emp - fan -. gen und wie be - gegn' ich dir?
O al - ler Welt Ver - lan - gen, o mei - ner See - len Zier!

The Evangelist returns with the biblical text, "And she brought forth her firstborn Son . . . . ,"

6. Evangelista

Und sie ge - bar ih - ren er - sten Sohn

and this is immediately followed by an accompanied chorale setting in which the bass soloist intersperses devotional, meditative statements in accompanied recitative style. This time the chorale is not harmonized but sung as a unison line by the sopranos (normally boys). This melody, less familiar to us today than it was to Lutherans in 1734, is set against the melodic layers of the two oboes *d'amore*.

7. Choral

A final aria shifts the mood from contemplation to one of celebration as the sounds of the opening return to continue the birthday celebration. The syncopation between trumpet and orchestra is a prominent feature of this opening, and the bass enters to proclaim,

Sovereign Lord and King Almighty,
Savior dear, behold how lightly
Holdest Thou all pride and state.

8. Aria

Finally, the chorus returns singing to the tune of the Christmas chorale, "Vom Himmel hoch" (From Heaven High), the words, "Ah, my dearest Jesus child. . . ."

9. Choral

Two centuries before Bach labored as a church musician in his beloved homeland, Martin Luther had chosen the chorale as the most appropriate vehicle for the congregation's communal expression of faith. Early in his career, Bach stated his goal of creating "a well-regulated church music to the honor of God." Like a preacher, he interpreted the texts he compiled with all the craft and art at his disposal. Taking the Lutheran chorale as his *cantus prius factus*, his pre-existent sacred melody, and coupling it with his skill, genius, and pious dedication, he composed works expressive of his age and for ours. Why he was held in no great esteem as a composer during his lifetime is a mystery that may never be solved, but it matters little to those of us today who have the opportunity of sharing his music in a way not possible at any other time in history. The *Christmas Oratorio* is both typical and unique, an example of his sacred music and an incomparable masterpiece.

22

The Arts at the Court of Louis XIV

Because the high point of baroque music came in the early eighteenth century, later than that of the other arts, we have temporarily stepped out of chronological order. We now return to France in the late seventeenth century to examine aspects of a culture that fused the baroque aesthetic with an espousal of reason, order, and clarity, as found in classical (Greco-Roman) art, a culture that came to be called *neoclassical*.

Louis XIV (1638–1715) and Absolutism

The most populous country in western Europe, reunited after the divisive religious wars of the late sixteenth century, sharing with England and Holland in the flourishing Atlantic trade, France was the most powerful country in Europe from the mid-seventeenth to the early nineteenth century. Under Louis XIV, France became dominant not only in politics but in cultural life as well. It was, however, a culture with a narrow base, created by and for the aristocracy and upper bourgeoisie, always oriented around the monarch (contrast the cultures of ancient Athens, the Middle Ages, and Africa), but one that impressed people from all social classes. This culture developed from the king's lifestyle at his court.

Absolutism as a form of government (manifested as absolute monarchy) began to take shape under Louis' predecessors, Henry IV and Louis XIII, but Louis XIV made it an unchangeable fact. He managed to transform France's traditionally restless, independent nobles into fawning courtiers eager to catch the smile of their king. As a child, Louis had witnessed the evils that seditious upper classes could inflict on society; now the central aim of his life was to transform these elements into loyal servants of the crown. A master showman, he created around him such an aura of grandeur that he became known as the Great Monarch. The upper nobility were expected to live at court, rather than in their own castles on their own lands. Louis moved his court from the palace of the Louvre in Paris to Versailles, twelve miles outside. There he built up a somewhat insulated world where he could entertain the nobles and keep an eye on them. The bourgeois, eager to buy their way into the nobility and to be presented at court, were not likely to cause any trouble; and the peasants and lower classes were so heavily taxed that they remained in an almost feudal stage of dependence. Louis saw to it that the monarchy became the primary source of privilege and honor in the society so that men would look to him as to the light. The "Sun King" was extolled as the center and source of all power, just as the sun was the center of the universe.

A noble from a once-powerful family—not at all pleased with the new absolutism—has left us a sometimes scathing, but nonetheless vivid and penetrating, portrayal of Louis and his court. The memoirs of the duke of Saint-Simon, although written in the last years of the Sun King's reign, are the best record that we have of what went on throughout. Here, for example, is Saint-Simon's account of why Louis built his palace at Versailles and how he lived there. The translation is by Bayle St. John.

LOUIS DE ROUVROY, DUC DE SAINT-SIMON

Versailles

He early showed a disinclination for Paris. The troubles that had taken place there during the minority[1] made him regard the place as dangerous; he wished, too, to render himself venerable by hiding himself from the eyes of the multitude; all these considerations fixed him at St. Germains[2] soon after the death of the Queen, his mother. It was to that place he began to attract the world by fêtes and gallantries, and by making it felt that he wished to be often seen.

His love for Madame de la Vallière,[3] which was at first kept secret, occasioned frequent excursions to Versailles, then a little card castle, which had been built by Louis XIII . . . the King, his son, slept there, so that he might be more in private with his mistress, pleasures unknown to the hero and just man, worthy son of Saint Louis, who built the little château.

These excursions of Louis XIV by degrees gave birth to those immense buildings he erected at Versailles; and their convenience for a numerous court, so different from the apartments at St. Germains, led him to take up his abode there entirely shortly after the death of the Queen. He built an infinite number of apartments, which were asked for by those who wished to pay their court to him; whereas at St. Germains nearly everybody was obliged to lodge in the town, and the few who found accommodation at the château were strangely inconvenienced.

The frequent fêtes, the private promenades at Versailles, the journeys, were means on which the King seized in order to distinguish or mortify the courtiers, and thus render them more assiduous in pleasing him. He felt that of real favours he had not enough to bestow; in order to keep up the spirit of devotion, he therefore unceasingly invented all sorts of ideal ones, little preferences and petty distinctions, which answered his purpose as well.

He was exceedingly jealous of the attention paid

---

[1] The "Fronde," a revolt of nobles against the power of the king.
[2] Another palace outside of Paris.
[3] Louis XIV's first mistress.

him. Not only did he notice the presence of the most distinguished courtiers, but those of inferior degree also. He looked to the right and to the left, not only upon rising but upon going to bed, at his meals, in passing through his apartments, or his gardens of Versailles, where alone the courtiers were allowed to follow him; he saw and noticed everybody; not one escaped him, not even those who hoped to remain unnoticed. He marked well all absentees from the court, found out the reason of their absence, and never lost an opportunity of acting towards them as the occasion might seem to justify. With some of the courtiers (the most distinguished), it was a demerit not to make the court their ordinary abode; with others 'twas a fault to come but rarely; for those who never or scarcely ever came it was certain disgrace. When their names were in any way mentioned, "I do not know them," the King would reply haughtily. Those who presented themselves but seldom were thus characterised: "They are people I never see;" these decrees were irrevocable. He could not bear people who liked Paris.

Every action of the day at court was performed with such ceremony and ritual that life must have seemed like a continuous formal ballet. Courtiers were present and assisted at *le lever du roi* and *le coucher du roi*, the king's getting up in the morning and going to bed at night. (The same words in French are used for the rising and setting of the sun.) Here is Saint-Simon's description of the king's rising:

Le Lever du Roi

At eight o'clock the chief valet de chambre on duty, who alone had slept in the royal chamber, and who had dressed himself, awoke the King. The chief physician, the chief surgeon, and the nurse (as long as she lived), entered at the same time. The latter kissed the King; the others rubbed and often changed his shirt, because he was in the habit of sweating a great deal. At the quarter, the grand chamberlain was called (or, in his absence, the first gentleman of the chamber), and those who had, what was called the *grandes entrées*. The chamberlain (or chief gentleman) drew back the cur-

tains which had been closed again, and presented the holy water from the vase, at the head of the bed. These gentlemen stayed but a moment, and that was the time to speak to the King, if any one had anything to ask of him; in which case the rest stood aside. When, contrary to custom, nobody had aught to say, they were there but for a few moments. He who had opened the curtains and presented the holy water, presented also a prayer-book. Then all passed into the cabinet of the council. A very short religious service being over, the King called, they re-entered. The same officer gave him his dressing-gown; immediately after, other privileged courtiers entered, and then everybody, in time to find the King putting on his shoes and stockings, for he did almost everything himself and with address and grace. Every other day we saw him shave himself; and he had a little short wig in which he always appeared, even in bed, and on medicine days. He often spoke of the chase, and sometimes said a word to somebody. No toilette table was near him; he had simply a mirror held before him.

As soon as he was dressed, he prayed to God, at the side of his bed, where all the clergy present knelt, the cardinals without cushions, all the laity remaining standing; and the captain of the guards came to the balustrade during the prayer, after which the King passed into his cabinet.

On Dancing

On Mardi Gras, there was a grand toilette of the Duchesse de Chartres, to which the King and all the Court came; and in the evening a grand ball, similar to that which had just taken place, except that the new Duchesse de Chartres was led out by the Duc de Bourgogne. Every one wore the same dress, and had the same partner as before.

I cannot pass over in silence a very ridiculous adventure which occurred at both of these balls. A son of Montbron, no more made to dance at Court than his father was to be chevalier of the order (to which, however, he was promoted in 1688), was among the company. He had been asked if he danced well; and he had replied with a confidence which made every one hope that the contrary was the case. Every one was satisfied. From the very first bow, he became confused, and he lost step at once. He tried to divert attention from his mistake by affected attitudes, and carrying his arms high; but this made him only more ridiculous, and excited bursts of laughter, which, in despite of the respect due to the person of the King (who likewise had great difficulty to hinder himself from laughing), degenerated at length into regular hooting. On the morrow, instead of flying the Court or holding his tongue, he excused himself by saying that the presence of the King had disconcerted him, and promised marvels for the ball which was to follow. He was one of my friends, and I felt for him. I should even have warned him against a second attempt, if the very different success I had met with had not made me fear that my advice would be taken in ill part. As soon as he began to dance at the second ball, those who were near stood up, those who were far off climbed wherever they could to get a sight; and the shouts of laughter were mingled with clapping of hands. Every one, even the King himself, laughed heartily, and most of us quite loud, so that I do not think any one was ever treated so before. Montbron disappeared immediately afterwards, and did not show himself again for a long time. It was a pity he exposed himself to this defeat, for he was an honourable and brave man.

Dancing became both a prime social pastime and a high art form under Louis XIV, and we will return to it. Let us examine now the framework in which this lifestyle was created: the palace at Versailles.

Versailles

The art and architecture of Versailles provided the setting for the spectacle of the monarchy of Louis XIV. It remains as the example of a place designed and refined to enhance the ideal of kingship and power.

The transformation of the medieval castle, secure from attack with its high walls and battlements, into an open palace tells the story of the transformation from a feudal way of life to the ascendancy of one ruler. When the court had an urban location, the rich and powerful built in the city. By the sixteenth century, however, in both Italy and France wealthy nobility and gentry had begun to build splendid country houses. In Italy the Venetian architect Palladio was the greatest designer of this type of residence (Fig. 22-1). In France sixteenth-century palatial architecture tended to grow from the local traditions with some influence from Renaissance Italy.

By the early seventeenth century the great country house, the château, had become a magnificent retreat for the summer; for hunting, games, and entertain-

22-1 Palladio, Villa Rotunda, Vicenza. (Alinari/Editorial Photocolor Archives)

22-2 Villa Vaux-le-Vicomte, Le Vau. (Giraudon, Paris)

ments; and for escape from life at the royal court. Louis XIII and his ministers had established a pattern that Louis XIV accepted and transformed. Vaux-le-Vicomte (1657–1661), built by Le Vau for one of Louis' ministers, was the most splendid and sumptuous of these residences (Fig. 22-2). With this (and the beautiful Louise de la Vallière) in mind, Louis XIV decided to enlarge the small hunting lodge at Versailles that had served Louis XIII. This extravaganza is based on the adaptation of the architectural language of Rome and the Renaissance.

The palace of Versailles was begun in 1669 by Le Vau, who incorporated the old brick and stone lodge into the new designs. Originally the building was a three-sided rectangle with the chief entrance on the east and the garden façade on the west with its courtyard (Fig. 22-3). Le Vau extended the wings east to create a courtyard on the entrance side; on the west garden façade he encased the building in the same pale, warm marble of the other sides, centering the courtyard with a six-columned portico and the ends of the flanking wings with smaller porticoes with paired columns. When Le Vau died in 1670, he was replaced by

Jules Hardouin Mansart. It was Mansart who gave the palace its present scale.

On the east side Mansart focused attention on the entrance by the convergence of three great avenues (Fig. 22-4). In the angles were the horseshoe-shaped stables. He also added the long flanking wings that run north and south. On the garden façade (Fig. 22-5) Mansart joined the wings with the Hall of Mirrors, and the façade became an unbroken expanse, punctuated by a central portico, like the original one.

As the garden façade was meant as the principal view, it is appropriate to examine it more closely. The ground floor has a deep substantial base and round arches for the windows. The masonry is fairly smooth, but deep grooves run parallel to the ground and break to create the *voussoirs*. The only other decoration is on the *keystones* of the arches; each has the relief of a head; the sequence depicts the ages of man. On the next level, which is slightly taller than the first, the arched windows are repeated and are separated by Ionic *pilasters* on bases that support the *entablature*. Each window is also framed by other pilasters and a profiled molding with decorative keystone. The central

Garden Facade

N

Entrance Facade

■ Le Roy	▨ Le Vau	▦ Mansart	▨ Gabriel
(Louis XIII)	(Louis XIV)	(Louis XIV)	(Louis XV)

22-3 Versailles (plan)

22-4 Versailles, aerial view. (French Government Tourist Office)

22-5 Versailles, garden façade. (Lauros-Giraudon, Paris)

portico and those on either side have Ionic columns and free-standing sculpture above the entablature. The masonry is smooth, the joints filled even with the surface. The third, attic story is lower in height; its rectangular windows with simple molding, pilaster, and balustrade with urns and sculpture act as a *cornice*, weighing down the whole flat-roofed block. All the details are familiar from the Greek, Roman, and Renaissance vocabularies. Their elaborate combination gives the wall rhythm and interest but only begins to suggest the complexity of weight, load, and plan that lies behind. In its strict continuity and order it also disguises scale. It is difficult to know how big it is, how tall, wide, or long. One cannot easily relate to the building, which is even more impressive as one walks around the palace. The exterior detailing is essentially continuous, and if one walks from long end to end, the distance is some six hundred yards or six football fields. From his bedroom on the east, facing the rising sun, the Sun King had an unimpeded view of three miles.

Begun with the work on the palace, the gardens were designed as its setting. André Le Notre, their designer, combined plantings, ponds, canals, fountains, and falls to enhance and repeat the symmetry and order of the palace. The long tree-lined or hedged walks and the intricately planted beds of brilliantly colored flowers provided the vistas, reflections, and light of outdoor rooms. Everywhere the court's formality was recalled in the total subjugation of nature to order and design, a formality that showed absolute control. Everywhere the Sun King's magnificence was proclaimed. The garden façade faced two great fountains: one featured the ancestors of Apollo; the other, on axis with the Hall of Mirrors and the long canal, was dedicated to Apollo himself, the god of light and sun (Fig. 22-6).

The Hall of Mirrors, which fills the central block of the west side, was the gathering place for the court and the site for balls and other performances (Fig. 22-7). Its great windows drew light from the expansive open vistas, and its mirrors reflected that light. At night, filled with candles, it glittered icily. On either end of this opulent vast room are the Salons of War and Peace. The ceilings and walls are decorated with allegorical paintings celebrating the deeds of Louis XIV. Le Brun, chief painter to the king, was responsible for this and for all the interior decoration. The paintings themselves, executed by swarms of assistants, are a bit mechanical and cold. Rather the rich marble paneled

22-6 Versailles, Fountain of Apollo. (Giraudon, Paris)

22-7 Versailles, Hall of Mirrors. (Giraudon, Paris)

walls, inlaid floors, and gilded pilasters and moldings attract our attention.

The Royal Chapel, added by Hardouin-Mansart between 1689 and 1710, gives us another experience of the palace (Fig. 22-8). Already the Sun King's power was waning; battles were lost, treasure spent. In his old age, when religion became more important, Louis abandoned all building, except for this light, very beautiful chapel. Its great height (lower floor for the court, gallery level for royalty) recalls the Gothic style, though the architectural members and details have their origin in antiquity and the Renaissance. Compare this with Brunelleschi's interior at San Lorenzo. (See Chapter 10 in Volume I.) What are the most significant departures from his ideals? Compare this with the Cornaro chapel.

The marble, gilded, painted, and paneled rooms of Versailles echoed with the feet of courtiers, ambassadors, and kings of France until the French revolution, but no one was truly accommodated except Louis XIV. This portrait bust by Bernini shows him shortly after his ascension (Fig. 22-9). The sensuous hair and mouth, the sharp-eyed gravity, the swirling drapery reveal the youthful, virile Sun King. The later portrait by Hyacinthe Rigaud gives us a better idea of the pomp and ceremony that defined the formal court (Fig. 22-10). The face is older, strong but sagging. The sweeping blue, gold, and ermine robes of state almost obscure the Sun King.

The overwhelming feeling at Versailles is domination: domination by order, symmetry, balance, and repetition; domination achieved by forcing grass, flowers, hedges, and trees into intricate patterns and by chan-

22-8 Versailles, Royal Chapel. (Lauros-Giraudon, Paris)

22-9 Bernini, *Louis XIV*. (Versailles—Alinari/Editorial Photocolor Archives)

22-10 Rigaud, *Portrait of Louis XIV*. (Louvre, Paris—Alinari/Editorial Photocolor Archives)

neling water into pools, fountains, and falls, subduing nature itself to Louis' ego. This architectural complex created by the classical vocabulary contradicts the intent of the vocabulary by its vast scale and its disregard for restraint and simplicity. In a similar way there is a conflict in our response to Versailles. It vacillates between respect for, and delight in, the intricate workmanship and a kind of horrified awe at the vast scale and richness, at this complex produced at great expense to the people of France. We sense that the glittering spectacle could not endure or be endured. Art and architecture had to become more and more accessible and essential to the rising bourgeoisie.

French Court Ballet and the Origins of Modern Theatrical Dancing

The showy, dramatic qualities of the palace at Versailles were appropriate to the highly theatrical rituals constituting life at court. Central to this life were the great festivals given in the gardens and halls at Versailles, where the nobles staged their own shows. It is then hardly surprising that in this world theatrical spectacles were the favorite form of entertainment and that the arts of ballet, opera, tragedy, and comedy reached new heights in France under the reign of Louis XIV.

Around the same time that baroque opera was developing in Italy, another new baroque art form was taking shape in France. The *ballet de cour* (court ballet) developed at the French court in the early seventeenth century but had its most splendid age under Louis XIV, who was himself an excellent dancer and took the starring role in a number of performances. The court ballet, though a short-lived art form, is nonetheless a crucial one because it is one of the important roots of both our social and our theatrical dancing. It demonstrates not only another facet of seventeenth-century art but also of something of the nature of dance itself.

Why do people dance? The urge springs from the same desire to express that motivates the other arts, but the medium is the most accessible—the human body. Dancing is in a sense "body language." We have all felt the need to express fear, sorrow, anger, love, and joy with gesture and with movement. This kind of expression is both preverbal and postverbal—one can express an emotion in movement before it can be put into words and also gesture feelings beyond the limits of words. Yet no real dancing is simply an acting out of feelings. It is related to body language as poetry is to conversation; that is, it is more concentrated and more stylized.

We have seen something of the function of dance and its relation to the other arts in the cultures studied in Volume I. Dancing in ancient Greece served a ceremonial or religious function that was incorporated into tragedy and comedy at the festival of Dionysus. King David, according to the Bible, "danced before the Lord," and dance enhanced medieval Christianity in religious dramas such as *The Play of Daniel*. It is certain, too, that medieval Europeans had secular folk dances to celebrate festivities such as harvest time. During the Renaissance, dance became less religious in function but remained linked with ceremony and festival, as Lorenzo de' Medici's carnivals show. Nearly all

African cultures place great value on dance, which remains a highly developed art form in modern Africa. We saw in the African section of Volume I how dance in Africa influences all the arts and how dance expresses dramatic and religious feeling in ceremonies such as the Gelede. While all of these cultures have had a direct or indirect impact on the way that we dance today, it is in seventeenth-century Europe that we find the origins of stage dancing as we know it.

Court ballet, the first theatrical dancing, evolved from court dances, many of which were themselves influenced by folk dances. Court dancing as a form of entertainment probably began in Italy. Manuals by dancing masters published in the fifteenth and sixteenth centuries make it clear that dancing was considered an essential social grace for courtiers. Since the young nobles spent so much of their time learning to dance well, there was little need to hire professional dancers for entertainment. Nobles entertained each other with "dinner ballets"—great feasts of several courses with a dance between each course. Balls became popular in all the courts of Europe, and nobles raged to learn the latest dances from Italy. A few, like "La Volta," scandalous to many because the gentleman lifted his lady in the air (but nonetheless danced by Queen Elizabeth), were couple dances (Fig. 22-11). Most, however, were dances for couples in large groups, intended to be danced as processions or in circles, lines, or other formations.

When Catherine de' Medici, great-granddaughter of Lorenzo, became queen of France through her marriage to Henry II, she brought many aspects of Italian culture to her new country. She was especially fond of dancing and feasts. Dancing masters at Catherine's court discovered that they could make dancers move in geometric patterns; they also experimented with imitative dances that mimed dramatic actions. As musicians, poets, and stage designers worked with dancing masters, the lavish spectacles known as court ballets were born.

Histories of theatrical dancing often open with *The Comic Ballet of the Queen*, a spectacle staged by Catherine's dancing master, Balthasar de Beaujoyeulx, at the Salle Bourbon in the Louvre palace in 1581. Like an all-star gala, it lasted from ten in the evening until three in the morning. It included drama, music, poetry, extravagant costumes, and an elaborate baroque stage set, as

22-11 Lord de l'Isle, *Queen Elizabeth I Dancing 'La Volta'*. (By permission of Viscount De L'Isle, VC, KG, from his collection at Penshurst Place, Kent, England)

well as dance. The ballet had a mythological subject but a political purpose: it was intended to impress upon the French people the triumph of reason and order (in the person of the king) over chaos and disorder. This and most of the court ballets following it were, like the palace at Versailles, excellent examples of the adoption of the French baroque style to the ideal of absolutism.

The theme of order and harmony that appears in many of the ballets was not, however, a mere political expedient. Dancing masters (or *choreographers*, as they came to be called) made high theoretical claims for their art, as Leonardo had done for painting. Dance, which united all the arts in the court ballet, was said to establish harmony among them. It reflected not only the unity of the arts but the grand design of nature as well. One choreographer concluded: "The Author of the Universe is the greatest Master of ballet."

The court ballet continued to grow in appeal throughout the seventeenth century. The prime minister under Louis XIII and XIV, Cardinal Mazarin, used this popularity for political purposes by impressing on the court the royal authority of the young Louis XIV through his performances. At the age of fifteen, Louis made his most celebrated appearance in the role of Apollo, the sun god, in *The Royal Ballet of Night* (1653). This is a typical piece of baroque theater in its mixtures of tones and genres, its extravagant scenery and costumes, its use of machines and surprises, and its ballet within a ballet, similar to a play within a play. The *entrées* (the term comes from the dinner ballet) included serious mythology, magical allegory, court dances, and comic and burlesque characters. A loose plot concerned with the events of a night holds it together. In the end the political purpose is manifest, for Louis appears to dance as the rising sun while the cast sings the glories of his realm. His title of Sun King derived from this role and the splendid costume that he wore (Fig. 22-12) while playing it.

As he grew to maturity, Louis continued both to dance himself and to encourage the production of more ballets. He was also an accomplished guitar player

22-12   Louis XIV as the Sun King in the *Ballet de la Nuit*. (Bibliothèque Nationale, Paris)

and fond of poetry and drama, but dance was his favorite of the arts. His dancing master was Pierre Beauchamps; his court musician the former Florentine, Jean-Baptiste Lully. They collaborated on some opera-ballets, but eventually these two arts separated. In 1661 Louis founded the Royal Academy of Dance and in 1669 the Royal Academy of Music, which became the Paris Opera. The dance academy was primarily for noble amateurs, but in 1672 Louis founded a school to train professional dancers; this date marks the beginning of stage dancing as we know it today. Beauchamps codified the five positions and other steps still taught in ballet classes. Dance in the ballroom and dance in the theater from then on went their separate ways.

Beauchamps and Lully did collaborate with the actor-director-playwright Molière in another type of production that flourished at the end of the century. The "comedy-ballet," of which we will read an example, *The Would-Be Gentleman*, represented a more impressive unity of the arts than did the court ballet. Molière, as we will see, is justly considered the father of modern comedy. To understand this art form, we must know something about drama in seventeenth-century France.

French Neoclassical Tragedy

Drama in France, in the early part of the seventeenth century, resembled the court ballet in its mixture of genres (tragedy, comedy, pastoral, and so on), its extravagant and complicated plots, and its sometimes unwieldly length. Later in the century, however, theoreticians and practitioners of the theater reacted against what they viewed as unbridled exuberance and attempted, in conformity with the reigning political absolutism, to impose universal standards on drama. Yet as in the palace at Versailles, classical standards of clarity, order, and harmony were often used in the service of qualities such as extremes of emotion, extravagance, *grandeur* and high-flown rhetoric that we might call baroque.

Classicism as an aesthetic first appeared in tragedy and in theories of tragedy. Basing their ideas on the Italian humanists' revival and imitations of Greek and Roman tragedy (see Chapter 9 in Volume I), French writers found rules that they believed must be followed in order to produce good tragedy. The rules that they set down became a kind of standard doctrine after they were accepted by the French Academy, founded in 1635. The academy, still in operation today, was charged with putting together theoretical works of importance to the French language: dictionaries, grammars, and treatises on rhetoric and poetics. It became in fact a kind of watchdog over matters of style and usage. Its members standardized the rules for tragedy when they pronounced judgment on the first important tragedy by Pierre Corneille, based on a Spanish work, entitled *The Cid* (1637). The members of the academy found the tragedy basically a good one but lacking in certain points. What were the standards by which they judged?

Most important to the "classical" ideal of tragedy were the so-called three unities: unity of time, place, and action. The tragedy was to take place in no more than twenty-four hours, in the same setting, and was to have only one plot. Related to these three basic unities was unity of tone—tragedy and comedy were not to appear in the same play. The characters of tragedy were to be nobles, kings and queens, who would speak in a dignified manner. No vulgar realism and no violent action could appear on the stage: such events necessary to the plot could be related by a messenger. Also, the events and characters could not be contemporary: they had to be far away either in time or space. In fact, most of the French classical tragedies were based on Greek or Roman history or mythology. And yet, the plots were to follow the rule of *verisimilitude*. They were not to be fantasies but to seem as if they could actually happen.

One can see how these rules might be applied to a Greek tragedy such as *Oedipus Rex*, but the French were in fact stricter than the Athenians; many Greek tragedies do not fit these standards. Certainly every play by Shakespeare would fail the French Academy's test. It is hard for us to understand now how such strict rules could be effectively applied to art; but French classicism did produce two great tragedians: Pierre Corneille (1606–1684), who admittedly did have some trouble with the rules; and Jean Racine (1639–1699), whose pure, compressed works seem to have benefited by the limits imposed on them. The grandeur and magnificence characteristic of all the art in the era of Louis XIV is evident in the tragedies of these two writers.

Corneille and Racine were (and are) considered by many to be the glories of their age; but when the influential literary critic Boileau was asked by Louis XIV to name the greatest contemporary writer, he replied, "Molière, Sire." Most people today would concur with that judgment, for while the two tragedians seem particularly French, the comedy writer Molière is universal. Yet Molière, too, was obliged to write in conformity with the standards of his day and, especially, for the pleasure of the king.

Molière (1622–1673), a Genius of Comedy   Jean-Baptiste Poquelin, who later assumed the stage name of Molière, was born to a solidly bourgeois Parisian family.

After receiving a good education, he abandoned a possible career in law to pursue two passions—the theater and the actress Madeleine Béjart. Molière and Mlle. Béjart together founded a company of actors, the *Illustre Théâtre*, in 1643. During the years in which the company toured France, Molière gained valuable experience as an actor, director, and manager. He also wrote and produced two of his own comedies, heavily influenced by the Italian *commedia dell'arte*, with its improvisations on stock characters, which he often saw during his travels. Like Shakespeare, Molière was not just a writer but a complete man of the theater.

The great breakthrough for the *Illustre Théâtre* came when the company pleased the king, performing before him at the Louvre. Louis then offered them a theater to play in, the Petit Bourbon, which they were to share with an Italian company. From then on, Molière turned more seriously to writing, though he continued to act in his own comedies throughout his lifetime (in fact, he died during a performance). Continuing to enjoy the protection and interest of the king, Molière staged his comedies not only at the Louvre but also at the palace at Versailles and at other castles. He thus became intimately involved in the atmosphere of festivity surrounding the court of Louis XIV, but his comedies reached a much wider audience. Common people, as well as bourgeois and nobles, attended them with great enthusiasm when they played in Paris. Molière was accused by certain purists of catering to the vulgar element of the audience, but it is exactly his wide human experience and his refusal to become too refined that helped to make him a great writer of comedy.

Molière's comedies range from rather gross farces, based on the stock character of the ridiculous dupe and almost slapstick effects, to subtle analyses of human character that are close to serious drama. His greatest originality lay in his ability to observe keenly the society and the people around him and to create from them characters both of their time and for all times and places. On the whole, his comedies observe the classical three unities originally laid down for tragedy, as well as other classical canons such as simplicity and verisimilitude, yet Molière did not hesitate to deviate from the rules when it suited his purposes. The only really important rule, he maintained, was to *please*. The audience, not the theoreticians, were the best judges. It was necessary, too, to please the king. Luckily, Louis was not a man of narrow tastes.

One of Molière's greatest comedies was written for a great festival at Versailles called "The Pleasures of the Enchanted Island" (Fig. 22-13) in 1664. The title character of the play, *Tartuffe*, is a religious hypocrite, and its proposed moral clearly favors good common sense against fanaticism. The play so shocked the religious elements of the court that the archbishop used his influence to persuade Louis to ban it; not until five years later was Molière free to produce it. Another of his most admired plays, *The Misanthrope*, is about a man who hates the pretensions and superficiality of upper-class society but is in love with a girl who accepts them fully. Both of these plays are centered around a complex character and are satirical studies of human life in society.

Le Bourgeois Gentilhomme, translated here as *The Would-Be Gentleman*, is not Molière's most complex or most literary play, but it remains a favorite on stage. The king himself suggested part of the subject of this spectacle, created for festivities at the royal hunting castle at Chambord in 1670. The preceding year Louis had established diplomatic relations with the Ottoman empire, receiving an ambassador from the Grand Turk Suleiman. This exotic embassy had so impressed the French court that Louis wanted a spectacle with a Turkish ceremony in it. He left the assignment and the actual planning to the musician Lully, the dancing master Beauchamps, and the comedian Molière.

The three had collaborated before on "comedy-ballets," but this was their most successful production. At first glance it seems an unlikely combination: what has the gross realism of comedy to do with the courtly and imaginary world of ballet? And yet it is just this contrast between solid reality and make-believe that is the subject of the comedy-ballet. As usual, Molière's comedy is centered around a character through whom he depicts a whole society. Monsieur Jourdain, the main figure here, comes from the most everyday "prosaic" milieu possible, the Parisian bourgeoisie. He is the very type of the self-made man—obviously shrewd and practical enough to have made himself a great deal of money. And yet this solid merchant is a man with a

22-13 Staging for an outdoor ballet at Versailles, *Alcina's Island*. (Crown copyright. Victoria and Albert Museum, London)

dream: he senses that there is a world of ideas, art, culture, and refinement out beyond his experience, and he longs to enter into it. For him, the dream world is summed up by one word, *gentleman*, which at that time meant a member of a particular social class, the nobility. The gentlemen are those with titles, taste, fine clothes, fine educations, and exquisite ladies—and Monsieur Jourdain feels that he now has the money to buy all these things. But Jourdain is also a man with very common human defects: pretentiousness, vanity, and egotism. These qualities receive the full force of Molière's satire; yet many readers and spectators feel a great deal of sympathy for this man with a dream. The dream world itself (as seen by Molière and the spectator, not by Jourdain) is hardly admirable: Molière's satiric comedy hits the cynicism and complacency of the petty nobility and the foppery of the artists and teachers as hard as it hits the bourgeois. (Naturally the king and the powerful nobles around him, Molière's patrons, are not attacked!) The only people with good sense, bourgeois and servants, are rather limited as characters.

The comedy-ballet combination admirably demonstrates the two realms of real world/dream world. At the end of the first act the music master and dance master put on a show that represents the world of culture to which Jourdain aspires. At the end of the second act the tailors who have brought the bourgeois "dream" clothes perform a dance. Song and dance accompany the dinner that Jourdain gives for his dream lady, the marquise, at the end of Act III. The "Turkish" ceremony at the end of Act IV brings Jourdain, now a complete dupe, into a fantasy world, and the entire play dissolves into fantasy with the long ballet at the end. It may be argued that the solid, clear, "real-seeming" prose comedy constitutes the classical element of the play and the fantasy-ballets its baroque element. This version is from the English translation published by John Watts, London, in 1739.

MOLIÈRE

The Would-Be Gentleman

CHARACTERS

M. JOURDAIN, *a self-made man*
MME JOURDAIN, *his wife*
LUCILE, *their daughter*

NICOLE, *their maid*
CLÉONTE, *a suitor to Lucile*
COVIELLE, *his valet, suitor to Nicole*
DORANTE, *a courtier*
DORIMÈNE, *a marchioness, widowed*
MUSIC MASTER AND PUPIL
DANCING MASTER
FENCING MASTER
PHILOSOPHY MASTER
MASTER TAILOR
JOURNEYMAN TAILORS
SINGERS AND MUSICIANS
PAGES AND LACKEYS

ACT I

THE SCENE. *Music Master, a Pupil of the Music Master (composing at a table in the middle of the stage), a Woman Singer, and two Men Singers; a Dancing Master and Dancers*

MUSIC MASTER (*to the musicians*)   Here, step into this hall, and sit there till he comes.

DANCING MASTER (*to the dancers*)   And you too, on this side.

MUSIC MASTER (*to his pupil*)   Is it done?

PUPIL   Yes.

MUSIC MASTER   Let's see. . . . 'Tis mighty well.

DANCING MASTER   Is it anything new?

MUSIC MASTER   Yes, 'tis an air for a serenade, which I set him to compose here while we wait till our gentleman's awake.

DANCING MASTER   May one see what it is?

MUSIC MASTER   You will hear it, with the dialogue, when he comes. He won't be long.

DANCING MASTER   We have no want of business, either of us, at present.

MUSIC MASTER   'Tis true. We have found a man here, just such a one as we both of us want. This same Monsieur Jourdain is a sweet income, with his visions of nobility and gallantry which he has got into his noddle, and it would be well for your capers and my crotchets, were all the world like him.

DANCING MASTER   Not altogether so well; I wish, for his sake, that he were better skilled than he is in the things we give him.

MUSIC MASTER   It is true he understands 'em ill, but he pays for 'em well. And that's what our art has more need of at present than of anything else.

DANCING MASTER   For my part, I own it to you, I regale a little upon glory. I am sensible of applause, and think it a very grievous punishment in the liberal arts to display one's self to fools and to expose our compositions to the barbarous judgment of the stupid. Talk no more of it, there is a pleasure in working for persons who are capable of relishing the delicacies of an art, who know how to give a kind reception to the beauties of a work, and, by titillating approbation, regale you for your labour. Yes, the most agreeable recompense one can receive for the things one does is to see them understood, to see 'em caressed with an applause that does you honour. There's nothing, in my opinion, which pays us better than this for all our fatigues. And the praises of connoisseurs give an exquisite delight.

MUSIC MASTER   I grant it, and I relish them as well as you. There is nothing certainly that tickles more than the applause you speak of, but one cannot live upon this incense. Sheer praises won't make a man easy. There must be something solid mixed withal, and the best method of praising is to praise with the open hand. This indeed is one whose understanding is very shallow, who speaks of everything awry, and cross of the grain, and never applauds but in contradiction to sense. But his money sets his judgment right. He has discernment in his purse. His praises are current coin; and this ignorant commoner is more worth to us, as you see, than that grand witty lord who introduced us here.

DANCING MASTER   There's something of truth in what you say; but I find you lean a little too much towards the pelf. And mere interest is something so base that an honest man should never discover an attachment to it.

MUSIC MASTER   For all that, you decently receive the money our spark gives you.

DANCING MASTER   Certainly; but I don't place all my happiness in that: and I wish that, with his fortune, he had also some good taste of things.

MUSIC MASTER   I wish the same; 'tis what we both labour at as much as we can. But, however, he gives us the opportunity of making ourselves known in the world; and he'll pay for others what others praise for him.

DANCING MASTER   Here he comes.

(*Enter* M. JOURDAIN *in a nightgown and cap, and two* LACKEYS)

M. JOURDAIN   Well, gentlemen? What have you there? Will you let me see your little drollery?

DANCING MASTER   How? What little drollery?

M. JOURDAIN   Why the—how do you call that thing? your prologue, or dialogue of songs and dancing.

DANCING MASTER   Ha, ha!

MUSIC MASTER   You see we are ready.

M. JOURDAIN   I have made you wait a little, but 'tis because I am to be dressed out to-day like your people of quality;[1] and my hosier has sent me a pair of silk stockings which I thought I should never have got on.

MUSIC MASTER   We are here only to wait your leisure.

M. JOURDAIN   I desire you'll both stay till they have brought me my clothes, that you may see me.

DANCING MASTER   As you please.

M. JOURDAIN   You shall see me most exactly equipped from head to foot.

MUSIC MASTER   We don't doubt it.

M. JOURDAIN   I have had this Indian thing made up for me.

DANCING MASTER   'Tis very handsome.

M. JOURDAIN   My tailor tells me that people of quality go thus in a morning.

MUSIC MASTER   It fits you to a miracle.

M. JOURDAIN   Why, ho! Fellow there! both my fellows!

FIRST LACKEY   Your pleasure, sir?

M. JOURDAIN   Nothing! 'Tis only to try whether you hear me readily. (*to the* MUSIC *and* DANCING MASTERS) What say you of my liveries?

DANCING MASTER   They are magnificent.

M. JOURDAIN   (*half-opens his gown and reveals a tight pair of breeches of scarlet velvet, and a green velvet jacket*)   Here again is a kind of dishabille to perform my exercises in a morning.

MUSIC MASTER   'Tis gallant.

M. JOURDAIN   Lackey!

FIRST LACKEY   Sir?

M. JOURDAIN   T'other lackey!

SECOND LACKEY   Sir?

---

[1] Jourdain's concern with dress is representative of the importance that he now gives to *appearance*. He judges something to be good or bad according to whether "people of quality" (the nobility) appear to have it or not.

M. JOURDAIN (*taking off his gown*)   Hold my gown. (*to the* MUSIC *and* DANCING MASTERS) Do you like me so?

DANCING MASTER   Mighty well; nothing can be better.

M. JOURDAIN   Now for your affair a little.

MUSIC MASTER   I should be glad first to let you hear an air (*pointing to his pupil*) he has just composed for the serenade which you gave me orders about. He is one of my pupils, who has an admirable talent for these sort of things.

M. JOURDAIN   Yes, but that should not have been put to a pupil to do; you were not too good for that business yourself.

MUSIC MASTER   You must not let the name of pupil impose upon you, sir. These sort of pupils know as much as the greatest masters, and the air is as good as can be made. Hear it only.

M. JOURDAIN (*to his servants*)   Give me my gown that I may hear the better.—Stay, I believe I shall be better without the gown.—No, give it me again, it will do better.

MUSICIAN
I languish night and day, nor sleeps my pain,
Since those fair eyes imposed the rigorous chain;
But tell me, Iris, what dire fate attends
Your enemies, if thus you treat your friends?

M. JOURDAIN   This song seems to me a little upon the dismal; it inclines one to sleep; I should be glad you could enliven it a little here and there.

MUSIC MASTER   'Tis necessary, sir, that the air should be suited to the words.

M. JOURDAIN   I was taught one perfectly pretty some time ago. Stay—um—how is it?

DANCING MASTER   In good troth, I don't know.

M. JOURDAIN   There's lamb in it.

DANCING MASTER   Lamb?

M. JOURDAIN   Yes—Ho!
I thought my dear Namby
  As gentle as fair-o:
I thought my dear Namby
  As mild as a lamb-y.
Oh dear, oh dear, oh dear-o!
For now the sad scold is a thousand times told,
More fierce than a tiger or bear-o.
Isn't it pretty?

MUSIC MASTER   The prettiest in the world.

DANCING MASTER   And you sing it well.

M. JOURDAIN   Yet I never learnt music.

MUSIC MASTER   You ought to learn it, sir, as you do dancing. They are two arts which have a strict connection one with the other.

DANCING MASTER   And which open the human mind to see the beauty of things.

M. JOURDAIN   What, do people of quality learn music too?

MUSIC MASTER   Yes, sir.

M. JOURDAIN   I'll learn it then. But I don't know how I shall find time. For, besides the fencing master who teaches me, I have also got me a philosophy master, who is to begin this morning.

MUSIC MASTER   Philosophy is something; but music, sir, music—

DANCING MASTER   Music and dancing—music and dancing, that is all that's necessary.

MUSIC MASTER   There's nothing so profitable in a state as music.

DANCING MASTER   There's nothing so necessary for men as dancing.

MUSIC MASTER   A state cannot subsist without music.

DANCING MASTER   Without dancing, a man can do nothing.

MUSIC MASTER   All the disorders, all the wars one sees in the world, happen only from not learning music.

DANCING MASTER   All the disasters of mankind, all the fatal misfortunes that histories are replete with, the blunders of politicians, the miscarriages of great commanders, all this comes from want of skill in dancing.

M. JOURDAIN   How so?

MUSIC MASTER   Does not war proceed from want of concord amongst men?

M. JOURDAIN   That's true.

MUSIC MASTER   And if all men learnt music, would not that be a means of keeping them better in tune, and of seeing universal peace in the world?

M. JOURDAIN   You're in the right.

DANCING MASTER   When a man has been guilty of a defect in his conduct—be it in the affairs of his family, or in the government of the state, or in the command of an army—don't we always say, such a one has made a false step in such an affair?

M. JOURDAIN   Yes, we say so.

DANCING MASTER   And can making a false step proceed from anything but not knowing how to dance?

M. JOURDAIN   'Tis true, and you are both in the right.[2]

DANCING MASTER   This is to let you see the excellence and advantage of dancing and music.

M. JOURDAIN   I now comprehend it.

MUSIC MASTER   Will you see each of our compositions?

M. JOURDAIN   Yes.

MUSIC MASTER   I have told you already that this is a slight essay which I formerly made upon the different passions that may be expressed by music.

M. JOURDAIN   Very well.

MUSIC MASTER (to the musicians)   Here, come forward. (to M. JOURDAIN) You are to imagine with yourself that they are dressed like shepherds.

M. JOURDAIN   Why always shepherds? One sees nothing but such stuff everywhere.

MUSIC MASTER   When we are to introduce persons as speaking in music, 'tis necessary to probability that we give in to the pastoral way. Singing has always been appropriated to shepherds; and it is by no means natural in dialogue that princes or citizens should sing their passions.

M. JOURDAIN   Be it so, be it so. Let's see.

(Dialogue in music between a Woman and two Men)

WOMAN   *The heart that must tyrannic love obey,*
A thousand fears and cares oppress.
Sweet are those sighs and languishments,
*   they say;*
Say what they will for me,
Nought is so sweet as liberty.

FIRST MAN   *Nothing so sweet as love's soft fire,*
Which can two glowing hearts inspire
With the same life, the same desire.
The loveless swain no happiness can
*   prove.*

From life take soothing love,
All pleasure you remove.

SECOND MAN   *Sweet were the wanton archer's sway,*
Would all with constancy obey;
But, cruel fate!
No nymph is true:
The faithless sex more worthy of our
*   hate,*
To love should bid eternally adieu.

FIRST MAN   *Pleasing heat!*

WOMAN   *Freedom blest!*

SECOND MAN   *Fair deceit!*

FIRST MAN   *O how I love thee!*

WOMAN   *How I approve thee!*

SECOND MAN   *I detest!*

FIRST MAN   *Against love's ardour quit this mortal*
*   hate.*

WOMAN   *Shepherd, myself I bind here,*
To show a faithful mate.

SECOND MAN   *Alas! but where to find her?*

WOMAN   *Our glory to retrieve,*
My heart I here bestow.

SECOND MAN   *But, nymph, can I believe*
That heart no change will know?

WOMAN   *Let experience decide,*
Who loves best of the two.

SECOND MAN   *And the perjured side*
May vengeance pursue.

ALL THREE   *Then let us kindle soft desire,*
Let us fan the amorous fire.
Ah! how sweet it is to love,
When hearts united constant prove!

M. JOURDAIN   Is this all?

MUSIC MASTER   Yes.

M. JOURDAIN   I find 'tis very concise, and there are some little sayings in it pretty enough.

DANCING MASTER   You have here, for my composition, a little essay of the finest movements, and the most beautiful attitudes with which a dance can possibly be varied.

M. JOURDAIN   Are they shepherds too?

DANCING MASTER   They're what you please. (to the dancers) Hola!

(Four dancers execute all the different movements and steps that the dancing master commands. This dance constitutes the first "intermission.")

---

[2] Molière mocks the pretentiousness of the two teachers here, but beneath the comedy is some serious contemporary thought on the benefits of the arts, with which Molière probably agreed. Jourdain, however, must be convinced by a strictly utilitarian argument that distorts the theory.

ACT II

THE SCENE.   *Monsieur Jourdain, Music Master, Dancing Master*

M. JOURDAIN   This is none of your stupid things, and these same fellows flutter it away bravely.

MUSIC MASTER   When the dance is mixed with the music, it will have a greater effect still, and you will see something gallant in the little entertainment we have prepared for you.

M. JOURDAIN   That's however for by and by; and the person for whom I have ordered all this, is to do me the honour of dining with me here.

DANCING MASTER   Everything's ready.

MUSIC MASTER   But in short, sir, this is not enough, 'tis necessary such a person as you, who live great and have an inclination to things that are handsome, should have a concert of music at your house every Wednesday, or every Thursday.

M. JOURDAIN   Why so? Have people of quality?

MUSIC MASTER   Yes, sir.

M. JOURDAIN   I'll have one then. Will it be fine?

MUSIC MASTER   Certainly. You must have three voices, a treble, a counter-tenor, and bass, which must be accompanied with a bass-viol, a theorbo-lute, and a harpsichord for the thorough-bass, with two violins to play the symphonies.

M. JOURDAIN   You must add also a trumpet-marine. The trumpet-marine is an instrument that pleases me, and is very harmonious.

MUSIC MASTER   Leave us to manage matters.

M. JOURDAIN   However, don't forget by and by to send the musicians to sing at table.

MUSIC MASTER   You shall have everything you should have.

M. JOURDAIN   But above all, let the entertainment be fine.

MUSIC MASTER   You will be pleased with it, and, amongst other things, with certain minuets you will find in it.

M. JOURDAIN   Ay, the minuets are my dance; and I have a mind you should see me dance 'em. Come, master.

DANCING MASTER   Your hat, sir, if you please.

(M. JOURDAIN *takes off his foot-boy's hat, and puts it on over his own nightcap; upon which his master takes him by the hand and makes him dance to a minuet-air which he sings)*

Tol, lol, lol, lol, lol, lol,
Tol, lol, lol,
     twice;
Tol, lol, lol; tol, lol.
     In time, if you please,
Tol, lol,
     the right leg.
Tol, lol, lol.
     Don't shake your shoulders so much.
Tol, lol, lol, lol, lol.
     Why, your arms are out of joint.
Tol, lol, lol, lol, lol.
     Hold up your head. Turn out your toes.
Tol, lol, lol.
     Your body erect.[1]

M. JOURDAIN   Heh?

MUSIC MASTER   Admirably well performed.

M. JOURDAIN   Now I think of it, teach me how I must bow to salute a marchioness; I shall have occasion for it by and by.

DANCING MASTER   How you must bow to salute a marchioness?

M. JOURDAIN   Yes, a marchioness whose name is Dorimène.

DANCING MASTER   Give me your hand.

M. JOURDAIN   No. You need only to do it, I shall remember it easily.

DANCING MASTER   If you would salute her with a great deal of respect, you must first of all make a bow and fall back, then advancing towards her, bow thrice, and at the last bow down to her very knees.

M. JOURDAIN   Do it a little. *(after the* DANCING MASTER *has made three bows)* Right.

(Enter a LACKEY *holding two foils)*

LACKEY   Sir, your fencing master is here.

---

[1] The minuet was the favorite social dance at court at this time, and continued to be so throughout the eighteenth century (both George Washington and Thomas Jefferson were very good at it). It is usually done in couples, with a bit of flirtation, and requires a good deal of precision and balance.

22-14 Scene from Act I of *Le Bourgeois Gentilhomme* (1951 Comèdie Française production) with Louis Seigneur and Jacques Charon. (Photo Lipnitzki-Viollet, Paris)

M. JOURDAIN   Bid him come in that he may give me a lesson. (*to the* MUSIC *and* DANCING MASTERS) I'd have you stay and see me perform.

(*Enter a* FENCING MASTER)

FENCING MASTER (*taking the two foils out of the* LACKEY'S *hand, and giving one to* M. JOURDAIN) Come, sir, your salute. Your body straight. A little bearing upon the left thigh. Your legs not so much a-straddle. Your feet both on a line. Your wrist opposite to your hip. The point of your sword over-against your shoulder. Your arm not quite so much extended. Your left hand on a level with your eye. Your left shoulder more square. Hold up your head. Your look bold. Advance. Your body steady. Beat carte, and push carte. One, two. Recover. Again with it, your foot firm. One, two. Leap back. When you make a pass, sir, 'tis necessary your sword should disengage first, and your body make as small a mark as possible. One, two. Come, beat tierce, and push the same. Advance. Your body firm. Advance. Quit after that manner. One, two. Recover. Repeat the same. One, two. Leap back. Parry, sir, parry.

(*The* FENCING MASTER *gives him two or three home-thrusts, crying, "Parry"*)

M. JOURDAIN   Ugh!

MUSIC MASTER   You do wonders.

FENCING MASTER   I have told you already—the whole secret of arms consists but in two things, in giving and not receiving. And as I showed you t'other day by demonstrative reason, it is impossible you should receive if you know how to turn your adversary's sword from the line of your body; which depends only upon a small motion of your wrist, either inward, or outward.

M. JOURDAIN   At that rate therefore, a man without any courage is sure to kill his man and not to be killed.

FENCING MASTER   Certainly. Don't you see the demonstration of it?

M. JOURDAIN   Yes.

FENCING MASTER   By this one may see of what consideration such persons as we should be esteemed in a state, and how highly the science of arms excels all the other useless sciences, such as dancing, music, and—

DANCING MASTER   Soft and fair, Monsieur *Sa, sa.* Don't speak of dancing but with respect.

MUSIC MASTER   Pray learn to treat the excellence of music in a handsomer manner.

FENCING MASTER   You're merry fellows, to pretend to compare your sciences with mine.

MUSIC MASTER   Do but see the importance of the creature!

DANCING MASTER   The droll animal there, with his leathern stomacher!

FENCING MASTER   My little master skipper, I shall make you skip as you should do. And you, my little master scraper, I shall make you sing to some tune.

DANCING MASTER   Monsieur Tick-tack, I shall teach you your trade.

M. JOURDAIN (*to the* DANCING MASTER)   Are you bewitched to quarrel with him, who understands tierce and carte, who knows how to kill a man by demonstrative reason?

DANCING MASTER   I laugh at his demonstrative reason, and his tierce and his carte.

M. JOURDAIN (*to the* DANCING MASTER)   Softly, I say.

FENCING MASTER (*to the* DANCING MASTER)   How? Master Impertinence!

M. JOURDAIN   Nay, my dear fencing master!

DANCING MASTER (*to the* FENCING MASTER)   How? You great dray-horse!

M. JOURDAIN   Nay, my dancing master.

FENCING MASTER   If I lay my—

M. JOURDAIN (*to the* FENCING MASTER)   Gently.

DANCING MASTER   If I lay my clutches on you—

M. JOURDAIN   Easily.

FENCING MASTER   I shall curry you with such an air—

M. JOURDAIN (*to the* FENCING MASTER)   For goodness' sake.

DANCING MASTER   I shall drub you after such a manner—

M. JOURDAIN (*to the* DANCING MASTER)   I beseech you.

MUSIC MASTER   Let us teach him a little how to speak.

M. JOURDAIN (*to the* MUSIC MASTER)   Lack-a-day, be quiet.

(*Enter a* PHILOSOPHY MASTER)

Hola, Monsieur Philosopher, you are come in the nick of time with your philosophy. Come, and make peace a little amongst these people here.

PHILOSOPHY MASTER   What's to do? What's the matter, gentlemen?

M. JOURDAIN   They have put themselves into such a passion about the preference of their professions as to call names, and would come to blows.

PHILOSOPHY MASTER   O fie, gentlemen, what need was there of all this fury? Have you not read the learned treatise upon anger, composed by Seneca? Is there anything more base and shameful than this passion, which makes a savage beast of a man? And should not reason be master of all our commotions?

DANCING MASTER   How, sir? Why he has just now been abusing us both, in despising dancing which is my employment, and music which is his profession.

PHILOSOPHY MASTER   A wise man is above all foul language that can be given him, and the grand answer one should make to all affronts is moderation and patience.

FENCING MASTER   They had both the assurance to compare their professions to mine.

PHILOSOPHY MASTER   Should this disturb you? Men should not dispute about vainglory and rank; that which perfectly distinguishes one from another is wisdom and virtue.

DANCING MASTER   I maintained to him that dancing was a science to which one cannot do sufficient honour.

MUSIC MASTER   And I, that music is one of those that all ages have revered.

FENCING MASTER   And I maintained against 'em both that the science of defence is the finest and most necessary of all sciences.

PHILOSOPHY MASTER   And what becomes of philosophy, then? You are all three very impertinent fellows, methinks, to speak with this arrogance before me; and impudently to give the name of science to things that one ought not to honour even with the name of art, that can't be comprised but under the name of a pitiful trade of gladiator, ballad-singer, and morris-dancer.

FENCING MASTER   Out, ye dog of a philosopher.

MUSIC MASTER   Hence, ye scoundrel of a pedant.

DANCING MASTER   Begone, ye arrant pedagogue.

(*The* PHILOSOPHER *falls upon them, they all three lay him on*)

PHILOSOPHY MASTER   How? Varlets as you are—

M. JOURDAIN   Monsieur Philosopher!

PHILOSOPHY MASTER   Infamous dogs! Rogues! Insolent curs!

M. JOURDAIN   Monsieur Philosopher!

FENCING MASTER   Plague on the animal!

M. JOURDAIN   Gentlemen!

PHILOSOPHY MASTER   Impudent villains!

M. JOURDAIN   Monsieur Philosopher!

DANCING MASTER   Deuce take the pack-saddled ass!

M. JOURDAIN   Gentlemen!

PHILOSOPHY MASTER   Profligate vermin!

M. JOURDAIN   Monsieur Philosopher!

MUSIC MASTER   The devil take the impertinent puppy!

M. JOURDAIN   Gentlemen!

PHILOSOPHY MASTER   Knaves! Ragamuffins! Traitors! Impostors!

M. JOURDAIN   Monsieur Philosopher! Gentlemen!

Monsieur Philosopher! Gentlemen! Monsieur Philosopher!

(*The four* MASTERS *beat each other out*)

Nay, beat your hearts out if you will, I shall neither meddle nor make with you, I shan't spoil my gown to part you. I should be a great fool to thrust myself among them, and receive some blow that might do me a mischief.[2]

(*Enter the* PHILOSOPHY MASTER)

PHILOSOPHY MASTER (*setting his band right*)   Now to our lesson.

M. JOURDAIN   Ah! Sir, I'm sorry for the blows they have given you.

PHILOSOPHY MASTER   'Tis nothing at all. A philosopher knows how to receive things in a proper manner; and I'll compose a satire against 'em, in the manner of Juvenal, that shall cut 'em most gloriously. Let that pass. What have you a mind to learn?

M. JOURDAIN   Everything I can, for I have all the desire in the world to be a scholar, and it vexes me that my father and mother had not made me study all the sciences when I was young.

PHILOSOPHY MASTER   'Tis a very reasonable sentiment. *Nam, sine doctrinâ vita est quasi mortis imago.* You understand that, and are acquainted with Latin, without doubt?

M. JOURDAIN   Yes; but act as if I were not acquainted with it. Explain me the meaning of that.

PHILOSOPHY MASTER   The meaning of it is, that without learning, life is as it were an image of death.[3]

M. JOURDAIN   That same Latin's in the right.

PHILOSOPHY MASTER   Have you not some principles, some rudiments of science?

M. JOURDAIN   Oh! yes, I can read and write.

PHILOSOPHY MASTER   Where would you please to have us begin? Would you have me teach you logic?

M. JOURDAIN   What may that same logic be?

PHILOSOPHY MASTER   It's that which teaches us the three operations of the mind.

M. JOURDAIN   What are those three operations of the mind?

PHILOSOPHY MASTER   The first, the second, and the third. The first is to conceive well, by means of universals. The second, to judge well, by means of categories. The third, to draw the conclusion right, by means of figures: Barbara, Celarent, Darii, Ferio, Baralipton, etc.

M. JOURDAIN   These words are too crabbed. This logic does not suit me by any means. Let's learn something else that's prettier.

PHILOSOPHY MASTER   Will you learn morality?

M. JOURDAIN   Morality?

PHILOSOPHY MASTER   Yes.

M. JOURDAIN   What means morality?

PHILOSOPHY MASTER   It treats of happiness, teaches men to moderate their passions, and—

M. JOURDAIN   No, no more of that. I'm as choleric as the devil, and there's no morality holds me; I will have my belly full of passion whenever I have a mind to it.

PHILOSOPHY MASTER   Would you learn physics?

M. JOURDAIN   What is it that physics treat of?

PHILOSOPHY MASTER   Physics are what explain the principles of things natural and the properties of bodies; which discourse of the nature of elements, of metals, of minerals, of stones, of plants, and animals, and teach us the cause of all the meteors; the rainbow, *ignes fatui*, comets, lightnings, thunder, thunder-bolts, rain, snow, hail, winds, and whirlwinds.

M. JOURDAIN   There's too much hurly-burly in this, too much confusion.

PHILOSOPHY MASTER   What would you have me teach you then?

M. JOURDAIN   Teach me orthography.

PHILOSOPHY MASTER   With all my heart.

M. JOURDAIN   Afterwards you may teach me the almanack, to know when there's a moon, and when not.

---

[2] Jourdain here shows solid middle-class sense, opposed to his "masters." How does each defend his art? Is there anything serious beneath their foolishness? Can you think of any modern equivalents to this squabble (college departments?)?

[3] How has this philosopher contradicted the image of the philosopher that he expounds? Here, again, Molière quotes something that he believes in while ridiculing the person who says it. What do you think of the philosophy master's teaching methods? Why is Jourdain so intimidated that he pretends to know Latin? How could you use this scene to illustrate the difference between a humanist and a pedant?

PHILOSOPHY MASTER   Be it so. To pursue this thought of yours right and treat this matter like a philosopher, we must begin, according to the order of things, with an exact knowledge of the nature of letters and the different manner of pronouncing them. And on this head I am to tell you that letters are divided into vowels, called vowels because they express the voice: and into consonants, so called because they sound with the vowels and only mark the different articulations of the voice. There are five vowels or voices, A, E, I, O, U.

M. JOURDAIN   I understand all that.

PHILOSOPHY MASTER   The vowel A is formed by opening the mouth very wide, A.

M. JOURDAIN   A, A. Yes.

PHILOSOPHY MASTER   The vowel E is formed by drawing the under-jaw a little nearer to the upper, A, E.

M. JOURDAIN   A, E. A, E. In troth it is. How pretty that is!

PHILOSOPHY MASTER   And the vowel I, by bringing the jaws still nearer one to the other, and stretching the two corners of the mouth towards the ears, A, E, I.

M. JOURDAIN   A, E, I, I, I, I. 'Tis true. Long live learning!

PHILOSOPHY MASTER   The vowel O is formed by re-opening the jaws and drawing the lips near at the two corners, the upper and the under, O.

M. JOURDAIN   O, O. There's nothing more just, A, E, I, O, I, O. 'Tis admirable! I, O, I, O.

PHILOSOPHY MASTER   The opening of the mouth makes exactly a little ring, which resembles an O.

M. JOURDAIN   O, O, O. You're right, O. How fine a thing it is but to know something!

PHILOSOPHY MASTER   The vowel U is formed by bringing the teeth near together without entirely joining them, and pouting out both your lips, bringing them also near together without absolutely joining 'em, U.

M. JOURDAIN   U, U. There's nothing more true, U.

PHILOSOPHY MASTER   Your two lips pout out, as if you were making faces. Whence it comes that if you would do that to anybody and make a jest of him, you need say nothing to him but U.

M. JOURDAIN   U, U. It's true. Ah! why did not I study sooner, that I might have known all this!

PHILOSOPHY MASTER   To-morrow we shall take a view of the other letters, which are the consonants.

M. JOURDAIN   Is there anything as curious in them, as in these?

PHILOSOPHY MASTER   Doubtless. The consonant D, for example, is pronounced by clapping the tip of your tongue above the upper teeth, DE.

M. JOURDAIN   DE, DE. 'Tis so. Oh! charming things! charming things!

PHILOSOPHY MASTER   The F, in leaning the upper teeth upon the lower lip, EF.

M. JOURDAIN   EF, EF. 'Tis truth. Ah! father and mother o' mine, how do I owe you a grudge!

PHILOSOPHY MASTER   And the R, in carrying the tip of the tongue up to the roof of your mouth; so that being grazed upon by the air which bursts out with a force, it yields to it, and returns always to the same part, making a kind of trill, R, ra.

M. JOURDAIN   R, r, ra. R, r, r, r, r, ra. That's true. What a clever man are you! And how have I lost time! R, r, r, ra.

PHILOSOPHY MASTER   I will explain to you all these curiosities to the bottom.

M. JOURDAIN   Pray do. But now, I must commit a secret to you. I'm in love with a person of great quality, and I should be glad you would help me to write something to her in a short *billet-doux*, which I'll drop at her feet.

PHILOSOPHY MASTER   Very well.

M. JOURDAIN   That will be very gallant, won't it?

PHILOSOPHY MASTER   Without doubt. Is it verse that you would write to her?

M. JOURDAIN   No, no, none of your verse.

PHILOSOPHY MASTER   You would only have prose?

M. JOURDAIN   No, I would neither have verse nor prose.

PHILOSOPHY MASTER   It must be one or t'other.

M. JOURDAIN   Why so?

PHILOSOPHY MASTER   Because, sir, there's nothing to express one's self by, but prose, or verse.

M. JOURDAIN   Is there nothing then but prose, or verse?

PHILOSOPHY MASTER   No, sir, whatever is not prose, is verse; and whatever is not verse, is prose.

M. JOURDAIN   And when one talks, what may that be then?

PHILOSOPHY MASTER   Prose.

M. JOURDAIN   How? When I say, Nicole, bring me my slippers, and give me my nightcap, is that prose?

PHILOSOPHY MASTER   Yes, sir.

M. JOURDAIN   On my conscience, I have spoken prose above these forty years without knowing anything of the matter;[4] and I have all the obligations in the world to you for informing me of this. I would therefore put into a letter to her: Beautiful marchioness, your fair eyes make me die with love; but I would have this placed in a gallant manner; and have a gentle turn.

PHILOSOPHY MASTER   Why, add that the fire of her eyes has reduced your heart to ashes: that you suffer for her night and day all the torments—

M. JOURDAIN   No, no, no, I won't have all that—I'll have nothing but what I told you. Beautiful marchioness, your fair eyes make me die with love.

PHILOSOPHY MASTER   You must by all means lengthen the thing out a little.

M. JOURDAIN   No, I tell you, I'll have none but those very words in the letter: but turned in a modish way, ranged handsomely as they should be. I desire you'd show me a little, that I may see the different manners in which one may place them.

PHILOSOPHY MASTER   One may place them first of all as you said: Beautiful marchioness, your fair eyes make me die for love. Or suppose: For love die me make, beautiful marchioness, your fair eyes. Or perhaps: Your eyes fair, for love me make, beautiful marchioness, die. Or suppose: Die your fair eyes, beautiful marchioness, for love me make. Or however: Me make your eyes fair die, beautiful marchioness, for love.

M. JOURDAIN   But of all these ways, which is the best?

PHILOSOPHY MASTER   That which you said: Beautiful marchioness, your fair eyes make me die for love.

M. JOURDAIN   Yet at the same time, I never studied it, and I made the whole of it at the first touch. I thank you with all my heart, and desire you would come in good time to-morrow.

PHILOSOPHY MASTER   I shall not fail.

---

[4] M. Jourdain's realization that he has been speaking prose all his life is cited in various contexts more often than anything else in the play. Why do you think this is so?

(*Exit* PHILOSOPHY MASTER)

M. JOURDAIN (*to his* LACKEY)   What? Are my clothes not come yet?

LACKEY   No, sir.

M. JOURDAIN   This cursed tailor makes me wait unreasonably, considering it's a day I have so much business in. I shall go mad. A quartan ague wring this villain of a tailor. D—l take the tailor. A plague choke the tailor. If I had him but here now, this detestable tailor, this dog of a tailor, this traitor of a tailor, I—

(*Enter a* MASTER TAILOR *and a* JOURNEYMAN TAILOR *bringing a suit of clothes for* M. JOURDAIN)

Oh! You're there. I was going to be in a passion with you.

MASTER TAILOR   I could not possibly come sooner, and I set twenty fellows to work at your clothes.

M. JOURDAIN   You have sent me a pair of silk hose so tight that I had all the difficulty in the world to get 'em on, and there are two stitches broke in 'em.

MASTER TAILOR   They'll grow rather too large.

M. JOURDAIN   Yes, if I break every day a loop or two. You have made me a pair of shoes too, that pinch me execrably.

MASTER TAILOR   Not at all, sir.

M. JOURDAIN   How, not at all?

MASTER TAILOR   No, they don't pinch you at all.

M. JOURDAIN   I tell you they do hurt me.

MASTER TAILOR   You fancy so.

M. JOURDAIN   I fancy so because I feel it. There's a fine reason indeed.

MASTER TAILOR   Hold, stay, here's one of the handsomest suits at court, and the best-matched. 'Tis a masterly work to invent a grave suit of clothes that should not be black, and I'll give the cleverest tailor in town six trials to equal it.

M. JOURDAIN   What a deuce have we here? You have put the flowers downwards.

MASTER TAILOR   Why, you did not tell me you would have 'em upwards.

M. JOURDAIN   Was there any need to tell you of that?

MASTER TAILOR   Yes, certainly. All the people of quality wear 'em in that way.

M. JOURDAIN   Do people of quality wear the flowers downwards?

MASTER TAILOR   Yes, sir.

M. JOURDAIN   Oh, 'tis very well, then.

MASTER TAILOR   If you please I'll put 'em upwards.

M. JOURDAIN   No, no.

MASTER TAILOR   You need only say the word.

M. JOURDAIN   No, I tell you, you have done right. Do you think my clothes will fit me?

MASTER TAILOR   A pretty question! I defy a painter with his pencil to draw you anything that shall fit more exact. I have a fellow at home who, for fitting a pair of breeches, is the greatest genius in the world; another who, for the cut of a doublet, is the hero of the age.

M. JOURDAIN   Are the peruke[5] and feather as they should be?

MASTER TAILOR   Everything's well.

M. JOURDAIN   (looking earnestly at the tailor's clothes)   Ah, hah! Monsieur Tailor, here's my stuff of the last suit you made for me. I know it very well.

MASTER TAILOR   The stuff appeared to me so handsome, that I had a mind to cut a coat out of it for myself.

M. JOURDAIN   Yes, but you should not have cabbaged it out of mine.

MASTER TAILOR   Will you put on your clothes?

M. JOURDAIN   Yes, give 'em me.

MASTER TAILOR   Stay; the matter must not go so. I have brought men along with me to dress you to music; these sort of suits are put on with ceremony. Soho? come in there, you.

(Enter four JOURNEYMEN TAILORS, dancing)

Put on this suit of the gentleman's, in the manner you do to people of quality.

(Two of the tailors pull off his straight breeches made for his exercises, and two others his waistcoat; then they put on his new suit to music, and M. JOURDAIN walks amongst them to show them his clothes to see whether they fit or no)

JOURNEYMAN TAILOR   My dear gentleman, please to give the tailor's men something to drink.

M. JOURDAIN   How do you call me?

_____
[5] Wig.

JOURNEYMAN TAILOR   My dear gentleman.

M. JOURDAIN   "My dear gentleman!" See what it is to dress like people of quality. You may go clothed like a commoner all your days, and they'll never call you "my dear gentleman." (gives them something) Stay, there's for "my dear gentleman."

JOURNEYMAN TAILOR   My lord, we are infinitely obliged to you.

M. JOURDAIN   My lord! Oh, ho! My lord! Stay, friend; "my lord" deserves something, "my lord" is none o' your petty words. Hold, there, "my lord" gives you that.

JOURNEYMAN TAILOR   My lord, we shall go drink your grace's health.

M. JOURDAIN   Your grace! oh, oh, oh! stay, don't go. Your grace, to me! (aside) I'faith if he goes as far as highness, he'll empty my purse. (aloud) Hold, there's for "my grace."

JOURNEYMAN TAILOR   My lord, we most humbly thank your grace for your liberality.

M. JOURDAIN   He did very well; I was going to give him all.

(The four JOURNEYMAN TAILORS perform a dance that constitutes the second intermission.)

ACT III

THE SCENE.   Monsieur Jourdain and his two Lackeys

M. JOURDAIN   Follow me, that I may go and show my clothes a little through the town; and especially take care, both of you, to walk immediately at my heels, that people may plainly see you belong to me.

LACKEYS   Yes, sir.

M. JOURDAIN   Call me Nicole, that I may give her some directions. You need not go—here she comes.

(Enter NICOLE)

Nicole?

NICOLE   Your pleasure, sir?

M. JOURDAIN   Harkee.

NICOLE (laughing)   Ha, ha, ha, ha, ha.

M. JOURDAIN   Who do ye laugh at?

NICOLE   Ha, ha, ha, ha, ha, ha.

M. JOURDAIN   What does this slut mean?

NICOLE   Ha, ha, ha. How you are bedizened! Ha, ha, ha.

M. JOURDAIN   How's that?

NICOLE   Oh! oh! my stars! ha, ha, ha, ha, ha.

M. JOURDAIN   What a jade is here! What! do ye make a jest of me?

NICOLE   No, no, sir, I should be very sorry to do so. Ha, ha, ha, ha, ha, ha.

M. JOURDAIN   I shall give ye a slap o' the chops, if you laugh any more.

NICOLE   Sir, I cannot help it. Ha, ha, ha, ha, ha, ha.

M. JOURDAIN   Won't ye have done?

NICOLE   Sir, I ask your pardon; but you are so comical, that I cannot hold from laughing. Ha, ha, ha.

M. JOURDAIN   Do but see the insolence!

NICOLE   You are so thoroughly droll there! Ha, ha.

M. JOURDAIN   I shall—

NICOLE   I beg you would excuse me. Ha, ha, ha, ha.

M. JOURDAIN   Hold, if you laugh again the least in the world, I protest and swear I'll give ye such a box o' the ear as ye never had in your life.

NICOLE   Well, sir, I have done; I won't laugh any more.

M. JOURDAIN   Take care you don't. You must clean out against by and by—

NICOLE   Ha, ha.

M. JOURDAIN   You must clean out as it should be—

NICOLE   Ha, ha.

M. JOURDAIN   I say, you must go clean out the hall, and—

NICOLE   Ha, ha.

M. JOURDAIN   Again?

NICOLE *(tumbles down with laughing)*   Hold, sir, beat me rather, and let me laugh my belly-full, that will do me more good. Ha, ha, ha, ha.[1]

M. JOURDAIN   I shall run mad!

NICOLE   For goodness' sake, sir, I beseech you let me laugh. Ha, ha, ha.

M. JOURDAIN   If I take you in hand—

NICOLE   Si-ir, I shall bu-urst, if I do—not laugh. Ha, ha, ha.

M. JOURDAIN   But did ever anybody see such a jade as that, who insolently laughs in my face, instead of receiving my orders!

NICOLE   What would you have me do, sir?

M. JOURDAIN   Why, take care to get ready my house for the company that's to come by and by.

NICOLE *(getting up)*   Ay, i'fakins, I've no more inclination to laugh; all your company makes such a litter here that the very word's enough to put one in an ill humour.

M. JOURDAIN   What! I ought to shut my doors against all the world for your sake?

NICOLE   You ought at least to shut it against certain people.

(Enter MME JOURDAIN*)*

MME JOURDAIN   Ah, hah! Here's some new story. What means this, husband, this same equipage? D'ye despise the world, that you harness yourself out in this manner? Have you a mind to make yourself a laughing-stock wherever ye go?

M. JOURDAIN   None but fools, wife, will laugh at me.

MME JOURDAIN   In truth, people have not stayed thus long to laugh; 'tis a good while ago that your ways have furnished all the world with a laugh.

M. JOURDAIN   Who is that "all the world," pray?

MME JOURDAIN   That "all the world" is a world perfectly in the right, and much wiser than yourself. For my part, I am shocked at the life you lead. I don't know what to call our house. One would swear 'twere carnival here all the year round; and from break o' day, for fear there should be any respite, there's nothing to be heard here but an uproar of fiddles and songsters which disturb the whole neighbourhood.

NICOLE   Madame says right. I shall never see my things set to rights again for that gang of folks that you bring to the house. They ransack every quarter of the town with their feet for dirt to bring here; and poor Frances is e'en almost slaved off her legs with scrubbing of the floors, which your pretty masters come to daub as regularly as the day comes.

M. JOURDAIN   Hey-day! our maid Nicole! you have a pretty nimble tongue of your own for a country-wench.

MME JOURDAIN   Nicole's in the right, and she has

---

[1] Here is a comic portrayal of Molière's deep belief in the therapeutic value of laughter for all human beings.

more sense than you have. I should be glad to know what you think to do with a dancing master, at your age?

NICOLE   And with a lubberly fencing master, that comes here with his stamping to shake the whole house, and tear up all the pavement of the hall.

M. JOURDAIN   Peace, our maid, and our wife.

MME JOURDAIN   What! will you learn to dance against the time you'll have no legs?

NICOLE   What! have you a mind to murder somebody?

M. JOURDAIN   Hold your prate; I tell you you are ignorant creatures, both of you, and don't know the advantage of all this.

MME JOURDAIN   You ought much rather to think of marrying your daughter, who is of age to be provided for.

M. JOURDAIN   I shall think of marrying my daughter when a suitable match presents itself; but I shall think too of learning the *belles sciences.*

NICOLE   I've heard say further, madame, that to pin the basket, he has got him a philosophy master to-day.

M. JOURDAIN   Very well. I've a mind to have wit, and to know how to reason upon things with your genteel people.

MME JOURDAIN   Won't you go to school one of these days, and be whipped at your age?

M. JOURDAIN   Why not? Would I were whipped this very instant before all the world, so I did but know what they learn at school!

NICOLE   Yes, forsooth, that would be a mighty advantage t'ye.

M. JOURDAIN   Without doubt.

MME JOURDAIN   This is all very necessary to the management of your house.[2]

M. JOURDAIN   Certainly. You talk, both of you, like asses, and I'm ashamed of your ignorance. (*to* MME JOURDAIN) For example, do you know, you, what it is you now speak?

MME JOURDAIN   Yes, I know that what I speak is very right, and that you ought to think of living in another manner.

M. JOURDAIN   I don't talk of that. I ask you what the words are that you now speak?

MME JOURDAIN   They are words that have a good deal of sense in them, and your conduct is by no means such.

M. JOURDAIN   I don't talk of that, I tell you. I ask you, what is that I now speak to you, which I say this very moment?

MME JOURDAIN   Mere stuff.

M. JOURDAIN   Pshaw, no, 'tis not that. That which we both of us say, the language we speak this instant?

MME JOURDAIN   Well?

M. JOURDAIN   How is it called?

MME JOURDAIN   'Tis called just what you please to call it.

M. JOURDAIN   'Tis prose, you ignorant creature.

MME JOURDAIN   Prose?

M. JOURDAIN   Yes, prose. Whatever is prose, is not verse; and whatever is not verse, is prose. Now, see what it is to study. And you, (*to* NICOLE) do you know very well how you must do to say U?

NICOLE   How?

M. JOURDAIN   Yes. What is it you do when you say U?

NICOLE   What?

M. JOURDAIN   Say U a little, to try.

NICOLE   Well, U.

M. JOURDAIN   What is it you do?

NICOLE   I say U.

M. JOURDAIN   Yes, but when you say U, what is it you do?

NICOLE   I do as you bid me.

M. JOURDAIN   O! what a strange thing it is to have to do with brutes! You pout out your lips, and bring your under-jaw to your upper, U, d'ye see? I make a mouth, U.

NICOLE   Yes, that's fine.

MME JOURDAIN   'Tis admirable!

M. JOURDAIN   'Tis quite another thing, had but you seen O, and DE, DE, and EF, EF.

MME JOURDAIN   What is all this ridiculous stuff?

NICOLE   What are we the better for all this?

M. JOURDAIN   It makes one mad, to see these ignorant women.

---

[2] Madame Jourdain, the voice of the middle class and Nicole, the voice of the lower class, represent good sense and honesty as opposed to Monsieur Jourdain's pretentiousness and the nobles' dishonesty. And yet, are they entirely in the right? Typically, Madame Jourdain can see no benefit in the arts unless they are directly *useful.*

MME JOURDAIN   Go, go, you should send all these folks apacking with their silly stuff.

NICOLE   And especially that great lubberly fencing master, who fills all my house with dust.

M. JOURDAIN   Hey-day! This fencing master sticks strangely in thy stomach. I'll let thee see thy impertinence presently.

(*He orders the foils to be brought, and gives one to* NI-COLE)

Stay, reason demonstrative, the line of the body. When they push in carte one need only do so; and when they push in tierce one need only do so. This is the way never to be killed; and is not that clever to be upon sure grounds, when one has an encounter with anybody? There, push at me a little, to try.

NICOLE   Well, how?

(NICOLE *gives him several thrusts*)

M. JOURDAIN   Gently! Hold! Oh! Softly; deuce take the hussy.

NICOLE   You bid me push.

M. JOURDAIN   Yes, but you push me in tierce before you push in carte, and you have not patience while I parry.

MME JOURDAIN   You are a fool, husband, with all these whims, and this is come to you since you have taken upon you to keep company with quality.

M. JOURDAIN   When I keep company with quality, I show my judgment; and that's much better than herding with your bourgeoisie.

MME JOURDAIN   Yes, truly, there's a great deal to be got by frequenting your nobility; and you have made fine work with that count you are so bewitched with.

M. JOURDAIN   Peace, take care what you say. Do you well know, wife, that you don't know whom you speak of when you speak of him? He's a man of more importance than you think of; a nobleman of consideration at court, who speaks to the king just for all the world as I speak to you. Is it not a thing that does me great honour, that you see a person of that quality come so often to my house, who calls me his dear friend and treats me as if I were his equal? He has more kindness for me than one would ever imagine, and he caresses me in such a manner before all the world that I myself am perfectly confounded at it.

MME JOURDAIN   Yes, he has a great kindness for you, and caresses you; but he borrows your money of you.

M. JOURDAIN   Well, and is it not a great honour to me to lend money to a man of that condition? And can I do less for a lord who calls me his dear friend?

MME JOURDAIN   And what is it this lord does for you?

M. JOURDAIN   Things that would astonish you if you did but know 'em.

MME JOURDAIN   And what may they be?

M. JOURDAIN   Peace, I can't explain myself. 'Tis sufficient that if I have lent him money, he'll pay it me honestly, and that before 'tis long.

MME JOURDAIN   Yes, stay you for that.

M. JOURDAIN   Certainly. Did he not tell me so?

MME JOURDAIN   Yes, yes, and he won't fail to disappoint you.

M. JOURDAIN   He swore to me on the faith of a gentleman.

MME JOURDAIN   A mere song.

M. JOURDAIN   Hey! You are mighty obstinate, wife of mine; I tell you he will keep his word with me, I am sure of it.

MME JOURDAIN   And I am sure that he will not, and all the court he makes to you is only to cajole you.

M. JOURDAIN   Hold your tongue. Here he comes.

MME JOURDAIN   That's all we shall have of him. He comes perhaps to borrow something more of you; the very sight of him gives me my dinner.

M. JOURDAIN   Hold your tongue, I say.

(*Enter* DORANTE)

DORANTE   My dear friend, Monsieur Jourdain, how do you do?

M. JOURDAIN   Very well, sir, to do you what little service I can.

DORANTE   And Madame Jourdain there, how does she do?

MME JOURDAIN   Madame Jourdain does as well as she can.

DORANTE   Hah! Monsieur Jourdain, you're dressed the most genteelly in the world!

M. JOURDAIN   As you see.

DORANTE   You have a very fine air with that dress,

and we have ne'er a young fellow at court that's better made than you.

M. JOURDAIN   He, he.

MME JOURDAIN (*aside*)   He scratches him where it itches.

DORANTE   Turn about. 'Tis most gallant.

MME JOURDAIN (*aside*)   Yes, as much of the fool behind as before.

DORANTE   'Faith, Monsieur Jourdain, I was strangely impatient to see you. You're the man in the world I most esteem, and I was talking of you again this morning at the king's levee.[3]

M. JOURDAIN   You do me a great deal of honour, sir. (*to* MME JOURDAIN) At the king's levee!

DORANTE   Come, be covered.[4]

M. JOURDAIN   Sir, I know the respect I owe you.

DORANTE   Lack-a-day, be covered; no ceremony, pray, between us two.

M. JOURDAIN   Sir—

DORANTE   Put on your hat, I tell you, Monsieur Jourdain; you are my friend.

M. JOURDAIN   Sir, I am your humble servant.

DORANTE   I won't be covered, if you won't.

M. JOURDAIN (*puts on his hat*)   I choose rather to be unmannerly than troublesome.

DORANTE   I am your debtor, you know.

MME JOURDAIN (*aside*)   Yes, we know it but too well.

DORANTE   You have generously lent me money upon several occasions; and have obliged me, most certainly, with the best grace in the world.

M. JOURDAIN   You jest, sir.

DORANTE   But I know how to repay what is lent me, and to be grateful for the favours done me.

M. JOURDAIN   I don't doubt it, sir.

DORANTE   I'm willing to get out of your books, and came hither to make up our accounts together.

M. JOURDAIN (*aside to* MME JOURDAIN)   Well, you see your impertinence, wife.

DORANTE   I'm one who loves to be out of debt as soon as possible.

M. JOURDAIN (*aside to* MME JOURDAIN)   I told you so.

DORANTE   Let's see a little what 'tis I owe you.

M. JOURDAIN (*aside to* MME JOURDAIN)   You there, with your ridiculous suspicions.

DORANTE   Do you remember right all the money you have lent me?

M. JOURDAIN   I believe so. I made a little memorandum of it. Here it is. Let you have at one time two hundred louis d'or.

DORANTE   'Tis true.

M. JOURDAIN   Another time, six-score.

DORANTE   Yes.

M. JOURDAIN   And another time a hundred and forty.

DORANTE   You are right.

M. JOURDAIN   These three articles make four hundred and sixty louis d'or, which come to five thousand and sixty livres.

DORANTE   The account is very right. Five thousand and sixty livres.

M. JOURDAIN   One thousand eight hundred and thirty-two livres to your plume-maker.

DORANTE   Just.

M. JOURDAIN   Two thousand seven hundred and four-score livres to your tailor.

DORANTE   'Tis true.

M. JOURDAIN   Four thousand three hundred and seventy-nine livres, twelve sols, and eight deniers to your tradesman.

DORANTE   Very well. Twelve sols, eight deniers. The account is just.

M. JOURDAIN   And a thousand seven hundred and forty-eight livres, seven sols, four deniers to your saddler.

DORANTE   'Tis all true. What does that come to?

M. JOURDAIN   Sum total, fifteen thousand eight hundred livres.

DORANTE   The sum total, and just. Fifteen thousand and eight hundred livres. To which add two hundred pistoles, which you are going to lend me, that will make exactly eighteen thousand francs, which I shall pay you the first opportunity.

MME JOURDAIN (*aside to* M. JOURDAIN)   Well, did I not guess how 'twould be!

M. JOURDAIN (*aside to* MME JOURDAIN)   Peace.

DORANTE   Will it incommode you to lend me what I tell you?

M. JOURDAIN   Oh! no.

---

[3] The king's levee—the ceremony of the king's morning rising, which courtiers attended (see Saint-Simon in Chapter 20).

[4] Put your hat back on.

MME JOURDAIN (*aside to* M. JOURDAIN) This man makes a mere milch cow of you.

M. JOURDAIN (*aside to* MME JOURDAIN) Hold your tongue.

DORANTE If this will incommode you, I'll seek it elsewhere.

M. JOURDAIN No, sir.

MME JOURDAIN (*aside to* M. JOURDAIN) He'll ne'er be satisfied till he has ruined you.

M. JOURDAIN (*aside to* MME JOURDAIN) Hold your tongue, I tell you.

DORANTE You need only tell me if this puts you to any straits.

M. JOURDAIN Not at all, sir.

MME JOURDAIN (*aside to* M. JOURDAIN) 'Tis a true wheedler.

M. JOURDAIN (*aside to* MME JOURDAIN) Hold your tongue then.

MME JOURDAIN (*aside to* M. JOURDAIN) He'll drain you to the last farthing.

M. JOURDAIN (*aside to* MME JOURDAIN) Will you hold your tongue?

DORANTE I've a good many people would be glad to lend it me, but as you are my very good friend, I thought I should wrong you if I asked it of anybody else.

M. JOURDAIN 'Tis too much honour, sir, you do me. I'll go fetch what you want.

MME JOURDAIN (*aside to* M. JOURDAIN) What! going to lend him still more?

M. JOURDAIN (*aside to* MME JOURDAIN) What can I do? Would you have me refuse a man of that rank, who spoke of me this morning at the king's levee?

MME JOURDAIN (*aside to* M. JOURDAIN) Go, you're a downright dupe.

(*Exit* M. JOURDAIN)

DORANTE You seem to me very melancholy. What ails you, Madame Jourdain?

MME JOURDAIN My head's bigger than my fist, even if it is not swelled.

DORANTE Where is Mademoiselle your daughter that I don't see her?

MME JOURDAIN Mademoiselle my daughter is pretty well where she is.

DORANTE How does she go on?

MME JOURDAIN She goes on her two legs.

DORANTE Won't you come with her, one of these days, and see the ball, and the play that's acted at court?

MME JOURDAIN Yes, truly, we've a great inclination to laugh, a great inclination to laugh have we.

DORANTE I fancy, Madame Jourdain, you had a great many sparks in your younger years, being so handsome and good-humoured as you were.

MME JOURDAIN Tredame, sir! what, is Madame Jourdain grown decrepit, and does her head totter already with a palsy?

DORANTE Odso, Madame Jourdain, I ask your pardon. I was not thinking that you are young. I'm very often absent. Pray excuse my impertinence.

(*Enter* M. JOURDAIN)

M. JOURDAIN (*to* DORANTE) Here's two hundred pieces for you, hard money.

DORANTE I do assure you, Monsieur Jourdain, I am absolutely yours; and I long to do you service at court.

M. JOURDAIN I'm infinitely obliged to you.

DORANTE If Madame Jourdain inclines to see the royal diversion, I'll get her the best places in the ballroom.

MME JOURDAIN Madame Jourdain kisses your hand.

DORANTE (*aside to* M. JOURDAIN) Our pretty marchioness, as I informed you in my letter, will be here by and by to partake of your ball and collation; I brought her, at last, to consent to the entertainment you design to give her.

M. JOURDAIN Let us draw to a distance a little, for a certain reason.

DORANTE 'Tis eight days since I saw you, and I gave you no tidings of the diamond you put into my hands to make her a present of, as from you; but the reason was, I had all the difficulty in the world to conquer her scruples, and 'twas no longer ago than to-day, that she resolved to accept of it.

M. JOURDAIN How did she like it?

DORANTE Marvellously; and I am much deceived if the beauty of this diamond has not an admirable effect upon her.

M. JOURDAIN Grant it, kind Heaven!

MME JOURDAIN (*to* NICOLE)   When he's once with him, he can never get rid of him.

DORANTE   I made her sensible in a proper manner of the richness of the present and the strength of your passion.

M. JOURDAIN   These kindnesses perfectly overwhelm me; I am in the greatest confusion in the world to see a person of your quality demean himself on my account as you do.

DORANTE   You jest sure. Does one ever stop at such sort of scruples among friends? And would not you do the same thing for me, if occasion offered?

M. JOURDAIN   Oh! certainly, and with all my soul.

MME JOURDAIN (*aside to* NICOLE)   How the sight of him torments me!

DORANTE   For my part, I never mind anything when a friend is to be served; and when you imparted to me the ardent passion you had entertained for the agreeable marchioness, with whom I was acquainted, you see that I made an immediate offer of my service.

M. JOURDAIN   'Tis true, these favours are what confound me.

MME JOURDAIN (*to* NICOLE)   What! will he never be gone?

NICOLE   They are mighty great together.

DORANTE   You've taken the right way to smite her. Women, above all things, love the expense we are at on their account; and your frequent serenades, your continual entertainments, that sumptuous firework she saw on the water, the diamond she received by way of present from you, and the regale you are now preparing—all this speaks much better in favour of your passion than all the things you yourself could possibly have said to her.

M. JOURDAIN   There's no expense I would not be at, if I could by that means find the way to her heart. A woman of quality has powerful charms for me, and 'tis an honour I would purchase at any rate.

MME JOURDAIN (*aside to* NICOLE)   What can they have to talk of so long together? Go softly, and listen a little.

DORANTE   By and by you will enjoy the pleasure of seeing her at your ease; your eyes will have full time to be satisfied.

M. JOURDAIN   To be at full liberty, I have ordered matters so that my wife shall dine with my sister, where she'll pass the whole afternoon.

DORANTE   You have done wisely, for your wife might have perplexed us a little. I have given the proper orders for you to the cook, and for everything necessary for the ball. 'Tis of my own invention; and provided the execution answers the plan, I am sure 'twill be—

M. JOURDAIN (*perceives that* NICOLE *listens, and gives her a box on the ear*)   Hey, you're very impertinent. (*to* DORANTE) Let us go if you please.

(*Exeunt* M. JOURDAIN *and* DORANTE)

NICOLE   I'faith, curiosity has cost me something; but I believe there's a snake in the grass, for they were talking of some affair which they were not willing you should be present at.

MME JOURDAIN   This is not the first time, Nicole, that I have had suspicions of my husband. I am the most deceived person in the world, or there is some amour in agitation, and I am labouring to discover what it should be. But let's think of my daughter. You know the love Cléonte has for her. He is a man who hits my fancy, and I have a mind to favour his addresses and help him to Lucile, if I can.

NICOLE   In truth, madame, I am the most ravished [5] creature in the world, to find you in these sentiments; for if the master hits your taste, the man hits mine no less; and I could wish our marriage might be concluded under favour of theirs.

MME JOURDAIN   Go, and talk with him about it, as from me, and tell him to come to me presently, that we may join in demanding my daughter of my husband.

NICOLE   I fly, madame, with joy, and I could not have received a more agreeable commission.

(*Exit* MME JOURDAIN)

I believe I shall very much rejoice their hearts.

(*Enter* CLÉONTE *and* COVIELLE)

Hah, most luckily met. I'm an ambassadress of joy, and I come—

---

[5] Delighted. Nicole wishes to marry Cléonte's servant.

CLÉONTE   Be gone, ye perfidious slut, and don't come to amuse me with thy traitorous speeches.

NICOLE   Is it thus you receive—

CLÉONTE   Be gone, I tell thee, and go directly and inform thy false mistress, that she never more, while she lives, shall impose upon the too simple Cléonte.

NICOLE   What whim is this? My dear Covielle, tell me a little what does this mean.

COVIELLE   Thy dear Covielle, wicked minx? Away quickly out of my sight, hussy, and leave me at quiet.

NICOLE   What! dost thou, too—

COVIELLE   Out o' my sight, I tell thee, and talk not to me, for thy life.

NICOLE   (aside)   Hey-day! What gadfly has stung 'em both? Well, I must march and inform my mistress of this pretty piece of history.

(Exit NICOLE)

CLÉONTE   What! treat a lover in this manner; and a lover the most constant, the most passionate of all lovers!

COVIELLE   'Tis a horrible trick they have served us both.

CLÉONTE   I discover all the ardour for her, all the tenderness one can imagine. I love nothing in the world but her, have nothing in my thoughts besides her. She is all my care, all my desire, all my joy. I speak of nought but her, think of nought but her, dream of nought but her, I breathe only for her, my heart lives wholly in her; and this is the worthy recompense of such a love! I am two days without seeing her, which are to me two horrible ages; I meet her accidentally, my heart feels all transported at the sight; joy sparkles in my face; I fly to her with ecstasy, and the faithless creature turns away her eyes, and brushes hastily by me, as if she had never seen me in her life!

COVIELLE   I say the same as you do.

CLÉONTE   Is it possible to see anything, Covielle, equal to this perfidy of the ungrateful Lucile?

COVIELLE   Or to that, sir, of the villainous jade Nicole?

CLÉONTE   After so many ardent sacrifices of sighs and vows that I have made to her charms!

COVIELLE   After so much assiduous sneaking, cares, and services that I have paid her in the kitchen!

CLÉONTE   So many tears that I have shed at her feet!

COVIELLE   So many buckets of water that I have drawn for her!

CLÉONTE   Such ardour as I have shown, in loving her more than myself!

COVIELLE   So much heat as I have endured, in turning the spit in her place!

CLÉONTE   She flies me with disdain!

COVIELLE   She turns her back upon me with impudence!

CLÉONTE   This is a perfidy worthy the greatest punishment.

COVIELLE   This a treachery that deserves a thousand boxes o' the ear.[6]

CLÉONTE   Prithee, never think to speak once more to me in her favour.

COVIELLE   I, sir? Marry, Heaven forbid.

CLÉONTE   Never come to excuse the action of this perfidious woman.

COVIELLE   Fear it not.

CLÉONTE   No, d'ye see, all discourses in her defence will signify nothing.

COVIELLE   Who dreams of such a thing?

CLÉONTE   I'm determined to continue my resentment against her, and break off all correspondence.

COVIELLE   I give my consent.

CLÉONTE   This same count that visits her, pleases perhaps her eye; and her fancy, I see plainly, is dazzled with quality. But I must, for my own honour, prevent the triumph of her inconstancy. I'll make as much haste as she can do towards the change which I see she's running into, and won't leave her all the glory of quitting me.

COVIELLE   'Tis very well said, and for my share, I enter into all your sentiments.

CLÉONTE   Second my resentments, and support my resolutions against all the remains of love that may yet plead for her. I conjure thee, say all the ill things of her thou canst. Paint me her person so as to make her despicable; and, in order to disgust me, mark me out well all the faults thou canst find in her.

COVIELLE   She, sir? A pretty mawkin, a fine piece to be so much enamoured with. I see nothing in her but

---

6 This scene has an operatic quality, as if the master and valet are singing a duet. How does each one reflect his social class?

what's very indifferent, and you might find a hundred persons more deserving of you. First of all she has little eyes.

CLÉONTE   That's true, she has little eyes; but they are full of fire, the most sparkling, the most piercing in the world, the most striking that one shall see.

COVIELLE   She has a wide mouth.

CLÉONTE   Yes; but one sees such graces in it, as one does not see in other mouths, and the sight of that mouth inspires desire: 'tis the most attractive, the most amorous in the world.

COVIELLE   As to her height, she's not tall.

CLÉONTE   No; but she's easy, and well-shaped.

COVIELLE   She affects a negligence in speaking and acting.

CLÉONTE   'Tis true; but all this has a gracefulness in her, and her ways are engaging; they have I don't know what charms that insinuate into our hearts.

COVIELLE   As to her wit—

CLÉONTE   Ah! Covielle, she has the most refined, the most delicate turn of wit.

COVIELLE   Her conversation—

CLÉONTE   Her conversation is charming.

COVIELLE   She's always grave.

CLÉONTE   Would you have flaunting pleasantry, a perpetual profuse mirth? And d'ye see anything more impertinent than those women who are always upon the giggle?

COVIELLE   But in short, she is the most capricious creature in the world.

CLÉONTE   Yes, she is capricious, I grant ye, but everything sits well upon fine women; we bear with everything from the fair.

COVIELLE   Since that's the case, I see plainly you desire always to love her.

CLÉONTE   I! I should love death sooner; and I am now going to hate her as much as ever I loved her.

COVIELLE   But how, if you think her so perfect?

CLÉONTE   Therein shall my vengeance be more glaring; therein shall I better display the force of my resolution in hating her, quitting her, most beautiful as she is; most charming, most amiable, as I think her. Here she is.

(*Enter* LUCILE *and* NICOLE)

NICOLE (*to* LUCILE)   For my part, I was perfectly

shocked at it.

LUCILE   It can be nothing else, Nicole, but what I said. But there he comes.

CLÉONTE (*to* COVIELLE)   I won't so much as speak to her.

COVIELLE   I'll follow your example.

LUCILE   What means this, Cléonte, what's the matter with you?

NICOLE   What ails thee, Covielle?

LUCILE   What trouble has seized you?

NICOLE   What cross humour possesses thee?

LUCILE   Are you dumb, Cléonte?

NICOLE   Hast thou lost thy speech, Covielle?

CLÉONTE   The abandoned creature!

COVIELLE   Oh! the Judas!

LUCILE   I see very well that the late meeting has disordered your mind.

CLÉONTE (*to* COVIELLE)   O, ho! She sees what she has done.

NICOLE   The reception of this morning has made thee take snuff.

COVIELLE (*to* CLÉONTE)   She has guessed where the shoe pinches.

LUCILE   Is it not true, Cléonte, that this is the reason of your being out of humour?

CLÉONTE   Yes, perfidious maid, that is it, since I must speak; and I can tell you that you shall not triumph, as you imagine, by your unfaithfulness, that I shall be beforehand in breaking with you, and you won't have the credit of discarding me. I shall, doubtless, have some difficulty in conquering the passion I have for you: 'twill cause me uneasiness; I shall suffer for a while; but I shall compass my point, and I would sooner stab myself to the heart than have the weakness of returning to you.

COVIELLE (*to* NICOLE)   As says the master, so says the man.

LUCILE   Here's a noise indeed about nothing. I'll tell you, Cléonte, the reason that made me avoid joining you this morning.

CLÉONTE (*endeavouring to go to avoid* LUCILE)   No, I'll hear nothing.

NICOLE (*to* COVIELLE)   I'll let thee into the cause that made us pass you so quick.

COVIELLE (*endeavouring to go to avoid* NICOLE)   I will hear nothing.

LUCILE (*following* CLÉONTE)   Know that this
    morning—
CLÉONTE (*walks about without regarding*
    LUCILE).   No, I tell you.
NICOLE (*following* COVIELLE)   Learn that—
COVIELLE (*walks about likewise without regarding*
    NICOLE)   No, traitress.
LUCILE   Hear me.
CLÉONTE   Not a bit.
NICOLE   Let me speak.
COVIELLE   I'm deaf.
LUCILE   Cléonte!
CLÉONTE   No.
NICOLE   Covielle!
COVIELLE   No.
LUCILE   Stay.
CLÉONTE   Idle stuff.
NICOLE   Hear me.
COVIELLE   No such thing.
LUCILE   One moment.
CLÉONTE   Not at all.
NICOLE   A little patience.
COVIELLE   A fiddle-stick.
LUCILE   Two words.
CLÉONTE   No, 'tis over.
NICOLE   One word.
COVIELLE   No more dealings.
LUCILE (*stopping*)   Well, since you won't hear me,
    keep your opinion, and do what you please.
NICOLE (*stopping likewise*)   Since that's thy way, e'en
    take it all just as it pleases thee.
CLÉONTE   Let's know the subject then of this fine
    reception.
LUCILE (*going in her turn to avoid* CLÉONTE)   I've no
    longer an inclination to tell it.
COVIELLE   Let us a little into this history.
NICOLE (*going likewise in her turn to avoid* COVIELLE)
    I won't inform thee now, not I.
CLÉONTE (*following* LUCILE)   Tell me—
LUCILE   No, I'll tell you nothing.
COVIELLE (*following* NICOLE)   Say—
NICOLE   No, I say nothing.
CLÉONTE   For goodness' sake.
LUCILE   No, I tell you.
COVIELLE   Of all charity.

NICOLE   Not a bit.
CLÉONTE   I beseech you.
LUCILE   Let me alone.
COVIELLE   I conjure thee.
NICOLE   Away with thee.
CLÉONTE   Lucile!
LUCILE   No.
COVIELLE   Nicole!
NICOLE   Not at all.
CLÉONTE   For Heaven's sake.
LUCILE   I will not.
COVIELLE   Speak to me.
NICOLE   Not a word.
CLÉONTE   Clear up my doubts.
LUCILE   No, I'll do nothing towards it.
COVIELLE   Cure my mind.
NICOLE   No, 'tis not my pleasure.
CLÉONTE   Well, since you are so little concerned to
    ease me of my pain, and to justify yourself as to the
    unworthy treatment my passion has received from
    you, ungrateful creature, 'tis the last time you shall
    see me, and I am going far from you to die of grief
    and love.
COVIELLE (*to* NICOLE)   And I'll follow his steps.
LUCILE (*to* CLÉONTE, *who is going*)   Cléonte!
NICOLE (*to* COVIELLE, *who follows his master*)
    Covielle!
CLÉONTE (*stopping*)   Hey?
COVIELLE (*likewise stopping*)   Your pleasure?
LUCILE   Whither do you go?
CLÉONTE   Where I told you.
COVIELLE   We go to die.
LUCILE   Do you go to die, Cléonte?
CLÉONTE   Yes, cruel, since you will have it so.
LUCILE   I? I have you die?
CLÉONTE   Yes, you would.
LUCILE   Who told you so?
CLÉONTE (*going up to* LUCILE)   Would you not have it
    so, since you would not clear up my suspicions?
LUCILE   Is that my fault? Would you but have given
    me the hearing, should I not have told you that the
    adventure you make such complaints about was
    occasioned this morning by the presence of an old
    aunt who will absolutely have it that the mere
    approach of a man is a dishonour to a girl, who is

perpetually lecturing us upon this head, and represents to us all mankind as so many devils, whom one ought to avoid.

NICOLE (*to* COVIELLE)   There's the whole secret of the affair.

CLÉONTE   Don't you deceive me, Lucile?

COVIELLE (*to* NICOLE)   Dost thou not put a trick upon me?

LUCILE (*to* CLÉONTE)   There's nothing more true.

NICOLE (*to* COVIELLE)   'Tis the very thing, as it is.

COVIELLE (*to* CLÉONTE)   Shall we surrender upon this?

CLÉONTE   Ah, Lucile, what art have you to calm my passions with a single word! How easily do we suffer ourselves to be persuaded by those we love!

COVIELLE   How easily is one wheedled by these plaguy animals! [7]

(*Enter* MME JOURDAIN)

MME JOURDAIN   I am very glad to see you, Cléonte, and you are here apropos. My husband's acoming; catch your opportunity quick, and demand Lucile in marriage.

CLÉONTE   Ah, madame, how sweet is that word, how it flatters my wishes! Could I receive an order more charming? a favour more precious?

(*Enter* M. JOURDAIN)

Sir, I was not willing to employ any other person to make a certain demand of you which I have long intended. It concerns me sufficiently to undertake it in my own person; and, without further circumlocution, I shall inform you that the honour of being your son-in-law is an illustrious favour which I beseech you to grant me.

M. JOURDAIN   Before I give you an answer, sir, I desire you would tell me whether you are a gentleman.

CLÉONTE   Sir, the generality of people don't hesitate much on this question. People speak out bluff, and with ease. They make no scruple of taking this title upon 'em, and custom now-a-days seems to authorise the theft. For my part, I confess to you, my sentiments in this matter are somewhat more delicate. I look upon all imposture as unworthy an honest man, and that there is cowardice in denying what Heaven has made us; in tricking ourselves out, to the eyes of the world, in a stolen title; in desiring to put ourselves off for what we are not. I am undoubtedly born of parents who have held honourable employments. I have had the honour of six years' service in the army; and I find myself of consequence enough to hold a tolerable rank in the world; but for all this I won't give myself a name, which others in my place would think they might pretend to, and I'll tell you frankly that I am no gentleman. [8]

M. JOURDAIN   Your hand, sir; my daughter is no wife for you.

CLÉONTE   How?

M. JOURDAIN   You are no gentleman, you shan't have my daughter.

MME JOURDAIN   What would you be at then with your gentlemen? D'ye think we sort of people are of the line of St. Louis? [9]

M. JOURDAIN   Hold your tongue, wife, I see you're acoming.

MME JOURDAIN   Are we either of us otherwise descended than of plain citizens?

M. JOURDAIN   There's a scandalous reflection for you!

MME JOURDAIN   And was not your father a tradesman as well as mine?

M. JOURDAIN   Plague take the woman! She never has done with this. If your father was a tradesman, so much was the worse for him; but as for mine, they are numskulls that say he was. All that I have to say to you is that I will have a gentleman for my son-in-law.

MME JOURDAIN   Your daughter should have a husband that's proper for her, and an honest man who is rich and well made would be much better for her than a gentleman who is deformed and a beggar.

NICOLE   That's very true. We have a young squire in

---

[7] This scene between the four lovers has been compared to a ballet because of its schematic, patterned quality. Can you imagine it danced or mimed?

[8] Cléonte, as opposed to Jourdain, accepts his station in life with neither pretense nor shame. It is a fact that many bourgeois were literally buying their way into the nobility at this time.

[9] Louis IX, King of France 1226–1270.

our town who is the most awkward looby, the veriest driveller that I ever set eyes on.

M. JOURDAIN   Hold your prate, Madame Impertinence. You are always thrusting yourself into conversation. I've means sufficient for my daughter, and want nothing but honour, and I will have her a marchioness.

MME JOURDAIN   A marchioness!

M. JOURDAIN   Yes, a marchioness.

MME JOURDAIN   Marry, Heaven preserve me from it!

M. JOURDAIN   'Tis a determined thing.

MME JOURDAIN   'Tis what I shall never consent to. Matches with people above one are always subject to grievous inconveniences. I don't like that a son-in-law should have it in his power to reproach my daughter with her parents, or that she should have children who should be ashamed to call me grandmother. Should she come and visit me with the equipage of a grand lady and, through inadvertency, miss curtsying to some of the neighbourhood, they would not fail, presently, saying a hundred idle things. Do but see, would they say, this lady marchioness, what haughty airs she gives herself! She's the daughter of Monsieur Jourdain, who was over and above happy, when she was a little one, to play children's play with us. She was not always so lofty as she is now; and her two grandfathers sold cloth near St. Innocent's Gate. They amassed great means for their children, which they are paying for now, perhaps very dear, in the other world. People don't generally grow so rich by being honest. I won't have all these tittle-tattle stories; in one word, I'll have a man who shall be beholden to me for my daughter, and to whom I can say, Sit you down there, son-in-law, and dine with me.

M. JOURDAIN   See there the sentiments of a little soul, to desire always to continue in a mean condition. Let me have no more replies; my daughter shall be a marchioness in spite of the world; and if you put me in a passion, I'll make her a duchess.

(*Exit* M. JOURDAIN)

MME JOURDAIN   Cléonte, don't be discouraged by all this. (*to* LUCILE) Follow me, daughter, and come tell your father resolutely that if you have not him, you won't marry anybody at all.

(*Exeunt* MME JOURDAIN, LUCILE, *and* NICOLE)

COVIELLE   You have made a pretty piece of work of it with your fine sentiments.

CLÉONTE   What wouldst thou have me do? I have a scrupulousness in this case that no precedents can conquer.

COVIELLE   You're in the wrong to be serious with such a man as that. Don't you see that he's a fool? And would it cost you anything to accommodate yourself to his chimeras?

CLÉONTE   You're in the right; but I did not dream it was necessary to bring your proofs of nobility, to be son-in-law to Monsieur Jourdain.

COVIELLE (*laughing*)   Ha, ha, ha.

CLÉONTE   What d'ye laugh at?

COVIELLE   At a thought that's come into my head to play our spark off and help you to obtain what you desire.

CLÉONTE   How?

COVIELLE   The thought is absolutely droll.

CLÉONTE   What is it?

COVIELLE   There was a certain masquerade performed a little while ago, which comes in here the best in the world; and which I intend to insert into a piece of roguery I design to make for our coxcomb. This whole affair looks a little like making a joke of him; but with him we may hazard everything. There's no need here to study finesse so much—he's a man who will play his part to a wonder, and will easily give in to all the sham tales we shall take in our heads to tell him. I have actors, I have habits all ready, only let me alone.

CLÉONTE   But inform me of it.

COVIELLE   I am going to let you into the whole of it. Let's retire; there he comes.

(*Exeunt* COVIELLE *and* CLÉONTE. *Enter* M. JOURDAIN)

M. JOURDAIN   What a deuce can this mean? They have nothing but great lords to reproach me with; and I for my part see nothing so fine as keeping company with your great lords; there's nothing but honour and civility among 'em, and I would it had cost me two fingers of a hand to have been born a count or a marquis.

(*Enter a* LACKEY)

LACKEY   Sir, here's the count, and a lady whom he's handing in.

M. JOURDAIN   Good lack-a-day, I have some orders to give. Tell 'em that I'm acoming in a minute.

(*Exit* M. JOURDAIN. *Enter* DORANTE *and* DORIMÈNE)

LACKEY   My master says that he's acoming in a minute.

(*Exit* LACKEY)

DORANTE   'Tis very well.

DORIMÈNE   I don't know, Dorante; I take a strange step here in suffering you to bring me to a house where I know nobody.

DORANTE   What place then, madame, would you have a lover choose to entertain you in, since, to avoid clamour, you neither allow of your own house nor mine?

DORIMÈNE   But you don't mention that I am every day insensibly engaged to receive too great proofs of your passion. In vain do I refuse things, you weary me out of resistance, and you have a civil kind of obstinacy which makes me come gently into whatsoever you please. Frequent visits commenced, declarations came next, which drew after them serenades and entertainments, which were followed by presents. I opposed all these things, but you are not disheartened, and you become master of my resolutions step by step. For my part, I can answer for nothing hereafter, and I believe in the end you will bring me to matrimony, from which I stood so far aloof.

DORANTE   Faith, madame, you ought to have been there already. You are a widow, and depend upon nobody but yourself. I am my own master, and love you more than my life. What does it stick at, then, that you should not, from this day forward, complete my happiness?

DORIMÈNE   Lack-a-day, Dorante, there must go a great many qualities on both sides, to make people live happily together; and two of the most reasonable persons in the world have often much ado to compose a union to both their satisfactions.

DORANTE   You're in the wrong, madame, to represent to yourself so many difficulties in this affair; and the experience you have had concludes nothing for the rest of the world.

DORIMÈNE   In short, I always abide by this. The expenses you put yourself to for me disturb me for two reasons; one is, they engage me more than I could wish; and the other is, I'm sure (no offence to you!) that you can't do this but you must incommode yourself, and I would not have you do that.

DORANTE   Fie, madame, these are trifles, and 'tis not by that—

DORIMÈNE   I know what I say; and, amongst other things, the diamond you forced me to take, is of value—

DORANTE   Nay, madame, pray don't enhance the value of a thing my love thinks unworthy of you: and permit—Here's the master of the house.

(*Enter* M. JOURDAIN)

M. JOURDAIN (*after having made two bows, finding himself too near* DORIMÈNE)   A little farther, madame.

DORIMÈNE   How?

M. JOURDAIN   One step, if you please.

DORIMÈNE   What then?

M. JOURDAIN   Fall back a little for the third.

DORANTE   Monsieur Jourdain, madame, knows the world.

M. JOURDAIN   Madame, 'tis a very great honour that I am fortunate enough to be so happy, but to have the felicity that you should have the goodness to grant me the favour, to do me the honour, to honour me with the favour of your presence; and had I also the merit to merit a merit like yours, and that Heaven—envious of my good—had granted me—the advantage of being worthy—of—

DORANTE   Monsieur Jourdain, enough of this; my lady does not love great compliments, and she knows you are a man of wit. (*aside to* DORIMÈNE) 'Tis a downright bourgeois, ridiculous enough, as you see, in his whole behaviour.

DORIMÈNE (*aside to* DORANTE)   It is not very difficult to perceive it.

DORANTE   Madame, this is a very good friend of mine.

M. JOURDAIN   'Tis too much honour you do me.

DORANTE   A very polite man.

DORIMÈNE   I have a great esteem for him.

M. JOURDAIN   I have done nothing yet, madame, to merit this favour.

DORANTE (*aside to* M. JOURDAIN)   Take good care however not to speak to her of the diamond you gave her.

M. JOURDAIN (*aside to* DORANTE)   Mayn't I ask her only how she likes it?

DORANTE (*aside to* M. JOURDAIN)   How! Take special care you don't. 'Twould be villainous of you; and to act like a man of gallantry, you should make as if it were not you who made the present. (*aloud*) Monsieur Jourdain, madame, says that he's in raptures to see you at his house.

DORIMÈNE   He does me a great deal of honour.

M. JOURDAIN (*aside to* DORANTE)   How am I obliged to you, sir, for speaking to her in that manner on my account!

DORANTE (*aside to* M. JOURDAIN)   I have had a most terrible difficulty to get her to come hither.

M. JOURDAIN (*aside to* DORANTE)   I don't know how to thank you enough for it.

DORANTE   He says, madame, that he thinks you the most charming person in the world.

DORIMÈNE   'Tis a great favour he does me.

M. JOURDAIN   Madame, it's you who do the favours, and—

DORANTE   Let's think of eating.

(*Enter a* LACKEY)

LACKEY (*to* M. JOURDAIN)   Everything is ready, sir.

DORANTE   Come, then, let us sit down to table; and fetch the musicians.[10]

(*Six cooks, who have prepared the feast, dance together for the third intermission. After this, they carry on a table covered with several dishes.*)

ACT IV

THE SCENE.   *Dorimène, Monsieur Jourdain, Dorante, three Musicians, Lackeys*

DORIMÈNE   How, Dorante? Why here's a most magnificent repast!

M. JOURDAIN   You are pleased to banter, madame; I would it were more worthy of your acceptance.

(DORIMÈNE, M. JOURDAIN, DORANTE *and three* MUSICIANS *sit down at the table*)

DORANTE   Monsieur Jourdain, madame, is in the right in what he says, and he obliges me in paying you, after so handsome a manner, the honours of his house. I agree with him that the repast is not worthy of you. As it was myself who ordered it, and I am not so clearly sighted in these affairs as certain of our friends, you have here no very learned feast; and you will find incongruities of good cheer in it, some barbarisms of good taste. Had our friend Damis had a hand here, everything had been done by rule; elegance and erudition would have run through the whole, and he would not have failed exaggerating all the regular pieces of the repast he gave you, and force you to own his great capacity in the science of good eating; he would have told you of bread *de rive*, with the golden kissing-crust, raised too all round with a crust that crumples tenderly in your teeth; of wine with a velvet sap, heightened with a smartness not too overpowering; of a breast of mutton stuffed with parsley; of a loin of veal *de rivière*, thus long, white, delicate, and which is a true almond paste between the teeth; of your partridges heightened with a surprising *goût*; and then by way of farce or entertainment, of a soup with jelly broth, fortified with a young plump turkey-pout, cantoned with pigeons, and garnished with white onions married to succory. But, for my part, I confess to you my ignorance; and, as Monsieur Jourdain has very well said, I wish the repast were more worthy of your acceptance.[1]

DORIMÈNE   I make no other answer to this compliment than eating as I do.

M. JOURDAIN   Ah! what pretty hands are there!

DORIMÈNE   The hands are so so, Monsieur Jourdain;

---

[10] This is a key scene of the play, prepared for in the first scene of Act I. What do we learn about the characters of Dorante and Dorimène here?

[1] This speech gives us a good idea of what a seventeenth-century court meal was like. The French were already famous for their cuisine.

but you mean to speak of the diamond, which is very pretty.

M. JOURDAIN   I, madame? Marry, Heaven forbid I should speak of it; I should not act like a gentleman of gallantry, and the diamond is a very trifle.

DORIMÈNE   You are wondrous nice.

M. JOURDAIN   You have too much goodness—

DORANTE (*having made signs to* M. JOURDAIN) Come, give some wine to Monsieur Jourdain, and to those gentlemen who will do us the favour to sing us a catch.

DORIMÈNE   You give a wondrous relish to the good cheer by mixing music with it; I am admirably well regaled here.

M. JOURDAIN   Madame, it is not—

DORANTE   Monsieur Jourdain, let us listen to these gentlemen, they'll entertain us with something better than all we can possibly say.

FIRST AND SECOND MUSICIANS (*together, each with a glass in his hand*)

Put it round, my dear Phyllis, invert the bright glass;
Oh what charms to the crystal those fingers impart!
You and Bacchus combined, all resistance surpass,
And with passion redoubled have ravished my heart.
'Twixt him, you, and me, my charmer, my fair,
Eternal affection let's swear.

At the touch of those lips how he sparkles more bright!
And his touch, in return, those lips does embellish:
I could quaff 'em all day, and drink bumpers all night.
What longing each gives me, what gusto, what relish!
'Twixt him, you, and me, my charmer, my fair,
Eternal affection let's swear.

SECOND AND THIRD MUSICIANS (*together*)

Since time flies so nimbly away,
Come drink, my dear boys, drink about;
Let's husband him well while we may,
For life may be gone before the mug's out.
When Charon has got us aboard,

Our drinking and wooing are past;
We ne'er to lose time can afford,
For drinking's a trade not always to last.

Let your puzzling rogues in the schools,
Dispute of the bonum of man;
Philosophers dry are but fools—
The secret is this: drink, drink off your can.
When Charon has got us aboard,
Our drinking and wooing are past;
We ne'er to lose time can afford,
For drinking's a trade not always to last.

ALL THREE (*together*)

Why bob there! some wine, boys! come fill the glass, fill,
Round and round let it go, till we bid it stand still.

DORIMÈNE   I don't think anything can be better sung; and 'tis extremely fine.

M. JOURDAIN   I see something here though, madame, much finer.

DORIMÈNE   Hey! Monsieur Jourdain is more gallant than I thought he was.

DORANTE   How, madame! who do you take Monsieur Jourdain for?

M. JOURDAIN   I wish she would take me for what I could name.

DORIMÈNE   Again?

DORANTE (*to* DORIMÈNE)   You don't know him.

M. JOURDAIN   She shall know me whenever she pleases.

DORIMÈNE   Oh! Too much.

DORANTE   He's one who has a repartee always at hand. But you don't see, madame, that Monsieur Jourdain eats all the pieces you have touched.

DORIMÈNE   Monsieur Jourdain is a man that I am charmed with.

M. JOURDAIN   If I could charm your heart, I should be—

(*Enter* MME JOURDAIN)

MME JOURDAIN   Hey-day! why here's a jolly company of you, and I see very well you did not expect me. It was for this pretty affair, then, Monsieur Husband o' mine, that you were in such a violent hurry to pack me off to dine with my sister; I just now found a play-house below, and here I find a dinner fit for a wedding. Thus it is you spend your money, and thus it is you feast the ladies in my absence, and present 'em with music and a play, whilst I'm sent abroad in the meantime.

DORANTE   What do you mean, Madame Jourdain? and what's your fancy to take it into your head that your husband spends his money, and that 'tis he who entertains my lady? Know, pray, that 'tis I do it, that he only lends me his house, and that you ought to consider a little better what you say.

M. JOURDAIN   Yes, Madame Impertinence, 'tis the count that presents the lady with all this, who is a person of quality. He does me the honour to borrow my house, and is pleased to let me be with him.

MME JOURDAIN   'Tis all stuff, this. I know what I know.

DORANTE   Madame Jourdain, take your best spectacles, take 'em.

MME JOURDAIN   I've no need of spectacles, sir, I see clear enough; I've smelt things out a great while ago, I am no ass. 'Tis base in you, who are a great lord, to lend a helping hand, as you do, to the follies of my husband. And you, madame, who are a great lady, 'tis neither handsome nor honest in you to sow dissension in a family, and to suffer my husband to be in love with you.

DORIMÈNE   What can be the meaning of all this? Go, Dorante, 'tis wrong in you to expose me to the silly visions of this raving woman.

DORANTE (following DORIMÈNE, who goes out)   Madame, why madame, where are you running?

M. JOURDAIN   Madame—My lord, make my excuses to her and endeavour to bring her back.

(Exit DORANTE)

(To MME JOURDAIN) Ah! impertinent creature as you are, these are your fine doings; you come and affront me in the face of all the world, and drive people of quality away from my house.

MME JOURDAIN   I value not their quality.

(LACKEYS take away the table)

M. JOURDAIN   I don't know what hinders me, you plaguy hussy, from splitting your skull with the fragments of the feast you came here to disturb.

MME JOURDAIN (going)   I despise all this. I defend my own rights, and I shall have all the wives on my side.

M. JOURDAIN   You do well to get out of the way of my fury.

(Exit MME JOURDAIN)

She came here at a most unlucky time. I was in the humour of saying fine things, and never did I find myself so witty. What have we got here?

(Enter COVIELLE, disguised)

COVIELLE   Sir, I don't know whether I have the honour to be known to you.

M. JOURDAIN   No, sir.

COVIELLE   I have seen you when you were not above thus tall.

M. JOURDAIN   Me?

COVIELLE   Yes. You were one of the prettiest children in the world; and all the ladies used to take you in their arms to kiss you.

M. JOURDAIN   To kiss me?

COVIELLE   Yes, I was an intimate friend of the late gentleman your father.

M. JOURDAIN   Of the late gentleman my father!

COVIELLE   Yes. He was a very honest gentleman.

M. JOURDAIN   What is't you say?

COVIELLE   I say that he was a very honest gentleman.

M. JOURDAIN   My father?

COVIELLE   Yes.

M. JOURDAIN   Did you know him very well?

COVIELLE   Certainly.

M. JOURDAIN   And did you know him for a gentleman?

COVIELLE   Without doubt.

M. JOURDAIN   I don't know then what the world means.

COVIELLE   How?

M. JOURDAIN   There is a stupid sort of people who would face me down that he was a tradesman.

COVIELLE   He a tradesman? 'Tis mere scandal; he never was one. All that he did was, that he was very obliging, very officious, and as he was a great connoisseur in stuffs, he used to pick them up everywhere, have 'em carried to his house, and gave 'em to his friends for money.

M. JOURDAIN   I'm very glad of your acquaintance, that

you may bear witness that my father was a gentleman.

COVIELLE   I'll maintain it in the face of all the world.

M. JOURDAIN   You will oblige me. What business brings you here?

COVIELLE   Since my acquaintance with the late gentleman your father, honest gentleman, as I was telling you, I have travelled round the world.

M. JOURDAIN   Round the world?

COVIELLE   Yes.

M. JOURDAIN   I fancy 'tis a huge way off, that same country.

COVIELLE   Most certainly. I have not been returned from these tedious travels of mine but four days. And because I have an interest in everything that concerns you, I come to tell you the best news in the world.

M. JOURDAIN   What?

COVIELLE   You know that the son of the Great Turk is here.

M. JOURDAIN   I? No.

COVIELLE   How? He has a most magnificent train. All the world goes to see him, and he has been received in this country as a person of importance.

M. JOURDAIN   In troth, I did not know that.

COVIELLE   What is of advantage to you in this affair is that he is in love with your daughter.

M. JOURDAIN   The son of the Great Turk?

COVIELLE   Yes, and wants to be your son-in-law.

M. JOURDAIN   My son-in-law, the son of the Great Turk?

COVIELLE   The son of the Great Turk your son-in-law. As I have been to see him, and perfectly understand his language, he held a conversation with me; and after some other discourse, says he to me: "Acciam croc soler, onch alla moustaph gidelum amanahem varahini oussere carbulath." That is to say, "Have you not seen a young handsome person, who is the daughter of Monsieur Jourdain, a gentleman of Paris?"

M. JOURDAIN   The son of the Great Turk said that of me?

COVIELLE   Yes, as I made answer to him that I knew you particularly well, and that I had seen your daughter. Ah, says he to me, "Marababa sahem"; that is to say, "Ah! how am I enamoured with her!"

M. JOURDAIN   "Marababa sahem" means: "Ah! how am I enamoured with her"?

COVIELLE   Yes.

M. JOURDAIN   Marry, you did well to tell me so, for as for my part, I should never have believed that "Marababa sahem" had meant, "Ah! how am I enamoured with her!" 'Tis an admirable language, this same Turkish!

COVIELLE   More admirable than one can believe. Do you know very well what is the meaning of "Cacaramouchen"?

M. JOURDAIN   "Cacaramouchen"? No.

COVIELLE   'Tis as if you should say, "My dear soul."

M. JOURDAIN   "Cacaramouchen" means, "My dear soul"?

COVIELLE   Yes.

M. JOURDAIN   Why, 'tis very wonderful! "Cacaramouchen—my dear soul." Would one ever have thought it? I am perfectly confounded at it.

COVIELLE   In short, to finish my embassy, he comes to demand your daughter in marriage; and to have a father-in-law who should be suitable to him, he designs to make you a Mamamouchi, which is a certain grand dignity of his country.

M. JOURDAIN   Mamamouchi?

COVIELLE   Yes, Mamamouchi; that is to say, in our language, a Paladin. Paladin is your ancient— Paladin, in short—there's nothing in the world more noble than this; and you will rank with the grandest lord upon earth.

M. JOURDAIN   The son of the Great Turk does me a great deal of honour, and I desire you would carry me to him, to return him my thanks.

COVIELLE   How? Why he's just acoming hither.

M. JOURDAIN   Is he acoming hither?

COVIELLE   Yes. And he brings all things along with him for the ceremony of your dignity.

M. JOURDAIN   He's main hasty.

COVIELLE   His love will suffer no delay.

M. JOURDAIN   All that perplexes me, in this case, is that my daughter is an obstinate hussy who has took into her head one Cléonte, and vows she'll marry no person besides him.

COVIELLE   She'll change her opinion when she sees the son of the Grand Turk; and then there happens here a very marvellous adventure, that is, that the son of the Grand Turk resembles this Cléonte, with a trifling difference. I just now came from him, they showed him me; and the love she bears for one may easily pass to the other, and—I hear him coming; there he is.

(Enter CLÉONTE, *like a Turk, and three* PAGES *holding up his gown*)

CLÉONTE   Ambousahim oqui boraf, Iordina, salamalequi.[2]

COVIELLE (*to* M. JOURDAIN)   That is to say, Monsieur Jourdain, "May your heart be all the year like a rose-tree in flower!" These are obliging ways of speaking in that country.

M. JOURDAIN   I am His Turkish Highness's most humble servant.

COVIELLE   Carigar camboto oustin moraf.

CLÉONTE   Oustin yoc catamalequi basum base alla moran.

COVIELLE   He says, "Heaven give you the strength of lions and the prudence of serpents!"

M. JOURDAIN   His Turkish Highness does me too much honour; and I wish him all manner of prosperity.

COVIELLE   Ossa binamin sadoc babally oracaf ouram.

CLÉONTE   Bel-men.

COVIELLE   He says that you should go quickly with him to prepare yourself for the ceremony, in order afterwards to see your daughter and to conclude the marriage.

M. JOURDAIN   So many things in two words?

COVIELLE   Yes, the Turkish language is much in that way; it says a great deal in a few words. Go quickly where he desires you.

(*Exeunt* M. JOURDAIN, CLÉONTE, *and* PAGES)

Ha, ha, ha. I'faith, this is all absolutely droll. What a dupe! Had he had his part by heart, he could not have played it better. O, ho!

(*Enter* DORANTE)

I beseech you, sir, lend us a helping hand here, in a certain affair which is in agitation.

DORANTE   Ah! ah! Covielle, who could have known thee? How art thou trimmed out there!

COVIELLE   You see, ha, ha!

DORANTE   What do ye laugh at?

COVIELLE   At a thing, sir, that well deserves it.

DORANTE   What?

COVIELLE   I could give you a good many times, sir, to guess the stratagem we are making use of with Monsieur Jourdain, to bring him over to give his daughter to my master.

DORANTE   I don't at all guess the stratagem, but I guess it will not fail of its effect, since you undertake it.

COVIELLE   I know, sir, you are not unacquainted with the animal.

DORANTE   Tell me what it is.

COVIELLE   Be at the trouble of withdrawing a little farther off, to make room for what I see acoming. You will see one part of the story whilst I give you a narration of the rest.

THE TURKISH CEREMONY

The Mufti, Dervishes, Turks (assisting the Mufti), Singers and Dancers

THE SCENE.   *Six Turks enter gravely, two and two, to the sound of instruments. They bear three carpets, with which they dance in several figures, and then lift them up very high. The Turks, singing, pass under the carpets and range themselves on each side of the stage. The Mufti, accompanied by Dervishes, closes the march.*

Then the Turks spread the carpets on the ground and kneel down upon them, the Mufti and the Dervishes standing in the middle of them; while the Mufti invokes Mahomet in dumb contortions and grimaces, the Turks prostrate themselves to the ground, singing Allah, raising their hands to heaven, singing Allah, and so continuing alternately to the end of the invocation, when they all rise up, singing Allahekber.

Then two Dervishes bring Monsieur Jourdain, clothed like a Turk, his head shaved, without a turban or sabre.

MUFTI (*to* M. JOURDAIN)
If thou understandest,
    Answer;
If thou dost not understand,
    Hold thy peace, hold thy peace.

I am Mufti,
    Thou! who thou art

---

[2] This is, of course, an invented language, but Molière has made it sound somewhat like Arabic.

I don't know:
   Hold thy peace, hold thy peace.

(Two DERVISHES *retire with* M. JOURDAIN)

  Say, Turk, who is this, An Anabaptist, an Anabaptist?
THE TURKS   No.
MUFTI   A Zwinglian?
THE TURKS   No.
MUFTI   A Coffite?
THE TURKS   No.
MUFTI   A Hussite? A Morist? A Fronist?
THE TURKS   No, no, no.
MUFTI   No, no, no. Is he a Pagan?
THE TURKS   No.
MUFTI   A Lutheran?
THE TURKS   No.
MUFTI   A Puritan?
THE TURKS   No.
MUFTI   A Brahmin? A Moffian? A Zurian?
THE TURKS   No, no, no.
MUFTI   No, no, no. A Mahometan, a Mahometan?
THE TURKS   There you have it, there you have it.
MUFTI   How is he called? How is he called?
THE TURKS   Jourdain, Jourdain.
MUFTI *(dancing)*   Jourdain! Jourdain!
THE TURKS   Jourdain, Jourdain.
MUFTI
  To Mahomet for Jourdain
  I pray night and day,
  That he would make a Paladin
  Of Jourdain, of Jourdain.
  Give him a turban, and give a sabre,
  With a galley and a brigantine,
  To defend Palestine.
  To Mahomet for Jourdain
  I pray night and day.[3]
  (to the Turks) Is Jourdain a good Turk?
THE TURKS   That he is, that he is.
MUFTI *(singing and dancing)*   *Ha, la ba, ba la chou,*
  ba la ba, ba la da.

  (*Exit* MUFTI)

THE TURKS   *Ha, la ba, ba la chou, ba la ba, ba la da.*

---

[3] The resemblance of Monsieur Jourdain's name to the Jordan river is used to make him "defender of Palestine."

THE SCENE. *The Mufti returns with the State Turban, which is of an immeasurable largeness, garnished with lighted wax candles, four or five rows deep, accompanied by two Dervishes, bearing the Alcoran, with comic caps garnished also with lighted candles.*

  The two other Dervishes lead up Monsieur Jourdain and place him on his knees with his hands to the ground so that his back, on which the Alcoran is placed, may serve for a desk to the Mufti, who makes a second burlesque invocation, knitting his eyebrows, striking his hands sometimes upon the Alcoran, and tossing over the leaves with precipitation, after which, lifting up his hands, and crying with a loud voice, Hoo.

  During this second invocation the assistant Turks, bowing down and raising themselves alternately, sing likewise, HOO, HOO, HOO.

M. JOURDAIN *(after they have taken the Alcoran off his back)*   Ouf!
MUFTI *(to* M. JOURDAIN)   Thou wilt not be a knave?
THE TURKS   No, no, no.
MUFTI   Not be a thief?
THE TURKS   No, no, no.
MUFTI *(to the* TURKS)   Give the turban.
THE TURKS
  Thou wilt not be a knave?
    No, no, no.
  Not be a thief?
    No, no, no.
  Give the turban.

(*The* TURKS, *dancing, put the turban on* M. JOURDAIN'S *head at the sound of the instruments*)

MUFTI *(giving the sabre to* M. JOURDAIN)
  Be brave, be no scoundrel,
  Take the sabre.
THE TURKS *(drawing their sabres)*
  Be brave, be no scoundrel,
  Take the sabre.

(*The* TURKS, *dancing, strike* M. JOURDAIN *several times with their sabres, to music*)

MUFTI
  Give, give
  The bastonade.
THE TURKS
  Give, give
  The bastonade.

(The TURKS, *dancing, give* M. JOURDAIN *several strokes with a cudgel, to music)*

MUFTI

Don't think it a shame,
This is the last affront.

THE TURKS

Don't think it a shame,
This is the last affront.

(The MUFTI *begins a third invocation. The* DERVISHES *support him with great respect, after which the* TURKS, *singing and dancing round the* MUFTI, *retire with him and lead off* MONSIEUR JOURDAIN.)*

ACT V

THE SCENE.   *Madame Jourdain, Monsieur Jourdain*

MME JOURDAIN   Bless us all! Mercy upon us! What have we got here? What a figure! What! dressed to go a-mumming, and is this a time to go masked? Speak therefore, what does this mean? Who has trussed you up in this manner?

M. JOURDAIN   Do but see the impertinent slut, to speak after this manner to a Mamamouchi.

MME JOURDAIN   How's that?

M. JOURDAIN   Yes, you must show me respect now I am just made a Mamamouchi.

MME JOURDAIN   What d'ye mean with your Mamamouchi?

M. JOURDAIN   Mamamouchi, I tell you. I am a Mamamouchi.

MME JOURDAIN   What beast is that?

M. JOURDAIN   Mamamouchi, that is to say, in our language, a Paladin.

MME JOURDAIN   A Paladin? Are you of an age to be a morris-dancer?[1]

M. JOURDAIN   What an ignoramus! I say, Paladin. 'Tis a dignity of which I have just now gone through the ceremony.

MME JOURDAIN   What ceremony then?

M. JOURDAIN   Mahameta per Jordina.

MME JOURDAIN   What does that mean?

M. JOURDAIN   Jordina, that is to say, Jourdain.

MME JOURDAIN   Well, how Jourdain?

M. JOURDAIN   Voler far un Paladina de Jordina.[2]

MME JOURDAIN   What?

M. JOURDAIN   Dar turbanta con galera.

MME JOURDAIN   What's the meaning of that?

M. JOURDAIN   Per deffender Palestina.

MME JOURDAIN   What is it you would say?

M. JOURDAIN   Dara, dara, bastonnara.

MME JOURDAIN   What is this same jargon?

M. JOURDAIN   Non tener honta, questa star l'ultima affronta.

MME JOURDAIN   What in the name of wonder can all this be?

M. JOURDAIN *(singing and dancing)*   Hou la ba, ba la chou, ba la ba, ba la da. *(falls down to the ground)*

MME JOURDAIN   Alas and well-a-day! My husband is turned fool.

M. JOURDAIN *(getting up and walking off)*   Peace! insolence, show respect to Monsieur Mamamouchi.

MME JOURDAIN *(alone)*   How could he lose his senses? I must run and prevent his going out. *(seeing* DORIMÈNE *and* DORANTE*)* So, so, here come the rest of our gang. I see nothing but vexation on all sides.

(Exit MME JOURDAIN. *Enter* DORANTE *and* DORIMÈNE*)*

DORANTE   Yes, madame, you'll see the merriest thing that can be seen; and I don't believe it's possible, in the whole world, to find another man so much a fool as this here. And besides, madame, we must endeavour to promote Cléonte's amour and to countenance his masquerade. He's a very pretty gentleman and deserves that one should interest one's self in his favour.

DORIMÈNE   I've a very great value for him, and he deserves good fortune.

DORANTE   Besides, we have here, madame, an entertainment that will suit us, and which we ought not to suffer to be lost; and I must by all means see whether my fancy will succeed.

DORIMÈNE   I saw there magnificent preparations, and these are things, Dorante, I can no longer suffer. Yes,

---

[1] In the original, "a ballet dancer." Morris dances were (and are) done in the English countryside, in costume.

[2] This "language," which resembles Italian, is used in the ceremony in the original.

I'm resolved to put a stop, at last, to your profusions; and to break off all the expenses you are at on my account, I have determined to marry you out of hand. This is the real secret of the affair, and all these things end, as you know, with marriage.

DORANTE   Ah! madame, is it possible you should form so kind a resolution in my favour?

DORIMÈNE   I only do it to prevent you from ruining yourself; and without this, I see plainly that before 'tis long you won't be worth a groat.

DORANTE   How am I obliged to you, madame, for the care you take to preserve my estate! 'Tis entirely at your service, as well as my heart, and you may use both of 'em just in the manner you please.

DORIMÈNE   I shall make a proper use of them both. But here comes your man; an admirable figure.

(Enter M. JOURDAIN)

DORANTE   Sir, my lady and I are come to pay our homage to your new dignity, and to rejoice with you at the marriage you are concluding betwixt your daughter and the son of the Grand Turk.

M. JOURDAIN (bowing first in the Turkish manner) Sir, I wish you the force of serpents and the wisdom of lions.

DORIMÈNE   I was exceeding glad to be one of the first, sir, who should come and congratulate you upon the high degree of glory to which you are raised.

M. JOURDAIN   Madame, I wish your rose-tree may flower all the year round; I am infinitely obliged to you for interesting yourselves in the honour that's paid me; and I am greatly rejoiced to see you returned hither, that I may make my most humble excuses for the impertinence of my wife.

DORIMÈNE   That's nothing at all, I can excuse a commotion of this kind in her; your heart ought to be precious to her, and 'tis not at all strange the possession of such a man as you are should give her some alarms.

M. JOURDAIN   The possession of my heart is a thing you have entirely gained.

DORANTE   You see, madame, that Monsieur Jourdain is none of those people whom prosperity blinds, and that he knows, in all his grandeur, how to own his friends.

DORIMÈNE   'Tis the mark of a truly generous soul.

DORANTE   Where is His Turkish Highness? We should be glad, as your friends, to pay our devoirs to him.

M. JOURDAIN   There he comes, and I have sent to bring my daughter to join hands with him.

(Enter CLÉONTE, in a Turkish habit)

DORANTE (to CLÉONTE)   Sir, we come to compliment Your Highness, as friends of the gentleman your father-in-law, and to assure you, with respect, of our most humble services.

M. JOURDAIN   Where's the dragoman, to tell him who you are and make him understand what you say? You shall see that he'll answer you, and he speaks Turkish marvellously. Hola! there; where the deuce is he gone? (to CLÉONTE)

Stref,

strif,

strof,

straf.

The gentleman is a

grande segnore, grande segnore, grande segnore;

and madame is a

granda dama, granda dama.

(Seeing he cannot make himself be understood)

Lack-a-day!

(to CLÉONTE) Sir, he be a French Mamamouchi, and madame a French Mamamouchess. I can't speak plainer. Good, here's the dragoman.

(Enter COVIELLE, disguised)

Where do you run? We can say nothing without you. (pointing to CLÉONTE) Inform him a little that the gentleman and lady are persons of great quality who come to pay their compliments to him, as friends of mine, and to assure him of their services. (to DORIMÈNE and DORANTE) You shall see how he will answer.

COVIELLE   Alabala crociam, acci boram alabamen.

CLÉONTE   Catalequi tubal ourin soter amalouchan.

M. JOURDAIN (to DORIMÈNE and DORANTE)   Do ye see?

COVIELLE   He says that the rain of prosperity waters, at all seasons, the garden of your family.

M. JOURDAIN   I told you that he speaks Turkish.

DORANTE   This is admirable.

(*Enter* LUCILE)

M. JOURDAIN   Come, daughter, come nearer, and give the gentleman your hand who does you the honour of demanding you in marriage.

LUCILE   What's the matter, father, how are you dressed here? What! are you playing a comedy?

M. JOURDAIN   No, no, 'tis no comedy, 'tis a very serious affair; and the most honourable for you that possibly can be wished. (*pointing to* CLÉONTE) This is the husband I bestow upon you.

LUCILE   Upon me, father?

M. JOURDAIN   Yes, upon you. Come, take him by the hand, and thank Heaven for your good fortune.

LUCILE   I won't marry.

M. JOURDAIN   I'll make you; am I not your father?

LUCILE   I won't do it.

M. JOURDAIN   Here's a noise indeed! Come, I tell you. Your hand here.

LUCILE   No, father, I've told you before that there's no power can oblige me to take any other husband than Cléonte; and I am determined upon all extremities rather than—(*discovering* CLÉONTE) 'Tis true that you are my father; I owe you absolute obedience; and you may dispose of me according to your pleasure.

M. JOURDAIN   Hah, I am charmed to see you return so readily to your duty; and it is a pleasure to me to have my daughter obedient.

(*Enter* MME JOURDAIN)

MME JOURDAIN   How, how, what does this mean? They tell me you design to marry your daughter to a mummer.[3]

M. JOURDAIN   Will you hold your tongue, impertinence? You're always coming to mix your extravagances with everything; there's no possibility of teaching you common sense.

MME JOURDAIN   'Tis you whom there's no teaching to be wise, and you go from folly to folly. What's your design, what would you do with this flock of people?

M. JOURDAIN   I design to marry my daughter to the son of the Grand Turk.

MME JOURDAIN   To the son of the Grand Turk?

M. JOURDAIN   Yes. (*pointing to* COVIELLE) Make your compliments to him by the dragoman there.

MME JOURDAIN   I have nothing to do with the dragoman, and I shall tell him plainly to his face that he shall have none of my daughter.

M. JOURDAIN   Will you hold your tongue once more?

DORANTE   What, Madame Jourdain, do you oppose such an honour as this? Do you refuse His Turkish Highness for a son-in-law?

MME JOURDAIN   Lack-a-day, sir, meddle you with your own affairs.

DORIMÈNE   'Tis a great honour, 'tis by no means to be rejected.

MME JOURDAIN   Madame, I desire you too not to give yourself any trouble about what no ways concerns you.

DORANTE   'Tis the friendship we have for you that makes us interest ourselves in what is of advantage to you.

MME JOURDAIN   I shall easily excuse your friendship.

DORANTE   There's your daughter consents to her father's pleasure.

MME JOURDAIN   My daughter consent to marry a Turk?

DORANTE   Certainly.

MME JOURDAIN   Can she forget Cléonte?

DORANTE   What would one not do to be a great lady?

MME JOURDAIN   I would strangle her with my own hands, had she done such a thing as this.

M. JOURDAIN   Here's tittle-tattle in abundance. I tell you this marriage shall be consummated.

MME JOURDAIN   And I tell you that it shall not be consummated.

M. JOURDAIN   What a noise is here?

LUCILE   Mother!

MME JOURDAIN   Go, you are a pitiful hussy.

M. JOURDAIN (*to* MME JOURDAIN)   What! do you scold her for being obedient to me?

MME JOURDAIN   Yes, she belongs to me as well as you.

COVIELLE (*to* MME JOURDAIN)   Madame.

MME JOURDAIN   What would you say to me, you?

COVIELLE   One word.

MME JOURDAIN   I've nothing to do with your word.

COVIELLE (*to* M. JOURDAIN)   Sir, would she hear me but one word in private, I'll promise you to make her

---

[3] An actor.

consent to what you have a mind.

MME JOURDAIN   I won't consent to it.

COVIELLE   Only hear me.

MME JOURDAIN   No.

M. JOURDAIN (*to* MME JOURDAIN)   Give him the hearing.

MME JOURDAIN   No, I won't hear him.

M. JOURDAIN   He'll tell you—

MME JOURDAIN   He shall tell me nothing.

M. JOURDAIN   Do but see the great obstinacy of the woman! Will it do you any harm to hear him?

COVIELLE   Only hear me; you may do what you please afterwards.

MME JOURDAIN   Well, what?

COVIELLE (*aside to* MME JOURDAIN)   We have made signs to you, madame, this hour. Don't you see plainly that all is done purely to accommodate ourselves to the visions of your husband; that we are imposing upon him under this disguise, and that it is Cléonte himself who is the son of the Great Turk?

MME JOURDAIN (*aside to* COVIELLE)   Oh, oh?

COVIELLE (*aside to* MME JOURDAIN)   And that 'tis me, Covielle, who am the dragoman?

MME JOURDAIN (*aside to* COVIELLE)   Oh! in that case, I give up.

COVIELLE (*aside to* MME JOURDAIN)   Don't seem to know anything of the matter.

MME JOURDAIN (*aloud*)   Yes, 'tis all done, I consent to the marriage.

M. JOURDAIN   Ay, all the world submits to reason. (*to* MME JOURDAIN) You would not hear him. I knew he would explain to you what the son of the Great Turk is.

MME JOURDAIN   He has explained it to me sufficiently, and I'm satisfied with it. Let us send for a notary.

DORANTE   'Tis well said. And, Madame Jourdain, that you may set your mind perfectly at rest, and that you should this day quit all jealousy which you may have entertained of the gentleman your husband, my lady and I shall make use of the same notary to marry us.

MME JOURDAIN   I consent to that too.

M. JOURDAIN (*aside to* DORANTE)   'Tis to make her believe.

DORANTE (*aside to* M. JOURDAIN)   We must by all means amuse her a little with this pretence.

M. JOURDAIN   Good, good. (*aloud*) Let somebody go for the notary.

DORANTE   In the meantime, till he comes and has drawn up the contracts, let us see our entertainment, and give His Turkish Highness the diversion of it.

M. JOURDAIN   Well advised; come let us take our places.

MME JOURDAIN   And Nicole?

M. JOURDAIN   I give her to the dragoman; and my wife, to whosoever pleases to take her.

COVIELLE   Sir, I thank you. (*aside*) If it's possible to find a greater fool than this, I'll go and publish it in Rome.

(The play ends with the "ballet des nations," a spectacle of music, singing, and dancing in which various nationalities are impersonated.)

COMMENTS AND QUESTIONS

1. Outline the plot of this comedy. Notice its simplicity. Some elements—the young lovers who wish to marry against the father's wishes, the marriages at the end—are stock features of comedy. How does Molière maintain interest?

2. Is anything really resolved in the end? Do you wonder about M. Jourdain's future? Could Molière have ended the comedy differently? More satisfactorily?

3. Do you feel that it is appropriate for each of the acts, and the whole show, to end with ballets? Why or why not?

4. What is Molière really ridiculing here, in your opinion? The bourgeoisie? The nobility? A particular type of character or character defect? The defects of an overcivilized society? Support your answer.

5. For which character do you feel the most sympathy? The least? There has always been considerable disagreement on this point—why?

6. How does a playwright succeed in portraying a character? What makes M. Jourdain memorable?

7. How does this play differ from and resemble other examples of comedy that we read in Volume I both as drama (*Lysistrata*) and as narrative ("The Miller's Tale")?

8. Could *The Would-Be Gentleman* be rewritten as a sentimental drama or as a tragedy? How and why does it make human weakness funny?

JEAN-BAPTISTE LULLY
Le Bourgeois Gentilhomme
(Beginning of the Overture)

A reduction demonstrating homophonic character and jagged rhythm

Lully's Music from *The Would-Be Gentleman*

Modern audiences view Molière's text as the most important element of this comedy-ballet, but the seventeenth-century audience thought of it as "a ballet composed of six *entrées* accompanied by comedy." [1] The music and dance were thus highly significant elements. The composer Lully enjoyed at the time a greater prestige than did Molière. He dominated French music from the time of his appointment as superintendent of Music of the Chamber in 1661 until his death in 1687, and his taste for magnificence is reflected in his compositions for the king: theater pieces with acting, dance, orchestra, costumes, and elaborate scenery. He directed two string orchestras—the *Grande Bande* or "The

---

[1] The music and the entire play in French can be heard on London Records, LL 1447.

(Beginning of the second section of the Overture)

King's 24 Violins" and the *Petite Bande*. Of course he wrote other music, but his operas and ballets stand out as the most characteristic of the types of music enjoyed at court at this time. In his comedy-ballets, Lully perfected all the elements of his mature style: appropriately pompous overtures for string orchestra; massive and spectacular choruses; rhythmically attractive dances that reflect the tastes of the French court; and musical recitatives suited to the French language.

Le Bourgeois Gentilhomme begins with a "French Overture," an instrumental form established by Lully for the introduction of large works—operas and ballets. It was also used as an independent composition and as an opening movement of an instrumental *suite, sonata,* or *concerto.* These compositions for the *24 Violons du Roi* are composed in two parts: the first section

Je lan - guis

becomes

Je lan - guis

and

la la ta ta la la

becomes

De - puis qu'à vos ri - gueurs

in duple *meter*, jagged *rhythm*, homophonic or *chordal texture*, and slow, majestic movement; the second section in triple meter, sprightly rhythm, and *fugal* or *contrapuntal texture*.

In listening to the opening section, one hears not only the jagged or dotted rhythm of the melodies but also an underlying pulse or beat of steady eighth notes, a stylistic feature of the period that some have referred to as the "baroque motor rhythm." This new sense of beat, like the jazz drummer's sense of time, pervades the music and infuses it with life and motion.

A clever baroque device occurs immediately after the conclusion of the overture. The play opens with a play within the play. We discover the composer at work at his harpsichord preparing music for the *comédie-ballet* to follow.

We see and hear him trying phrases, accepting and rejecting passages, humming and strumming, and otherwise reworking a number heard later in its polished form, *Je languis nuit et jour* ("I pine night and day."). Actually, Lully is not giving us a true glimpse into the composer's workshop, for the unfinished version is as complete, correct, and baroque as the shorter final song; but he gives the impression of something not real, and that is very characteristic of French baroque theater. It delighted Louis XIV and is capable of delighting audiences today.

Molière's story line, of course, outlines the formal structure of the entire comedy-ballet, but, according to taste, Lully inserts favorite court dances throughout. Here are some examples:

Sarabande

Bourrée

Gavotte

Turkish March

Both Lully and Louis took music seriously. For political reasons, the court composer had to do his best to please his sovereign, as inferior performance was rewarded harshly. On the other hand, for political reasons, too, Louis XIV took his court entertainments most seriously. Besides satisfying his vanity and love of pleasure, they helped to perpetuate the mystique of absolutist monarchy. Keeping the nobles and even the bourgeoisie pleasantly entertained was another way of keeping them in their place.

THE SEVENTEENTH CENTURY: CONTINUITIES

No historical period is more complex and contradictory than the one we have just studied. Every general statement made about seventeenth-century culture almost seems to generate an equally valid opposite. Perhaps this is because the first half of the century, at least, was a time of tremendous change, of birth and growth. By the second half of the century, Europe was established as a world power and had become more stable at home, culturally as well as politically. Let us review briefly some of the often conflicting aspects of the seventeenth century and their significance.

Religion   In the area of religion, Europe by 1650 was divided into Catholic and Protestant territories, which have more or less survived as such into the present. Protestantism evolved from a revolutionary movement into an establishment or series of establishments, each with its own set of orthodox beliefs. With the subsidence of religious warfare came a growing indifference to religion and a secular view of the world. Attempts by new reform movements among Catholics and Protestants could not halt the trend.

Science   The rapid developments in science were in part responsible for this increasing nonreligious view of the world. First the revolutionary Copernican theory and then experiments conducted by men such as Newton and Galileo taught people to trust their own minds or senses rather than the decrees of authority. Bacon condemned what he conceived of as the traditional deductive approach to nature and called for a new method based on principles derived directly from observation. By use of this method, he believed, a new age of discovery could begin. Eventually man would be able to understand and control his surroundings. In practice, at least, many thinkers of the century treated nature itself as a self-regulating, autonomous machine: God was needed only to explain how the world came into being in the first place. But some felt uneasy about

living in such a world. A few experienced a kind of terror. If earth was no longer perceived as the center of the universe, the position of man also had to be rethought.

Economics   The seventeenth century witnessed a new stage in the development of a highly important modern economic institution: industrial capitalism. The desire for world markets and wealth led to the exploitation of African and American cultures by Europeans. Whereas in the sixteenth century, America had furnished Europe with precious metals primarily, in the seventeenth the American colonies supplied important agricultural products and raw materials. The colonies became an important outlet for European investment. Slaves were a significant cost factor here. In turn, trade with the New World and Africa stimulated intracontinental trade in Europe as well. The new economic interests were another influence in the growth of secularism.

Politics   The rapid accumulation of wealth allowed many middle-class people, "would-be gentlemen," literally to buy their way into the nobility. After very unsettled political conditions in the first half of the century, after 1650 the European monarchs (most strikingly Louis XIV) learned how to keep the upper classes politically subservient; royal absolutism became the political order of the day. Absolutism was the means by which strong central government was established in most of Europe. Accordingly, the modern state owes more to absolutism than to republican or constitutional monarchical forms.

Drawing on the mechanistic model prevalent in the new sciences and terrified of anarchy, Hobbes intended to come to the aid of absolutism with his *Leviathan*. Only by surrendering their individual wills to a will jointly created through a common convenant could mankind know the peace and security sought by the life force in each person. The justification for Leviathan's absolute power was purely utilitarian: he could claim obedience only so long as he provided the security for which he had been created.

If rejected by contemporary defenders for absolutism, Hobbes's *Leviathan*, in basing political theory on enlightened self-interest, clearly predicted the direction of the modern age. For the next two centuries, self-interest became recognized generally as the basic motive in human action. Almost as a necessary counterpoise to this strong individualism, Hobbes insisted on the need for a superior will with absolute power that men, out of self-interest, must obey to keep from killing one another. Here, too, he was a harbinger of the modern world, which has witnessed a steady increase in the power wielded by the state over the lives of individuals.

The Baroque Style   The baroque style in the arts in many ways reflects the turmoil, contradictions, and dynamism of the age in which it flourished. Exuberance is perhaps its most overriding quality. We have seen in many instances that baroque art is characterized by intense sensuality combined with intense spirituality, by a realistic depiction of everyday life along with a love of fantasy and illusion, by a delight in the material aspects of life with a sense of the impermanence of life in this world. Aesthetically, we have seen that the concept *baroque* may include the neoclassical —a classicism expanded to create a sense of magnificence and grandeur. This classicism fitted well with the increase in political stability in the last half of the century.

Performing Arts   Theatricality is characteristic of much of seventeenth-century culture. The Catholic mass became more like a show as churches came to resemble theaters; Bernini transformed Rome into something like a huge theater. Louis XIV, the master showman, built a showplace and ran his court ritual like a ballet. It is not surprising that the theatrical arts rose to great importance during this period. The first theaters that we can call modern were built in Italy and influenced those in other parts of Europe. Two forms of modern stage entertainment, the opera and the ballet, came into being in the seventeenth century; Handel developed the *oratorio* into a form that could be used for a popular show. Greek and Roman tragedies were reborn in neoclassical form with the dramas of Corneille and Racine. Molière, with his ability to depict characters both everyday and universal, created the first truly modern comedies. The combined arts of dance, drama, and music make Molière's comedy-ballets enchanting spectacles as well as incisive commentaries on human nature. A stage piece like *The Would-Be Gentleman*, with its play between reality and fantasy, is another illustration of the diverse richness of seventeenth-century art.

The grandeur, magnificence, and exuberance that characterize the baroque style are nowhere more apparent than in Handel's *Messiah*. Yet many knowing musicians turn to Bach, not Handel, as the culmination of the era. In truth, both composers, and their works, were at the same time typical and extraordinary in their day and ours. Musically speaking, we have extended the limit of the seventeenth century into the mid-eighteenth because of the longer duration of musical baroque. The early eighteenth century, which saw a flowering of great religious music, was on the whole for the other humanities a most nonreligious time. We will see the secular spirit that developed in the seventeenth century take a more profound hold on Western culture in the eighteenth as the larger-than-life dimensions of baroque art are reduced to a more "reasonable" level.

PART SIX
Reason, Revolution, Romanticism: The Eighteenth and Early Nineteenth Centuries

Plate I Pieter Breughel the Elder, *Haymaking*, 1565. (National Gallery of Prague)

Plate II El Greco, *View of Toledo*. Oil on canvas. (The Metropolitan Museum of Art, Bequest of Mrs. H. O. Havemeyer, 1929. The H. O. Havemeyer Collection.)

Plate III Caravaggio, *The Calling of Saint Matthew*. Church of San Luigi dei Francesi, Rome. (Scala/Art Resource)

Plate IV Rubens, *The Garden of Love*.

Plate VI Rembrandt, *Self-Portrait*, c. 1660.
(The Iveagh Bequest, Kenwood/English Heritage)

Plate V Rembrandt, *Syndics of the Drapers Guild.*
(Rijksmuseum, Amsterdam)

Plate VII Rembrandt, *Return of the Prodigal Son.*
(The Hermitage Museum, Leningrad)

23

The European Enlightenment

꒜

A Pre-revolutionary Movement   If the modern world was initiated in the seventeenth century, it was brought into being in the eighteenth. The thinkers formed by the Scientific Revolution taught reliance on individual experience or reason rather than on authority and tradition. Within the age of absolutism, seeds were being planted for a cultural, and eventually political, revolution that would destroy everything the age stood for. France, which dominated Europe culturally and politically throughout the eighteenth century, began the period with Louis XIV, king by the grace of God, and ended it with General Napoleon, sovereign by popular support. In the interim Louis' royal line, the Bourbon family, was swept away by the earthshaking revolution of 1789, which toppled in its turn one European crowned head after the other. The ideas originating in France also had a profound impact on the formation of a new republic across the Atlantic.

EUROPE in 1715

The Philosophes

The intellectual movement that came to be known as the Enlightenment was led by a group of diverse, individualistic Frenchmen who are usually labeled together as the *philosophes*. Although the word literally means "philosopher," these men were not on the whole creators of new philosophical systems. Rather, they were propagandists for a general set of ideas that they believed would bring "light" to their generation and so improve the life of the human race as a whole. Primarily middle-class, skilled and prolific writers, the philosophes reached their public through the burgeoning printed media—not only books and pamphlets but also the newly introduced weekly newspaper and monthly journal. Their mission would have been impossible in prior centuries when the level of literacy was low even in the upper class. The philosophes were able to reach a wide, literate upper- and middle-class public, but not the poor. The lower classes throughout the eighteenth century remained, in general, as oppressed as before, though they joined the bourgeoisie at the end to overthrow the monarchy and to enthrone the goddess of reason. The philosophes had a rather abstract, if genuine, concern for the poor, but they associated primarily with the polished, witty, urbane men and women who frequented the Parisian *salons*. Paris was now replacing Versailles as the center of cultural life.

The *Salon* The Hôtel de Soubise, designed by Germain Boffrand and begun in 1732, is an example of the smaller and more intimate quarters fashioned for the nobility in Paris (Fig. 23-1). Located on small and sometimes awkwardly shaped urban sites, these buildings had a fairly simple exterior; the architects and clients concentrated on the interiors, where the salon was used for small gatherings that replaced the great festivities of the court. The salons were run primarily by women—Madame du Deffand and Madame Geoffrin were two of the most celebrated—and the sexes conversed and exchanged ideas on an equal footing. These conversations were also means for spreading ideas. As the century progressed, educated men and women everywhere strove to be recognized as "enlightened"; even the sovereigns of Europe sought to win the title of "enlightened monarch."

Foundations of the Enlightenment: John Locke How did the Enlightenment develop, and what were its common tenets? Essentially the French philosophes' conceptions of the sources of knowledge were confused. They claimed to be empiricists, deriving their ideas from experience, but they also espoused a belief in natural rights determined by examination of the human conscience. In *rationalist* fashion they used these natural rights as criteria for judging both the society and government of their time. The confusions in their thought, however, were in a sense inherited from the late seventeenth-century English philosopher Locke, from whom they took much of the methodological approach.

23–1 Hôtel de Soubise, Paris. (Giraudon, Paris)

John Locke (1632–1704) was the author of two fundamental tracts, *Essay on Human Understanding* and *Essay Concerning the True Original Extent and End of Civil Government*. In the tradition of Bacon, Locke held in his *Essay on Human Understanding* that all knowledge comes from sense perception. The mind begins as a blank slate, a *tabula rasa*, and what the mind comes to know is a product of combining perceptions and reflection on those combinations. What this in effect meant was that man was a product of his environment: change the environment and the man is changed. Inspired in his turn by the scientific discoveries taking place in his time, Locke attempted to establish laws of human behavior by *inductive* means.

Like his countryman Hobbes a few decades earlier, Locke begins his *Essay Concerning Civil Government* by assuming that originally people lived in a state of nature before the existence of government. Locke had the Indians living in the New World very much in mind. Whereas Hobbes saw primitive people as locked in an endless struggle for self-preservation, isolated and hostile to one another, Locke viewed them in nowhere near such dire circumstances. For Locke, people in that state possessed by nature certain rights to life, liberty, and property. These natural rights could not be proved by experience but were deduced by an examination of the conscience. Because people are by nature sociable, society existed in the state of nature, even without government. Nonetheless, because individuals could not adequately protect all their rights without government, they created the state to guarantee them. Whereas Hobbes's people gave up all liberty to escape their miserable predicament, Locke's people created a state with limited power, one whose executive was closely watched by a legislature. If however, the state ceased to perform the express functions for which it was created and began to rob and oppress its citizens, then Locke advocated revolution and the creation of a new government.

The Philosophes' Political and Religious Doctrines   *Empiricism* and a rationalistic doctrine of natural rights formed the core of the Enlightenment. With a few exceptions the philosophes believed that all men were essentially equal—in that they all possessed reason. As a creature of reason and equal to every other man by nature, every individual had the right to life, liberty, and a happy life. Associated with these natural rights were others like the right to freedom of speech and to religious liberty. The philosophes deplored the intolerance to Protestants still practiced by the Catholic church in France; in fact they viewed the Church itself as a source of superstition, ignorance, and subservience. Priests and others in the hierarchy served to benight, rather than to enlighten the multitudes. A philosophe motto, "Crush the infamous!" *(Écrasez l'infâme)* referred to all irrational and superstitious forces but was directed primarily against the Church.

Although the philosophes supported tolerance for Protestants, they had little respect for any Christian doctrines. They called their own form of religion *deism.* Drawing heavily on the conception of God fostered by Descartes and the Scientific Revolution, they held that God has created the world and set it running on its own, as a watchmaker makes a watch. Heaven and hell were not to be found in the hereafter but on

this earth. If human beings would follow their God-given reason rather than their momentary passions, they could create a world in which everyone would enjoy felicity and peace.

Although their ideas were to influence the revolution, the majority of the philosophes were politically proponents of *despotism*, or rule by one enlightened man, harking back to Plato's notion of the philosopher-king. Turgot, a philosophe and one of Louis XV's ministers, declared: "Give me five years of despotism and I will make France free." Given the situation in France, the greatest concern was to establish a basic equality among the classes and to eliminate privilege; the only way to do this practically was to give the central government absolute control of reform. In England where, despite the existence of classes, there was a basic equality before the law, Locke stressed constitutional monarchy; in France the worst source of oppression came from the privileged classes and groups. If there was to be toleration and freedom of the press in France, it would have to come from the king: the Church and other interest groups were violently opposed to such freedoms.

The reason that Frenchmen did not enjoy natural rights in the present was the fault of evil institutions. Men are good, but corrupted institutions have damaged them. Reform the institutions and men will improve. Indeed they believed that if the proper institutions could be designed, men might eventually perfect themselves. Thus, the philosophes introduced a doctrine of progress. They placed great hope in the reform of the state because they saw it as a central means for reforming all the other institutions of society.

Diderot and the Encyclopedia   The philosophes were the first to broadcast an idea both widely accepted and under attack today: progress through education. If human beings are to be enlightened, to be able to use their reason to unmask lies and superstitions, then they must *know*. To this end, one of the most intelligent and versatile of their number, Denis Diderot (1713–1784), conceived and directed the compiling of a vast encyclopedia called *Dictionnaire Raisonné des Sciences, des Arts et des Métiers.* French authorities saw the whole idea as dangerous—twice they suppressed the Encyclopedia. It contained articles, written by philosophes and others, on everything from how to make wallpaper to the definition of God. It was full of information on science and technology. Eighteenth-century socialites, as well as the philosophes, were passionate amateur scientists, often performing experiments for company after dinner in their elegant salons.

Voltaire (1694–1778)   A contributor to the Encyclopedia and the giant of the French Enlightenment, whose life spanned most of the eighteenth century, was François Arouet, better known under his pen name Voltaire. Probably no other writer was so adored and so hated during his lifetime. Not a profoundly original thinker, he was endowed with an ability to see through hypocrisy and delusion and a witty, satiric style that he used mercilessly against his enemies and anti-Enlightenment forces.

23–2 Marianne Loir, *Portrait de la Marquise de Châtelet*. (Musée et Galerie des Beaux-Arts, Bordeaux/photo© Alain Danvers)

Son of a bourgeois lawyer and an aspiring poet, the young Voltaire wanted nothing so much as to ingratiate himself with the court nobility; with his wit, intelligence, and good education, he accomplished this. Becoming well known as a writer of neoclassical tragedies, he discovered that in spite of his talents he was not socially equal to aristocrats when one of them had him publicly beaten and then thrown into the infamous French prison, the Bastille. He also suffered from an inefficient censorship law, which arbitrarily swooped down on a victim and punished him with imprisonment or exile. After his release from the Bastille, Voltaire was sent into exile in England, where he found a constitutional government, an enlightened noble class that obeyed the law, a tolerant spirit, and the works of John Locke. It was Voltaire who introduced Locke's ideas into France. He also brought back to France the idea that its government and society could, indeed should, be changed. But Voltaire's *Philosophical Letters* (1734) on his impressions of England were seized by the French censors; the philosophe then sought a safe haven in northeastern France at Cirey, with his friend and mistress for the next ten years, Emilie du Châtelet.

Madame du Châtelet herself deserves attention as one of the liberated women of eighteenth-century France. Her portrait (Fig. 23-2), by a woman, Marianne Loir, reveals a subtle intelligence and love of learning coupled with a smile—typical features of the Enlightenment. Forced into an early marriage with an unintellectual nobleman, she astonished Parisian society by exiling herself to a small town to devote herself to intellectual pursuits. She was a mathematician who wrote several treatises on natural philosophy as well as mathematics. While Voltaire lived with her, they observed a rigid schedule filled with scientific experiments, studies, and theatrical performances put on by themselves and their visitors. Another of Voltaire's ambitions while at Cirey was to write history in a manner worthy of a scientific age. With the desire to create a record of the advance of civilization and to deal with all of the creations of the human mind—art, literature, science, business, and politics—Voltaire composed *The Century of Louis XIV*, still a classic of its kind.

In 1750 Voltaire left his country haven to live at the

court of Frederick the Great of Prussia, a man whom many of the philosophes saw as the prototype of the "enlightened despot." Eventually he settled on an estate that he bought at Ferney, just outside Geneva but in France, where he became an enthusiastic farmer. It is there that he wrote, apparently with astounding speed, the most famous of what he called his "philosophical tales," *Candide*. One can see the influence of the satisfaction of cultivating the earth after suffering the vicissitudes of life in the tale's conclusion. Voltaire devoted the rest of his life not only to farming and writing but also to espousing various causes in the name of enlightened justice. He exposed some of the miseries of the French peasants who lived around him and took up the cause of Jean Calas, an aged French Protestant executed by torture after being falsely charged with murdering his son because he had converted to Catholicism. Voltaire exposed the facts of the scandal in his *Treatise on Toleration*. A deist, Voltaire made the plea for tolerance in matters of religion, along with the demand for social justice, a constant throughout his life.

The old Voltaire, admirably portrayed in a statue by the sculptor Houdon (Fig. 23-3) was confident that he had witnessed the triumph of reason in his lifetime. "It is certain," he wrote, "that the knowledge of nature, the skeptical attitude toward old fables dignified by the name of history, a healthy metaphysic freed from the absurdities of the schools, are the fruits of that century when reason was perfected."

He was to see Paris only once more, and to die there, but because he would not "retract his errors" to a priest, his body was not allowed to be buried on consecrated ground. Thirteen years after his death, after the revolution that he did not live to see, his body was brought back to Paris and interred in the Pantheon. Skeptical and cynical as he was, he undoubtedly would not have approved of the revolution. Yet the crowds that came to honor him in 1790 inscribed on his tomb: "He taught us to be free."

Voltaire's life was thus an active one that spanned almost the entire eighteenth century. The products of his pen were many: poetry, philosophy, history, tragedies, pamphlets, essays, and the genre for which he is now best remembered, the philosophical tale. Characteristically of the Enlightenment, his talents were best

23-3 Houdon, *Bust of Voltaire*. (Louvre, Paris)

suited to forms in which he could exercise his quick, sharp style and especially his gift for satire. The progress of Voltaire's thought may be roughly divided into the periods before and after 1755, when a significant event occurred. The earthquake at Lisbon on November 1, the worst natural disaster in Europe in centuries, killed an estimated fifty thousand people. If Voltaire's earlier thought had been characterized by an unshakable belief in progress and in the benefits of civilization, he was now forced to reevaluate his position. His "Poem on the Disaster of Lisbon" expresses compassion for the suffering of humanity but disgust for the proponents of the doctrine of optimism. He was to develop this vision more fully in *Candide*, written in 1758 and published in 1759.

One of the targets of Voltaire's satire in *Candide* was the doctrine of the German philosopher Gottfried Wilhelm Leibnitz (1646-1716). This doctrine, which came to be known as optimism, postulated that God, having an infinite choice of worlds to create, had decided to create a world containing evil as well as good because evil is necessary in order for certain goods, such as free will, to exist. The world that we live in is thus "the best of all possible worlds." Voltaire, who had earlier espoused this philosophy, saw it after the Lisbon earthquake as naive and distorting.

If *Candide* were only a satire on an outmoded philosophical doctrine, it would have long ago been forgotten. But it is also a great adventure story and, at the same time, because of its flagrant improbabilities, a parody of the adventure story and the romance. It contains a utopian vision—the country of El Dorado, significantly in the New World—which shows Voltaire's basic faith in human nature, but it viciously satirizes human pretensions, greed, and fanaticism. In the end, it is a testimony to neither optimism nor pessimism but to the ability of the indomitable human spirit to adapt itself and to do what it can to better life on earth. The following version has been somewhat abridged.

VOLTAIRE

Candide

(translated by T. Smollett, revised by James Thornton)

CHAPTER I

HOW CANDIDE WAS BROUGHT UP IN A MAGNIFICENT CASTLE, AND HOW HE WAS DRIVEN FROM THENCE

In the country of Westphalia, in the castle of the most noble Baron of Thunder-ten-tronckh, lived a youth whom nature had endowed with a most sweet disposition. His face was the true index of his mind. He had a solid judgment joined to the most unaffected simplicity; and hence, I presume, he had his name of Candide. The old servants of the house suspected him to have been the son of the Baron's sister, by a mighty good sort of a gentleman of the neighbourhood, whom that young lady refused to marry, because he could produce no more than threescore and eleven quarterings in his arms;[1] the rest of the genealogical tree belonging to the family having been lost through the injuries of time.

The Baron was one of the most powerful lords in Westphalia; for his castle had not only a gate, but even windows; and his great hall was hung with tapestry. He used to hunt with his mastiffs and spaniels instead of greyhounds; his groom served him for huntsman; and the parson of the parish officiated as grand almoner.[2] He was called "My Lord" by all his people, and he never told a story but every one laughed at it.

My lady Baroness weighed three hundred and fifty pounds, consequently was a person of no small consideration; and then she did the honours of the house with a dignity that commanded universal respect. Her daughter Cunegund was about seventeen years of age, fresh coloured, comely, plump, and desirable. The Baron's son seemed to be a youth in every respect worthy of his father. Pangloss the preceptor was the oracle of the family, and little Candide listened to his instructions with all the simplicity natural to his age and disposition.

Master Pangloss taught the metaphysico-theologo-cosmolo-nigology. He could prove to admiration that there is no effect without a cause; and that, in this best of all possible worlds, the Baron's castle was the most magnificent of all castles, and my lady the best of all possible baronesses.

"It is demonstrable," said he, "that things cannot be otherwise than they are; for as all things have been created for some end, they must necessarily be created for the best end. Observe, for instance, the nose is formed for spectacles, therefore we wear spectacles. The legs are visibly designed for stockings, accordingly we wear stockings. Stones were made to be hewn, and to construct castles, therefore my lord has a magnificent castle; for the greatest baron in the province ought to be the best lodged. Swine were intended to be eaten; therefore we eat pork all the year round: and they who assert that everything is right do not express themselves correctly; they should say, that everything is best."

Candide listened attentively, and believed implicitly; for he thought Miss Cunegund excessively handsome, though he never had the courage to tell her so. He concluded that next to the happiness of being Baron of Thunder-ten-tronckh, the next was that of being Miss Cunegund, the next that of seeing her every day, and the last that of hearing the doctrine of Master

---

[1] He could not prove that he was entirely of a noble lineage.

[2] The one who officially distributes alms.

Pangloss, the greatest philosopher of the whole province, and consequently of the whole world.

One day, when Miss Cunegund went to take a walk in a little neighbouring wood, which was called a park, she saw, through the bushes, the sage Doctor Pangloss giving a lecture in experimental physics to her mother's chambermaid, a little brown wench, very pretty, and very tractable. As Miss Cunegund had a great disposition for the sciences, she observed with the utmost attention the experiments which were repeated before her eyes; she perfectly well understood the force of the doctor's reasoning upon causes and effects.[3] She retired greatly flurried, quite pensive, and filled with the desire of knowledge, imagining that she might be a sufficing reason[3] for young Candide, and he for her.

On her way back she happened to meet Candide; she blushed, he blushed also: she wished him a good morning in a faltering tone; he returned the salute, without knowing what he said. The next day, as they were rising from dinner, Cunegund and Candide slipped behind the screen; She dropped her handkerchief, the young man picked it up. She innocently took hold of his hand, and he as innocently kissed hers with a warmth, a sensibility, a grace—all very extraordinary; their lips met; their eyes sparkled; their knees trembled; their hands strayed. The Baron of Thunder-ten-tronckh chanced to come by; he beheld the cause and effect, and, without hesitation, saluted Candide with some notable kicks on the breech, and drove him out of doors. Miss Cunegund fainted away, and, as soon as she came to herself, the Baroness boxed her ears. Thus a general consternation was spread over this most magnificent and most agreeable of all possible castles.

CHAPTER II

WHAT BEFELL CANDIDE AMONG THE BULGARIANS

Candide, thus driven out of this terrestrial paradise, wandered a long time, without knowing where he went; sometimes he raised his eyes, all bedewed with tears, towards heaven, and sometimes he cast a melancholy look towards the magnificent castle where dwelt the fairest of young baronesses. He laid himself down

___
[3] Allusions to the terminology of Leibnitz.

to sleep in a furrow, heartbroken and supperless. The snow fell in great flakes, and, in the morning when he awoke, he was almost frozen to death; however, he made shift to crawl to the next town, which was called Waldberghoff-trarbkdikdorff, without a penny in his pocket, and half dead with hunger and fatigue. He took up his stand at the door of an inn. He had not been long there, before two men dressed in blue fixed their eyes steadfastly upon him.

"Faith, comrade," said one of them to the other, "yonder is a well-made young fellow, and of the right size."

Thereupon they made up to Candide, and with the greatest civility and politeness invited him to dine with them.

"Gentlemen," replied Candide, with a most engaging modesty, "you do me much honour, but, upon my word, I have no money."

"Money, Sir!" said one of the men in blue to him, "young persons of your appearance and merit never pay anything; why, are not you five feet five inches high?"

"Yes, gentlemen, that is really my size," replied he, with a low bow.

"Come then, Sir, sit down along with us; we will not only pay your reckoning, but will never suffer such a clever young fellow as you to want money. Mankind were born to assist one another."

"You are perfectly right, gentlemen," said Candide; "that is precisely the doctrine of Master Pangloss; and I am convinced that everything is for the best."

His generous companions next entreated him to accept of a few crowns, which he readily complied with, at the same time offering them his note for the payment, which they refused, and sat down to table.

"Have you not a great affection for _____"

"O yes!" he replied, "I have a great affection for the lovely Miss Cunegund."

"May be so," replied one of the men, "but that is not the question! We are asking you whether you have not a great affection for the King of the Bulgarians?"

"For the King of the Bulgarians!" said Candide. "Not at all. Why, I never saw him in my life."

"Is it possible! Oh, he is a most charming king! Come, we must drink his health."

"With all my heart, gentlemen," Candide said, and he tossed off his glass.

"Bravo!" cried the blues; "you are now the support, the defender, the hero of the Bulgarians; your fortune is made; you are on the high road to glory."

So saying, they put him in irons, and carried him away to the regiment. There he was made to wheel about to the right, to the left, to draw his ramrod, to return his ramrod, to present, to fire, to march, and they gave him thirty blows with a cane; the next day he performed his exercise a little better, and they gave him but twenty; the day following he came off with ten, and was looked upon as a young fellow of surprising genius by all his comrades.

Candide was struck with amazement, and could not for the soul of him conceive how he came to be a hero. One fine spring morning, he took it into his head to take a walk, and he marched straight forward, conceiving it to be a privilege of the human species, as well as of the brute creation, to make use of their legs how and when they pleased. He had not gone above two leagues when he was overtaken by four other heroes, six feet high, who bound him neck and heels, and carried him to a dungeon. A court-martial sat upon him, and he was asked which he liked best, either to run the gauntlet six and thirty times through the whole regiment, or to have his brains blown out with a dozen musket-balls. In vain did he remonstrate to them that the human will is free, and that he chose neither; they obliged him to make a choice, and he determined, in virtue of that divine gift called free will, to run the gauntlet six and thirty times. He had gone through his discipline twice, and the regiment being composed of two thousand men, they composed for him exactly four thousand strokes, which laid bare all his muscles and nerves, from the nape of his neck to his rump. As they were preparing to make him set out the third time, our young hero, unable to support it any longer, begged as a favour they would be so obliging as to shoot him through the head. The favour being granted, a bandage was tied over his eyes, and he was made to kneel down. At that very instant, his Bulgarian Majesty, happening to pass by, inquired into the delinquent's crime, and being a prince of great penetration, he found, from what he heard of Candide, that he was a young metaphysician, entirely ignorant of the world; and therefore, out of his great clemency, he condescended to pardon him, for which his name will be celebrated in every journal, and in every age. A skilful surgeon made a cure of Candide in three weeks, by means of emollient unguents prescribed by Dioscorides.[4] His sores were now skinned over, and he was able to march, when the King of the Bulgarians gave battle to the King of the Abares.[5]

CHAPTER III

HOW CANDIDE ESCAPED FROM THE BULGARIANS, AND WHAT BEFELL HIM AFTERWARDS

Never was anything so gallant, so well accoutred, so brilliant, and so finely disposed as the two armies. The trumpets, fifes, hautboys, drums, and cannon, made such harmony as never was heard in hell itself. The entertainment began by a discharge of cannon, which, in the twinkling of an eye, laid flat about six thousand men on each side. The musket bullets swept away, out of the best of all possible worlds, nine or ten thousand scoundrels that infested its surface. The bayonet was next the sufficient reason for the deaths of several thousands. The whole might amount to thirty thousand souls. Candide trembled like a philosopher, and concealed himself as well as he could during this heroic butchery.

At length, while the two kings were causing *Te Deum* to be sung in each of their camps, Candide took a resolution to go and reason somewhere else upon causes and effects. After passing over heaps of dead or dying men, the first place he came to was a neighbouring village, in the Abarian territories, which had been burnt to the ground by the Bulgarians in accordance with international law. Here lay a number of old men covered with wounds, who beheld their wives dying with their throats cut, and hugging their children to their breasts all stained with blood. There several young virgins, whose bellies had been ripped open after they had satisfied the natural necessities of the Bulgarian heroes, breathed their last; while others, half burnt in the flames, begged to be dispatched out of the world.

---

[4] A physician in ancient Greece.
[5] King of the Bulgarians refers to Frederick the Great of Prussia and Abares to the French-Austrian coalition.

The ground about them was covered with the brains, arms, and legs of dead men.

Candide made all the haste he could to another village, which belonged to the Bulgarians, and there he found that the heroic Abares had enacted the same tragedy. From thence continuing to walk over palpitating limbs, or through ruined buildings, at length he arrived beyond the theatre of war, with a little provision in his pouch, and Miss Cunegund's image in his heart. When he arrived in Holland his provisions failed him; but having heard that the inhabitants of that country were all rich and Christians, he made himself sure of being treated by them in the same manner as at the Baron's castle, before he had been driven from thence through the power of Miss Cunegund's bright eyes.

He asked charity of several grave-looking people, who one and all answered him that if he continued to follow this trade, they would have him sent to the house of correction, where he should be taught to earn his bread.

He next addressed himself to a person who had just been haranguing a numerous assembly for a whole hour on the subject of charity. The orator, squinting at him under his broad-brimmed hat, asked him sternly, what brought him thither? and whether he was for the good cause?

"Sir," said Candide, in a submissive manner, "I conceive there can be no effect with a cause; everything is necessarily concatenated and arranged for the best. It was necessary that I should be banished the presence of Miss Cunegund; that I should afterwards run the gauntlet; and it is necessary I should beg my bread, till I am able to earn it: all this could not have been otherwise."

"Hark ye, friend," said the orator, "do you hold the Pope to be Antichrist?"

"Truly, I never heard anything about it," said Candide; "but whether he is or not, I am in want of something to eat."

"Thou deservest not to eat or to drink," replied the orator, "wretch, monster that thou art! hence! avoid my sight, nor ever come near me again while thou livest."

The orator's wife happened to put her head out of the window at that instant, when, seeing a man who doubted whether the Pope was Antichrist, she discharged upon his head a chamber-pot full of ———. Good heavens, to what excess does religious zeal transport the female kind!

A man who had never been christened, an honest Anabaptist, named James, was witness to the cruel and ignominious treatment showed to one of his brethren, to a rational, two-footed, unfledged being. Moved with pity, he carried him to his own house, cleaned him up, gave him meat and drink, and made him a present of two florins, at the same time proposing to instruct him in his own trade of weaving Persian silks which are fabricated in Holland. Candide threw himself at his feet, crying:

"Now I am convinced that Master Pangloss told me truth, when he said that everything was for the best in this world; for I am infinitely more affected by your extraordinary generosity than by the inhumanity of that gentleman in the black cloak and his wife."

The next day, as Candide was walking out, he met a beggar all covered with scabs, his eyes were sunk in his head, the end of his nose was eaten off, his mouth drawn on one side, his teeth as black as coal, snuffling and coughing most violently, and every time he attempted to spit, out dropped a tooth.

CHAPTER IV

HOW CANDIDE FOUND HIS OLD
MASTER IN PHILOSOPHY, DR.
PANGLOSS, AGAIN, AND WHAT
HAPPENED TO THEM

Candide, divided between compassion and horror, but giving way to the former, bestowed on this shocking figure the two florins which the honest Anabaptist James had just before given to him. The spectre looked at him very earnestly, shed tears, and threw his arms about his neck. Candide started back aghast.

"Alas!" said the one wretch to the other, "don't you know your dear Pangloss?"

"What do I hear? Is it you, my dear master! you I behold in this piteous plight? What dreadful misfortune has befallen you? What has made you leave the most magnificent and delightful of all castles? What is become of Miss Cunegund, the mirror of young ladies, and nature's masterpiece?"

"Oh Lord!" cried Pangloss, "I am so weak I cannot stand."

Thereupon Candide instantly led him to the Anabaptist's stable, and procured him something to eat. As soon as Pangloss had a little refreshed himself, Candide began to repeat his inquiries concerning Miss Cunegund.

"She is dead," replied the other.

Candide immediately fainted away: his friend recovered him by the help of a little bad vinegar which he found by chance in the stable. Candide opened his eyes.

"Dead! Miss Cunegund dead!" he said. "Ah, where is the best of worlds now? But of what illness did she die? Was it for grief upon seeing her father kick me out of his magnificent castle?"

"No," replied Pangloss; "her belly was ripped open by the Bulgarian soldiers, after they had ravished her as much as it was possible for damsel to be ravished: they knocked the Baron her father on the head for attempting to defend her; my lady her mother was cut in pieces; my poor pupil was served just in the same manner as his sister; and as for the castle, they have not left one stone upon another; they have destroyed all the ducks, and the sheep, the barns, and the trees: but we have had our revenge, for the Abares have done the very same thing in a neighbouring barony, which belonged to a Bulgarian lord."

At hearing this, Candide fainted away a second time; but, having come to himself again, he said all that it became him to say; he inquired into the cause and effect, as well as into the sufficing reason, that had reduced Pangloss to so miserable a condition.

"Alas!" replied the other, 'it was love: love, the comfort of the human species; love, the preserver of the universe, the soul of all sensible beings; love! tender love!"[6]

"Alas," replied Candide, "I have had some knowledge of love myself, this sovereign of hearts, this soul of souls; yet it never cost me more than a kiss, and twenty kicks on the backside. But how could this beautiful cause produce in you so hideous an effect?"

Pangloss made answer in these terms: "O my dear Candide, you must remember Pacquette, that pretty wench, who waited on our noble Baroness; in her arms I tasted the pleasures of paradise, which produced these hell-torments with which you see me devoured. She was infected with the disease, and perhaps is since dead of it; she received this present of a learned cordelier, who derived it from the fountain-head; he was indebted for it to an old countess, who had it of a captain of horse, who had it of a marchioness, who had it of a page; the page had it of a Jesuit, who, during his novitiate, had it in a direct line from one of the fellow-adventurers of Christopher Columbus; for my part I shall give it to nobody, I am a dying man."

"O Pangloss," cried Candide, "what a strange genealogy is this! Is not the devil the root of it?"

"Not at all," replied the great man, "it was a thing unavoidable, a necessary ingredient in the best of worlds; for if Columbus had not, in an island of America, caught this disease, which contaminates the source of generation, and frequently impedes propagation itself, and is evidently opposite to the great end of nature, we should have had neither chocolate nor cochineal. It is also to be observed that, even to the present time, in this continent of ours, this malady, like our religious controversies, is peculiar to ourselves. The Turks, the Indians, the Persians, the Chinese, the Siamese, and the Japanese are entirely unacquainted with it; but there is a sufficing reason for them to know it in a few centuries. In the meantime, it is making prodigious progress among us, especially in those armies composed of well-disciplined hirelings, who determine the fate of nations; for we may safely affirm that, when an army of thirty thousand men fights to another equal in number, there are about twenty thousand of them poxed on each side."

"Very surprising, indeed," said Candide, "but you must get cured."

"How can I?" said Pangloss: "my dear friend, I have not a penny in the world; and you know one cannot be bled, or have a clyster, without a fee."

This last speech had its effect on Candide; he flew to the charitable Anabaptist James, he flung himself at his feet, and gave him so touching a picture of the miserable situation of his friend, that the good man, without any further hesitation, agreed to take Dr. Pangloss into his house, and to pay for his cure. The cure was effected with only the loss of one eye and an ear. As he wrote a

---

[6] Pangloss has syphillis.

good hand and understood accounts tolerably well, the Anabaptist made him his book-keeper. At the expiration of two months, being obliged to go to Lisbon, about some mercantile affairs, he took the two philosophers with him in the same ship; Pangloss, during the voyage, explained to him how everything was so constituted that it could not be better. James did not quite agree with him on this point.

"Mankind," said he, "must, in some things, have deviated from their original innocence; for they were not born wolves, and yet they worry one another like those beasts of prey. God never gave them twenty-four pounders nor bayonets, and yet they have made cannon and bayonets to destroy one another. To this account I might add, not only bankruptcies, but the law, which seizes on the effects of bankrupts, only to cheat the creditors."

All this was indispensably necessary," replied the one-eyed doctor; "for private misfortunes are public benefits; so that the more private misfortunes there are, the greater is the general good."

While he was arguing in this manner, the sky was overcast, the winds blew from the four quarters of the compass, and the ship was assailed by a most terrible tempest, within sight of the port of Lisbon.

CHAPTER V

A TEMPEST, A SHIPWRECK, AN EARTHQUAKE; AND WHAT ELSE BEFELL DR. PANGLOSS, CANDIDE, AND JAMES THE ANABAPTIST

One half of the passengers, weakened and half dead with the inconceivable anguish which the rolling of a vessel at sea occasions to the nerves and all the humours of the body, tossed about in opposite directions, were lost to all sense of the danger that surrounded them. The other made loud outcries, or betook themselves to their prayers; the sails were blown into shivers, and the masts were brought by the board. The vessel leaked. Every one was busily employed, but nobody could be either heard or obeyed. The Anabaptist, being upon deck, lent a helping hand as well as the rest, when a brutish sailor gave him a blow, and laid him speechless; but, with the violence of the blow, the tar himself tumbled head foremost overboard, and fell upon a piece of the broken mast, which he immediately grasped.

Honest James flew to his assistance, and hauled him in again, but, in the attempt, was thrown overboard himself in sight of the sailor, who left him to perish without taking the least notice of him. Candide, who beheld all that passed, and saw his benefactor one moment rising above water, and the next swallowed up by the merciless waves, was preparing to jump after him; but was prevented by the philosopher Pangloss, who demonstrated to him that the coast of Lisbon had been made on purpose for the Anabaptist to be drowned there. While he was proving his argument à priori, the ship foundered, and the whole crew perished, except Pangloss, Candide, and the brute of a sailor who had been the means of drowning the good Anabaptist. The villain swam ashore; but Pangloss and Candide got to land upon a plank.

As soon as they had recovered a little, they walked towards Lisbon; with what little money they had left they thought to save themselves from starving after having escaped drowning.

Scarce had they done lamenting the loss of their benefactor and set foot in the city, when they perceived the earth to tremble under their feet, and the sea, swelling and foaming in the harbour, dash in pieces the vessels that were riding at anchor. Large sheets of flames and cinders covered the streets and public places; the houses tottered, and were tumbled topsy-turvy, even to their foundations, which were themselves destroyed, and thirty thousand inhabitants of both sexes, young and old, were buried beneath the ruins.

The sailor, whistling and swearing, cried, "Damm it, there's something to be got here."

"What can be the suffing reason of this phenomenon?" said Pangloss.

"It is certainly the day of judgment," said Candide.

The sailor, defying death in the pursuit of plunder, rushed into the midst of the ruin, where he found some money, with which he got drunk, and after he had slept himself sober, he purchased the favours of the first good-natured wench that came his way, amidst the ruins of demolished houses, and the groans of half-buried and expiring persons. Pangloss pulled him by the sleeve.

"Friend," said he, "this is not right, you trespass against the universal reason, and have mistaken your time."

"Death and zounds!" answered the other, "I am a

sailor, and born at Batavia, and have trampled four times upon the crucifix in as many voyages to Japan: you are come to a good hand with your universal reason."

Candide, who had been wounded by some pieces of stone that fell from the houses, lay stretched in the street, almost covered with rubbish.

"For God's sake," said he to Pangloss, "get me a little wine and oil. I am dying."

"This concussion of the earth is no new thing," replied Pangloss, "the city of Lima,[7] in America, experienced the same last year; the same cause, the same effects: there is certainly a train of sulphur all the way under ground from Lima to Lisbon."

"Nothing more probable," said Candide; "but, for the love of God, a little oil and wine."

"Probable!" replied the philosopher, "I maintain that the thing is demonstrable."

Candide fainted away, and Pangloss fetched him some water from a neighbouring spring.

The next day, in searching among the ruins, they found some eatables with which they repaired their exhausted strength. After this, they assisted the inhabitants in relieving the distressed and wounded. Some, whom they had humanely assisted, gave them as good a dinner as could be expected under such terrible circumstances. The repast, indeed, was mournful, and the company moistened their bread with their tears; but Pangloss endeavoured to comfort them under this affliction by affirming that things could not be otherwise than they were.

"For," said he, "all this is for the very best end; for if there is a volcano at Lisbon, it could be on no other spot; for it is impossible for things not to be as they are, for everything is for the best."

By his side sat a little man dressed in black, who was one of the familiars of the Inquisition.[8] This person, taking him up with great politeness, said, "Possibly, my good Sir, you do not believe in original sin; for if everything is best, there could have been no such thing as the fall or punishment of man."

"I humbly ask your Excellency's pardon," answered Pangloss, still more politely; "for the fall of man, and the curse consequent thereupon necessarily entered into the system of the best of worlds."

"That is as much as to say, Sir," rejoined the familiar, "you do not believe in free will."

"Your Excellency will be so good as to excuse me," said Pangloss; "free will is consistent with absolute necessity; for it was necessary we should be free, for in that the will ———"

Pangloss was in the midst of his proposition, when the familiar made a sign to the attendant who was helping him to a glass of port wine.

CHAPTER VI

HOW THE PORTUGUESE MADE A SUBERB AUTO-DA-FÉ[9] TO PREVENT ANY FUTURE EARTHQUAKES, AND HOW CANDIDE UNDERWENT PUBLIC FLAGELLATION

After the earthquake which had destroyed three-quarters of the city of Lisbon, the sages of that country could think of no means more effectual to preserve the kingdom from utter ruin, than to entertain the people with an *auto-da-fé*, it having been decided by the University of Coimbra that burning a few people alive by a slow fire, and with great ceremony, is an infallible secret to prevent earthquakes.

In consequence thereof they had seized on a Biscayan for marrying his godmother, and on two Portuguese for taking out the bacon of a larded pullet chicken they were eating.[10] After dinner, they came and secured Dr. Pangloss, and his pupil Candide; the one for speaking his mind, and the other for seeming to approve what he had said. They were conducted to separate apartments, extremely cool, where they were never incommoded with the sun. Eight days afterwards they were each dressed in a *fanbenito*,[11] and their heads were adorned with paper mitres. The mitre and *fanbenito* worn by Candide were painted with flames reversed, and with

---

[7] There had been an earthquake in Peru in 1746.

[8] The Spanish Inquisition was created by Ferdinand and Isabella in 1478 to deal with heresy especially among recently converted Jews and Moors in Spain. With the conquests in the New World agencies of the Inquisition were established there as well. "Familiars" were its policemen.

[9] Literally "act of faith." Public executions, often by burning, of heretics by the Inquisition.

[10] Thus they were thought to be Jews. How does Voltaire satirize religious intolerance?

[11] A kind of garment worn by the prisoners of the Inquisition.

devils that had neither tails nor claws; but Dr. Pangloss's devils had both tails and claws, and his flames were upright. In these habits they marched in procession, and heard a very pathetic sermon, which was followed by a chant, beautifully intoned. Candide was flogged in regular cadence, while the chant was being sung; the Biscayan, and the two men who would not eat bacon, were burnt, and Pangloss was hanged, although this is not a common custom at these solemnities. The same day there was another earthquake, which made most dreadful havoc.

Candide, amazed, terrified, confounded, astonished, and trembling from head to foot, said to himself, "If this is the best of all possible worlds, what are the others? If I had only been whipped, I could have put up with it, as I did among the Bulgarians; but, O my dear Pangloss! thou greatest of philosophers! that ever I should live to see thee hanged, without knowing for what! O my dear Anabaptist, thou best of men, that it should be thy fate to be drowned in the very harbour! O Miss Cunegund, you mirror of young ladies! that it should be your fate to have your belly ripped open."

He was making the best of his way from the place where he had been preached to, whipped, absolved, and received benediction, when he was accosted by an old woman, who said to him, "Take courage, my son, and follow me."

CHAPTER VII

HOW THE OLD WOMAN TOOK CARE OF CANDIDE, AND HOW HE FOUND THE OBJECT OF HIS LOVE

Candide followed the old woman, though without taking courage, to a decayed house where she gave him a pot of pomatum to anoint his sores, showed him a very neat bed, with a suit of clothes hanging up by it; and set victuals and drink before him.

"There," said she, "eat, drink, and sleep, and may our blessed Lady of Atocha, and the great St. Anthony of Padua, and the illustrious St. James of Compostella, take you under their protection. I shall be back tomorrow."

Candide, struck with amazement at what he had seen, at what he had suffered, and still more with the charity of the old woman, would have shown his acknowledgment by kissing her hand.

"It is not my hand you ought to kiss," said the old woman, "I shall be back to-morrow. Anoint your back, eat, and take your rest."

Candide, notwithstanding so many disasters, ate and slept. The next morning, the old woman brought him his breakfast; examined his back, and rubbed it herself with another ointment. She returned at the proper time, and brought him his dinner; and at night she visited him again with his supper. The next day she observed the same ceremonies.

"Who are you?" said Candide to her. "What god has inspired you with so much goodness? What return can I ever make you?"

The good old beldame kept a profound silence. In the evening she returned, but without his supper.

"Come along with me," said she, "but do not speak a word."

She took him by the arm, and walked with him about a quarter of a mile into the country, till they came to a lonely house surrounded with moats and gardens. The old woman knocked at a little door, which was immediately opened, and she showed him up a pair of back stairs into a small, but richly furnished apartment. There she made him sit down on a brocaded sofa, shut the door upon him, and left him. Candide thought himself in a trance; he looked upon his whole life hitherto as a frightful dream, and the present moment as a very agreeable one.

The old woman soon returned, supporting with great difficulty a young lady, who appeared scarce able to stand. She was of a majestic mien and stature; her dress was rich, and glittering with diamonds, and her face was covered with a veil.

"Take off that veil," said the old woman to Candide.

The young man approached, and, with a trembling hand, took off her veil. What a happy moment! What surprise! He thought he beheld Miss Cunegund; he did behold her, it was she herself. His strength failed him, he could not utter a word, he fell at her feet. Cunegund fainted upon the sofa. The old woman bedewed them with spirits; they recovered; they began to speak. At first they could express themselves only in broken accents; their questions and answers were alternately interrupted with sighs, tears, and exclamations. The old woman desired them to make less noise; and left them together.

"Good heavens!" cried Candide, "is it you? Is it Miss

Cunegund I behold, and alive? Do I find you again in Portugal? Then you have not been ravished? They did not rip open your belly, as the philosopher Pangloss informed me?"

"Indeed but they did," replied Miss Cunegund; "but these two accidents do not always prove mortal."

"But were your father and mother killed?"

"Alas!" answered she, "it is but too true!" and she wept.

"And your brother?"

"And my brother also."

"And how did you come to Portugal? And how did you know of my being here? And by what strange adventure did you contrive to have me brought into this house?"

"I will tell you all," replied the lady, "but first you must acquaint me with all that has befallen you since the innocent kiss you gave me, and the rude kicking you received."

Candide, with the greatest submission, obeyed her, and though he was still wrapped in amazement, though his voice was low and tremulous, though his back pained him, yet he gave her a most ingenuous account of everything that had befallen him since the moment of their separation. Cunegund, with her eyes uplifted to heaven, shed tears when he related the death of the good Anabaptist James, and of Pangloss; after which, she thus related her adventures to Candide, who lost not one syllable she uttered, and seemed to devour her with his eyes all the time she was speaking.

CHAPTER VIII

THE HISTORY OF CUNEGUND

"I was in bed and fast asleep, when it pleased heaven to send the Bulgarians to our delightful castle of Thunder-ten-tronckh, where they murdered my father and brother, and cut my mother in pieces. A tall Bulgarian soldier, six feet high, perceiving that I had fainted away at this sight, attempted to ravish me; the operation brought me to my senses. I cried, I struggled, I bit, I scratched, I would have torn the tall Bulgarian's eyes out, not knowing that what had happened at my father's castle was a customary thing. The brutal soldier gave me a cut in the left groin with his hanger, the mark of which I still carry."

"I hope I shall see it," said Candide, with all imaginable simplicity.

"You shall," said Cunegund; "but let me proceed."

"Pray do," replied Candide.

She continued. "A Bulgarian captain came in and saw me weltering in my blood, and the soldier still as busy as if no one had been present. The officer, enraged at the fellow's want of respect to him, killed him with one stroke of his sabre as he lay upon me. This captain took care of me, had me cured, and carried me prisoner of war to his quarters. I washed what little linen he was master of, and dressed his victuals: he thought me very pretty, it must be confessed; neither can I deny that he was well made, and had a white soft skin, but he was very stupid, and knew nothing of philosophy: it might plainly be perceived that he had not been educated under Doctor Pangloss. In three month's time, having gamed away all his money, and being grown tired of me, he sold me to a Jew, named Don Issachar, who traded Holland and Portugal, and was passionately fond of women. This Jew showed me great kindness in hopes to gain my favours; but he never could prevail on me. A modest woman may be once ravished; but her virtue is greatly strengthened thereby. In order to make sure of me, he brought me to this country house you now see. I had hitherto believed that nothing could equal the beauty of the castle of Thunder-ten-tronckh; but I found I was mistaken.

"The Grand Inquisitor saw me one day at mass, ogled me all the time of service, and, when it was over, sent to let me know he wanted to speak with me about some private business. I was conducted to his palace, where I told him of my parentage: he represented to me how much it was beneath a person of my birth to belong to an Israelite. He caused a proposal to be made to Don Issachar that he should resign me to his lordship. Don Issachar, being the court banker, and a man of credit, was not easily to be prevailed upon. His lordship threatened him with an *auto-da-fé*; in short, my Jew was frightened into a compromise, and it was agreed between them that the house and myself should belong to both in common; that the Jew should have Monday, Wednesday, and the Sabbath to himself; and the Inquisitor the other days of the week. This agreement has lasted almost six months; but not without several disputes, whether the space from Saturday night to Sunday morning belonged to the old or the new law. For my part, I have hitherto withstood them both, and truly I believe this is the very reason why they both still love me.

"At length, to turn aside the scourge of earthquakes, and to intimidate Don Issachar, my lord Inquisitor was pleased to celebrate an *auto-da-fé*. He did me the honour to invite me to the ceremony. I had a very good seat; and refreshments were offered the ladies between mass and the execution. I was dreadfully shocked at the burning of the two Jews, and the honest Biscayan who married his godmother; but how great was my surprise, my consternation, and concern, when I beheld a figure so like Pangloss, dressed in a *sanbenito* and mitre! I rubbed my eyes, I looked at him attentively. I saw him hanged, and I fainted away: scarce had I recovered my senses, when I beheld you stark naked; this was the height of horror, grief, and despair. I must confess to you for a truth, that your skin is far whiter and more blooming than that of the Bulgarian captain. This spectacle worked me up to a pitch of distraction. I screamed out, and would have said, "Hold, barbarians!" but my voice failed me; and indeed my cries would have been useless. After you had been severely whipped I said to myself, "How is it possible that the lovely Candide and the sage Pangloss should be at Lisbon, the one to receive a hundred lashes, and the other to be hanged by order of my lord Inquisitor, of whom I am so great a favourite? Pangloss deceived me most cruelly, in saying that everything is fittest and best."

"Thus agitated and perplexed, now distracted and lost, now half dead with grief, I revolved in my mind the murder of my father, mother, and brother; the insolence of the rascally Bulgarian soldier; the wound he gave me in the groin; my servitude; my being a cook wench to my Bulgarian captain; my subjection to the villainous Don Issachar, and my cruel Inquisitor; the hanging of Doctor Pangloss; the *Miserere* sung while you were whipped; and particularly the kiss I gave you behind the screen the last day I ever beheld you. I returned thanks to God for having brought you to the place where I was, after so many trials. I charged the old woman who attends me to bring you hither, as soon as possible. She has carried out my orders well, and I now enjoy the inexpressible satisfaction of seeing you, hearing you, and speaking to you. But you must certainly be half dead with hunger; I myself have got a good appetite, and so let us sit down to supper."

Upon this the two lovers immediately placed themselves at table, and, after having supped, they returned to seat themselves again on the magnificent sofa already mentioned; they were there when Signor Don Issachar, one of the masters of the house, entered unexpectedly; it was the Sabbath day, and he came to enjoy his privilege, and sigh forth his tender passion.

Chapter IX: Candide kills both Don Issachar and the Inquisitor in self-defense. The old woman procures some horses, and on them Candide escapes with her and Cunegund to the town of Aracena in the mountains of Sierra Morena.

CHAPTER X

IN WHAT DISTRESS CANDIDE, CUNEGUND, AND THE OLD WOMAN ARRIVE AT CADIZ; AND OF THEIR EMBARKATION

"Who could it be who has robbed me of my moidores and jewels?" exclaimed Miss Cunegund, all bathed in tears. "How shall we live? What shall we do? Where shall I find Inquisitors and Jews who can give me more?"

"Alas!" said the old woman, "I have a shrewd suspicion of a reverend father cordelier, who lay last night in the same inn with us at Badajoz: God forbid I should condemn any one wrongfully, but he came into our room twice, and he set off in the morning long before us."

"Alas!" said Candide, "Pangloss has often demonstrated to me that the goods of this world are common to all men, and that every one has an equal right to the enjoyment of them; but, according to these principles, the cordelier ought to have left us enough to carry us to the end of our journey. Have you nothing at all left, my beautiful Cunegund?"

"Not a sou," replied she.

"What is to be done then?" said Candide.

"Sell one of the horses," replied the old woman, "I will get behind my young lady though I have only one buttock to ride on, and we shall reach Cadiz, never fear."

In the same inn there was a Benedictine prior who bought the horse very cheap. Candide, Cunegund, and the old woman, after passing through Lucena, Chellas, and Lebrija, arrived at length at Cadiz. A fleet was then getting ready, and troops were assembling in order to reduce the reverend fathers, the Jesuits of Paraguay, who were accused of having excited one of the Indian tribes, in the neighbourhood of the town of the Holy Sacrament, to revolt against the Kings of Spain and Portugal. Candide, having been in the Bulgarian service, performed the military exercise of that nation before the general of this little army with so intrepid an air, and with such agility and expedition that he gave him the command of a company of foot. Being now made a captain, he embarked with Miss Cunegund, the old woman, two valets, and the two Andalusian horses which had belonged to the Grand Inquisitor of Portugal.

During their voyage they amused themselves with many profound reasonings on poor Pangloss's philosophy.

"We are now going into another world," said Candide, "and surely it must be there that everything is best; for I must confess that we have had some little reason to complain of what passes in ours, both as to the physical and moral part."

"Though I have a sincere love for you," said Miss Cunegund, "yet I still shudder at the reflection of what I have seen and experienced."

"All will be well," replied Candide, "the sea of this new world is already better than our European seas: it is smoother, and the winds blow more regularly."

"God grant it," said Cunegund; "but I have met with such terrible treatment in this that I have almost lost all hopes of a better."

"What murmuring and complaining is here indeed!" cried the old woman. "If you had suffered half what I have done, there might be some reason for it."

Miss Cunegund could scarcely refrain from laughing at the good old woman, and thought it droll enough to pretend to a greater share of misfortunes than herself.

"Alas! my good dame," said she, "unless you have been ravished by two Bulgarians, have received two deep wounds in your belly, have seen two of your own castles demolished, and beheld two fathers and two mothers barbarously murdered before your eyes, and, to sum up all, have had two lovers whipped at an *auto-da-fé*, I cannot see how you could be more unfortunate than me. Add to this, though born a baroness and bear-

ing seventy-two quarterings, I have been reduced to a cook-wench."

"Miss," replied the old woman, "you do not know my family as yet; but if I were to show you my backside, you would not talk in this manner, but suspend your judgment."

This speech raised a high curiosity in Candide and Cunegund; and the old woman continued as follows.

Chapters XI and XII: The old woman tells the story of her life. Once an extraordinarily beautiful princess, she suffered a series of misadventures, including kidnapping, rape, and slavery.

Chapter XIII: Candide, Cunegund, and the old woman arrive in Buenos Aires, where the haughty governor falls in love with Cunegund and offers to marry her. Since the friends have no money, the old woman advises Cunegund to do so and tells Candide he must leave.

CHAPTER XIV

THE RECEPTION CANDIDE AND CACAMBO MET WITH AMONG THE JESUITS IN PARAGUAY

Candide has brought with him from Cadiz such a footman as one often meets with on the coasts of Spain and in the colonies. He was the fourth part of a Spaniard, of a mongrel breed, and born in Tucuman.[12] He had successively gone through the profession of a choirboy, sexton, sailor, monk, pedlar, soldier, and lackey. His name was Cacambo; he had a great affection for his master because his master was a mighty good man. He immediately saddled the two Andalusian horses.

"Come, my good master," he said, "let us follow the old woman's advice, and make all the haste we can from this place, without staying to look behind us."

Candide burst into a flood of tears.

"O my dear Cunegund, must I then be compelled to quit you, just as the Governor was going to honour us with his presence at our wedding! Cunegund, so long lost, and found again, what will become of you?"

"Lord!" said Cacambo, "she must do as well as she

---

[12] Part of Argentina.

can; women are never at a loss. God takes care of them, and so let us make the best of our way."

"But whither wilt thou carry me? Where can we go? What can we do without Cunegund?" cried the disconsolate Candide.

"By St. James of Compostella," said Cacambo, "you were going to fight against the Jesuits of Paraguay; now, let us go and fight for them: I know the road perfectly well; I'll conduct you to their kingdom; they will be delighted with a captain that understands the Bulgarian exercise; you will certainly make a prodigious fortune. If we cannot find our account in one world, we may in another. It is a great pleasure to see new objects, and perform new exploits."

"Then you have been in Paraguay?" said Candide.

"Ay, marry, have I," replied Cacambo: "I was a scout in the College of the Assumption, and I am as well acquainted with the new government of Los Padres[13] as I am with the streets of Cadiz. Oh, it is an admirable government, that is most certain! The kingdom is at present upwards of three hundred leagues in diameter, and divided into thirty provinces; the fathers are there masters of everything, and the people have no money at all; this is that masterpiece of justice and reason. For my part, I see nothing so divine as the good fathers, who wage war in this part of the world against the King of Spain and the King of Portugal, at the same time that they hear the confessions of those very princes in Europe; who kill Spaniards in America, and send them to Heaven in Madrid. This pleases me exceedingly, but let us push forward; you are going to be most fortunate of all mortals. How charmed will those fathers be to hear that a captain who understands the Bulgarian exercise is coming among them!"

As soon as they reached the first barrier, Cacambo called to the advance guard, and told them a captain wanted to speak to my Lord the General. Notice was given to the main guard, and immediately a Paraguayan officer ran to throw himself at the feet of the Commandant to impart this news to him. Candide and Cacambo were immediately disarmed, and their two Andalusian horses were seized. The two strangers were now conducted between two files of musketeers, the Commandant was at the farther end with a three-cornered cap on his head, his gown tucked up, a sword by his side, and a half-pike in his hand; he made a sign, and instantly four-and-twenty soldiers drew up round the newcomers. A sergeant told them that they must wait, the Commandant could not speak to them; and that the Reverend Father Provincial did not suffer any Spaniard to open his mouth but in his presence, or to stay above three hours in the province.

"And where is the Reverend Father Provincial?" said Cacambo.

"He is just come from mass, and is at the parade," replied the sergeant, "and in about three hours' time, you may possibly have the honour to kiss his spurs."

"But," said Cacambo, "the captain, who, as well as myself, is perishing with hunger, is no Spaniard, but a German; therefore, pray, might we not be permitted to break our fast till we can be introduced to his Reverence?"

The sergeant immediately went, and acquainted the Commandant with what he heard.

"God be praised," said the Reverend Commandant, "since he is a German, I will hear what he has to say; let him be brought to my arbour."

Immediately they conducted Candide to a beautiful pavilion, adorned with a colonnade of green and gold marble, and with trellises of vines, which served as a kind of cage for parrots, humming-birds, fly-birds, guinea-hens, and all other curious kinds of birds. An excellent breakfast was provided in vessels of gold; and while the Paraguayans were eating coarse Indian corn out of wooden dishes in the open air, and exposed to the burning heat of the sun, the Reverend Father Commandant retired to his cool arbour.

He was a very handsome young man, round-faced, fair, and fresh-coloured, his eyebrows were finely arched, he had a piercing eye, the tips of his ears were red, his lips vermilion, and he had a bold and commanding air; but such a boldness as neither resembled that of a Spaniard nor of a Jesuit. He ordered Candide and Cacambo to have their arms restored to them, together with their two Andalusian horses. Cacambo gave the poor beasts some oats to eat close by the arbour, keeping a strict eye upon them all the while for fear of surprise.

---

[13] "The Fathers"—that is, the Jesuits.

Candide having kissed the hem of the Commandant's robe, they sat down to table.

"It seems you are a German?" said the Jesuit to him in that language.

"Yes, Reverend Father," answered Candide.

As they pronounced these words, they looked at each other with great amazement, and with an emotion that neither could conceal.

"From what part of Germany do you come?" said the Jesuit.

"From the dirty province of Westphalia," answered Candide: "I was born in the castle of Thunder-ten-tronckh."

"Oh heavens! is it possible?" said the Commandant.

"What a miracle!" cried Candide.

"Can it be you?" said the Commandant.

On this they both retired a few steps backwards, then embraced, and let fall a shower of tears.

"Is it you then, Reverend Father? You are the brother of the fair Cunegund? you who were slain by the Bulgarians! you the Baron's son! you a Jesuit in Paraguay! I must confess this is a strange world we live in. O Pangloss! Pangloss! what joy would this have given you, if you had not been hanged."

The Commandant dismissed the negro slaves, and the Paraguayans who were presenting them with liquor in crystal goblets. He returned thanks to God and St. Ignatius[14] a thousand times; he clasped Candide in his arms, and both their faces were bathed in tears.

"You will be more surprised, more affected, more transported," said Candide, "when I tell you that Miss Cunegund, your sister, whose belly was supposed to have been ripped open, is in perfect health."

"Where?"

"In your neighbourhood, with the Governor of Buenos Ayres; and I myself was going to fight against you."

Every word they uttered during this long conversation was productive of some new matter of astonishment. Their souls fluttered on their tongues, listened in their ears, and sparkled in their eyes. Like true Germans, they continued a long time at table, waiting

for the Reverend Father Provincial; and the Commandant spoke to his dear Candide as follows:

CHAPTER XV

HOW CANDIDE KILLED THE BROTHER OF HIS DEAR CUNEGUND

"Never while I live shall I lose the remembrance of that horrible day on which I saw my father and mother barbarously butchered before my eyes, and my sister ravished. When the Bulgarians retired, we found no sign of my dear sister; but the bodies of my father, mother, and myself, with two servant maids, and three little boys with their throats cut, were thrown into a cart, to be buried in a chapel belonging to the Jesuits, within two leagues of our family seat. A Jesuit sprinkled us with some holy water, which was confoundedly salt, and a few drops of it went into my eyes: the father perceived that my eyelids stirred a little; he put his hand on my breast, and felt my heart beat; upon which he gave me proper assistance, and at the end of three weeks I was perfectly recovered. You know, my dear Candide, I was very handsome; I became still more so, and the Reverend Father Croust, Superior of the House, took a great fancy to me; he gave me a novice's habit, and some years afterwards I was sent to Rome. Our general stood in need of new levies of young German Jesuits. The sovereigns of Paraguay admit as few Spanish Jesuits as possible; they prefer those of other nations, as being more obedient to command. The Reverend Father General looked upon me as a proper person to work in that vineyard. I set out in company with a Pole and a Tyrolese. Upon my arrival, I was honoured with a subdeaconship and a lieutenancy. Now I am colonel and priest. We shall give a warm reception to the King of Spain's troops; I can assure you, they will be well excommunicated and beaten. Providence has sent you hither to assist us. But is it true that my dear sister Cunegund is in the neighbourhood with the Governor of Buenos Ayres?"

Candide swore that nothing could be more true; and the tears began again to trickle down their cheeks.

The Baron knew no end of embracing Candide: he called him his brother, his deliverer.

"Perhaps," said he, "my dear Candide, we shall be

---

[14]Ignatius Loyola, founder of the Jesuit order.

fortunate enough to enter the town sword in hand, and rescue my sister Cunegund."

"Ah! that would crown my wishes," replied Candide, "for I intended to marry her; and I hope shall still be able to do so."

"Insolent fellow! " replied the Baron. "You! you have the impudence to marry my sister, who bears seventy-two quarterings! I think you have an insufferable degree of assurance to dare so much as to mention such an audacious design to me."

Candide, thunder-struck at the oddness of this speech, answered, "Reverend Father, all the quarterings in the world are of no significance. I have delivered your sister from a Jew and an Inquisitor; she is under many obligations to me, and she is resolved to give me her hand. Master Pangloss always told me that mankind are by nature equal. Therefore, you may depend upon it, that I will marry your sister."

"We shall see about that, villain! " said the Jesuit Baron of Thunder-ten-Tronckh, and struck him across the face with the flat side of his sword.

Candide, in an instant, drew his rapier, and plunged it up to the hilt in the Jesuit's body; but, in pulling it out reeking hot, he burst into tears.

"Good God! " cried he, "I have killed my old master, my friend, my brother-in-law; I am the mildest man in the world, and yet I have already killed three men; and of these three two were priests."

Cacambo, standing sentry near the door of the arbour, instantly ran up.

"Nothing remains," said his master, "but to sell our lives as dearly as possible; they will undoubtedly look into the arbour; we must die sword in hand."

Cacambo, who had seen many of these kind of adventures, was not discouraged! He stripped the Baron of his Jesuit's habit, and put it upon Candide, then gave him the dead man's three-cornered cap, and made him mount on horseback. All this was done as quick as thought.

"Gallop, master," cried Cacambo; "everybody will take you for a Jesuit going to give orders; and we shall have passed the frontiers before they are able to overtake us."

He flew as he spoke these words, crying out aloud in Spanish, "Make way, make way for the Reverend Father Colonel."

CHAPTER XVI

WHAT HAPPENED TO OUR TWO TRAVELERS WITH TWO GIRLS, TWO MONKEYS, AND THE SAVAGES, CALLED OREILLONS

Candide and his servant had already passed the frontiers before it was known that the German Jesuit was dead. The wary Cacambo had taken care to fill his wallet with bread, chocolate, ham, fruit, and a few bottles of wine. They penetrated with their Andalusian horses into a strange country where they could discover no beaten path. At length, a beautiful meadow, intersected with streams, opened to their view. Our two travelers allowed their steeds to graze. Cacambo urged his master to take some food, and he set him an example.

"How can you desire me to eat ham, when I have killed the son of my Lord the Baron, and am doomed never more to see the beautiful Cunegund? What will it avail me to prolong a wretched life that might be spent far from her in remorse and despair; and then, what will the *Journal of Trevoux*[15] say?"

While he was making these reflections, he still continued eating. The sun was now on the point of setting, when the ears of our two wanderers were assailed with cries which seemed to be uttered by a female voice. They could not tell whether these were cries of grief or joy: however, they instantly started up, full of that uneasiness and apprehension which a strange place inspires. The cries proceeded from two young women who were tripping stark naked on the edge of the prairie, while two monkeys followed close at their heels biting their buttocks. Candide was touched with compassion; he had learned to shoot while he was among the Bulgarians, and he could hit a filbert in a hedge without touching a leaf. Accordingly, he took up his double-barrelled Spanish musket, pulled the trigger, and laid the two monkeys lifeless on the ground.

"God be praised, my dear Cacambo, I have rescued two poor girls from a most perilous situation: if I have committed a sin in killing an Inquisitor and a Jesuit, I made ample amends by saving the lives of these two

---

[15] A periodical critique on the works of the learned, executed by Jesuits in France.

girls. Who knows but they may be young ladies of a good family, and that this assistance I have been so happy to give them may procure us great advantage in this country."

He was about to continue, when he felt himself struck speechless at seeing the two girls embracing the dead bodies of the monkeys in the tenderest manner, bathing their wounds with their tears, and rending the air with the most doleful lamentations.

"Really," said he to Cacambo, "I should not have expected to see such a prodigious share of good nature."

"Master," replied Cacambo, "you have made a precious piece of work of it; do you know that you have killed the lovers of these two ladies!"

"Their lovers! Cacambo, you are jesting! it cannot be! I can never believe it."

"Dear Sir," replied Cacambo, "you are surprised at everything; why should you think it so strange that there should be a country where monkeys insinuate themselves into the good graces of the ladies? They are the fourth part of a man as I am the fourth part of a Spaniard."

"Alas!" replied Candide, "I remember to have heard Master Pangloss say that such accidents as these frequently came to pass in former times, and that these commixtures are productive of centaurs, fauns, and satyrs; and that many of the ancients had seen such monsters: but I looked upon the whole as fabulous."

"Now you are convinced," said Cacambo, "that it is very true, and you see what use is made of those creatures by persons who have not had a proper education: all I am afraid of is that these same ladies will play us some ugly trick."

These judicious reflections operated so far on Candide, as to make him quit the meadow and strike into a thicket. There he and Cacambo supped, and after heartily cursing the Grand Inquisitor, the Governor of Buenos Ayres, and the Baron, they fell asleep on the ground. When they awoke, they were surprised to find that they could not move; the reason was that the Oreillons[16] who inhabit that country, and to whom the

two girls had denounced them, had bound them with cords made of the bark of trees. They were surrounded by fifty naked Oreillons armed with bows and arrows, clubs, and hatchets of flint; some were making a fire under a large cauldron; and others were preparing spits, crying out one and all, "A Jesuit! a Jesuit! We shall be revenged; we shall have excellent cheer; let us eat this Jesuit; let us eat him up."

"I told you, master," cried Cacambo mournfully, "that those two wenches would play us some scurvy trick."

Candide seeing the cauldron and the spits, cried out, "I suppose they are going either to boil or roast us. Ah! what would Master Pangloss say if he were to see how pure nature is formed! Everything is right: it may be so: but I must confess it is something hard to be bereft of Miss Cunegund, and to be spitted by these Oreillons."

Cacambo, who never lost his presence of mind in distress, said to the disconsolate Candide, "Do not despair; I understand a little of the jargon of these people; I will speak to them."

"Ay, pray do," said Candide, "and be sure you make them sensible of the horrid barbarity of boiling and roasting human creatures, and how little of Christianity there is in such practices."

"Gentlemen," said Cacambo, "you think perhaps you are going to feast upon a Jesuit; if so, it is mighty well; nothing can be more agreeable to justice than thus to treat your enemies. Indeed, the law of nature teaches us to kill our neighbour, and accordingly we find this practised all over the world; and if we do not indulge ourselves in eating human flesh, it is because we have much better fare; but you have not such resources as we have; it is certainly much better judged to feast upon your enemies than to abandon to the fowls of the air the fruits of your victory. But surely, gentlemen, you would not choose to eat your friends. You imagine you are going to roast a Jesuit, whereas my master is your friend, your defender, and you are going to spit the very man who has been destroying your enemies: as to myself, I am your countryman; this gentleman is my master, and so far from being a Jesuit, he has very lately killed one of that order, whose spoils he now wears, and which have probably occasioned your mistake. To convince you of the truth of what I say, take the habit he now has on, and carry it to the

[16] *Orejones* in Spanish, so called because they elongated their earlobes with ornaments.

first barrier of the Jesuits' kingdom, and inquire whether my master did not kill one of their officers. There will be little or no time lost by this, and you may still reserve our bodies in your power to feast on, if you should find what we have told you to be false. But, on the contrary, if you find it to be true, I am persuaded you are too well acquainted with the principles of the laws of society, humanity, and justice, not to use us courteously.''

This speech appeared very reasonable to the Oreillons; they deputed two of their people with all expedition to inquire into the truth of this affair. The two delegates acquitted themselves of their commission like men of sense, and soon returned with good tidings. Upon this the Oreillons released their two prisoners, showed them all sorts of civilities, offered them girls, gave them refreshments, and reconducted them to the confines of their country, crying before them all the way, in token of joy, ''He is no Jesuit, he is no Jesuit.''

Candide could not help admiring the cause of his deliverance.

''What men! what manners! '' cried he: ''if I had not fortunately run my sword up to the hilt in the body of Miss Cunegund's brother, I should have infallibly been eaten alive. But, after all, pure nature is an excellent thing; since these people, instead of eating me, showed me a thousand civilities, as soon as they knew I was not a Jesuit.''

CHAPTER XVII

CANDIDE AND HIS SERVANT ARRIVE IN THE COUNTRY OF EL DORADO.[17] WHAT THEY SAW THERE

When they got to the frontiers of the Oreillons, Cacambo said to Candide, ''You see, this hemisphere is no better than the other: take my advice, and let us return to Europe by the shortest way possible.''

''But how can we get back? '' said Candide; ''and whither shall we go? To my own country? the Bulgarians and the Abares are laying that waste with fire and sword. Or shall we go to Portugal? there I shall be burnt; and if we abide here, we are every moment in danger of being spitted. But how can I bring myself to quit that part of the world where Miss Cunegund has her residence? ''

''Let us turn towards Cayenne,''[18] said Cacambo; ''there we shall meet with some Frenchmen; for you know those gentry ramble all over the world; perhaps they will assist us, and God will look with pity on our distress.''

It was not so easy to get to Cayenne. They knew pretty nearly whereabouts it lay; but the mountains, rivers, precipices, robbers, savages, were dreadful obstacles in the way. Their horses died with fatigue, and their provisions were at an end. They subsisted a whole month upon wild fruit, till at length they came to a river bordered with cocoa-nut palms, the sight of which at once sustained life and hope.

Cacambo, who was always giving as good advice as the old woman herself, said to Candide, ''You see there is no holding out any longer; we have traveled enough on foot. I see an empty canoe near the river-side; let us fill it with cocoa-nuts, get into it, and go down with the stream; a river always leads to some inhabited place. If we do not meet with agreeable things, we shall at least meet with something new.''

''Agreed,'' replied Candide; ''let us recommend ourselves to Providence.''

They rowed a few leagues down the river, the banks of which were in some places covered with flowers; in others barren; in some parts smooth and level, and in others steep and rugged. The stream widened as they went further on, till at length it passed under one of the frightful rocks whose summits seemed to reach the clouds. Here our two travelers had the courage to commit themselves to the stream beneath this vault, which, contracting in this part, hurried them along with a dreadful noise and rapidity. At the end of four-and-twenty hours, they saw daylight again; but their canoe was dashed to pieces against the rocks. They were obliged to creep along, from rock to rock, for the space of a league, till at last a spacious plain presented itself to their sight, bound by inaccessible mountains. The country appeared cultivated equally for pleasure, and to produce the necessaries of life. The useful and

---

[17] The legendary ''land of gold'' in the New World.

[18] In French Guiana.

agreeable were here equally blended. The roads were covered, or rather adorned, with carriages formed of glittering materials, in which were men and women of a surprising beauty, drawn with great rapidity by red sheep of a very large size, surpassed in speed the finest coursers of Andalusia, Tetuan, or Mequinez.[19]

"Here is a country, however," said Candide, "preferable to Westphalia."

He and Cacambo landed near the first village they saw, at the entrance of which they perceived some children covered with tattered garments of the richest brocade, playing at quoits. Our two inhabitants of the other hemisphere amused themselves greatly with what they saw. The quoits were large round pieces, yellow, red, and green, which cast a most glorious lustre. Our travelers picked some of them up, and they proved to be gold, emeralds, rubies, and diamonds, the least of which would have been the greatest ornament to the superb throne of the great Mogul.

"Without doubt," said Cacambo, "those children must be the king's sons, that are playing at quoits."

As he was uttering those words, the schoolmaster of the village appeared, who came to call them to school.

"There," said Candide, "is the preceptor of the royal family."

The little ragamuffins immediately quitted their game, leaving the quoits on the ground with all their other playthings. Candide gathered them up, ran to the schoolmaster, and, with a most respectful bow, presented them to him, giving him to understand by signs that their Royal Highnesses had forgotten their gold and precious stones. The schoolmaster, with a smile, flung them upon the ground, then having examined Candide from head to foot with an air of great surprise, went on his way.

Our travelers took care, however, to gather up the gold, the rubies, and the emeralds.

"Where are we?" cried Candide. "The king's children in this country must have an excellent education, since they are taught to show such a contempt for gold and precious stones."

Cacambo was as much surprised as his master.

They at length drew near the first house in the vil-lage, which was built after the manner of a European palace. There was a crowd of people round the door, and a still greater number in the house. The sound of the most delightful musical instruments was heard, and the most agreeable smell came from the kitchen. Cacambo went up to the door, and heard those within talking in the Peruvian language, which was his mother tongue; for every one knows that Cacambo was born in a village of Tucuman where no other language is spoken.

"I will be your interpreter here," said he to Candide, "let us go in; this is an eating-house."

Immediately two waiters, and two servant-girls, dressed in cloth of gold, and their hair braided with ribbons of tissue, accosted the strangers, and invited them to sit down to the ordinary. Their dinner consisted of four dishes of different soups, each garnished with two young paroquets, a large dish of bouille that weighed two hundredweight, two roasted monkeys of a delicious flavour, three hundred humming-birds in one dish, and six hundred fly-birds in another; some excellent ragouts, delicate tarts, and the whole served up in dishes of rock-crystal. Several sorts of liquors, extracted from the sugar-cane, were handed about by the servants who attended.

Most of the company were chapmen and wagoners, all extremely polite: they asked Cacambo a few questions, with the utmost discretion and circumspection; and replied to his in a most obliging and satisfactory manner.

As soon as dinner was over, both Candide and Cacambo thought they would pay very handsomely for their entertainment by laying down two of those large gold pieces which they had picked off the ground; but the landlord and landlady burst into a fit of laughing and held their sides for some time before they were able to speak.

"Gentlemen," said the landlord, "I plainly perceive you are strangers, and such we are not accustomed to see; pardon us, therefore, for laughing when you offered us the common pebbles of our highways for payment of your reckoning. To be sure, you have none of the coin of this kingdom; but there is no necessity to have any money at all to dine in this house. All the inns, which are established for the convenience of those who carry on the trade of this nation, are maintained by the gov-

---

[19] Province of Spain and two towns in Morocco.

ernment. You have found but very indifferent entertainment here, because this is only a poor village; but in almost every other of these public houses you will meet with a reception worthy of persons of your merit."

Cacambo explained the whole of this speech of the landlord to Candide, who listened to it with the same astonishment with which his friend communicated it.

"What sort of a country is this," said the one to the other, that is unknown to all the world, and in which Nature had everywhere so different an appearance from what she has in ours? Possibly this is that part of the globe where everything is right, for there must certainly be some such place; and, for all that Master Pangloss could say, I often perceived that things went very ill in Westphalia."

CHAPTER XVIII

WHAT THEY SAW IN THE COUNTRY OF EL DORADO

Cacambo vented all his curiosity upon the landlord by a thousand different questions.

The honest man answered him thus: "I am very ignorant, Sir, but I am contented with my ignorance; however, we have in this neighbourhood an old man retired from court, who is the most learned and communicative person in the whole kingdom."

He then directed Cacambo to the old man; Candide acted now only a second character, and attended his servant. They entered a quite plain house, for the door was nothing but silver, and the ceiling was only of beaten gold, but wrought in so elegant a taste as to vie with the richest. The antechamber, indeed, was only incrusted with rubies and emeralds; but the order in which everything was disposed made amends for this great simplicity.

The old man received the strangers on a sofa, which was stuffed with humming-birds' feathers; and ordered his servants to present them with liquors in golden goblets, after which he satisfied their curiosity in the following terms:

"I am now one hundred and seventy-two years old; and I learnt of my late father who was equerry to the king the amazing revolutions of Peru, to which he had been an eye-witness. This kingdom is the ancient patrimony of the Incas, who very imprudently quitted it to conquer another part of the world, and were at length conquered and destroyed themselves by the Spaniards.

"Those princes of their family who remained in their native country acted more wisely. They ordained, with the consent of their whole nation, that none of the inhabitants of our little kingdom should ever quit it; and to this wise ordinance we owe the preservation of our innocence and happiness. The Spaniards had some confused notion of this country, to which they gave the name of El Dorado; and Sir Walter Raleigh, an Englishman, actually came very near it, about a hundred years ago: but the inaccessible rocks and precipices with which our country is surrounded on all sides have hitherto secured us from the rapacious fury of the people of Europe, who have an unaccountable fondness for the pebbles and dirt of our land, for the sake of which they would murder us all to the very last man."

The conversation lasted some time and turned chiefly on the form of government, the customs, the women, the public diversions, and the arts. At length, Candide, who had always had a taste for metaphysics, asked whether the people of that country had any religion.

The old man reddened a little at this question.

"Can you doubt it?" said he. "Do you take us for wretches lost to all sense of gratitude?"

Cacambo asked in a respectful manner what was the established religion of El Dorado. The old man blushed again.

"Can there be two religions then?" he said. "Ours, I apprehend, is the religion of the whole world; we worship God from morning till night."

"Do you worship but one God?" said Cacambo, who still acted as the interpreter of Candide's doubts.

"Certainly," said the old man; "there are not two, nor three, nor four Gods. I must confess the people of your world ask very extraordinary questions."

However, Candide could not refrain from making many more inquiries of the old man; he wanted to know in what manner they prayed to God in El Dorado.

"We do not pray to him at all," said the reverend sage; "we have nothing to ask of him, he has given us all we want, and we give 'im thanks incessantly."

Candide had a curiosity to see some of their priests,

and desired Cacambo to ask the old man where they were.

At this he, smiling, said, "My friends, we are all of us priests; the King and all the heads of families sing solemn hymns of thanksgiving every morning, accompanied by five or six thousand musicians."

"What!" said Cacambo, "have you no monks among you, to dispute, to govern, to intrigue, and to burn people who are not of the same opinion with themselves?"

"Do you take us for fools?" said the old man. "Here we are all of one opinion, and know not what you mean by your monks."

During the whole of this discourse Candide was in raptures, and he said to himself:

"What a prodigious difference is there between this place and Westphalia, and this house and the Baron's castle! If our friend Pangloss had seen El Dorado, he would no longer have said that the castle of Thunder-ten-Tronckh was the finest of all possible edifices: there is nothing like seeing the world, that's certain."

This long conversation being ended, the old man ordered six sheep to be harnessed, and put to the coach, and sent twelve of his servants to escort the travellers to Court.

"Excuse me," said he, "for not waiting on you in person; my age deprives me of that honour. The King will receive you in such a manner that you will have no reason to complain; and doubtless you will make a proper allowance for the customs of the country, if they should not happen altogether to please you."

Candide and Cacambo got into the coach, the six sheep flew, and in less than a quarter of an hour they arrived at the King's palace, which was situated at the further end of the capital. At the entrance was a portal two hundred and twenty feet high, and one hundred wide; but it is impossible for words to express the materials of which it was built. The reader, however, will readily conceive they must have a prodigious superiority over the pebbles and sand which we call gold and precious stones.

Twenty beautiful young virgins-in-waiting received Candide and Cacambo at their alighting from the coach, conducted them to the bath, and clad them in robes woven of the down of humming-birds; after this they were introduced by the great officers of the crown of both sexes to the King's apartment, between two files of musicians, each file consisting of a thousand, according to the custom of the country. When they drew near to the presence chamber, Cacambo asked one of the officers in what manner they were to pay their obeisance to his Majesty: whether it was the custom to fall upon their knees, or to prostrate themselves upon the ground? whether they were to put their hands upon their heads, or behind their backs? whether they were to lick the dust off the floor? in short, what was the ceremony usual on such occasions?

"The custom," said the great officer, "is to embrace the King, and kiss him on each cheek."

Candide and Cacambo accordingly threw their arms round his Majesty's neck; and he received them in the most gracious manner imaginable, and very politely asked them to sup with him.

While supper was preparing, orders were given to show them the city, where they saw public structures that reared their lofty heads to the clouds; the market-places decorated with a thousand columns; fountains of spring water, besides others of rose water, and of liquors drawn from the sugar-cane, incessantly flowing in the great squares; these were paved with a kind of precious stone that emitted an odour like that of cloves and cinnamon. Candide asked to see the high court of justice, the parliament; but was answered that they have none in that country, being utter strangers to lawsuits. He then inquired, if they had any prisons; they replied, "None." But what gave him at once the greatest surprise and pleasure was the Palace of Sciences, where he saw a gallery two thousand feet long, filled with the various apparatus of mathematics and natural philosophy.

After having spent the whole afternoon in seeing only about the thousandth part of the city, they were brought back to the King's palace. Candide sat down at the table with his Majesty, his servant Cacambo, and several ladies of the Court. Never was entertainment more elegant, nor could any one possibly show more wit than his Majesty displayed while they were at supper. Cacambo explained all the King's *bons mots* to Candide, and although they were translated they still appeared to be *bons mots*. Of all the things that surprised Candide, this was not the least. They spent a whole month in this hospitable place, during which time Candide was continually saying to Cacambo:

"I own, my friend, once more, that the castle where I was born is a mere nothing in comparison with the place where we now are; but still Miss Cunegund is not here, and you yourself have doubtless some mistress in Europe. If we remain here, we shall only be as others are: whereas, if we return to our own world with only a dozen of El Dorado sheep, loaded with the pebbles of this country, we shall be richer than all the kings in Europe; we shall no longer need to stand in awe of the Inquisitors; and we may easily recover Miss Cunegund."

This speech pleased Cacambo. A fondness for roving, for making a figure in their own country, and for boasting of what they had seen in their travels, was so strong in our two wanderers that they resolved to be no longer happy; and demanded permission of his Majesty to quit the country.

"You are about to do a rash and silly action," said the King; "I am sensible my kingdom is an inconsiderable spot; but when people are tolerably at their ease in any place, I should think it would be their interest to remain there. Most assuredly, I have no right to detain you or any strangers against your wills; this is an act of tyranny to which our manners and our laws are equally repugnant: all men are free; you have an undoubted liberty to depart whenever you please, but you will have many difficulties in passing the frontiers. It is impossible to ascend that rapid river which runs under high and vaulted rocks, and by which you were conveyed hither by a miracle. The mountains by which my kingdom is hemmed in on all sides are ten thousand feet high, and perfectly perpendicular; they are above ten leagues over each, and the descent from them is one continued precipice. However, since you are determined to leave us, I will immediately give orders to the superintendent of machines to cause one to be made that will convey you safely. When they have conducted you to the back of the mountains, nobody can attend you further; for my subjects have made a vow never to quit the kingdom, and they are too prudent to break it. Ask me whatever else you please."

"All we shall ask of your Majesty," said Cacambo, "is a few sheep laden with provisions, pebbles, and the clay of your country."

The King smiled at the request, and said, "I cannot imagine what pleasure you Europeans find in our yellow clay; but take away as much of it as you will, and much good may it do you."

He immediately gave orders to his engineers to make a machine to hoist these two extraordinary men out of the kingdom. Three thousand good mathematicians went to work and finished it in about fifteen days; and it did not cost more than twenty millions sterling of that country's money. Candide and Cacambo were placed on this machine, and they took with them two large red sheep, bridled and saddled, to ride upon when they got on the other side of the mountains; twenty others to serve as pack-horses for carrying provisions; thirty laden with presents of whatever was most curious in the country; and fifty with gold, diamonds, and other precious stones. The King embraced the two wanderers with the greatest cordiality.

It was a curious sight to behold the manner of their setting off, and the ingenious method by which they and their sheep were hoisted to the top of the mountains. The mathematicians and engineers took leave of them as soon as they had conveyed them to a place of safety, and Candide was wholly occupied with the thoughts of presenting his sheep to Miss Cunegund.

"Now," said he, "thanks to heaven, we have more than sufficient to pay the Governor of Buenos Ayres for Miss Cunegund, if she is redeemable. Let us make the best of our way to Cayenne, where we will take ship, and then we may at leisure think of what kingdom we shall purchase."

CHAPTER XIX

WHAT HAPPENED TO THEM AT
SURINAM, AND HOW CANDIDE
BECAME ACQUAINTED WITH MARTIN

Our travellers' first day's journey was very pleasant; they were elated with the prospect of possessing more riches than were to be found in Europe, Asia, and Africa together. Candide, in amorous transports, cut the name of Miss Cunegund on the trees. The second day, two of their sheep sank into a morass, and were swallowed up with their loads; two more died of fatigue some few days afterwards; seven or eight perished with hunger in a desert, and others, at different times, tumbled down precipices; so that, after travelling about a hundred days, they had only two sheep left.

Said Candide to Cacambo, "You see, my dear friend, how perishable the riches of this world are; there is nothing solid but virtue and the joy of seeing Miss Cunegund again."

"Very true," said Cacambo; "but we have still two sheep remaining, with more treasure than ever the King of Spain will be possessed of; and I espy a town at a distance, which I take to be Surinam, a town belonging to the Dutch. We are now at the end of our troubles, and at the beginning of happiness."

As they drew near the town, they saw a negro stretched on the ground with only one half of his habit, which was a pair of blue cotton drawers; for the poor man had lost his left leg, and his right hand.

"Good God," said Candide in Dutch, "what dost thou here, friend, in this deplorable condition?"

"I am waiting for my master Mynheer Vanderdendur, the famous trader," answered the negro.

"Was it Mynheer Vanderdendur that used you in this cruel manner?"

"Yes, Sir," said the negro; "it is the custom here. They give a pair of cotton drawers twice a year, and that is all our covering. When we labour in the sugar-works, and the mill happens to snatch hold of a finger, they instantly chop off our hand; and when we attempt to run away, they cut off a leg. Both these cases have happened to me, and it is at this expense that you eat sugar in Europe; and yet when my mother sold me for ten pattacoons on the coast of Guinea, she said to me, 'My dear child, bless our fetishes; adore them for ever; they will make thee live happy; thou hast the honour to be a slave to our lords the whites, by which thou wilt make the fortune of us thy parents.' Alas! I know not whether I have made their fortunes; but they have not made mine: dogs, monkeys, and parrots, are a thousand times less wretched than me. The Dutch fetishes who converted me tell me every Sunday that, blacks and whites, we are all children of Adam. As for me, I do not understand any thing of genealogies; but if what these preachers say is true, we are all second cousins; and you must allow, that is is impossible to be worse treated by our relations than we are."

"O Pangloss!" cried out Candide, "such horrid doings never entered thy imagination. Here is an end of the matter; I find myself, after all, obliged to renounce thy Optimism."

"Optimism!" said Cacambo, "what is that?"

"Alas!" replied Candide, "it is the obstinacy of maintaining that everything is best when it is worst": and so saying, he turned his eyes towards the poor negro, and shed a flood of tears; and in this weeping mood he entered the town of Surinam.

Immediately upon their arrival, our travellers inquired if there was any vessel in the harbour which they might send to Buenos Ayres. The person they addressed themselves to happened to be the master of a Spanish bark, who offered to agree with them on moderate terms, and appointed them a meeting at a public-house. Thither Candide and his faithful Cacambo went to wait for him, taking with them their two sheep.

Candide, who was all frankness and sincerity, made an ingenuous recital of his adventures to the Spaniard, declaring to him at the same time his resolution of carrying off Miss Cunegund.

"In that case," said the shipmaster, "I'll take good care not to take you to Buenos Ayres. It would prove a hanging matter to us all. The fair Cunegund is the Governor's favourite mistress."

These words were like a clap of thunder to Candide; he wept bitterly for a long time, and, taking Cacambo aside, he said to him:

"I'll tell you, my dear friend, what you must do. We have each of us in our pockets to the value of five or six millions in diamonds; you are cleverer at these matters than I; you must go to Buenos Ayres and bring off Miss Cunegund. If the Governor makes any difficulty, give him a million; if he holds out, give him two; as you have not killed an Inquisitor, they will have no suspicion of you: I'll fit out another ship and go to Venice, where I will wait for you: Venice is a free country, where we shall have nothing to fear from Bulgarians, Abares, Jews, or Inquisitors."

Cacambo greatly applauded this wise resolution. He was inconsolable at the thought of parting with so good a master, who treated him more like an intimate friend than a servant; but the pleasure of being able to do him a service soon got the better of his sorrow. They embraced each other with a flood of tears. Candide charged him not to forget the old woman. Cacambo set out the same day. This Cacambo was a very honest fellow.

Candide continued some days longer at Surinam,

waiting for any captain to carry him and his two remaining sheep to Italy. He hired domestics and purchased many things necessary for a long voyage; at length, Mynheer Vanderdendur, skipper of a large Dutch vessel, came and offered his service.

"What will you take," said Candide, "to carry me, my servants, my baggage, and these two sheep you see here, direct to Venice?"

The skipper asked ten thousand piastres; and Candide agreed to his demand without hesitation.

"Oh, ho!" said the cunning Vanderdendur to himself, "this stranger must be very rich; he agrees to give me ten thousand piastres without hesitation."

Returning a little while after, he told Candide that upon second consideration he could not undertake the voyage for less than twenty thousand.

"Very well, you shall have them," said Candide.

"Zounds!" said the skipper to himself, "this man agrees to pay twenty thousand piastres with as much ease as ten."

Accordingly he went back again, and told him roundly that he would not carry him to Venice for less than thirty thousand piastres.

"Then you shall have thirty thousand," said Candide.

"Odso!" said the Dutchman once more to himself, "thirty thousand piastres seem a trifle to this man. Those sheep must certainly be laden with an immense treasure. I'll stop here and ask no more; but make him pay down the thirty thousand piastres, and then we shall see."

Candide sold two small diamonds, the least of which was worth more than all the skipper asked. He paid him before-hand, and the two sheep were put on board, and Candide followed in a small boat to join the vessel in the road. The skipper took his opportunity, hoisted his sails, and put out to sea with a favourable wind. Candide, confounded and amazed, soon lost sight of the ship.

"Alas!" said he, "this is a trick like those in our old world!"

He returned back to the shore overwhelmed with grief; and, indeed, he had lost what would have been the fortune of twenty monarchs.

Immediately upon his landing, he applied to the Dutch magistrate: being transported with passion, he thundered at the door; which being opened, he went in, told his case, and talked a little louder than was necessary. The magistrate began with fining him ten thousand piastres for his petulance, and then listened very patiently to what he had to say, promised to examine into the affair at the skipper's return, and ordered him to pay ten thousand piastres more for the fees of the court.

This treatment put Candide out of all patience: it is true, he had suffered misfortunes a thousand times more grievous; but the cool insolence of the judge and of the skipper who robbed him raised his choler and threw him into a deep melancholy. The villainy of mankind presented itself to his mind in all its deformity, and his soul was a prey to the most gloomy ideas. After some time, hearing that the captain of a French ship was ready to set sail for Bordeaux, as he had no more sheep loaded with diamonds to put on board, he hired the cabin at the usual price; and made it known in the town that he would pay the passage and board of any honest man who would give him his company during the voyage; besides making him a present of ten thousand piastres, on condition that such person was the most dissatisfied with his condition and the most unfortunate in the whole province.

Upon this there appeared such a crowd of candidates that a large fleet could not have contained them. Candide, willing to choose from among those who appeared most likely to answer his intention, selected twenty, who seemed to him the most sociable, and who all pretended to merit the preference. He invited them to his inn, and promised to treat them with a supper, on condition that every man should bind himself by an oath to relate his own history. He declared at the same time that he would make choice of that person who should appear to him the most deserving of compassion, and the most justly dissatisfied with his condition of life; and that he would make a present to the rest.

This extraordinary assembly continued sitting till four in the morning. Candide, while he was listening to their adventures, called to mind what the old woman had said to him on their voyage to Buenos Ayres, and the wager she had laid that there was not a person on board the ship but had met with some great misfortune. Every story he heard put him in mind of Pangloss.

"My old master," said he, "would be confoundedly put to it to demonstrate his favourite system. Would he were here! Certainly if everything is for the best, it is in El Dorado, and not in the other parts of the world."

At length he determined in favour of a poor scholar who had laboured ten years for the booksellers at Amsterdam, being of opinion that no employment could be more detestable.

This scholar, who was in fact a very honest man, had been robbed by his wife, beaten by his son, and forsaken by his daughter, who had run away with a Portuguese. He had been likewise deprived of a small employment on which he subsisted, and he was persecuted by the clergy of Surinam, who took him for a Socinian.[20] It must be acknowledged that the other competitors were, at least, as wretched as he; but Candide was in hopes that the company of a man of letters would relieve the tediousness of the voyage. All the other candidates complained that Candide had done them great injustice; but he stopped their mouths by a present of a hundred piastres to each.

CHAPTER XX

WHAT BEFELL CANDIDE AND MARTIN ON THEIR VOYAGE

The old scholar, whose name was Martin, took shipping with Candide for Bordeaux. They both had seen and suffered a great deal; and if the ship had been destined to sail from Surinam to Japan round the Cape of Good Hope, they could have found sufficient entertainment for each other during the whole voyage in discoursing upon moral and natural evil.

Candide, however, had one advantage over Martin: he lived in the pleasing hopes of seeing Miss Cunegund once more; whereas the poor philosopher had nothing to hope for. Besides, Candide had money and jewels, and, notwithstanding he had lost a hundred red sheep, laden with the greatest treasure on the earth, and though he still smarted from the reflection of the Dutch skipper's knavery, yet when he considered what he had still left, and repeated the name of Cunegund, especially after meal-times, he included to Pangloss's doctrine.

"And pray," said he to Martin, "what is your opinion of the whole of this system? What notion have you of moral and natural evil?"

"Sir," replied Martin, "our priests accused me of being a Socinian; but the real truth is, I am a Manichaean."[21]

"Nay, now you are jesting," said Candide; "there are no Manichaeans existing at present in the world."

"And yet I am one," said Martin; "but I cannot help it; I cannot for the soul of me think otherwise."

"Surely the devil must be in you," said Candide.

"He concerns himself so much," replied Martin, "in the affairs of this world that it is very probable he may be in me as well as everywhere else; but I must confess, when I cast my eye on this globe, or rather globule, I cannot help thinking that God has abandoned it to some malignant being. I always except El Dorado. I scarce ever knew a city that did not wish the destruction of its neighbouring city; nor a family that did not desire to exterminate some other family. The poor, in all parts of the world, bear an inveterate hatred to the rich, even while they creep and cringe to them; and the rich treat the poor like sheep, whose wool and flesh they barter for money: a million of regimented assassins traverse Europe from one end to the other to get their bread by regular depredation and murder, because it is the most gentleman-like profession. Even in those cities which seem to enjoy the blessings of peace, and where the arts flourish, the inhabitants are devoured with envy, care, and anxiety, which are greater plagues than any experienced in a town besieged. Private chagrins are still more dreadful than public calamities. In a word, I have seen and suffered so much, that I am a Manichaean."

"And yet there is some good in the world," replied Candide.

"May be," said Martin, "but it has escaped my knowledge."

---

[20] A heresy resembling modern Unitarianism.

[21] A believer in the doctrine (considered heretical) that good and evil are forces of equal strength in the universe.

"While they were deeply engaged in this dispute they heard the report of cannon, which redoubled every moment. Each took out his glass, and they espied two ships warmly engaged at the distance of about three miles. The wind brought them both so near the French ship that those on board her had the pleasure of seeing the fight with great ease. At last one of the two vessels gave the other a shot between wind and water, which sank her outright. Then could Candide and Martin plainly perceive a hundred men on the deck of the vessel which was sinking, who, with hands uplifted to heaven, sent forth piercing cries, and were in a moment swallowed up by the waves.

"Well," said Martin, "you now see in what manner mankind treat each other."

"It is certain," said Candide, "that there is something diabolical in this affair."

As he was speaking thus, he saw something of a shining red hue, which swam close to the vessel. The boat was hoisted out to see what it might be, when it proved to be one of his sheep. Candide felt more joy at the recovery of this one animal than he did grief when he lost the other hundred, though laden with the large diamonds of El Dorado.

The French captain quickly perceived that the victorious ship belonged to the crown of Spain; that the other which sank was a Dutch pirate, and the very same captain who had robbed Candide. The immense riches which this villain had amassed were buried with him in the deep, and only this one sheep saved out of the whole.

"You see," said Candide to Martin, "that vice is sometimes punished: this villain, the Dutch skipper, has met with the fate he deserved."

"Very true," said Martin; "but why should the passengers be doomed also to destruction? God has punished the knave, and the devil has drowned the rest."

The French and Spanish ships continued their cruise, and Candide and Martin their conversation. They disputed fourteen days successively, at the end of which they were just as far advanced as the first moment they began. However, they had the satisfaction of disputing, of communicating their ideas, and of mutually comforting each other. Candide embraced his sheep.

"Since I have found thee again," said he, "I may possibly find my Cunegund once more."

CHAPTER XXI

CANDIDE AND MARTIN, WHILE THUS REASONING WITH EACH OTHER, DRAW NEAR TO THE COAST OF FRANCE

At length they sighted the coast of France.

"Pray, Mr. Martin," said Candide, "have you ever been in France?"

"Yes, Sir," said Martin, "I have been in several provinces of that kingdom. In some, one half of the people are madmen; in some, they are too artful; in others, again, they are in general either very good-natured or very brutal; while in others, they affect to be witty, and in all, their ruling passion is love, the next is slander, and the last is to talk nonsense."

"But pray, Mr. Martin, were you ever in Paris?"

"Yes, Sir, I have been in that city, and it is a place that contains the several species just described; it is a chaos, a confused multitude, where everyone seeks for pleasure without being able to find it; at least, as far as I have observed during my short stay in that city. At my arrival, I was robbed of all I had in the world by pickpockets and sharpers, at the fair of St. Germain. I was taken up myself for a robber, and confined in prison a whole week; after that I hired myself as corrector to a press in order to get a little money towards defraying my expenses back to Holland on foot. I knew the whole tribe of scribblers, malcontents, and religious convulsionaries. It is said the people of that city are very polite; I believe they may be so."

"For my part, I have no curiosity to see France," said Candide, "you may easily conceive, my friend, that, after spending a month at El Dorado, I can desire to behold nothing upon earth but Miss Cunegund; I am going to wait for her at Venice; I intend to pass through France on my way to Italy; will you not bear me company?"

"With all my heart," said Martin: "they say Venice is agreeable to none but noble Venetians; but that, nevertheless, strangers are well received there when they have plenty of money; now I have none, but you have, therefore I will attend you wherever you please."

"Now we are upon this subject," said Candide, "do you think that the earth was originally sea, as we read in that great book which belongs to the captain of the ship?"

"I believe nothing of it," replied Martin, "any more than I do of the many other chimeras which have been related to us for some time past."

"But then, to what end," said Candide, "was the world formed?"

"To make us mad," said Martin.

"Are you not surprised," continued Candide, "at the love which the two girls in the country of the Oreillons had for those two monkeys?—You know I have told you the story."

"Surprised!" replied Martin, "not in the least; I see nothing strange in this passion. I have seen so many extraordinary things, that there is nothing extraordinary to me now."

"Do you think," said Candide, "that mankind always massacred each other as they do now? Were they always guilty of lies, fraud, treachery, ingratitude, inconstancy, envy, ambition, and cruelty? Were they always thieves, fools, cowards, gluttons, drunkards, misers, calumniators, debauchees, fanatics, and hypocrites?"

"Do you believe," said Martin, "that hawks have always been accustomed to eat pigeons when they came in their way?"

"Doubtless," said Candide.

"Well then," replied Martin, "that hawks have always had the same nature, why should you pretend that mankind change theirs?"

"Oh!" said Candide, "there is a great deal of difference, for free will . . ."

Reasoning thus, they arrived at Bordeaux.

Chapter XXII: The recounting of Candide's and Martin's sojourn in France gives Voltaire an opportunity to satirize the cynicism and the dishonesty of Parisian society.

CHAPTER XXIII

CANDIDE AND MARTIN TOUCH UPON THE ENGLISH COAST; WHAT THEY SAW THERE

"Ah Pangloss! Pangloss! Ah, Martin! Martin! Ah, my dear Miss Cunegund! What sort of a world is this? Thus exclaimed Candide, as soon as he had got on board the Dutch ship.

"Why, something very foolish, and very abominable," said Martin.

"You are acquainted with England," said Candide; "are they as great fools in that country as in France?"

"Yes, but in a different manner," answered Martin.

"You know that these two nations are at war about a few acres of snow in the neighbourhood of Canada, and that they have expended much greater sums in the contest than all Canada is worth.[22] To say exactly whether there are a greater number fit to be inhabitants of a mad-house in the one country than the other, exceeds the limits of my imperfect capacity; I know, in general, that the people we are going to visit, are of a very dark and gloomy disposition." . . .

[*Candide and Martin find a ship to take them to Venice.*]

CHAPTER XXIV

OF PACQUETTE AND FRIAR GIROFLÉE

Upon their arrival at Venice, he went in search of Cacambo at every inn and coffee-house, and among all the ladies of pleasure; but could hear nothing of him. He sent every day to inquire of every ship and every vessel that came in: still no news of Cacambo.

"It is strange!" said he to Martin, "very strange! that I should have had time to sail from Surinam to Bordeaux; to travel from thence to Paris, to Dieppe, to Portsmouth; to sail along the coast of Portugal and Spain, and up the Mediterranean, to spend some months in Venice; and that my lovely Cunegund should not have arrived. Instead of her, I only met with a Parisian imposter, and a rascally Abbé of Périgord. Cunegund is actually dead, and I have nothing to do but to follow her. Alas! how much better would it have been for me to have remained in the paradise of El Dorado than to have returned to this cursed Europe! You are in the right, my dear Martin; you are certainly in the right; all is misery and deceit."

He fell into a deep melancholy, and neither went to the opera in vogue, nor partook of any of the diversions of the Carnival; not a woman caused him even a moment's temptation.

Martin said to him, "Upon my word, I think you are very simple to imagine that a rascally valet, with five

---

[22] The French and Indian War (1754–1763).

or six millions in his pocket, would go in search of your mistress to the further end of the world, and bring her to Venice to meet you. If he finds her, he will take her for himself; if he does not, he will take another. Let me advise you to forget your valet Cacambo, and your mistress Cunegund."

Martin's speech was not consoling. Candide's melancholy increased, and Martin never left proving to him that there is very little virtue or happiness in this world; except, perhaps, in El Dorado where hardly anybody can gain admittance.

While they were disputing on this important subject, and still expecting Miss Cunegund, Candide perceived a young Theatine friar in St. Mark's Place, with a girl under his arm. The Theatine looked fresh-coloured, plump, and vigorous; his eyes sparkled; his air and gait were bold and lofty. The girl was very pretty, and was singing a song; and every now and then gave her Theatine an amorous ogle and wantonly pinched his ruddy cheeks.

"You will at least allow," said Candide to Martin, "that these two are happy. Hitherto I have met with none but unfortunate people in the whole habitable globe, except in El Dorado; but, as to this couple, I would venture to lay a wager they are happy."

"Done," said Martin; "they are not, for what you will."

"Well, we have only to ask them to dine with us," said Candide, "and you will see whether I am mistaken or not."

Thereupon he accosted them, and with great politeness invited them to his inn to eat some macaroni, with Lombard partridges and caviare, and to drink a bottle of Montepulciano, Lacrima Christi, Cyprus and Samos wine. The girl blushed; the Theatine accepted the invitation, and she followed him, eyeing Candide every now and then with a mixture of suprise and confusion, while the tears stole down her cheeks. No sooner did she enter his apartment than she cried out:

"How, Mr. Candide, have you quite forgotten poor Pacquette? Do you not know her again?"

Candide, who had not regarded her with any degree of attention before, being wholly occupied with the thoughts of his dear Cunegund, exclaimed:

"Ah! is it you, child? Was it you that reduced Dr. Pangloss to that fine condition I saw him in?"

"Alas! Sir," answered Pacquette, "it was I, indeed. I find you are acquainted with everything; and I have been informed of all the misfortunes that happened to the whole family of my lady Baroness and the fair Cunegund. But I can safely swear to you that my lot was no less deplorable; I was innocence itself when you saw me last. A cordelier, who was my confessor, easily seduced me; the consequences proved terrible. I was obliged to leave the castle some time after the Baron kicked you out by the backside from there; and if a famous surgeon had not taken compassion on me, I had been a dead woman. Gratitude obliged me to live with him some time as a mistress: his wife, who was a very devil for jealousy, beat me unmercifully every day. Oh! she was a perfect fury. The doctor himself was the most ugly of all mortals, and I the most wretched creature existing, to be continually beaten for a man whom I did not love. You are sensible, Sir, how dangerous it was for an ill-natured woman to be married to a physician. Incensed at the behaviour of his wife, he one day gave her so affectionate a remedy for a slight cold she had caught, that she died in less than two hours in most dreadful convulsions. Her relations prosecuted the husband, who was obliged to fly, and I was sent to prison. My innocence would not have saved me, if I had not been tolerably handsome. The judge gave me my liberty on condition he should succeed the doctor. However, I was soon supplanted by a rival, turned off without a farthing, and obliged to continue the abominable trade which you men think so pleasing, but which to us unhappy creatures is the most dreadful of all sufferings. At length I came to follow the business at Venice. Ah! Sir, did you but know what it is to be obliged to lie indifferently with old tradesmen, with counsellors, with monks, gondoliers, and abbés; to be exposed to all their insolence and abuse; to find it often necessary to borrow a petticoat, only that it may be taken up by some disagreeable wretch; to be robbed by one gallant of what we get from another; to be subject to the extortions of civil magistrates; and to have for ever before one's eyes the prospect of old age, a hospital, or a dunghill, you would conclude that I am one of the most unhappy wretches breathing."

Thus did Pacquette unbosom herself to honest Candide in his closet, in the presence of Martin, who took occasion to say to him:

"You see I have half won the wager already."

Friar Giroflée was all this time in the parlour refreshing himself with a glass or two of wine till dinner was ready.

"But," said Candide to Pacquette, "you looked so gay and content, when I met you, you were singing, and caressing the Theatine with so much fondness that I absolutely thought you as happy as you say you are now miserable."

"Ah! dear Sir," said Pacquette, "this is one of the miseries of the trade; yesterday I was stripped and beaten by an officer; yet to-day I must appear good-humoured and gay to please a friar."

Candide was convinced, and acknowledged that Martin was in the right. They sat down to table with Pacquette and the Theatine; the entertainment was very agreeable, and towards the end they began to converse together with some freedom.

"Father," said Candide, to the friar, "you seem to me to enjoy a state of happiness that even kings might envy; joy and health are painted in your countenance. You have a tight pretty wench to divert you; and you seem to be perfectly well contented with your condition as a Theatine."

"Faith, Sir," said Friar Giroflée, "I wish with all my soul the Theatines were every one of them at the bottom of the sea. I have been tempted a thousand times to set fire to the convent and go and turn Turk. My parents obliged me, at the age of fifteen, to put on this detestable habit only to increase the fortune of an elder brother of mine, whom God confound! Jealousy, discord, and fury reside in our convent. It is true, I have preached some paltry sermons, by which I have got a little money, half of which the prior robs me of, and the remainder helps to pay my girls; but, at night, when I go hence to my convent, I am ready to dash my brains against the walls of the dormitory; and this is the case with all the rest of our fraternity."

Martin, turning towards Candide, with his usual indifference, said, "Well, what think you now? Have I won the wager entirely?"

Candide gave two thousand piastres to Pacquette, and a thousand to Friar Giroflée, saying, "I will answer that this will make them happy."

"I am not of your opinion," said Martin; "perhaps this money will only make them much more wretched."

"Be that as it may," said Candide, "one thing comforts me; I see that one often meets with those whom we expected never to see again; so that, perhaps, as I have found my red sheep and Pacquette, I may be lucky enough to find Miss Cunegund also."

"I wish," said Martin, "she one day may make you happy, but I doubt it much."

"You are very hard of belief," said Candide.

"It is because," said Martin, "I have seen the world."

"Observe those gondoliers," said Candide; "are they not perpetually singing?"

"You do not see them," answered Martin, "at home with their wives and brats. The doge has his chagrin, gondoliers theirs. Nevertheless, in the main, I look upon the gondolier's life as preferable to that of the doge; but the difference is so trifling that it is not worth the trouble of examining into."

"I have heard great talk," said Candide, "of the senator Pococurante, who lives in that fine house at the Brenta, where, they say, he entertains foreigners in the most polite manner. They claim that this man is a perfect stranger to uneasiness."

"I should be glad to see so extraordinary a being," said Martin.

Candide thereupon sent a messenger to Signor Pococurante, desiring permission to wait on him the next day.

Chapter XXV: Candide and Martin pay a visit to Signor Pococurante, a noble Venetian whose name means "little caring." As they question him about ancient and modern writers, this man seems to show that he is above everything by cynically dismissing it all. Martin points out that his dislike of everything he possesses reveals his unhappiness.

Chapter XXVI: Candide and Martin have supper with six strangers who all turn out to be kings who have lost their thrones and have come to spend carnival in Venice.

CHAPTER XXVII

CANDIDE'S VOYAGE TO CONSTANTINOPLE

The trusty Cacambo had already engaged the captain of the Turkish ship that was to carry Sultan Achmet back to Constantinople, to take Candide and Martin on board. Accordingly, they both embarked, after paying their obeisance to his miserable Highness. As they were going on board, Candide said to Martin:

"You see we supped in company with six dethroned kings, and to one of them I gave charity. Perhaps there may be a great many other princes still more unfortunate. For my part, I have lost only a hundred sheep, and am now going to fly to the arms of Cunegund. My dear Martin, I must insist on it, that Pangloss was in the right. All is for the best."

"I wish it may be," said Martin.

"But this was an odd adventure we met with at Venice. I do not think there ever was an instance before, of six dethroned monarchs supping together at a public inn."

"This is no more extraordinary," said Martin, "than most of what has happened to us. It is a very common thing for kings to be dethroned; and as for our having the honour to sup with six of them, it is a mere accident, not deserving our attention. What does it matter with whom one sups, provided one has good fare?"

As soon as Candide set his foot on board the vessel, he flew to his old friend and servant Cacambo; and throwing his arms about his neck, embraced him with transports of joy.

"Well," said he, "what news of Cunegund? Does she still continue the paragon of beauty? Does she love me still? How is she? You have, doubtless, purchased a palace for her at Constantinople?"

"My dear master," replied Cacambo, "Cunegund washes dishes on the banks of the Propontis, in the house of a prince who has very few to wash. She is at present a slave in the family of an ancient sovereign, named Ragotsky, whom the Grand Turk allows three crowns a day to maintain him in his exile; but the most melancholy circumstance of all is, that she has lost her beauty and turned horrible ugly."

"Ugly or handsome," said Candide, "I am a man of honour; and, as such, am obliged to love her still. But how could she possibly have been reduced to so abject a condition, when I sent five or six millions to her by you?"

"Lord bless me," said Cacambo, "was not I obliged to give two millions to Senor Don Fernando d'Ibaraa y Figueora y Mascarenas y Lampourdos y Souza, Governor of Buenos Ayres, for liberty to take Miss Cunegund away with me? and then did not a brave fellow of a pirate very gallantly strip us of all the rest? and then did not this same pirate carry us with him to Cape Matapan, to Milo, to Nicaria, to Samos, to Petra, to the Dardanelles, to Marmora, to Scutari? Cunegund and the old woman are now servants to the prince I have told you of; and I myself am slave to the dethroned Sultan."

"What a chain of terrible calamities!" exclaimed Candide. "But, after all, I have still some diamonds left, with which I can easily procure Cunegund's liberty. It is a pity she is grown so very ugly."

Then turning to Martin, "What think you, friend," said he, "whose condition is most to be pitied, the Emperor Achmet's, the Emperor Ivan's, King Charles Edward's,[23] or mine?"

"Faith, I cannot resolve your question," said Martin, "unless I had been in the breasts of you all."

"Ah!" cried Candide, "was Pangloss here now, he would have known, and satisfied me at once."

"I know not," said Martin, "in what balance your Pangloss could have weighed the misfortunes of mankind, and have set a just estimation on their sufferings. All that I pretend to know of the matter is that there are millions of men on the earth whose conditions are an hundred times more pitiable than those of King Charles Edward, the Emperor Ivan, or Sultan Achmet."

"Why, that may be," answered Candide.

In a few days they reached the Bosphorus; and the first thing Candide did was to pay a high ransom for Cacambo: then, without losing time, he and his companions went on board a galley, in order to search for his Cunegund, on the banks of the Propontis, notwithstanding she was grown so ugly.

There were two slaves among the crew of the galley, who rowed very ill, and to whose bare backs the master of the vessel frequently applied a lash of oxhide. Candide, from natural sympathy, looked at these two slaves more attentively than at any of the rest, and drew near them with a look of pity. Their features,

---

[23] The deposed kings Candide and Martin met in Venice.

though greatly disfigured, appeared to him to bear a strong resemblance with those of Pangloss and the unhappy Baron Jesuit, Miss Cunegund's brother. This idea affected him with grief and compassion: he examined them more attentively than before.

"In troth," said he, turning to Martin, "if I had not seen my master Pangloss fairly hanged, and had not myself been unlucky enough to run the Baron through the body, I could believe these are they rowing in the galley."

No sooner had Candide uttered the names of the Baron and Pangloss than the two slaves gave a great cry, ceased rowing, and let fall their oars out of their hands. The master of the vessel, seeing this, ran up to them, and redoubled the discipline of the lash.

"Hold, hold," cried Candide, "I will give you what money you ask for these two persons."

"Good heavens! it is Candide," said one of the men.

"Candide!" cried the other.

"Do I dream," said Candide, "or am I awake? Am I actually on board this galley? Is this my lord Baron, whom I killed? and that my master Pangloss, whom I saw hanged?"

"It is I! it is I!" cried they both together.

"What! is this your great philosopher?" said Martin.

"My dear Sir," said Candide to the master of the galley, "how much do you ask for the ransom of the Baron of Thunder-ten-tronckh, who is one of the first barons of the empire, and of Mr. Pangloss, the most profound metaphysician in Germany?"

"Why then, Christian cur," replied the Turkish captain, "since these two dogs of Christian slaves are barons and metaphysicians, who no doubt are of high rank in their own country, thou shalt give me fifty thousand sequins."

"You shall have them, Sir: carry me back as quick as thought to Constantinople, and you shall receive the money immediately. No! carry me first to Miss Cunegund."

The captain, upon Candide's first proposal, had already tacked about, and he made the crew apply their oars so effectively that the vessel flew through the water quicker than a bird cleaves the air.

Candide bestowed a thousand embraces on the Baron and Pangloss.

"And so then, my dear Baron, I did not kill you? and you, my dear Pangloss, are come to life again after your hanging? But how came you slaves on board a Turkish galley?"

"And is it true that my dear sister is in this country?" said the Baron.

"Yes," said Cacambo.

"And do I once again behold my dear Candide?" said Pangloss.

Candide presented Martin and Cacambo to them; they embraced each other, and all spoke together. The galley flew like lightning, and now they were got back to the port. Candide instantly sent for a Jew, to whom he sold for fifty thousand sequins a diamond richly worth one hundred thousand, though the fellow swore to him all the time, by Abraham, that he gave him the most he could possibly afford. He no sooner got the money into his hands than he paid it down for the ransom of the Baron and Pangloss. The latter flung himself at the feet of his deliverer, and bathed him with his tears: the former thanked him with a gracious nod, and promised to return him the money at the first opportunity.

"But is it possible," said he, "that my sister should be in Turkey?"

"Nothing is more possible," answered Cacambo; "for she scours the dishes in the house of a Transylvanian prince."

Candide sent directly for two Jews, and sold more diamonds to them; and then he set out with his companions in another galley, to deliver Cunegund from slavery.

CHAPTER XXVIII

WHAT BEFELL CANDIDE, CUNEGUND, PANGLOSS, MARTIN, &C.

"Pardon," said Candide to the Baron; "once more let me intreat your pardon, Reverend Father, for running you through the body."

"Say no more about it," replied the Baron; "I was a little too hasty I must own: but as you seem to be anxious to know by what accident I came to be a slave on board the galley where you saw me, I will inform you. After I had been cured of the wound you gave me, by the apothecary of the College, I was attacked and carried off by a party of Spanish troops, who clapped me up in prison in Buenos Ayres, at the very time my sister was setting out from there. I asked leave to return to Rome, to the general of my Order, who appointed me chaplain to the French Ambassador at Constantinople. I had not been a week in my new office, when I happened to meet one evening with a young Icoglan, extremely handsome and well made. The weather was very hot; the young man had an inclination to bathe. I took the opportunity to bathe likewise. I did not know it was a crime for a Christian to be found naked in company with a young Turk. A cadi[24] ordered me to receive a hundred blows on the soles of my feet, and sent me to the galleys. I do not believe that there was ever an act of more flagrant injustice. But I would fain know how my sister came to be a scullion to a Transylvanian prince who has taken refuge among the Turks?"

"But how happens it that I behold you again, my dear Pangloss?" said Candide.

"It is true," answered Pangloss, "you saw me hanged, though I ought properly to have been burnt; but you may remember that it rained extremely hard when they were going to roast me. The storm was so violent that they found it impossible to light the fire; so they hanged me because they could do no better. A surgeon purchased my body, carried it home, and prepared to dissect me. He began by making a crucial incision from my navel to the clavicle. It is impossible for any one to have been more lamely hanged than I had been. The executioner of the Holy Inquisition was a subdeacon, and knew how to burn people very well, but as for hanging, he was a novice at it, being quite out of the way of his practice; the cord being wet, and not slipping properly, the noose did not join. In short, I still continued to breathe; the crucial incision made me scream to such a degree that my surgeon fell flat upon his back; and imagining it was the devil he was dissecting, ran away, and in his fright tumbled downstairs. His wife hearing the noise flew from the next room, and, seeing me stretched upon the table with my crucial incision, was still more terrified than her husband.

She took to her heels and fell over him. When they had a little recovered themselves, I heard her say to her husband, 'My dear, how could you think of dissecting an heretic? Don't you know that the devil is always in them? I'll run directly to a priest to come and drive the evil spirit out.' I trembled from head to foot at hearing her talk in this manner, and exerted what little strength I had left to cry out, 'Have mercy on me!' At length the Portuguese barber took courage, sewed up my wound, and his wife nursed me; and I was upon my legs in a fortnight's time. The barber got me a place as lackey to a Knight of Malta who was going to Venice; but finding my master had no money to pay me my wages, I entered into the service of a Venetian merchant, and went with him to Constantinople.

"One day I happened to enter a mosque, where I saw no one but an old imam[25] and a very pretty young female devotee, who was saying her prayers; her neck was quite bare, and in her bosom she had a beautiful nosegay of tulips, roses, anemones, ranunculuses, hyacinths, and auriculas. She let fall her nosegay. I ran immediately to take it up, and presented it to her with a most respectful bow. I was so long in delivering it, that the imam began to be angry; and, perceiving I was a Christian, he cried out for help; they carried me before the cadi, who ordered me to receive one hundred bastinadoes, and sent me to the galleys. I was chained in the very galley, and to the very same bench with my lord the Baron. On board this galley there were four young men belonging to Marseilles, five Neapolitan priests, and two monks of Corfu, who told us that the like adventures happened every day. The Baron pretended that he had been worse used than myself; and I insisted that there was far less harm in taking up a nosegay, and putting it into a woman's bosom, than to be found stark naked with a young Icoglan. We were continually in dispute, and received twenty lashes a-day with a thong, when the concatenation of sublunary events brought you on board our galley to ransom us from slavery."

"Well, my dear Pangloss," said Candide to him, "when you were hanged, dissected, whipped, and tug-

_____
[24] A Moslem judge.

_____
[25] A priest.

ging at the oar, did you continue to think that every thing in this world happens for the best?"

"I have always abided by my first opinion," answered Pangloss; "for, after all, I am a philosopher; and it would not become me to retract my sentiments; especially, as Leibnitz could not be in the wrong; and that pre-established harmony is the finest thing in the world, as well as the *plenum* and the *materia subtilis*."[26]

CHAPTER XXIX

IN WHAT MANNER CANDIDE FOUND CUNEGUND AND THE OLD WOMAN AGAIN

While Candide, the Baron, Pangloss, Martin, and Cacambo were relating their several adventures, and reasoning on the contingent or non-contingent events of this world; while they were disputing on causes and effects, on moral and physical evil, on free will and necessity, and on the consolation that may be felt by a person when a slave and chained to an oar in a Turkish galley, they arrived at the house of the Transylvanian prince on the coasts of the Propontis. The first objects they beheld there were Miss Cunegund and the old woman, who were hanging some table-cloths on a line to dry.

The Baron turned pale at the sight. Even the tender Candide, that affectionate lover, upon seeing his fair Cunegund all sun-burnt, with blear eyes, a withered neck, wrinkled face and arms, all covered with a red scurf, started back with horror; but, recovering himself, he advanced towards her out of good manners. She embraced Candide and her brother; they embraced the old woman, and Candide ransomed them both.

There was a small farm in the neighbourhood, which the old woman proposed to Candide to make a shift with till the company should meet with a more favourable destiny. Cunegund, not knowing that she was grown ugly, as no one had informed her of it, reminded Candide of his promise in so peremptory a manner that the simple lad did not dare to refuse her;

he then acquainted the Baron that he was going to marry his sister.

"I will never suffer," said the Baron, "my sister to be guilty of an action so derogatory to her birth and family; nor will I bear this insolence on your part: no, I never will be reproached that my nephews are not qualified for the first ecclesiastical dignities in Germany; nor shall a sister of mine ever be the wife of any person below the rank of a baron of the Empire."

Cunegund flung herself at her brother's feet, and bedewed them with her tears, but he still continued inflexible.

"Thou foolish fellow," said Candide, "have I not delivered thee from the galleys, paid thy ransom, and thy sister's too who was a scullion, and is very ugly, and yet I condescend to marry her? and shalt thou make claim to oppose the match? If I were to listen only to the dictates of my anger, I should kill thee again."

"Thou mayest kill me again," said the Baron, "but thou shalt not marry my sister while I am living."

CHAPTER XXX

CONCLUSION

Candide had, in truth, no great inclination to marry Cunegund; but the extreme impertinence of the baron determined him to conclude the match; and Cunegund pressed him so warmly that he could not recant. He consulted Pangloss, Martin, and the faithful Cacambo. Pangloss composed a fine memorial, by which he proved that the Baron had no right over his sister; and that she might, according to all the laws of the Empire, marry Candide with the left hand.[27] Martin concluded that they should throw the Baron into the sea: Cacambo decided that he must be delivered to the Turkish captain and sent to the galleys; after which he should be conveyed by the first ship to the Father General at Rome. This advice was found to be very good; the old woman approved of it, and not a syllable was said to his sister; the business was executed for a little money: and they had the pleasure of tricking a Jesuit and punishing the pride of a German baron.

---

[26] Terms used by Leibnitz.

[27] That is, Candide would not assume his wife's rank.

It was altogether natural to imagine that after undergoing so many disasters, Candide married to his mistress, and living with the philosopher Pangloss, the philosopher Martin, the prudent Cacambo, and the old woman, having besides brought home so many diamonds from the country of the ancient Incas, would lead the most agreeable life in the world. But he had been so much cheated by the Jews that he had nothing else left but his little farm; his wife, every day growing more and more ugly, became ill-natured and insupportable; the old woman was infirm, and more bad-tempered yet than Cunegund. Cacambo, who worked in the garden, and carried the produce of it to sell at Constantinople, was past his labour, and cursed his fate. Pangloss despaired of making a figure in any of the German universities. And as to Martin, he was firmly persuaded that a person is equally ill-situated everywhere. He took things with patience. Candide, Martin, and Pangloss disputed sometimes about metaphysics and morality. Boats were often seen passing under the windows of the farm fraught with effendis, pashas, and cadis,[28] that were going into banishment to Lemnos, Mytilene, and Erzeroum. And other cadis, pashas, and effendis were seen coming back to succeed the place of the exiles, and were driven out in their turns. They saw several heads very curiously stuffed with straw, being carried as presents to the Sublime Porte.[29] Such sights gave occasion to frequent dissertations; and when no disputes were carried on, the irksomeness was so excessive that the old woman ventured one day to say to them:

"I would be glad to know which is worst, to be ravished a hundred times by negro pirates, to have one buttock cut off, to run the gauntlet among the Bulgarians, to be whipped and hanged at an *auto-da-fé*, to be dissected, to be chained to an oar in a galley, and in short to experience all the miseries through which every one of us hath passed,—or to remain here doing nothing?"

"This," said Candide, "is a big question."

This discourse gave birth to new reflections, and Martin especially concluded that man was born to live in the convulsions of disquiet, or in the lethargy of idleness. Though Candide did not absolutely agree to this; yet he was sure of nothing. Pangloss avowed that he had undergone dreadful sufferings; but having once maintained that everything went on as well as possible, he still maintained it, and at the same time believed nothing of it.

There was one thing which, more than ever, confirmed Martin in his detestable principles, made Candide hesitate, and embarrassed Pangloss. This was the arrival of Pacquette and Friar Giroflée one day at their farm. This couple had been in the utmost distress; they had very speedily made away with their three thousand piastres; they had parted, been reconciled; quarrelled again, been thrown into prison; had made their escape, and at last Brother Giroflée turned Turk. Pacquette still continued to follow her trade wherever she came; but she got little or nothing by it.

"I foresaw very well," said Martin to Candide, "that your presents would soon be squandered, and only make them more miserable. You and Cacambo have spent millions of piastres, and yet you are not more happy than Brother Giroflée and Pacquette."

"Ah!" said Pangloss to Pacquette. "It is heaven who has brought you here among us, my poor child! Do you know that you have cost me the tip of my nose, one eye, and one ear? What a handsome shape is here! and what is this world!"

This new adventure engaged them more deeply than ever in philosophical disputations.

In the neighbourhood lived a very famous dervish,[30] who passed for the best philosopher in Turkey; him they went to consult: Pangloss, who was their spokesman, addressed him thus:

"Master, we come to intreat you to tell us why so strange an animal as man has been formed?"

"Why do you trouble your head about it?" said the dervish. "Is it any business of yours?"

"But, my Reverend Father," said Candide, "there is a horrible deal of evil on the earth."

"What signifies it," said the dervish, "whether there is evil or good? When his Highness sends a ship to

---

[28] Turkish officials.
[29] The gate of the Sultan's palace.

[30] A Moslem friar.

Egypt, does he trouble his head whether the rats in the vessel are at their ease or not?"

"What must then be done?" said Pangloss.

"Be silent," answered the dervish.

"I flattered myself," replied Pangloss, "that we should have the pleasure of arguing with you on causes and effects, on the best of possible worlds, the origin of evil, the nature of the soul, and the pre-established harmony."

At these words the dervish shut the door in their faces.

During this conversation, news was spread abroad that two viziers of the bench and the mufti[31] had just been strangled at Constantinople, and several of their friends impaled. This catastrophe made a great noise for some hours. Pangloss, Candide, and Martin, as they were returning to the little farm, met with a good-looking old man, who was taking the air at his door, under an alcove formed of orange-trees. Pangloss, who was as inquisitive as he was argumentative, asked him what was the name of the mufti who was lately strangled.

"I cannot tell," answered the good old man; "I never knew the name of any mufti or vizier breathing. I am entirely ignorant of the event you speak of; I presume, that in general, such as are concerned in public affairs sometimes come to a miserable end; and that they deserve it: but I never inquire what is happening at Constantinople; I am content with sending thither the produce of the garden which I cultivate."

After saying these words, he invited the strangers to come into his house. His two daughters and two sons presented them with diverse sorts of iced sherbet of their own making; besides *caymac*, heightened with the peel of candied citrons, oranges, lemons, pineapples, pistachio-nuts, and Mocha coffee unadulterated with the bad coffee of Batavia or the West Indies. After which the two daughters of this good mussulman perfumed the beards of Candide, Pangloss, and Martin.

"You must certainly have a vast estate," said Candide to the Turk.

"I have no more than twenty acres of ground," he replied, "the whole of which I cultivate myself with the help of my children; and our labour keeps off from us three great evils, idleness, vice, and want."

Candide, as he was returning home, made profound reflections on the Turk's discourse.

"This good old man," he said to Pangloss and Martin, "appears to me to have chosen for himself a lot much preferable to that of the six kings with whom we had the honour to sup."

"Human grandeur," said Pangloss, "is very dangerous. if we believe the testimonies of almost all philosophers; for we find Eglon, King of the Moabites, was assassinated by Ehud; Absalom was hanged by the hair of his head, and run through with three darts; King Nadab, son of Jeroboam, was slain by Baasha; King Elah by Zimri; Ahaziah by Jehu; Athaliah by Jehoiada; the Kings Jehoiakim, Jechoniah, and Zedekiah were led into captivity: I need not tell you what was the fate of Croesus, Astyages, Darius, Dionysius of Syracuse, Pyrrhus, Perseus, Hannibal, Jugurtha, Ariovistus, Caesar, Pompey, Nero, Otho, Vitellius, Domitian, Richard II of England, Edward II, Henry VI, Richard III, Mary Stuart, Charles I, the three Henrys of France, and the Emperor Henry IV."

"Neither need you tell me," said Candide, "that we must take care of our garden."

"You are in the right," said Pangloss; "for when man was put into the Garden of Eden, it was with an intent to dress it: and this proves that man was not born to be idle."

"Work then without disputing," said Martin; "it is the only way to render life supportable."

The little society, one and all, entered into this laudable design; and set themselves to exert their different talents. The little piece of ground yielded them a plentiful crop. Cunegund indeed was very ugly, but she became an excellent hand at pastry-work; Pacquette embroidered; the old woman had the care of the linen. There was none, down to Brother Giroflée, but did some service; he was a very good carpenter, and became an honest man. Pangloss used now and then to say to Candide:

"There is a concatenation of all events in the best of possible worlds; for, in short, had you not been kicked out of a fine castle by the backside for the love of Miss Cunegund, had you not been put into the Inquisition, had you not travelled over America on foot, had you

---

[31] Officials of the Moslem legal system.

not run the Baron through the body, and had you not lost all your sheep which you brought from the good country of El Dorado, you would not have been here to eat preserved citrons and pistachio-nuts."

"Excellently observed," answered Candide; "but let us take care of our garden."

QUESTIONS

1. Voltaire has in part followed the model of the "picaresque" tale, developed in seventeenth-century Spain, that recounts the adventures of a young man wandering through the world. How does the use of an innocent, truthful, "candid" hero allow Voltaire to satirize some of the world's follies?
2. What events in the tale are most improbable? Do these add to or detract from its effectiveness? How?
3. To what extent are the characters realistic? Why are they not as "well rounded" as those in a realist novel, for example?
4. What are some of the specific objects of Voltaire's satire? How would you describe generally the human characteristics that he most scorns?
5. Find specific passages most representative of Voltaire's satiric technique and attempt to analyze his method. Compare it with those of Horace and Juvenal in Volume I.
6. What different philosophies of life are represented in the tale and by which characters? Does Voltaire side entirely with any of them? What philosophy of life emerges from *Candide*?
7. How do you interpret Candide's final sentence?

Montesquieu (1689–1755)

One of the greatest objections leveled against the philosophes by later generations is that they had no appreciation for the effect of history on man. Too analytical, they saw man in the abstract and were therefore unable to effect reform within a historical context. One perceptive critic of the eighteenth century, the Baron de Montesquieu, attacked this neglect of history on the very same grounds. His belief was that men are basically a product of history and that constitutions must be tailored to meet the conditions and historical traditions of the particular society.

Yet Montesquieu himself is usually regarded as a philosophe on the grounds that despite his historical interests he, like most of the others in the movement, was a deist, a believer in natural rights, and a reformer, especially of the penal code. Though he was also an empiricist, he included history as a vital part of the human experience; his insistence on history as an important factor when considering reforms of society and government led him to be politically conservative. A member of the privileged provincial nobility, he was both by self-interest and conviction antagonistic to political reforms predicated on the belief that the past could simply be wiped away. Frankly fearing for personal liberty in a state ruled by a despot no matter how enlightened, he found Locke's theory of an executive checked by a legislature very appealing. Admiring English government but basically misunderstanding its constitutional machinery, Montesquieu developed a theory of separation of powers among legislative, judicial, and executive agencies; he insisted that the individual could be free only where the power of one of these branches of government was checked by the other two. Of almost no importance in France, the theory had tremendous influence in the conception of the United States Constitution.

An issue dealt with by Montesquieu in *The Spirit of the Laws*, which did not take effect in America until much later, was the question of slavery. Seventeenth-century absolutists and capitalists had accepted slavery in the course of their trade; Montesquieu and other philosophes, scrutinizing the institution under the light of reason, found it unnatural and evil. It is clear that slavery would be abhorrent to those who believe in the natural rights of human beings. (We will examine the paradox of its continuation in the new, "enlightened" United States in the next chapter.) The translation is by Thomas Nugent.

MONTESQUIEU

from *The Spirit of the Laws*

OF CIVIL SLAVERY

Slavery, properly so called, is the establishment of a right which gives to one man such a power over another as renders him absolute master of his life and fortune. The state of slavery is in its own nature bad. It is neither useful to the master nor to the slave; not to the slave, because he can do nothing through a motive of virtue; nor to the master, because by having an unlimited authority over his slaves he insensibly accustoms himself to the want of all moral virtues, and thence becomes fierce, hasty, severe, choleric, voluptuous, and cruel.

In despotic countries, where they are already in a state of political servitude, civil slavery is more tolerable than in other governments. Every one ought to be satisfied in those countries with necessaries and life. Hence the condition of a slave is hardly more burdensome than that of a subject.

But in a monarchical government, where it is of the utmost importance that human nature should not be debased or dispirited, there ought to be no slavery. In democracies, where they are all upon equality; and in aristocracies, where the laws ought to use their utmost endeavors to procure as great an equality as the nature of the government will permit, slavery is contrary to the spirit of the constitution: it only contributes to give a power and luxury to the citizens which they ought not to have. . . .

Knowledge humanizes mankind, and reason inclines to mildness; but prejudices eradicate every tender disposition.

ANOTHER ORIGIN OF THE RIGHT OF SLAVERY

I would as soon say that religion gives its professors a right to enslave those who dissent from it, in order to render its propagation more easy.

This was the notion that encouraged the ravagers of America in their iniquity. Under the influence of this idea they founded their right of enslaving so many nations; for these robbers, who would absolutely be both robbers and Christians, were superlatively devout.

Louis XIII was extremely uneasy at a law by which all the negroes of his colonies were to be made slaves; but it being strongly urged to him as the readiest means for their conversion, he acquiesced without further scruple.

OF THE SLAVERY OF THE NEGROES

Were I to vindicate our right to make slaves of the negroes, these should be my arguments:—

The Europeans, having extirpated the Americans, were obliged to make slaves of the Africans, for clearing such vast tracts of land.

Sugar would be too dear if the plants which produce it were cultivated by any other than slaves.

These creatures are all over black, and with such a flat nose that they can scarcely be pitied.

It is hardly to be believed that God, who is a wise Being, should place a soul, especially a good soul, in such a black, ugly body.

It is so natural to look upon color as the criterion of human nature, that the Asiatics, among whom eunuchs are employed, always deprive the blacks of their resemblance to us by a more opprobrious distinction.

The color of the skin may be determined by that of the hair, which, among the Egyptians, the best philosophers in the world, was of such importance that they put to death all the red-haired men who fell into their hands.

The negroes prefer a glass necklace to that gold which polite nations so highly value. Can there be a greater proof of their wanting common sense?

It is impossible for us to suppose these creatures to be men, because, allowing them to be men, a suspicion would follow that we ourselves are not Christians.

Weak minds exaggerate too much the wrong done to the Africans. For were the case as they state it, would the European powers, who make so many needless conventions among themselves, have failed to enter into a general one, in behalf of humanity and compassion?

QUESTIONS

1. How do you think Montesquieu's arguments would strike an eighteenth-century public?
2. Explain the use of irony in the last section. Is it effective?
3. How does Montesquieu turn to ridicule statements that were undoubtedly believed by many?
4. Compare Montesquieu's satire on European "civilization" to that of Montaigne in Volume I.

Rousseau (1712–1778)

Jean-Jacques Rousseau is in many ways, a paradoxical figure who in some ways belongs with the philosophes and in others may be seen as a precursor of romanticism. Of humble origins, Rousseau was born in the city-state of Geneva, in Switzerland; he came to Paris at the age of thirty after fifteen years of living a vagabond existence. An insecure, unhappy man, suffering from a sense of persecution and an embarrassing urinary problem, Rousseau found the source of his problems in the artificiality of society. Among the many contradictions of his life was his writing in praise of the simple, virtuous life in Geneva while he continued to live in Paris.

In two essays that brought him his first literary honors, *The Discourse on the Arts and Sciences* (1749) and *On the Origins of Inequality among Men* (1755), he attacked the corruptions of society and characterized the progress that men had made in the arts and sciences as contributing to this degeneration. Accordingly, he idealized the state of nature, the time when men were originally free. Although he did not deny the rational capacity of men, Rousseau believed that the deepest part of the human being was at the level of the instincts and that by nature men are loving, sympathetic, and kind. When Voltaire finished reading *On the Origins*, he commented that Rousseau's work made him feel like getting down on four legs.

In the society of his own time Rousseau idealized the lower classes, who seemed to him to be living closest to the natural life. In works like *Émile*, a treatise on "natural" education, and his novel, *The New Heloise*, he depicted the beauties of the simple life led amid nature. So popular were these works by the last quarter of the century that all over France the upper classes, including the queen herself, entertained themselves by dressing as shepherds and peasants, picnicking and playing in the woods and fields. It became fashionable to speak of one's feelings in public, to act "naturally," and to idealize the poor.

Rousseau's most important work on political theory, *The Social Contract* (1762) reflects the contradictions found in this paradoxical figure, whose tortured genius endeavored to reconcile into a system his philosophe inheritance with his own intense experience of life. Terminology like "contract" and "state of nature" is that of Locke and Voltaire. On man's emerging from the state of nature to set up a government, the philosophes commonly spoke of a contract being made among the members of the society and the government that they created. This contract was to stipulate the duties and limitations of the government and to afford a legal basis for destroying the government if it violated the terms.

In Rousseau's hands the language of the Enlightenment remains, but the meanings are very different. Whereas previously he had seen man as good in the state of nature and subsequently corrupted by evil institutions, in this work man in nature is depicted as a brute driven by his impulses and appetite. His man, however, is less self-conscious and rational in the state of nature than is Hobbes's man, and the transformation of the individual personality once in the state is much greater. For Rousseau, man becomes truly human only when living in a civil society: "By dint of being exercised, his sentiments become ennobled and his whole soul becomes so elevated that, but for the fact that misuse of the new conditions still, at times, degrades him to a point below that from which he has emerged, he would unceasingly bless the day which freed him for ever from his ancient state, and turned him from a limited and stupid animal into an intelligent being and a man." Against his own earlier view and that of earlier philosophes, Rousseau maintains that the state is not a creation of fully formed men, but rather that men become men only by living in a community. There is no interest in returning to a state of nature; man's task is to create a better society where one's humanity can be fully realized.

Moreover, for Rousseau the contract is not an agreement between a society and its government but between the various free individuals in the state of nature to create the society itself. Driven by the desire for self-preservation, brutish and lonely men unite themselves out of fear and voluntarily surrender their natural freedom in exchange for the benefits of social life. Merging their individual wills into a "general will," they agree to obey everything that "will" decrees. Rousseau's ideal society is small enough so that the collective body of the citizens can assemble to express the general will, which rules that state. The actual government consists just of administrators who carry out its orders. Rousseau probably had in mind a society like the city-state of Geneva where he grew up. But whereas Geneva was governed by an *aristocracy*, Rousseau's ideal state was a *democracy*. The translations are by Henry J. Tozer.

JEAN-JACQUES ROUSSEAU

from *The Social Contract*

THE SOCIAL PACT

I assume that men have reached a point at which the obstacles that endanger their preservation in the state of nature overcome by their resistance the forces which each individual can exert with a view to maintaining himself in that state. Then this primitive condition can no longer subsist, and the human race would perish unless it changed its mode of existence.

Now, as men cannot create any new forces, but only combine and direct those that exist, they have no other means of self-preservation than to form by aggregation a sum of forces which may overcome the resistance, to put them in action by a single motive power, and to make them work in concert.

This sum of forces can be produced only by the combination of many; but the strength and freedom of each man being the chief instruments of his preservation, how can he pledge them without injuring himself, and without neglecting the cares which he owes to himself? This difficulty, applied to my subject, may be expressed in these terms:

"To find a form of association which may defend and protect with the whole force of the community the person and property of every associate, and by means of which each, coalescing with all, may nevertheless obey only himself, and remain as free as before." Such is the fundamental problem of which the social contract furnishes the solution.

The clauses of this contract are so determined by the nature of the act that the slightest modification would render them vain and ineffectual; so that, although they have never perhaps been formally enunciated, they are everywhere the same, everywhere tacitly admitted and recognised, until, the social pact being violated, each man regains his original rights and recovers his natural liberty, whilst losing the conventional liberty for which he renounced it.

These clauses, rightly understood, are reducible to one only, viz. the total alienation to the whole community of each associate with all rights; for, in the first place, since each gives himself up entirely, the conditions are equal for all; and, the conditions being equal for all, no one has any interest in making them burdensome to others.

Further, the alienation being made without reserve, the union is as perfect as it can be, and an individual associate can no longer claim anything; for, if any rights were left to individuals, since there would be no common superior who could judge between them and the public, each being on some point his own judge, would soon claim to be so on all; the state of nature would still subsist, and the association would necessarily become tyrannical or useless.

In short, each giving himself to all, gives himself to nobody; and as there is not one associate over whom we do not acquire the same rights which we concede to him over ourselves, we gain the equivalent of all that we lose, and more power to preserve what we have.

If, then, we set aside what is not of the essence of the social contract, we shall find that it is reducible to the following terms: "Each of us puts in common his person and his whole power under the supreme direction of the general will; and in return we receive every member as an indivisible part of the whole."

Forthwith, instead of the individual personalities of all the contracting parties, this act of association produces a moral and collective body, which is composed of as many members as the assembly has voices, and which receives from this same act its unity, its common self, its life, and its will. This public person, which is thus formed by the union of all the individual members, formerly took the name of "city" and now takes that of "republic" or "body politic," which is called by its members "State" when it is passive, "sovereign" when it is active, "power" when it is compared to similar bodies. With regard to the associates, they take collectively the name of "people," and are called individually "citizens," as participating in the sovereign power, and "subjects," as subjected to the laws of the State. But these terms are often confused and are mistaken one for another; it is sufficient to know how to distinguish them when they are used with complete precision.

QUESTIONS

1. What societies do not have a social contract? Why?

2. Why must the individual give up all his rights on entering the contract?
3. Why, after the creation of the social contract, does each individual remain as free as before?
4. What limitations are there on the actions of the community in regard to the individual? What kind of laws can the community not make?

What is the general will? One thing is clear: for Rousseau it is not the will of the majority. Often the vote of the multitude reflects only the combined self-interest of every individual and not the public interest. For Rousseau the general will is mysteriously found in each citizen below the level of his individual selfish will. It is the common will that seeks the good of the whole community; when it speaks, it reflects the true interests even of those who violently opposed its decision. In the case of citizens who differ with the general will, they are literally forced to be free, that is, to accept what the deepest part of their being really wants.

WHETHER THE GENERAL WILL CAN ERR

It follows from what precedes that the general will is always right and always tends to the public advantage; but it does not follow that the resolutions of the people have always the same rectitude. Men always desire their own good, but do not always discern it; the people are never corrupted, though often deceived, and it is only then that they seem to will what is evil.

There is often a great deal of difference between the will of all and the general will; the latter regards only the common interest, while the former has regard to private interests, and is merely a sum of particular wills; but take away from these same wills the pluses and minuses which cancel one another, and the general will remains as the sum of the differences.

If the people came to a resolution when adequately informed and without any communication among the citizens, the general will would always result from the great number of slight differences, and the resolution would always be good. But when factions, partial associations, are formed to the detriment of the whole society, the will of each of these associations becomes general with reference to its members, and particular with reference to the State; it may then be said that

there are no longer as many voters as there are men, but only as many voters as there are associations. The differences become less numerous and yield a less general result. Lastly, when one of these associations becomes so great that it predominates over all the rest, you no longer have as the result a sum of small differences, but a single difference; there is then no longer a general will, and the opinion which prevails is only a particular opinion.

It is important, then, in order to have a clear declaration of the general will, that there should be no partial association in the State, and that every citizen should express only his own opinion.

QUESTIONS

1. Why does Rousseau feel as he does about political parties?
2. How did most philosophes regard such organizations? Why?
3. What does Rousseau mean by natural rights? Who determines the limits of these rights in society?
4. How does Rousseau's general will differ from the will of Leviathan in Hobbes? Do you see a difference in the way the two philosophers explain why the citizen obeys the government?

Voltaire and other philosophes envisaged men as atoms of rationality alike all over the earth. Rousseau saw man rather as essentially a bundle of feelings and instincts determined to a large extent by the society in which he lives. For Rousseau an individual's community was not simply a convenience; rather, it provided the framework in which the individual realized himself. But for full personal development to occur, every member of the community had to participate in deliberations. Only in this way could the collective, or general, will be expressed and the good of all best be served. Of course, by maintaining that even the will of the majority does not necessarily express that will, he left the door open for the rise of a demagogue who knew better what the people needed than they did themselves. At various times, and with valid reasons, Rousseau has been called the father of democracy, socialism, communism, nationalism, and fascism.

23-4 Joseph Wright, *Experiment with the Air-Pump*. (The Tate Gallery, London)

23-5 Boucher, *Diana after the Hunt*. (Musée Cognacq-Jay/Photographie Bulloz, Paris)

177

Aspects of Painting in the Enlightenment

Many of the tendencies found in the philosophes—the movement from the nobility to the bourgeois, from the grandiose to the petite, from tragedy to satire, as well as the interests in science and in society—are reflected in the art of the early eighteenth century. An example of the new middle class passion for science and homemade experiments may be seen in the painting *Experiment with the Air-Pump* (1768) by an Englishman, Joseph Wright (Fig. 23-4). Exhibited in London, it would have appealed to Diderot and Voltaire, for it records a scientific experiment in explicit detail. The air pump, on the table in the center of the composition, has been purchased by a prosperous bourgeois to entertain and to educate. The glass globe contains a dove that will die when the air is pumped from the globe to create a vacuum. The two young girls are sad, but the others, youths and elders, watch with interest. The surfaces and textures of objects are rendered with extreme *verisimilitude*—the painter is as observant as the scientist.

Paintings such as this indicate one characteristic of eighteenth-century art: the decline in importance of the art of the court. Another type, a more intimate and sensual art, replaced the neoclassicism of Le Brun and his school. Watteau's *Pilgrimage to Cythera* (Color Plate V) is thematically the progeny of Rubens' *Garden of Love* (Color Plate II). Yet these couples who move through the forest of the enchanted island of Venus are

23-6   Greuze, *The Village Bride*. (Louvre, Paris)

not arriving, but leaving, to return to the real world. Watteau has given a sense of melancholy to the beautiful but shallow world of entertainments and parties that seemed more and more to occupy the life of the nobility.

Boucher, who followed Watteau, continued the decorative and intimate character of his art while adding a more sexual, sensuous content (Fig. 23-5). The golden colors, the flesh tones and textures, and the delightful abandon of these figures are the subject. Mythological or other themes are only an excuse for these handsome paintings that celebrate the life of the senses.

The philosophe Diderot, who also wrote essays on contemporary art, was not impressed by these frivolous objects. Diderot's taste ran rather toward *genre* painting—scenes from everyday life among the peasants and the lower classes. In particular he praised Chardin and Greuze, two painters whose work have only the most superficial elements in common. Chardin imparts to his subjects, whether a maid, a mother and child, or a still life, a monumental and quiet objectivity that recalls Vermeer (Color Plate IX). His pictures of still-life subjects seem constructed from a careful, loving observation of nature that renders textures, surfaces, and light with verisimilitude (Color Plate VI). Order and harmony are extracted from the simple events and objects of the middle classes. We know that Chardin meant his pictures to educate and to instruct in virtue, but the depiction of objects seems to mean as much to him as the portrayal of a moral. It was Chardin's naturalism that so appealed to Diderot; yet, in contrast to Vermeer, Chardin's paint has a creamy sensual surface that is as covertly appealing as his objects.

Greuze's work appealed to Diderot because his scenes suggested narratives that praised virtue or had a didactic moral. Too frequently these scenes also had a marked sentimentalizing attitude toward the event. *The Village Bride,* shown in the Salon of 1761, is a sample of his work. A youthful bride watches while the dowry is negotiated, the grandfather admonishes, the mother is pensive, the hen in the foreground protects her chicks (Fig. 23-6). These sweet, clean, honest, virtuous, natural peasants provide a vivid contrast to what we know of life. But these pictures appealed to the upper bourgeoisie of the mid-eighteenth century, who saw in these peasants natural virtue.

24

The Enlightenment in the United States

Political events in North America in the last four decades of the eighteenth century fascinated European observers. While the French philosophes were forced to adapt their goals for improving the human condition to the circumstances of a very traditional social and political structure, English-speaking North America presented the situation of a new people in an underdeveloped land largely untrammeled by the weight of past institutions. Once the colonists had thrown off the control imposed on their society by the imperial system of the mother country, the possibilities for political creativity and experimentation seemed limitless. As the new nation emerged from the endless deliberations of the political leadership, European intellectuals watched intently for signs to determine whether the American republic, the most populous and geographically extensive republican government in the history of the world, would succeed or fail.

The history of the creation of the United States, following more than a century of colonial development, can be divided into three basic phases. The first phase began with the defeat of French armies in the New World by combined British and colonial forces, part of a worldwide struggle between rival European powers. When British officials then tried to impose increased taxes upon the growing colonies to help cover the rising military and administrative costs of the empire, the colonists resisted in increasing numbers and finally declared themselves politically independent in 1776. The second phase comprises the period from the first years of the war until the creation of the Constitution in 1787, when the dominant minds in America attempted to devise some sort of lasting union among the thirteen loosely confederated states. The final period is that of the first decades after ratification of the Constitution (which went into effect in 1789) as Americans endeavored to make the new government work in the face of forces for decentralization that threatened at times to pull the new federal structure apart.

American Religion   Christianity in pre-Revolutionary America was the most important cultural and intellectual force in colonial life. Among whites, the predominant allegiance of the colonists was to some form of Protestantism. Even in Maryland, originally founded as a Catholic refuge, Protestants were in the vast majority. The few Jews in the colonies resided largely in the coastal towns. Missionary associations of various churches had achieved little success with the rapidly dwindling Indian population, but from the 1730s on Afro-Americans converted in large numbers. By the Revolution conversion among the enslaved population, now principally being carried out by blacks themselves, created a significant mass of black Christians in the colonies. The black churches, however, retained many elements of religious practices from the African religious heritage.

The beginning of the conversion of blacks on a large scale in the 1730s was only one aspect of a great religious revival that swept the English colonies in that and the succeeding decade. Known as the Great Awakening, the movement started in New Jersey, was taken up by Jonathan Edwards (1703-1758), a Congregational minister in Northampton, Connecticut, and within the next few years was spread by a series of fiery preachers

the entire length of the Atlantic coast.

Americans in these years were responding to a deeply felt sense that their churches were becoming too institutionalized and too committed to doctrine while the passion of belief that nourished the emotional life of the believer was draining away. By arousing religious feelings at the expense of catechisms and utilizing emotion rather than reasoned argument, the preachers of the Great Awakening, a movement that cut across all doctrinal lines, exercised an enormous appeal, especially on those with little education. The spiritual malaise was so general, however, that large numbers from all classes were attracted to the revival movement.

The following excerpt is taken from Jonathan Edwards's *A Faithful Narrative of the Surprising Work of God* (1737), in which Edwards first describes the effect of his revivalist preaching on his congregation and then the diffusion of its effect to the surrounding countryside in the Connecticut Valley. Edwards tells us that he had resolved to preach from the pulpit with no ambiguity that mankind is saved by faith alone, that human beings have absolutely no power to ensure, or even to cooperate in, their own salvation. These sermons had a dazzling and surprising effect.

JONATHAN EDWARDS

From *A Faithful Narrative of the Surprising Work of God*

Although great fault was found with meddling with the controversy in the pulpit, by such a person, at that time, and though it was ridiculed by many elsewhere; yet it proved a word spoken in season here; and was most evidently attended with a very remarkable blessing of heaven to the souls of the people in this town. They received thence a general satisfaction with respect to the main thing in question, which they had in trembling doubts and concern about; and their minds were engaged the more earnestly to seek that they might come to be accepted of God, and saved in the way of the gospel, which had been made evident to them to be the true and only way. And then it was, in the latter part of December [1734], that the Spirit of God began extraordinarily to set in, and wonderfully to work amongst us; and there were, to all appearance, savingly converted, and some of them wrought upon in a very remarkable manner.

Particularly, I was surprised with the relation of a young woman, who had been one of the greatest company keepers in the whole town: when she came to me, I had never heard that she was become in any wise serious, but by the conversation I then had with her, it appeared to me, that what she gave an account of, was a glorious work of God's infinite power and sovereign grace; and that God had given her a new heart, truly broken and sanctified. I could not then doubt of it, and have seen much in my acquaintance with her since to confirm it.

Though the work was glorious, yet I was filled with concern about the effect it might have upon others: I was ready to conclude (though too rashly) that some would be hardened by it, in carelessness and looseness of life; and would take occasion from it to open their mouths, in reproaches of religion.[1] But the event was the reverse, to a wonderful degree; God made it, I suppose, the greatest occasion of awakening to others, of any thing that ever came to pass in the town. I have had abundant opportunity to know the effect it had, by my private conversation with many. The news of it seemed to be almost like a flash of lightning, upon the hearts of young people, all over the town, and upon many others. Those persons amongst us, who used to be farthest from seriousness, and that I most feared would make an ill improvement of it, seemed greatly to be awakened with it; many went to talk with her, concerning what she had met with; and what appeared in her seemed to be to the satisfaction of all that did so.

Presently upon this, a great and earnest concern about the great things of religion, and the eternal world, became universal in all parts of the town, and among persons of all degrees, and all ages; the noise amongst the dry bones waxed louder and louder: all other talk but about spiritual and eternal things was soon thrown by; all the conversation in all companies, and upon all occasions, was upon these things only, unless so much as was necessary for people carrying on their ordinary secular business. Other discourse than of the things of religion, would scarcely be tolerated in any company. The minds of people were wonderfully taken off from the world; it was treated amongst us as a thing of very little consequence: they seem to follow their worldly business, more as a part of their duty, than from any disposition they had to it; the temptation now seemed to be on that hand, to neglect worldly affairs too much, and to spend too much time in the immediate exercise of religion: which thing was exceedingly misrepresented by reports that were spread in distant parts of the land, as though the people here had wholly thrown by all worldly business, and betook themselves entirely to reading and praying, and such like religious exercises. . . .

This work of God, as it was carried on, and the number of true saints multiplied, soon made a glorious alteration in the town; so that in the spring and summer following, anno 1735, the town seemed to be full of the presence of God: it never was so full of love, nor so full of joy; and yet so full of distress as it was then. There were remarkable tokens of God's presence in almost every house. It was a time of joy in families on the account of salvation's being brought unto them; parents rejoicing over their children as new born, and husbands over their wives, and wives over their husbands. *The goings of God were then seen in his sanctuary, God's day was a delight, and his tabernacles were amiable.* Our public assemblies were then beautiful; the congregation was alive in God's service, every one earnestly intent on the public worship, every hearer eager to drink in the words of the minister as they came from his mouth; the assembly in general were, from time to time, in tears while the word was preached; some weeping with sorrow and distress, others with joy and love, others with pity and concern for the souls of their neighbors. . . .

When this work of God first appeared, and was so extraordinarily carried on amongst us in the winter, others round about us, seemed not to know what to make of it; and there were many that scoffed at, and ridiculed it; and some compared what we called conversion to certain distempers. But it was very observable of many, that occasionally came amongst us from abroad, with disregardful hearts, that what they saw here cured them of such a temper of mind: strangers were generally surprised to find things so much beyond

---

[1] Edwards feared that when people were told that they could do nothing to help in their own salvation, they would abandon themselves to pleasure or curse God for his injustice in robbing them of the power of their will.

what they had heard, and were wont to tell others that the state of the town could not be conceived of by those that had not seen it. The notice that was taken of it by the people that came to town on occasion of the court, that sat here in the beginning of March, was very observable. And those that came from the neighborhood to our public lectures, were for the most part remarkably affected. Many that came to town, on one occasion or other, had their consciences smitten, and awakened, and went home with wounded hearts, and with those impressions that never wore off till they had hopefully a saving issue; and those that before had serious thoughts, had their awakenings and convictions greatly increased. And there were many instances of persons that came from abroad, on visits, or on business, that had not been long here before, to all appearance, they were savingly wrought upon, and partook of that shower of divine blessing that God rained down here, and went home rejoicing; till at length the same work began evidently to appear and prevail in several other towns in the county.

In the month of March, the people in South Hadley began to be seized with deep concern about the things of religion; which very soon became universal: and the work of God has been very wonderful there; not much, if any thing, short of what it has been here, in proportion to the bigness of the place. About the same time it began to break forth in the west part of Suffield (where it has also been very great), and it soon spread into all parts of the town. It next appeared at Sunderland, and soon overspread the town; and I believe was for a season, not less remarkable than it was here. About the same time it began to appear in a part of Deerfield, called Green River, and afterwards filled the town, and there has been a glorious work there: it began also to be manifest in the south part of Hatfield, in a place called the Hill, and after that the whole town, in the second week in April, seemed to be seized, as it were at once, with concern about the things of religion: and the work of God has been great there. There has been also a very general awakening at West Springfield, and Long Meadow; and in Enfield, there was, for a time, a pretty general concern amongst some that before had been very loose persons. About the same time that this appeared at Enfield, the Rev. Mr. Bull of Westfield informed me, that there had been a great alternation

there, and that more had been done in one week there than in seven years before.—Something of this work likewise appeared in the first precinct in Springfield, principally in the north and south extremes of the parish. And in Hadley old town, there gradually appeared so much of a work of God on souls, as at another time would have been thought worthy of much notice. For a short time there was also a very great and general concern, of the like nature, at Northfield. And wherever this concern appeared, it seemed not to be in vain: but in every place God brought saving blessings with them, and his word attended with his Spirit (as we have all reason to think) returned not void. It might well be said at that time in all parts of the country, *Who are these that fly as a cloud, and as doves to their windows!* . .

This remarkable pouring out of the Spirit of God, which thus extended from one end to the other of this country, was not confined to it, but many places in Connecticut have partook in the same mercy: as for instance, the first parish in Windsor, under the pastoral care of the Reverend Mr. Marsh, was thus blest about the same time, as we in Northampton, while we had no knowledge of each other's circumstances. . . .

But this shower of Divine blessing has been yet more extensive: there was no small degree of it in some parts of the Jerseys; as I was informed when I was at New-York (in a long journey I took at that time of the year for my health), by some people of the Jerseys, whom I saw: especially the Rev. Mr. William Tennent, a minister, who seemed to have such things much at heart, told me of a very great awakening of many in a place called the Mountains, under the ministry of one Mr. Cross; and of a very considerable revival of religion in another place under the ministry of his brother the Rev. Mr. Gilbert Tennent; and also at another place, under the ministry of a very pious young gentleman, a Dutch minister, whose name as I remember, was Freelinghousen.

Effect of the Great Awakening The Great Awakening had a tremendously disruptive effect on established religion in the colonies, dividing congregations into Old Light and New Light groups. The activity of itinerant preachers tended to destroy the identification of churches with particular territories, and because the preachers of the Awakening were marked more by charismatic gifts than by education or status, it undermined the authority of the traditional clergy. The intensity of the Great Awakening abated after 1750, but its effects on American religion were long lasting.

This revival movement contributed to bringing into question two fundamental beliefs of traditional Christianity: that religious conformity was necessary and that the state should lend financial and other support to a particular church. Although some states continued to use tax money to support a designated church or churches, the competition for membership in the spiritual market in the second half of the eighteenth century could not be prevented, and in practice freedom of conscience for all religions became the rule. Unlike European countries, in which the established church had a guaranteed membership and religion tended to be taken for granted, in the British colonies the competition for souls fostered an almost continuous spirit of revival and a rich variety of choices. Consequently, by the time of the Revolution, the Christian churches were highly decentralized and largely voluntary in membership, and reflected the evolution of republican feeling in a broad sector of the population.

European Influences   From the early eighteenth century the dominant stream of ideas shaping politics in America was English. The *empiricism* of English thinkers like Bacon and Newton made a strong impact on Americans, and theory was reinforced by a pioneer culture that respected labor and practical know-how. Products of a highly mobile society with a flexible social structure, the colonists worked well together at the local level in meeting their common needs. The validity of Locke's doctrine of natural rights of man seemed borne out by their experience. Beginning as they did in a new environment, the colonists tended to view critically any limitation on their freedom of action unless it could be justified in terms of personal advantage. With the executive power firmly in the hands of British governors, they also found Locke's emphasis on the duty of legislative assemblies to supervise the executive authority to their liking. Characteristically, the Declaration of Independence, which claimed rights to life,

liberty, and the pursuit of happiness to be self-evident, justified severance with England on the grounds of George III's tyranny, not because of oppression by Parliament. Furthermore, the Declaration of Independence and the Constitution echo Locke in their statements that governments derive their just powers from the consent of the governed and that when governments exceed their power, the people have the right to institute new governments.

French philosophes were, on the whole, ardent supporters of the American revolution. They admired versatile diplomats like Benjamin Franklin and Thomas Jefferson, both of whom lived for long periods in France, as the kind of "enlightened" men that the New World could produce. Men like Turgot, a *philosophe* minister of Louis XV, used their influence at court to bring the French government into the war on the rebels' side in 1778, and the French intervention was decisive. On the intellectual level, Montesquieu doubtless had the most significant influence on American political thought in the revolutionary period. His conception of a balance of power among the legislative, executive, and judicial branches of government suited the American distrust of the executive and made the Constitution more attractive to many who looked on a strong executive as a potential threat to individual freedom. In the 1780s and 1790s, however, Rousseau's democratic theories provided ammunition against elitist conceptions of political authority held by most American thinkers. For example, property qualifications for voting rights were reduced at this time.

To an extent, the ease with which Americans accepted the ideas of the philosophes stemmed from the fact that much of the philosophy of the French thinkers had been inspired by the English political experience, which Americans had inherited. But more than this, the increasingly voluntaristic character of American religion made Christianity in the colonies compatible with most of their ideas. In France, as we have seen, intellectuals attacked the privileged church as obscurantist and as the champion of political oppression. Religion itself became tainted by association. On the other hand, in religiously pluralistic America, the enlightenment lost its anti-religious bias. Whereas in France the enlightenment doctrine of religious toleration aimed at subverting the hold of the Catholic church on French culture, in America this doctrine was introduced to justify a practical situation created by the existence of conflicting religious groups.

American Federalism   Federalism, perhaps the United States' most original contribution to the theory and practice of republican government, owed little to either the French or the English; it was born of necessity. Under no circumstances able to induce strong, independent state governments to become mere agencies of the central government, the writers of the Constitution established a principle of separation of powers between the central government and the states. Such a system of power division was to have a great future because it permitted unification of large areas of land and supported regional diversity while still limiting the power of local opposition.

The Heritage of Ancient Rome   No account of the ideology of the American revolutionary epoch would be complete without acknowledging the extent to which these patriots thought of themselves and were considered by their European sympathizers as the heirs to the republican tradition of ancient Rome. Since the Renaissance the educated class of the Western world had been deeply imbued with classical culture; one aspect of that culture, clearly defined since the early fifteenth century (see Volume I) was its *republican* tradition. The leaders of the revolution appeared to contemporaries as the simple, honest descendants of Roman statesmen like Cato, or the general, Cincinnatus, who left his own plow to lead an army against the enemies of the Roman republic. Americans often signed their letters of protest against English tyranny with Roman names, and Washington and other officers of the revolutionary army took part in a controversial Society of Cincinnatus. In their struggle for liberty, these patriots (from Latin *patria*—homeland) seemed the modern counterparts of Roman heroes like Horatio and Brutus. The architects of the Constitution drew on words of Latin derivation like *president* and *senate*, and the Great Seal of the new nation and its coinage were marked with Latin phrases and classical emblems (Fig. 24-1). Houdon's statue of Washington in the capital at Richmond dramatically illustrates these associations of the new republic with the old. In 1786 the French

24-1   Great Seal of the United States. (Bureau of Engraving and Printing, U.S. Department of the Treasury)

24-2   Houdon, *George Washington*. (Virginia State Library)

sculptor represented the future president of the United States in modern dress; but he stands beside the Roman *fasces*, a bundle of rods symbolic of power and union, in a pose based on that of a classical statue (Fig. 24-2).

Thomas Jefferson The figure who best represents the American Enlightenment is Thomas Jefferson (1743–1826). Jefferson combined the Old World's tradition of scholarship and philosophy with the New World's practicality and readiness to experiment. Both philosopher and plantation manager, he was at home in the salons of Paris and the still untamed parts of Virginia. Like the French philosophes, he combined wide learning in the classical humanities with a lively interest in recent scientific developments. He regarded the republic of letters and ideas as an international one.

In addition to his career as a politician, Jefferson was an excellent writer, an educator, a farmer, and an architect. One of his masterpieces is his home near Charlottesville, Virginia, which he called Monticello ("the little mountain"). The house itself is symbolic of the nature of the American Enlightenment. Jefferson used the *Palladian* Villa Rotunda as his model (Fig. 22-1), but the plan of the interior exhibits a functional adaptation of the symmetrical plan to his own particular needs (Fig. 24-3). Similarly, the building originally designed for stone execution is rendered in red brick with white wooden trim—an elegant, rich contrast to the building's general simplicity of shape. These adaptations to use and surroundings do not, however, detract from the *portico* and *dome*, the two forms that link it with Greek democracy and the Roman republic. Facing westward, to the wilderness, dominating but sympathetic to the landscape, the house is almost a metaphor for the man—aristocratic, cosmopolitan, inventive, practical—a farmer and a philosopher.

Designing his own tomb for the grounds at Monticello, Jefferson composed the following inscription: "Here was buried Thomas Jefferson, author of the Declaration of American Independence, of the Statute of Virginia for Religious Freedom, and Father of the University of Virginia." He apparently did not consider that being the third president of the United States was

24-3 Jefferson, Monticello, west front. (Thomas Jefferson Memorial Foundation)

among his most significant accomplishments. Those that he lists are excellent examples of the application of the principles of the Enlightenment to the American experience.

The Declaration of Independence   The Declaration, written largely by Jefferson and approved by the Continental Congress on July 4, 1776, is a statement of political philosophy as well as an act of rebellion. It is in fact typical of the American Enlightenment that theory and its practical application are combined in the same document. The Declaration may be divided into two distinct parts: the first sets forth principles of democratic government and proves, in the abstract, philosophical terms of the Enlightenment, the right of the colonies to rebel. The second part is a specific list of grievances against the king of Great Britain, George III.

Because of its ready availability, we will not print the entire Declaration here. A close reading of the first two paragraphs, however, reveals the purpose of the document and a theoretical basis for rebellion.

> When, in the course of human events, it becomes necessary for one people to dissolve the political bands which have connected them with another, and to assume, among the powers of the earth, the separate and equal station to which the laws of nature and of nature's God entitle them, a decent respect to the Opinions of mankind requires that they should declare the causes which impel them to the separation.
>
> We hold these truths to be self-evident: That all men are created equal; that they are endowed by their Creator with certain unalienable rights; that among these are life, liberty & the pursuit of happiness; that to secure these rights governments are instituted among men, deriving their just powers from the consent of the governed; that whenever any form of government becomes destructive of these ends, it is the right of the people to alter or to abolish it, and to institute new government, laying its foundation on such principles and organizing its powers in such form, as to them shall seem most likely to effect their safety and happiness.

COMMENTS AND QUESTIONS

1. Is there any religious basis for the rebellion? Does it seem to be Christian?
2. How do the expressions "laws of nature," "nature's God," and "truths" that are "self-evident" reflect values of the Enlightenment?

3. Did the American political system in fact guarantee the "unalienable rights" that Jefferson lists? What do you think that he meant by "the pursuit of happiness"? By "all men are created equal"?
4. How do Jefferson's political ideals differ from, or resemble, those of Thucydides or Bruni? (See Vol. I.)
5. Do the principles of the Enlightenment found here (such as self-evident truths) seem a valid basis from which to argue legal and moral questions today?

The questions raised here may be applied to the entire Declaration. The second part of the document purports to show, by the list of grievances, that George III deliberately and malevolently attempted to establish an "absolute tyranny" over the colonies. It is consistent with Jefferson's idea of a government that derives its powers from the "consent of the governed" that he blames all sorts of evils on the tyrannical will of the king. The last of Jefferson's charges, omitted by the Congress in the final draft of the Declaration, was an indictment against the enslavement of Africans.

> He has waged cruel war against human nature itself, violating its most sacred rights of life and liberty in the persons of a distant people who never offended him, captivating and carrying them into slavery in another hemisphere, or to incur miserable death in their transportation thither. This piratical warfare, the opprobrium of *infidel* powers, is the warfare of the *Christian* king of Great Britain. Determined to keep open a market where MEN should be bought and sold, he has prostituted his negative for suppressing every legislative attempt to prohibit or to restrain this execrable commerce; and that this assemblage of horrors might want no fact of distinguished die, he is now exciting these very people to rise in arms among us, and to purchase that liberty of which *he* deprived them, by murdering the people upon whom *he* also obtruded them; thus paying off former crimes committed against the *liberties* of one people, with crimes which he urges them to commit against the *lives* of another.

QUESTIONS

1. How does Jefferson's application of the principles of the Enlightenment to the question of slavery differ from and/or resemble that of Montesquieu?
2. Does it make good historical sense to blame the existence of slavery and the slave trade on George III?
3. What important factors does Jefferson omit?

Jefferson's own position on slavery was fraught with ambiguity. He owned many slaves on his plantation at Monticello. After the death of his wife he probably lived with a mulatto woman, one of his slaves, who bore him several children. He seems to have been tormented by his contradictory feelings that slavery was a moral wrong and would eventually be abolished, but that the time was not yet ripe for black Americans to be free. Recent biographies of Jefferson wrestle with this and other contradictions in this multifaceted man.

The Virginia Statute The second accomplishment on which Jefferson prided himself, the *Virginia Statute of Religious Liberty* (October 1785), is in the spirit of Voltaire's *Treatise on Toleration*. The statute was part of the constitution of the state of Virginia, which served as a model for other state constitutions.

THOMAS JEFFERSON

The Virginia Statute of Religious Liberty

AN ACT FOR ESTABLISHING RELIGIOUS FREEDOM

I. Whereas Almighty God hath created the mind free; that all attempts to influence it by temporal punishments or burthens, or by civil incapacitations, tend only to beget habits of hypocrisy and meanness, and are a departure from the plan of the Holy author of our religion, who being Lord both of body and mind, yet chose not to propagate it by coercions on either, as was in his Almighty power to do; that the impious presumption of legislators and rulers, civil as well as ecclesiastical, who being themselves but fallible and uninspired men, have assumed dominion over the faith of others, setting up their own opinions and modes of thinking as the only true and infallible, and as such endeavouring to impose them on others, hath established and maintained false religions over the greatest part of the world, and through all time; that to compel a man to furnish contributions of money for the propagation of opinions which he disbelieves, is sinful and tyrannical; that even the forcing him to support this or that teacher of his own religious persuasion, is depriving him of the comfortable liberty of giving his contributions to the particular pastor whose morals he would make his pattern, and whose powers he feels most persuasive to righteousness, and is withdrawing from the ministry those temporary rewards, which proceeding from an approbation of their personal conduct, are an additional incitement to earnest and unremitting labours for the instruction of mankind; that our civil rights have no dependence on our religious opinions, any more than our opinions in physics or geometry; that therefore the proscribing any citizen as unworthy the public confidence by laying upon him an incapacity of being called to offices of trust and emolument, unless he profess or renounce this or that religious opinion, is depriving him injuriously of those privileges and advantages to which in common with his fellow-citizens he has a natural right; that it tends only to corrupt the principles of that religion it is meant to encourage, by bribing with a monopoly of worldly honours and emoluments, those who will externally profess and conform to it; that though indeed these are criminal who do not withstand such temptation, yet neither are those innocent who lay the bait in their way; that to suffer the civil magistrate to intrude his powers into the field of opinion, and to restrain the profession or propagation of principles on supposition of their ill tendency, is a dangerous fallacy, which at once destroys all religious liberty, because he being of course judge of that tendency will make his opinions the rule of judgment, and approve or condemn the sentiments of others only as they shall square with or differ from his own; that it is time enough for the rightful purposes of civil government, for its officers to interfere when principles break out into overt acts against peace and good order; and finally, that truth is great and will prevail if left to herself, that she is the proper and sufficient antagonist to error, and has nothing to fear from the conflict, unless by human interposition disarmed of her natural weapons, free argument and debate, errors ceasing to be dangerous when it is permitted freely to contradict them.

II. Be it enacted by the General Assembly, that no man shall be compelled to frequent or support any religious worship, place or ministry whatsoever, nor shall be enforced, restrained, molested, or burthened in his body or goods, nor shall otherwise suffer on account of his religious opinions or belief; but that all men shall be free to profess, and by argument to maintain their opinion in matters of religion, and that the same shall in no wise diminish, enlarge or affect their civil capacities.

III. And though we well know that this Assembly, elected by the people for the ordinary purposes of legislation only, have no power to restrain the acts of succeeding Assemblies, constituted with powers equal to our own, and that therefore to declare this Act to be irrevocable would be of no effect in law; yet as we are free to declare, and do declare, that the rights hereby asserted are of the natural rights of mankind, and that if any Act shall hereafter be passed to repeal the present, or to narrow its operation, such Act will be an infringement of natural right.

QUESTIONS

1. On what basis does Jefferson seek to establish religious tolerance?

2. Is he critical of Christianity? How?
3. What does Jefferson mean by *truth*, and what are his criteria for determining what is true?
4. Does his optimistic belief that truth will inevitably triumph over error strike you as typical of the Enlightenment? As typically American?
5. What specific human rights does Jefferson consider "natural"?

Jefferson remained a nominal Anglican until the end of his life but continued to combat what he considered to be superstitions and unnecessary dogmas in Christianity. He respected Jesus as a great moral teacher but did not necessarily believe him to be divine. He did his own edition of the Bible, cutting out references to miracles. Unitarians today consider Jefferson one of their forefathers. In an "unenlightened" age a century or two earlier, he would have been arrested as a heretic.

24-4 Jefferson, University of Virginia. 1856 engraving by C. Bohn. (University of Virginia Library)

The University of Virginia In keeping with Jefferson's beliefs, his third monumental project, the University of Virginia, was the only early university not to be associated with a church. Jefferson viewed this "academical village" as an opportunity not only to create an ideal educational environment but also to improve the tastes of the Americans who would be educated there (Fig. 24-4).

Jefferson had always scorned the architecture of Williamsburg, where he was educated, and had tried to mold taste with his designs for the capitol of Virginia at Richmond (Fig. 24-5). He used no Renaissance models, sources. Having seen engravings of the Maison Carrée in Nîmes, he adopted it for the new capitol.

That the pure temple form was not immediately adopted nationally can be seen by comparing it with the State House in Boston, designed by Charles Bulfinch in 1795 (Fig. 24-6). The sources of the State House are from the English Renaissance as well as from Rome. Both buildings, however, provided strong images of the state.

24–5   Jefferson, Capitol, Richmond. (Virginia State Library)

24–6   Bulfinch, Boston State House. (Courtesy of the Boston Public Library, Print Department)

24–7   Jefferson, University of Virginia, Pavilion and Colonnade. (University of Virginia Library)

This belief, that art and architecture reinforce and perpetuate strong, appropriate images for ideals was much in Jefferson's mind when the university was laid out. The heart of the university is a rectangular quadrangle bounded on each of its long sides by a one-story covered colonnade broken at intervals by the two-story houses of the professors. Students lived in rooms off the colonnades; professors held classes downstairs in their living quarters (Fig. 24-7). The east end of the quad is closed by the domed, porticoed rotunda—the library (Fig. 24-8). Suggested by Benjamin Latrobe, another important architect, the rotunda acted as the focus and capstone, while the west end of the campus was open to the mountains. This very regular pattern for the central campus was relieved by the dining rooms, kitchens, and other service facilities located behind the two parallel rows of colonnades. There were found gardens (which students were expected to help work), pathways, and private walks for the students, who would participate in the educative life in the main quad but still have time for meditation, contemplation and studies, close to nature.

The rotunda and professors' houses were carefully detailed with what Jefferson considered the best forms

24–8   Jefferson, University of Virginia, Rotunda. (University of Virginia Library)

of the classical *orders*; the Corinthian was reserved for the interior of the rotunda. All are used in correct proportion and with their correct *entablatures* and *moldings*. Jefferson drew on ancient and Renaissance treatises in his planning.

The architecture of the campus reflects the two areas in which students were supposed to grow to become successful men—the active and the contemplative lives. Conspicuously absent is a chapel or church—religion was to be a personal, private affair. Unlike Harvard, Yale, or Princeton, this early university of the new republic was a monument to free thought.

The ideal behind the University of Virginia was, in typical Enlightenment fashion, universal. "Enlighten the people generally," Jefferson wrote, "and oppressions of body and mind will vanish like evil spirits at the dawn of day." Practically, however, because of the nature of the education planned, it could accommodate only an elite few. Women of all races, blacks, and white males from poor familes were excluded. Jefferson, though he educated his daughters, held in fact very conventional ideas regarding women: they should not mix in politics or public meetings or be outspoken in any way; their proper place was in the domestic sphere. The educated elite, who alone were fit to rule the American nation in Jefferson's view, would have been limited to white men of some means if his plan had remained the pattern. Fortunately, as is the case with most important thinkers, Jefferson's ideas outgrew his era's limitations and eventually served the causes of the struggles in which we are still involved.

The product of Jefferson's old age and retirement years, the University of Virginia opened its doors in 1824 when its founder was eighty-one. It was perhaps natural that the revolutionary, politician, and diplomat should retire into creating an ideal world on a reduced scale. This edifice for the education of the New World elite stands today as a manifestation of the styles and ideals of the Enlightenment, as interpreted by the New World's best example of Enlightenment thinking.

25

The Classical Style in Music, the Development of Opera, and Mozart's *Don Giovanni*

The baroque style in music, as stated earlier, lasted well into the eighteenth century, but the second half of the century saw the development of a musical style better suited to the ideals of the Enlightenment. This period of calm, lightening, balancing, and simplifying, this brief and splendid era, is one that music historians have labelled *classic*. It reached its height in the works of two towering geniuses: Josef Haydn and Wolfgang Amadeus Mozart. The music of Mozart forsook the intricate counterpoint and long-winded phrases of the baroque master Bach. The compositions of Haydn consistently employed distinct phrases and sections in new structures that achieved unity and balance through readily perceived contrasts of melodies and harmonies. Composers seemed to find a regularity in their musical language that brought a logical coherence to works both tiny and grandiose. They worked primarily with the short, articulated phrase; they strove for structural symmetry; and they contrasted the rhythmic activities of the melody and the harmony in such a way that "tune" and "harmony" became distinct entities. New instruments developed, as they always had in the past; but, more importantly, old instruments changed character so that eventually the piano would replace the harpsichord and clavichord and the violin would replace the viol. This came about because the new bourgeoisie created a market for music, calling it from the patron's chamber to the public concert hall. As *dynamics* became louder, the music became more appropriate for performance before large audiences. It was at this time that the symphony orchestra emerged as a primary musical medium upon which compositional ideas might be sounded in concert.

We will study the form of the classical symphony in the next chapter as we look at a work that breaks the classical limits to announce the romantic style: Beethoven's *Ninth Symphony*. Here we intend to focus on one of the greatest works of the classical period and one of the greatest operas ever written. First, however, it is necessary to understand the development of this form combining drama, spectacle, and music.

Opera

Opera as we know it today has a long continuous history that dates back to a group of Florentine aristocrats who met at the home of Count Giovanni de' Bardi in the late 16th century. He was host to this group of Italian humanists known as the Camerata, a group of friends who met as an intellectual club to discuss cultural—primarily literary—matters. However, most of the men were musical amateurs and three—Vincenzo Galilei, Giulio Caccini, and Pietro Strozzi—were musicians of the highest order. In the Camerata's attempt to understand classical Greek drama and the power music apparently held to sway the emotions of the ancient Greeks, they laid the groundwork for the development of a music drama soon to be called Opera. Their search for cultural roots brought them back to classical Greece, but one must not overlook the fact that there has been a continuous interest in the West in the relationship of musical matters (appropriate themes, modes, rhythms, and so forth) to textual significance and dramatic events.

Even Gregorian chants may be seen as a musical amplification and ornamentation of the drama of the liturgy. The Mass, after all, is the repeated symbolic action of the last days of Christ on earth. In the later Middle Ages, we saw that more overt musical drama developed within the Church when we studied the *Play of Daniel* (Vol. I, pp. 216–26). Then, in the Renaissance, the development of oratorio and opera heralded the dawn of the Baroque period. The music of the first opera that resulted from the efforts of the Camerata is lost, but we saw a sample of the declamatory style developed to "imitate" Greek music drama in the passage from Jacopo Peri's *Euridice*, the earliest opera (1600) for which complete music has survived (see p. 62). The first masterpiece in this genre followed soon after, Claudio Monteverdi's *L'Orfeo* (1607), and the next two centuries saw a rapid expansion of interest and remarkable growth, change, and development in nearly all technical aspects of the genre: libretto, scenery, costume, dance, and music—orchestration, forms, vocal virtuosity, and so on. The growth of opera took place throughout Europe, not just in Italy, and important contributors were Lully in France (for example, *Le Bourgeois Gentilhomme*, pp. 125–28), Henry Purcell in England, Giovanni Pergolesi and Alessandro Scarlatti in Italy, and Handel in Germany and England (for example, the *Messiah*). Even though he was German and wrote for German audiences, Handel composed Italian operas in the Italian style.

The word *opera* comes from the Italian *opera in musica* (work in music) and it may be defined as a drama, either tragic or comic, sung throughout and presented on stage with scenery and action. The emphasis is on the solo voice, and, like the oratorio, which borrowed the forms from opera, it employs arias and recitatives. Because opera, of all the musical or dramatic forms, is the most difficult and expensive to produce, it has always been associated with the upper strata of social life. Often, the mere fact of being able to support an operatic production—that is, sponsor a big, ostentatious display—has been compensation enough for a great many noble and wealthy patrons. Likewise, to be able to understand and appreciate this art form has been, and still is, a prestige symbol with the general public.

The successful composer and producer of opera has

also traditionally received special rewards because of its difficulty, expense, and elite clientele. In the second half of the eighteenth century, such a composer was Wolfgang Amadeus Mozart—child prodigy, court figure, true genius, and perhaps the most universal composer in the history of Western music. In 1769, Sigismund, Count of Schrattenbach and Archbishop of Salzburg, gave orders for Mozart's first opera, *La Finta Semplice,* to be performed in the palace. Wolfgang was thirteen and had written it when he was twelve! After the performance, Sigismund appointed the young Mozart Kapellmeister, an important court position. This opera was not Mozart's first stage composition, for he had composed the singspiel, *Bastien und Bastienne,* a year earlier. As fine as these early compositions are, they are still youthful works and only serve as a prelude to the towering monuments of his mature years. The opera, *Don Giovanni* (Don Juan), is one such masterpiece.

By 1787, the year of *Don Giovanni,* opera was a popular form among the elite of Austria, and Mozart was riding on the success of *Le Nozze di Figaro* (*The Marriage of Figaro*) produced in Prague the preceding winter. The classical style in music was established, and opera as a formal structure was well defined and commonly understood. When Mozart asked his librettist, Lorenzo da Ponte, for a new opera to follow *Figaro,* da Ponte was already busy with two other commissions. It may have been for this reason that he seized on the story of Don Juan, for he could rework a well-known tale more quickly than compose a new one.

The Don Juan Theme

Tirso de Molina's *The Trickster of Seville* (Chapter 20) fired the imaginations of many imitators, notably in the Italian *commedia dell ' arte* ("improvised theater") in which Don Juan began to appear not so much as an overconfident aristocrat but more as a wicked and scheming character, in revolt against both society and religion. His next important literary incarnation is in Molière's play *Don Juan* (1665). There the hero appears as a character type prevalent in the French neoclassical period: the libertine. Refined and sophisticated, a cynical philosopher of free love rather than an unrepentant

deceiver, Molière's Don Juan apparently has no religious beliefs. The eighteenth century, a time of increased freedom between the sexes, saw portrayals of a scheming seducer who pursued women as if in a military campaign and who cared for nothing but his own pleasure. By then, Don Juan had a real life counterpart in Italy—the famous Casanova. In the Romantic period, as we shall see later, he was to take on yet another form.

Da Ponte's and Mozart's collaborative work was not the first opera on Don Juan (Giovanni is the Italian equivalent of John or Juan) but it is the one that has made the legend immortal. Da Ponte was able to combine the vitality and passion of Tirso's hero with the wit and scheming intelligence of the Don Juans of Molière and his successors. Although the basic story line of Tirso's play remains, da Ponte has added some characters and events, eliminated some, and changed almost everyone's name. With his development of the character of the Don's servant, now called Leporello, he was able to merge the comic with the serious in original ways (as when Leporello sings under the table during Don Giovanni's supper with the statue). It is true that, as in most operas, there are some improbable incidents and the action does not always follow smoothly. This is more than compensated for, however, by the genius of Mozart.

In *Don Giovanni* perhaps even more than in his earlier operas, Mozart shows his ability to assume the personality and state of mind of his principal characters and his genius to create music suitable to each. Indeed, the music changes mood and character, reflecting the attitude and frame of mind of the singer. In fact, Mozart creates character in musical terms in the same way that Shakespeare does with vocabulary and poetic structures. This is remarkable enough in the parts in which only one character appears on stage at a time, but his virtuosity is particularly apparent in the scenes in which several characters appear together, usually in conflict. It is at these times that the element of "symphonic development" enters as an important ingredient in Mozart's style. It is through this polyphonic interweaving of the voice and orchestra that the characterization comes to life.

Don Giovanni: The Rake Punished

A Comic Opera in Two Acts

Poetry by LORENZO DA PONTE
Music by WOLFGANG AMADEUS MOZART[1]

Don Giovanni (Baritone) is a Spanish nobleman who is both courageous and self-indulgent. With bravado he defies convention, propriety, and established authority, and with gusto he pursues, seduces, and subsequently abandons all women who cross his path. This opera represents the end of a dazzlingly successful career of seduction. It portrays not the successes but rather the failures, and it ends with a heroic rejection of compromise, along with the terrible penalty exacted for the Don's refusal of penitence.

We learn that before the story begins, *Donna Anna* (Soprano) was successful in rejecting the forceful advances of Don Giovanni, but, because this event took place in the dark, she is unaware of the identity of her assailant. Don Giovanni is served by *Leporello* (Bass), a resourceful but cowardly scoundrel. In contrast to Don Giovanni, Donna Anna's fiancé, *Don Octavio* (Tenor), is a somewhat pale character. But *Donna Elvira* (Soprano) is not. She is a lady from Burgos who truly loves Don Giovanni and vainly hopes to reform him. Even through the pain of having been loved and deserted by the Don, she tries to win him back and save his soul. Donna Elvira is almost as striking a character as the Don himself, for she refuses to accept the code of conduct laid down by society. Even though she is of the nobility and has been wronged by Don Giovanni, she considers herself to be his wife, follows him around, and tries to save him, not from the mores of society, but from the evil within himself.

Three lesser but important roles complete the cast of characters: *Commendatore* (Bass) is Donna Anna's father and he is killed in the first scene by Don Giovanni while trying to avenge his daughter's honor. *Zerlina* (Soprano) is just one more conquest for the Don. She is an attractive peasant girl who is seduced on the very eve of her wedding day, and *Masetto* (Bass) is the country bumpkin to whom she is engaged. Mozart also gives dramatic substance to the *Chorus*, which sings and dances as peasants in Act I and personifies devils in Act II.

The opera begins with an orchestral Overture, a symphonic composition in its own right. It has a slow (andante) introduction. The massive opening chords establish the key of D minor and use a syncopated rhythm to begin the forward motion and give the listener a feeling of disquiet.

Soon the syncopations move at twice the speed, and the forward movement becomes more intense. Shifting harmonies, expressive dissonances, and the hypnotic syncopated figure help set the mood for the music that follows.

---

[1] Mozart himself conducted the first performance in Prague in 1787, and the audience responded with cheers.

The notes are subdivided again, and the speed increases with running passages that crescendo and decrescendo (grow louder and softer) in sequence.

Suddenly the tempo changes, the mood becomes more lively as the mode shifts to major, and the principal theme is introduced. This is the exposition section, and Mozart displays his musical prowess in sonata form, a musical construction in three sections—exposition, development, and recapitulation—in which two contrasting musical ideas are pitted against each other, developed, and brought together for resolution. The rising first theme

Molto Allegro

is followed by a descending and less lyrical second theme.

The conflicting personalities of the music in this opening movement undergo a dramatic development not unlike the drama that will take place on the stage later. In music, the development involves changes of key, interworkings of themes and fragments of themes, orchestration changes, contrasts of dynamics, and the general interplay of musical elements that give life to an extended composition. The overture is a beginning, and before the final resolution it flows without pause into the opening song of Leporello. The curtain rises on the Don's servant, wrapped in his cloak and pacing back and forth in the darkness outside the house of Donna Anna.

LEPORELLO:

 Notte e giorno faticar
 Per chi nulla sa gradir;
 Pioggia e vento sopportar,
 Mangiar male e mal dormir!

 Night and day I slave away
 For one who's never pleased.
 Through wind and rain I earn my pay
 Of rotten food and troubled sleep.

 ´ ˘ ´ ˘ ´ ˘ ´ [-car]
 ˘ ˘ ´ ˘ ´ ˘ ´ [-dir]
 ´ ˘ ´ ˘ ´ ˘ ´ [-tar]
 ´ ˘ ´ ˘ ´ ˘ ˘ [-mir]

Don Giovanni suddenly appears, having been forced to make a hasty exit from the house of Donna Anna. She pursues him, and the commotion wakes her father, the Commandant. He challenges Don Giovanni who, at first reluctant to duel the old man, succumbs to vanity and murders her father. Others rush to the scene of the crime, but Don Giovanni and Leporello escape. The scene closes with Don Octavio promising to avenge the deed.

The scene changes to another street, where the Don and Leporello chatter about his habits. An angry Donna Elvira appears, and we learn that she pursues him because he seduced her with a promise of marriage. She sings her aria

DONNA ELVIRA:

 Ah! chi mi dice mai
 Quel barbaro dov'è,
 Che per mio scorno amai
 Che mi mancò di fè?

 Oh, who can tell me now
 Where to find the cad I seek,
 Whom, to my shame, I gave my love,
 Who betrayed and left me there?

 ´ ˘ ˘ ´ ´ ˘ [-i]
 ´ ´ ˘ ´ ˘ ´ [-v'è]
 ´ ˘ ˘ ´ ´ ˘ [-i]
 ´ ´ ˘ ´ ˘ ` [fè]

Donna Elvira

p

Ah! chi mi di - ce ma - i quel bar - ba - ro dov'-è

Don Giovanni slips out, leaving Leporello to explain the facts of his master's life to her. In a rollicking song he points out that, to date, his master has already seduced 2,065 women, 1,003 of them in Spain. No matter how serious the crime, the worldly audience cannot help laughing. And this is *opera buffa* at its best, a tradition reaching back to seventeenth-century Italy and forward at least as far as Gilbert and Sullivan. For those who know *The Mikado*, it becomes obvious that Leporello's aria serves as the model for Pooh Bah's "I've got a little list!" Still, the astute drama critic would realize this gesture of open confession is somewhat out of character for the trusted servant.

LEPORELLO:

Madamina, il catalogo è questo	Little lady, this is a list
Delle belle che amò il padron mio:	Of the beauties my master loved:
Un catalogo egli è che ho fatt'io;	A catalogue I compiled;
Osservate, leggete con me.	Take a look, read along with me.
In Italia seicentoquaranta,	In Italy, six hundred and forty,
In Alemagna duecentotrentuna,	In Germany two hundred thirty-one.
Cento in Francia, in Turchia novantuna,	One hundred in France, ninety-one in Turkey,
Ma in Ispagna son già mille e tre.	But in Spain, already one thousand and three.
V'han fra queste contadine,	Among these are peasant girls,
Cameriere, cittadine,	Maidservants, city girls,
V'han contesse, baronesse,	Countesses, baronesses,
Marchesane, principesse,	Noble ladies, even princesses.
E v'han donne d'ogni grado,	Women of every rank,
D'ogni forma, d'ogni età.	Of every size, of every age.
Nella bionda egli ha l'usanza	With blonds, it is his habit
Di lodar la gentilezza;	To praise their kindness;
Nella bruna la costanza;	With brunettes their faithfulness;
Nella bianca la dolcezza;	Or the white-haired's sweetness.
Vuol d'inverno la grassotta,	In the winter he likes fat ones,
Vuol d'estate la magrotta;	In the summer, he likes them thin.
È la grande maestosa,	He calls the tall ones stately,
La piccina è ognor vezzosa;	A tiny one always dainty;
Delle vecchie fa conquista	Even the elderly he seduces for
Pel piacer di porle in lista;	The pleasure of adding to the list.
Sua passion predominante	His greatest passion
È la giovin principiante;	Is the young beginner;
Non si picca se sia ricca,	It doesn't matter if she's rich,
Se sia brutta, se sia bella;	If she's ugly or a beauty;
Purchè porti la gonnella,	Because if she wears a skirt,
Voi sapete quel che fa.	You know what he does.

The scene changes. A group of gay young country people are celebrating the forthcoming marriage of Zerlina and Masetto. When Don Giovanni and Leporello join the group, the Don loses no time in beginning his seduction of Zerlina. He promises a party at the villa and orders Masetto to lead the others there. He, of course, will escort the bride-to-be. Masetto is not fooled, but he fears disobeying the nobleman. As soon as they are gone, Don Giovanni promises to marry Zerlina in a lovely duet. Mozart's mastery of both the classic principles of formal balance and the dramatist's need to set the words of a love duet for a simple country maid in appropriate sounds is clearly demonstrated here. The duet's formal scheme of A B A C is combined with simple melodies, clear harmonies, and uncomplicated rhythms.

Don Giovanni

Là   ci da-rem la ma - no,   là   mi di-rai   di   si.

DON GIOVANNI
  Là ci darem la mano,
  Là mi dirai di sì
  Vedi, non è lontano,
  Partiam, ben mio, da qui.

There we'll hold hands,
There you'll whisper "yes,"
See, it's not far,
Let's go there, my dear.

ZERLINA
  Vorrei, e non vorrei. . . .
  Mi trema un poco il cor. . . .
  Felice, è ver, sarei:
  Ma può burlarmi ancor.

I'd like to but I dare not,
My heart trembles a bit,
It's true, I would be happy:
But might he be tricking me?

A

DON GIOVANNI
  Vieni, mio bel diletto!

Come, my dearly beloved!

ZERLINA
  Mi fa pietà Masetto!

I'm sorry for Masetto!

B

DON GIOVANNI
  Io cangerò tua sorte.

I'll change your way of life.

ZERLINA
  Presto . . . non son più forte.

Quickly . . . I'm not very strong.

[repeat of beginning in dialogue form]

TOGETHER
  Andiam, andiam, mio bene,
  A ristorar le pene
  D'un innocente amor!

C

Let's go, let's go, my dearest,
To soothe the ache
Of an innocent love!

Before the two can slip away, Donna Elvira appears and exposes the Don's real intentions. She takes the girl with her, and Donna Anna and Don Octavio enter to enlist Don Giovanni's aid in the search for her father's murderer. Donna Elvira returns to expose her faithless lover again, and Donna Anna begins to suspect the possible guilt of Don Giovanni.

Donna Elvira leaves, and she is followed by a much-irritated Don Giovanni. Donna Anna confides her suspicions to Don Octavio, and they talk the circumstances through in a recitative.

DONNA ANNA:
Don Ottavio . . . son morta!

Don Octavio, I shall die!

DON OCTAVIO:
Cos'è stato?

What's happened?

DONNA ANNA:
Per pietà, soccorretemi.

For pity's sake, help me.

DON OCTAVIO:
Mio bene, fate coraggio.

My dearest, be brave.

DONNA ANNA:
Oh Dei! quegli è il carnefice del padre mio!

Oh God! There goes my father's executioner!

DON OCTAVIO:
Che dite?

What did you say?

DONNA ANNA:
Non dubitate più. Gli ultimi accenti, che l'empio proferì, tutta la voce richiamà nel cor mio di quell'indegno che nel mio appartamento. . . .

There's no doubt about it. His parting words, the quality of his voice, bring back the memory of that vile beast who, in my chamber. . . .

DON OCTAVIO:
Oh ciel! possibile che sotto il sacro manto d'amicizia. . . .
Ma come fu, narratemi lo strano avvenimento.

Oh heaven! Could it be that under the sacred cloak of friendship. . . .
But what happened? Describe this bizarre affair.

DONNA ANNA:
Era già alquanto avanzata la notte, quando nelle mie stanze, ove soletta mi trovai per sventura, entrar io vidi in un mantello avvolto un uom che al primo istante avea preso per voi; ma riconobbi poi che un inganno era il mio. . . .

It was already quite late when into my room, where unluckily I happened to be alone, I saw a man enter all wrapped in a cloak. At first, I mistook him for you: But I soon found out how mistaken I was. . . .

DON OCTAVIO:
Stelle; seguite.

Great heavens! Go on.

DONNA ANNA:

Tacito a me s'appressa, e mi vuol abbracciar; sciogliermi cerco, ei più mi stringe; io grido; non vien alcun; con una mano cerca d'impedire la voce, e coll'altra m'afferra stretta cosi, che già mi credo vinta.

Silently he came next to me, and drew me to him: I tried to free myself, but he only drew me closer. I screamed, but no one came: With one hand, he tried to stifle my voice, and with the other, he held me so tight I thought I must die.

DON OCTAVIO:

Perfido! E alfin?

Horrible! And then?

DONNA ANNA:

Alfine il duol, l'orrore dell'infame attentato accrebbe sì la lena mia che a forza di svincolarmi, torcermi e piegarmi, da lui mi sciolsi.

Finally, the shame, the horror of this vile affront, so strengthened me that by struggling, twisting, and turning I was able to break loose from him.

DON OCTAVIO:

Ahimè! Respiro.

Thank God! I can breathe again.

DONNA ANNA:

Allora rinforzo i stridi miei, chiamo soccorso, fugge il fellon; arditamente il seguo fin nella strada per fermarlo, e sono assalitrice ed assalita: il padre v'accorre, vuol conoscerlo, e l'indegno che del povero vecchio era più forte, compie il misfatto suo col dargli morte.

Then I redoubled my screaming. I yelled for help, and the criminal raced out: boldly I chased him out to the street to stop him and began hitting my assailant: my father challenged him, wanting to know his identity. But the wretch, who was stronger than my poor old father, ended his night of crime by killing him.

She then cries for vengeance in a magnificent *Da capo* aria, with coda. (*Da capo* means "go back to the beginning." Therefore, the aria, which has two musical sec-tions (A B), gains its classical, rounded binary form when the first section is repeated (A B A). Then, with a little extension (coda) it closes.

Donna Anna

Or sai   chi   l'o - no - re   ra - pi - re'a   me vol - se,

DONNA ANNA:
Or sai chi l'onore
Rapire a me volse:
Chi fu il traditore,
Che il padre mi tolse:
Vendetta ti chiedo,
La chiede il tuo cor.

Now you know who tried
To take from me my honor,
Who was my betrayer,
Who took my father's life:
I ask you for vengeance,
Your heart asks it too.

Rammenta la piaga	Remember the wound
Del misero seno:	In his poor breast:
Rimira di sangue	If the wrath of a just fury
Coperto il terreno,	Ever weakens in you,
Se l'ira in te langue	Remember the pool of blood
D'un giusto furor.	Covering the ground.

D.C. (*da* capo—A again) and Coda

Donna Anna leaves, and Don Octavio sings of his love for her as well as his determination to discover the truth. He must either redeem his friend, Don Giovanni, or avenge his love.

In the next scene, the Don is fully recovered and goes on as though nothing has happened. He is preparing the party for Masetto and Zerlina, and he's laying plans for his next conquest.

Don Giovanni

Fin ch'han dal vi - no cal - da la te - sta,

DON GIOVANNI:

Fin ch'han dal vino	Go and prepare
Calda la testa,	A lavish affair
Una gran festa	With plenty of wine
Fa preparar.	To make the heads spin.
Se trovi in piazza	If you find some young lady
Qualche ragazza,	Standing out in the square
Teco ancor quella	Invite her too,
Cerca menar.	Try to bring her along.
Senza alcun ordine	Let the dancing be
La danza sia:	Free and unrestricted:
Chi il minuetto,	Let them dance
Chi la follia,	Here a minuet,
Chi l'alemanna	Here a folia,
Farai ballar.	There an allamande.
Ed io frattanto	And in the meantime,
Dall'altro canto	To a different song,
Con questa e quella	I'll make love
Vo' amoreggiar.	To this one and that one.
Ah! La mia lista	Ah! Tomorrow morning
Doman mattina	You will have to add
D'una decina	A dozen names
Devi aumentar.	To my little list.

In the garden, Masetto scolds Zerlina and she begs his forgiveness. He is not thoroughly convinced of her faithfulness, but Don Giovanni turns the tables by reproaching Masetto for having left his bride. The three enter the house, and Donna Anna, Donna Elvira, and Don Octavio appear, masked. Leporello invites them to the party and then engages Masetto, so that the Don can try once again to seduce Zerlina. They move into another room, but she begins to scream. The Don tries to bluff his way out by rushing from the room, sword in hand, pretending it was Leporello who was annoying her. No one believes the story this time, but the fearless Don brazens his way out through the crowd, pushing Leporello in front of him.

Act II opens with Don Giovanni and Leporello standing before the Inn in which Donna Elvira is staying. The Don has a mandolin in his hand, because he wants to seduce Donna Elvira's maid. Knowing that Donna Elvira still loves him, he disguises Leporello as himself, by exchanging clothes with his servant, so that Leporello will lead her off and leave him a little free time with the maid. As soon as this is accomplished, Don Giovanni serenades the maid with one of the most charming songs in the opera.

Don Giovanni

Deh vie - ni al - la fi - ne-stra, o mi - o te-so - ro,

DON GIOVANNI:

Deh! vieni alla finestra,
  o mio tesoro.
Deh, vieni a consolar
  il pianto mio.
Se neghi a me di dar
  qualche ristoro,
Davanti agli occhi tuoi
  morir vogl'io.

Tu ch'hai la bocca dolce
  più del miele,
Tu che il zucchero porti
  in mezzo al core,
Non esser, gioia mia,
  con me crudele,
Lasciati almen vedere,
  o bell'amore!

O come to the window,
  my treasure,
O come and dispel
  my tears.
If you refuse
  to save me,
I will die
  before your eyes.

Your lips are sweeter
  than honey,
Your heart, the essence
  of sweet,
Do not be cruel
  my gladness,
At least let me see you,
  my love.

But the Don is doomed to yet another failure, for before she can come to him, Masetto returns with a band of armed friends. Pretending to be Leporello, the Don sends Masetto's companions off on a wild goose chase, then tricks the not-too-bright Masetto into giving him his weapons, and beats him severely before making his escape. Zerlina returns, comforts her bruised fiancé, and promises never to be unfaithful again.

The scene changes to a dark courtyard before Donna Anna's house. Donna Elvira tries to make love to Leporello, whom she believes to be Don Giovanni, and Leporello seeks a way to escape. Suddenly, he is cornered by all of the Don's enemies, and he reveals his identity to save himself. They are irate at discovering that they have been tricked again, and seizing the opportunity, Leporello bolts away from them. Finally, Don Octavio promises to avenge them all and sings of his love for Donna Anna.

Although most of the drama of this scene is second rate—few in the audience really believe that Leporello can imitate Don Giovanni well enough to deceive the one woman who knows, understands, and truly loves him, or that Leporello could simply run away from this furious group of armed men—the music is not. Following a brief recitative, each of the characters, in turn, expresses his thoughts with a brief melodic line characteristic of that particular personage. Gradually the parts begin to combine until the five—Donna Anna, Zerlina, Donna Elvira, Don Octavio, and Masetto—group their musical forces against the line of Leporello in a sextet that is excellent musical drama. As they blend together in song, each maintains his distinct musical identity.

LEPORELLO (recitative):
    Di molte faci il lume s'avvicina, . . .

I see the light of torches coming near, . . .

DONNA ELVIRA (1st solo in sextet):
    Sola, sola in buio loco, palpitar il cor mi sento, . . .

All alone in this dark spot I feel the beating of my heart. . . .

LEPORELLO (2nd solo in sextet):
    Più che cerco, men ritrovo
    Questa porta sciagurata. . . .

The more I search, the less I find.
Where is this stupid doorway? . . .

DON OCTAVIO (3rd solo in sextet):
  Tergi il ciglio, o vita mia!
  E da calma al tuo dolore; . . .

Stop your crying, my beloved,
And calm your sadness; . . .

In time, Zerlina and Masetto are introduced into the fabric, too.

When all are properly entered, the five side against Leporello.

LEPORELLO:

. . . .

Viver lasciatemi, per carità!

. . . .

Let me live, I beg you!

THE OTHERS:

Dei! Leporello!

Che inganno è questo? . . .

What? Leporello!

What trick is this? . . .

Also, when the group are about to punish Leporello, he stops the action with an aria that both seeks their

pity and gives him time to move toward a convenient gate.

Leporello

Ah   pie - tà,   Si - gno - ri   miei,   ah   pie - tà,   pie - tà   di   me,

LEPORELLO:

Ah! Pietà signori miei!

Do ragione a voi . . . a lei. . . .

Ma il delitto mio non è.

Il padron con prepotenza

L'innocenza mi rubò.

Donna Elvira! Compatite;

Già capite come andò.

Di Masetto non so nulla,

Vel dirà questa fanciulla;

E un'oretta circum circa

Che con lei girando vo.

A voi, signore, non dico niente.

Certo timore . . . certo accidente. . . .

Di fuori chiaro . . . di dentro scuro. . . .

Non c'è riparo . . . la porta, il muro. . . .

Io me ne vo da quel lato. . . .

Poi qui celato, l'affar si sa. . . .

Ma s'io sapeva, fuggia per qua! . . .

Oh! Have mercy my lords!

You are right, sir . . . and you. . . .

But the real fault is not mine.

My master, with threats,

Robbed me of my innocence.

Donna Elvira! Forgive me!

You know what happened.

Of Masetto, I know nothing.

This lady can confirm it:

For about an hour

I've been walking with her.

To you, sir, I can say nothing.

Partly fear . . . partly chance. . . .

It was light out but dark here.

No way out, the door, the wall,

I couldn't get out of here. . . .

Then I hid myself, you know all.

But had I known this, I'd have run from here! (flees)

Even though we are no more likely to believe that Don Octavio will live up to his word this time, since he

has failed in the past, his sincerity, and his lovely tenor voice, are beautifully displayed in his aria:

Don Octavio

Il   mio te - so - ro   in - tan - to   an - da - te,

DON OCTAVIO:

Il mio tesoro intanto
Andate a consolar:
E del bel ciglio il pianto
Cercate d'asciugar.
Ditele che i suoi torti
A vendicar io vado;
Che sol di stragi e morti
Nunzio voglio tornar.

Meanwhile, go and console
My dearest treasure:
And from her beautiful eyes,
Try and dry the tears.
Tell her I go
To avenge her wrongs:
I will return to announce
His punishment and death.

The scene changes to an enclosed cemetery with several equestrian statues, including that of the Commendatore. Don Giovanni enters, laughing about the night's events, and is quickly followed by a distressed Leporello. The Don chides him and tells about another escapade with a girl on his escape route. She mistook him for Leporello, showed affection, and was just about to be compromised by the Don when he heard pursuers coming and decided to run. Leporello is serious, but the Don is clever and unconcerned. Leporello says:

LEPORELLO:

Ma se fosse costei stata mia moglie?

But supposing she had been my wife?

And the Don laughingly replies:

DON GIOVANNI:

Meglio ancora!

Better still!

Then one of the most dramatic moments in the opera takes place, for the statue speaks!

COMMENDATORE:

Di rider finirai prima dell'aurora.

Your laughter will be silenced before morning.

From this moment on, the intense conflict between Don Giovanni's personal libertine philosophy and the morality of heaven and earth is personified in the struggle between the Don and the Commendatore. Leporello is frightened beyond reason when the marble statue speaks and nods, but Don Giovanni disdainfully orders his servant to invite the statue to dinner.

A brief respite takes place when the scene changes to a room in Donna Anna's house. Don Octavio tells her to calm down; The murder will be avenged. They should bow to the will of Providence, and she should soothe his longings by marrying him tomorrow. Donna Anna is affronted, Don Octavio calls her cruel, and she sets him straight in her recitative and aria:

DONNA ANNA:

(Recitative)
Crudele? Ah no! mio bene!
. . . .

(Aria)
Non mi dir, bell'idol mio, Che son io crudel con te

I cruel? Oh no, my dear!
. . . .

Don't tell me, my love,
That I am cruel to you:
. . . .

Dramatically, there is not much point to this scene, other than providing time for a set change to Don Giovanni's dining hall. But musically, this aria gives Donna Anna an opportunity to display her coloratura vocal wares for the last time before the finale. She sings an embellished line, as follows:

Donna Anna

sen - ti - rà

DONNA ANNA:
Forse un giorno il cielo ancora
Sentirà pietà di me.

Perhaps, one day, heaven will again
Feel merciful for me.

In the next scene, the curtain rises to show the dining room in Don Giovanni's house. The table is laid, and the Don, Leporello, servants, and a few musicians await the guest. Don Giovanni begins eating and jokes with Leporello and the musicians. Donna Elvira enters, pleads her love, and asks him to change. He only mocks her. Fearful screaming outside announces the approach of the invited guest. Leporello hides under the table while the Don opens the door. He invites the Commandant to the table, and the statue slowly and grotesquely moves upstage. After a brief verbal repartee, the statue says:

COMMENDATORE:
  Tu m'invitasti a cena:
  Il tuo dovere or sai,
  Rispondimi; verrai
  Tu a cenar meco?

  You invited me to supper;
  You know what you must do,
  So answer me: will you
  Come and dine with me?

Don Giovanni is no coward. He takes the hand offered by the statue, and he is trapped. The statue demands repentance; Don Giovanni refuses. Flames leap up, a chasm opens, and the trombone voices of hell speak out. Before he is pulled to the torments of the underworld, Don Giovanni cries out:

Don Giovanni

Chi l'a - ni - ma   mi la - ce-ra!   chi m'a - gi - ta   le vi - sce-re!

DON GIOVANNI:
  Chi l'anima mi lacera!
  Chi m'agita le viscere!
  Che strazio! ohimè! che smania!
  Che inferno! che terror!

  My soul is torn in agony!
  My body is in torture!
  What torment! Ah, what madness!
  The fires of hell! The terror!

The flames rise and the chorus sings

CHORUS:
  Tutto a tue colpe è poco:
  Vieni; c'è un mal peggior.

  For all your sins, this is nothing:
  Come! worse torments await below!

Were the opera to end here, it would have the elements of tragedy. The hero, Don Giovanni, recognizes his sins and goes to pay the price. But Mozart and da Ponte did not set out to moralize, but to entertain a pleasure-seeking audience. And with their final scene,

they turn the drama from tragedy to comedy. As Don Giovanni disappears from the stage into the great abyss, all the principals emerge on the stage with officials and the entire cast. They ask for the criminal, learn of his fate, and quickly proceed to announce:

Don Octavio:
Donna Anna:
Donna Elvira:
Zerlina and Masetto:
Leporello:

I want to get married.
Give me a year.
I'm off to a convent.
Let's go home to dinner.
I'll go to the Inn and find a better master.

And together, everyone sings and dances the moral of the tale:

TUTTI:
  Questo è il fin di chi fa mal!
  E de' perfidi la morte
  Alla vita è sempre ugual.

  This is the evil doer's end.
  Death is the payment for great sin.
  Always was and always will be.

Created towards the end of the Enlightenment and on the eve of the French Revolution, *Don Giovanni* reflects the Enlightenment's reliance on reason and individual experience rather than on authority and tradition. Despite the final outcome, the opera is not without sympathy for the hero, for it balances the comic and tragic aspects of real human experience. Yet in presenting Don Giovanni as a man who lives without restraint and who views the well-being of others as incidental to the pleasure-seeking principle, Mozart and da Ponte seem to warn against the perils of supreme individualism. In keeping with the spirit of an age that could produce a treatise on toleration and the American Declaration of Independence and Constitution, the composer and the poet acknowledge the responsibilities of the individual and the possibility of retribution for acts that deny the rights of other individuals. *Don Gio-*

vanni portrays this dilemma, a situation modern psychology would call the conflict of the id and superego, the struggle between immediate gratification and deferred pleasure for the greater good of both society and the individual. Yet, it is not a sermon, but a work of art and an entertainment, a masterpiece of music and poetry by Wolfgang Amadeus Mozart and Lorenzo da Ponte.

Many fine recordings of *Don Giovanni* are, and will always be, available. One that can be recommended for both its fine performance and technical brilliance as well as the quality of the book that accompanies the set is produced by Deutsche Grammophon (2711 006). It stars Dietrich Fischer-Dieskau as Don Giovanni and is conducted by Karl Böhm. The film of the opera (EAV G1VH 6885) made on location in Italy is also recommended.

26

Romanticism: Revolution, Individualism, and Nature

The delicate balance between the demands of enlightened reason and those of passionate individualism was not to have a long supremacy in European culture. The philosophes' demands for a more just and equal society were to culminate in an upheaval of which they probably would not have approved and that was to change the face of Europe forever: the French Revolution.

The American Revolution, far less bloody, had in a sense served as a prelude to the French one. The American experiment demonstrated to Europeans that Enlightenment ideas could be realized in practice. The Declaration of Independence and the Virginia Statute of Religious Liberty were not abstract treatises but statements by a government of its official beliefs and policies. Heretofore, the principles of limited government and a system of checks endorsed by the American Constitution had been considered by most Europeans to be connected with feudal privilege and aristocratic domination. This is why many of the philosophes had espoused absolute monarchy. America seemed to prove that this kind of constitutional structure could in fact foster the freedom and equality sought by Enlightenment thinkers.

The French Revolution

Causes of the Revolution   The American example was particularly important for France. The most populous country in Europe and among the most prosperous, France in the last half of the eighteenth century was a troubled society. The death of Louis XIV in 1715 had brought to the throne a five-year-old boy, Louis XV (1710–1776). Largely unconcerned with government, Louis was primarily interested in women, eating, and lock making. His son, Louis XVI (1754–1793), though well-meaning, was weak and popularly seen as dominated by his wife, Marie Antoinette.

Neither of these monarchs, consequently, played a guiding role in the political life of the nation. A succession of ministers of varying ability governed the country, and policy lacked the consistency an active monarch could have given it. Indicative of the shift in political focus is the increasing marginalization of Versailles as the center of French culture and the return of Paris to that position.

In retrospect, historians after the French Revolution came to speak of France in the eighteenth century as the *ancien régime* (the "old order"). All phases of French life were dominated by an outmoded social structure that endured primarily because it was legally defined and protected. All Frenchmen except the royal family were divided into three classes: the clergy, the nobility, and the third estate, by far the largest of the three, comprising the peasants, the artisans of the towns, and the middle class or *bourgeois*. Of France's 24,000,000 people, only about 2 percent belonged to the clergy and nobility. Yet in a society where land remained the greatest form of wealth, the other 98 percent owned only 60 percent of the landed property. This social group was the greatest force in causing the revolution.

But there was a greater source of discontent among the third estate. The clergy and nobility paid almost no taxes. Moreover, while giving little or nothing to support it, the nobility enjoyed all the highest offices in the government; they also constituted the officer corps of the army. As for the clergy, this class had the right to levy a tax, for its maintenance, on all agricultural goods produced by the third estate.

What made the situation volatile was that for most of the eighteenth century the economy was expanding. Bankers, merchants, and other members of the middle class had accumulated great wealth, and many of the peasants were prosperous. Traditionally there had been various avenues by which successful members of the third estate could work their way into the nobility, but in the course of the eighteenth century these avenues had gradually been shut off by an aristocracy resolved not to dilute its membership further. The upper bourgeois, therefore, felt excluded from the social and financial privileges to which their success entitled them.

Economic prosperity also entailed rising prices and higher living costs. The nobility and clergy, barred by law from entering commerce or industry to reap the profits of the boom, increasingly came to insist on their economic rights over the third estate. Indeed, this was the heyday of lawyers employed by the upper classes to dredge up old, long-neglected rights over the peasantry. Moreover, although the bourgeois and the upper peasantry were profiting throughout most of the eighteenth century, the lower classes, at least in the last half of the century, saw their wages rise more slowly than prices and their standard of living fall.

The most immediate cause of the revolution, which began in the summer of 1789, was the government's financial crisis. Because some of the wealthiest elements in the country were exempt from taxation, the state could not balance its budget. An important element in the French public debt was the expense incurred by helping the Americans in their revolt against England. For years the enlightened advisers of the French king had endeavored to abolish the tax privileges of the clergy and the nobility, but these two orders had solidly resisted the effort. The king could proclaim the necessary laws, but the courts, completely controlled by the nobility, would never enforce them. Finally, in 1788, the royal government simply abolished the old court system and created a new one.

The result was an aristocratic revolt: the army officers and the king's officials at Paris and in the provinces refused to serve, and the whole state was brought to a halt. Unable to persevere in the attempt at reform, the king (Louis XVI) acceded to noble demands that, for the first time since 1614, a National Assembly be called to settle the nations's problems. The nobility clearly intended to gain more control over the king's government through an assembly that, by tradition, gave them and the clergy (dominated by the aristocracy) two votes, against one for the third estate.

Beginning of the Revolution The Assembly met in May 1789 at Versailles, but in the months preceding the meeting, the third estate, growing conscious of its massive power, resolved to use the Assembly as a means of abolishing legal classes. Refusing their places in the Royal Assembly, where they were given one of the three votes, the delegates of the third estate declared themselves to be the Assembly of the Nation and defied the monarchy. Though Louis XVI called troops to Versailles at the end of June, he hesitated to arrest the disobedient delegates. In the atmosphere of tension prevailing over the next weeks, the common people of Paris rose on July 14, 1789, stormed and captured the Bastille (the king's prison in the city), and the revolution was on. The terrified king ordered the nobility and clergy to join with the third estate; those who had not already joined out of sympathy or gone home did so.

One of the first steps of the new one-house National Assembly was the publication of a Declaration of the Rights of Man and the Citizen on August 26, 1789. Like the American Bill of Rights, its provisions emphasized the freedom and equality of every man. Subsequently, all privilege was abolished and the church's property confiscated; henceforth, the clergy was to receive salaries from the state. The leaders of the Assembly at this stage were determined to make France a constitutional monarchy like that of England. Before the new constitution could be approved, however, the would-be constitutional monarch, Louis XVI, fled in June 1791. Despite his capture, the position of the leadership was undercut, and the Jacbins or republicans seized power in the National Assembly in September 1791. The king, however, was not officially deposed until August 1792, when France was declared a republic.

The Jacobins The Jacobins were interested in more than transforming the French monarchy into a republic; they also wished to topple the crowned heads all over Europe and republicanize the subcontinent. Their rise to power naturally brought on conflict with the rest of Europe, and from the spring of 1792 France was at war. When the war began badly and the politicians blamed the defeat of the army on treachery behind the lines, the pursuit of traitors was underway. Starting in May 1793, the radical Jacobins, a group of ruthless idealists, displaced the more moderate leadership.

Robespierre Whereas the moderate Jacobins had aimed at establishing a republic governed by an electorate with modest property qualifications, the radical Jacobins wanted an eventual democratic republic. Their leader Robespierre believed that, before this could be brought about, a dictatorship representing Rousseau's general will must destroy all the reactionaries. His dictatorship took the form of an executive committee of twelve men called the Committee of Public Safety. He introduced the Reign of Terror, which lasted over a year. A new device, the guillotine, was introduced to expedite the execution of traitors to the revolution, including the king and queen. Nevertheless, by July 1794, France was tired of blood, and the assembly, now called the National Convention, had Robespierre arrested and guillotined.

The government emerging from the reaction was dominated by large property owners. The fragility of its control, with radicals to the left and royalists on the right, was to an extent balanced by the success that French armies were having on the battlefield. Actually, after a bad start, the French by the fall of 1792 were having one victory after another. By mid-1794 they had occupied what is now Belgium, the Netherlands, and Germany up to the Rhine as well as parts of northern Italy. In large part their success derived from the fact that the volunteer armies were enormous as opposed to the small professional armies of their opponents. Under the command of officers who held their commissions because of merit rather than family position, highly motivated by intense patriotic zeal, the French soldiers were irresistible. Everywhere they went they were welcomed by revolutionaries opposed to the local regime

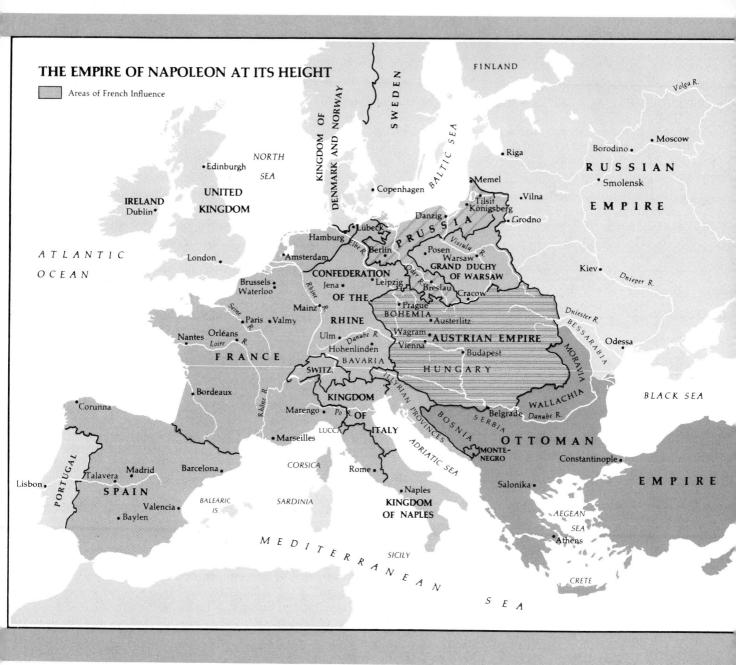

THE EMPIRE OF NAPOLEON AT ITS HEIGHT

Areas of French Influence

FINLAND

SWEDEN

KINGDOM OF DENMARK AND NORWAY

NORTH SEA

BALTIC SEA

Edinburgh

IRELAND
Dublin

UNITED
KINGDOM

ATLANTIC
OCEAN

London

Copenhagen

Riga

Memel

Moscow

Borodino

RUSSIAN

Smolensk

EMPIRE

Vilna

Tilsit
Königsberg

Danzig

Grodno

PRUSSIA

Lübeck

Hamburg

Berlin

Amsterdam

Elbe R.

Posen

Vistula R.

Kiev

Brussels
Waterloo

CONFEDERATION

Leipzig

Oder R.

Warsaw

GRAND DUCHY
OF WARSAW

Dnieper R.

Jena

Breslau

Cracow

OF THE

Mainz

Rhine R.

Prague

Dniester R.

Paris

Valmy

RHINE

BOHEMIA

Austerlitz

BESSARABIA

Odessa

Nantes

Orléans

Loire R.

Seine R.

Ulm

Danube R.

Wagram

Hohenlinden

Vienna

AUSTRIAN EMPIRE

MORAVIA

FRANCE

BAVARIA

Budapest

Bordeaux

SWITZ.

Rhône R.

HUNGARY

ILLYRIAN PROVINCES

WALLACHIA

BLACK SEA

KINGDOM OF

Marengo

Po R.

Belgrade

Danube R.

LUCCA

ITALY

SERBIA

Marseilles

BOSNIA

Corunna

CORSICA

Rome

ADRIATIC SEA

OTTOMAN

MONTE-
NEGRO

Constantinople

Lisbon

Talavera

Madrid

Barcelona

SPAIN

Naples

Salonika

EMPIRE

PORTUGAL

BALEARIC
IS.

SARDINIA

KINGDOM
OF NAPLES

AEGEAN
SEA

Valencia

Baylen

MEDITERRANEAN

SICILY

Athens

SEA

CRETE

---

of despotism and privilege. French conquest meant the abolition of a legal class system and the establishment of a more equitable law code and social system.

Napoleon Bonaparte By 1796 one of the revolutionary generals, Napoleon Bonaparte, had distinguished himself above the others by a brilliant invasion of Italy and a swift capture of most of the northern part of the peninsula. Born in 1769 of minor Corsican nobility, Napoleon would probably never have risen above the rank of captain in the old aristocratic French army. But, as it was in the new army, he was a general by the age of twenty-five. Not only a military genius but a brilliant statesman as well, Napoleon in 1797 purged the leadership of the conservative government that had come in after the Reign of Terror. In 1799, after an invasion of Egypt that stirred the imagination of all Europe, Napoleon abolished the whole government and declared himself the First Consul of France.

Napoleon had been deeply influenced by the Enlightenment. He has been referred to as "the last of the Enlightened despots," and he once said of himself: "I am the revolution." Napoleon believed that the real concern of the French was not so much political liberty as social equality. Political participation was for them secondary to their desire for a society where all men were equal before the law and where advancement derived from merit. While Napoleon's constitution provided for a parliamentary government with universal male suffrage, there could be no question that Napoleon governed France.

Napoleon established a meritocracy in the bureaucracy and army, and he reformed laws to enable more equality. His fiscal system was run by professionals, and there were no tax exemptions. On the whole, it is fair to say that Napoleon realized in his government most of the goals of the Enlightenment: those dealing with political freedom had always been secondary in any case.

Between 1799 and 1814 Napoleon, who took the title of emperor of the French in 1802, almost succeeded in conquering all of continental Europe. But when he penetrated Russia as far as Moscow in 1812, this invasion cost him dearly; 500,000 men never returned, and from this point on, his fortune waned.

With the heavy loss in troops and resistance to French war taxation growing among the subject peoples, Napoleon decided to surrender to an allied coalition of England, Austria, Russia, and Prussia. He abdicated and was sent in exile to Elba off the Italian coast in 1814. With hopes of turning the tables, he appeared again in France early in 1815. The French rallied, his old soldiers gathered again, and in the spring of 1815 he fought and lost the great battle of Waterloo. Defeated, he was exiled this time to Saint Helena in the Atlantic Ocean, and a brother of Louis XVI was made king of France by the allies.

Effects of the Revolution The French revolution and its aftermath, however, left a lasting mark on Western Europe. No longer could rulers fight with the small professional armies of the past: the levy *en masse* was an absolute necessity in a new age of war. Rulers had to put arms in the hands of their subjects. Despite their conservative temper and fear of reform, kings, including the new French monarch, could not reimpose the old legal class structure where it had been abolished. The law codes destroying legal privilege in these areas were permanent. Moreover, French nationalism had proven infectious. At first welcomed as liberators by many in the conquered countries, the French ended by creating a national feeling directed against them in Germany, Italy, Spain, and elsewhere. Until later in the nineteenth century, however, nationalism would be considered the property of liberals wishing to imitate the French. After that time monarchs would learn how to use it for their own purposes. Although the allies reduced France to her boundaries before 1789, the French were considered as the most dangerous people of Europe until 1870. The figure of Napoleon, the keen rationalist, became a symbol of the creative, mysterious, and at times demonic personality that fascinated the first generation of the nineteenth century.

The Art of the French Revolution: Jacques-Louis David (1748–1825)

Just as the leaders of the American revolution instigated the search for a new visual and architectural language for the new republic, so the French revolution and its aftermath profoundly affected art in France and England. The citizens of France, like those of the United States, first adopted the severe classical style of republican Rome; Napoleon, however, preferred to imitate the empire. The foremost painter of the revolutionary and Napoleonic eras was Jacques Louis David. David revolted strongly against the sensual elegance of the court style as exemplified by the paintings of Boucher (Fig. 23-5) and Fragonard. He sought to renew art by contact with the art of Rome and the Italian High Renaissance. While in Italy he painted his first important picture in this fresh style. Displayed in his Roman studio, *The Oath of the Horatii* (1784–85) combined qualities from the 16th and 17th centuries to convey what some saw as revolutionary sentiments. Based on a story from Livy, *The Oath* places loyalty to the state above all other concerns, even those of family. The painting shows heroic male figures in a stark architectural setting. As in *The Death of Marat* (p. 162), the figures are somewhat idealized but retain a degree of intense realism through an almost photographic rendering of flesh and muscle. Such detail makes them highly convincing. Colors are cool; the harsh light isolates form and gesture. Crisp and clear, the figures seem like a sculpted bas relief.

Returning to Paris where his style was immediately recognized as revolutionary, though not necessarily politically so, David nevertheless moved away from the sentiments of the Royal Academy that had sent him to Rome. In *The Death of Socrates* (1787) he explored the theme of injustice by a government fearing the truth. This picture and others like it were celebrated as manifestos of those virtues most lacking in monarchial France and their artist became a leading revolutionary painter.

David was commissioned by the Committee of Public Safety to make three paintings of revolutionary heroes; only one of them was finished, *The Death of Marat* (Fig. 26-1). It portrays the murder of the Jacobin Marat by Charlotte Corday, from a rival revolutionary group. Sending a note to Marat, she gained access to him while, seated in a medicinal bath, he received petitioners. She stabbed him when he could offer no resistance. An almost ludicrous scene is transformed by David into the final act of a great tragedy. The dead revolutionary still lies in his draped tub, the focus of a cold, dramatic light. His wound gapes, blood stains his drapery and the water, and his limp arm and hand fall to the floor, his pen permanently stilled. The figure is rendered with sculptural intensity. Though there is a pervasive sense of reality, the body bears no marks of the skin disease that forced him to sit in the tub. His face shows little age, no anguish. In the contrast between reality and abstraction, David creates a magnificent tension—a tension like that between reason and intuition, calculation and passion.

Recognizing this formidable talent, Napoleon made David the pageant master of the consular government and then of the empire. In his *Napoleon Crossing the Alps* (Fig. 26-2) David's abstract clarity has given way to an ideal image. The youthful general, astride a rearing horse, his cloak blowing in the wind as he gestures forward, has become a romantic hero comparable to Hannibal and Charlemagne, whose names are carved in

26-1 David, *The Death of Marat*. (Musées Royaux des Beaux-Arts © A.C.L. Bruxelles)

the rocks. This is not a real general; it is how all generals might see themselves—indeed how men might envision a hero—commanding, youthful, virile, clean, shiny, and dry, in spite of cold, snow, and the hell of war.

The revolution in style begun by David would take on new forms with the birth of the sensibility called *romantic*.

Romanticism: A Revolutionary Movement

The two great revolutions of the eighteenth century, the American and the French, were followed not only by upheavals altering the course of European politics but also by rapid changes in other spheres of life: taste, feeling, thought, behavior, social and domestic relations. The varied, often contradictory cultural movement that swept over Europe and America and became known as romanticism had profound effects on the hu-

26-2 David, *Napoleon Crossing the Alps*, Versailles Museum. (Cliché des Musées Nationaux France © S.P.A.D.E.M., 1980)

manities—effects still very much felt in the contemporary world. The individualism, sense of isolation, and alienation of which we are now so aware have their roots in the Renaissance and Reformation period, but they were cultivated and brought to flower by the romantics.

Romanticism as a movement may be said to have originated in Germany, but the word *romantic* first appeared in England in the mid-eighteenth century. It originated from an association with medieval "romances," the (predominately French) stories of knights and ladies. As the word became coined in all European languages, it took on connotations of fanciful, picturesque, rugged, spontaneous, natural, and sentimental. During the early nineteenth century it was applied to groups of rebellious young artists promoting creativity, individualism, and free expression of emotion in opposition to classical canons and the regulations and stan-

dards based on "enlightened" reason that their parents' generation had espoused. For the romantics, life and art were one: as they threw out the old standards for art, so they lived their lives with bohemian freedom, following their passions or imagination rather than their reason or the "artificial" rules of society. Artistic and political ideals also intertwined: the French writer Victor Hugo called romanticism "liberalism in literature" and proclaimed that words, like postrevolutionary human beings, were now free from tyranny. By the middle of the century, however, many romantics had grown conservative, Catholic, or nationalistic, or they had retreated into an asocial dream world. This was partly because of the political scene in Europe: many who had first adored Napoleon as the bearer of the revolution became disillusioned with Napoleon the emperor. Yet some romantics were intensely conservative from the beginning, looking back toward the Middle Ages as an ideal period of order and spirituality. (The liberals, too, liked medieval themes but for other reasons.) It is impossible to attribute an exact beginning and end to this complex, varied, pan-European and American movement; but the French revolution gave impetus to its latent beginnings, and it died out in most places before 1850. In Slavic countries, however, the romantic movement in literature (and in nationalistic politics) continued longer, and romantic music flourished in Germany, France, and Italy throughout the nineteenth century. It is hardly possible to attempt a global history or definition of romanticism here. We will concentrate instead on the artistic expression of some major romantic themes: in this chapter, revolution, the hero, and nature; and in the following chapter, women and love.

Enlightened Ideas, Romantic Style

The American and French revolutions fired the imaginations of the romantics as they had seemed at first to confirm the reasonableness of the philosophes. Jean-Jacques Rousseau is the single most important figure for understanding the transition between the Enlightenment and romanticism Revered as a forefather of the revolution because of his analyses of social injustice and his "enlightened" beliefs in the dignity and freedom of man, Rousseau was the first in French letters to promote feeling above reason and nature above institutions. Above all, he raised the unique, individual self to a position of prime importance. The individualism propounded by Rousseau seemed to be the philosophical foundation of the new American republic, the largest territory ever ruled by a government proclaiming men to be free and equal.

Liberty, Equality, Fraternity   Liberty, equality, and fraternity, the catchwords of the French revolution, were taken by the romantics to apply to all aspects of life. Ironically, it was outside of France that these ideals first took hold as a cultural force. It is in Germany and in England that we first see poets celebrating the ideals of the revolution, and it is there, too, that other signs of budding romanticism first show themselves. Germany's two greatest writers, Johann Wolfgang von Goethe (1749–1832) and Friedrich Schiller (1759–1805), spanned Neoclassicism and romanticism in their careers. Schiller's fervent belief in man's rights to dignity and freedom and his lofty hopes for universal brotherhood place him in the transition between the Enlightenment and romanticism. His poem "Ode to Joy," written on the eve of the French revolution, is a passionate statement of those beliefs and hopes that were stirring at the time. Immortalized by Beethoven in his Ninth Symphony some thirty years later, it has become one of the great statements of romanticism.

Ludwig von Beethoven (1770–1827)

The late eighteenth and early nineteenth centuries saw the flowering of German music as well as of German literature. Beethoven, like Goethe and Schiller, is a gigantic figure whose works rise above categories like classical or romantic but include elements of both. Like many of his generation, he was at first stirred by the ideals of the French revolution and by their embodiment in Napoleon, and later disillusioned. Beethoven had both feet firmly planted in the fertile soil of classicism but was able to reach out with both hands to grapple with the giant problems of romanticism: the meaning of life, the values of human existence, the powers of man, and the importance of the individual.

What does romanticism in music really mean? What are the musical features that inform our ears about the interests and ideals of Beethoven and the nineteenth-century composers who followed him? To search for answers to these questions, let us look into a single masterpiece that fuses classical and romantic styles—the values of the Enlightenment and the passions of the romantic revolutionaries. Let us try to learn from Beethoven's last and most monumental symphony, his Symphony in D Minor, opus 125, a work familiarly known as the Ninth Symphony.

Like all classical symphonies, Beethoven's Ninth is divided into four movements, and they follow a traditional pattern: the first and fourth movements are energetic, moving at a lively speed; the second and third movements offer contrast, one slow and the other a dance form related to the classical dance called the minuet. This four-movement, balanced structure developed as a means to create a large-scale work (a half hour or more) capable of capturing intellectual attention for long periods of time using musical means only. In other words, the composers were seeking an answer to a compositional problem: if we exclude extramusical ideas and effects (such as a church service, a dance, a festival, and programmatic ideas), how can we keep from losing the listener's attention if we play a continuous piece of music for a very long time? Haydn, Mozart, and their mid-eighteenth century contemporaries solved the problem by designing symphonies that had distinct movements related by key, contrasted by mood, and subdivided by various formal designs that developed contrasting melodies in a variety of ways. Their large works lasted up to thirty or even forty minutes; Beethoven's Ninth lasts almost two hours! His first movement continues as long as do most complete classical symphonies. Although Beethoven's concept of form was classical, his expansion of dimensions, his breaking of boundaries, was romantic.

Classical composers had a knack for the well-turned phrase, a neat tune of four or eight measures' duration whose shape had character and individuality and was capable of expansion or development as the piece progressed. Classical melodies had musical characteristics that allowed these tunes, usually, to be categorized as antecedent-consequent phrases; that is, the first half is answered and completed by the second half. A good example of this type of theme is Mozart's opening theme from his Symphony no. 40 in G minor (K.550), where both halves are similar but different, ascending and descending, opening and closing. In fact, Mozart's sense of balance was so certain and ingrained that the entire phrase can be seen as the antecedent of the next four-measure phrase.

This analytical game can be played even further, if we choose, for the two-to-two and four-to-four measure relationships can be carried even further by viewing the first eight measures as antecedent to the second eight measures. This is possible with Mozart and his G Minor symphony; it is not possible with the opening theme of Beethoven's Ninth.

Beethoven's "tune" is hardly a melody at all; it is a series of short *motives* laid out along a descending *arpeggiated* chord and a brief closing figure.

Opening musical figure (combination of motives)

Closing figure of first phrase

From small germinal ideas, Beethoven sculpts larger forms; from almost tuneless groups of notes, Beethoven creates tonal music of a relentless, soul-searching nature. Each fragment of melody is taken in turn, examined, dissected, synthesized, and reissued in a new shape within a fresh context at a later time. The rhythm of the closing fragment

becomes a driving melody for the bass instruments at one point:

and a lyrical, sweet passage for French horn at another.

In other words, even these few processes we have discussed here sound the death knell for the ease, grace, and regularity of classical music. In time the classical forms will even be replaced or set aside, but for Beethoven it was enough to fragment the old and pile smaller blocks into larger structures.

Those who already are familiar with the Ninth Symphony will say that this analysis has been deceptive thus far, for the Ninth is also called the Choral Symphony and is unlike its classical predecessors if for no

other reason than that. Additionally, they might add that a chorus and vocal soloists require text and that words bring extramusical ideas immediately into play. True enough, but in the Ninth Symphony of Beethoven, the vocalists do not begin their work until the last movement. An hour of instrumental music has been performed before they sing their first note. To understand the Ninth, we must first grasp the meaning of this creation on purely musical terms, for it is a complex instrumental construction with a choral and literary element added to it. Without the chorus, it would still be a classical-romantic symphony. The chorus does not make it romantic; the notes do. Without an understanding of the first three movements, the fourth would be diminished. Beethoven binds the beginning to the end, for he takes the opening motive from the beginning of the symphony to play in the introduction to the fourth, or choral, movement; likewise he takes the melody of the scherzo, or second movement, for use in the finale's introduction. The restatement of earlier ideas in a Beethoven symphony is not merely saying the same thing twice; rather, it is a reiteration of initial ideas now seen in the new light cast from all the music that has been played since the ideas were first stated. Had the remainder of the symphony not been performed—that is, had the first three movements been omitted—the music of the opening of the last movement would be extraneous and the finale reduced to a skillfully orchestrated choral piece. Beethoven's way made it the crowning gem of a symphonic career. The Ninth Symphony looks both ways—back to the past and forward into the future.

Since this work is indeed a choral symphony, we must look carefully at the poem, for surely a composer's preoccupation with text is the critical event that starts the compositional process for a choral setting. In Beethoven's case it was truly a preoccupation. From a letter of 1793 written by a Viennese admirer, Bartolomeus Fischenich, when the composer was only twenty-three years old, we learn that the young musician intended to set Schiller's *Freude* (Joy) poem stanza by stanza; the Ninth Symphony was completed in 1824. Obviously Beethoven was not actively working on this symphony for thirty-one years, but the Schiller poem seems to have been tucked within the composer's mind throughout the period of the Napoleonic exploits in France, a series of events that strongly molded Beethoven's philosophy. In fact, this poem gains even greater significance if the noted British composer, Ralph Vaughan Williams, is correct, for he relates:

> When I was young I was told that Schiller originally wrote his Ode to "Freedom" (*Freiheit*), not "Joy" (*Freude*), and that Beethoven knew of this when he composed the music. I have never been able to find any confirmation of this legend, but we may profitably keep it at the back of our minds when we play or sing or read, or hear this great Symphony.[1]

There is no doubt that Schiller's poem exemplifies the romantic spirit in Europe and was capable of holding special meaning for Beethoven.

Alle Menschen werden Brueder,
  Wo dein sanfter Fluegel weilt.
(Men throughout the world are brothers,
  In the haven of thy wings.)

Napoleon, until he named himself Emperor, had been a hero for Beethoven, a leader of common men against the tyranny of the rich, the oppression of the aristocracy. Beethoven did not like his indebtedness to the patronage of the rich; recognizing personal worth and artistic genius to be far superior to accident of birth, he struggled constantly throughout his life to assert his independence, his freedom. To him freedom was the greatest joy, and Schiller's poem expressed in words what he felt in his soul and was capable of translating into music. (Only the portion of the poem used by Beethoven is printed below; Louis Untermeyer is the translator.)

---

[1] Ralph Vaughan Williams, *Some Thoughts on Beethoven's Choral Symphony with Writings on Other Musical Subjects* (London: Oxford University Press, 1953), p. 13.

FRIEDRICH SCHILLER   *Hymn to Joy* ————————————————————————————————— •

Baritone: O Freunde, nicht diese Toene!
Sondern lasst uns angenehmere anstimmen, und
freudenvollere.

Baritone: O friends, friends, not these sounds!
Let us sing something more pleasant, more
full of gladness. O Joy, let us praise thee!

(Baritone Solo, Quartet and Chorus)

Freude, schoener Goetterfunken,	Joy, thou source of light immortal,
Tochter aus Elysium,	Daughter of Elysium,
Wir betreten feuer-trunken,	Touched with fire, to the portal
Himmlische, dein Heiligthum!	Of thy radiant shrine we come.
Deine Zauber binden wieder,	Thy pure magic frees all others
Was die Mode streng getheilt;	Held in Custom's rigid rings;
Alle Menschen werden Brueder,	Men throughout the world are brothers
Wo dein sanfter Fluegel weilt.	In the haven of thy wings.

Wem der grosse Wurf gelungen,	He who knows the pride and pleasure
Eines Freundes Freund zu sein,	Of a friendship firm and strong,
Wer ein holdes Weib errungen,	He who has a wife to treasure,
Mische seinen Jubel ein!	Let him swell our mighty song.

Ja, wer auch nur eine Seele	If there is a single being
Sein nennt auf dem Erdenrund!	Who can call a heart his own,
Und wer's nie gekonnt, der stehle	And denies it—then, unseeing,
Weinend sich aus diesem Bund!	Let him go and weep alone.

Freude trinken alle Wesen	Joy is drunk by all God's creatures
An den Bruesten der Natur;	Straight from earth's abundant breast;
Alle Guten, alle Boesen	Good and bad, all things are nature's,
Folgen ihrer Rosenspur.	And with blameless joy are blessed.
Kuesse gab sie uns und Reben,	Joy gives love and wine; her gladness
Einen Freund, geprueft im Tod;	Makes the universe her zone,
Wollust ward dem Wurm gegeben,	From the worm that feels spring's madness
Und der Cherub steht vor Gott.	To the angel near God's throne.

(Tenor Solo and Chorus)

Froh, wie seine Sonnen fliegen	Glad, as when the suns run glorious
Durch des Himmels praecht'gen Plan,	Through the deep and dazzling skies,
Laufet, Brueder, eure Bahn,	Brothers, run with shining eyes—
Freudig, wie ein Held zum Siegen.	Heroes, happy and victorious.

Freude, schoener Gotterfunken,	Joy, thou source of light immortal,
Tochter aus Elysium,	Daughter of Elysium,
Wir betreten feuer-trunken,	Touched with fire, to the portal
Himmlische, dein Heiligthum!	Of thy radiant shrine we come.
Deine Zauber binden wieder,	Thy pure magic frees all others
Was die Mode streng getheilt;	Held in Custom's rigid rings;
Alle Menschen werden Brueder,	Men throughout the world are brothers
Wo dein sanfter Fluegel weilt.	In the haven of thy wings.

(Quartet and Chorus)

Seid umschlungen, Millionen!	Millions, myriads, rise and gather!
Diesen Kuss der ganzen Welt!	Share this universal kiss!
Brueder, ueber'm Sternenzelt	Brothers, in a heaven of bliss,
Muss ein lieber Vater wohnen.	Smiles the world's all-loving Father.
Ihr stuerzt nieder, Millionen?	Do the millions, His creation,
Ahnest du den Schoepfer, Welt?	Know Him and His works of love?
Such ihn ueber'm Sternenzelt!	Seek Him! In the heights above
Ueber Sternen muss er wohnen.	Is His starry habitation!

Beethoven's chorus, singing their heads off in a "fire-drunk" jubilation, celebrate the human spirit; they are singing a great song for all peoples, nations, and languages. And as the fervor builds and the orchestral and vocal sounds sweep you away, the listener is unlikely to notice that this great romantic outpouring is framed by Beethoven's simplest, and most classical, melody:

The simplicity of the *theme*, the clarity of its form (A–A–B–A–B–A), the unpretentious nature of its harmony and rhythm make it a song for the common man, and that it has become. The works of Beethoven live today because, in addition to their sheer beauty and historical importance, they symbolize those values that we cherish now. In the words of Romain Rolland:

> The music of Beethoven is the daughter of the same forces of imperious Nature that had just sought an outlet in the man of Rousseau's *Confessions*. Each of them is the flowering of a new season. . . . [Beethoven], too, like the eagle on his rock, goes into exile on an island lost in the expanse of the seas—more truly lost than that island in the Atlan-

tic, for he does not hear even the waves breaking on the rocks. He is immured. And when out of the silence there rises the song of the Ego of the last ten years of his life, it is no longer the same Ego; he has renounced the empire of men; he is with his God.[2]

Individualism and the Romantic Hero From the romantic version of revolutionary ideals—as from the writings of the transitional Rousseau—there devel-

---

[2] Romain Rolland, *Beethoven the Creator*, trans. Ernest Newman (New York: Harper & Brothers, 1929), pp. 25ff.

oped a new sense of the value of the unique individual. Rousseau's confession, "If I am not better than other men, *at least* I am different!" would be unthinkable to a classicist. Schiller, who could write a hymn to the brotherhood of man, could also write a play *The Robbers* with an individualistic outlaw as hero. Men like Beethoven, and for that matter Napoleon, embodied the romantic doctrine of individual, unique, "titanic" genius.

But the romantic hero could also be a forlorn individual, solitary and alienated. Although the "suffering" type of romantic hero may wander off to commune with nature or commit suicide, the "titanic" type of rebel attempts to take destiny into his own hands. Prometheus, the deity from Greek mythology who stole the secret of fire from the gods to bring it to man and who defied Zeus himself, was a favorite subject of romantic verse and drama. The romantics' Prometheus goes beyond their model, the Prometheus of the Greek tragedian Aeschylus. Prometheus combines two aspects of the romantic hero that may be separate and contradictory elsewhere: he is both a self-willed individual and a benefactor of mankind. Shelley's verse drama *Prometheus Unbound* is the most extended treatment of this theme; Byron's short lyric "Prometheus" (pp. 232–233) is an early model for what came to be known as the Byronic hero. The second poem of Byron's printed here, in which the poet seems to feel his life is over at thirty-six, portrays a suffering type of hero but offers a solution in dedication to revolution. But Byron was capable of mocking his own heroic types with a comic antihero, Don Juan.

The poet George Gordon, Lord Byron, is a good example of a romantic who lived as well as wrote his romanticism. Spectacularly handsome, he was involved in many unhappy love affairs. He wandered restlessly over Europe and finally died while fighting for a liberal cause, the war of the Greeks against their oppressors, the Turks. Byron's literary heroes, particularly his Childe Harold, Manfred, and Cain, are rebellious individuals with a passionate belief in individual freedom. They are men of powerful emotions and a genius that may at times appear satanic. There is a "dark" side to the Byronic hero that we may see in some of the characters created in his wake, such as Melville's Captain Ahab. The "gothic" hero and the mad scientist, two other romantic types, may be seen as offshoots of the

Byronic hero. The most famous of the latter, Victor Frankenstein, was created by Mary Godwin Shelley, a close friend of Byron. She called her novel *Frankenstein, or the Modern Prometheus*.

Perhaps the most enduring romantic hero-rebel, one who goes beyond romanticism, is Goethe's Faust, in the long dramatic poem of that title. Faust's rebellion is really against human limits, or finitude. He embarks on a quest after the absolute: absolute knowledge, power, and love, and in the process puts his soul in the hands of the devil. He refuses to accept any limits on his individuality until the end of the poem, when he also becomes a benefactor of mankind.

The various types of romantic individuals took hold of the imaginations of Americans as well as Europeans. It is possible to see in the romantic hero a kind of literary prototype for the "robber barons" of the later nineteenth century. The romantic period was the time when American literature came into its own. Ralph Waldo Emerson celebrated the heroic, "self-reliant" individual; Herman Melville and Edgar Allan Poe portrayed the darker side of the soul. A different and perhaps more typically American romantic individualism emerged in the poetry of Walt Whitman. In his long poem, "Song of Myself," part of which is printed here, he celebrates his unique self in an attempt to break down the artificial barriers that society creates between human beings. An unheroic, but no less significant sense of individual uniqueness is expressed in the extraordinary poetry of Emily Dickinson.

Nature and "Natural People"

For the "enlightened" European or American, the word *nature* meant essentially human nature, and man's natural place was among his fellow human beings. Human institutions might be corrupt, but they could be changed for the better. Civilization brought with it many ills, but it was still humanity's greatest achievement. Yet as early as the eighteenth century, we witness a kind of disillusionment with Western civilization and urban life and a curiosity about "uncivilized" peoples that came to be known as the "noble savage" craze. With this came a yearning for unspoiled natural scenery—forests, lakes, mountains, the ocean.

Once again, Rousseau is a pivotal figure here. Just as he went beyond a doctrine of liberty to one of individuality, so he went beyond a critique of the faults of civilized society to a radical questioning of its value. The romantics, who followed Rousseau, eulogized the free and "natural" life of the American Indian as superior to that of the decadent European, although few seemed to understand the social and economic threat that the new republic posed to him. The social ideals promoted by the revolutions *were* used by romantics, first British and later American, in the service of the antislavery cause that culminated in the abolitionist movement. In the romantic view, the black African was a proud, noble individual who had suffered the oppression and tyranny of the old order of Europe, an order that was now to be overthrown on all levels. The romantic liberals championed the cause of the peasant, the worker, the poor, and the oppressed; they looked with contempt on the rich bourgeois, smug and materialistic. Naturally the champions of the oppressed tended to, as we would say, "romanticize" those that they perceived as victims, sometimes endowing them with sublime, superhuman characters. They were, in fact, more interested in lofty ideals than in everyday reality. Out of the revolution, they believed, a new order would be born that would bring with it the creative freedom of the individual and the brotherhood of all mankind.

Rousseau influenced not only the idealization of "natural" people but also the tendency of the "misunderstood," unhappy, and yearning urban romantic to seek solitude and solace in the natural world. In his *Reveries of a Solitary Walker*, Rousseau describes the beauty of the Swiss landscape, its mountains and lakes, and his feeling of communing with it. He also describes his joy in abandoning himself to "pure sensation" as he experiences the lapping of a mountain lake's waves. To be able to abandon thought and feel oneself in unison with nature: a romantic ideal is born.

Ideas like returning to nature and living a natural (that is, nonartificial, nonurban) life began in the romantic period to acquire the connotations that they have today. Changes in fashion were indicative of the trend. Partly because of Rousseau, women abandoned corsets and stiffened skirts for loose, flowing, "natural" attire, while the formal, symmetrical French garden (as at Versailles) gave way to the more luxuriant, chaotic, and "natural" English garden. Hiking and mountain climbing became for the first time popular pastimes in Europe. The vine-covered cottage replaced the palace as dream house. The life of the simple peasant was prized (at least in theory) above that of the sophisticated city dweller; and feeling, or richness of sensation, above intellectual capacity. There was even a concern for what we could call conservation and ecology. The New Englander Henry David Thoreau actually carried out a solitary back-to-nature experiment, which he described both practically and emotionally in *Walden*.

The celebration of nature in romantic art took on varying aspects, corresponding to the individualistic temperaments of the artists. Romantic artists tended to depict nature as reflecting the sensations of their own souls. For some she consoled; to others she seemed indifferent. To some she was picturesque; to others fearful and sublime. Some romantics, weary of cold and sterile eighteenth-century deism, found their religious yearnings satisfied in their relations with the natural world. Those drawn back to a devout Christianity found God's bounty and goodness reflected in nature; those who shunned organized religion tended toward a kind of pantheism, worshiping the spirit of nature itself. Coleridge's poetry emphasizes the mystical, uplifting aspects of nature. A poet like Keats, on the other hand, renders through language the pure sensuous feelings of an autumn day or a summer night, sensations comparable to those rendered in paint by the artist J.M.W. Turner. Emily Dickinson's close observations of natural phenomena sometimes reveal nature as a soothing mother and sometimes as a terrifying foreboder of death. In music we find composers imitating the sounds and feelings of nature with new orchestral textures. Beethoven's Pastoral Symphony (No. 6) renders a wide range of moods from the natural world—sublime, mysterious, joyful, humble—and it even imitates a thunderstorm. In painting, landscapes came into vogue. Like the romantic poets, romantic landscape painters often attempted to render the communion between human emotion and nature. The painters John Constable and Jean Francois Millet, when juxtaposed with the poet William Wordsworth, exemplify some aspects of the romantic vision of nature common to both visual art and poetry.

John Constable (1776–1837) Keen observers the world around them, Constable and Wordsworth were more taken with the humble, everyday aspects of nature than with its sublime or mystical ones. Both were profoundly attached to their native countryside. Constable recorded his pleasure in simple phenomena: "The sound of water escaping from mill dams, willows, old rotten planks, slimy posts, brickwork. I love such things." The statement would have been inconceivable to a Renaissance or Neoclassical artist. It reveals not only a sensitivity to the textures of ordinary objects but also (especially in the escaping water and the rotten plants) a concern with mutability, the ways in which time changes things. Constable's pursuit of a means to capture his experience of the natural world led him to study clouds, rain, light, and the weather. His early pictures are not far removed from the perpetual sunlight or storm of seventeenth- and eighteenth-century pictures; but, as his ideas and abilities mature, we see him open the landscape to capture the broken light of moving air and clouds. Colors become more intense, and the surface of paint is dense and wet. His brushstrokes give trees a shimmer and clouds a sense of movement

and energy. Constable painted only those things that he knew and loved. The River Stour was completely familiar to him and he took comfort and refreshment from its mossy banks, bridges, and surrounding countryside (Color Plate XIII).

William Wordsworth (1770–1850) A poem by Wordsworth, written on his return to a spot near the medieval ruins of Tintern Abbey, in many ways parallels Constable's painting. The primary theme of both works is man's relationship to nature. "Lines Composed a Few Miles above Tintern Abbey" paints a landscape in its first stanza and meditates on the poet's interaction with it in the rest of the poem. But the landscape painted by Wordsworth is not a simple one; it is superimposed, as in a double-exposure photograph. From the first lines the reader is aware that Wordsworth is *also* viewing this scene with the memory of how he viewed it five years previously. A sense of the passage of time is imposed on the place. Because of this dual perception, the poet is able to reexperience his feelings as they were five years ago. At that time he was able to enjoy the purely sensational effects of nature; now he finds that the recollection, as well as the new vision of the natural landscape, has a profound effect on his moral and intellectual being. Both of these perceptions are conveyed to the reader. Another dimension is added as the poet looks, through the person of his sister Dorothy, into the future. The sensations from nature that they experience in the present will be sublimated and perpetuated as "lovely forms" in her mind's "mansion." In Wordsworth's mention of the possibility of his own death while his sister is still alive, we experience no sense of dread, or even sadness, but a sense of life as continuity. The life and death of the individual are part of the processes of nature. Still, it is through the individual's consciousness and judgment that nature is given meaning. Wordsworth's poem, like Constable's painting, brings out the interdependence between man's life cycle and nature.

Beauty, for Wordsworth, could also be found in the simple people who inhabited his countryside. One of Wordsworth's ideals was to let his poems speak for the inarticulate, to express the poetry latent in the woodsman, the peasant, or the country girl: such a poem is his "Solitary Reaper." Here again Wordsworth emphasizes the beauty to be found in the familiar and the near

26–3   Millet, *The Sower*, (Courtesy Museum of Fine Arts, Boston. Gift of Quincy A. Shaw)

at hand. The young girl reaping is a part of nature, yet her song—whether of past events or eternal emotions—gives a continuity and a temporality to the natural world that it would not otherwise have. At the end the suggestion is made that the poet will perpetuate her song into the future.

Jean François Millet (1814–1875)   A painter who saw the same poetry in simple people at their country tasks was the Frenchman Jean François Millet. Millet portrayed the French peasantry as virtuous, humane, and monumentally enduring. In his picture *The Sower* (Fig. 26-3) the figure is huge, the gesture simple, the colors earthy and rich. Unlike the romantic hero or heroine, the romantic peasant in poem and painting is anonymous and eternal, rather than individualistic. Like Wordsworth, Millet emphasizes the harmony between the workers of the field and their natural surroundings.

Romantic Lyric Poetry

Romantic writers were prolific in all *genres*—fiction, drama, and poetry—but the movement is perhaps best remembered for its achievements in poetry. The individualistic, subjective, and emotional bent of romanticism made the *lyric* a congenial form. In contrast to the period of the Enlightenment, the romantic era was one of the great ages of lyricism. This was true all over Europe, but especially in Germany and in England. American poetry also flourished in this period. Because it is so abundant, of such greatness, and representative of the themes discussed, we have limited our literary selections to lyric poetry written in English.

WILLIAM WORDSWORTH (1770—1850)

from *The Prelude*

RESIDENCE IN FRANCE

Oh! pleasant exercise of hope and joy!
For mighty were the auxiliars which then stood
Upon our side, we who were strong in love!
Bliss was it in that dawn to be alive,
But to be young was very heaven!—Oh! times,
In which the meagre, stale, forbidding ways
Of custom, law, and statute, took at once

The attraction of a country in romance!
When Reason seemed the most to assert her rights,
When most intent on making of herself
A prime Enchantress—to assist the work
Which then was going forward in her name!
Not favoured spots alone, but the whole earth,
The beauty wore of promise, that which sets
(As at some moments might not be unfelt
Among the bowers of paradise itself)
The budding rose above the rose full blown.
What temper at the prospect did not wake
To happiness unthought of? The inert
Were roused, and lively natures rapt away!
They who had fed their childhood upon dreams,
The playfellows of fancy, who had made
All powers of swiftness, subtilty, and strength
Their ministers,—who in lordly wise had stirred
Among the grandest objects of the sense,
And dealt with whatsoever they found there
As if they had within some lurking right
To wield it;—they, too, who, of gentle mood,
Had watched all gentle motions, and to these
Had fitted their own thoughts, schemers more mild,
And in the region of their peaceful selves;—
Now was it that *both* found, the meek and lofty
Did both find, helpers to their heart's desire,
And stuff at hand, plastic as they could wish;
Were called upon to exercise their skill,
Not in Utopia, subterranean fields,
Or some secreted island, Heaven knows where!
But in the very world, which is the world
Of all of us,—the place where in the end
We find our happiness, or not at all!

QUESTIONS

1. Whose viewpoint of the French revolution does Wordsworth give here?
2. What is romantic in his interpretation of the revolution?

The Solitary Reaper

Behold her, single in the field,
Yon solitary Highland Lass!
Reaping and singing by herself;
Stop here, or gently pass!

Alone she cuts and binds the grain,
And sings a melancholy strain;
O listen! for the Vale profound
Is overflowing with the sound.

No Nightingale did ever chaunt
More welcome notes to weary bands
Of travellers in some shady haunt,
Among Arabian sands:
A voice so thrilling ne'er was heard
In spring-time from the Cuckoo-bird,
Breaking the silence of the seas
Among the farthest Hebrides.

Will no one tell me what she sings?—
Perhaps the plaintive numbers flow
For old, unhappy, far-off things,
And battles long ago:
Or is it some more humble lay,
Familiar matter of to-day?
Some natural sorrow, loss, or pain,
That has been, and may be again?

Whate'er the theme, the Maiden sang
As if her song could have no ending;
I saw her singing at her work,
And o'er the sickle bending;—
I listened, motionless and still;
And, as I mounted up the hill,
The music in my heart I bore,
Long after it was heard no more.

Lines

COMPOSED A FEW MILES ABOVE
TINTERN ABBEY ON REVISITING THE
BANKS OF THE WYE DURING A TOUR,
JULY 13, 1798[1]

Five years have passed; five summers, with the
    length
Of five long winters! and again I hear
These waters, rolling from their mountain-springs
With a soft inland murmur. Once again

---

[1] Wordsworth wrote this poem at the age of twenty-eight; he had
first visited the ruins of the medieval abbey five years earlier
while on a solitary walking tour.

Do I behold these steep and lofty cliffs,
That on a wild secluded scene impress
Thoughts of more deep seclusion; and connect
The landscape with the quiet of the sky.
The day is come when I again repose
Here, under this dark sycamore, and view
These plots of cottage-ground, these orchard tufts,
Which at this season, with their unripe fruits,
Are clad in one green hue, and lose themselves
'Mid groves and copses. Once again I see
These hedge-rows, hardly hedge-rows, little lines
Of sportive wood run wild: these pastoral farms,
Green to the very door; and wreaths of smoke
Sent up, in silence, from among the trees!
With some uncertain notice, as might seem
Of vagrant dwellers in the houseless woods,
Or of some hermit's cave, where by his fire
The hermit sits alone.
                    These beauteous forms,
Through a long absence, have not been to me
As is a landscape to a blind man's eye;
But oft, in lonely rooms, and 'mid the din
Of towns and cities, I have owed to them,
In hours of weariness, sensations sweet,
Felt in the blood, and felt along the heart;
And passing even into my purer mind,
With tranquil restoration—feelings too
Of unremembered pleasure: such, perhaps,
As have no slight or trivial influence
On that best portion of a good man's life,
His little, nameless, unremembered acts
Of kindness and of love. Nor less, I trust,
To them I may have owed another gift,
Of aspect more sublime; that blessèd mood,
In which the burthen of the mystery,
In which the heavy and the weary weight
Of all this unintelligible world,
Is lightened—that serene and blessèd mood,
In which the affections gently lead us on—
Until, the breath of this corporeal frame
And even the motion of our human blood
Almost suspended, we are laid asleep
In body, and become a living soul;
While with an eye made quiet by the power
Of harmony, and the deep power of joy,
We see into the life of things.
                            If this

Be but a vain belief, yet, oh! how oft—
In darkness and amid the many shapes
Of joyless daylight; when the fretful stir
Unprofitable, and the fever of the world,
Have hung upon the beatings of my heart—
How oft, in spirit, have I turned to thee,
O sylvan Wye! thou wanderer through the woods,
How often has my spirit turned to thee!

   And now, with gleams of half-extinguished
      thought,
With many recognitions dim and faint,
And somewhat of a sad perplexity,
The picture of the mind revives again;
While here I stand, not only with the sense
Of present pleasure, but with pleasing thoughts
That in this moment there is life and food
For future years. And so I dare to hope,
Though changed, no doubt, from what I was when
      first
I came among these hills; when like a roe
I bounded o'er the mountains, by the sides
Of the deep rivers, and the lonely streams,
Wherever nature led: more like a man
Flying from something that he dreads than one
Who sought the thing he loved. For nature then
(The coarser pleasures of my boyish days,
And their glad animal movements all gone by)
To me was all in all—I cannot paint
What then I was. The sounding cataract
Haunted me like a passion; the tall rock,
The mountain, and the deep and gloomy wood,
Their colors and their forms, were then to me
An appetite; a feeling and a love,
That had no need of a remoter charm,
By thought supplied, nor any interest
Unborrowed from the eye. That time is past,
And all its aching joys are now no more,
And all its dizzy raptures. Not for this
Faint I, nor mourn nor murmur; other gifts
Have followed; for such loss, I would believe,
Abundant recompense. For I have learned
To look on nature, not as in the hour
Of thoughtless youth; but hearing oftentimes
The still, sad music of humanity,
Nor harsh nor grating, though of ample power
To chasten and subdue. And I have felt

A presence that disturbs me with the joy
Of elevated thoughts; a sense sublime
Of something far more deeply interfused,
Whose dwelling is the light of setting suns,
And the round ocean and the living air,
And the blue sky, and in the mind of man:
A motion and a spirit, that impels
All thinking things, all objects of all thought,
And rolls through all things. Therefore am I still
A lover of the meadows and the woods
And mountains; and of all that we behold
From this green earth; of all the mighty world
Of eye, and ear—both what they half create,
And what perceive; well pleased to recognize
In nature and the language of the sense
The anchor of my purest thoughts, the nurse,
The guide, the guardian of my heart, and soul
Of all my moral being
               Nor perchance,
If I were not thus taught, should I the more
Suffer my genial spirits to decay:
For thou art with me here upon the banks
Of this fair river; thou my dearest Friend,[2]
My dear, dear Friend; and in thy voice I catch
The language of my former heart, and read
My former pleasures in the shooting lights
Of thy wild eyes. Oh! yet a little while
May I behold in thee what I was once,
My dear, dear Sister! and this prayer I make,
Knowing that Nature never did betray
The heart that loved her; 'tis her privilege,
Through all the years of this our life, to lead
From joy to joy: for she can so inform
The mind that is within us, so impress
With quietness and beauty, and so feed
With lofty thoughts, that neither evil tongues,
Rash judgments, nor the sneers of selfish men,
Nor greetings where no kindness is, nor all
The dreary intercourse of daily life,
Shall e'er prevail against us, or disturb
Our cheerful faith that all which we behold
Is full of blessings. Therefore let the moon
Shine on thee in thy solitary walk;
And let the misty mountain-winds be free
To blow against thee: and, in after years,

---

[2]His sister Dorothy.

When these wild ecstasies shall be matured
Into a sober pleasure; when thy mind
Shall be a mansion for all lovely forms,
Thy memory be as a dwelling-place
For all sweet sounds and harmonies; oh! then,
If solitude, or fear, or pain, or grief,
Should be thy portion, with what healing thoughts
Of tender joy wilt thou remember me,
And these my exhortations! Nor, perchance—
If I should be where I no more can hear
Thy voice, nor catch from thy wild eyes these
        gleams
Of past existence—wilt thou then forget
That on the banks of this delightful stream
We stood together; and that I, so long
A worshiper of Nature, hither came
Unwearied in that service; rather say
With warmer love—oh! with far deeper zeal
Of holier love. Nor wilt thou then forget,
That after many wanderings, many years
Of absence, these steep woods and lofty cliffs,
And this green pastoral landscape, were to me
More dear, both for themselves and for thy sake!

QUESTIONS

1. Find all of the places with the word *nature* in the poem. Does it always have the same meaning? How would you define Wordsworth's conception of nature?
2. How does the poet describe the moral effect that nature has on him?
3. With what images does he convey the differences between his present and former selves?
4. What is the role of his sister in the poem?
5. Do you find any other points of comparison with Constable? What are the different processes that a painter and a poet must go through to render a landscape?

GEORGE GORDON, LORD BYRON (1788–1824)

Prometheus

I

Titan! to whose immortal eyes
    The sufferings of mortality,

Seen in their sad reality,
Were not as things that gods despise;
What was thy pity's recompense?
A silent suffering, and intense;
The rock, the vulture, and the chain,
All that the proud can feel of pain,
The agony they do not show,
The suffocating sense of woe,
    Which speaks but in its loneliness,
And then is jealous lest the sky
Should have a listener, nor will sigh
    Until its voice is echoless.

II

Titan! to thee the strife was given
    Between the suffering and the will,
    Which torture where they cannot kill;
And the inexorable Heaven,
And the deaf tyranny of Fate,
The ruling principle of Hate,
Which for its pleasure doth create
The things it may annihilate,
Refused thee even the boon to die:
The wretched gift eternity
Was thine—and thou hast borne it well.
All that the Thunderer wrung from thee
Was but the menace which flung back
On him the torments of thy rack;
The fate thou didst so well foresee,
But would not to appease him tell;
And in thy Silence was his Sentence,
And in his Soul a vain repentance,
And evil dread so ill dissembled,
That in his hand the lightnings trembled.

III

Thy Godlike crime was to be kind,
    To render with thy precepts less
    The sum of human wretchedness,
And strengthen Man with his own mind;
But baffled as thou wert from high,
Still in thy patient energy,
In the endurance, and repulse
    Of thine impenetrable Spirit,
Which Earth and Heaven could not convulse,
    A mighty lesson we inherit:
Thou art a symbol and a sign

To Mortals of their fate and force;
Like thee, Man is in part divine,
    A troubled stream from a pure source;
And Man in portions can foresee
His own funereal destiny;
His wretchedness, and his resistance,
And his sad unallied existence:
To which his Spirit may oppose
Itself—and equal to all woes,
    And a firm will, and a deep sense,
Which even in torture can descry
    Its own concenter'd recompense,
Triumphant where it dares defy,
And making Death a Victory.

QUESTIONS

1. Look up the myth of Prometheus if you are not familiar with it. How has Byron reinterpreted it?
2. What is the *meter* of the verse used here? How
   would you describe the language of the poem? How
   are both appropriate to the subject matter?
3. Of what is Prometheus a "symbol and a sign"? What
   makes him a hero? Would he be a fitting heroic symbol for our times?

On This Day I Complete My Thirty-Sixth Year

MISSOLONGHI,[1] JANUARY 22, 1824

'Tis time this heart should be unmoved,
    Since others it hath ceased to move:
Yet, though I cannot be beloved,
        Still let me love!

My days are in the yellow leaf;
    The flowers and fruits of love are gone;
The worm, the canker, and the grief
        Are mine alone!

---

[1] Town in Greece where Byron had gone to help the Greeks in their
war for independence from Turkey. Less than three months later he
died there.

The fire that on my bosom preys
    Is lone as some volcanic isle;
No torch is kindled at its blaze—
        A funeral pile.

The hope, the fear, the jealous care,
    The exalted portion of the pain
And power of love, I cannot share,
        But wear the chain.

But 'tis not *thus*—and 'tis not *here*—
    Such thoughts should shake my soul, nor *now*,
Where glory decks the hero's bier,
        Or binds his brow.

The sword, the banner, and the field,
    Glory and Greece, around me see!
The Spartan, born upon his shield,
        Was not more free.

Awake! (not Greece—she *is* awake!)
    Awake, my spirit! Think through *whom*
Thy life-blood tracks its parent lake,
        And then strike home!

Tread those reviving passions down,
    Unworthy manhood!—unto thee
Indifferent should the smile or frown
        Of beauty be.

If thou regrett'st thy youth, *why live?*
    The land of honorable death
Is here:—up to the field, and give
        Away thy breath!

Seek out—less often sought than found—
    A soldier's grave, for thee the best;
Then look around, and choose thy ground,
        And take thy rest.

QUESTIONS

1. What two typically romantic states of mind does Byron contrast in this poem?
2. How is political commitment understood as individual salvation?

JOHN KEATS (1795–1821)

Ode to a Nightingale

MY HEART aches, and a drowsy numbness pains
  My sense, as though of hemlock[1] I had drunk,
Or emptied some dull opiate to the drains
  One minute past, and Lethe-wards[2] had sunk:
'Tis not through envy of thy happy lot,
  But being too happy in thy happiness,—
    That thou, light-winged Dryad of the trees,
      In some melodious plot
Of beechen green, and shadows numberless,
  Singest of summer in full-throated ease.

O for a draught of vintage, that hath been
  Cool'd a long age in the deep-delved earth,
Tasting of Flora[3] and the country-green,
  Dance, and Provençal song,[4] and sun-burnt mirth!
O for a beaker full of the warm South,[5]
  Full of the true, the blushful Hippocrene,[6]
    With beaded bubbles winking at the brim,
      And purple-stained mouth;
That I might drink, and leave the world unseen,
  And with thee fade away into the forest dim:

Fade far away, dissolve, and quite forget
  What thou among the leaves hast never known,
The weariness, the fever, and the fret
  Here, where men sit and hear each other groan;
Where palsy shakes a few, sad, last grey hairs,
  Where youth grows pale, and spectre-thin, and
    dies;
      Where but to think is to be full of sorrow
        And leaden-eyed despairs;
Where beauty cannot keep her lustrous eyes,
  Or new Love pine at them beyond to-morrow.

Away! away! for I will fly to thee,
  Not charioted by Bacchus and his pards,

But on the viewless wings of Poesy,
  Though the dull brain perplexes and retards:
Already with thee! tender is the night,
  And haply the Queen-Moon is on her throne,
    Cluster'd around by all her starry Fays;
      But here there is no light,
Save what from heaven is with the breezes blown
  Through verdurous glooms and winding mossy
  ways.

I cannot see what flowers are at my feet,
  Nor what soft incense hangs upon the boughs,
But, in embalmed darkness, guess each sweet
  Wherewith the seasonable month endows
The grass, the thicket, and the fruit-tree wild;
  White hawthorn, and the pastoral eglantine;
    Fast-fading violets cover'd up in leaves;
      And mid-May's eldest child,
The coming musk-rose, full of dewy wine,
  The murmurous haunt of flies on summer eves.

Darkling[7] I listen; and for many a time
  I have been half in love with easeful Death,
Call'd him soft names in many a mused rhyme,
  To take into the air my quiet breath;
Now more than ever seems it rich to die,
  To cease upon the midnight with no pain,
    While thou art pouring forth thy soul abroad
      In such an ecstasy!
Still wouldst thou sing, and I have ears in vain—
  To thy high requiem become a sod.

Thou wast not born for death, immortal Bird!
  No hungry generations tread thee down;
The voice I hear this passing night was heard
  In ancient days by emperor and clown:
Perhaps the self-same song that found a path
  Through the sad heart of Ruth, when, sick for
  home,
    She stood in tears amid the alien corn;
      The same that oft-times hath
Charm'd magic casements, opening on the foam
  Of perilous seas, in faery lands forlorn.

Forlorn! the very word is like a bell
  To toll me back from thee to my sole self.

---

[1] A poison.
[2] Towards Lethe, the river of forgetfulness in the classical underworld.
[3] Goddess of flowers and spring. (See Botticelli's *Primavera*, Vol. I,
  pp. 308–9 and 330 and Color Plate VIII.)
[4] Troubadour songs from southern France.
[5] Wine.
[6] Fountain of the Muses.

---

[7] As it grows dark.

Adieu! the fancy cannot cheat so well
    As she is famed to do, deceiving elf.
Adieu! adieu! thy plaintive anthem fades
    Past the near meadows, over the still stream,
        Up the hill-side; and now 'tis buried deep
            In the next valley-glades:
Was it a vision, or a waking dream?
    Fled is that music:—do I wake or sleep?

QUESTIONS

1. What is the feeling of the poet toward the nightingale? What attractions does it represent?
2. What different sensations (tactile, visual, auditory,
   and so forth) are represented in the poem, and how?
3. Compare Keats' attitudes toward and representation
   of nature with Wordsworth's.
4. Compare Keats' sensuous expression of colors and
   textures to Turner's (see Color Plate XIV).

WALT WHITMAN (1819–1892)

From *Song of Myself*

1

I celebrate myself, and sing myself,
And what I assume you shall assume,
For every atom belonging to me as good belongs to
    you.

I loafe and invite my soul,
I lean and loafe at my ease observing a spear of
    summer grass.

My tongue, every atom of my blood, form'd from
    this soil, this air,
Born here of parents born here from parents the
    same, and their parents the same,
I, now thirty-seven years old in perfect health begin,
Hoping to cease not till death.

Creeds and schools in abeyance,
Retiring back a while sufficed at what they are, but
    never forgotten,
I harbor for good or bad, I permit to speak at every
    hazard,
Nature without check with original energy.

24

Walt Whitman, a kosmos, of Manhattan the son,
Turbulent, fleshy, sensual, eating, drinking and
        breeding,
No sentimentalist, no stander above men and
        women or apart from them,
No more modest than immodest.

Unscrew the locks from the doors!
Unscrew the doors themselves from their jambs!

Whoever degrades another degrades me,
And whatever is done or said returns at last to me.

Through me the afflatus surging and surging,
    through me the current and index.

I speak the pass-word primeval, I give the sign of
        democracy,
By God! I will accept nothing which all cannot have
        their counterpart of on the same terms.

Through me many long dumb voices,
Voices of the interminable generation of prisoners
        and slaves,
Voices of the diseas'd and despairing and of thieves
        and dwarfs,
Voices of cycles of preparation and accretion,
And of the threads that connect the stars, and of
        wombs and of the father-stuff,
And of the rights of them the others are down upon,
Of the deform'd, trivial, flat, foolish, despised,
Fog in the air, beetles rolling balls of dung.

Through me forbidden voices,
Voices of sexes and lusts, voices veil'd and I remove
        the veil,
Voices indecent by me clarified and transfigur'd.

I do not press my fingers across my mouth,
I keep as delicate around the bowels as around the
        head and heart,
Copulation is no more rank to me than death is.

I believe in the flesh and the appetites,
Seeing, hearing, feeling, are miracles, and each part
    and tag of me is a miracle.

Divine am I inside and out, and I make holy
    whatever I touch or am touch'd from,
The scent of these arm-pits aroma finer than prayer,
This head more than churches, bibles, and all the
    creeds.

If I worship one thing more than another it shall be
    the spread of my own body, or any part of it,
Translucent mould of me it shall be you!
Shaded ledges and rests it shall be you!
Firm masculine colter it shall be you!
Whatever goes to the tilth of me it shall be you!
You my rich blood! your milky stream pale
    strippings of my life!
Breast that presses against other breasts it shall be you!
My brain it shall be your occult convolutions!
Root of wash'd sweet-flag! timorous pond-snipe! nest
    of guarded duplicate eggs! it shall be you!
Mix'd tussled hay of head, beard, brawn, it shall be
    you!
Trickling sap of maple, fibre of manly wheat, it shall
    be you!
Sun so generous it shall be you!
Vapors lighting and shading my face it shall be you!
You sweaty brooks and dews it shall be you!
Winds whose soft-trickling genitals rub against me it
    shall be you!
Broad muscular fields, branches of live oak, loving
    lounger in my winding paths, it shall be you!
Hands I have taken, face I have kiss'd, mortal I have
    ever touch'd, it shall be you

I dote on myself, there is that lot of me and all so
    luscious,
Each moment and whatever happens thrills me with
    joy,
I cannot tell how my ankles bend, nor whence the
    cause of my faintest wish,
Nor the cause of the friendship I emit, nor the cause
    of the friendship I take again.

That I walk up my stoop, I pause to consider if it
    really be,

A morning-glory at my window satisfies me more
    than the metaphysics of books.
To behold the day-break!
The little light fades the immense and diaphanous
    shadows,
The air tastes good to my palate.

Hefts of the moving world at innocent gambols
    silently rising, freshly exuding,
Scooting obliquely high and low.

Something I cannot see puts upward libidinous
    prongs,
Seas of bright juice suffuse heaven.

The earth by the sky staid with, the daily close of
    their junction,
The heav'd challenge from the east that moment
    over my head,
The mocking taunt, See then whether you shall be
    master!

QUESTIONS

1. Why and how does Whitman "celebrate" and "sing"
   himself? In what different connections does he view
   the self?
2. In what sense is this a democratic poem?
3. What "unpoetic" subject matters does Whitman
   treat? How might he have shocked his readers?
4. Whitman was the first American poet to make extensive use of *free verse*, that is, lines that are not
   predetermined by any metrical scheme. Why is free
   verse appropriate to this poem?
5. Can you find patterns of sound and rhythms in this
   verse? What is their effect?
6. What seems to be Whitman's idea of his role as a
   poet?

EMILY DICKINSON (1830-1886)

I

A narrow fellow in the grass
Occasionally rides;
You may have met him,—did you not?
His notice sudden is.

The grass divides as with a comb,
A spotted shaft is seen;
And then it closes at your feet
And opens further on.

He likes a boggy acre,
A floor too cool for corn.
Yet when a child, and barefoot,
I more than once, at morn,

Have passed, I thought, a whip-lash
Unbraiding in the sun,—
When, stooping to secure it,
It wrinkled, and was gone.

Several of nature's people
I know, and they know me;
I feel for them a transport
Of cordiality;

But never met this fellow,
Attended or alone,
Without a tighter breathing,
And zero at the bone.

II

The leaves, like women, interchange
  Sagacious confidence;
Somewhat of nods, and somewhat of
  Portentous inference,

The parties in both cases
  Enjoining secrecy,—
Inviolable compact
  To notoriety.

III

I dreaded that first robin so,
But he is mastered now,
And I'm accustomed to him grown,—
He hurts a little, though.

I thought if I could only live
Till that first shout got by,
Not all pianos in the woods
Had power to mangle me.

I dared not meet the daffodils,
For fear their yellow gown
Would pierce me with a fashion
So foreign to my own.

I wished the grass would hurry,
So when 'twas time to see,
He'd be too tall, the tallest one
Could stretch to look at me.

I could not bear the bees should come,
I wished they'd stay away
In those dim countries where they go:
What word had they for me?

They're here, though; not a creature failed,
No blossom stayed away
In gentle deference to me,
The Queen of Calvary.

Each one salutes me as he goes,
And I my childish plumes
Lift, in bereaved acknowledgment
Of their unthinking drums.

IV

I'm nobody! Who are you?
Are you nobody, too?
Then there's a pair of us—don't tell!
They'd banish us, you know.

How dreary to be somebody!
How public, like a frog
To tell your name the livelong day
To an admiring bog!

QUESTIONS

1. How would you describe Emily Dickinson's view of nature? Compare it to that of Wordsworth, Keats, and Whitman.
2. How, if at all, does the fact that Emily Dickinson is a woman influence her perception of individuality?

Art: Revolution, Individualism, and Nature

We have seen how the painter David turned from neoclassicism to portray Napoleon as a romantic hero. The revolutionary ideals of liberty, equality, and fraternity had a profound influence on developing romanticism in the visual arts as in literature. There were also inventions and advances that affected art internally. The development of photography; the scientific study of light, color, and perception; and the opening of Japan and China to the Western world all had immediate repercussions in painting, sculpture, and the graphic arts.

Architecture was challenged by the growing diversification of life and human needs. Commissions for palaces and churches were replaced by industrial, commercial, and transportation needs. Hospitals, housing, and prisons were demanded as never before. The manufacture of iron, then steel, glass, and finally concrete provided new building possibilities and problems without precedent. Both the private individual and governments experienced the stress of a burgeoning economy and rapidly increasing population. Systems of transportation, water, waste disposal, marketing, and housing taxed cities beyond their limits, and the vast slum became a familiar reality.

Not only were the artist and architect challenged by these things but also the systems of education and patronage experienced pressures that were either absorbed or ignored. In France the academy that had produced David and his pupils also produced a number of artists who revolted against the doctrines of Davidian classicism; they began searching for a form and content expressive of revolutionary and romantic ideals. Three painters who typify, in different ways, the search for new forms and means of expression are the Spaniard Francisco Goya; the Frenchman Eugene Delacroix; and the Englishman J.M.W. Turner.

Francisco Goya (1746–1828) Goya was a successful and celebrated painter in the court of Charles IV. He had begun his career as a designer of tapestries whose subjects, the amusements of the court life, document the end of an era with elegance and beauty. There was, however, a toughness and tenacity about Goya that was first revealed in a series of etchings, *Los Caprichos*

26-4   Goya, *The Sleep of Reason Produces Monsters.* (Courtesy Museum of Fine Arts, Boston. Bequest of William P. Babcock)

(*Human Follies*), executed in 1795–1796. Of this collection perhaps the most famous is one of the first, *The Sleep of Reason Produces Monsters* (Fig. 26-4). The title is a complex one. A sleeping man dreams of horrible winged creatures who hover about his head. Reason, when she flees, permits the appearance of the dark, demonic undisciplined self; but a rigid and inflexible Reason produces the monsters of revolution, too. Technically Goya draws on traditional conventions but transforms them into an awful assemblage of shadow and texture.

While serving as the court painter, he experienced the horror of the French invasion of Spain with its guerrilla warfare. Spanish royalists fought the invaders, republicans fought the royalists, and the invaders and the ensuing chaos reduced the populace to a terror-filled mob. No longer reserved for armies and generals,

26-5 Goya, *The Disasters of War; I Saw This.* (Courtesy of the Boston Public Library, Print Department)

26-7 Goya, *The Shootings of the Third of May, 1808.*

war decimated the entire population. There was looting, rape, pillage, and plunder. These years are recorded in the etchings *The Disasters of War*. Probably made from scenes he witnessed, the pictures reveal violence, brutality, and man's monstrous inhumanity. Figure 26-5, *I Saw This*, shows a family wrenched apart. In Figure 26-6 a man stumbles on a tumbled mass of bodies; the sight and smell make him retch.

After the war Goya was commissioned to commemorate the events of May 2 and 3, 1808, when the citizenry of Madrid had attacked the soldiers of Napoleon in the Puerta del Sol. That night and the next day citizens were rounded up and summarily shot in a gesture of reprisal. *The Shootings of the Third of May, 1808* is among the most brilliant images that Goya created (Fig. 26-7). The huddled citizens, unarmed and frightened, and the anonymous rank of surging soldiery spotlighted by a flaring lamp resemble a nightmare. The open mouths and astonished faces, the blood and gore are without precedent. The loosely handled paint is rapidly brushed, while the earthy tones, cream, and reds focus our eyes into the center foreground, where the pose of the figure with upraised arms alludes to Christ and an attitude of innocence. This is a court of no resort; no pleading protects women or children. Death is stark, awful, ignominious. The romantic revolt against tyranny is the theme, but Napoleon is the villain rather than the hero.

Eugène Delacroix (1798–1863) Goya's work was known in France and was not without influence. But for the French romantic painter Eugène Delacroix, considered a revolutionary by his peers and teachers, war's terrifying nature was still susceptible to the romanticizing distance of place, if not time. Delacroix's painting *The Massacres of Scios* (Fig. 26-8) recounts an event similar in nature to the murders in Madrid, but the event is presented as a scene from a poetic drama. The figures are drawn from Renaissance types: their deaths seem to be those of passive resignation. There is little immediate violence. The men are handsome and noble, the women are splendidly beautiful in old age or youth, the costumes are magnificent, and the horse is glorious. Yet Delacroix was condemned for his intensity of presentation and for the looseness of his brilliant paint. Compared to the hard coldness of David and his follow-

26-8 Delacroix, *The Massacres of Scios*. (Louvre, Paris/photo © ARCH. PHOT. PARIS—S.P.A.D.E.M., 1980)

ers, Delacroix's work was considered a direct threat to the classicism of the academy.

In his painting *Liberty at the Barricades* (Fig. 26-9), a scene from the 1830 revolution, Delacroix uses a bare-breasted female to personify Liberty. The diagonal composition and the piled-up bodies recall Rubens and the monumental compositions of the baroque. Nevertheless, Delacroix, who painted nudes, animals, and scenes from the Bible, mythology, and the tales of Sir Walter Scott, exemplifies a romantic response to the strictures of the past. His emotion-filled canvases, brilliant in color and heavy with paint, are his attempt to make an art in response to his personal temperament and imagination.

Baudelaire, the French poet and critic, praised Delacroix for his imagination and energy, finding in his work an individual temperament given free reign to speak directly to the emotions and dreams of others. Yet Delacroix's work seems reserved and controlled when compared to the elemental passion tapped in Goya's work.

We can understand this only when we remember

26-9 Delacroix, *Liberty at the Barricades. (Louvre, Paris/photo © ARCH. PHOT. PARIS—S.P.A.D.E.M., 1980)*

that Delacroix revered the art of the past, seeking to preserve it while giving it new values, whereas Goya seemed absolutely unable to incorporate his feelings and ideas in the old traditions. It is this split between reverence for the past and a passion for new ways of thinking, seeing, and feeling that characterizes the romantic period.

Delacroix drew on the images of the past as sources for form and for inspiration. He also used photographs as a means to study poses and gestures, and he developed theories about color and light that influenced his work enormously. But his interest was nevertheless in the narrative, which by its very nature depends on human figures as the *dramatis personae.*

Other painters looked at the natural world and found there the inspiration for new approaches to painting and to the landscape. In France, Corot, Millet, and others sought nature in the farmland and the forests of Barbizon. In England, J.M.W. Turner, like John Constable (see pp. 227–28), drew revolutionary ideas from his observations of nature.

J.M.W. Turner (1775–1851) Joseph Mallord William Turner began by painting the studied landscapes that one associates with early-nineteenth-century academic work, but even those showed an intense interest in light (Fig. 26-10). By the 1840s, however, Turner had transformed the light, air, and motion of the observed world into a visibly fragmented and energy-charged painted surface. *Rain, Steam and Speed, The Great Western Railway* (Color Plate XIV), painted in 1845, was, according to Turner, a literal account of an event—a train in a snow storm—that Turner himself had witnessed. However, it was not accepted by the public, who considered the thin veils of paint "tinted steam". Untroubled by popular opinion, Turner continued to explore similar subjects—sometimes with a narrative or moral, but more often concentrating on light. The light of the sun was energy creating, and countless fluid, light-filled and layered canvases convey an almost tragic obsession that is mitigated only by Turner's success in achieving a sense of the fluctuating, ephemeral world of light that his studies of nature re-

26-10   J.M.W. Turner, *Mortlake Terrace: Early Summer Morning.* (The Frick Collection)

vealed. Not until the Impressionists—indeed, many would argue, not until the completely nonobjective paintings of the twentieth century—have there been other works similar enough to Turner's to form a basis for comparison. But he, like Constable, took his inspiration from the natural, external world, not from the internal world of the mind or from the hermetic world of paintings about painting, which was to become characteristic of the "romanticism" of the twentieth century.

27

The Romantic Woman
And Romantic Love

❧

We saw in the last chapter how the ideals of revolution and individualism and the idealization of "nature" and "natural man" influenced the arts in the romantic period. Another aspect of the complex romantic sensibility was its fervent interest in questions regarding the nature of women and the nature of love. In the romantic era—in life as well as in art—women undoubtedly assumed a new importance, a role more influential than in any previous cultural epoch in the West. Yet the positions assumed by women in society and as artists and the images of women in art created by men seem, from our modern point of view, contradictory. Liberated and autonomous, predatory and dangerous, domestic and subservient, ethereal and mystical; all are aspects of the image of romantic woman.

Pre-Romantic Feminism: Mary Wollstonecraft (1759–1797)

We have seen that aristocratic and some upper middle-class women played an influential role in the salons and other intellectual circles of eighteenth-century society, particularly in France. It is clear, however, that the educated woman who considered herself equal to men remained the exception rather than the rule and that in general women were expected to limit their education to domestic arts along with a few "accomplishments," such as singing, to interest themselves primarily in fashion, gossip, and flirtation, and not to meddle in the affairs of men. Rousseau, the radical thinker whose ideas challenged so many of the fundamental assumptions of his society, remained fundamentally conventional in his attitudes toward women. In his treatise on education entitled *Emile,* in which he proposes many of the theories that underlie modern ideas on "progressive" education with regard to boys, he maintains that women's role is to be subservient to men and that women's education should be structured accordingly:

> For this reason the education of women should always be relative to men. To please, to be useful to us, to make us love and esteem them, to educate us when young, and take care of us when grown up, to advise us, to console us, to render our lives easy and agreeable—these are the duties of women at all times, and what they should be taught in their infancy.[1]

Despite the fact that Rousseau's attitude represented the norm, the eighteenth century witnessed several challenges to the inferior status of women. In England, Lady Mary Wortley, whose pen name was "Sophia," referred to women's social position as one of "slaves" and argued for better education and more independence for her sex. The rhetoric of the French Revolution supplied fuel for the feminist fire. In France, Olympe de Gouges attempted to extend the Revolution's doctrine of the Rights of Man by publishing a pamphlet entitled *Declaration of the Rights of Woman and of the Female Citizen* in 1791. Advocates for better education for

women included the philosophe Condorcet, the English writer Catherine Macaulay, and Mary Wollstonecraft.

Wollstonecraft's *A Vindication of the Rights of Woman,* published in 1792, in many way prefigures some of the feminist ideas that have become common currency in our own time. A middle-class woman who shared the Enlightenment thinkers' disdain for the "decadent" aristocracy, Wollstonecraft worked as a governess and a teacher, attempted to found a school, and lived for a while in Paris, where she fell in love with an American. She eventually married her old friend, the English social thinker William Godwin, and had with him a daughter, Mary Wollstonecraft Godwin. She died of "childbed fever" at the age of thirty-six. Wollstonecraft's stated aim in her treatise was "to persuade women to endeavour to acquire strength, both of mind and body. . . . " The chapter reprinted here is representative in its incorporation of revolutionary ideas, its rather dismal portrayal of the lives of contemporary women, and its advocacy of both domestic virtue and educational and professional achievement.

MARY WOLLSTONECRAFT

From *A Vindication of the Rights of Woman*

CHAPTER IX

OF THE PERNICIOUS EFFECTS WHICH ARISE FROM THE UNNATURAL DISTINCTIONS ESTABLISHED IN SOCIETY

From the respect paid to property flow, as from a poisoned fountain, most of the evils and vices which render this world such a dreary scene to the contemplative mind. For it is in the most polished society that noisome reptiles and venomous serpents lurk under the rank herbage; and there is voluptuousness pampered by the still sultry air, which relaxes every good disposition before it ripens into virtue.

One class presses on another; for all are aiming to procure respect on account of their property: and property, once gained, will procure the respect due only to

---

[1] Jean-Jacques Rousseau, *L'Emile or A Treatise on Education,* ed. W. H. Payne (New York and London, 1906), p. 263.

talents and virtue. Men neglect the duties incumbent on man, yet are treated like demi-gods; religion is also separated from morality by a ceremonial veil, yet men wonder that the world is almost, literally speaking, a den of sharpers or oppressors.

There is a homely proverb, which speaks a shrewd truth, that whoever the devil finds idle he will employ. And what but habitual idleness can hereditary wealth and titles produce? For man is so constituted that he can only attain a proper use of his faculties by exercising them, and will not exercise them unless necessity, of some kind, first set the wheels in motion. Virtue likewise can only be acquired by the discharge of relative duties; but the importance of these sacred duties will scarcely be felt by the being who is cajoled out of his humanity by the flattery of sycophants. There must be more equality established in society, or morality will never gain ground, and this virtuous equality will not rest firmly even when founded on a rock, if one half of mankind be chained to its bottom by fate, for they will be continually undermining it through ignorance or pride.

It is vain to expect virtue from women till they are, in some degree, independent of men; nay, it is vain to expect that strength of natural affection, which would make them good wives and mothers. Whilst they are absolutely dependent on their husbands they will be cunning, mean, and selfish, and the men who can be gratified by the fawning fondness of spaniel-like affection, have not much delicacy, for love is not to be bought, in any sense of the words, its silken wings are instantly shrivelled up when any thing beside a return in kind is sought. Yet whilst wealth enervates men; and women live, as it were, by their personal charms, how can we expect them to discharge those ennobling duties which equally require exertion and self-denial. Hereditary property sophisticates[1] the mind, and the unfortunate victims to it, if I may so express myself, swathed from their birth, seldom exert the locomotive faculty of body or mind; and, thus viewing every thing through one medium, and that a false one, they are unable to discern in what true merit and happiness consist. False, indeed, must be the light when the drap-

ery of situation hides the man, and makes him stalk in masquerade, dragging from one scene of dissipation to another the nerveless limbs that hang with stupid listlessness, and rolling round the vacant eye which plainly tells us that there is no mind at home.

I mean, therefore, to infer that the society is not properly organized which does not compel men and women to discharge their respective duties, by making it the only way to acquire that countenance from their fellow-creatures, which every human being wishes some way to attain. The respect, consequently, which is paid to wealth and mere personal charms, is a true north-east blast, that blights the tender blossoms of affection and virtue. Nature has wisely attached affections to duties, to sweeten toil, and to give that vigour to the exertions of reason which only the heart can give. But, the affection which is put on merely because it is the appropriated insignia of a certain character, when its duties are not fulfilled, is one of the empty compliments which vice and folly are obliged to pay to virtue and the real nature of things.

To illustrate my opinion, I need only observe, that when a woman is admired for her beauty, and suffers herself to be so far intoxicated by the admiration she receives, as to neglect to discharge the indispensable duty of a mother, she sins against herself by neglecting to cultivate an affection that would equally tend to make her useful and happy. True happiness, I mean all the contentment, and virtuous satisfaction, that can be snatched in this imperfect state, must arise from well regulated affections; and an affection includes a duty. Men are not aware of the misery they cause, and the vicious weakness they cherish, by only inciting women to render themselves pleasing; they do not consider that they thus make natural and artificial duties clash, by sacrificing the comfort and respectability of a woman's life to voluptuous notions of beauty, when in nature they all harmonize.

Cold would be the heart of a husband, were he not rendered unnatural by early debauchery, who did not feel more delight at seeing his child suckled by its mother, than the most artful wanton tricks could ever raise; yet this natural way of cementing the matrimonial tie, and twisting esteem with fonder recollections, wealth leads women to spurn. To preserve their beauty, and wear the flowery crown of the day, which gives

---

[1] Corrupts.

them a kind of right to reign for a short time over the sex, they neglect to stamp impressions on their husbands' hearts, that would be remembered with more tenderness when the snow on the head began to chill the bosom, than even their virgin charms. The maternal solicitude of a reasonable affectionate woman is very interesting, and the chastened dignity with which a mother returns the caresses that she and her child receive from a father who has been fulfilling the serious duties of his station, is not only a respectable, but a beautiful sight. So singular, indeed, are my feelings, and I have endeavoured not to catch factitious ones, that after having been fatigued with the sight of insipid grandeur and the slavish ceremonies that with cumberous pomp supplied the place of domestic affections, I have turned to some other scene to relieve my eye by resting it on the refreshing green every where scattered by nature. I have then viewed with pleasure a woman nursing her children, and discharging the duties of her station with, perhaps, merely a servant maid to take off her hands the servile part of the household business. I have seen her prepare herself and children, with only the luxury of cleanliness, to receive her husband, who returning weary home in the evening found smiling babes and a clean hearth. My heart has loitered in the midst of the group, and has even throbbed with sympathetic emotion, when the scraping of the well known foot has raised a pleasing tumult.

Whilst my benevolence has been gratified by contemplating this artless picture, I have thought that a couple of this description, equally necessary and independent of each other, because each fulfilled the respective duties of their station, possessed all that life could give.—Raised sufficiently above abject poverty not to be obliged to weigh the consequence of every farthing they spend, and having sufficient to prevent their attending to a frigid system of œconomy, which narrows both heart and mind. I declare, so vulgar are my conceptions, that I know not what is wanted to render this the happiest as well as the most respectable situation in the world, but a taste for literature, to throw a little variety and interest into social converse, and some superfluous money to give to the needy and to buy books. For it is not pleasant when the heart is opened by compassion and the head active in arranging plans of usefulness, to have a prim urchin continually

twitching back the elbow to prevent the hand from drawing out an almost empty purse, whispering at the same time some prudential maxim about the priority of justice.

Destructive, however, as riches and inherited honours are to the human character, women are more debased and cramped, if possible, by them, than men, because men may still, in some degree, unfold their faculties by becoming soldiers and statesmen.

As soldiers, I grant, they can now only gather, for the most part, vain glorious laurels, whilst they adjust to a hair the European balance, taking especial care that no bleak northern nook or sound incline the beam. But the days of true heroism are over, when a citizen fought for his country like a Fabricius[2] or a Washington, and then returned to his farm to let his virtuous fervour run in a more placid, but not a less salutary, stream. No, our British heroes are oftener sent from the gaming table than from the plow; and their passions have been rather inflamed by hanging with dumb suspense on the turn of a die, than sublimated by panting after the adventurous march of virtue in the historic page.

The statesman, it is true, might with more propriety quit the Faro Bank, or card-table, to guide the helm, for he has still but to shuffle and trick. The whole system of British politics, if system it may courteously be called, consisting in multiplying dependents and contriving taxes which grind the poor to pamper the rich; thus a war, or any wild goose chace, is, as the vulgar use the phrase, a lucky turn-up of patronage for the minister, whose chief merit is the art of keeping himself in place. It is not necessary then that he should have bowels for[3] the poor, so he can secure for his family the odd trick. Or should some shew of respect, for what is termed with ignorant ostentation an Englishman's birth-right, be expedient to bubble the gruff mastiff that he has to lead by the nose, he can make an empty shew, very safely, by giving his single voice, and suffering his light squadron to file off to the other side. And when a question of humanity is agitated he may dip a sop in the milk of human kindness, to silence Cerberus, and talk of the interest which his heart takes in an attempt to make the earth no longer cry for

---

[2] Roman general (third century B.C.).
[3] Compassion for.

vengeance as it sucks in its children's blood, though his cold hand may at the very moment rivet their chains, by sanctioning the abominable traffick. A minister is no longer a minister, than while he can carry a point, which he is determined to carry.—Yet it is not necessary that a minister should feel like a man, when a bold push might shake his seat.

But, to have done with these episodical observations, let me return to the more specious slavery which chains the very soul of woman, keeping her for ever under the bondage of ignorance.

The preposterous distinctions of rank, which render civilization a curse, by dividing the world between voluptuous tyrants, and cunning envious dependents, corrupt, almost equally, every class of people, because respectability is not attached to the discharge of the relative duties of life, but to the station, and when the duties are not fulfilled the affections cannot gain sufficient strength to fortify the virtue of which they are the natural reward. Still there are some loop-holes out of which a man may creep, and dare to think and act for himself; but for a woman it is an herculean task, because she has difficulties peculiar to her sex to overcome, which require almost superhuman powers.

A truly benevolent legislator always endeavours to make it the interest of each individual to be virtuous; and thus private virtue becoming the cement of public happiness, an orderly whole is consolidated by the tendency of all the parts towards a common centre. But, the private or public virtue of woman is very problematical; for Rousseau, and a numerous list of male writers, insist that she should all her life be subjected to a severe restraint, that of propriety. Why subject her to propriety—blind propriety, if she be capable of acting from a nobler spring, if she be an heir of immortality? Is sugar always to be produced by vital blood? Is one half of the human species, like the poor African slaves, to be subject to prejudices that brutalize them, when principles would be a surer guard, only to sweeten the cup of man? Is not this indirectly to deny woman reason? for a gift is a mockery, if it be unfit for use.

Women are, in common with men, rendered weak and luxurious by the relaxing pleasures which wealth procures; but added to this they are made slaves to their persons, and must render them alluring that man may lend them his reason to guide their tottering steps

aright. Or should they be ambitious, they must govern their tyrants by sinister tricks, for without rights there cannot be any incumbent duties. The laws respecting woman, . . . make an absurd unit of a man and his wife;[4] and then, by the easy transition of only considering him as responsible, she is reduced to a mere cypher.

The being who discharges the duties of its station is independent; and, speaking of women at large, their first duty is to themselves as rational creatures, and the next, in point of importance, as citizens, is that, which includes so many, of a mother. The rank in life which dispenses with their fulfilling this duty necessarily degrades them by making them mere dolls. Or, should they turn to something more important than merely fitting drapery upon a smooth block, their minds are only occupied by some soft platonic attachment; or, the actual management of an intrigue may keep their thoughts in motion; for when they neglect domestic duties, they have it not in their power to take the field and march and countermarch like soldiers, or wrangle in the senate to keep their faculties from rusting.

I know that, as a proof of the inferiority of the sex, Rousseau has exultingly exclaimed, How can they leave the nursery for the camp!—And the camp has by some moralists been termed the school of the most heroic virtues; though, I think, it would puzzle a keen casuist to prove the reasonableness of the greater number of wars that have dubbed heroes. I do not mean to consider this question critically; because, having frequently viewed these freaks of ambition as the first natural mode of civilization, when the ground must be torn up, and the woods cleared by fire and sword, I do not choose to call them pests; but surely the present system of war has little connection with virtue of any denomination, being rather the school of *finesse* and effeminacy, than of fortitude.

Yet, if defensive war, the only justifiable war, in the present advanced state of society, where virtue can shew its face and ripen amidst the rigours which purify the air on the mountain's top, were alone to be adopted as just and glorious, the true heroism of antiquity might again animate female bosoms.—But fair and

---

[4] According to English law at the time, the husband was the only legally responsible person in a family unit.

softly, gentle reader, male or female, do not alarm thyself, for though I have compared the character of a modern soldier with that of a civilized woman, I am not going to advise them to turn their distaff into a musket, though I sincerely wish to see the bayonet converted into a pruning-hook. I only recreated an imagination, fatigued by contemplating the vices and follies which all proceed from a feculent stream of wealth that has muddied the pure rills of natural affection, by supposing that society will some time or other be so constituted, that man must necessarily fulfil the duties of a citizen, or be despised, and that while he was employed in any of the departments of civil life, his wife, also an active citizen, should be equally intent to manage her family, educate her children, and assist her neighbours.

But, to render her really virtuous and useful, she must not, if she discharge her civil duties, want, individually, the protection of civil laws; she must not be dependent on her husband's bounty for her subsistence during his life, or support after his death—for how can a being be generous who has nothing of its own? or, virtuous, who is not free? The wife, in the present state of things, who is faithful to her husband, and neither suckles nor educates her children, scarcely deserves the name of a wife, and has no right to that of a citizen. But take away natural rights, and duties become null.

Women then must be considered as only the wanton solace of men, when they become so weak in mind and body, that they cannot exert themselves, unless to pursue some frothy pleasure, or to invent some frivolous fashion. What can be a more melancholy sight to a thinking mind, than to look into the numerous carriages that drive helter-skelter about this metropolis in a morning full of pale-faced creatures who are flying from themselves. I have often wished, with Dr. Johnson, to place some of them in a little shop with half a dozen children looking up to their languid countenances for support. I am much mistaken, if some latent vigour would not soon give health and spirit to their eyes, and some lines drawn by the exercise of reason on the blank cheeks, which before were only undulated by dimples, might restore lost dignity to the character, or rather enable it to attain the true dignity of its nature. Virtue is not to be acquired even by speculation, much less by the negative supineness that wealth naturally generates.

Besides, when poverty is more disgraceful than even vice, is not morality cut to the quick? Still to avoid misconstruction, though I consider that women in the common walks of life are called to fulfil the duties of wives and mothers, by religion and reason, I cannot help lamenting that women of a superiour cast have not a road open by which they can pursue more extensive plans of usefulness and independence. I may excite laughter, by dropping an hint, which I mean to pursue, some future time, for I really think that women ought to have representatives, instead of being arbitrarily governed without having any direct share allowed them in the deliberations of government.

But, as the whole system of representation is now, in this country, only a convenient handle for despotism, they need not complain, for they are as well represented as a numerous class of hard working mechanics, who pay for the support of royalty when they can scarcely stop their children's mouths with bread. How are they represented whose very sweat supports the splendid stud of an heir apparent, or varnishes the chariot of some female favourite who looks down on shame? Taxes on the very necessaries of life, enable an endless tribe of idle princes and princesses to pass with stupid pomp before a gaping crowd, who almost worship the very parade which costs them so dear. This is mere gothic grandeur, something like the barbarous useless parade of having sentinels on horseback at Whitehall, which I could never view without a mixture of contempt and indignation.

How strangely must the mind be sophisticated when this sort of state impresses it! But, till these monuments of folly are levelled by virtue, similar follies will leaven the whole mass. For the same character, in some degree, will prevail in the aggregate of society: and the refinements of luxury, or the vicious repinings of envious poverty, will equally banish virtue from society, considered as the characteristic of that society, or only allow it to appear as one of the stripes of the harlequin coat, worn by the civilized man.

In the superior ranks of life, every duty is done by deputies, as if duties could ever be waved, and the vain pleasures which consequent idleness forces the rich to pursue, appear so enticing to the next rank, that the numerous scramblers for wealth sacrifice every thing to tread on their heels. The most sacred trusts are then considered as sinecures, because they were procured by interest, and only sought to enable a man to keep *good company*. Women, in particular, all want to be ladies. Which is simply to have nothing to do, but listlessly to go they scarcely care where, for they cannot tell what.

But what have women to do in society? I may be asked, but to loiter with easy grace; surely you would not condemn them all to suckle fools and chronicle small beer![5] No. Women might certainly study the art of healing, and be physicians as well as nurses. And midwifery, decency seems to allot to them, though I am afraid the word midwife, in our dictionaries, will soon give place to *accoucheur*,[6] and one proof of the former delicacy of the sex be effaced from the language.

They might, also, study politics, and settle their benevolence on the broadest basis; for the reading of history will scarcely be more useful than the perusal of romances, if read as mere biography; if the character of the times, the political improvements, arts, &c. be not observed. In short, if it be not considered as the history of man; and not of particular men, who filled a niche in the temple of fame, and dropped into the black rolling stream of time, that silently sweeps all before it, into the shapeless void called—eternity.—For shape, can it be called, 'that shape hath none?[7]

Business of various kinds, they might likewise pursue, if they were educated in a more orderly manner, which might save many from common and legal prostitution. Women would not then marry for a support, as men accept of places under government, and neglect the implied duties; nor would an attempt to earn their own subsistence, a most laudable one! sink them almost to the level of those poor abandoned creatures who live by prostitution. For are not milliners and mantua-makers[8] reckoned the next class? The few employments open to women, so far from being liberal, are menial; and when a superiour education enables them to take charge of the education of children as governesses, they are not treated like the tutors of sons, though even clerical tutors are not always treated in a manner calculated to render them respectable in the eyes of their pupils, to say nothing of the private com-

fort of the individual. But as women educated like gentlewomen, are never designed for the humiliating situation which necessity sometimes forces them to fill; these situations are considered in the light of a degradation; and they know little of the human heart, who need to be told, that nothing so painfully sharpens sensibility as such a fall in life.

Some of these women might be restrained from marrying by a proper spirit or delicacy, and others may not have had it in their power to escape in this pitiful way from servitude; is not that government then very defective, and very unmindful of the happiness of one half of its members, that does not provide for honest, independent women, by encouraging them to fill respectable stations? But in order to render their private virtue a public benefit, they must have a civil existence in the state, married or single; else we shall continually see some worthy woman, whose sensibility has been rendered painfully acute by undeserved contempt, droop like 'the lily broken down by a plow-share.'

It is a melancholy truth; yet such is the blessed effect of civilization! the most respectable women are the most oppressed; and, unless they have understandings far superiour to the common run of understandings, taking in both sexes, they must, from being treated like contemptible beings, become contemptible. How many women thus waste life away the prey of discontent, who might have practised as physicians, regulated a farm, managed a shop, and stood erect, supported by their own industry, instead of hanging their heads surcharged with the dew of sensibility, that consumes the beauty to which it at first gave lustre; nay, I doubt whether pity and love are so near akin as poets feign, for I have seldom seen much compassion excited by the helplessness of females, unless they were fair; then, perhaps, pity was the soft handmaid of love, or the harbinger of lust.

How much more respectable is the woman who earns her own bread by fulfilling any duty, than the most accomplished beauty!—beauty did I say?—so sensible am I of the beauty of moral loveliness, or the harmonious propriety that attunes the passions of a well-regulated mind, that I blush at making the comparison; yet I sigh to think how few women aim at attaining this respectability by withdrawing from the giddy whirl of pleasure, or the indolent calm that stupifies the good sort of women it sucks in.

---

[5] *Othello* II. i. 160.
[6] "The birther," a male doctor.
[7] *Paradise Lost* II. 666–67.
[8] Dressmakers.

Proud of their weakness, however, they must always be protected, guarded from care, and all the rough toils that dignify the mind.—If this be the fiat of fate, if they will make themselves insignificant and contemptible, sweetly to waste 'life away,' let them not expect to be valued when their beauty fades, for it is the fate of the fairest flowers to be admired and pulled to pieces by the careless hand that plucked them. In how many ways do I wish, from the purest benevolence, to impress this truth on my sex; yet I fear that they will not listen to a truth that dear bought experience has brought home to many an agitated bosom, nor willingly resign the privileges of rank and sex for the privileges of humanity, to which those have no claim who do not discharge its duties.

Those writers are particularly useful, in my opinion, who make man feel for man, independent of the station he fills, or the drapery of factitious sentiments. I then would fain convince reasonable men of the importance of some of my remarks, and prevail on them to weigh dispassionately the whole tenor of my observations.—I appeal to their understandings; and, as a fellow-creature, claim, in the name of my sex, some interest in their hearts. I entreat them to assist to emancipate their companion, to make her a *help meet* for them!

Would men but generously snap our chains, and be content with rational fellowship instead of slavish obedience, they would find us more observant daughters, more affectionate sisters, more faithful wives, more reasonable mothers—in a word, better citizens. We should then love them with true affection, because we should learn to respect ourselves; and the peace of mind of a worthy man would not be interrupted by the idle vanity of his wife, nor the babes sent to nestle in a strange bosom,[9] having never found a home in their mother's.

QUESTIONS

1. How does Wollstonecraft's concept of "unnatural distinctions" reveal Enlightenment thinking?
2. What influence of the French Revolution can you find in this passage?

---

[9] That of a wet-nurse.

3. Why does Wollstonecraft place so much importance on women nursing their own children?
4. What accounts for women's inferior status in society? What are Wollstonecraft's remedies?
5. Does Wollstonecraft seem too hard on the women of her own time?
6. Compare Wollstonecraft's views to those of present-day feminists.

Romantic Women Novelists

Mary Wollstonecraft Godwin (who married the poet Shelley) followed in her mother's footsteps in that she became a writer, but she typified the shift from the Enlightenment to romanticism, writing novels of fantasy rather than treatises. Her *Frankenstein* as we mentioned in Chapter 26, has become a classic in its genre. The early nineteenth century saw a veritable outbreak of female writers, primarily novelists, struggling against restrictions imposed on them by family and society, in order to live freely as human beings and as artists. Many of them published under male pen names. In England, there were the Brontë sisters and Mary Ann Evans ("George Eliot"); in France, Germaine Necker (known as "Madame de Staël") and Aurore Dupin ("George Sand"). The United States produced the outspoken Margaret Fuller and the reclusive Emily Dickinson. The two Frenchwomen were particularly concerned in their novels with the nature and destinies of women. Sand was a liberated woman in her lifestyle, which included a passionate affair with the composer Chopin; but, with typical romantic contradiction, she exalts the simple, virtuous wife in many of her works. Her *Lélia* is nonetheless an apology for free love. Mme. de Staël's Corinne, in the novel by that name, is a poetic genius who suffers and dies of unrequited love. Her statement on poetic inspiration is remarkable not only for its portrayal of women, but for its typically romantic exaltation of inspired genius:

Sometimes . . . my impassioned excitement carries me beyond myself; teaches me to find in nature and my own heart such daring truths and forcible expressions as solitary meditation could never have engendered. My enthusiasm then seems supernatural: a spirit speaks within me far greater than my own; it often happens that I abandon the measure of verse to explain my thoughts in prose.... Sometimes my lyre, by a simple national air, may complete the effect which flies from the control of words. In truth, I feel myself a poet, less when a happy choice of rhymes, of syllables, of figures, may dazzle my auditors, than when my spirit soars disdainful of all selfish baseness; when godlike deeds appear easy to me, 'tis then my verse is at its best. I am ... a poet while I admire or hate, not by my personal feelings nor in my own cause, but for the sake of human dignity and the glory of the world.... I cannot touch on any of the themes that affect me, without that kind of thrill which is the source of ideal beauty in the arts, of religion in the recluse, generosity in heroes and disinterestedness among men.

How far we are here from the neoclassical conception of the role of the artist and the composition of the work of art! Corinne's portrayal of herself is comparable to that of an allegorical figure, like Delacroix's *Liberty at the Barricades.*

Romantic Love and Female Types

Literature and the other arts continued nevertheless to be dominated by men in the romantic period, and so it is primarily woman as viewed by man that has given us the various images of woman in romantic art. These range from the idealized simple, domestic, virtuous girl and mother to the ethereal beauty, inspirer of lofty ideas, to the she-devil, temptress or *femme fatale* who seduces and ruins innocent young men. All these types may inspire romantic love, an all-consuming passion that can never be fulfilled (if it is, it usually leads to disillusionment and a new object) and often causes the hero extreme misery or even death. The romantic sufferer and the romantic lover are often one and the same, as we will see in the selection from Goethe's romantic novel *The Sorrows of Young Werther*. Werther, a lover of nature and poetry but a misfit in society, is obsessed with love for a married woman, Charlotte. Unable to find any kind of satisfaction in this world, he finally commits suicide. Young people all over Europe identified with Werther, both in their art and their lives. The novel actually provoked a rash of suicides. Romantic sufferers, pursuing an ideal, impossible love, felt themselves to be born in the wrong place at the wrong time, sensitive geniuses inevitably misunderstood by a crass society.

GOETHE

From *The Sorrows of Young Werther*

[The following passage describes the meeting of Werther with Charlotte, who is bethrothed to Albert. The entire novel—except for the end, after Werther's suicide—is written in the form of letters from Werther to his friend Wilhelm.]

I could not restrain myself—go to her I must. I have just returned, Wilhelm; and whilst I am taking supper I will write to you. What a delight it was for my soul to see her in the midst of her dear, beautiful children,—eight brothers and sisters!

But, if I proceed thus, you will be no wiser at the end of my letter than you were at the beginning. Attend, then, and I will compel myself to give you the details.

I mentioned to you the other day that I had become acquainted with S——, the district judge, and that he had invited me to go and visit him in his retirement, or rather in his little kingdom. But I neglected going, and perhaps should never have gone, if chance had not discovered to me the treasure which lay concealed in that retired spot. Some of our young people had proposed giving a ball in the country, at which I consented to be present. I offered my hand for the evening to a pretty and agreeable, but rather commonplace, sort of girl from the immediate neighborhood; and it was agreed that I should engage a carriage, and call upon Charlotte, with my partner and her aunt, to convey them to the ball. My companion informed me, as we drove along through the park to the hunting-lodge, that I should make the acquaintance of a very charming young lady. "Take care," added the aunt, "that you do not lose your heart."—"Why?" said I. "Because she is already engaged to a very worthy man," she replied, "who is gone to settle his affairs upon the death of his father, and will succeed to a very considerable inheritance." This information possessed no interest for me. When we arrived at the gate, the sun was setting behind the tops of the mountains. The atmosphere was heavy; and the ladies expressed their fears of an approaching storm, as masses of low black clouds were gathering in the horizon. I relieved their anxieties by pretending to be weather-wise, although I myself had some apprehensions lest our pleasure should be interrupted.

I alighted; and a maid came to the door, and requested us to wait a moment for her mistress. I walked across the court to a well-built house, and, ascending the flight of steps in front, opened the dor, and saw before me the most charming spectacle I had ever witnessed. Six children, from eleven to two years old, were running about the hall, and surrounding a lady of middle height, with a lovely figure, dressed in a robe of simple white, trimmed with pink ribbons. She was holding a rye loaf in her hand, and was cutting slices for the little ones all round, in proportion to their age and appetite. She performed her task in a graceful and affectionate manner; each claimant awaiting his turn with outstretched hands, and boisterously shouting his thanks. Some of them ran away at once, to enjoy their evening meal; whilst others, of a gentler disposition, retired to the courtyard to see the strangers, and to survey the carriage in which their Charlotte was to drive away. "Pray forgive me for giving you the trouble to come for me, and for keeping the ladies waiting: but dressing, and arranging some household duties before I leave, had made me forget my children's supper; and they do not like to take it from any one but me." I uttered some indifferent compliment: but my whole soul was absorbed by her air, her voice, her manner; and I had scarcely recovered myself when she ran into her room to fetch her gloves and fan. The young ones threw inquiring glances at me from a distance; whilst I approached the youngest, a most delicious little creature. He drew back; and Charlotte, entering at the very moment, said, "Louis, shake hands with your cousin." The little fellow obeyed willingly; and I could not resist giving him a hearty kiss, notwithstanding his rather dirty face. "Cousin," said I to Charlotte, as I handed her down, "do you think I deserve the happiness of being related to you? " She replied, with a ready smile, "Oh! I have such a number of cousins, that I should be sorry if you were the most undeserving of them." In taking leave, she desired her next sister, Sophy, a girl about eleven years old, to take great care of the children, and to say good-by to papa for her when he came home from his ride. She enjoined to the little ones to obey their sister Sophy as they would herself, upon which some promised that they would; but a little fair-haired girl, about six years old, looked discontented, and said, "But Sophy is not you, Charlotte; and

we like you best." The two eldest boys had clambered up the carriage; and, at my request, she permitted them to accompany us a little way through the forest, upon their promising to sit very still, and hold fast.

We were hardly seated, and the ladies had scarcely exchanged compliments, making the usual remarks upon each other's dress, and upon the company they expected to meet, when Charlotte stopped the carriage, and made her brothers get down. They insisted upon kissing her hands once more; which the eldest did with all the tenderness of a youth of fifteen, but the other in a lighter and more careless manner. She desired them again to give her love to the children, and we drove off.

The aunt inquired of Charlotte whether she had finished the book she had last sent her. "No," said Charlotte; "I did not like it: you can have it again. And the one before was not much better." I was surprised, upon asking the title, to hear that it was[1]——. I found penetration and character in every thing she said: every expression seemed to brighten her features with new charms,—with new rays of genius,—which unfolded by degrees, as she felt herself understood.

"When I was younger," she observed, "I loved nothing so much as romances. Nothing could equal my delight when, on some holiday, I could settle down quietly in a corner, and enter with my whole heart and soul into the joys or sorrows of some fictitious Leonora. I do not deny that they even possess some charms for me yet. But I read so seldom, that I prefer books suited exactly to my taste. And I like those authors best whose scenes describe my own situation in life,—and the friends who are about me, whose stories touch me with interest, from resembling my own homely existence,—which, without being absolutely paradise, is, on the whole, a source of indescribable happiness." . . .

We talked of the pleasures of dancing. "If it is a fault to love it," said Charlotte, "I am ready to confess that I prize it above all other amusements. If any thing dis-

---

[1] We feel obliged to suppress the passage in the letter, to prevent any one from feeling aggrieved; although no author need pay much attention to the opinion of a mere gril, or that of an unsteady young man. [Author's note]

turbs me, I go to the piano, play an air to which I have danced, and all goes right again directly."

You, who know me, can fancy how steadfastly I gazed upon her rich dark eyes during these remarks, how my very soul gloated over her warm lips and fresh, glowing cheeks, how I became quite lost in the delightful meaning of her words, so much so, that I scarcely heard the actual expressions. In short, I alighted from the carriage like a person in a dream, and was so lost to the dim world around me, that I scarcely heard the music which resounded from the illuminated ballroom. . . .

We set off, and, at first, delighted ourselves with the usual graceful motions of the arms. With what grace, with what ease, she moved! When the waltz commenced, and the dancers whirled round each other in the giddy maze, there was some confusion, owing to the incapacity of some of the dancers. We judiciously remained still, allowing the others to weary themselves; and, when the awkward dancers had withdrawn, we joined in, and kept it up famously together with one other couple,—Andran and his partner. Never did I dance more lightly. I felt myself more than mortal, holding this loveliest of creatures in my arms, flying with her as rapidly as the wind, till I lost sight of every other object; and O Wilhelm, I vowed at that moment, that a maiden whom I loved, or for whom I felt the slightest attachment, never, never should waltz with any one else but with me, if I went to perdition for it!—you will understand this.

[Charlotte eventually marries Albert, and Werther takes up residence near them. He sees Charlotte every day. While she is fond of him, she remains true to her husband. Werther's unrequited passion finally drives him insane.]

Unhappy being that I am! Why do I thus deceive myself? What is to come of all this wild, aimless, endless passion? I cannot pray except to her. My imagination sees nothing but her: all surrounding objects are of no account, except as they relate to her. In this dreamy state I enjoy many happy hours, till at length I feel compelled to tear myself away from her. Ah, Wilhelm, to what does not my heart often compel me! When I have spent several hours in her company, till I feel

completely absorbed by her figure, her grace, the divine expression of her thoughts, my mind becomes gradually excited to the highest excess, my sight grows dim, my hearing confused, my breathing oppressed as if by the hand of a murderer, and my beating heart seeks to obtain relief for my aching senses. I am sometimes unconscious whether I really exist. If in such moments I find no sympathy, and Charlotte does not allow me to enjoy the melancholy consolation of bathing her hand with my tears, I feel compelled to tear myself from her, when I either wander through the country, climb some precipitous cliff, or force a path through the trackless thicket, where I am lacerated and torn by thorns and briers; and thence I find relief. Sometimes I lie stretched on the ground, overcome with fatigue and dying with thirst; sometimes, late in the night, when the moon shines above me, I recline against an aged tree in some sequestered forest, to rest my weary limbs, when, exhausted and worn, I sleep till break of day. O Wilhelm! the hermit's cell, his sackcloth, and girdle of thorns would be luxury and indulgence compared with what I suffer. Adieu! I see no end to this wretchedness except the grave.

[Werther leaves Charlotte and Albert for a while but is driven to return. Feeling that the whole world is against him, he shoots himself with one of Albert's pistols.]

QUESTIONS

1. Describe Werther's initial perception of Charlotte. What ideal of woman does she represent?
2. Compare the passage on dancing to the ballet *Giselle*, described on p. 257. Note that the waltz was at this time a new and shocking dance.
3. Analyze the last passage. What are the symptoms of romantic love? How does the sufferer find relief? Would Werther's passion really be satisfied if he married Charlotte?

Throughout American romantic fiction—the novels of James Fenimore Cooper, Hawthorne, and Melville offer some examples—one can find examples of blonde heroines who inspire the hero to noble thoughts and chaste love and brunettes who inevitably bring out his "darker" passions. In France, the type of the fatal woman, the *femme fatale,* is exemplified in Prosper Mérimée's story *Carmen,* about a young man led to ruin by an enticing, fickle Spanish gypsy. This mythical character was developed further in the opera *Carmen* by Bizet. Romantic opera—*La Bohème* and *La Traviata* are other examples—is indeed full of free living women who inspire consuming passions. Music, many romantics were convinced, could express the passion of love better than any other art could. Words by themselves were too limited. In early nineteenth-century Germany an extraordinary cooperation between poets and composers resulted in a new art form, the *Lied* (art song), or the song cycle. One of the best known of the cycles on the theme of love is *Dichterliebe* ("The Love of a Poet") by the poet Heinrich Heine and the composer Robert Schumann. The culminating portrayal of romantic love in music is Richard Wagner's opera *Tristan und Isolde,* taking its subject from the literature that gave romantic love its prototype, the medieval romance. The music portrays the soaring passions of the lovers and the only climax possible—death.

Some of the many facets of romantic love and of the romantic view of women are illustrated in the following poems.

JOHN KEATS

La Belle Dame sans Merci[1]

A Ballad

O what can ail thee, knight-at-arms,
　　Alone and palely loitering?
The sedge has withered from the lake,
　　And no birds sing.

O what can ail thee, knight-at-arms,
　　So haggard and so woe-begone?
The squirrel's granary is full,
　　And the harvest's done.

I see a lily on thy brow,
　　With anguish moist and fever dew,

And on thy cheeks a fading rose
　　Fast withereth too.

I met a lady in the meads,[2]
　　Full beautiful—a faery's child,
Her hair was long, her foot was light,
　　And her eyes were wild.

I made a garland for her head,
　　And bracelets too, and fragrant zone;[3]
She looked at me as she did love,
　　And made sweet moan.

I set her on my pacing steed,
　　And nothing else saw all day long,
For sidelong would she bend, and sing
　　A faery's song.

She found me roots of relish sweet,
　　And honey wild, and manna dew,
And sure in language strange she said,
　　"I love thee true."

She took me to her elfin grot,
　　And there she wept, and sighed full sore,
And there I shut her wild wild eyes
　　With kisses four.

And there she lulléd me asleep,
　　And there I dreamed—Ah! woe betide!
The latest[4] dream I ever dreamed
　　On the cold hill side.

I saw pale kings and princes too,
　　Pale warriors, death-pale were they all;
They cried—"La Belle Dame sans Merci
　　Hath thee in thrall!"

I saw their starved lips in the gloom,
　　With horrid warning gapéd wide,
And I awoke and found me here,
　　On the cold hill's side.

---

[1] "The beautiful lady without pity."

[2] Meadows.
[3] Belt.
[4] Last.

And this is why I sojourn here,
  Alone and palely loitering,
Though the sedge has withered from the lake,
  And no birds sing.

PERCY BYSSHE SHELLEY

LINES: WHEN THE LAMP IS SHATTERED

I

When the lamp is shattered
  The light in the dust lies dead—
When the cloud is scattered
  The rainbow's glory is shed.
When the lute is broken,
  Sweet tones are remembered not;
When the lips have spoken,
  Loved accents are soon forgot.

II

As music and splendour
  Survive not the lamp and the lute,
The heart's echoes render
  No song when the spirit is mute:—
No song but sad dirges,
  Like the wind through a ruined cell,
Or the mournful surges
  That ring the dead seaman's knell.

III

When hearts have once mingled,
  Love first leaves the well-built nest;
The weak one is singled
  To endure what it once possessed.
O Love! who bewailest
  The frailty of all things here,
Why choose you the frailest
  For your cradle, your home, and your bier?

IV

Its passions will rock thee
  As the storms rock the ravens on high;
Bright reason will mock thee,
  Like the sun from a wintry sky.
From thy nest every rafter
  Will rot, and thine eagle home

Leave thee naked to laughter,
  When leaves fall and cold winds come.

EMILY DICKINSON

Wild nights! Wild nights!
  Were I with thee,
Wild nights should be
  Our luxury!

Futile the winds
  To a heart in port,—
Done with the compass,
  Done with the chart.

Rowing in Eden!
  Ah! the sea!
Might I but moor
  To-night in thee!

GEORGE GORDON, LORD BYRON

SHE WALKS IN BEAUTY

I

She walks in beauty, like the night
  Of cloudless climes and starry skies;
And all that's best of dark and bright
  Meet in her aspect and her eyes:
Thus mellow'd to that tender light
  Which heaven to gaudy day denies.

II

One shade the more, one ray the less,
  Had half impair'd the nameless grace
Which waves in every raven tress,
  Or softly lightens o'er her face;
Where thoughts serenely sweet express
  How pure, how dear their dwelling-place.

III

And on that cheek, and o'er that brow,
  So soft, so calm, yet eloquent,
The smiles that win, the tints that glow,
  But tell of days in goodness spent,
A mind at peace with all below,
  A heart whose love is innocent!

HEINRICH HEINE[1]

You Are Just Like a Flower

You are just like a flower
So fair and chaste and dear;
Looking at you, sweet sadness
Invades my heart with fear.

I feel I should be folding
My hands upon your hair,
Praying that God may keep you
So dear and chaste and fair.

A Young Man Loves a Maiden

A young man loves a maiden
Whose heart for another sighed;
This other loves another
Who then becomes his bride.

The maiden takes the first man
Who happens to come her way
Just out of spite and anger;
The youth is left in dismay.

It is an old old story
And yet it's always new;
And to whomever it happens
't will break his heart in two.

QUESTIONS

1. What are the different aspects of romantic love that appear in these poems?
2. Compare romantic love to courtly love (see Vol. I, Chapter 8).
3. How has romantic love influenced modern expressions of love? What is different?

---

[1] If possible, listen to both of Heine's lyrics set to the music of Robert Schumann in his *Dichterliebe* ("Love of a Poet") song cycle.

27-1 *Carlotta Grisi in Giselle,* from the lithograph by J. Bouvier. (Crown Copyright, Victoria and Albert Museum, London)

The Romantic Ballet

A romantic art form that gave great importance to women, both as artists and as mythical figures, and to romantic love was the ballet. The Neoclassical stage ballet of the eighteenth century, like the *ballet de cour* of the seventeenth, showed an equality of roles between the sexes but gave some predominance to men in the execution of showy steps. In the romantic ballet, however, the first female dancer of the company—the *prima ballerina*—upstaged everyone. Dancing on the tip of the toes, or *pointe,* and airy tulle costumes appeared at this time. Men were sometimes reduced to machines to lift the ethereal creatures in the air. The popular notion of ballet as a woman's art, as it still is in most of the best-known ballets still performed, dates from the romantic period. Romanticism in ballet, as in the other arts, stressed exoticism, fantasy, nature, and, of course, love; an unrealizable love for an evanescent lady or a "fatal" love for a heartless temptress.

Paris, with London a close second, was the center of

romantic ballet. It was there, at the opera, that the stars—the Italians Maria Taglioni and Carlotta Grisi and the Viennese Fanny Essler—became for their admirers legendary, almost goddess-like. The poet Théophile Gautier, an admirer of the art of dance, wrote the story for the greatest romantic ballet, *Giselle*, one that is still popular with modern audiences. Based on a German legend, the ballet recounts the story of a young country girl who loves to dance and falls in love with a shepherd boy. Her mother foretells her fate: "Unhappy child! You will dance forever, you will kill yourself, and, when you are dead, you will become a *Wili* (a dancing spirit)." Giselle pays no heed, but the prophecy comes true. It turns out that the shepherd whom she loves is really a duke in disguise and, when Giselle learns that he is in reality engaged to a noble lady, she kills herself. We then see the *Wilis* dancing around Giselle's grave, coaxing her spirit out to become one of them. The duke, in tears, returns to her tomb, and is almost danced to death by the *Wilis*. After a frenzied dance and a passionate love scene, Giselle returns to the grave and the duke is consoled by his noble fiancée. Carlotta Grisi, according to Gautier, danced this role "with a perfection, lightness, boldness, and a chaste and refined seductiveness, which places her in the first rank . . . she was nature and artlessness personified." The contemporary lithograph (Fig. 27-1) suggests an ethereal, floating creature, idealized and unearthly.

FROM THE ENLIGHTENMENT TO ROMANTICISM: CONTINUITIES

The two great political revolutions at the end of the eighteenth century, the French and the American, not only transformed the leading philosophies of government in Western Europe but dramatically altered some basic conceptions about the nature of human beings as well. In terms of the humanities, these revolutions embodied the ideas of the Enlightenment while exciting the passions of romanticism.

Enlightenment Ideals   The primarily middle-class philosophes challenged once and for all the medieval belief that everyone had his place in a hierarchical society, a belief that still held sway in the absolutist seventeenth century. Human beings, they argued, were "naturally" equal and thus were entitled to certain natural rights. Thomas Jefferson, in a sense an American philosophe, defined these as life, liberty, and the pursuit of happiness. The writers and the artists of the Enlightenment submitted everything—social customs and institutions, religious beliefs, passions—to the cold light of reason.

The Enlightenment belief that the human predicament was largely the product of bad institutions raised tremendous expectations regarding the possibilities of improving human beings and their society through institutional reforms. Although Voltaire's El Dorado was not intended as a model for imitation, other philosophes were deeply engaged in drawing up sketches of model societies, which they took very seriously. Within limits, this belief in human-engineered progress provided a healthy incentive to reform what were seen as present evils. But this belief could also justify something like the Reign of Terror during the French Revolution. An idealist, Robespierre felt perfectly justified in destroying thousands of human beings in the name of a brighter tomorrow. Unfortunately, he was not to be the last of this type.

Enlightenment Style   If the seventeenth century was an age for the grandiose in the arts, the eighteenth was an age for the petite and the well ordered. Neoclassicism, no longer inspired by the baroque sense of splendor, became in the Enlightenment less ornate and somewhat colder and more mechanical. Eighteenth-century artists were more interested in sensuality than in love, in humble virtues more than in religious yearnings.

Classical composers such as Mozart and Haydn made use of short phrases and strived to achieve unity, balance, and symmetry, forsaking the complex fugues of the baroque era. Architecture, such as the government buildings in Washington, D.C., and Jefferson's ideal "academic village," reflected the inspiration of classical Rome and a belief in order and rationality. Like classical Rome, with Horace and Juvenal, European literature in the eighteenth century reflected a strong predilection for satire and thus for examining human folly and pretensions under the light of reason. Voltaire's *Candide,* with its short, witty, sometimes biting humor and its distrust of metaphysical abstraction, represents well the style of the Enlightenment.

In our post-Freudian era we may view the Enlightenment's understanding of human nature with some skepticism. People cannot be defined primarily as atoms of reason, as some of the philosophes seemed to suppose. We cannot share all of their optimism about progress through education and science. Yet many of the ideals formulated during the Enlightenment are still the basis of many of our society's assumptions. Toleration of the beliefs of others, human equality, basic human rights, the freedom to think for oneself, and even less widespread notions such as equal legal and social rights for women—all of these have had considerable impact on our way of thinking.

Romantic Changes   The romantics adapted the ideals of the Enlightenment to their own purposes. Rejecting the belief that reason is the primary human faculty, they developed a current of sentimentality already present in the eighteenth century. The transitional Jean-Jacques Rousseau makes the Enlightenment's belief in the natural goodness of human beings the basis for a romantic apology for feeling above reason and for the supremacy of the unique individual, thus laying the basis for the misunderstood romantic sufferer and the titanic romantic hero. Napoleon, the rationalistic administrator, becomes, as in David's painting, the passionate, dashing, almost superhuman general, comparable to Byron's Prometheus, the savior of mankind.

Rousseau's mature thought made an important contribution to nascent nationalism, which began to take shape in the early decades of the nineteenth century, in a sense inspired by French aggression. Whereas the Enlightenment conceived of human beings as essentially a universal race, the proponents of nationalism saw them as divided into linguistically and culturally defined groupings. Each of these groupings had its own particular characteristics and its own political will. Further, each political will had a right to self-government.

Nothing could have been more congenial to the nationalist position than Rousseau's idea that human beings become human only by virtue of membership in a particular community. To it they owe their values and the character of their intellectual and emotional lives. Moreover, created in a very real sense by their cultures, human beings have, as their very essense, a general will, which they share with other members of the community. It was easy for nineteenth-century nationalists to identify this general will as the will of the nation and to envisage it as struggling for life against other general wills that would attempt to oppress it.

Romantic Style   We have seen how the rationalistic goals of liberty, equality, and fraternity became pas-

sionate statements in the hands of romantic artists. Open to the entire range of human emotions, the romantics also tended to plumb the depths as well as the heights of experience. Goya, for example, who had lived through the disasters of a brutal war rather than with the theories of revolution, portrayed the demonic side of human nature while showing an intense compassion for the victims of exploitation and tyranny. The desire to portray the extremes and varieties of human passions greatly enriched the range and textures of romatic visual, literary, and musical art. The artists' need for individuality of expression also caused then to find the neat balances and rules of Neoclassical art insufficient. Beethoven expanded both classical structures and orchestration, Delacroix experimented with color and composition, the English romantic poets opened poetry to music and to the sensuous imagery of painting, Whitman abandoned the meters and vocabulary considered suitable for poetry, and Dickinson found highly personal images and rhymes.

Romantic Continuities   Romantic exuberance for social causes and for nature, as well as romantic individualism and emotionalism, are still with us. The modern concept of the artist as a supersensitive being—more likely to be misunderstood by, and at odds with, his society than in harmony with it—was born with the romantics. The romantic concept of love and the romantic views of women have also, for good or ill, profoundly influenced our own.

We have seen that love, for the romantics, resembled an infinite yearning that could never really be satisfied by a finite human being. Romantic lovers in literature and life were doomed to desire the unattainable and to suffer—or to throw themselves into one passionate love affair after another. They viewed a stable marriage and family life either as too bourgeois and constricting or as a kind of dreamy ideal.

In ways that are often contradictory, women became a romantic preoccupation. A romantic lover might idealize a domestic and virtuous young girl as a mysterious and ethereal creature; he might be destroyed by a *femme fatale* or temptress. The romantic ballet, with the predominance it gave to the ballerina, reinforced the idealization of women. At the same time, women began to explore, in their own way, the romantic ideal of individual freedom. The notion of women's liberation, a philosophical ideal with Mary Wollstonecraft, became a way of life for some romantic women.

The modern reverence for unspoiled nature began in the romantic period. The romantics were particularly prone to see their own emotions reflected in the natural world or to look on nature as a mother, a consolation for their troubles. Many romantics shunned organized religions, finding a substitute in the worship of nature, but even orthodox Christians found that they could approach God through immersion in His works. As they idealized nature, the romantics idealized the simple life of the "natural" peasant, unspoiled by the corruptions of the modern world. For many of those would mean a dramatic uprooting. It would also necessitate new responses in thought and style from the humanities.

Plate IX Vermeer, *The Kitchenmaid.*
(Rijksmuseum, Amsterdam)

Plate VIII Vermeer, *The Little Street (Street in Delft).*
(Rijksmuseum, Amsterdam)

Plate XI Watteau, *Pilgrimage to Cythera*. (Clichés Musées Nationaux, Paris)

Plate XII Jean-Baptiste-Siméon Chardin, *The Morning Toilet*. (Nationalmuseum, Stockholm)

Plate XIII Constable, *Dedham Vale with the House Called "Dedham Valley"*. (The Tate Gallery, London)

Plate XIV Turner, *Rain, Steam and Speed,
The Great Western Railway*. (Reproduced by
courtesy of the Trustees, The National
Gallery, London)

Plate XV Monet, *The Bridge at Argenteuil*.
(Neue Pinakothek, München/Artothek)

PART SEVEN

Industrialism and The Humanities: The Middle and Late Nineteenth Century

28

The Industrial Revolution and New Social Thought

By the beginning of the nineteenth century, while Keats was musing on his nightingale and Wordsworth was celebrating the English countryside and his solitary reaper, the face of rural England was in a state of transformation. Eighteenth-century country towns like Manchester were fast becoming makeshift cities for hundreds of thousands of poor workers who sought employment in the new factories whose belching smokestacks polluted the landscape for miles around. A few years before Wordsworth's death in 1850, engineers laid down the iron rails that were to bring the first trains across the wheat fields.

The Industrial Revolution could easily be considered the most important event in the history of the human race. In all previous societies known to man, periods of population growth were necessarily succeeded by periods of contraction caused by disease and starvation. After 1750, however, the productive capacity of the world rapidly increased to the point where population could expand unceasingly and at the same time enjoy an improved standard of living. What the so-called revolution entailed was basically the massive substitution of machines and new techniques of production for human labor. The result was that, depending on the commodity, the output of the individual worker expanded five, fifty, a hundred, and even a thousand or more times, causing accumulations of goods undreamed of earlier. That human beings in such a world continued to live in dire poverty came to appear either as the fault of a backward regional system of production or as an unjust method of distributing the rewards—or a combination of both.

The Industrial Revolution was not, of course, an event like the political revolution in France that took place within a few years' time. It exerted its effect on different areas at different times. By 1785 clearly underway in the British Isles, significant industrial development occurred on the continent only after 1815, and before 1900 it still remained limited to Western Europe, parts of North America, and Japan. Even today certain parts of the world have yet to undergo their industrial revolution.

England in the Lead   There are a number of reasons for English precedence in industrial development. By the early eighteenth century Englishmen (with the Dutch) had the highest standard of living in the world. After approximately a century of applying innovative techniques, English agricultural producers were able to supply food cheaply and in abundance while still making a profit. This efficiency in agriculture also liberated a large percentage of the working population for other pursuits. English government compared with continental monarchies was inexpensive, and the low tax burden left most of the money in the pockets of those who earned it. There was consequently a good deal of money available for investment and consumption. Moreover, whereas absolutist monarchies on the continent regulated economic life closely, productive enterprise in England was relatively free; personal initiative and experimentation were encouraged. Finally, in the coming age of the machine, England was particularly favored with its enormous deposits of a cheap fuel, coal.

The breakthrough in industrialism first came in cotton, a cloth industry that, compared with wool or silk, was very new. Because of its low cost relative to that of wool and silk, the market for cotton cloth was large, and it happened that cotton could be worked more easily by machine than by hand. By the late eighteenth century the demand for cotton cloth both in England and abroad was such that the raw material came into short supply. Eli Whitney's cotton gin remedied the major bottleneck in production of raw cotton, and the plantation economy of the American South soared from the 1790s on.

The mechanization of cotton production encouraged invention and investment in other areas of the economy. By the end of the eighteenth century the English had developed a relatively efficient steam engine, were able to mine coal and manufacture steel in impressive quantities, and were increasingly utilizing new chemical discoveries for industrial purposes. The nineteenth century in Europe was marked by the continued progress of British industry and by the desperate efforts of continental and American competitors to imitate and catch up with Britain.

Social Effects of Industrialization   The social consequences of industrialization were enormous. Within decades hundreds of thousands of workers moved into the industrial centers, overwhelming the capacity of the cities to absorb them. Shanty towns grew up on the outskirts where the new workers lived in crowded unsanitary conditions. The machines not only demanded regimentation of work but also reduced the need for skill or physical force. Especially in the cloth industry most operations involved in mechanized production could be performed by children, who were cheaper to hire than adults. By the middle 1820s a small boy working two looms could produce fifteen times more than an adult laborer working by hand.

Unable to support the family even with both mother and father working, parents were forced to send their children into the factories. Children four and five years of age worked from twelve to sixteen hours, six days a week, for pennies. Often forbidden to sit down during their hours of work, they were subject to the brutality of the overseer for the slightest infraction. In the case of babies too young to work, desperate parents, unable to pay for babysitters, resorted to "Mother's Helper" to drug the baby from early morning until late at night when they returned home. In the seething tenements of workers' quarters, twisted bodies and early death were common.

Included in the report of the "Committee on Factory Children's Labour," 1831–1832, was the following interview with a certain Samuel Coulson.

5047. At what time in the morning, in the brisk[1] time, did those girls go to the mills?

In the brisk time, for about six weeks, they have gone at 3 o'clock in the morning, and ended at 10, or nearly half past at night.

5049. What intervals were allowed for rest or refreshment during those nineteen hours of labour?

Breakfast a quarter of an hour, and dinner half an hour, and drinking a quarter of an hour.

5051. Was any of that time taken up in cleaning the machinery?

They generally had to do what they call dry down; sometimes this took the whole of the time at breakfast or drinking, and they were to get their dinner or breakfast as they could; if not, it was brought home.

5054. Had you not great difficulty in awakening your children to this excessive labour?

Yes, in the early time we had them to take up asleep and shake them, when we got them on the floor to dress them, before we could get them off to their work; but not so in the common hours.

5056. Supposing they had been a little too late, what would have been the consequence during the long hours?

They were quartered in the longest hours, the same as in the shortest time.

5057. What do you mean by quartering?

A quarter was taken off.

5058. If they had been how much too late?

Five minutes.

5059. What was the length of time they could be in bed during those long hours?

It was near 11 o'clock before we could get them into bed after getting a little victuals, and then at morning my mistress used to stop up all night, for fear that we could not get them ready for the time; sometimes we have gone to bed, and one of us generally awoke.

5060. What time did you get them up in the morning?

In general me or my mistress got up at 2 o'clock to dress them.

5061. So that they had not above four hours' sleep at this time?

No, they had not.

5062. For how long together was it?

About six weeks it held; it was only done when the throng was very much on; it was not often that.

5063. The common hours of labour were from 6 in the morning till half-past eight at night?

Yes.

5064. With the same intervals for food?

Yes, just the same.

5065. Were the children excessively fatigued by this labour?

Many times; we have cried often when we have given them the little victualling we had to give them; we had to shake them, and they have fallen to sleep with the victuals in their mouths many a time.

5066. Had any of them any accident in consequence of this labour?

Yes, my eldest daughter when she went first there; she had been about five weeks, and used to fettle the frames when they were running, and my eldest girl agreed with one of the others to fettle hers that time, that she would do her work; while she was learning more about the work, the overlooker came by and said, "Ann, what are you doing there?" she said, "I am doing it for my companion, in order that I may know more about it," he said, "Let go, drop it this minute," and the cog caught her forefinger nail, and screwed it off below the knuckle, and she was five weeks in Leeds Infirmary.

5067. Has she lost that finger?

It is cut off at the second joint.

5068. Were her wages paid during that time?

As soon as the accident happened the wages were totally stopped; indeed, I did not know which way to get her cured, and I do not know how it would have been cured but for the Infirmary.

5069. Were the wages stopped at the half-day?

She was stopped a quarter of a day; it was done about four o'clock.

5072. Did this excessive term of labour occasion much cruelty also?

Yes, with being so very much fatigued the strap was very frequently used.

5073. Have any of your children been strapped?

Yes, every one.

---

[1] Busy.

Despite the terrible conditions of life suggested in reports like this, many historians maintain that, on the whole, conditions of the laboring poor in England improved with the Industrial Revolution. Many of the poor preferred the urban slums to those in the rural districts where their misery was compounded by chronic underemployment and hunger.

Liberalism

Indeed, while no doubt regretting the sufferings of the poor, an important group of English and continental thinkers called the liberals believed that these were minor evils compared with the greater good attained by industrialization. Espousing the Enlightenment values of liberty and equality, thinkers like Adam Smith and David Ricardo argued that there was a kind of law of human nature: if individuals were allowed to follow their own self-enlightened interest, the general good and liberty of all would best be served. The state should interfere as little as possible with the exercise of individual judgment, aside from keeping order and protecting property; the economy as well as other aspects of society should be in the control of private citizens. Wages would always tend to the subsistence level because, when workers rise above this, they have more children who devour the surplus, thus forcing the family income down again. However, in a free society, the liberals argued optimistically, individuals with initiative have the opportunity of leaving this condition and joining the ranks of the successful.

Although thinkers of this stamp violently opposed it, public opinion in the 1830s and 1840s finally forced the English government to pass legislation to remedy the worst abuses. As the continent came to industrialize, government there, too, stepped in to ameliorate the condition of workers to a degree. Some of the major proponents of this legislation belonged to a new breed of liberals. These thinkers had come to realize that, if liberty and equality were truly the goals of a society, the major threats to those principles did not come so much from the government as from private pressures. A worker's freedom was essentially limited to starving or accepting the conditions offered him by an employer. The role of government, as they began to conceive it, was that of a mediator, which through its laws would prevent the oppression of one individual by another. The ideal remained, as earlier, to foster individual freedom, but the experience of the first fifty years of industrialism had shown that, paradoxically, freedom had in certain respects to be restricted by legislation in order to maximize it for everyone. The new liberals also moved gradually to the position that the lower classes must also be given the vote. Political power was not, as for earlier liberals, a privilege achieved by the successful; rather, it was a basic right. Thus, the newer liberalism endeavored to incorporate the workers into the establishment.

From the opening decades of the nineteenth century, however, there were critics of the industrial economy who believed that the major source of its evils came from the fact of private property. As long as the principle of private property was regarded as sacred, no amount of legislation, even by a government in which workers participated, could guarantee a just society. To a varying degree these critics maintained that basic industry and essential services should be taken out of private hands and operated by the community for the common welfare. Some of these thinkers, like Charles Fourier (1772–1837) went further, devising utopian communities where each would do the work for which he or she was best suited and would receive the fruits of the collective labor according to need.

Friedrich Engels and Karl Marx

In 1844, a young German socialist and friend of Karl Marx named Friedrich Engels (1820–1895) set himself the task of describing living conditions in the cities of England, the most advanced industrial country in Europe. What Engels exposed in *The Condition of the Working Class in England*, published in 1845, were urban conglomerations sharply divided into neighborhoods for the rich and the poor, the exploiters and the exploited, the high livers and the downtrodden. For Engels, these unjust social and economic conditions were a result of capitalism and could be changed only by a socialist revolution. The phenomenon of the modern city with its subhuman living conditions, its despair and alienation as well as its teeming life, will become, as we shall see, a theme that haunts the imaginations of late-nineteenth- and early-twentieth-century artists and writers. The following passage was translated by Florence Kelley Wischnewetzky.

FRIEDRICH ENGELS

From *The Condition of the Working Class in England in 1844*

CHAPTER 2

THE GREAT TOWNS.

A Town, such as London, where a man may wander for hours together without reaching the beginning of the end, without meeting the slightest hint which could lead to the inference that there is open country within reach, is a strange thing. This colossal centralisation, this heaping together of two and a half millions of human beings at one point, has multiplied the power of this two and a half millions a hundred-fold; has raised London to the commercial capital of the world, created the giant docks and assembled the thousand vessels that continually cover the Thames. I know nothing more imposing than the view which the Thames offers during the ascent from the sea to London Bridge. The masses of buildings, the wharves on both sides, especially from Woolwich upwards, the countless ships along both shores, crowding ever closer and closer together, until, at last, only a narrow passage remains in the middle of the river, a passage through which hundreds of steamers shoot by one another; all this is so vast, so impressive, that a man cannot collect himself, but is lost in the marvel of England's greatness before he sets foot upon English soil.[1]

But the sacrifices which all this has cost become apparent later. After roaming the streets of the capital a day or two, making headway with difficulty through the human turmoil and the endless lines of vehicles, after visiting the slums of the metropolis, one realises for the first time that these Londoners have been forced to sacrifice the best qualities of their human nature, to bring to pass all the marvels of civilisation which crowd their city; that a hundred powers which slumbered within them have remained inactive, have been suppressed in order that a few might be developed more fully and multiply through union with those of others. The very turmoil of the streets has something repulsive, something against which human nature rebels. The hundreds of thousands of all classes and ranks crowding past each other, are they not all human beings with the same qualities and powers, and with the same interest in being happy? And have they not, in the end, to seek happiness in the same way, by the same means? And still they crowd by one another as though they had nothing in common, nothing to do with one another, and their only agreement is the tacit one, that each keep to his own side of the pavement, so as not to delay the opposing streams of the crowd, while it occurs to no man to honour another with so much as a glance. The brutal indifference, the unfeeling isolation of each in his private interest becomes the more repellant and offensive, the more these individuals are crowded together, within a limited space. And, however much one may be aware that this isolation of the individual, this narrow self-seeking is the fundamental principle of our society everywhere, it is nowhere so shamelessly barefaced, so self-conscious as just here in the crowding of the great city. The dissolution of mankind into monads, of which each one has a separate principle, the world of atoms, is here carried out to its utmost extreme. . . .

What is true of London, is true of Manchester, Birmingham, Leeds, is true of all great towns. Everywhere barbarous indifference, hard egotism on one hand, and nameless misery on the other, everywhere social warfare, every man's house in a state of siege, everywhere reciprocal plundering under the protection of the law, and all so shameless, so openly avowed that one shrinks before the consequences of our social state as they manifest themselves here undisguised, and can only wonder that the whole crazy fabric still hangs together. . . .

Every great city has one or more slums, where the working-class is crowded together. True, poverty often dwells in hidden alleys close to the palaces of the rich; but, in general, a separate territory has been assigned to it, where, removed from the sight of the happier classes, it may struggle along as it can. These slums are pretty equally arranged in all the great towns of England, the worst houses in the worst quarters of the towns; usually one or two-storied cottages in long

---

[1] This applies to the time of sailing vessels. The Thames now is a dreary collection of ugly steamers.—F.E.

rows, perhaps with cellars used as dwellings, almost always irregularly built. These houses of three or four rooms and a kitchen form, throughout England, some parts of London excepted, the general dwellings of the working-class. The streets are generally unpaved, rough, dirty, filled with vegetable and animal refuse, without sewers or gutters, but supplied with foul, stagnant pools instead. Moreover, ventilation is impeded by the bad, confused method of building of the whole quarter, and since many human beings here live crowded into a small space, the atmosphere that prevails in these working-men's quarters may readily be imagined. Further, the streets serve as drying grounds in fine weather; lines are stretched across from house to house, and hung with wet clothing.

Let us investigate some of the slums in their order. London comes first, and in London the famous rookery of St. Giles which is now, at last, about to be penetrated by a couple of broad streets. St. Giles is in the midst of the most populous part of the town, surrounded by broad, splendid avenues in which the gay world of London idles about, in the immediate neighbourhood of Oxford Street, Regent Street, of Trafalgar Square and the Strand. It is a disorderly collection of tall, three or four-storied houses, with narrow, crooked, filthy streets, in which there is quite as much life as in the great thoroughfares of the town, except that, here, people of the working-class only are to be seen. A vegetable market is held in the street, baskets with vegetables and fruits, naturally all bad and hardly fit to use, obstruct the sidewalk still further, and from these, as well as from the fish-dealers' stalls, arises a horrible smell. The houses are occupied from cellar to garret, filthy within and without, and their appearance is such that no human being could possibly wish to live in them. But all this is nothing in comparison with the dwellings in the narrow courts and alleys between the streets, entered by covered passages between the houses, in which the filth and tottering ruin surpass all description. Scarcely a whole window-pane can be found, the walls are crumbling, doorposts and window-frames loose and broken, doors of old boards nailed together, or altogether wanting in this thieves' quarter, where no doors are needed, there being nothing to steal. Heaps of garbage and ashes lie in all directions, and the foul liquids emptied before the doors gather in stinking pools. Here live the poorest of the poor, the worst paid workers with thieves and the victims of prostitution indiscriminately huddled together, the majority Irish, or of Irish extraction, and those who have not yet sunk in the whirlpool of moral ruin which surrounds them, sinking daily deeper, losing daily more and more of their power to resist the demoralizing influence of want, filth, and evil surroundings.

Nor is St. Giles the only London slum. In the immense tangle of streets, there are hundreds and thousands of alleys and courts lined with houses too bad for anyone to live in, who can still spend anything whatsoever upon a dwelling fit for human beings. Close to the splendid houses of the rich such a lurking-place of the bitterest poverty may often be found. So, a short time ago, on the occasion of a coroner's inquest, a region close to Portman Square, one of the very respectable squares, was characterised as an abode "of a multitude of Irish demoralised by poverty and filth." So, too, may be found in streets, such as Long Acre and others, which, though not fashionable, are yet "respectable," a great number of cellar dwellings out of which puny children and half-starved, ragged women emerge into the light of day. In the immediate neighbourhood of Drury Lane Theatre, the second in London, are some of the worst streets of the whole metropolis, Charles, King, and Park Streets, in which the houses are inhabited from cellar to garret exclusively by poor families. In the parishes of St. John and St. Margaret there lived in 1840, according to the *Journal of the Statistical Society*, 5,366 working-men's families in 5,294 "dwellings" (if they deserve the name!), men, women, and children thrown together without distinction of age or sex, 26, 830 persons all told; and of these families three-fourths possessed but one room. In the aristocratic parish of St. George, Hanover Square, there lived, according to the same authority, 1,465 working-men's families, nearly 6,000 persons, under similar conditions, and here, too, more than two-thirds of the whole number crowded together at the rate of one family in one room. And how the poverty of these unfortunates, among whom even thieves find nothing to steal, is exploited by the property-holding class in lawful ways! The abominable dwellings in Drury Lane, just mentioned, bring in the following rents: two cellar dwellings, 3s.; one room, ground-floor, 4s.; second-storey,

4s. 6d.; third-floor, 4s.; garret-room, 3s. weekly, so that the starving occupants of Charles Street alone, pay the house-owners a yearly tribute of £2,000, and the 5,336 families above mentioned in Westminister, a yearly rent of £40,000. . . .

But in spite of all this, they who have some kind of a shelter are fortunate, fortunate in comparison with the utterly homeless. In London fifty thousand human beings get up every morning, not knowing where they are to lay their heads at night. The luckiest of this multitude, those who succeed in keeping a penny or two until evening, enter a lodging-house, such as abound in every great city, where they find a bed. But what a bed! These houses are filled with beds from cellar to garret, four, five, six beds in a room; as many as can be crowded in. Into every bed four, five, or six human beings are piled, as many as can be packed in, sick and well, young and old, drunk and sober, men and women, just as they come, indiscriminately. Then come strife, blows, wounds, or, if these bed-fellows agree, so much the worse; thefts are arranged and things done which our language, grown more humane than our deeds, refuses to record. And those who cannot pay for such a refuge? They sleep where they find a place in passages, arcades, in corners where the police and the owners leave them undisturbed. A few individuals find their way to the refuges which are managed, here and there, by private charity, others sleep on the benches in the parks close under the windows of Queen Victoria. Let us hear the London *Times*:

It appears from the report of the proceedings at Marlborough Street Police Court in our columns of yesterday, that there is an average number of 50 human beings of all ages, who huddle together in the parks every night, having no other shelter than what is supplied by the trees and a few hollows of the embankment. Of these, the majority are young girls who have been seduced from the country by the soldiers and turned loose on the world in all the destitution of friendless penury, and all the recklessness of early vice.

This is truly horrible! Poor there must be everywhere. Indigence will find its way and set up its hideous state in the heart of a great and luxurious city. Amid the thousand narrow lanes and by-streets of a populous metropolis there must always, we fear, be much suffering—much that offends the eye—much that lurks unseen.

But that within the precincts of wealth, gaiety, and fashion, nigh the regal grandeur of St. James, close on the palatial splendour of Bayswater, on the confines of the old and new aristocratic quarters, in a district where the cautious refinement of modern design has refrained from creating one single tenement for poverty; which seems, as it were, dedicated to the exclusive enjoyment of wealth, that *there* want, and famine, and disease, and vice should stalk in all their kindred horrors, consuming body by body, soul by soul!

It is indeed a monstrous state of things! Enjoyment the most absolute, that bodily ease, intellectual excitement, or the more innocent pleasures of sense can supply to man's craving, brought in close contact with the most unmitigated misery! Wealth, from its bright saloons, laughing—an insolently heedless laugh—at the unknown wounds of want! Pleasure, cruelly but unconsciously mocking the pain that moans below! All contrary things mocking one another—all contrary, save the vice which tempts and the vice which is tempted!

But let all men remember this—that within the most courtly precincts of the richest city of God's earth, there may be found, night after night, winter after winter, women—young in years—old in sin and suffering—outcasts from society—ROTTING FROM FAMINE, FILTH, AND DISEASE. Let them remember this, and learn not to theorise but to act. God knows, there is much room for action nowadays.[2] . . .

QUESTIONS

1. For Engels, the existence of slums and homeless people is a direct result of the unbridled development of industrial capitalism. What arguments can be made for and against this view?
2. What techniques of description does Engels use to elicit the reader's sympathy?
3. To what extent do the conditions that Engels describes exist today?
4. What, for Engels, are the dehumanizing characteristics of the modern city? The theme of the city will become an important one for many nineteenth- and twentieth-century writers. Keep Engels's view in mind as we study literary and artistic representations of the city in succeeding chapters.

---

[2]*Times*, Oct. 12th, 1843.

Like Engels, the German philosopher Karl Marx (1818–1883), who also spent much of his life in London, felt a sense of moral outrage at a system of distribution in which millions, living on the borderline of subsistence, slaved so that a few thousand could wallow in luxury and indolence. Marx expressed his theories primarily in philosophical and economic language, most notably in *Das Kapital*, his analysis of the capitalist system and of its inevitable downfall. Along with Engels, Marx believed that bourgeois capitalism was a necessary stage in a historical development in which justice, in the form of true communism, would triumph.

Human history for Marx was characterized by a series of economic organizations, the more recent evolving out of the preceding as a result of class conflict. Slavery, the economic system of the ancient world, was brought to an end because of slave revolts. The ancient economy was replaced by a feudal one in which serfs, who were not slaves because they were tied to the land and could not be sold, worked for the benefit of the landlords. According to Marx, the continued oppression of the serf by feudal lords induced numbers of these laborers to flee. These runaways constituted the founders of the medieval merchant class. From the sixteenth century on, this merchant class, or bourgeoisie, gained increasing power until finally in England in the 1640s, in France in 1789, and in Germany in 1848, they were successful in overthrowing the feudal order and establishing themselves as the masters of the economy. The Industrial Revolution was the triumph of the new oppressors; the development of the factory brought into being a new class of oppressed, the proletariat. These were the workers, men, women and children, who possessed nothing but the labor of their bodies.

In Marx's theory, fierce competition among the capitalists—those who control the means of production and the goods—would result in the concentration of wealth into fewer and fewer hands and the swelling of the worker ranks by bourgeois who go under. At the same time the need to keep up profit margins in a situation of limited markets encourages more intensive exploitation of the workers. Whereas formerly the oppressed classes had been widely diffused, by its very nature industrialism brings them together; then they

gradually become aware of the injustice of the system and of their own power.

Marx firmly believed that the conflicts between classes were nearing a crisis point. A revolution of the masses against the exploiters was inevitable. When that occurred, Marx thought, the course of human history would change. Because the proletariat made up the vast majority of the people, this revolution would mark the end of class struggle and a new society would result, where all would live in harmony with one another.

Although Marx developed his theories in more elaborate form in his later writings, *The Communist Manifesto*, composed in 1848, represents his basic positions most eloquently. Written in collaboration with Engels, the work was published in the very year when Europe was swept by a revolutionary fervor that threatened to destroy most of its major monarchies. In the long run all of the revolutions failed, and in none of them did Marx's thought serve as a platform for a significant group of revolutionaries. Marxism did not become a major ideological force until the twentieth century. (The following selections from *The Communist Manifesto* were translated by Samuel Moore.)

KARL MARX AND FRIEDRICH ENGELS

From *The Communist Manifesto*

INTRODUCTION

A spectre is haunting Europe—the spectre of Communism. All the powers of old Europe have entered into a holy alliance to exorcise this spectre: Pope and Czar, Metternich and Guizot, French Radicals and German political police.

Where is the party in opposition that has not been decried as communistic by its opponents in power? Where is the Opposition that has not hurled back the branding reproach of Communism, against the more advanced opposition parties as well as against its reactionary adversaries?

Two things result from this fact:

1. Communism is already acknowledged by all European powers to be itself a power.

2. It is high time that Communists should openly, in the face of the whole world, publish their views, their aims, their tendencies, and meet this nursery tale of

the spectre of Communism with a manifesto of the party itself.

To this end, Communists of various nationalities have assembled in London, and sketched the following manifesto, to be published in the English, French, German, Italian, Flemish and Danish languages.

CHAPTER I
BOURGEOIS AND PROLETARIANS

The history of all hitherto existing society is the history of class struggles.

Freeman and slave, patrician and plebeian, lord and serf, guild-master and journeyman, in a word, oppressor and oppressed, stood in constant opposition to one another, carried on an uninterrupted, now hidden, now open fight, a fight that each time ended, either in a revolutionary reconstitution of society at large, or in the common ruin of the contending classes.

In the earlier epochs of history, we find almost everywhere a complicated arrangement of society into various orders, a manifold gradation of social rank. In ancient Rome we have patricians, knights, plebeians, slaves; in the Middle Ages, feudal lords, vassals, guild-masters, journeymen, apprentices, serfs; in almost all of these classes, again, subordinate gradations.

The modern bourgeois society that has sprouted from the ruins of feudal society has not done away with class antagonisms. It has but established new classes, new conditions of oppression, new forms of struggle in place of the old ones.

Our epoch, the epoch of the bourgeoisie, possesses, however, this distinctive feature: it has simplified the class antagonisms. Society as a whole is more and more splitting up into two great hostile camps, into two great classes directly facing each other—bourgeoisie and proletariat.

From the serfs of the Middle Ages sprang the chartered Burghers of the earliest towns. From these burgesses the first elements of the bourgeoisie were developed.

The discovery of America, the rounding of the Cape, opened up fresh ground for the rising bourgeoisie. The East-Indian and Chinese markets, the colonization of America, trade with the colonies, the increase in the means of exchange and in commodities generally, gave to commerce, to navigation, to industry, an impulse

never before known, and thereby, to the revolutionary element in the tottering feudal society, a rapid development.

The feudal system of industry, in which industrial production was monopolized by closed guilds, now no longer sufficed for the growing wants of the new markets. The manufacturing system took its place. The guild-masters were pushed aside by the manufacturing middle class; division of labour between the different corporate guilds vanished in the face of division of labour in each single workshop.

Meantime the markets kept ever growing, the demand ever rising. Even manufacture no longer sufficed. Thereupon, steam and machinery revolutionized industrial production. The place of manufacture was taken by the giant, modern industry, the place of the industrial middle class by industrial millionaires, the leaders of whole industrial armies, the modern bourgeois.

Modern industry has established the world market, for which the discovery of America paved the way. This market has given an immense development to commerce, to navigation, to communication by land. This development has, in its turn, reacted on the extension of industry; and in proportion as industry, commerce, navigation, railways extended, in the same proportion the bourgeoisie developed, increased its capital, and pushed into the background every class handed down from the Middle Ages.

We see, therefore, how the modern bourgeoisie is itself the product of a long course of development, of a series of revolutions in the modes of production and of exchange.

Each step in the development of the bourgeoisie was accompanied by a corresponding political advance of that class. An oppressed class under the sway of the feudal nobility, it became an armed and self-governing association in the medieval commune; here independent urban republic (as in Italy and Germany), there taxable "third estate" of the monarchy (as in France); afterwards, in the period of manufacture proper, serving either the semi-feudal or the absolute monarchy as a counterpoise against the nobility, and, in fact, cornerstone of the great monarchies in general, the bourgeoisie has at last, since the establishment of modern industry and of the world market, conquered for itself, in the modern parliamentary State, exclusive political sway. The executive of the modern State is but a committee for managing the common affairs of the whole bourgeoisie.

The bourgeoisie, historically, has played a most revolutionary part.

The bourgeoisie, wherever it has got the upper hand, has put an end to all feudal, patriarchal, idyllic relations. It has pitilessly torn asunder the motley feudal ties that bound man to his "natural superiors," and has left no other nexus between man and man than naked self-interest, than callous "cash payment." It has drowned the most heavenly ecstasies of religious fervour, of chivalrous enthusiasm, of Philistine sentimentalism, in the icy water of egotistic calculation. It has resolved personal worth in exchange value and in place of the numberless indefeasible chartered freedoms has set up that single, unconscionable freedom—Free Trade. In one word, for exploitation veiled by religious and political illusions it has substituted naked, shameless, direct, brutal exploitation. . . .

The need of a constantly-expanding market for its products chases the bourgeoisie over the whole surface of the globe. It must get a footing everywhere, settle everywhere, establish connections everywhere.

The bourgeoisie has through its exploitation of the world market given a cosmopolitan character to production and consumption in every country. To the great chagrin of reactionaries, it has drawn from under the feet of industry the national ground on which it stood. Old established national industries have been destroyed and are still being destroyed every day. They are dislodged by new industries, whose introduction becomes a life and death question for all civilized nations, by industries that no longer work up indigenous raw material, but raw material drawn from the remotest zones; industries whose products are consumed, not only at home, but in every quarter of the globe. In place of the old wants, satisfied by the production of the country, we find new wants, requiring for their satisfaction the products of distant lands and climes. In place of the old local and national seclusion and self-sufficiency, we have exchange in every direction, universal interdependence of nations. And as in material, so also in intellectual production. The intellectual creations of individual nations become common property.

National onesidedness and narrowmindedness become more and more impossible, and from the numerous national and local literatures there arises a world literature.

The bourgeoisie, by the rapid improvement of all instruments of production, by the immensely facilitated means of communication, draws all, even the most barbarian, nations into civilization. The cheap prices of its commodities are the heavy artillery with which it batters down all Chinese walls, with which it forces the barbarians' intensely obstinate hatred of foreigners to capitulate. It compels all nations, on pain of extinction, to adopt the bourgeois mode of production; it compels them to introduce what it calls civilization into their midst, i.e., to become bourgeois themselves. In one word, it creates a world after its own image. . . .

We see then: the means of production and of exchange, on whose foundation the bourgeoisie built itself up, were generated in feudal society. At a certain stage in the development of these means of production and of exchange, the conditions under which feudal society produced and exchanged, the feudal organization of agriculture and manufacturing industry, in one word, the feudal relations of property, became no longer compatible with the already developed productive forces; they hindered production instead of promoting it; they became so many fetters. They had to be burst asunder; they were burst asunder.

Into their place stepped free competition, accompanied by a social and political constitution adapted to it, and by the economical and political sway of the bourgeois class.

A similar movement is going on before our own eyes. Modern bourgeois society with its relations of production, of exchange and of property, a society that has conjured up such gigantic means of production and of exchange, is like the sorcerer who is no longer able to control the powers of the nether world whom he has called up by his spells. For many a decade past the history of industry and commerce is but the history of the revolt of modern productive forces against modern conditions of production, against the property relations that are the conditions for the existence of the bourgeoisie and of its rule. It is enough to mention the commercial crises that by their periodical return put the existence of the entire bourgeois society on its trial, each time more threateningly. In these crises a great part, not only of the existing products, but also of the previously-created productive forces, are periodically destroyed. In these crises there breaks out an epidemic that, in all earlier epochs, would have seemed an absurdity—the epidemic of over-production. Society suddenly finds itself put back into a state of momentary barbarism; it appears as if a famine, a universal war of devastation, had cut off the supply of every means of subsistence; industry and commerce seem to be destroyed. And why? Because there is too much civilization, too much means of subsistence, too much industry, too much commerce. The productive forces at the disposal of society no longer tend to promote bourgeois civilization and bourgeois property; on the contrary, they have become too powerful for these relations, by which they are fettered, and so soon as they overcome these fetters, they bring disorder into the whole of bourgeois society, endanger the existence of bourgeois property. The conditions of bourgeois society are too narrow to contain the wealth created by them. And how does the bourgeoisie get over these crises? On the one hand by enforced destruction of a mass of productive forces; on the other, by the conquest of new markets, and by the more thorough exploitation of the old ones. That is to say, by paving the way for more extensive and more destructive crises, and by diminishing the means whereby crises are prevented.

The weapons with which the bourgeoisie felled feudalism to the ground are now turned against the bourgeoisie itself.

But not only has the bourgeoisie forged the weapons that bring death to itself; it has also called into existence the men who are to wield those weapons—the modern working class—the proletarians.

In proportion as the bourgeoisie, i.e., capital, is developed, in the same proportion is the proletariat developed—the modern class of workers, who live only so long as they find work, and who find work only so long as their labour increases capital. These workmen, who must sell themselves piecemeal, are a commodity, like every other article of commerce, and are consequently exposed to all the vicissitudes of competition, to all the fluctuations of the market.

Owing to the extensive use of machinery and to division of labour, the work of the proletarians has lost all independent character, and, consequently, all charm for the workman. He becomes a mere appendage of the machine, and it is only the most simple, most monotonous, and most easily acquired knack, that is required of him. Hence, the cost of production of a workman is restricted, almost entirely, to the means of subsistence that he requires for his maintenance, and for the propagation of his race. But the price of a commodity, and therefore also of labour, is equal to its cost of production. In proportion, therefore, as the repulsiveness of the work increases, the wage decreases. Nay, more, in proportion as the use of machinery and division of labour increases, in the same proportion the burden of toil also increases, whether by prolongation of the working hours, by increase of the work exacted in a given time, or by increased speed of the machinery, etc.

Modern industry has converted the little workshop of the patriarchal master into the great factory of the industrial capitalist. Masses of labourers, crowded into the factory, are organized like soldiers. As privates of the industrial army they are placed under the command of a perfect hierarchy of officers and sergeants. Not only are they slaves of the bourgeois class, and of the bourgeois State; they are daily and hourly enslaved by the machine, by the overlooker, and, above all, by the individual bourgeois manufacturer himself. The more openly this despotism proclaims gain to be its end and aim, the more petty, the more hateful and the more embittering it is.

The less the skill and exertion of strength implied in manual labour, in other words, the more modern industry becomes developed, the more is the labour of men superseded by that of women. Differences of age and sex have no longer any distinctive social validity for the working class. All are instruments of labour, more or less expensive to use, according to their age and sex.

No sooner is the exploitation of the labourer by the manufacturer so far at an end that he receives his wages in cash, than he is set upon by the other portions of the bourgeoisie, the landlord, the shopkeeper, the pawnbroker, etc.

The former lower strata of the middle class—the small manufacturers, traders and persons living on small incomes, the handicraftsmen and peasants—all these sink gradually into the proletariat, partly because their diminutive capital does not suffice for the scale on which modern industry is carried on and is swamped in the competition with the large capitalists, partly because their specialized skill is rendered worthless by new methods of production. Thus the proletariat is recruited from all classes of the population.

But with the development of industry the proletariat not only increases in number; it becomes concentrated in greater masses, its strength grows, and it feels that strength more. The various interests and conditions of life within the ranks of the proletariat are more and more equalized, in proportion as machinery obliterates all distinctions of labour, and nearly everywhere reduces wages to the same low level. The growing competition among the bourgeois, and the resulting commercial crises, make the wages of the workers ever more fluctuating. The unceasing improvement of machinery, ever more rapidly developing, makes their livelihood more and more precarious; the collisions between individual workmen and individual bourgeois take more and more the character of collisions between two classes. Thereupon the workers begin to form combinations against the bourgeois; they club together in order to keep up the rate of wages; they themselves found permanent associations in order to make provision beforehand for these occasional revolts. Here and there the contest breaks out into riots. Now and then the workers are victorious, but only for a time. The real fruit of their battles lies, not in the immediate result, but in the ever-expanding union of the workers. This union is helped on by the improved means of communication that are created by modern industry and that place the workers of different localities in contact with one another. It was just this contact that was needed to centralize the numerous local struggles, all of the same character, into one national struggle between classes. But every class struggle is a political struggle. And that union, to attain which the Burghers of the Middle Ages, with their miserable highways, required centuries, the modern proletarians, thanks to railways, achieve in a few years.

This organization of the proletarians into a class, and consequently into a political party, is continually being upset again by the competition between the workers themselves. But it ever rises up again, stronger, firmer, mightier. It compels legislative recognition of particular interests of the workers, by taking advantage of the divisions among the bourgeoisie itself. Thus the ten-hours' bill in England was carried.

Altogether, collisions between the classes of the old society further in many ways the course of development of the proletariat. The bourgeoisie finds itself involved in a constant battle. At first with the aristocracy; later on, with those portions of the bourgeoisie itself, whose interests have become antagonistic to the progress of industry; at all times with the bourgeoisie of foreign countries. In all these battles it sees itself compelled to appeal to the proletariat, to ask for its help, and thus, to drag it into the political arena. The bourgeoisie itself, therefore, supplies the proletariat with its own elements of political and general education, in other words, it furnishes the proletariat with weapons for fighting the bourgeoisie.

Further, as we have already seen, entire sections of the ruling classes are, by the advance of industry, precipitated into the proletariat, or are at least threatened in their conditions of existence. These also supply the proletariat with fresh elements of enlightenment and progress.

Finally, in times when the class struggle nears the decisive hour, the process of dissolution going on within the ruling class, in fact within the whole range of old society, assumes such a violent, glaring character, that a small section of the ruling class cuts itself adrift, and joins the revolutionary class, the class that holds the future in its hands. Just as, therefore, at an earlier period, a section of the nobility went over to the bourgeoisie, so now a portion of the bourgeoisie goes over to the proletariat, and in particular, a portion of the bourgeois ideologists who have raised themselves to the level of comprehending theoretically the historical movement as a whole.

Of all the classes that stand face to face with the bourgeoisie today, the proletariat alone is a really revolutionary class. The other classes decay and finally disappear in the face of modern industry; the proletariat is its special and essential product.

The lower middle class, the small manufacturer, the shopkeeper, the artisan, the peasant, all these fight against the bourgeoisie, to save from extinction their existence as fractions of the middle class. They are therefore not revolutionary, but conservative. Nay, more, they are reactionary, for they try to roll back the wheel of history. If by chance they are revolutionary, they are so only in view of their impending transfer into the proletariat; they thus defend not their present, but their future interests; they desert their own standpoint to place themselves at that of the proletariat.

The "dangerous class," the social scum, that passively rotting mass thrown off by the lowest layers of old society, may, here and there, be swept into the movement by a proletarian revolution; its conditions of life, however, prepare it far more for the part of a bribed tool of reactionary intrigue.

In the conditions of the proletariat, those of old society at large are already virtually swamped. The proletarian is without property; his relation to his wife and children has no longer anything in common with the bourgeois family relations; modern industrial labour, modern subjection to capital, the same in England as in France, in America as in Germany, has stripped him of every trace of national character. Law, morality, religion, are to him so many bourgeois prejudices, behind which lurk in ambush just as many bourgeois interests.

All the preceding classes that got the upper hand sought to fortify their already-acquired status by subjecting society at large to their conditions of appropriation. The proletarians cannot become masters of the productive forces of society except by abolishing their own previous mode of appropriation, and thereby also every other previous mode of appropriation. They have nothing of their own to secure and to fortify; their mission is to destroy all previous securities for, and insurances of, individual property.

All previous historical movements were movements of minorities, or in the interest of minorities. The proletarian movement is the self-conscious, independent movement of the immense majority, in the interest of the immense majority. The proletariat, the lowest stratum of our present society, cannot stir, cannot raise itself up, without the whole superincumbent strata of official society being sprung into the air.

Though not in substance, yet in form, the struggle of the proletariat with the bourgeoisie is at first a national struggle. The proletariat of each country must, of course, first of all settle matters with its own bourgeoisie.

In depicting the most general phases of the development of the proletariat, we traced the more or less veiled civil war, raging within existing society, up to the point where that war breaks out into open revolution, and where the violent overthrow of the bourgeoisie lays the foundation for the sway of the proletariat.

Hitherto, every form of society has been based, as we have already seen, on the antagonism of oppressing and oppressed classes. But in order to oppress a class, certain conditions must be assured to it under which it can, at least, continue its slavish existence. The serf, in the period of serfdom, raised himself to membership in the commune, just as the petty bourgeois, under the yoke of feudal absolutism, managed to develop into a bourgeois. The modern labourer, on the contrary, instead of rising with the progress of industry, sinks deeper and deeper below the conditions of existence of his own class. He becomes a pauper, and pauperism develops more rapidly than population and wealth. And here it becomes evident that the bourgeoisie is unfit to rule because it is incompetent to assure an existence to its slave within his slavery, because it cannot help letting him sink into such a state that it has to feed him, instead of being fed by him. Society can no longer live under this bourgeoisie; in other words, its existence is no longer compatible with society.

The essential condition for the existence and for the sway of the bourgeois class is the accumulation of wealth in the hands of private individuals, the formation and augmentation of capital; the condition for capital is wage-labour. Wage-labour rests exclusively on competition between the labourers. The advance of industry, whose involuntary promoter is the bourgeoisie, replaces the isolation of the labourers, due to competition, by their revolutionary combination, due to association. The development of modern industry, therefore, cuts from under the feet of the bourgeoisie the very foundation on which it produces and appropriates products. What the bourgeoisie therefore produces, above all, are its own grave-diggers. Its fall and the victory of the proletariat are equally inevitable.

QUESTIONS

1. How does Marx explain the triumph of the bourgeois over the feudal aristocracy?
2. What is the function of the state under bourgeois rule?
3. Why is bourgeois supremacy antinationalistic?

4. What does Marx mean when he writes that the productive forces of society have become too powerful for the conditions of bourgeois property?

5. Why is the wage of a worker roughly equal to his level of subsistence?

6. In what way does the bourgeoisie produce "its own grave-diggers"?

7. In what sense are all the enemies of the bourgeois save the proletariat reactionary?

8. What did Marx foresee and what did he not foresee?

Marx feels that the duty of communists is to help workers become more intensely conscious of their status and to weld them into a political class. While Marx himself favored trade unions, he urged the workers not to be content with better wages and better conditions of work. Joining the system in this way would undermine the solidarity of the movement and, while improving the lot of certain individuals, would leave the mass of proletarians in their misery. The communist was dedicated to the destruction of private property, which was the primary tool in the hands of the bourgeoisie for the subjection of the lower class. Also slated for destruction was the state, which was the political means by which the bourgeois protected their property and controlled the workers. Once bourgeois property had been eliminated and the classless society achieved, social conflict would end and there would be no need for the oppressive power of the state.

Although Marx believed that certain members of the bourgeoisie like himself could work themselves free from their class allegiances, on the whole he maintained that individual mentalities were determined by the economic class to which they belonged. Accordingly, the agencies of historical change were not for him individuals but rather classes. Nevertheless, Marx remained to the end a child of the Enlightenment. His final goal for humanity remained the attainment of personal liberty and equality. He was committed to the belief that once the forces of exploitation were annihilated, men would be rational enough to live as brothers and sisters, sharing the goods of their labor. Indeed, his faith in the power of rationality and the essential goodness of man was even greater than that of the philosophes, for he thought that men in the final stage would live in freedom and equality even without the presence of a government.

The Growth of Material Progress Paradoxically, Marxism enjoyed its greatest success in those countries where industrialism was only getting underway and where agriculture remained the dominant occupation. This was the case in Russia in 1917 and in China in the years immediately following World War II. In Western Europe and America, however, Marx's fears were realized. In the course of the century after the publication of *The Communist Manifesto*, workers proved more concerned with immediate material gains than with ultimate goals and found that these could be accomplished with greater ease and security through trade unionism and participation in the established political system than through revolution. Although the capitalist economy suffered periodic setbacks, some of great magnitude like the Depression of the 1930s, on the whole the working population of the Western world experienced a steady increase in its standard of living. Rather than polarizing between the extremes of rich bourgeois and proletariat, industrial society witnessed an enormous expansion of the middle class. Large numbers of workers were drawn into its ranks, or at least many were led to believe they belonged there. Belief in progress, scientific and technological as well as economic, came to be characteristic of all social classes in the late nineteenth century.

People rich and poor flocked to the Great Exhibition in London in 1851 at the astounding Crystal Palace, which they viewed as a marvel of engineering and a symbol of an optimistic age of technological achievement. Science created new wonders in daily life at an astounding rate. The railroad, the steamship, the telegraph and telephone, electricity, and the internal combustion engine convinced most people that scientific invention was fundamentally helpful to mankind and that continuous progress was inevitable. Workers' awareness of continuing economic inequalities and social injustices was largely overcome by a trust in future improvement and in the efficacy of political action within the system.

Women's Rights

While Marx was publishing his *Communist Manifesto* in 1848, a group of women met peacefully at Seneca Falls, New York, in an effort to organize the fight for woman's suffrage. In the *Manifesto*, Marx had argued that for the bourgeois, women, including the wives of the bourgeois themselves, were merely instruments of production. Women supporters of the numerous antislavery societies in Europe and America had by this time already begun a campaign to broaden the goals of these organizations to include the liberation of supposedly free women. For instance, until the 1840s women could not receive a college degree nor could they own real estate in their own name in most states of the United States. But the battle was joined!

Perhaps the most eloquent of the early writings arguing for the equality of women and against the injustice of their present status was John Stuart Mill's *The Subjection of Women* written in 1861. One of the finest, most decent spirits of his age, Mill (1806–1873) was the son of John Mill, one of the leaders of early liberalism. A disciple of his father in his youth, Mill gradually grew disillusioned with a philosophy that, while committed to the freedom and equality of men, could permit the degradation of the poor and even justify it as part of the law of nature. As a writer and later a member of Parliament, he defended the rights of individuals against the oppression of the majority but at the same time urged the government to interfere when powerful individuals inflicted injury on society as a whole by abusing those same rights. Earlier liberals for him had been too selective in their espousal of the principles of liberty and equality. Conveniently they had stopped short of ensuring such freedoms when they would interfere with their own prejudices or economic and political interests. This respect for individual personality at all levels made Mill a vigorous opponent of slavery and, in his maturity, a champion of women's rights as well.

JOHN STUART MILL

From *The Subjection of Women*

The object of this Essay is to explain as clearly as I am able the grounds of an opinion which I have held from the very earliest period when I had formed any opinions at all on social or political matters, and which, instead of being weakened or modified, has been constantly growing stronger by the progress of reflection and the experience of life. That the principle which regulates the existing social relations between the two sexes—the legal subordination of one sex to the other—is wrong in itself, and now one of the chief hindrances to human improvement; and that it ought to be replaced by a principle of perfect equality, admitting no power or privilege on the one side, nor disability on the other. . . . It is one of the characteristic prejudices of the reaction of the nineteenth century against the eighteenth, to accord to the unreasoning elements in human nature the infallibility which the eighteenth century is supposed to have ascribed to the reasoning elements. For the apotheosis of Reason we have substituted that of Instinct; and we call everything instinct which we find in ourselves and for which we cannot trace any rational foundation. This idolatry, infinitely more degrading than the other, and the most pernicious of the false worships of the present day, of all of which it is now the main support, will probably hold its ground until it gives way before a sound psychology laying bare the real root of much that is bowed down to as the intention of Nature and the ordinance of God. As regards the present question, I am willing to accept the unfavourable conditions which the prejudice assigns to me. I consent that established custom, and the general feeling, should be deemed conclusive against me, unless that custom and feeling from age to age can be shown to have owed their existence to other causes than their soundness, and to have derived their power from the worse rather than the better parts of human nature. I am willing that judgment should go against me, unless I can show that my judge has been tampered with. The concession is not so great as it might appear; for to prove this, is by far the easiest portion of my task.

The generality of a practice is in some cases a strong presumption that it is, or at all events once was, conducive to laudable ends. This is the case, when the practice was first adopted, or afterwards kept up, as a means to such ends, and was grounded on experience of the mode in which they could be most effectually attained. If the authority of men over women, when first established, had been the result of a conscientious comparison between different modes of constituting the government of society; if, after trying various other modes of social organisation—the government of women over men, equality between the two, and such mixed and divided modes of government as might be invented—it had been decided, on the testimony of experience, that the mode in which women are wholly under the rule of men, having no share at all in public concerns, and each in private being under the legal obligation of obedience to the man with whom she has associated her destiny, was the arrangement most conducive to the happiness and well-being of both; its general adoption might then be fairly thought to be some evidence that, at the time when it was adopted, it was the best: though even then the considerations which recommended it may, like so many other primeval social facts of the greatest importance, have subsequently, in the course of ages, ceased to exist. But the state of the case is in every respect the reverse of this. In the first place, the opinion in favour of the present system, which entirely subordinates the weaker sex to the stronger, rests upon theory only; for there never has been trial made of any other: so that experience, in the sense in which it is vulgarly opposed to theory, cannot be pretended to have pronounced any verdict. And in the second place, the adoption of this system of inequality never was the result of deliberation, or forethought, or any social ideas, or any notion whatever of what conduced to the benefit of humanity or the good order of society. It arose simply from the fact that from the very earliest twilight of human society, every woman (owing to the value attached to her by men, combined with her inferiority in muscular strength) was found in a state of bondage to some man. Laws and systems of polity always begin by recognising the relations they find already existing between individuals. They convert what was a mere physical fact into a legal right, give it the sanction of society, and principally aim at the substitution of public and organised means of asserting and protecting these rights, instead of the irregular and lawless conflict of physical strength. Those who had already been compelled to obedience became in this manner legally bound to it. Slavery, from being a mere affair of force between the master and the slave, became regularised and a matter of compact among the masters, who, binding themselves to one another for common protection, guaranteed by their collective strength the private possessions of each, including his slaves. In early times, the great majority of the male sex were slaves, as well as the whole of the female. And many ages elapsed, some of them ages of high cultivation, before any thinker was bold enough to question the rightfulness, and the absolute social necessity, either of the one slavery or of the other. By degrees such thinkers did arise; and (the general progress of society assisting) the slavery of the male sex has, in all the countries of Christian Europe at least (though, in one of them, only within the last few years) been at length abolished, and that of the female sex has been gradually changed into a milder form of dependence. But this dependence, as it exists at present, is not an original institution, taking a fresh start from considerations of justice and social expediency—it is the primitive state of slavery lasting on, through successive mitigations and modifications occasioned by the same causes which have softened the general manners, and brought all human relations more under the control of justice and the influence of humanity. It has not lost the taint of its brutal origin. No presumption in its favour, therefore, can be drawn from the fact of its existence. The only such presumption which it could be supposed to have, must be grounded on its having lasted till now, when so many other things which came down from the same odious source have been done away with. And this, indeed, is what makes it strange to ordinary ears, to hear it asserted that the inequality of rights between men and women has no other source than the law of the strongest. . . .

If people are mostly so little aware how completely, during the greater part of the duration of our species, the law of force was the avowed rule of general conduct, any other being only a special and exceptional consequence of peculiar ties—and from how very recent a date it is that the affairs of society in general have been even pretended to be regulated according to any moral law; as little do people remember or consider, how institutions and customs which never had any ground but the law of force, last on into ages and states of general opinion which never would have permitted their first establishment. Less than forty years ago, Englishmen might still by law hold human beings in bondage as saleable property: within the present century they might kidnap them and carry them off, and work them literally to death. This absolutely extreme case of the law of force, condemned by those who can tolerate almost every other form of arbitrary power, and which, of all others presents features the most revolting to the feelings of all who look at it from an impartial position, was the law of civilised and Christian England within the memory of persons now living: and in one half of Anglo-Saxon America three or four years ago, not only did slavery exist, but the slave-trade, and the breeding of slaves expressly for it, was a general practice between slave-states. Yet not only was there a greater strength of sentiment against it, but, in England at least, a less amount either of feeling or of interest in favour of it, than of any other of the customary abuses of force: for its motive was the love of gain, unmixed and undisguised; and those who profited by it were a very small numerical fraction of the country, while the natural feeling of all who were not personally interested in it, was unmitigated abhorrence. So extreme an instance makes it almost superfluous to refer to any other: but consider the long duration of absolute monarchy. In England at present it is the almost universal conviction that military despotism is a case of the law of force, having no other origin or justification. Yet in all the great nations of Europe except England it either still exists, or has only just ceased to exist, and has even now a strong party favourable to it in all ranks of the people, especially among persons of station and consequence. Such is the power of an established system, even when far from universal; when not only in almost every period of history there have been great and well-known examples of the contrary system, but these have almost invariably been afforded by the most illustrious and most prosperous communities. In this case, too, the possessor of the undue power, the person directly interested in it, is only one person, while those who are subject to it and suffer from it are literally all the rest. The yoke is naturally and necessarily humiliating to all persons, except the one who is on the throne, together with, at most, the one who expects to succeed to it. How different are these cases from that of the power of men over women! I am not now prejudging the question of its justifiableness. I am showing how vastly more permanent it could not but be, even if not justifiable, than these other dominations which have nevertheless lasted down to our own time. Whatever gratification of pride there is in the possession of power, and whatever personal interest in its exercise, is in this case not confined to a limited class, but common to the whole male sex. Instead of being, to most of its support-

ers, a thing desirable chiefly in the abstract, or, like the political ends usually contended for by factions, of little private importance to any but the leaders; it comes home to the person and hearth of every male head of a family, and of everyone who looks forward to being so. The clodhopper exercises, or is to exercise, his share of the power equally with the highest nobleman. And the case is that in which the desire of power is the strongest: for everyone who desires power, desires it most over those who are nearest to him, with whom his life is passed, with whom he has most concerns in common, and in whom any independence of his authority is oftenest likely to interfere with his individual preferences. If, in the other cases specified, powers manifestly grounded only on force, and having so much less to support them, are so slowly and with so much difficulty got rid of, much more must it be so with this, even if it rests on no better foundation than those. We must consider, too, that the possessors of the power have facilities in this case, greater than in any other, to prevent any uprising against it. Every one of the subjects lives under the very eye, and almost, it may be said, in the hands, of one of the masters—in closer intimacy with him than with any of her fellow-subjects; with no means of combining against him, no power of even locally overmastering him, and, on the other hand, with the strongest motives for seeking his favour and avoiding to give him offence. In struggles for political emancipation, everybody knows how often its champions are bought off by bribes, or daunted by terrors. In the case of women, each individual of the subject-class is in a chronic state of bribery and intimidation combined. In setting up the standard of resistance, a large number of the leaders, and still more of the followers, must make an almost complete sacrifice of the pleasures or the alleviations of their own individual lot. If ever any system of privilege and enforced subjection had its yoke tightly riveted on the necks of those who are kept down by it, this has. I have not yet shown that it is a wrong system: but everyone who is capable of thinking on the subject must see that even if it is, it was certain to outlast all other forms of unjust authority. And when some of the grossest of the other forms still exist in many civilised countries, and have only recently been got rid of in others, it would be strange if that which is so much the deepest rooted had yet been perceptibly shaken anywhere. There is more reason to wonder that the protests and testimonies against it should have been so numerous and so weighty as they are.

Some will object, that a comparison cannot fairly be made between the government of the male sex and the forms of unjust power which I have adduced in illustration of it, since these are arbitrary, and the effect of mere usurpation, while it on the contrary is natural. But was there ever any domination which did not appear natural to those who possessed it? There was a time when the division of mankind into two classes, a small one of masters and a numerous one of slaves, appeared, even to the most cultivated minds, to be natural, and the only natural, condition of the human race. No less an intellect, and one which contributed no less to the progress of human thought, than Aristotle, held this opinion without doubt or misgiving; and rested it on the same premises on which the same assertion in regard to the dominion of men over women is usually based, namely that there are different natures among mankind, free natures, and slave natures; that the Greeks were of a free nature, the barbarian races of Thracians and Asiatics of a slave nature. But why need I go back to Aristotle? Did not the slave-owners of the Southern United States maintain the same doctrine, with all the fanaticism with which men cling to the theories that justify their passions and legitimate their personal interests? Did they not call heaven and earth to witness that the dominion of the white man over the black is natural, that the black race is by nature incapable of freedom, and marked out for slavery? some even going so far as to say that the freedom of manual labourers is an unnatural order of things anywhere. Again, the theorists of absolute monarchy have always affirmed it to be the only natural form of government; issuing from the patriarchal, which was the primitive and spontaneous form of society, framed on the model of the paternal, which is anterior to society itself, and, as they contend, the most natural authority of all. . . .

But, it will be said, the rule of men over women differs from all these others in not being a rule of force: it is accepted voluntarily; women make no complaint, and are consenting parties to it. In the first place, a great number of women do not accept it. Ever since there have been women able to make their sentiments known by their writings (the only mode of publicity which society permits to them), an increasing number of them have recorded protests against their present social condition: and recently many thousands of them, headed by the most eminent women known to the public, have petitioned Parliament for their admission to the Parliamentary Suffrage. The claim of women to be educated as solidly, and in the same branches of knowledge, as men, is urged with growing intensity, and with a great prospect of success; while the demand for their admission into professions and occupations hitherto closed against them, becomes every year more urgent. Though there are not in this country, as there are in the United States, periodical conventions and an organised party to agitate for the Rights of Women, there is a numerous and active society organised and managed by women, for the more limited object of obtaining the political franchise. Nor is it only in our own country and in America that women are beginning to protest, more or less collectively, against the disabilities under which they labour. France, and Italy, and Switzerland, and Russia now afford examples of the same thing. How many more women there are who silently cherish similar aspirations, no one can possibly know; but there are abundant tokens how many *would* cherish them, were they not so strenuously taught to repress them as contrary to the proprieties of their sex. It must be remembered, also, that no enslaved class ever asked for complete liberty at once. . . .

All causes, social and natural, combine to make it unlikely that women should be collectively rebellious to the power of men. They are so far in a position different from all other subject classes, that their masters require something more from them than actual service. Men do not want solely the obedience of women, they want their sentiments. All men, except the most brutish, desire to have, in the woman most nearly connected with them, not a forced slave but a willing one, not a slave merely, but a favourite. They have therefore put everything in practice to enslave their minds. The masters of all other slaves rely, for maintaining obedience, on fear; either fear of themselves, or religious fears. The masters of women wanted more than simple obedience, and they turned the whole force of education to effect their purpose. All women are brought up from the very earliest years in the belief that their ideal of character is the very opposite to that of men; not self-will, and government by self-control, but submission, and yielding to the control of others. All the moralities tell them that it is the duty of women, and all the current sentimentalities that it is their nature, to live for others; to make complete abnegation of themselves, and to have no life but in their affections. And by their affections are meant the only ones they are allowed to have—those to the men with whom they are connected, or to the children who constitute an additional and indefeasible tie between them and a man. When we put together three things—first, the natural attraction between opposite sexes; secondly, the wife's entire dependence on the husband, every privilege or pleasure she has being either his gift, or depending entirely on his will; and lastly, that the principal object of human pursuit, consideration, and all objects of social ambition, can in general be sought or obtained by her only through him, it would be a miracle if the object of being attractive to men had not become the polar star of feminine education and formation of character. And, this great means of influence over the minds of women having been acquired, an instinct of selfishness made men avail themselves of it to the utmost as a means of holding women in subjection, by representing to them meekness, submissiveness, and resignation of all individual will into the hands of a man, as an essential part of sexual attractiveness. Can it be doubted that any of the other yokes which mankind have succeeded in breaking, would have subsisted till now if the same means had existed, and had been so sedulously used, to bow down their minds to it? If it had been made the object of the life of every young plebeian to find personal favour in the eyes of some patrician, of every young serf with some seigneur; if domestication with him, and a share of his personal affections, had been held out as the prize which they all should look out for, the most gifted and aspiring being able to reckon on the most desirable prizes; and if, when this prize had been obtained, they had been shut out by a wall of brass from all interests not centring in him, all feelings and desires but those which he shared or inculcated; would not serfs and seigneurs, plebeians and patricians, have been as broadly distinguished at this day as men and women are? and would not all but a thinker here and there, have believed the distinction to be a fundamental and unalterable fact in human nature?

The preceding considerations are amply sufficient to show that custom, however universal it may be, affords in this case no presumption, and ought not to create any prejudice, in favour of the arrangements which place women in social and political subjection to men. But I may go farther, and maintain that the course of history, and the tendencies of progressive human society, afford not only no presumption in favour of this system of inequality of rights, but a strong one against it; and that, so far as the whole course of human improvement up to the time, the whole stream of modern tendencies, warrants any inference on the subject, it is, that this relic of the past is discordant with the future, and must necessarily disappear.

For, what is the peculiar character of the modern world—the difference which chiefly distinguishes modern institutions, modern social ideas, modern life itself, from those of times long past? It is, that human beings are no longer born to their place in life, and chained down by an inexorable bond to the place they are born to, but are free to employ their faculties, and such favourable chances as offer, to achieve the lot which may appear to them most desirable. Human society of old was constituted on a very different principle. All were born to a fixed social position, and were mostly kept in it by law, or interdicted from any means by which they could emerge from it. As some men are born white and others black, so some were born slaves and others freemen and citizens; some were born patricians, others plebeians; some were born feudal nobles, others commoners and *roturiers*. A slave or serf could never make himself free, nor, except by the will of his master, become so. . . .

In modern Europe, and most in those parts of it which have participated most largely in all other modern improvements, diametrically opposite doctrines now prevail. Law and government do not undertake to prescribe by whom any social or industrial operation shall or shall not be conducted, or what modes of conducting them shall be lawful. These things are left to the unfettered choice of individuals. Even the laws which required that workmen should serve an apprenticeship, have in this country been repealed: there being ample assurance that in all cases in which an apprenticeship is necessary, its necessity will suffice to enforce it. The old theory was, that the least possible should be left to the choice of the individual agent; that all he had to do should, as far as practicable, be laid down for him by superior wisdom. Left to himself he was sure to go wrong. The modern conviction, the fruit of a thousand years of experience, is, that things in which the individual is the person directly interested, never go right but as they are left to his own discretion; and that any regulation of them by authority, except to protect the rights of others, is sure to be mischievous. . . .

If this general principle of social and economical science is not true; if individuals, with such help as they can derive from the opinion of those who know them, are not better judges than the law and the government, of their own capacities and vocation; the world cannot too soon abandon this principle, and return to the old system of regulations and disabilities. But if the principle is true, we ought to act as if we believed it, and not to ordain that to be born a girl instead of a boy, any more than to be born black instead of white, or a commoner instead of a nobleman, shall decide the person's position through all life—shall interdict people from all the more elevated social positions, and from all, except a few, respectable occupations. . . .

At present, in the more improved countries, the disabilities of women are the only case, save one, in which laws and institutions take persons at their birth, and ordain that they shall never in all their lives be allowed to compete for certain things. The one exception is that of royalty. Persons still are born to the throne; no one, not of the reigning family, can ever occupy it, and no one even of that family can, by any means but the course of hereditary succession, attain it. All other dignities and social advantages are open to the whole male sex: many indeed are only attainable by wealth, but wealth may be striven for by anyone, and is actually obtained by many men of the very humblest origin. The difficulties, to the majority, are indeed insuperable without the aid of fortunate accidents; but no male human being is under any legal ban: neither law nor opinion superadd artificial obstacles to the natural ones. . . .

Neither does it avail anything to say that the *nature* of the two sexes adapts them to their present functions and position, and renders these appropriate to them. Standing on the ground of common sense and the constitution of the human mind, I deny that anyone knows, or can know, the nature of the two sexes, as long as they have only been seen in their present relation to one another. If men had ever been found in so-

ciety without women, or women without men, or if there had been a society of men and women in which the women were not under the control of the men, something might have been positively known about the mental and moral differences which may be inherent in the nature of each. What is now called the nature of women is an eminently artificial thing—the result of forced repression in some directions, unnatural stimulation in others. It may be asserted without scruple, that no other class of dependents have had their character so entirely distorted from its natural proportions by their relation with their masters; for, if conquered and slave races have been, in some respects, more forcibly repressed, whatever in them has not been crushed down by an iron heel has generally been let alone, and if left with any liberty of development, it has developed itself according to its own laws; but in the case of women, a hot-house and stove cultivation has always been carried on of some of the capabilities of their nature, for the benefit and pleasure of their masters. Then, because certain products of the general vital force sprout luxuriantly and reach a great development in this heated atmosphere and under this active nurture and watering, while other shoots from the same root, which are left outside in the wintry air, with ice purposely heaped all round them, have a stunted growth, and some are burnt off with fire and disappear; men, with that inability to recognise their own work which distinguishes the unanalytic mind, indolently believe that the tree grows of itself in the way they have made it grow, and that it would die if one half of it were not kept in a vapour bath and the other half in the snow. . . .

Hence, in regard to that most difficult question, what are the natural differences between the two sexes—a subject on which it is impossible in the present state of society to obtain complete and correct knowledge—while almost everybody dogmatises upon it, almost all neglect and make light of the only means by which any partial insight can be obtained into it. This is, an analytic study of the most important department of psychology, the laws of the influence of circumstances on character. For, however great and apparently ineradicable the moral and intellectual differences between men and women might be, the evidence of there being natural differences could only be negative. Those only could be inferred to be natural which could not possibly be artificial—the residuum, after deducting every characteristic of either sex which can admit of being explained from education or external circumstances. The profoundest knowledge of the laws of the formation of character is indispensable to entitle anyone to affirm even that there is any difference, much more what the difference is, between the two sexes considered as moral and rational beings; and since no one, as yet, has that knowledge (for there is hardly any subject which, in proportion to its importance, has been so little studied), no one is thus far entitled to any positive opinion on the subject. Conjectures are all that can at present be made; conjectures more or less probable, according as more or less authorised by such knowledge as we yet have of the laws of psychology, as applied to the formation of character. . . . We may safely assert that the knowledge which men can acquire of women, even as they have been and are, without reference to what they might be, is wretchedly imperfect and superficial, and always will be so, until women themselves have told all that they have to tell.

And this time has not come; nor will it come otherwise than gradually. It is but of yesterday that women have either been qualified by literary accomplishments, or permitted by society, to tell anything to the general public. As yet very few of them dare tell anything, which men, on whom their literary success depends, are unwilling to hear. Let us remember in what manner, up to a very recent time, the expression, even by a male author, of uncustomary opinions, or what are deemed eccentric feelings, usually was, and in some degree still is, received; and we may form some faint conception under what impediments a woman, who is brought up to think custom and opinion her sovereign rule, attempts to express in books anything drawn from the depths of her own nature. The greatest woman who has left writings behind her sufficient to give her an eminent rank in the literature of her country, thought it necessary to prefix as a motto to her boldest work, "Un homme peut braver l'opinion; une femme doit s'y soumettre." [1] The greater part of what women write about women is mere sycophancy to men. In the case

of unmarried women, much of it seems only intended to increase their chance of a husband. Many, both married and unmarried, overstep the mark, and inculcate a servility beyond what is desired or relished by any man, except the very vulgarest. But this is not so often the case as, even at a quite late period, it still was. Literary women are becoming more free-spoken, and more willing to express their real sentiments. Unfortunately, in this country especially, they are themselves such artificial products, that their sentiments are compounded of a small element of individual observation and consciousness, and a very large one of acquired associations. This will be less and less the case, but it will remain true to a great extent, as long as social institutions do not admit the same free development of originality in women which is possible to men. When that time comes, and not before, we shall see, and not merely hear, as much as it is necessary to know of the nature of women, and the adaptation of other things to it. . . .

One thing we may be certain of—that what is contrary to women's nature to do, they never will be made to do by simply giving their nature free play. The anxiety of mankind to interfere in behalf of nature, for fear lest nature should not succeed in effecting its purpose, is an altogether unnecessary solicitude. What women by nature cannot do, it is quite superfluous to forbid them from doing. What they can do, but not so well as the men who are their competitors, competition suffices to exclude them from; since nobody asks for protective duties and bounties in favour of women; it is only asked that the present bounties and protective duties in favour of men should be recalled. If women have a greater natural inclination for some things than for others, there is no need of laws or social inculcation to make the majority of them do the former in preference to the latter. Whatever women's services are most wanted for, the free play of competition will hold out the strongest inducements to them to undertake. And, as the words imply, they are most wanted for the things for which they are most fit; by the apportionment of which to them, the collective faculties of the two sexes can be applied on the whole with the greatest sum of valuable result.

The general opinion of men is supposed to be, that the natural vocation of a woman is that of a wife and mother. I say, is supposed to be, because, judging from

---

[1] Title-page of Mme de Staël's *Delphine.* "A man can go against public opinion; a woman must submit herself to it."

acts—from the whole of the present constitution of society—one might infer that their opinion was the direct contrary. They might be supposed to think that the alleged natural vocation of women was of all things the most repugnant to their nature; insomuch that if they are free to do anything else—if any other means of living or occupation of their time and faculties, is open, which has any chance of appearing desirable to them—there will not be enough of them who will be willing to accept the condition said to be natural to them. If this is the real opinion of men in general, it would be well that it should be spoken out. I should like to hear somebody openly enunciating the doctrine (it is already implied in much that is written on the subject)—"It is necessary to society that women should marry and produce children. They will not do so unless they are compelled. Therefore it is necessary to compel them." The merits of the case would then be clearly defined. It would be exactly that of the slaveholders of South Carolina and Louisiana. "It is necessary that cotton and sugar should be grown. White men cannot produce them. Negroes will not, for any wages which we choose to give. *Ergo* they must be compelled." An illustration still closer to the point is that of impressment. Sailors must absolutely be had to defend the country. It often happens that they will not voluntarily enlist. Therefore there must be the power of forcing them. How often has this logic been used! and, but for one flaw in it, without doubt it would have been successful up to this day. But it is open to the retort— First pay the sailors the honest value of their labour. When you have made it as well worth their while to serve you, as to work for other employers, you will have no more difficulty than others have in obtaining their services. To this there is no logical answer except "I will not": and as people are now not only ashamed, but are not desirous, to rob the labourer of his hire, impressment is no longer advocated. Those who attempt to force women into marriage by closing all other doors against them, lay themselves open to a similar retort. If they mean what they say, their opinion must evidently be, that men do not render the married condition so desirable to women, as to induce them to accept it for its own recommendations. It is not a sign of one's thinking the boon one offers very attractive, when one allows only Hobson's choice, "that or none." And here,

I believe, is the clue to the feelings of those men, who have a real antipathy to the equal freedom of women. I believe they are afraid, not lest women should be unwilling to marry, for I do not think that anyone in reality has that apprehension; but lest they should insist that marriage should be on equal conditions; lest all women of spirit and capacity should prefer doing almost anything else, not in their own eyes degrading, rather than marry, when marrying is giving themselves a master, and a master too of all their earthly possessions. And truly, if this consequence were necessarily incident to marriage, I think that the apprehension would be very well founded. I agree in thinking it probable that few women, capable of anything else, would, unless under an irresistible *entraînement*, rendering them for the time insensible to anything but itself, choose such a lot, when any other means were open to them of filling a conventionally honourable place in life: and if men are determined that the law of marriage shall be a law of despotism, they are quite right, in point of mere policy, in leaving to women only Hobson's choice. But, in that case, all that has been done in the modern world to relax the chain on the minds of women, has been a mistake. They never should have been allowed to receive a literary education. Women who read, much more women who write, are, in the existing constitution of things, a contradiction and a disturbing element: and it was wrong to bring women up with any acquirements but those of an odalisque, or of a domestic servant.

QUESTIONS

1. List the arguments that Mill says have been made in favor of the subjection of women and explain how he answers each of these.
2. Compare Mill's portrayal of women's condition and his arguments for women's equality with those of Mary Wollstonecraft in Chapter 27.
3. What ideas of liberalism are reflected in this passage?
4. What comparisons does Mill make between the condition of women and slavery? How valid are these parallels in your opinion?
5. How do Mill's analyses of, and remedies for, an oppressed class differ from those of Marx?

6. How relevant are the injustices that Mill points out and the solutions that he offers to the condition of present-day women?

The struggle begun by Mill's generation for equal rights for women was to last for many years. In the crucial matter of suffrage, for instance, women were not to have the vote in Canada until 1917, in the United States and England until 1920 and 1928 respectively; in France they were denied this basic right until after World War II. This chronology follows by fifty to a hundred years the granting of voting rights to all males in the various countries of Western Europe and America. Even after voting rights were won, however, large areas remained in which women experienced discrimination. The women's movement that began around 1970 represents an ongoing determination to eliminate inequalities.

29

Art and Literature in the Industrial World: Realism

꒳

Artists, as well as social thinkers, were forced to come to terms with the industrialization of society. The conventions and enthusiasms that had permitted an artist to create the gentle *Experiment with a Vacuum Pump* (Fig. 23-4) were no longer appropriate in an age in which scientific progress had produced the vast, dehumanizing factories of Leeds and Birmingham. Nor did the idealizing and exotic tendencies of romanticism deal adequately with the problems of the mid-nineteenth century. Industrialism and its social consequences necessitated profound changes in *all* the arts, but our examples will be drawn from painting and architecture.

Architecture

Nineteenth-century architects were hesitant in their attempts to create a new architectural language for their age. In 1847 Professor Donaldson, speaking at a meeting of the Architectural Association (an important English architectural school) said, "The great question is, are we to have an architecture of our period, a distinct, individual, palpable style of the 19th century?" Romanticism had produced a series of revivals: Gothic, Romanesque, Renaissance. It is difficult for us to imagine the controversies that raged as to which style was the most correct or appropriate for particular needs. By mid-century, the architect tended to elect forms based on associations with the functions of the building, hence, Gothic for churches and Italian Renaissance for banks and businesses. Yet the new functions, needs, and materials of architecture posed new problems and demanded new solutions, which were more frequently offered by engineers and builders than by architects. An example of such a new problem and a new solution is the Crystal Palace, created for the Great Exhibition of 1851 in London (Fig. 29-1).

A call for designs for the main exhibition hall, one-third of a mile long, produced a variety of solutions that would take too long to build, were too costly and would be impossible to light. However, Joseph Paxton, gardener of the earl of Chatworth, proposed a modular glass box made of cast and wrought iron framing and glass. All the parts could be prefabricated, shipped by rail, and erected on the site in Hyde Park. On July 16, 1850, an agreement was signed between the commissioners of the exhibition, the engineers, and the glass manufacturers. The completed hall was handed over on January 31, 1851, ready for the installation of exhibits. Lighted naturally, cooled by giant louvered windows that could be opened mechanically, the Crystal Palace was truly a marvel (though John Ruskin, the English architectural critic, refused to call it architecture). Today we see it as a modern solution to a difficulty without reliance on the visual or technical formulas of traditional architecture.

Similar requirements—limited land, money, and time; the need for adequate space and light—were the conditions that created the tall office building in Chicago in the last decades of the nineteenth century. Tall

29-1 Crystal Palace. *(Illustrated London News,* Sept. 6, 1851)

29-2 William Lebaron Jenny, Chicago Home Insurance Building.
(Chicago Architectural Photographing Company)

29-3 Burnham & Root, Reliance Building, Chicago.
(Chicago Architectural Photographing Company)

buildings had become possible with the invention of the elevator, fireproofing, and the perfection of iron and steel framing. Yet many architects tended to clothe these stacks of floors in Greek, Gothic, or Renaissance details (Fig. 29-2). It was as if they could not decide what a tall building should look like. Should it express height, the cells of the floors? Should it resemble a column with shaft, base, and capital? After the fire of 1871 destroyed the heart of commercial Chicago, the architects of that city were faced with problems demanding innovation. The Reliance Building (Fig. 29-3) is the cul-

mination of a number of ideas. Built in the summer of 1891, it is a self-supporting metal cage with glass infill. It was simple to erect and maintain. The walls were great expanses of glass, some fixed, some movable panels, providing light and ventilation for the offices lining each side of its central corridor. Visually, the building is a very clear expression of its function, which is to be tall, slablike, economical, and useful. There are no classical orders, no pointed arches. Chicagoans pointed with pride to the development of the "Commercial Style," but some critics felt that its simple expression of function through form was too commercial, too expedient. It would not be until after World War I that the hold of tradition would be completely broken.

Painting: Realism

In architecture, as in any art, it is never enough to solve a problem. Building forms have a profound effect on the quality of life; painting and sculpture reflect, comment on, and affect the future of the arts and of man. In mid-century what seemed most real and most important was progress and economic expansion. In painting the consequences of industrialism made the problems perceived by Delacroix, Goya, and Constable seem more acute. Again and again the artist found himself asking, what should he paint, for whom, and how? Some painters found that industrialism itself provided fascinating subject matter. The English painter William Turner interpreted the technology that had revolutionized transportation in *Rain, Steam and Speed, The Great Western Railway* (Color Plate VIII). Painted in 1845, it was, according to Turner, a literal account of an event that he had witnessed during a storm while riding on a train. The public, however, could not readily accept the modern, "unartistic" subject matter, and Turner's methods were not to the liking of the public, who were used to the smooth surfaces and academic perfection of most successful painting.

Gustave Courbet (1819–1877)   The questions of what one should paint and how one should paint it are issues that were central to the development of art in the nineteenth century. Turner and Constable represented one kind of revolt from the accepted academic painting that was a natural descendent of the art of the seventeenth and eighteenth centuries. Another kind of revolt was that represented by the French painter Gustave Courbet and the collection of artists who thought of themselves as realists. This group, which included landscape painters as well as figure and genre painters, succeeded in dominating trends in painting in the third quarter of the nineteenth century. In an 1855 manifesto, Courbet, the pioneer in the movement, stated his principal aims as a realist to be "to translate the customs, the ideas, the appearances of my epoch." The artist was to paint what he saw. For Courbet, this meant

depicting the ugly as well as the beautiful. In his view the lower classes were more important than the upper social groups because it was on their labor that modern life was founded. Born in the French countryside, Courbet was the personification of the swaggering, tough but independent socialist. In rendering the harsh reality of his peasant subjects, Courbet depicted life in the country in a way far removed from romantic idealization of it. Courbet was a realist primarily because of his subject matter and his attitudes, but he was not concerned with rendering the details and textures of every object. For this reason he usually painted in his studio, only doing sketches out-of-doors. More traditional painters criticized his strong colors and his heavily layered paint, which he sometimes applied with a palette knife, a most unconventional process. The total effect of his work, however, was shocking only to those who preferred older styles of painting.

Ford Madox Brown (1821–1893)   In England the painter Ford Madox Brown, like Courbet, chose subjects that had philosophical or social relevance for the day. His paintings were filled with the minutiae of life. Brown, like Constable, worked out-of-doors, drawing his subjects from nature in an attempt to create an intensified illusion of reality. His large painting, *Work*, 1862–1865 (Fig. 29-4) shows a sharp contrast between busy laborers and elegant passers-by. To the right, watching the scene is the English philosopher Carlyle, who wrote about the dignity of labor. Beside Carlyle is Frederick D. Maurice, who helped to found the Working Men's College, an institution dedicated to combating social ills and raising working men's status through education. *Work* is certainly more than a picture of Hampstead on a sunny day.

Compare this painting with *The Stonebreakers*, painted in 1849 by Courbet (Fig. 29-5). Begin by deciding what you consider "realism." Does it have to do with the subject matter or the way in which the subject is presented? How does the stonebreaker differ from the workers in *Work*? Which is more anonymous? Which portrays workers more authentically? Which picture rouses a greater response? Why? Does Courbet's focus on two figures intensify or detract from the scene? Do you think the two pictures have a moral? What is that moral? Are location, time of day, and condition of the weather as important as they were to Constable?

29-4 Above. Ford Madox Brown, *Work*. (Courtesy of the City of Manchester Art Galleries)

29-5 Right. Gustave Courbet, *The Stonebreakers*. (Staatliche Kunstsammlugen, Dresden, Gemäldegalerie Neue Meister; Deutsche Fotothek Dresden)

Thomas Eakins (1844–1916)   Born in Philadelphia, Eakins studied at the Pennsylvania Academy then traveled abroad to France and Spain, where he was profoundly affected by the work of Velasquez. When he returned home in 1870 he began to produce the intense, ordered, and descriptive paintings that are characteristic of his particular style of realism. He worked out-of-doors sketching and studying light, air, and the movement of both over figures and ground. In his *Max Schmitt in a Single Scull* (Fig. 29-6) Eakins, portrayed in the far boat, pulls away from his more famous friend whose skill at racing had made him an important figure in the Philadelphia area. Schmitt is seen in the near ground and the effort and concentration that characterize the sport have lapsed into a momentary pause that permits us to see Schmitt and the setting as if in a single moment in time. Eakins' ability to capture a moment in time should be compared with that of Monet, the French impressionist who will be considered in the next chapter.

Photography

The problem with being a realist painter is no better revealed than when one compares a photograph with a painting. The social and economic forces that influenced the realists also produced the technological revolution that produced new ways in which pictures could be made. Although Courbet, Ford Madox Brown, and Eakins might call themselves "realists" they could not compete with the ability of the camera to give an account of the thing seen. Invented in the first decades of

29-6   Thomas Eakins, *Max Schmitt in a Single Scull.* (The Metropolitan Museum of Art, Purchase, 1934 Alfred N. Punnett Fund and Gift of George D. Pratt)

29-7   Edward Muybridge, *Studies in Animal Locomotion*. (International Museum of Photography at George Eastman House)

the nineteenth century (the earliest photograph dates from ca. 1826), by the 1850s it seemed that the camera could capture more detail and information than the eye could see or the hand record. If realism was to be defined by painterly conventions that rendered everything as it was seen, then painting was in danger of being replaced. If, however, realism was an attitude that was defined by an honesty toward subject matter and a willingness to seek subject matter in the everyday life and experience of people, then photography was much less threatening—the artist could rely on his skill in creating a convincing painting. Artists responded with some of both, and some artists saw photography as a tool that they, too, might use. Eakins, and the Frenchman Edgar Degas both used Edward Muybridge's *Studies in Animal Locomotion* (Fig. 29-7), the first important publication of both the human figure and animals in motion, as caught by time-lapse photography, as a means to study forms in action. Eventually photographers, too would seek to have their work accepted as art.

Realism in Literature

Writers in the industrial world, like artists, felt the need to portray as exactly as possible real life around them. As Courbet called for realism in painting, the French critic Duranty urged writers to strive for "the exact, complete, and sincere reproduction of the social milieu in which we live." Writers who considered themselves realists reacted against the fantastic, exotic, and ideal elements in romanticism, although in many of the greatest nineteenth-century works of literature, realism and romanticism coexist. If romanticism produced great *lyrics*, realism, as might be expected, produced great *novels*, for the novel, of all literary genres, is most capable of representing the varied dimensions of a society and its characters. If the middle to late nineteenth century was the great age of the realistic novel, there are still many writers who practice this art today. Although realism has been severely questioned in the twentieth century, it has not entirely died out. Realistic novels are still popular in the United States; and in the Soviet Union, China, and other communist countries, "socialist realism" is still the only officially accepted style for novelists.

One reason for the success of realism as a literary style in the nineteenth century was the increase in literacy among people in the middle and lower classes and the diffusion of journalism. Many novels were published in serial form in the cheap and easily accessible newspapers and journals. The new reading public was not interested in kings, gods, or ideal types; they preferred to read about people like themselves in surroundings like their own.

Realism could be considered a literary school only in France, where it had its fervent proponents and its detractors, its practitioners and its critics. The greatest realistic novelists there were Stendhal and Balzac. The latter, in his series of novels entitled *The Human Comedy* (obviously in contrast to *The Divine Comedy*) attempted a complete portrayal of French nineteenth-century society, creating memorable characters in the process. In England, Charles Dickens, George Eliot, and William Thackeray are examples of realistic novelists. Realism in the United States began later than in Europe, but it had a considerable impact on American fiction that continues to the present day. Henry James studied the French realists for his own benefit; William Dean Howells wrote against "romantic lies" in literature in favor of realism, which portrays "men and women as they actually are, actuated by the motives and the passions in the measure we all know." Stephen Crane, who portrayed the harsher aspects of the Civil War, was another great American realist.

What are the basic characteristics of realism? As Howells' statement indicates, a belief in the possibility of realism implies a belief in an objective reality. Realism can be both material and psychological. It uses words to depict the way that things look and feel and the way that people act. Very often, the things influence or represent the people. The realist believes in "realistically" motivated characters who do not act in unexpected ways. Wishing to exclude nothing, realistic writers pay much attention to detail, especially the more sordid or shocking aspects of human life. Although nineteenth-century realists claimed to be objective in their portrayal of actual life, many of them reveal in their writings their profound convictions on contemporary social issues. The impact of industrialism on cities and on human life, particularly the wretched condition of the urban poor, was a particularly apt subject for socially concerned realists.

Charles Dickens (1812–1870)   Dickens, a great literary success through his serial novels widely diffused in journals, was one of the most vivid portrayers of the new cities, the characters of all social strata within them, and the alienating effects of industrial capitalism. Because of his improbable plots and grotesque, almost monstrous characters, he cannot be called a consistently realistic novelist; still, he does to a great extent reproduce the material, social, and psychological environment of his time. This selection from *The Old Curiosity Shop* describes the arrival of the novel's heroine, little Nell, and her grandfather in the English mill town of Birmingham.

CHARLES DICKENS

From *The Old Curiosity Shop*

In all their journeying, they had never longed so ardently, they had never so pined and wearied, for the freedom of pure air and open country, as now. No, not even on that memorable morning, when, deserting their old home, they abandoned themselves to the mercies of a strange world, and left all the dumb and senseless things they had known and loved, behind—not even then, had they so yearned for the fresh solitudes of wood, hillside, and field, as now; when the noise and dirt and vapour of the great manufacturing town, reeking with lean misery and hungry wretchedness, hemmed them in on every side, and seemed to shut out hope, and render escape impossible.

"Two days and nights!" thought the child. "He said two days and nights we should have to spend among such scenes as these. Oh! if we live to reach the country once again, if we get clear of these dreadful places, though it is only to lie down and die, with what a grateful heart I shall thank God for so much mercy!''

With thoughts like this, and with some vague design of travelling to a great distance among streams and mountains, where only very poor and simple people lived, and where they might maintain themselves by very humble helping work in farms, free from such terrors as that from which they fled—the child, with no resource but the poor man's gift, and no encouragement but that which flowed from her own heart, and its sense of the truth and right of what she did, nerved herself to this last journey and boldly pursued her task.

"We shall be very slow to-day, dear," she said, as they toiled painfully through the streets; "my feet are sore, and I have pains in all my limbs from the wet of yesterday. I saw that he looked at us and thought of that, when he said how long we should be upon the road."

"It was a dreary way he told us of," returned her grandfather, piteously. "Is there no other road? Will you not let me go some other way than this?"

"Places lie beyond these," said the child, firmly, "where we may live in peace, and be tempted to do no harm. We will take the road that promises to have that end, and we would not turn out of it, if it were a hundred times worse than our fears lead us to expect. We would not, dear, would we?"

"No," replied the old man, wavering in his voice, no less than in his manner. "No. Let us go on. I am ready. I am quite ready, Nell."

The child walked with more difficulty than she had led her companion to expect, for the pains that racked her joints were of no common severity, and every exertion increased them. But they wrung from her no complaint, or look of suffering; and, though the two travellers proceeded very slowly, they did proceed; and clearing the town in course of time, began to feel that they were fairly on their way.

A long suburb of red brick houses,—some with patches of garden ground, where coal-dust and factory smoke darkened the shrinking leaves, and coarse rank flowers; and where the struggling vegetation sickened and sank under the hot breath of kiln and furnace, making them by its presence seem yet more blighting and unwholesome than in the town itself,—a long, flat, straggling suburb passed, they came by slow degrees upon a cheerless region, where not a blade of grass was seen to grow; where not a bud put forth its promise in the spring; where nothing green could live but on the surface of the stagnant pools, which here and there lay idly sweltering by the black roadside.

Advancing more and more into the shadow of this mournful place, its dark depressing influence stole upon their spirits, and filled them with a dismal gloom. On every side, and as far as the eye could see into the heavy distance, tall chimneys, crowding on each other, and presenting that endless repetition of the same dull, ugly form, which is the horror of oppressive dreams, poured out their plague of smoke, obscured the light, and made foul the melancholy air. On mounds of ashes by the wayside, sheltered only by a few rough boards, or rotten pent-house roofs, strange engines spun and writhed like tortured creatures; clanking their iron chains, shrieking in their rapid whirl from time to time as though in torment unendurable, and making the ground tremble with their agonies. Dismantled houses here and there appeared, tottering to the earth, propped up by fragments of others that had fallen down, unroofed, windowless, blackened, desolate, but yet inhabited. Men, women, children, wan in their looks and ragged in attire, tended the engines, fed their tributary fires, begged upon the road, or scowled half-naked from the doorless houses. Then came more of the wrathful monsters, whose like they almost seemed to be in their wildness and their untamed air, screeching and turning round and round again; and still, before, behind, and to the right and left, was the same interminable perspective of brick towers, never ceasing in their black vomit, blasting all things living or inanimate, shutting out the face of day, and closing in on all these horrors with a dense dark cloud.

But night-time in this dreadful spot!—night, when the smoke was changed to fire; when every chimney spirted up its flame; and places, that had been dark vaults all day, now shone red-hot, with figures moving to and fro within their blazing jaws, and calling to one another with hoarse cries—night, when the noise of every strange machine was aggravated by the darkness; when the people near them looked wilder and more savage; when bands of unemployed labourers paraded in the roads, or clustered by torchlight round their leaders, who told them in stern language of their wrongs, and urged them on to frightful cries and threats; when maddened men, armed with sword and firebrand, spurning the tears and prayers of women who would restrain them, rushed forth on errands of terror and destruction, to work no ruin half so surely as their own—night, when carts came rumbling by, filled with rude coffins (for contagious disease and death had been busy with the living crops); when orphans cried, and distracted women shrieked and followed in their wake—night, when some called for bread, and some for drink to drown their cares; and some with tears, and some with staggering feet, and some with bloodshot eyes, went brooding home—night, which, unlike the night that Heaven sends on earth, brought with it no peace, nor quiet, nor signs of blessed sleep—who shall tell the terrors of the night to that young wandering child!

And yet she lay down, with nothing between her and the sky; and, with no fear for herself, for she was past it now, put up a prayer for the poor old man. So very weak and spent she felt, so very calm and unresisting, that she had no thought of any wants of her own, but prayed that God would raise up some friend for *him*. She tried to recall the way they had come, and to look in the direction where the fire by which they had slept last night was burning. She had forgotten to ask the name of the poor man, their friend, and when she had remembered him in her prayers, it seemed ungrateful not to turn one look towards the spot where he was watching.

A penny loaf was all they had had that day. It was very little, but even hunger was forgotten in the strange tranquillity that crept over her senses. She lay down very gently, and, with a quiet smile upon her face, fell into a slumber. It was not like sleep—and yet it must have been, or why those pleasant dreams of the little scholar all night long!

Morning came. Much weaker, diminished powers even of sight and hearing, and yet the child made no complaint—perhaps would have made none, even if she had not that inducement to be silent, travelling by her side. She felt a hopelessness of their ever being extricated together from that forlorn place, a dull conviction that she was very ill, perhaps dying; but no fear or anxiety.

A loathing of food, that she was not conscious of until they expended their last penny in the purchase of another loaf, prevented her partaking even of this poor repast. Her grandfather ate greedily, which she was glad to see.

Their way lay through the same scenes as yesterday, with no variety or improvement. There was the same thick air, difficult to breathe; the same blighted ground, the same hopeless prospect, the same misery and distress. Objects appeared more dim, the noise less, the path more rugged and uneven, for sometimes she stumbled, and became roused, as it were, in the effort to prevent herself from falling. Poor child! the cause was in her tottering feet.

Towards the afternoon, her grandfather complained bitterly of hunger. She approached one of the wretched hovels by the wayside, and knocked with her hand upon the door.

"What would you have here?" said a gaunt miserable man, opening it.

"Charity. A morsel of bread."

"Do you see that?" returned the man hoarsely, pointing to a kind of bundle on the ground. "That's a dead child. I and five hundred other men were thrown out of work three months ago. That is my third dead child, and last. Do you think I have charity to bestow, or a morsel of bread to spare?"

The child recoiled from the door, and it closed upon her. Impelled by strong necessity, she knocked at another: a neighbouring one, which, yielding to the slight pressure of her hand, flew open.

It seemed that a couple of poor families lived in this hovel, for two women, each among children of her own, occupied different portions of the room. In the centre stood a grave gentleman in black who appeared to have just entered, and who held by the arm a boy.

"Here, woman," he said, "here's your deaf and dumb son. You may thank me for restoring him to you. He was brought before me this morning, charged with theft; and with any other boy it would have gone hard, I assure you. But as I had compassion on his infirmities, and thought he might have learnt no better, I have managed to bring him back to you. Take more care of him for the future."

"And won't you give me back *my* son!" said the other woman, hastily rising and confronting him. "Won't you give me back *my* son, sir, who was transported for the same offence!"

"Was *he* deaf and dumb, woman?" asked the gentleman sternly.

"Was he not, sir?"

"You know he was not."

"He was," cried the woman. "He was deaf, dumb, and blind, to all that was good and right, from his cradle. Her boy may have learnt no better! where did mine learn better? where could he? who was there to teach him better, or where was it to be learnt?"

"Peace, woman," said the gentleman, "your boy was in possession of all his senses."

"He was," cried the mother; "and he was the more easy to be led astray because he had them. If you save this boy because he may not know right from wrong, why did you not save mine who was never taught the difference? You gentlemen have as good a right to punish her boy, that God has kept in ignorance of sound and speech, as you have to punish mine, that you kept in ignorance yourselves. How many of the girls and boys—ah, men and women too—that are brought before you and you don't pity, are deaf and dumb in their minds, and go wrong in that state, and are punished in that state, body and soul, while you gentlemen are quarrelling among yourselves whether they ought to learn this or that?—Be a just man, sir, and give me back my son."

"You are desperate," said the gentleman, taking out his snuff-box, "and I am sorry for you."

"I *am* desperate," returned the woman, "and you have made me so. Give me back my son, to work for these helpless children. Be a just man, sir, and for God's sake, as you have had mercy upon this boy, give me back my son!"

The child had seen and heard enough to know that this was not a place at which to ask for alms. She led the old man softly from the door, and they pursued their journey.

QUESTIONS

1. What contrast does Dickens make between the city and the country in this passage? What are the techniques that produce this contrast?
2. Is Dickens' description an entirely objective one? What subjective elements do you find in it?
3. What relationship is established between the industrial environment and the people who inhabit it? How?
4. Compare Engels's description of London in Chapter 28 with Dickens's description of Birmingham. What do the social philosopher and the novelist have in common? What differentiates them?
5. Compare this passage with Courbet's paintings. Can realistic art ever be an exact reproduction of reality? Why or why not? What conventions do realistic artists use?

Since no excerpts can possibly convey the world created by any of the great nineteenth-century realistic novels, the student is urged to read at least one in its entirety. The passage from *The Old Curiosity Shop* does exemplify a characteristic of realism that was to become more and more important toward the end of the nineteenth century: the determination of human character by the material and social environment. As this belief evolved into a so-called scientific credo, the movement known as *naturalism* replaced realism. The naturalists, more interested in the new theories of Charles Darwin on human evolution than on Courbet's ideas on the reproduction of reality, tried to establish cause-and-effect laws in their novels. Certain conditions in the environment, they demonstrated, will produce certain traits in human beings. The foremost practitioner of naturalism in France was Émile Zola; he found an avid follower in the American Theodore Dreiser. As late as 1940, the black American writer Richard Wright produced a great naturalistic novel, *Native Son*, which demonstrates how a young black man becomes a criminal through the influence of the racist society in which he lives.

30

Developments in the Late Nineteenth Century: Beyond Realism

❧

The years corresponding to the reign of Queen Victoria in England (1837–1901) produced a number of radical changes in the ways that people in the West viewed themselves and their environment. As industrialism became a fact of life, prevailing attitudes became more and more materialistic. Marx had taught human beings to see themselves as controlled by economic forces, although they could help to shape these forces for the cause of social justice. Some liberal thinkers envisaged a future time when the steady progress of capitalistic industry would create a society in which everyone would be surrounded by mechanical conveniences and physical comfort. Living in a world where every year seemed to witness dramatic technical achievements, the middle-class European or American (if he did not accept the predictions of Marx) had every reason to feel smug about himself and his society.

EUROPE in 1871

Charles Darwin (1809–1882) In the pure, as opposed to the applied, sciences, more fundamental changes were taking place. Among the most important of these were the evolutionary theories put forth by Charles Darwin. Darwin, who published his *Origin of Species* in 1859 and *The Descent of Man* in 1871, showed through his scientific observations of the "lower" animals that man was an integral part of their world. By evolution he meant that species are mutable: that each class of living organisms has developed through a series of gradual changes from a different one that preceded it. Species developed through mutations in inherited characteristics. Those inheriting the most useful characteristics—for fighting, food gathering, or mating—survived; the others died out. Thus life was basically a struggle for existence. The "survival of the fittest" was brought about through "natural selection." Man was one of those species that had evolved from the primate family and had managed to survive.

The protest against Darwin and his theories, which lasted well into the twentieth century, was very great indeed. Fundamentalist religious groups denounced him for proposing a theory of creation contrary to the one in Genesis; other moralists and religious authorities claimed that he had turned man into a monkey and undermined the foundations of human dignity, morality, and religion. The most upsetting concept in Darwin's theory of evolution was its concept of life as a scene of struggle and survival, of "nature red in tooth and claw." Nature could no longer be seen as the harmonious work of the Supreme Being or the motherly source of consolation for wounded emotions. Constant flux, change, relativity of existence, and the elimination of the weak were in the natural order of things.

Herbert Spencer (1820–1903)   Nonscientific Darwin enthusiasts did not hesitate to apply his theories to human society. Herbert Spencer proclaimed a doctrine of agnosticism (the impossibility of knowing the existence of God with certainty) and what came to be known as "social Darwinism." Spencer argued that society, like the natural world, was governed by the principle of evolution. There, too, the fittest survived and the weak went under. Social evolution was headed toward the increased freedom of the individual, and governments had no business interfering in the "natural" economic processes or protecting the weak and unfit. In stressing the freedom of individual struggle in the economic process, Spencer seemed to give a scientific confirmation to the doctrines of early liberalism. His ideas had a particularly great influence in the United States, where the individualistic capitalism that led to the "robber barons" was booming. Thus the nineteenth-century bourgeois managed to assimilate even the radical theories of evolution into their materialistic, self-satisfied view of the world.

Friedrich Nietzsche (1844–1900)   Yet other philosophers and artists raised their voices loudly against this view of human nature and society. The highly influential German Nietzsche, a poetic more than a systematic

philosopher, adapted evolutionary theories to purposes quite different from Spencer's. He denounced his bourgeois contemporaries for their hypocrisy, their stale morality, and their rationalism. He also saw human nature in terms of evolution toward freedom and elimination of weakness, but the freedom that interested him was spiritual and intellectual rather than economic and material. Rather than being satisfied with Western culture as he found it, he attacked not only its present state but also what we have seen to be its roots: the Greco-Roman and Judeo-Christian traditions. The Greek emphasis on reason as exemplified by Socrates worked against the healthy vitality of the instincts, according to Nietzsche. He did admire an aspect of Greek culture that, he felt, modern times had neglected—the irrational or "Dionysian" strain represented by ancient tragedy. Nietzsche advocated a revolt against the limits of reason and reasonableness and a return to greater sources of personal and cultural power in the irrational and in myth. The moral values of Jews and Christians he found to be the expressions of weaklings or of "slaves." Christian ideas such as "pity," "turning the other cheek," or "sin" were for Nietzsche notions designed to keep people in their place instead of allowing free individuals to realize themselves to their full potential.

Nietzsche's thought, interpreted in various ways, has been influential on a variety of modern doctrines. Following his profound doubts about Western culture, some thinkers turned to the Orient or to Africa in an effort to find new sources of vitality for their own times. Others, following an opposite line of thought, derived racist ideas from Nietzsche, seeing in his theory of human evolution toward the free, noble "superman" a justification for beliefs in the superiority of the white or Aryan race. The Nazis interpreted Nietzsche in this way. Nietzsche's thought has been deeply influential on the philosophical school of existentialism, both in its Christian and atheistic forms. Although Nietzsche's works are best read in their entirety, people tend to remember his stunning aphorisms. A few of the influential ones, taken from *The Antichrist, Beyond Good and Evil, Thus Spake Zarathustra* and *Will to Power*, are printed below. Consider each one for its implications and possible impact on modern culture and thought.

FRIEDRICH NIETZSCHE

Quotations

The Christian religion grew upon a soil of such utter falsification, where the deepest instincts of the ruling factions were opposed to nature and natural values to such an extent, that Christianity became a death struggle against reality which has never been surpassed.

Nothing is more pathological in our pathological modernity than this disease of Christian pity.

What is good? All that elevates the feeling of power, the will to power, the power itself in man.

What is bad? All that proceeds from weakness.

Life is an instinct of growth, for survival, for the accumulation of forces, for power.

Morality is the best of all devices for leading mankind by the nose.

Woman was God's second mistake.

I call Christianity the one great curse, the one intrinsic depravity, . . . the one immortal blemish on the human race.

Life itself is *Will to Power*; self-preservation is only one of the indirect and most frequent results thereof.

The noble soul has reverence for itself.

The Christian faith from the beginning, is sacrifice: the sacrifice of all freedom, all pride, all self-confidence of spirit; it is at the same time subjection, self-derision, and self-mutilation.

There are no eternal facts, as there are no absolute truths.

I teach you the Superman. Man is something that is to be surpassed. What have you done to surpass him?

All the gods are dead; so we now want the superman to live.

God is dead! God remains dead! And we have killed Him!

He who must be a creator in good and evil—verily, he must first be a destroyer, and break values into pieces.

The man who has won his freedom . . . tramples ruthlessly upon that contemptible kind of comfort which tea-grocers, Christians, cows, women, Englishmen and other democrats worship in their dreams.

The world is beautiful, but has a disease called Man.

The Christian resolve to find the world evil and ugly has made the world evil and ugly.

Beyond Realism: Fyodor Dostoevsky (1821–1881)

Another radical critique of materialistic and rationalistic Western society came from the Russian writer Dostoevsky. Dostoevsky, who was to have a major impact on Western literature and thought in the twentieth century, considered himself as a Russian outside the traditions of Western Europe and thus able to view them more critically. He envisioned a major role for Russia in the destiny of the West. History has proved him right in a way that he would not have approved.

Dostoevsky began his intellectual career as a socialist, associating with one of many groups of young Russians interested in the new doctrines from Europe. For this, the tsarist regime arrested him, sending him off to imprisonment in Siberia. He was at first sentenced to death, but the sentence was commuted at the last minute. During his stay in the Siberian prison, an experience that he recounted later in *The House of the Dead*, Dostoevsky underwent a reconversion to a mystical, Russian Orthodox Christianity. He also gained insight from observing the various criminals and political prisoners around him. In his later novels Dostoevsky portrayed characters in the extremes of moral degradation on the one hand and spiritual illumination on the other. The achievement of salvation through doubt, suffering, and even crime became one of his major themes. Like Nietzsche, Dostoevsky praised the extremes of human existence and deplored the safe, smug middle road; but, unlike Nietzsche, he believed that mankind could be saved through faith in Christ.

The much acclaimed Crystal Palace became in Dostoevsky's first major work, *Notes from the Underground* (1864), a symbol of the utopia of those who believe in the doctrines of progress through science and materialism. The kind of happiness represented by the Crystal Palace (Fig. 29-1) could, according to Dostoevsky, be achieved only through the loss of human freedom. Freedom, not political or economic but spiritual freedom of choice, is for Dostoevsky man's precious possession. Man should be free to follow his irrational yearnings, his caprice, in order to develop his spiritual nature fully. Man in Dostoevsky's view is not naturally good, as the optimists of both the eighteenth and the nineteenth centuries believed, but fallen and yet free to choose faith in Christ. Such a choice made for reasons of certainty or stability would be, however, a false one. The choice for Christ should be made irrationally, or suprarationally, through faith, taking upon oneself the burden of humanity since "everybody is guilty for all and before all." Dostoevsky came to believe that only the Russian people and the Russian church had preserved Christianity in its pure form, and he prophesied a messianic role for Russia. The West, whether materialistic or socialistic or Catholic, was for him in complete decay. Roman Catholicism he viewed as a kind of herd religion, an attempt to force belief and conformity through authority.

Dostoevsky develops these themes in his four great novels, *Crime and Punishment* (1866), *The Idiot* (1868), *The Possessed* (1871), and *The Brothers Karamazov* (1880). There his ideas are given flesh and blood through the complexity and fullness of his tortured, extremist characters and the settings in which they play out their destinies. In his ability to create living characters, Dostoevsky is in the tradition of the great European realists and indeed one of the masters of realism; yet his belief in human freedom puts him in direct opposition to the naturalists, who portrayed man as conditioned by social and material conditions. His supreme interest in the exploration of the human soul makes Dostoevsky break through the bounds of a style limited to everyday life and "realistic" character motivation. Influenced by Dickens, he developed aspects of the grotesque already present in the English novelist's works. For Dostoevsky, reality, in art as in life, extended beyond realism. In a letter of 1869 he wrote, "I have my own view of art, and that which the majority call fantastic and exceptional is for me the very essence of reality."

It is perhaps not too surprising, then, that at the heart of *The Brothers Karamazov*, in many ways a realistic novel about nineteenth-century Russia, lies a fantastic story recounting the return of Christ to the earth during the *Inquisition* in sixteenth-century Spain. The story is told by one of the Karamazov brothers, Ivan, to his younger brother Alyosha. Ivan, with whom Dostoevsky shows great sympathy, is an atheist, or at least one who cannot accept the revelations of Christianity though he struggles with them desperately. Alyosha, in contrast, is a novice in a monastery and a pure-souled believer. Before telling the story that he calls "The Grand Inquisitor," Ivan makes two pronouncements, both of which have been widely quoted and commented on by twentieth-century thinkers. In the first, Ivan reasons that if God and the immortality of the individual soul do not exist, "everything is permitted." Without such a foundation, there can be no universal morality, and man is free to create his own. In the second, Ivan finds the existence of human suffering a just cause for revolt against God. If God can permit innocent children to be tortured to death, Ivan asks, how can he be just? What Ivan cannot accept is the world as he finds it, the world that God has made. Ivan demands justice on his own terms.

The Grand Inquisitor in Ivan's story represents the established Church, the Roman Church, but also what Ivan would consider an authentic view of most human beings as weak, slavish, and needing authority. In the Inquisitor's view, Christ neither loved nor understood men because He believed them capable of freely chosen faith without the assurances of material comfort and proof. The arguments of the Grand Inquisitor are strong ones; they have caused many readers to believe that Dostoevsky, in spite of his professed intentions, was really on his side. What is at stake here are two fundamentally different conceptions of human nature and of religion that Dostoevsky has set against each other with exquisite balance. The selection is taken from Constance Garnett's translation of *The Brothers Karamazov*.

FYODOR DOSTOEVSKY

The Grand Inquisitor

"Even this must have a preface—that is, a literary preface," laughed Ivan, "and I am a poor hand at making one. You see, my action takes place in the sixteenth century, and at that time, as you probably learnt at school, it was customary in poetry to bring down heavenly powers on earth. Not to speak of Dante, in France, clerks, as well as the monks in the monasteries, used to give regular performances in which the Madonna, the saints, the angels, Christ, and God Himself were brought on the stage. In those days it was done in all simplicity. In Victor Hugo's 'Notre Dame de Paris' an edifying and gratuitous spectacle was provided for the people in the Hotel de Ville of Paris in the reign of Louis XI. in honour of the birth of the dauphin. It was called *Le bon jugement de la très sainte et gracieuse Vierge Marie,* and she appears herself on the stage and pronounces her *bon jugement.* Similar plays, chiefly from the Old Testament, were occasionally performed in Moscow too, up to the times of Peter the Great. But besides plays there were all sorts of legends and ballads scattered about the world, in which the saints and angels and all the powers of Heaven took part when required. In our monasteries the monks busied themselves in translating, copying, and even composing such poems—and even under the Tatars. There is, for instance, one such poem (of course, from the Greek), 'The Wanderings of Our Lady through Hell,' with descriptions as bold as Dante's. Our Lady visits Hell, and the Archangel Michael leads her through the torments. She sees the sinners and their punishment. There she sees among others one noteworthy set of sinners in a burning lake; some of them sink to the bottom of the lake so that they can't swim out, and 'these God forgets'—an expression of extraordinary depth and force. And so Our Lady, shocked and weeping, falls before the throne of God and begs for mercy for all in Hell—for all she has seen there, and indiscriminately. Her conversation with God is immensely interesting. She beseeches Him, she will not desist, and when God points to the hands and feet of her Son, nailed to the Cross, and asks, 'How can I forgive His tormentors?' she bids all the saints, all the martyrs, all the angels and archangels to fall down with her and pray for mercy on all without distinction. It ends by her winning from God a respite of suffering every year from Good Friday till Trinity day, and the sinners at once raise a cry of thankfulness from Hell, chanting, 'Thou art just, O Lord, in this judgment.' Well, my poem would have been of that kind if it had appeared at that time. He comes on the scene in my poem, but He says nothing, only appears and passes on. Fifteen centuries have passed since He promised to come in His glory, fifteen centuries since His prophet wrote, 'Behold, I come quickly'; 'Of that day and that hour knoweth no man, neither the Son, but the Father,' as He Himself predicted on earth. But humanity awaits him with the same faith and with the same love. Oh, with greater faith, for it is fifteen centuries since man has ceased to see signs from Heaven.

No signs from Heaven come to-day
To add to what the heart doth say.

There was nothing left but faith in what the heart doth say. It is true there were many miracles in those days. There were saints who performed miraculous cures; some holy people, according to their biographies, were visited by the Queen of Heaven herself. But the devil did not slumber, and doubts were already arising among men of the truth of these miracles. And just then there appeared in the north of Germany a terrible new heresy. 'A huge star like to a torch' (that is, to a church) 'fell on the sources of the waters and they became bitter.' These heretics began blasphemously denying miracles. But those who remained faithful were all the more ardent in their faith. The tears of humanity rose up to Him as before, awaiting His coming, loved Him, hoped for Him, yearned to suffer and die for Him as before. And so many ages mankind had prayed with faith and fervour, 'O Lord our God, hasten Thy coming,' so many ages called upon Him, that in His infinite mercy He deigned to come down to His servants. Before that day He had come down, He had visited some holy men, martyrs and hermits, as is written in their 'Lives.' Among us, Tyutchev, with absolute faith in the truth of his words, bore witness that

Bearing the Cross, in slavish dress
Weary and worn, the Heavenly King
Our mother, Russia, came to bless,
And through our land went wandering.

And that certainly was so, I assure you.

"And behold, He deigned to appear for a moment to the people, to the tortured, suffering people, sunk in iniquity, but loving Him like children. My story is laid in Spain, in Seville, in the most terrible time of the Inquisition, when fires were lighted every day to the glory of God, and 'in the splendid *auto da fé* the wicked heretics were burnt.' Oh, of course, this was not the coming in which He will appear according to His promise at the end of time in all His heavenly glory, and which will be sudden 'as lightning flashing from east to west.' No, He visited His children only for a moment, and there where the flames were crackling round the heretics. In His infinite mercy He came once more among men in that human shape in which He walked among men for three years fifteen centuries ago. He came down to the 'hot pavement' of the southern town in which on the day before almost a hundred heretics had, *ad majorem gloriam Dei*, been burnt by the cardinal, the Grand Inquisitor, in a magnificent *auto da fé*, in the presence of the king, the court, the knights, the cardinals, the most charming ladies of the court, and the whole population of Seville.

"He came softly, unobserved, and yet, strange to say, every one recognised Him. That might be one of the best passages in the poem. I mean, why they recognised Him. The people are irresistibly drawn to Him, they surround Him, they flock about Him, follow Him. He moves silently in their midst with a gentle smile of infinite compassion. The sun of love burns in His heart, light and power shine from His eyes, and their radiance, shed on the people, stirs their hearts with responsive love. He holds out His hands to them, blesses them, and a healing virtue comes from contact with Him, even with His garments. An old man in the crowd, blind from childhood, cries out, 'O Lord, heal me and I shall see Thee!' and, as it were, scales fall from his eyes and the blind man sees Him. The crowd weeps and kisses the earth under His feet. Children throw flowers before Him, sing, and cry hosannah. 'It is He—it is He!' all repeat. 'It must be He, it can be no one but Him!' He stops at the steps of the Seville cathedral at the moment when the weeping mourners are bringing in a little open white coffin. In it lies a child of seven, the only daughter of a prominent citizen. The dead child lies hidden in flowers. 'He will raise your child,' the crowd shouts to the weeping mother. The priest, coming to meet the coffin, looks perplexed, and frowns, but the mother of the dead child throws herself at His feet with a wail. 'If it is Thou, raise my child!' she cries, holding out her hands to Him. The procession halts, the coffin is laid on the steps at His feet. He looks with compassion, and His lips once more softly pronounce, 'Maiden, arise!' and the maiden arises. The little girl sits up in the coffin and looks round, smiling with wide-open wondering eyes, holding a bunch of white roses they had put in her hand.

"There are cries, sobs, confusion among the people, and at that moment the cardinal himself, the Grand In-

quisitor, passes by the cathedral. He is an old man, almost ninety, tall and erect, with a withered face and sunken eyes, in which there is still a gleam of light. He is not dressed in his gorgeous cardinal's robes, as he was the day before, when he was burning the enemies of the Roman Church—at that moment he was wearing his coarse, old, monk's cassock. At a distance behind him come his gloomy assistants and slaves and the 'holy guard.' He stops at the sight of the crowd and watches it from a distance. He sees everything; he sees them set the coffin down at His feet, sees the child rise up, and his face darkens. He knits his thick grey brows and his eyes gleam with a sinister fire. He holds out his finger and bids the guards take Him. And such is his power, so completely are the people cowed into submission and trembling obedience to him, that the crowd immediately make way for the guards, and in the midst of deathlike silence they lay hands on Him and lead Him away. The crowd instantly bows down to the earth, like one man, before the old inquisitor. He blesses the people in silence and passes on. The guards lead their prisoner to the close, gloomy vaulted prison in the ancient palace of the Holy Inquisition and shut Him in it. The day passes and is followed by the dark, burning 'breathless' night of Seville. The air is 'fragrant with laurel and lemon.' In the pitch darkness the iron door of the prison is suddenly opened and the Grand Inquisitor himself comes in with a light in his hand. He is alone; the door is closed at once behind him. He stands in the doorway and for a minute or two gazes into His face. At last he goes up slowly, sets the light on the table and speaks.

" 'Is it Thou? Thou?' but receiving no answer, he adds at once, 'Don't answer, be silent. What canst Thou say, indeed? I know too well what Thou wouldst say. And Thou hast no right to add anything to what Thou hadst said of old. Why, then, art Thou come to hinder us? For Thou hast come to hinder us, and Thou knowest that. But dost Thou know what will be to-morrow? I know not who Thou art and care not to know whether it is Thou or only a semblance of Him, but to-morrow I shall condemn Thee and burn Thee at the stake as the worst of heretics. And the very people who have to-day kissed Thy feet, to-morrow at the faintest sign from me will rush to heap up the embers of Thy fire. Knowest Thou that? Yes, maybe Thou knowest it,' he added with thoughtful penetration, never for a moment taking his eyes off the Prisoner."

"I don't quite understand, Ivan. What does it mean?" Alyosha, who had been listening in silence, said with a smile. "Is it simply a wild fantasy, or a mistake on the part of the old man—some impossible *qui pro quo?*"

"Take it as the last," said Ivan, laughing, "if you are so corrupted by modern realism and can't stand anything fantastic. If you like it to be a case of mistaken identity, let it be so. It is true," he went on, laughing, "the old man was ninety, and he might well be crazy over his set idea. He might have been struck by the appearance of the Prisoner. It might, in fact, be simply his ravings, the delusion of an old man of ninety, over-excited by the *auto da fé* of a hundred heretics the day before. But does it matter to us after all whether it was a mistake of identity or a wild fantasy? All that matters is that the old man should speak out, should speak openly of what he has thought in silence for ninety years."

"And the Prisoner too is silent? Does He look at him and not say a word?"

"That's inevitable in any case," Ivan laughed again. "The old man has told Him He hasn't the right to add anything to what He has said of old. One may say it is the most fundamental feature of Roman Catholicism, in my opinion at least. 'All has been given by Thee to the Pope,' they say, 'and all, therefore, is still in the Pope's hands, and there is no need for Thee to come now at all. Thou must not meddle for the time, at least.' That's how they speak and write too—the Jesuits, at any rate. I have read it myself in the works of their theologians. 'Hast Thou the right to reveal to us one of the mysteries of that world from which Thou hast come?' my old man asks Him, and answers the question for Him. 'No, Thou hast not; that Thou mayest not add to what has been said of old, and mayest not take from men the freedom which Thou didst exalt when Thou wast on earth. Whatsoever Thou revealest anew will encroach on men's freedom of faith; for it will be manifest as a miracle, and the freedom of their faith was dearer to Thee than anything in those days fifteen hundred years ago. Didst Thou not often say then, "I will make you free"? But now Thou has seen these "free" men,' the old man adds suddenly, with a pensive smile. 'Yes, we've paid dearly for it,' he

goes on, looking sternly at Him, 'but at last we have completed that work in Thy name. For fifteen centuries we have been wrestling with Thy freedom, but now it is ended and over for good. Dost Thou not believe that it's over for good? Thou lookest meekly at me and deignest not even to be wroth with me. But let me tell Thee that now, to-day, people are more persuaded than ever that they have perfect freedom, yet they have brought their freedom to us and laid it humbly at our feet. But that has been our doing. Was this what Thou didst? Was this Thy freedom?' "

"I don't understand again," Alyosha broke in. "Is he ironical, is he jesting?"

"Not a bit of it! He claims it as a merit for himself and his Church that at last they have vanquished freedom and have done so to make men happy. 'For now' (he is speaking of the Inquisition, of course) 'for the first time it has become possible to think of the happiness of men. Man was created a rebel; and how can rebels be happy? Thou wast warned,' he says to Him. 'Thou hast had no lack of admonitions and warnings, but Thou didst not listen to those warnings; Thou didst reject the only way by which men might be made happy. But, fortunately, departing Thou didst hand on the work to us. Thou has promised, Thou hast established by Thy word, Thou has given to us the right to bind and to unbind, and now, of course, Thou canst not think of taking it away. Why, then, hast Thou come to hinder us?' "

"And what's the meaning of 'no lack of admonitions and warnings'?" asked Alyosha.

"Why, that's the chief part of what the old man must say."

" 'The wise and dread Spirit, the spirit of self-destruction and nonexistence,' the old man goes on, 'the great spirit talked with Thee in the wilderness, and we are told in the books that he "tempted" Thee. Is that so? And could anything truer be said than what he revealed to Thee in three questions and what Thou didst reject, and what in the books is called "the temptation"? And yet if there has ever been on earth a real stupendous miracle, it took place on that day, on the day of the three temptations. The statement of those three questions was itself the miracle. If it were possible to imagine simply for the sake of argument that those three questions of the dread spirit had perished utterly from the books, and that we had to restore them and to invent them anew, and to do so had gathered together all the wise men of the earth—rulers, chief priests, learned men, philosophers, poets—and had set them the task to invent three questions, such as would not only fit the occasion, but express in three words, three human phrases, the whole future history of the world and of humanity—dost Thou believe that all the wisdom of the earth united could have invented anything in depth and force equal to the three questions which were actually put to Thee then by the wise and mighty spirit in the wilderness? From those questions alone, from the miracle of their statement, we can see that we have here to do not with the fleeting human intelligence, but with the absolute and eternal. For in those three questions the whole subsequent history of mankind is, as it were, brought together into one whole, and foretold, and in them are united all the unsolved historical contradictions of human nature. At the time it could not be so clear, since the future was unknown; but now that fifteen hundred years have passed, we see that everything in those three questions was so justly divined and foretold, and has been so truly fulfilled, that nothing can be added to them or taken from them.

" 'Judge Thyself who was right—Thou or he who questioned Thee then? Remember the first question; its meaning, in other words, was this: "Thou wouldst go into the world, and art going with empty hands, with some promise of freedom which men in their simplicity and their natural unruliness cannot even understand, which they fear and dread—for nothing has ever been more insupportable for a man and a human society than freedom. But seest Thou these stones in this parched and barren wilderness? Turn them into bread, and mankind will run after Thee like a flock of sheep, grateful and obedient, though for ever trembling, lest Thou withdraw Thy hand and deny them Thy bread." But Thou wouldst not deprive man of freedom and didst reject the offer, thinking, what is that freedom worth, if obedience is bought with bread? Thou didst reply that man lives not by bread alone. But dost Thou know that for the sake of that earthly bread the spirit of the earth will rise up against Thee and will strive with Thee and overcome Thee, and all will follow him, crying, "Who can compare with this beast? He has given us fire from heaven!" Dost Thou know that the

ages will pass, and humanity will proclaim by the lips of their sages that there is no crime, and therefore no sin; there is only hunger? "Feed men, and then ask of them virtue!" that's what they'll write on the banner, which they will raise against Thee, and with which they will destroy Thy temple. Where Thy temple stood will rise a new building; the terrible tower of Babel will be built again, and though, like the one of old, it will not be finished, yet Thou mightest have prevented that new tower and have cut short the sufferings of men for a thousand years; for they will come back to us after a thousand years of agony with their tower. They will seek us again, hidden underground in the catacombs, for we shall be again persecuted and tortured. They will find us and cry to us, "Feed us, for those who have promised us fire from heaven haven't given it!" And then we shall finish building their tower, for he finishes the building who feeds them. And we alone shall feed them in Thy name, declaring falsely that it is in Thy name. Oh, never, never can they feed themselves without us! No science will give them bread so long as they remain free. In the end they will lay their freedom at our feet, and say to us, "Make us your slaves, but feed us." They will understand themselves, at last, that freedom and bread enough for all are inconceivable together, for never, never will they be able to share between them! They will be convinced, too, that they can never be free, for they are weak, vicious, worthless and rebellious. Thou didst promise them the bread of Heaven, but, I repeat again, can it compare with earthly bread in the eyes of the weak, ever sinful and ignoble race of man? And if for the sake of the bread of Heaven thousands and tens of thousands shall follow Thee, what is to become of the millions and tens of thousands of millions of creatures who will not have the strength to forego the earthly bread for the sake of the heavenly? Or dost Thou care only for the tens of thousands of the great and strong, while the millions, numerous as the sands of the sea, who are weak but love Thee, must exist only for the sake of the great and strong? No, we care for the weak too. They are sinful and rebellious, but in the end they too will become obedient. They will marvel at us and look on us as gods, because we are ready to endure the freedom which they have found so dreadful and to rule over them—so awful it will seem to them to be free. But we shall tell them that we are Thy servants and rule them in Thy name. We shall deceive them again, for we will not let Thee come to us again. That deception will be our suffering, for we shall be forced to lie.

" 'This is the significance of the first question in the wilderness, and this is what Thou hast rejected for the sake of that freedom which Thou hast exalted above everything. Yet in this question lies hid the great secret of this world. Choosing "bread," Thou wouldst have satisfied the universal and everlasting craving of humanity—to find some one to worship. So long as man remains free he strives for nothing so incessantly and so painfully as to find some one to worship. But man seeks to worship what is established beyond dispute, so that all men would agree at once to worship it. For these pitiful creatures are concerned not only to find what one or the other can worship, but to find something that all would believe in and worship; what is essential is that all may be *together* in it. This craving for *community* of worship is the chief misery of every man individually and of all humanity from the beginning of time. For the sake of common worship they've slain each other with the sword. They have set up gods and challenged one another, "Put away your gods and come and worship ours, or we will kill you and your gods!" And so it will be to the end of the world, even when gods disappear from the earth; they will fall down before idols just the same. Thou didst know, Thou couldst not but have known, this fundamental secret of human nature, but Thou didst reject the one infallible banner which was offered Thee to make all men bow down to Thee alone—the banner of earthly bread; and Thou hast rejected it for the sake of freedom and the bread of Heaven. Behold what Thou didst further. And all again in the name of freedom! I tell Thee that man is tormented by no greater anxiety than to find some one quickly to whom he can hand over that gift of freedom with which the ill-fated creature is born. But only one who can appease their conscience can take over their freedom. In bread there was offered Thee an invincible banner; give bread, and man will worship Thee, for nothing is more certain than bread. But if some one else gains possession of his conscience—oh! then he will cast away Thy bread and follow after him who has ensnared his conscience. In that Thou wast right. For the secret of man's being is not

only to live but to have something to live for. Without a stable conception of the object of life, man would not consent to go on living, and would rather destroy himself than remain on earth, though he had bread in abundance. That is true. But what happened? Instead of taking men's freedom from them, Thou didst make it greater than ever! Didst Thou forget that man prefers peace, and even death, to freedom of choice in the knowledge of good and evil? Nothing is more seductive for man than his freedom of conscience, but nothing is a greater cause of suffering. And behold, instead of giving a firm foundation for setting the conscience of man at rest for ever, Thou didst choose all that is exceptional, vague and enigmatic; Thou didst choose what was utterly beyond the strength of men, acting as though Thou didst not love them at all—Thou who didst come to give Thy life for them! Instead of taking possession of men's freedom, Thou didst increase it, and burdened the spiritual kingdom of mankind with its sufferings for ever. Thou didst desire man's free love, that he should follow Thee freely, enticed and taken captive by Thee. In place of the rigid ancient law, man must hereafter with free heart decide for himself what is good and what is evil, having only Thy image before him as his guide. But didst Thou not know he would at last reject even Thy image and Thy truth, if he is weighed down with the fearful burden of free choice? They will cry aloud at last that the truth is not in Thee, for they could not have been left in greater confusion and suffering than Thou hast caused, laying upon them so many cares and unanswerable problems.

" 'So that, in truth, Thou didst Thyself lay the foundation for the destruction of Thy kingdom, and no one is more to blame for it. Yet what was offered Thee? There are three powers, three powers alone, able to conquer and to hold captive for ever the conscience of these impotent rebels for their happiness—those forces are miracle, mystery and authority. Thou hast rejected all three and hast set the example for doing so. When the wise and dread spirit set Thee on the pinnacle of the temple and said to Thee, "If Thou wouldst know whether Thou art the Son of God then cast Thyself down, for it is written: the angels shall hold him up lest he fall and bruise himself, and Thou shalt know then whether Thou art the Son of God and shalt prove then how great is Thy faith in Thy Father." But Thou didst refuse and wouldst not cast Thyself down. Oh! of course, Thou didst proudly and well like God; but the weak, unruly race of men, are they gods? Oh, Thou didst know then that in taking one step, in making one movement to cast Thyself down, Thou wouldst be tempting God and have lost all Thy faith in Him, and wouldst have been dashed to pieces against that earth which Thou didst come to save. And the wise spirit that tempted Thee would have rejoiced. But I ask again, are there many like Thee? And couldst Thou believe for one moment that men, too, could face such a temptation? Is the nature of men such, that they can reject miracle, and at the great moments of their life, the moments of their deepest, most agonising spiritual difficulties, cling only to the free verdict of the heart? Oh, Thou didst know that Thy deed would be recorded in books, would be handed down to remote times and the utmost ends of the earth, and Thou didst hope that man, following Thee, would cling to God and not ask for a miracle. But Thou didst not know that when man rejects miracle he rejects God too; for man seeks not so much God as the miraculous. And as man cannot bear to be without the miraculous, he will create new miracles of his own for himself, and will worship deeds of sorcery and witchcraft, though he might be a hundred times over a rebel, heretic and infidel. Thou didst not come down from the Cross when they shouted to Thee, mocking and reviling Thee, "Come down from the cross and we will believe that Thou art He." Thou didst not come down, for again Thou wouldst not enslave man by a miracle, and didst crave faith given freely, not based on miracle. Thou didst crave for free love and not the base raptures of the slave before the might that has overawed him for ever. But Thou didst think too highly of men therein, for they are slaves, of course, though rebellious by nature. Look round and judge; fifteen centuries have passed, look upon them. Whom hast Thou raised up to Thyself? I swear, man is weaker and baser by nature than Thou hast believed him! Can he, can he do what Thou didst? By showing him so much respect, Thou didst, as it were, cease to feel for him, for Thou didst ask far too much from him—Thou who hast loved him more than Thyself! Respecting him less, Thou wouldst have asked less of him. That would have been more like love, for his burden would have been lighter. He is weak and vile.

What though he is everywhere now rebelling against our power, and proud of his rebellion? It is the pride of a child and a schoolboy. They are little children rioting and barring out the teacher at school. But their childish delight will end; it will cost them dear. They will cast down temples and drench the earth with blood. But they will see at last, the foolish children, that, though they are rebels, they are impotent rebels, unable to keep up their own rebellion. Bathed in their foolish tears, they will recognise at last that He who created them rebels must have meant to mock at them. They will say this in despair, and their utterance will be a blasphemy which will make them more unhappy still, for man's nature cannot bear blasphemy, and in the end always avenges it on itself. And so unrest, confusion and unhappiness—that is the present lot of man after Thou didst bear so much for their freedom! Thy great prophet tells in vision and in image, that he saw all those who took part in the first resurrection and that there were of each tribe twelve thousand. But if there were so many of them, they must have been not men but gods. They had borne Thy cross, they had endured scores of years in the barren, hungry wilderness, living upon locusts and roots—and Thou mayest indeed point with pride at those children of freedom, of free love, of free and splendid sacrifice for Thy name. But remember that they were only some thousands; and what of the rest? And how are the other weak ones to blame, because they could not endure what the strong have endured? How is the weak soul to blame that it is unable to receive such terrible gifts? Canst Thou have simply come to the elect and for the elect? But if so, it is a mystery and we cannot understand it. And if it is a mystery, we too have a right to preach a mystery, and to teach them that it's not the free judgment of their hearts, not love that matters, but a mystery which they must follow blindly, even against their conscience. So we have done. We have corrected Thy work and have founded it upon *miracle*, *mystery* and *authority*. And men rejoiced that they were again led like sheep, and that the terrible gift that had brought them such suffering, was, at last, lifted from their hearts. Were we right teaching them this? Speak! Did we not love mankind, so meekly acknowledging their feebleness, lovingly lightening their burden, and permitting their weak nature even sin with our sanction?

Why hast Thou come now to hinder us? And why dost Thou look silently and searchingly at me with Thy mild eyes? Be angry. I don't want Thy love, for I love Thee not. And what use is it for me to hide anything from Thee? Don't I know to Whom I am speaking? All that I can say is known to Thee already. And is it for me to conceal from Thee our mystery? Perhaps it is Thy will to hear it from my lips. Listen, then. We are not working with Thee, but with *him*—that is our mystery. It's long—eight centuries—since we have been on *his* side and not on Thine. Just eight centuries ago, we took from him what Thou didst reject with scorn, that last gift he offered Thee, showing Thee all the kingdoms of the earth. We took from him Rome and the sword of Caesar, and proclaimed ourselves sole rulers of the earth, though hitherto we have not been able to complete our work. But whose fault is that? Oh, the work is only beginning, but it has begun. It has long to await completion and the earth has yet much to suffer, but we shall triumph and shall be Caesar's, and then we shall plan the universal happiness of man. But Thou mightest have taken even then the sword of Caesar. Why didst Thou reject that last gift? Hadst Thou accepted that last counsel of the mighty spirit, Thou wouldst have accomplished all that man seeks on earth—that is, some one to worship, some one to keep his conscience, and some means of uniting all in one unanimous and harmonious ant-heap, for the craving for universal unity is the third and last anguish of men. Mankind as a whole has always striven to organise a universal state. There have been many great nations with great histories, but the more highly they were developed the more unhappy they were, for they felt more acutely than other people the craving for worldwide union. The great conquerors, Timours and Ghenghis-Khans, whirled like hurricanes over the face of the earth striving to subdue its people, and they too were but the unconscious expression of the same craving for universal unity. Hadst Thou taken the world and Caesar's purple, Thou wouldst have founded the universal state and have given universal peace. For who can rule men if not he who holds their conscience and their bread in his hands. We have taken the sword of Caesar, and in taking it, of course, have rejected Thee and followed *him*. Oh, ages are yet to come of the confusion of free thought, of their science and cannibalism. For

having begun to build their tower of Babel without us, they will end, of course, with cannibalism. But then the beast will crawl to us and lick our feet and spatter them with tears of blood. And we shall sit upon the beast and raise the cup, and on it will be written, "Mystery." But then, and only then, the reign of peace and happiness will come for men. Thou art proud of Thine elect, but Thou hast only the elect, while we give rest to all. And besides, how many of those elect, those mighty ones who could become elect, have grown weary waiting for Thee, and have transferred and will transfer the powers of their spirit and the warmth of their heart to the other camp, and end by raising their *free* banner against Thee. Thou didst Thyself lift up that banner. But with us all will be happy and will no more rebel nor destroy one another as under Thy freedom. Oh, we shall persuade them that they will only become free when they renounce their freedom to us and submit to us. And shall we be right or shall we be lying? They will be convinced that we are right, for they will remember the horrors of slavery and confusion to which Thy freedom brought them. Freedom, free thought and science, will lead them into such straits and will bring them face to face with such marvels and insoluble mysteries, that some of them, the fierce and rebellious, will destroy themselves, others, rebellious but weak, will destroy one another, while the rest, weak and unhappy, will crawl fawning to our feet and whine to us: "Yes, you were right, you alone possess His mystery, and we come back to you, save us from ourselves!"

" 'Receiving bread from us, they will see clearly that we take the bread made by their hands from them, to give it to them, without any miracle. They will see that we do not change the stones to bread, but in truth they will be more thankful for taking it from our hands than for the bread itself! For they will remember only too well that in old days, without our help, even the bread they made turned to stones in their hands, while since they have come back to us, the very stones have turned to bread in their hands. Too, too well they know the value of complete submission! And until men know that, they will be unhappy. Who is most to blame for their not knowing it, speak? Who scattered the flock and sent it astray on unknown paths? But the flock will come together again and will submit once more, and then it will be once for all. Then we shall give them the quiet humble happiness of weak creatures such as they are by nature. Oh, we shall persuade them at last not to be proud, for Thou didst lift them up and thereby taught them to be proud. We shall show them that they are weak, that they are only pitiful children, but that childlike happiness is the sweetest of all. They will become timid and will look to us and huddle close to us in fear, as chicks to the hen. They will marvel at us and will be awe-stricken before us, and will be proud at our being so powerful and clever, that we have been able to subdue such a turbulent flock of thousands of millions. They will tremble impotently before our wrath, their minds will grow fearful, they will be quick to shed tears like women and children, but they will be just as ready at a sign from us to pass to laughter and rejoicing, to happy mirth and childish song. Yes, we shall set them to work, but in their leisure hours we shall make their life like a child's game, with children's songs and innocent dance. Oh, we shall allow them even sin, they are weak and helpless, and they will love us like children because we allow them to sin. We shall tell them that every sin will be expiated, if it is done with our permission, that we allow them to sin because we love them, and the punishment for these sins we take upon ourselves. And we shall take it upon ourselves, and they will adore us as their saviour who have taken on themselves their sins before God. And they will have no secrets from us. We shall allow or forbid them to live with their wives and mistresses, to have or not to have children—according to whether they have been obedient or disobedient—and they will submit to us gladly and cheerfully. The most painful secrets of their conscience, all, all they will bring to us, and we shall have an answer for all. And they will be glad to believe our answer, for it will save them from the great anxiety and terrible agony they endure at present in making a free decision for themselves. And all will be happy, all the millions of creatures except the hundred thousand who rule over them. For only we, we who guard the mystery, shall be unhappy. There will be thousands of millions of happy babes, and a hundred thousand sufferers who have taken upon themselves the curse of the knowledge of good and evil. Peacefully they will die, peacefully they will expire in Thy name, and beyond the grave they will find nothing but death. But we shall keep the secret, and for their happiness we shall allure them with the reward of heaven and eternity. Though if there were anything in the other world, it certainly would not be for such as they. It is prophesied that Thou wilt come again in victory, Thou wilt come with Thy chosen, the proud and strong, but we will say that they have only saved themselves, but we have saved all. We are told that the harlot who sits upon the beast, and holds in her hands the *mystery*, shall be put to shame, that the weak will rise up again, and will rend her royal purple and will strip naked her loathsome body. But then I will stand up and point out to Thee the thousand millions of happy children who have known no sin. And we who have taken their sins upon us for their happiness will stand up before Thee and say: "Judge us if Thou canst and darest." Know that I fear Thee not. Know that I too have been in the wilderness, I too have lived on roots and locusts, I too prized the freedom with which Thou hast blessed men, and I too was striving to stand among Thy elect, among the strong and powerful, thirsting "to make up the number." But I awakened and would not serve madness. I turned back and joined the ranks of those *who have corrected Thy work*. I left the proud and went back to the humble, for the happiness of the humble. What I say to Thee will come to pass, and our dominion will be built up. I repeat, to-morrow Thou shalt see that obedient flock who at a sign from me will hasten to heap up the hot cinders about the pile on which I shall burn Thee for coming to hinder us. For if any one has ever deserved our fires, it is Thou. To-morrow I shall burn Thee. Dixi.'"

Ivan stopped. He was carried away as he talked and spoke with excitement; when he had finished, he suddenly smiled.

Alyosha had listened in silence; towards the end he was greatly moved and seemed several times on the point of interrupting, but restrained himself. Now his words came with a rush.

"But ... that's absurd!" he cried, flushing. "Your poem is in praise of Jesus, not in blame of Him—as you meant it to be. And who will believe you about freedom? Is that the way to understand it? That's not the idea of it in the Orthodox Church ... That's Rome, and not even the whole of Rome, it's false—those are the worst of the Catholics, the Inquisitors, the Jesuits!... And there could not be such a fantastic creature as your Inquisitor. What are these sins of mankind they take on themselves? Who are these keepers of the mystery who have taken some curse upon themselves for the happiness of mankind? When have they been seen? We know the Jesuits, they are spoken ill of, but surely they are not what you describe? They are not that at all, not at all.... They are simply the Romish army for the earthly sovereignty of the world in the future, with the Pontiff of Rome for Emperor... that's their ideal, but there's no sort of mystery or lofty melancholy about it.... It's simple lust of power, of filthy earthly gain, of domination—something like a universal serfdom with them as masters—that's all they stand for. They don't even believe in God perhaps. Your suffering inquisitor is a mere fantasy."

"Stay, stay," laughed Ivan, "how hot you are! A fantasy you say, let it be so! Of course it's a fantasy. But allow me to say: do you really think that the Roman Catholic movement of the last centuries is actually nothing but the lust of power, of filthy earthly gain? Is that Father Païssy's teaching?"

"No, no, on the contrary, Father Païssy did once say something rather the same as you... but of course it's not the same, not a bit the same," Alyosha hastily corrected himself.

"A precious admission, in spite of your 'not a bit the same.' I ask you why your Jesuits and Inquisitors have united simply for vile material gain? Why can there not be among them one martyr oppressed by great sorrow and loving humanity? You see, only suppose that there was one such man among all those who desire nothing but filthy material gain—if there's only one like my old inquisitor, who had himself eaten roots in the desert and made frenzied efforts to subdue his flesh to make himself free and perfect. But yet all his life he loved humanity, and suddenly his eyes were opened, and he saw that it is no great moral blessedness to attain perfection and freedom, if at the same time one gains the conviction that millions of God's creatures have been created as a mockery, that they will never be capable of using their freedom, that these poor rebels can never turn into giants to complete the tower, that it was not for such geese that the great idealist dreamt his dream of harmony. Seeing all that he turned back and

joined—the clever people. Surely that could have happened?"

"Joined whom, what clever people?" cried Alyosha, completely carried away. "They have no such great cleverness and no mysteries and secrets.... Perhaps nothing but Atheism, that's all their secret. Your inquisitor does not believe in God, that's his secret!"

"What if it is so! At last you have guessed it. It's perfectly true that that's the whole secret, but isn't that suffering, at least for a man like that, who has wasted his whole life in the desert and yet could not shake off his incurable love of humanity? In his old age he reached the clear conviction that nothing but the advice of the great dread spirit could build up any tolerable sort of life for the feeble, unruly 'incomplete, empirical creatures created in jest.' And so, convinced of this, he sees that he must follow the counsel of the wise spirit, the dread spirit of death and destruction, and therefore accept lying and deception, and lead men consciously to death and destruction, and yet deceive them all the way so that they may not notice where they are being led, that the poor blind creatures may at least on the way think themselves happy. And note, the deception is in the name of Him in Whose ideal the old man had so fervently believed all his life long. Is not that tragic? And if only one such stood at the head of the whole army 'filled with the lust of power only for the sake of filthy gain'—would not one such be enough to make a tragedy? More than that, one such standing at the head is enough to create the actual leading idea of the Roman Church with all its armies and Jesuits, its highest idea. I tell you frankly that I firmly believe that there has always been such a man among those who stood at the head of the movement. Who knows, there may have been some such even among the Roman Popes. Who knows, perhaps the spirit of that accursed old man who loves mankind so obstinately in his own way, is to be found even now in a whole multitude of such old men, existing not by chance but by agreement, as a secret league formed long ago for the guarding of the mystery, to guard it from the weak and the unhappy, so as to make them happy. No doubt it is so, and so it must be indeed. I fancy that even among the Masons there's something of the same mystery at the bottom, and that's why the Catholics so detest the Masons as their rivals breaking up the unity of the idea, while it is so essential that there should be one flock and one shepherd. . . . But from the way I defend my idea I might be an author impatient of your criticism. Enough of it."

"You are perhaps a Mason yourself!" broke suddenly from Alyosha. "You don't believe in God," he added, speaking this time very sorrowfully. He fancied besides that his brother was looking at him ironically. "How does your poem end?" he asked, suddenly looking down. "Or was it the end?"

"I meant to end it like this. When the Inquisitor ceased speaking he waited some time for his Prisoner to answer him. His silence weighed down upon him. He saw that the Prisoner had listened intently all the time, looking gently in his face and evidently not wishing to reply. The old man longed for Him to say something, however bitter and terrible. But He suddenly approached the old man in silence and softly kissed him on his bloodless aged lips. That was all his answer. The old man shuddered. His lips moved. He went to the door, opened it, and said to Him: 'Go, and come no more. . . . Come not at all, never, never!' And he let Him out into the dark alleys of the town. The Prisoner went away."

"And the old man?"

"The kiss glows in his heart, but the old man adheres to his idea."

"And you with him, you too?" cried Alyosha, mournfully.

Ivan laughed.

"Why, it's all nonsense, Alyosha. It's only a senseless poem of a senseless student, who could never write two lines of verse. Why do you take it so seriously? Surely you don't suppose I am going straight off to the Jesuits, to join the men who are correcting His work? Good Lord, it's no business of mine. I told you, all I want is to live on to thirty, and then . . . dash the cup to the ground!"

"But the little sticky leaves, and the precious tombs, and the blue sky, and the woman you love! How will you live, how will you love them?" Alyosha cried sorrowfully. "With such a hell in your heart and your head, how can you? No, that's just what you are going away for, to join them . . . if not, you will kill yourself,

you can't endure it!"

"There is a strength to endure everything," Ivan said with a cold smile.

"What strength?"

"The strength of the Karamazovs—the strength of the Karamazov baseness."

"To sink into debauchery, to stifle your soul with corruption, yes?"

"Possibly even that . . . only perhaps till I am thirty I shall escape it, and then."

"How will you escape it? By what will you escape it? That's impossible with your ideas."

"In the Karamazov way, again."

" 'Everything is lawful,' you mean? Everything is lawful, is that it?"

Ivan scowled, and all at once turned strangely pale.

"Ah, you've caught up yesterday's phrase, which so offended Miüsov—and which Dmitri pounced upon so naïvely and paraphrased!" he smiled queerly. "Yes, if you like, 'everything is lawful' since the word has been said. I won't deny it. And Mitya's version isn't bad."

Alyosha looked at him in silence.

"I thought that going away from here I have you at least," Ivan said suddenly, with unexpected feeling; "but now I see that there is no place for me even in your heart, my dear hermit. The formula, 'all is lawful,' I won't renounce—will you renounce me for that, yes?"

Alyosha got up, went to him and softly kissed him on the lips.

"That's plagiarism," cried Ivan, highly delighted. "You stole that from my poem. Thank you though. Get up, Alyosha, it's time we were going, both of us."

QUESTIONS

1. Reconstruct, as precisely as you can, the line of argument followed by the Grand Inquisitor. How does he arrive at the conclusions that Christ has caused human beings to suffer, that He is indifferent and unconcerned toward the masses of people, and that He is a heretic?

2. Describe the Grand Inquisitor's concept of human nature. Why does he believe that human beings fear freedom?

3. Does Christ answer the arguments of the Grand In-

quisitor? If so, in what way? How does His view of human nature differ?

4. Whose side is the author on, in your opinion?
5. Which view of human nature seems truer to you? Which one has history borne out?

From Realism to Symbolism in Painting

By the middle of the nineteenth century, realism was perceived by some artists as a limitation as well as an inspiration. Like the novelists and poets who came to feel that "reality" lay beyond the grasp of "realism," painters began to experiment with ways of rendering reality that went beyond the representational or photographic. The first school of painters to experiment along these lines was called, by a hostile art critic, "impressionist." Between the harsh "reality" of Courbet's *Stonebreakers* and the thrilling light of Monet's *The Bridge at Argenteuil* (Color Plate IX) lie years of experimentation by artists, painting both out-of-doors and in the studio, trying paints, brushes, sketches, and colors to achieve the sense of momentariness that is so characteristic of the impressionist painters.

Whenever the artist has to discover new ways of making the images that fascinate him, old habits first have to be broken, old ways of seeing altered. This is not easy. Often (as we shall see in the case of African art in the early twentieth century) the influence of the art of a foreign culture can be a profoundly liberating one. For Edouard Manet and the "impressionists," the printmakers of Japan provided a major source of inspiration for change. Prints came to the west as wrapping paper. Usually woodblock, in two or three colors, these prints, of everyday events, comic happenings, satire, the theater, represented a completely new way of seeing the world and accounting for it. The Japanese printmaker was essentially not interested in creating a reproduction of the experienced event but in creating an image that focused attention by simplification—thus eliminating any need to reproduce natural light and shade, space, or textures. Rhythmic patterns, flat colors, abstraction, and stylization are characteristics of these art objects. To the artists in France, these prints (see Fig. 30-1) were a complete revelation. They proved it was possible to make successful art without attempting to copy nature. Artists from Manet on looked at prints and sometimes

adapted them to their particular needs. Thus as industrialization brought problems, it also brought information that was as new and revolutionary as technology itself.

Edouard Manet (1832–1883)   In the development of impressionism, Manet played the role of a transitional figure. Though born into the Parisian upper middle class, Manet was not a conscious rebel like Courbet, but he did approach the subject matter suggested by the realists with different artistic tools. From his studies of seventeenth-century art, particularly Velasquez, his viewing of the newly imported Japanese prints, and a knowledge of photography, Manet set out to create a personal style for recording the public and private pursuits of his milieu. Using what photography had shown

30-1   Suzuki Harunobu (1725–1770), *Suzumegai*. Japanese woodblock print illustrating a poem by the same name. (Courtesy, Museum of Fine Arts, Boston. Asiatic Curators Fund in memory of Marjorie K. Hussey.)

30-2 Edouard Manet, *Olympia* (Louvre, Paris/© ARCH. PHOT. PARIS—S.P.A.D.E.M., 1980)

him, he set his subjects in a strong, harsh light that tended to flatten them against their background, even as a photograph eliminates much three-dimensionality. Unlike the photograph, which does not discriminate among objects, however, Manet concentrated on the firm contours of his subjects. He utilized sharp contrasts of light and dark to create a strong sense of three-dimensionality, unlike the surface modeling or tonal adjustments of earlier pictures.

Manet's painting *Olympia* (Fig. 30-2), exhibited in the Salon of the Refused in 1863 (a countershow to the government-sanctioned Salon), typifies his emerging style. The idea of a reclining nude is a very old one in art, but this one is different. Who is this woman? What is her profession? Is Manet being critical or patronizing? Why or why not? Paris was shocked by this rather pert lady who engaged the viewer with her direct, quizzical look. It is certain that she is no Venus; she is too pres-

ent and familiar. The flat white of the sheets and the creamy flat paint that delineates her body end in harsh dark edges and folds. The black servant and black cat seem to emphasize the black/white impact of the picture. The bouquet of flowers, brilliant slashes of painting, recalls the sensation of flowers seen in passing. The elimination of detail, the surface textures, the harsh contrasts, together with Olympia's direct, unselfconscious gaze, create the sensation of a scene glimpsed for an instant, but captured, arrested permanently.

These early paintings, which recall photography's impact and the remembrance of things past (Venus, for instance), reveal Manet's hesitancy in creating his personal style. More and more, however, he was able to compose freely, reducing gesture and pose to that which was most telling, most relevatory for a particular moment or personality. His later pictures were also coloristically richer. This later concern with color was in

315

30-3 Claude Monet, *Impression: Sunrise*. (Musée Marmottan/© S.P.A.D.E.M., 1980/photo Routhier, Studio Lourmell 77, Paris)

part due to the influence of young painters who were, properly speaking, members of the impressionist group. Manet in turn played an important role in influencing them to paint contemporary life in an appropriate way. Yet whereas Manet's subjects were almost always human beings, viewed with detachment, objectivity, and minimal setting, the impressionists' major interest was in landscape.

Impressionism

Claude Monet, August Renoir, and Camille Pissarro were the chief creators of impressionism. Painting land-scapes out-of-doors, these men became committed to recording the illusive effects of sunlight on objects. They had some knowledge of the sciences of color and optics; but when we study their paintings made between 1860 and 1880, we observe that their search for a painterly language unfolds experimentally and unevenly. Consider your own experience of a landscape. The color is vivid; details attract your eyes as they shift, adjusting to the brightness, concentrating, shifting, focusing. Even as this occurs, the scene itself is changing, for clouds, sun, air, and people move and transform what you are seeing even as you see it. If you pause only for a moment, the light/dark contrasts give

30-4 Claude Monet, *Waterlilies,* sunrise section. (Cliché des Musées Nationaux, Paris/© S.P.A.D.E.M., 1980)

you the needed information of the location of things; but if you stay to observe, you become aware of the vibrant, changing color and light.

To translate this experience onto the canvas, the painters first realized that they must eliminate black, brown, and gray from their palettes. Natural light is the product of the *hues* of the spectrum: red, orange, yellow, green, blue, and purple. Like Constable, the impressionists realized that a local color, like green grass, could be made more intense by painting it not as a flat green but as a mottled combination of green and its components, blue and yellow. Moreover, they began to take into account not only the colors of objects themselves but also the fact that objects take on the colors of objects adjacent to them, reflecting some of that color back into the air. Next they realized that shadows are not simply black, brown, or gray but rather the contrasting color of light on the object. Realizing then that all objects, light, and air are reflected, refracted waves of color that the eye perceives and joins into patterns and volumes, they considered it appropriate that the brushstroke should also be fragmented and short, in commas, dots, and dashes. In addition, this kind of brushstroke gave the pictures a sense of immediacy and tension suggesting a rapid, feverish execution. Landscapes, seascapes (Color Plate XV), and people on

boats and in gardens celebrate the apparent conquest of the momentary that is also a real experience. Monet's *Impression: Sunrise,* painted in 1873, gave the movement its name and was exhibited at the first impressionist exhibition of 1874 (Fig. 30-3). Like Courbet and Manet, these painters met with a hostile reception: their works were "crude and unfinished." Today we see the pictures made by Monet and his colleagues in the 1870s and 1880s as monuments to the splendor of the natural world. As the impressionists continued their experiments, each of their styles changed in different ways.

Monet remained most true to impressionism's ideal of recording the fleeting transformations of sunlight on objects. Resorting to numerous canvases, each to record a different hour of the day, Monet's almost scientific obsession caused him to concentrate on a few subjects, year after year. A series of huge paintings entitled *Waterlilies,* for example, contains his impressions of a pond at different times of day. Compare a canvas of waterlilies (Fig. 30-4) with *Impression: Sunrise.* Where are Monet's references to the visual world? How are the objects of his interest defined? Does time of day make a difference in your perception of the two works? Compare the brushstrokes and the surfaces. In which painting do you sense more clearly the presence of the artist?

317

Why? Are the pond and lilies really important? It would seem that the waterlilies become known to us now only as a concept; they are our link with reality that succumbs to Monet's intensely personal way of seeing and organizing experience.

Waterlilies represents an extremity of the artistic movement that started with realism. What began as an attempt to paint the world "as it is" has become a recording of a subjective view of the world. This approach to art will produce new, more complex, and elaborate languages with which to apprehend and render experience.

Postimpressionism and Symbolism   With Monet's *Waterlilies* we witness a delicate balance between the need to paint what is seen and the need to paint what is felt. If the impressionists went beyond realism in their representation of the visual world, their successors broke with the tenets of realism altogether. From about 1870 onward, a growing segment of artists, along with poets and musicians, tended to think that the function of art was *not* to represent, or even to interpret, the everyday, normal world, but rather to create its own world and its own meaning. Traditional religion, most believed, was outmoded; its images were no longer valid for modern people. The philosophies of materialism—whether Marxist or liberal—failed to satisfy spiritual and aesthetic needs. Left to fill the vacuum was art—not art for or about something else, but art for its own sake. Thus art became a kind of new religion. The movement began in France with painters usually grouped together under the rubric "postimpressionist," with writers who came to be known as Symbolists, and with musicians, such as Claude Debussy and Maurice Ravel, who were associated with them. This end-of-the-century trend was followed in England by aesthetic or "dandies" such as Oscar Wilde and Aubrey Beardsley. Germany, Italy, and Spain produced their own Symbolist, and later, decadent, schools. In the United States, where realism had taken a strong hold, Symbolism, and the view of art as religion, did not have any appreciable effect until the early twentieth century. Here we will study the trend briefly through a few French paintings and poems.

Van Gogh (1853–1890)   The Dutchman Vincent Van Gogh came at first to Paris to make his painting career. Oppressed by the inhumanity and materialism of city life, however, he moved to Arles in southern France. As a response to the pain and suffering that man brought into the world, Van Gogh wished to paint pictures that would be comforting and uplifting. He presents aspects of nature such as the sun, a flower, or a plowed field in a way that does not emphasize their photographic reality, but intensifies our experience of them through the use of strong, pure colors and a vigorous brushstroke. Compare Van Gogh's *Sower* (Fig. 30-5) with that of Millet (Fig. 26-3). Pay particular attention to the differences created by tone and texture. What is the role of the bare tree? What does the sun stand for? How does it relate to the sower?

Van Gogh's *The Night Café* (Fig. 30-6) is obviously neither a realistic nor an impressionistic rendering of an apparently familiar subject: a café with a billiard table, chairs and smaller tables arranged around the walls, a bar, a host. But what of this place? The space seems empty and somehow threatening; the lamps have strangely glowing halos, and the patrons are anonymous bodies. Van Gogh, unlike the impressionist painters who were primarily interested in rendering account of the surface appearance of things, wished to penetrate beneath the surface. Writing of this painting, Van Gogh said, "I have tried to express humanity's terrible passions by using red and green." This basic color scheme produces intense contrasts perceptible in the black and white reproduction, and heightens the emotions that seem to emanate from the scene. What are those emotions; what do they convey; how? What is man's plight as Van Gogh describes it here?

Though Van Gogh believed strongly in the redemptive power of art, he remained, unlike most end-of-the-century artists, a convinced Christian. His was a deep and tortured nature, not unlike that of Dostoevsky's characters. At the end of his life he went mad. The fine line between genius and madness was never more evident than in this period.

Paul Gauguin (1848–1903)   Gauguin avoided both religious torments and rampant materialism by leaving his native France for Tahiti, where he found a natural,

30-5 Van Gogh, *The Sower*. (Collection National Museum Vincent Van Gogh, Amsterdam)

30-6 Van Gogh, *The Night Café*. (Yale University Art Gallery. Bequest of Stephen Carlton Clark, B.A. 1903)

319

instinctive culture free from inhibitions and greed. The faraway Pacific island also provided him with an unfamiliar subject matter that forces the viewer to concentrate on the experience of the picture rather than on the familiar narrative or object. In a letter to a friend he explains *The Spirit of the Dead Watching* (Fig. 30-7).

PAUL GAUGUIN

Manao Tupapau (The Spirit of the Dead Watching) 1892

From the manuscript "Cahier pour Aline," Tahiti, 1893

A young Tahitian girl is lying on her stomach, showing part of her frightened face. She rests on a bed covered by a blue *pareu* and a light chrome yellow sheet. A violet purple background, sown with flowers glowing like electric sparks; a strange figure sits beside the bed.

Captured by a form, a movement, I paint them with no other preoccupation than to execute a nude figure. As it is, it is a slightly indecent study of a nude, and yet I wish to make of it a chaste picture and imbue it with the spirit of the native, its character and tradition.

The *pareu* being intimately connected with the life of a Tahitian, I use it as a bedspread. The bark cloth sheet must be yellow, because in this color it arouses something unexpected for the spectator, and because it suggests lamplight. This, however, prevents me from making an actual effect of a lamp. I need a background of terror; purple is clearly indicated. And now the musical part of the picture is laid out.

What can a young native girl be doing completely nude on a bed, and in this somewhat difficult position? Preparing herself for making love? That is certainly in character, but it is indecent, and I do not wish it to be so. Sleeping? The amorous activity would then be over, and that is still indecent. I see here only fear. What kind of fear? Certainly not the fear of Susanna surprised by the elders. That kind of fear does not exist in Oceania.

The *tupapau* (Spirit of the Dead) is clearly indicated. For the natives it is a constant dread. A lamp is always lighted at night. No one ever goes out on the paths on a moonless night without a lantern, and even then they travel in groups.

Once I have found my *tupapau* I devote my atten-

tion completely to it and make it the motif of my picture. The nude sinks to a secondary level.

What can a spirit mean to a Tahitian? She knows neither the theatre nor the reading of novels, and when she thinks of a dead person she thinks necessarily of someone she has already seen. My spirit can only be an ordinary little woman. Her hand is outstretched as if to seize a prey.

My decorative sense leads me to strew the background with flowers. These flowers are the phosphorescent flowers of the *tupapau;* they are the sign that the spirit nears you. Tahitian beliefs.

The title *Manao tupapau* has two meanings, either the girl thinks of the spirit, or the spirit thinks of her.

To sum up: The musical part: undulating horizontal lines; harmonies of orange and blue, united by the yellows and purples (their derivatives) lit by greenish sparks. The literary part: the spirit of a living person linked to the spirit of the dead. Night and Day.

This genesis is written for those who must always know the *why* and the *wherefore.*

Otherwise it is simply a study of an Oceanian nude.

This letter reveals Gauguin's active search for an abstract pictorial language that can communicate with the viewer. While we cannot decipher all the meanings of his painting, *Whence Come We? Who Are We? Where Are We Going?* (Fig. 30-8), the juxtaposition of rich blues, golds, lavenders, and purples creates a sense of melancholy languidness. The juxtaposition of youth and old age, lovers and strangers combines and harmonizes in a mysterious landscape. The plaintive cry of the title registers clearly.

Though Van Gogh and Gauguin did not share identical aims, their concern with the value of line, color, and form to express a personal view of human truths demonstrates a common understanding of the power of the purely formal, abstract elements of art. This philosophy helps us to understand the rationale that will permit the painter to eliminate the familiar visual world from the canvas altogether.

Cézanne (1836–1906) Among the postimpressionists was another man of great genius, Paul Cézanne, who was older than the other two but whose work matured in the same years. His goal was to formulate a painterly

30-7 Right. Gauguin, *The Spirit of the Dead Watching.* (Albright-Know Art Gallery, Buffalo, New York. A. Conger Goodyear Collection, 1965)

30-8 Below. Gauguin, *Whence Come We? Who Are We? Where Are We Going?* (Courtesy Museum of Fine Arts, Boston, Arthur Tompkins Residuary Fund)

language that would give an account of nature. He distrusted the implicit subjectivism and emotionalism of Van Gogh and Gauguin, and he felt that impressionism created ephemeral works. He wanted to make art universal and independent, timeless, and free of subjectivity and emotionalism.

Cézanne liked to paint several versions of the same subject, such as Mont Sainte-Victoire in southern France. The version reproduced here (Color Plate XVI) shows his technique of using bright, intense colors, applied in varying thicknesses, sometimes even reduced to transparency. Cézanne has alluded to the natural experience of the out-of-doors, but there is none of the transient quality of an impressionist picture. Each object—trees, housetops, road, bridge, mountain, sky—exists in space, separated by air and distance from us and from each other. Each object has weight and volume; but there is no consistent single point *perspective*, no consistent shadow pattern. Objects in the middle and background do not diminish in clarity as they do in traditional painting. Rather, the painted surface is made up of blocks of color; when the color changes, our eyes see that change as a change in direction toward or away from us. We follow the changes from a smoother foreground into a more complex middle and background. The overlapping colored blocks also establish the perception of behind and beside, which the mind tells us are sensations of distance and space, volume and weight. We can identify objects, but Cézanne does not attempt to emulate the texture of objects. Rather, he paints a characteristic contour, color, and mass, drawing on all our knowledge of, and associations with, that object. Mont Sainte-Victoire is a particular mountain made of rugged, substantial, colored blocks that suggest the concepts of height, weight, mass, and, therefore, mountain. The pine tree that spreads over the foreground surface, enveloping the mountain and sky, is not only that tree but every experience of the graceful, linear, light-filtering pine, whose branches and needles flatten against the sky and through which the sky literally shines. The same process has been applied to all objects; they are particular and universal. It is Cézanne's experience of the world, but it is made up of the experiences of seeing that may be everyone's.

Cézanne had always wanted to paint nature and to thereby portray the essential integrity of each object;

yet he also wished to integrate each object into the framework that gives it meaning. The forest recedes when we concentrate on one tree, but we *know* that the other trees are there, acting with it to give it meaning. As our focus changes, the importance of one object is transferred to another object; it is this process of seeing that Cézanne has recorded, presenting an experience parallel to that in nature. Rather than creating the illusion of a window on the world, he wanted the canvas and paint to be present in their own right while acting as *abstract* equivalents for the seen world. This sounds difficult and as a painterly ideal it is; but as a convention it resembles those used by medieval or Renaissance artists to portray their world. What makes Cézanne's approach different is that he does not want to represent a medieval world of profound religious mystery or a Renaissance world of idealized and ordered harmonies, but the personal experience of seeing, in which to see is to know, because we come to know by focusing our attention from object to object. Cézanne makes us aware of the processes by which we see, and we enjoy his paintings because they are abstract arrangements of color and form that are pleasing and stimulating in their own right, without reference to the particular or specific world.

The Poet and the City: Baudelaire

If one poet can be said to have been the initiator of modern poetry, it is probably the Frenchman Charles Baudelaire (1821–1867). An art critic as well as a poet, Baudelaire was extremely sensitive to the achievements of the best painters of his time, particularly Eugène Delacroix. Although he died before the major works of the impressionists and symbolists had been created, he shared with them the understanding that the artist's task is to portray outward reality through inner vision. His poem "Correspondances" is often considered a kind of pre-symbolist manifesto. Of Manet, he wrote (in *Esthetic Curiosities*) that he "combined with a definite taste for reality, modern reality—which is already a good sign—that ample, lively, sensitive, and daring imagination without which, it must be said, all the best faculties are only servants without a master, agents without a government." The description might be applied to Baudelaire's own poetry as well.

Baudelaire's publication of his collection of poetry entitled *Les Fleurs du mal* (*The Flowers of Evil*) in 1857 shocked the bourgeois public, and some of the poems in it were subsequently banned. A city dweller all of his life, Baudelaire saw in his native Paris some of the same conditions that Engels and Dickens had observed in the industrialized cities of England: the gap between the smug, comfortable bourgeoisie and the marginalized poor, the dehumanized nature of the crowd, the alienations of modern life. But Baudelaire was a poet, not a reformer. His task, as the title of his collection states, was to bring flowers from evil; to create beauty by exploring the very depths of the ugliness of modern life. His Paris was the city recently transformed by Haussmann's majestic urban renewal, with its wide new boulevards and elegant neoclassical facades. His era was Napoleon III's Second Empire, which was dominated by materialism and greed. Baudelaire's vision of the modern city resembles that of Dante in the *Inferno* (see Volume 1), in that it becomes a symbolic representation of infinite spiritual loss. Behind the shiny new products of materialistic progress are to be found the squalor and poverty that reveal unpleasant truths about the human condition. This vision of the city is found especially in the section of *Les Fleurs du mal* entitled "Tableaux Parisiens," from which the three selections following "Correspondances" are taken.

CHARLES BAUDELAIRE (1821–1867)

Correspondances ————————————————— •

La nature est un temple où de vivants piliers
Laissent parfois sortir de confuses paroles;
L'homme y passe à travers des forêts de symboles
Qui l'observent avec des regards familiers.

Comme de longs échos qui de loin se confondent
Dans une ténébreuse et profonde unité,
Vaste comme la nuit et comme la clarté,
Les parfums, les couleurs et les sons se répondent.

Il est des parfums frais comme des chairs d'enfants,
Doux comme les hautbois, verts comme les prairies,
—Et d'autres, corrompus, riches et triomphants,

Ayant l'expansion des choses infinies,
Comme l'ambre, le musc, le benjoin et l'encens,
Qui chantent les transports de l'esprit et des sens.

Correspondences ————————————————— •
(*translated by Henri Peyre*)

Nature is a temple where living columns
Sometimes murmur indistinct words (allow confused
     words to escape);
There man passes through forests of symbols
That watch him with familiar glances.

Like prolonged echoes that mingle in the distance,
In a shadowy and profound unity,
Vast as night and as the light of day,
Perfumes, colors, and sounds respond to (answer to)
     one another.

There are perfumes, fresh as the flesh of children,
Sweet as oboe music, green as meadows,
—Others [are] corrupt, rich, and triumphant,

Having the expansion of things infinite,
Like amber, musk, benzoin, and frankincense,
Which sing the raptures of spirit and of sense.

QUESTIONS

1. What does the word *symbols* mean here?
2. How is the theme of *synaesthesia* (the relationships between the five senses) treated in this poem?

3. How does Baudelaire give the impression that all things are related through analogy? How can the poet perceive this better than the scientist can?

A Une Passante ———————————•

La rue assourdissante autour de moi hurlait. Longue,
    mince, en grand deuil, douleur majestueuse,
Une femme passa, d'une main fastueuse
Soulevant, balançant le feston et l'ourlet;

Agile et noble, avec sa jambe de statue.
Moi, je buvais, crispé comme un extravagant,
Dans son œil, ciel livide où germe l'ouragan,
La douceur qui fascine et le plaisir qui tue.

Ue élair . . . puis la nuit!—Fugitive beauté
Dont le regard m'a fait soudainement renaître,
Ne te verrai-je plus que dans l'éternité?

Ailleurs, bien loin d'ici ! trop tard ! *jamais* peut-être!
Car j'ignore où tu fuis, tu ne sais où je vais,
O toi que j'eusse aimée, ô toi qui le savais!

To A Passer-By ———————————•

(translated by C. F. MacIntyre)

Amid the deafening traffic of the town,
Tall, slender, in deep mourning, with majesty,
A woman passed, raising, with dignity
In her poised hand, the flounces of her gown;

Graceful, noble, with a statue's form.
And I drank, trembling as a madman thrills,
From her eyes, ashen sky where brooded storm,
The softness that fascinates, the pleasure that kills.

A flash . . . then night !—O lovely fugitive,
I am suddenly reborn from your swift glance;
Shall I never see you till eternity?

Somewhere, far off ! too late ! *never*, perchance!
Neither knows where the other goes or lives;
We might have loved, and you knew this might be!

QUESTIONS

1. Why do you think Baudelaire uses the sonnet form in this poem? Note the rhyme scheme in the original.
2. Do you recognize any aspects of romantic love in this poem?

3. What is the tone of this poem, and how does Baudelaire convey it?
4. What role does the city play in this brief "love story"?

The Swan

TO VICTOR HUGO

(translated by Anthony Hecht)

I

Andromache, I think of you. The little stream,
A yellowing mirror that onetime beheld
The huge solemnity of your widow's grief,
That other Simois your tears have swelled)[1]

Suddenly flooded the memory's dark soil
As I was crossing the new *Place du Carrousel.*[2]
The old Paris is gone (the face of a town)
Is more changeable than the heart of mortal man).

I see what seem the ghosts of these royal barracks,
The rough-hewn capitals, the columns waiting to
    crack,
Weeds, and the big rocks greened with standing
    water,
And at the window, a jumble of bric-a-brac.

---

[1] Allusion to Book III of Virgil's *Aeneid*. Andromache, the widow of the Trojan general Hector, and now a captive in Greece, weeps into the stream she calls "Simois" after a Trojan river.

[2] An interior courtyard of the Louvre palace.

One time a menagerie was on display there,
And there I saw one morning at the hour
Of cold and clarity when Labor rises
And brooms make little cyclones of soot in the air

A swan that had escaped out of his cage,
And there, web-footed on the dry sidewalk,
Dragged his white plumes over the cobblestones,
Lifting his beak at the gutter as if to talk,

And bathing his wings in the sifting city dust,
His heart full of some cool, remembered lake,
Said, "Water, when will you rain? Where is your
     thunder?"
I can see him now, straining his twitching neck

Skyward again and again, like the man in Ovid,[3]
Toward an ironic heaven as blank as slate,
And trapped in a ruinous myth, he lifts his head
As if God were the object of his hate.

        II

Paris changes, but nothing of my melancholy
Gives way. Foundations, scaffoldings, tackle and
     blocks,
And the old suburbs drift off into allegory,
While my frailest memories take on the weight of
     rocks.

And so at the Louvre one image weighs me down:
I think of my great swan, the imbecile strain
Of his head, noble and foolish as all the exiled,
Eaten by ceaseless needs—and once again

Of you, Andromache, from a great husband's arms
Fallen to the whip and mounted lust of Pyrrhus,
And slumped in a heap beside an empty tomb,
(Poor widow of Hector, and bride of Helenus)[4]

And think of the consumptive negress, stamping
In mud, emaciate, and trying to see
The vanished coconuts of hidden Africa
Behind the thickening granite of the mist;

Of whoever has lost what cannot be found again,
Ever, ever; of those who lap up the tears
And nurse at the teats of that motherly she-wolf,
     Sorrow;
Of orphans drying like flowers in empty jars.

So in that forest where my mind is exiled
One memory sounds like brass in the ancient war:
I think of sailors washed up on uncharted islands,
Of prisoners, the conquered, and more, so many
     more.

QUESTIONS

1. How does Baudelaire portray the old and the new Paris in this poem?
2. What different figures represent the theme of exile, and how?
3. What does the swan symbolize?
4. Do you see any relationship between the alienation and dehumanization of city life as portrayed by Engels and Dickens and by Baudelaire's poetry?

The Seven Old Men

TO VICTOR HUGO

(translated by Roy Campbell)

Ant-seething city, city full of dreams,
Where ghosts by daylight tug the passer's sleeve.
Mystery, like sap, through all its conduit-streams,
Quickens the dread Colossus that they weave.

One early morning, in the street's sad mud,
Whose houses, by the fog increased in height,
Seemed wharves along a riverside in flood:
When with a scene to match the actor's plight,

---

[3] Allusion to Ovid's *Metamorphoses* I. 85: "The creator gave man a face turned toward the sun so that he could look directly at it."
[4] Pyrrhus, the greek general, abducted Andromache to Troy and married her to Helenus.

Foul yellow mist had filled the whole of space:
Steeling my nerves to play a hero's part,
I coaxed my weary soul with me to pace
The backstreets shaken by each lumbering cart.

A wretch appeared whose tattered, yellow clothing,
Matching the colour of the raining sky,
Could make it shower down alms—but for the
    loathing
Malevolence that glittered in his eye.

The pupils of his eyes, with bile injected,
Seemed with their glance to make the frost more
    raw.
Stiff as a sword, his long red beard projected,
Like that of Judas, level with his jaw.

He was not bent, but broken, with the spine
Forming a sharp right-angle to the straight,
So that his stick, to finish the design,
Gave him the stature and the crazy gait

Of a three-footed Jew, or crippled hound.
He plunged his soles into the slush as though
To crush the dead; and to the world around
Seemed less of an indifferent than a foe.

His image followed him (back, stick, and beard
In nothing differed), spawned from the same hole,
A centenarian twin. Both spectres steered
With the same gait to the same unknown goal.

To what foul plot was I exposed? of what
Humiliating hazard made the jeer?
For seven times (I counted) was begot
This sinister, self-multiplying fear!

Let him mark well who laughs at my despair
With no fraternal shudder in reply . . .
Those seven loathsome monsters had the air,
Though rotting through, of what can never die.

Disgusting Phoenix,[1] his own son and father!
Could I have watched an eighth instalment spawn
Ironic, fateful, grim—nor perished rather?
But from that hellish cortege I'd withdrawn.

Preplexed as drunkards when their sight is doubled,
I locked my room, sick, fevered, chilled with fright:
With all my spirit sorely hurt and troubled
By so ridiculous yet strange a sight.

Vainly my reason for the helm was striving:
The tempest of my efforts made a scorn.
My soul like a dismasted wreck went driving
Over a monstrous sea without a bourn.

----

[1] The mythical bird reborn from his own ashes.

QUESTIONS

1. Which elements of Baudelaire's description of the city and of the old men are realistic? In what ways do they go beyond realism?
2. What effect does the apparition of the seven old men have upon the poet? What might they symbolize?

INDUSTRIALISM
AND THE HUMANITIES: CONTINUITIES

The effects of industrialism on our modern world have been almost incalculable. In addition to restructuring the economic and social fabric of Western society, the so-called Industrial Revolution contributed significantly to the ways in which human beings perceive themselves and their world.

Social, Political, and Scientific Thought Much of the social and political thought of the nineteenth century takes the new conditions into account by extending the egalitarian ideas of the Enlightenment into the economic sphere. Early liberal stress on individual initiative in the market place was clearly an outgrowth of Enlightenment principles, but the cost of laissez-faire capitalism in human suffering, as Friedrich Engels's vivid descriptions of working-class life demonstrate, had to be reckoned with. Among the various socialist thinkers, Karl Marx, whose theories have produced societies that might astound him, understood best the economic, social, and human consequences of industrialism.

Whereas most nineteenth-century socialist thought approached the problems of society from a collective viewpoint—seeing man not so much as an individual but as a member of a group or class—the new liberalism from the middle decades of the century endeavored to foster social and economic justice while preserving an individualistic perspective. Its call for selective government intervention in the market place was based on the belief that such regulation would enhance the liberty of all while preventing the tyranny of the few. These newer liberals also urged extension of the suffrage to members of the lower classes in the furtherance of Enlightenment goals. John Stuart Mill maintained that this goal necessitated recognition of the rights of women as well as of men. Present-day women's liberation movements owe much to Mill's arguments.

In any event, the pragmatic philosophy of the newer liberals, together with the preference of the lower classes for immediate economic gains, prevented the social revolution predicted by Marx and other radical thinkers. The overall tendency in Western industrial societies by the end of the century was toward the amelioration of the living conditions of the lower classes and the rapid increase in the number of middle-class families.

Scientific and technological developments also contributed to changes in human perceptions. The evolutionary theories of Charles Darwin profoundly upset traditional religious and humanistic notions of man's unique position in creation. The notion of life as evolutionary, together with the increasing standard of living, generally tended to support belief in inevitable progress and to encourage an overriding interest in the material aspects of life.

Realism in the Arts Artists responded to these conditions in various ways. While romanticism remained the dominant trend in music until the very end of the nineteenth century, the style called realism came to dominate painting and literature around 1850. Realist artists and writers felt that the times called for depicting the world as in its beauty. The invention and development of photography seemed in many ways to replace what the realists were trying to accomplish. Stressing the effects of the environment on individual characters, the realists and, even more so, the naturalists, were often harshly critical of the social and psychological consequences of industrialism.

Architects tended either to escape from the modern world by building in revival styles like Greek classical or Gothic, or to respond enthusiastically to the new technological possibilities. Unlike the often critical realistic painting and fiction, buildings like the Crystal Palace in London and the early skyscrapers in Chicago are testimonies to a dynamic capitalistic society, proud of itself and its accomplishments.

Beyond Realism   During the closing decades of the nineteenth century many prominent artists and thinkers were reacting against both the assurance that life could be portrayed as it seemed, "realistically," and the widespread contemporary self-satisfaction with material progress. Although still in the realist tradition, Dostoevsky maintained that reality was to be found more in the human soul than in the external environment. Nietzsche, who accepted Dostoevsky's emphasis on the irrational and spiritual but not his religious beliefs, insisted on the moral and intellectual weakness of Judaism and Christianity and proclaimed: "God is dead!" As a solution to the problems of man without God, he advocated the free development of all human potentialities in the individual "superman."

In painting, Edouard Manet served as a kind of bridge between realism and the style that became known as impressionism. Using the discoveries of photography and through experimenting with light, the impressionists became more interested in rendering subjective "impressions" of the visible world than in attempting to portray objective reality. The post-impressionist artists and the Symbolist poets veered even more sharply from the tenets of realism. The function of art became not to reproduce the crass material world but to create a purer—and indeed, *truer*—world. Extending the romantic vision, these artists imposed a persona, symbolic world of nature.   By the end of the century, art seemed to many to fill the vacuum left by religion.

The City   The rapid growth of industrialism brought with it the equally rapid and unplanned development of what we have come to call urban sprawl. Cut off from the natural rhythms of rural living and from the reassurances of an ancestral homeland, millions of new city dwellers, although less likely to starve than they would have been in the country, came to experience not only the miserable living conditions but also the rootlessness and alienation endemic to city life. Social thinkers such as Engels described the sense of inhumanity present in city crowds composed of the indifferent well off and the indigent and homeless. Novelists and poets such as Dickens, Dostoevsky, and Baudelaire expressed the hell-like nature of the city. For Baudelaire and the symbolist poets who followed him, the city became not so much a reality to be rendered objectively as an outward manifestation of the exploration of inner dreams and nightmares. The love-hate relationship with city life and the rift between ordinary external reality and poetic reality was to expand dramatically in the works of artists and writers of the early twentieth century.

PART EIGHT

Discontinuities: The Early Twentieth Century

31

A Culture in Self-Doubt

In 1900, continuity snapped . . .

HENRY ADAMS

On or about December, 1910, human nature changed.

VIRGINIA WOOLF

Developments in Science and Politics

The study of the humanities makes it evident that change—in forms, styles, ideas, outlooks, and especially in the apprehension of the nature of reality—is inevitable. The values and the truths of one generation cannot be those of the generation that succeeds it; the children must grow away from or revolt against the parents. We have seen that in certain periods change in the humanities comes about gradually, while in others it seems to erupt violently. No culture in the history of the world, however, has experienced either the extent or the intensity of change as that which the West has seen in our own century. Changes in Western culture have had profound repercussions on the rest of the world, and the rest of the world has in turn challenged the West's claim to leadership.

As the quotations heading this chapter indicate, it seemed to artists and thinkers in the early 1900s that the twentieth century had broken in a new and radical way with previous tradition. A radical break in the arts became evident with a series of new styles which can all be loosely grouped under the name *modernism*. We will look at some examples of this trend shortly; first let us examine briefly some of the intellectual and social developments that contributed toward making this period one of discontinuity.

Scientific Developments   In the pure sciences, a series of astounding new discoveries altered the scientific picture of the natural world as radically as had Newtonian physics in the seventeenth century and Darwinian biology in the nineteenth. Among the more important was Max Planck's discovery at the turn of the century that atoms emit energy not with continuity but in separate units. A few years later Albert Einstein (1879–1955) initially expounded his theory of relativity: that space, time, and motion are not absolute (as Newtonian physics had assumed), but rather that all are relative to the observer's position. The Newtonian conceptions appeared inapplicable to the atom or the universe where movement was measured at the speed of light.

There are, however, two essential differences between this scientific revolution and the two previous ones. First, whereas the intelligent layman could read Newton and Darwin and gain a fairly good understanding of their theories, it was and is impossible for someone without scientific training to have more than a superficial understanding of the discoveries of Planck and Einstein. Secondly, whereas Newton offered a rational picture of the world and evolution stressed progressive continuity between one species and another, the new physics seemed to postulate a world without continuity or absolutes, a world in which nothing was certain. Even without a scientific knowledge of physics, twentieth-century human beings are well aware that a world composed of subatomic particles, a world in which matter and energy, space and time, interpenetrate, a world in which scientific laws are given names like

"relativity" (Einstein) or "uncertainty" (Werner Heisenberg), is a world in which nothing is as it appears to be to the human senses.

In the social sciences, too, certainties of the past gave way to uncertainties or relativities. Developments in anthropology emphasized the relativity of cultural values. The new science of psychology (launched in the 1870s) showed, first through the work of the Russian Ivan Pavlov, that human beings could be conditioned by their environment to elicit certain responses, thus that they did not act primarily from reason and conscious decision. Foremost in upsetting traditional notions about human nature was the work of Sigmund Freud. Freud's theories that our actions and behavior are rooted in our unconscious, rather than our conscious mind, seemed to many a more pessimistic view of human nature than Darwin's theories about our ancestry. We will examine Freud's work in more detail.

What the early twentieth century witnessed was what Nietzsche had prophesied: a radical questioning of the Greco-Roman and Judeo-Christian roots of our culture. Reason and authority, humanism and faith, the pillars of these cultures, were undermined as never before. Yet the great minds who contributed most to this upheaval, Einstein and Freud (we could add the earlier Marx), were of Jewish backgrounds and steeped in humanistic culture.

Colonialism   At the same time that Western culture appeared to be casting doubts on itself, the Western powers, particularly England and France, expanded colonization in Africa, Asia, and America. The years after 1880 witnessed an increasingly bitter competition between European powers to establish their flags over as many colonies in the world as possible.

The effect of this late colonialism was devastating for the life of those areas occupied. True, the Europeans brought with them some of the benefits of communication, transportation, and scientific advancement, but the cost in terms of the social and cultural life of Asiatic and African people was tremendous. This rapid change—the disintegration of a traditional society—is graphically chronicled by the Nigerian writer Chinua Achebe in his *Things Fall Apart*. The influence, however, was not all one-way. Especially in the visual arts in the decades before World War I, western Europeans,

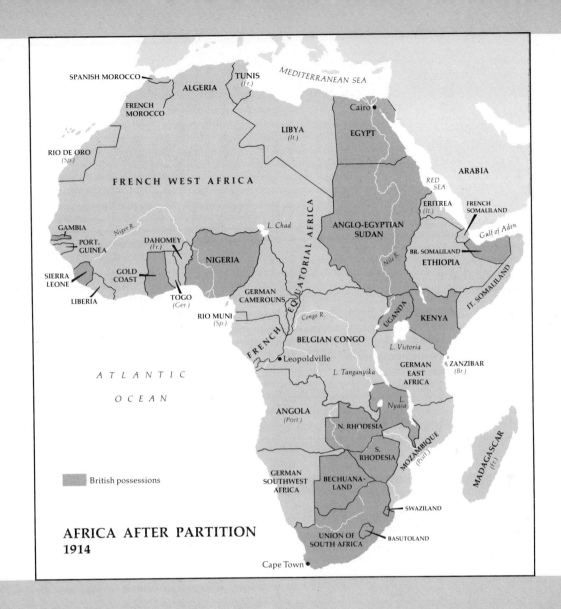

AFRICA AFTER PARTITION 1914

SPANISH MOROCCO

TUNIS
(Fr.)

MEDITERRANEAN SEA

ALGERIA

FRENCH
MOROCCO

LIBYA
(It.)

Cairo •

EGYPT

RIO DE ORO
(Sp.)

FRENCH WEST AFRICA

ARABIA

RED
SEA

ERITREA
(It.)

FRENCH
SOMALILAND

GAMBIA

Niger R.

L. Chad

ANGLO-EGYPTIAN
SUDAN

Gulf of Aden

PORT.
GUINEA

DAHOMEY
(Fr.)

NIGERIA

BR. SOMALILAND

ETHIOPIA

Nile R.

SIERRA
LEONE

GOLD
COAST

LIBERIA

TOGO
(Ger.)

GERMAN
CAMEROUNS

RIO MUNI
(Sp.)

Congo R.

UGANDA

KENYA

IT. SOMALILAND

ATLANTIC

OCEAN

FRENCH EQUATORIAL AFRICA

BELGIAN CONGO

• Leopoldville

L. Victoria

GERMAN
EAST
AFRICA

ZANZIBAR
(Br.)

L. Tanganyika

ANGOLA
(Port.)

L.
Nyasa

N. RHODESIA

MOZAMBIQUE
(Port.)

MADAGASCAR
(Fr.)

S.
RHODESIA

GERMAN
SOUTHWEST
AFRICA

BECHUANA-
LAND

British possessions

SWAZILAND

UNION OF
SOUTH AFRICA

BASUTOLAND

Cape Town •

questioning their own culture, proved receptive to the civilization of the colonized peoples.

World War I By the first decade of the twentieth century, after all the desirable opportunities for colonial expansion were realized, the focus of international competition came back to the European continent itself. World War I started in 1914 in an almost careless mood with plumes and full-dress parades; but within the first year it became a war fought in muddy trenches with interminable days and nights of waiting alternating with sudden attacks, sometimes costing thousands of lives for a few square yards of ground gained. The growth of industrialism had made possible an exquisite technology of destruction: the tank, the machine gun, the airplane, and poison gas. The following poem, "Dulce et Decorum Est," by Wilfred Owen, describes the horror of a gas attack at the front. The poem constitutes a commentary on the ancient Latin patriotic motto in the last two lines: "It is sweet and becoming to die for one's country." The poet himself was killed at age twenty-five a week before the war ended.

WILFRED OWEN

Dulce Et Decorum Est

Bent double, like old beggars under sacks,
Knock-kneed, coughing like hags, we cursed through
    sludge,
Till on the haunting flares we turned our backs
And towards our distant rest began to trudge.
Men marched asleep. Many had lost their boots
But limped on, blood-shod. All went lame; all blind;
Drunk with fatigue; deaf even to the hoots
Of disappointed shells that dropped behind.

Gas! Gas! Quick, boys!—An ecstasy of fumbling,
Fitting the clumsy helmets just in time;
But someone still was yelling out and stumbling
And floundering like a man in fire or lime.—
Dim, through the misty panes and thick green light
As under a green sea, I saw him drowning.

In all my dreams, before my helpless sight,
He plunges at me, guttering, choking, drowning.

If in some smothering dreams you too could pace
Behind the wagon that we flung him in,
And watch the white eyes writhing in his face,
His hanging face, like a devil's sick of sin;
If you could hear, at every jolt, the blood
Come gargling from the froth-corrupted lungs,
Obscene as cancer, bitter as the cud
Of vile, incurable sores on innocent tongues,—
My friend, you would not tell with such high zest
To children ardent for some desperate glory,
The old Lie: Dulce et decorum est
Pro patria mori.

At the outset the Central Powers—Germany, Austria-Hungary, and Turkey—opposed the Allies: Great Britain, France, and Russia. Italy joined the latter three in 1915. The loss of Russia in 1917 because of a civil war was balanced by the entrance of the United States on the Allied side. Although the Central Powers put up a vigorous fight for more than a year, by late 1918 the Allies were victorious.

Europeans on both sides became almost immediately aware that the war had, if anything, aggravated long-standing problems. The losses in men, land, and property were enormous, and it was difficult to say that anything had been gained. At Versailles in 1919, where the peace settlement was worked out, the major European powers, primarily France and England, intentionally set out to so cripple Germany that it could not again pose a threat to the victors. Parts of its territory were taken away, and the newly established democratic government, the Weimar Republic, was burdened with paying an astronomical reparations debt to its former enemies. Restrictions were placed on the size of the Germany army. While the fledgling government in Germany suffered peculiar handicaps, democracy there, as in the half-dozen new countries created out of the old Austro-Hungarian empire, also suffered from the lack of any sort of republican tradition. Most, though not all, of these governments created by the victors in the lands of the vanquished had little popular support in their own country. The weakness of these new states therefore made the whole political atmosphere unstable.

The League of Nations

To ensure that this war really had been "a war to end all wars," the victors at Versailles, led by Woodrow Wilson, the American President, drew up a covenant, or constitution, for an international organization designed to defend the independence of every member nation. Created in January 1920 at Geneva, Switzerland, the League of Nations from the very beginning was weakened by the refusal of the most powerful nation in the world, the United States, to participate in its operations. Throughout its life in the years between the two World Wars, the League was further hampered by conflicting interpretations of its purposes by member nations and by its inability to take decisive action when a powerful nation was party to a dispute.

Decline of the West Europe in the early 1920s was worn out and discouraged. Symptomatic of the weariness and sense of decline was the work of Otto Spengler (1880–1936) with its ominous title, *The Decline of the West*. For Spengler, Western culture was in

FINLAND

NORWAY

SWEDEN

NORTH SEA

BALTIC SEA

ESTONIA

LATVIA

UNION OF SOVIET SOCIALIST REPUBLICS

Moscow •

N. IRELAND

IRELAND

DENMARK

SCHLESWIG-
HOLSTEIN

MEMEL

LITHUANIA

GREAT BRITAIN

EAST
PRUSSIA

London •

NETHERLANDS

Berlin •

POLISH CORRIDOR

• Warsaw

POLAND

ATLANTIC OCEAN

BELGIUM

GERMANY

UPPER SILESIA

EUPEN, MALMEDY

LUXEMBOURG

• Paris

SAAR

Prague •

CZECHOSLOVAKIA

ALSACE-LORRAINE

Danube R.

FRANCE

SWITZ-
ERLAND

Vienna •

BESSARABIA

AUSTRIA

Budapest •

TYROL

HUNGARY

TRANSYLVANIA

ISTRIA

RUMANIA

PORTUGAL

ITALY

YUGOSLAVIA

Belgrade •

Bucharest •

BLACK SEA

Madrid •

SPAIN

• Rome

BULGARIA

ALBANIA

GREECE

TURKEY

TERRITORIAL CHANGES IN EUROPE
After World War I

old age, its ruling classes were timid and not so much governing as administrating. Without faith and self-discipline the forces of anarchy would grow in the society and, unless strong leaders arose, it would continue its path of decline.

The new governments formed out of the defeated states proved highly unstable. The war had created a cooperative spirit between workers and bosses, but, with the war over, social conflicts increased markedly. Capitalists nervously eyed developments in Russia, where a communist state came into being infused with missionary zeal. Would the workers in the capitalist countries heed the call for revolt? Many expected another dreaded war but it was felt more than likely that that war would not be an affair of nations but of classes.

The Roaring Twenties

The postwar mood in the United States contrasted starkly with that in Europe. While many Europeans looked gloomily at the future of the human race, Americans exuded optimism. Unwilling to play its role as the key power in international relations, the United

States was not reluctant to assert its economic predominance. The magic word of the decade of the 1920s was *credit*: a generous policy of lending against future earnings led to an enormous expansion of production. The first generation of installment-plan buyers in America found within its reach a range of luxuries, now considered necessities, that could be had on the promise of payment later. Because the country was the leading financial and industrial power, the economic system of other nations eventually became drawn into the same upward draft. When in 1929 panic struck Wall Street, the bubble burst and the world's economy shriveled; production statistics dropped, millions were thrown out of work, and the Great Depression of the 1930s was launched.

Politics in the 1930s: Communism and Fascism

The collapse of the world economy had its effect on almost every area of the globe but nowhere was it as marked as in the highly developed economic countries of Western Europe and the United States. Breadlines, starving sharecroppers and dispossessed families constituted only the obvious results of the financial disaster. In such circumstances, the gulf between the haves and the have-nots in society became glaringly obvious, with a corresponding intensification of social tension.

The sense of shock and dismay brought on by the economic crisis led to a broad questioning of traditional political values both in the United States and abroad. Could free enterprise and democracy survive? Almost totally independent of Western capitalism, the socialistic economy of the Soviet Union—although it had problems of its own—was insulated from the shock. In capitalistic countries millions of peasants and workers, either unemployed or threatened with unemployment, looked to communism as a way out of a depression in which they were the chief sufferers.

On the other hand, large numbers of people—many members of the middle classes as well as peasants and urban workers—turned to the radical right, especially to fascism, for a solution. Partly motivated by a fear of communism, partly by an antipathy toward big business that reduced the artisan to a laborer and threatened the shopkeeper with competition, they felt the appeal of a conservative right stressing the old values of

thrift, industry, national traditions, and loyalty to the country.

Communism is similar to fascism in that it is a totalitarian political philosophy that sees the individual as having historical existence only in terms of a larger group. For the communist the larger group is the class; for the fascist it is the nation. Just as the communists declare that an individual's mentality is determined by the class to which he belongs, so the fascists claim that one's basic outlook derives from one's nationality. What we call reason, therefore, is relative to each nation. Like Rousseau's general will, the national will of the fascist is the deepest part of every member of the national group. Whereas the communists view class conflict as inevitable, the fascists see struggle between national wills as the central characteristic of human history. Indeed, national wills are defined primarily in their conflict with other nations. However, in contrast to communism, which tends to play down the importance of individual leaders in accomplishing its goals, for fascism the leader is the one who best senses the national will and, therefore, can effectively direct the people to realizing the nation's destiny.

In contrast with fascism elsewhere in Europe, German fascism had a peculiarly racial bias. Adolf Hitler (1889–1945), the leader of the movement in Germany from the 1920s, viewed German nationalism as a manifestation of superior Aryan culture. Many anthropologists believe that the Aryans were a large *linguistic* group originating in north-central Europe that around 3000 B.C. began migrating southward, eastward, and westward. For Hitler the Aryans constituted a *racial* group and one naturally superior to all other "races." Although he regarded all non-Aryans as inferior, he despised the Jews particularly, because he considered them cultural parasites, enemies of creative societies, and a people intent on dominating the world. His book *Mein Kampf (My Battle)*, published in two volumes in 1925 and 1926, respectively, called for state action not only to purify the Aryan race from racial corruption but also to build a master race by eliminating mental and physical handicaps through birth control. After seizing power in 1933, Hitler proceeded to carry out his program through massive sterilization campaigns and concentration camps. The following selections from *Mein Kampf* were translated by Ralph Manheim.

ADOLF HITLER

From *Mein Kampf*

THE JEWS

The mightiest counterpart to the Aryan is represented by the Jew. In hardly any people in the world is the instinct of self-preservation developed more strongly than in the so-called "chosen." Of this, the mere fact of the survival of this race may be considered the best proof. Where is the people which in the last two thousand years has been exposed to so slight changes of inner disposition, character, etc., as the Jewish people? What people, finally, has gone through greater upheavals than this one—and nevertheless issued from the mightiest catastrophes of mankind unchanged? What an infinitely tough will to live and preserve the species speaks from these facts!

The mental qualities of the Jew have been schooled in the course of many centuries. Today he passes as "smart," and this in a certain sense he has been at all times. But his intelligence is not the result of his own development, but of visual instruction through foreigners.

Since the Jew—for reasons which will at once become apparent—was never in possession of a culture of his own, the foundations of his intellectual work were always provided by others. His intellect at all times developed through the cultural world surrounding him.

The reverse process never took place.

For if the Jewish people's instinct of self-preservation is not smaller but larger than that of other peoples, if his intellectual faculties can easily arouse the impression that they are equal to the intellectual gifts of other races, he lacks completely the most essential requirement for a cultured people, the idealistic attitude.

In the Jewish people the will to self-sacrifice does not go beyond the individual's naked instinct of self-preservation. Their apparently great sense of solidarity is based on the very primitive herd instinct that is seen in many other living creatures in this world. It is a noteworthy fact that the herd instinct leads to mutual support only as long as a common danger makes this seem useful or inevitable. The same pack of wolves which has just fallen on its prey together disintegrates when hunger abates into its individual beasts. The same is true of horses which try to defend themselves against an assailant in a body, but scatter again as soon as the danger is past. . . .

If the Jews were alone in this world, they would stifle in filth and offal; they would try to get ahead of one another in hate-filled struggle and exterminate one another, in so far as the absolute absence of all sense of self-sacrifice, expressing itself in their cowardice, did not turn battle into comedy here too.

So it is absolutely wrong to infer any ideal sense of sacrifice in the Jews from the fact that they stand together in struggle, or, better expressed, in the plundering of their fellow men. . . .

Hence the Jewish people, despite all apparent intellectual qualities, is without any true culture, and especially without any culture of its own. For what sham culture the Jew today possesses is the property of other peoples, and for the most part it is ruined in his hands.

No, the Jew possesses no culture-creating force of any sort, since the idealism, without which there is no true higher development of man, is not present in him and never was present. Hence his intellect will never have a constructive effect, but will be destructive, and in very rare cases perhaps will at most be stimulating, but then as the prototype of the "force which always wants evil and nevertheless creates good." Not through him does any progress of mankind occur, but in spite of him.

THE STATE

The folkish state[1] must make up for what everyone else today has neglected in this field. *It must set race in the center of all life. It must take care to keep it pure. It must declare the child to be the most precious treasure of the people. It must see to it that only the healthy beget children; that there is only one disgrace: despite one's own sickness and deficiencies, to bring children into the world, and one highest honor: to renounce doing so. And conversely it must be considered reprehensible: to withhold healthy children from the nation. Here the state must act as the guardian of a millennial future in the face of which the wishes and the selfishness of the individual must appear as noth-*

---

[1] A state designed to serve the needs of a race capable of culture—i.e., the Aryans.

ing and submit. It must put the most modern medical means in the service of this knowledge. It must declare unfit for propagation all who are in any way visibly sick or who have inherited a disease and can therefore pass it on, and put this into actual practice. Conversely, it must take care that the fertility of the healthy woman is not limited by the financial irresponsibility of a state régime which turns the blessing of children into a curse for the parents. It must put an end to that lazy, nay criminal, indifference with which the social premises for a fecund family are treated today, and must instead feel itself to be the highest guardian of this most precious blessing of a people. Its concern belongs more to the child than to the adult. . . .

In the folkish state, finally, the folkish philosophy of life must succeed in bringing about that nobler age in which men no longer are concerned with breeding dogs, horses, and cats, but in elevating man himself, an age in which the one knowingly and silently renounces, the other joyfully sacrifices and gives.

That this is possible may not be denied in a world where hundreds and hundreds of thousands of people voluntarily submit to celibacy, obligated and bound by nothing except the injunction of the Church.

Should the same renunciation not be possible if this injunction is replaced by the admonition finally to put an end to the constant and continuous original sin of racial poisoning, and to give the Almighty Creator beings such as He Himself created?

COMMENTS AND QUESTIONS

1. How does Hitler characterize the intelligence of Jews?
2. Why could the Jews never found their own state? By implication, why does Hitler believe the Aryans capable of creating a powerful state?
3. What result has the Weimar Republic's indifference to controlling birth produced?
4. What policies for remedying the "racial poisoning" suggest themselves?

Caught between extreme movements on the right and left, European democratic political parties were hard put to deal with enemies who would not play ac-

cording to the rules. Already in the early years after World War I, Benito Mussolini in Italy had successfully used the threat of communism to destroy the government and to establish a fascist state. Now, in the early 1930s, it was Germany's turn. With six million unemployed—including their families about 40 percent of the German population was involved—Germany in 1932 was ripe for a violent change. Adolf Hitler and his National Socialist (Nazi) party utilized every trick in the election of that year to present the choice as one between communism and the forces of order. Particularly virulent were the Nazi attacks on the Jews as the authors of the Depression and the source of Germany's major ills. (This was a new element in fascism not found in Mussolini's Italy.) The result was a plurality for the Nazi party in the popular assembly, the Reichstag. Hitler was appointed chancellor, or prime minister, by the president of the Weimar Republic; within the next few years he acted to destroy any political opposition and to make Germany a fascist state. By the mid-1930s the notorious concentration camps were in operation to house political dissidents and Jews. Then Hitler embarked on his promise to the German people to undo the provisions of the Treaty of Versailles.

The Spanish Civil War   In the mid-1930s fascist Italy and Germany had an opportunity to face communist Russia in a trial war where both sides could test their weapons and the fascists their soldiers. In 1936 a combined group of high-ranking army officers, Catholic traditionalists, fascists (Falangists) and monarchists, supported by the Church hierarchy, revolted against the legally elected republican government in an effort to prevent the application of a reform program aimed primarily against the large landholders. General Francisco Franco took command of the right-wing groups, the Nationalists, at an early stage and requested the assistance of Italy and Germany in fighting the civil war. The principal ally of the republicans, or Loyalists, was the Soviet union, but groups of sympathizers from America and Europe came as volunteers to help the cause as well. The Western democracies themselves, however, remained neutral. Fought with vicious cruelty on both sides, the war lasted almost three years. The distance of the Soviet Union from the fighting gave the

Nationalists an advantage in allies. The powerful German and Italian air forces were used for merciless bombing of the cities occupied by the enemy.

By 1939, when the civil war ended with a Nationalist victory, the hope of the Allies in World War I "to make the world safe for democracy" seemed in large part frustrated. Spain became one of the seventeen European nations out of twenty-seven to fall under the rule of a dictator. The League of Nations, essentially an international debating forum, was powerless to enforce international law and agreements. Not only were Germany and Italy aggressively menacing the remaining democratic powers, but, moreover, in August of that year Germany and Russia dumbfounded the world by signing a nonaggression pact. This meant that the burden for stopping the designs of the Axis powers (the term taken by Germany and Italy for their alliance) fell on Great Britain and France, neither of whom wanted war nor was prepared for it.

Sigmund Freud (1856–1939)

The debacle of world War I and the precarious character of peace in the postwar years led Sigmund Freud, like Spengler and others of that generation, to meditate on the nature of civilization. As a psychologist rather than a historian, Freud was primarily interested in the conflicts between individuals and their society, and reflection led him to trace the origins of civilized life back to its source in the human psyche. Freud's thought is represented here with a selection from his central work on this theme, *Civilization and Its Discontents* (1930). In order to assess his considerable impact on modern culture, however, it is also necessary to know something of the development of his ideas before that work. We will summarize this development briefly.

Depth Psychology   A Viennese neurologist, Freud left his first vocation to develop what came to be called "depth psychology." This depth psychology claimed to furnish a key to the exploration of the unconscious mind and, through this, a renewed knowledge of the conscious mind, with wider application to the understanding of literature, art, religion, and culture. The first dynamic psychiatry had been, in the main, the sys-

tematization of observations made on hypnotized patients. With Freud's method of free association, a new approach was introduced. The patient, relaxed on a couch, was told the basic rule: to tell whatever came to his mind, no matter how futile, absurd, embarrassing, or even offensive it seemed.

Three Parts of Mind   Much of Freud's understanding of the human individual rests on his contention that mental life is produced by the interaction of three psychic agencies: the ego, the id, and the super-ego. The *ego* was defined as "the coordinated organization of mental processes in a person." The *id* was not very different from what Freud had originally described as the unconscious, the seat of both the repressed material and the drives, to which had been added the unconscious fantasies and unconscious feelings, notably guilt feelings. The *super-ego* is the watchful, judging, punishing agency in the individual, the source of social and religious feelings in mankind.

The main aspects of depth psychology were Freud's dream theory and his theory of parapraxis, or faulty behavior, that is, slips of the tongue and erroneously carried-out actions. These theories were elaborated simultaneously and presented in two of his best-known books, *The Interpretation of Dreams* in 1900 and *The Psychopathology of Everyday Life* in 1904.

Dreams   Freud's theory of dreams has been told so often that it has become common knowledge. Among the many trivial events of the day, the dream chooses the one that shows some relationship to a childhood memory; and, as Freud puts it, the dream stands with one foot in the present and one foot in childhood. Thus one is led from the latent content still farther back to a childhood memory expressing an unfulfilled wish of that remote time. Here Freud introduced the notion he had found in his self-analysis and in his patients, the *Oedipus complex:* the little boy, wanting to possess his mother, wishes to get rid of his father; but he is frightened of this threatening rival and of castration as a punishment for his incestuous feelings toward the mother. Such is, Freud says, the terrible secret that every man keeps in the recesses of his heart, repressed and forgotten, and which appears in a veiled form in a dream every night. Freud named this complex from the

Greek myth on which Sophocles built his tragedy. Freud postulated a similar trauma for women, the *Electra complex*, in which the little girl desires to have children by her father and to kill her mother. A great reader in the humanities, Freud was well aware that profound psychological truths had been expressed in literature and art before being formulated scientifically.

The dream, for Freud, is essentially a fulfillment of a repressed, unacceptable sexual wish. When controls of consciousness are relaxed, waking acts, too, can reveal repressed wishes or desires. Such acts include forgetting proper names, slips of the tongue and speech blunders, mistakes in reading and writing, acts of physical clumsiness, and intellectual errors.

Pleasure Principle and Instincts   Also important in Freud's thinking are his theories of the pleasure principle and of the instincts, *Thanatos* and *Eros*, as discussed in his *Beyond the Pleasure Principle* (1920). The pleasure principle may be understood as man's constant attempt to achieve pleasure and to avoid pain. As for his dualistic theory of instincts, Freud contended that Eros included the sexual instincts, most of the egoistic or self-preservative impulses, and those drives and forces that enhanced and unified life. Thanatos, on the other hand, included the tendency to self-punishment in the individual as well as those impulses that denied life and disrupted civilized existence. Thus Freud hypothesized that perhaps there was some innate tendency in the psychobiological make-up of man that overrides the pleasure principle. Or, expressed another way, since the aim of the instincts (according to Freud's older definition) was to diminish tension and since this was also his definition of pleasure, the ultimate pleasure was not life or Eros, but Thanatos, stasis or death. There is no doubt that the experience of World War I influenced Freud's concept of the "death wish."

Freud on Religion, Culture, and Literature
Soon after he had conceived his psychoanalytic theory, Freud expanded his reflection upon the fields of religion, sociology, cultural history, art, and literature. In 1907 he compared obsessive compulsive symptoms of neurotics with religious rituals and creeds, concluding that religion was a universal obsessional neurosis and that obsession was an individualized religion. Twenty years later, in *The Future of an Illusion*, Freud defined religion as an illusion inspired by infantile belief in the omnipotence of thought, a universal neurosis, a kind of narcotic that hampers the free exercise of intelligence, something that man will have to give up. With *Totem and Taboo* Freud undertook to retrace the origin, not only of religion but of human culture as well, trying to find a link between the individual Oedipus complex and the prehistory of mankind.

Whereas Freud found religion harmful, he deemed art and literature beneficial to man. *The Interpretation of Dreams* contains two major ideas that have an impact on art and the criticism of art: the conception of the unconscious and the theory of the pleasure principle. Freud sees the work of art as the expression of a wish and the artist as a neurotic. Like the neurotic, the artist yearns for honor, power, wealth, fame, and the love of women; however, he does not have the necessary means toward achieving these goals. Therefore, he turns his back on reality, transferring his interests to the expression of his wishes in fantasy as creation. Art thus becomes, in Freud's view, something like a public dream, an occasion to contemplate the unconscious. "Dostoevsky and Parricide," "Leonardo da Vinci," and "The Moses of Michelangelo" are only three of the many works by Freud that reveal this psychoanalytical approach to the work of art.

Civilization and Its Discontents   In his essay of 1930, *Civilization and Its Discontents*, Freud applies psychoanalytical methods to the study of civilization. He begins by asking the question: why do so many people blame the fact of human unhappiness on civilization and technical progress? Would we in fact be better off in a "free" primitive state? Freud analyzes the clash between individual instincts, creative and destructive, and the restrictive forces of overripe Western civilization. He nevertheless argues that all societies, even the most primitive, impose restrictions and taboos and that human cultures in fact develop through the sublimation of instinctual drives. Eros, the drive for individual happiness, may clash with social necessities, but it also takes the form of the urge that causes human beings to seek to bind together, first in families and then in larger social groups. The other basic instinct, *Thanatos,* conceptualized by Freud shortly after World War I, occurs both in the form of an individual "death wish" and as aggression toward others. It constantly threatens the destruction of both self and society. Freud concludes, pessimistically, that civilization of necessity had to channel and restrain people's instinctual strivings if both individuals and civilization were to survive. Unlike Marx and the tradition of Western radicalism emerging from the Enlightenment, Freud saw no possibility for a radically different future for the majority of mankind. His philosophic outlook is often thought of as a secular variant of the doctrine of original sin or as a modern version of the tragic vision.

The selection here (translated from the German by James Strachey) reflects Freud's view that the meaning of culture is the struggle between Eros and Thanatos (Death) as it works itself out in human society. "This struggle," he says, "is what all life essentially consists of and the evolution of civilization may therefore be simply described as the struggle for the life of the human species."

SIGMUND FREUD

From *Civilization and Its Discontents*

The assumption of the existence of an instinct of death or destruction has met with resistance even in analytic circles; I am aware that there is a frequent inclination rather to ascribe whatever is dangerous and hostile in love to an original bipolarity in its own nature. To begin with it was only tentatively that I put forward the views I have developed here, but in the course of time they have gained such a hold upon me that I can no longer think in any other way. To my mind, they are far more serviceable from a theoretical standpoint than any other possible ones; they provide that simplification, without either ignoring or doing violence to the facts, for which we strive in scientific work. I know that in sadism and masochism we have always seen before us manifestations of the destructive instinct (directed outwards and inwards), strongly alloyed with eroticism but I can no longer understand how we can have overlooked the ubiquity of non-erotic

aggressivity and destructiveness and can have failed to give it its due place in our interpretation of life. (The desire for destruction when it is directed *inwards* mostly eludes our perception, of course, unless it is tinged with erotism.) I remember my own defensive attitude when the idea of an instinct of destruction first emerged in psycho-analytic literature, and how long it took before I became receptive to it. That others should have shown, and still show, the same attitude of rejection surprises me less. For "little children do not like it"[1] when there is talk of the inborn human inclination to "badness", to aggressiveness and destructiveness, and so to cruelty as well. God has made them in the image of His own perfection; nobody wants to be reminded how hard it is to reconcile the undeniable existence of evil—despite the protestations of Christian Science—with His all-powerfulness or His all-goodness. The Devil would be the best way out as an excuse for God; in that way he would be playing the same part as an agent of economic discharge as the Jew does in the world of the Aryan ideal. But even so, one can hold God responsible for the existence of the Devil just as well as for the existence of the wickedness which the Devil embodies. In view of these difficulties, each of us will be well advised, on some suitable occasion, to make a low bow to the deeply moral nature of mankind; it will help us to be generally popular and much will be forgiven us for it.

The name "libido" can once more be used to denote the manifestations of the power of Eros in order to distinguish them from the energy of the death instinct. It must be confessed that we have much greater difficulty in grasping that instinct; we can only suspect it, as it were, as something in the background behind Eros, and it escapes detection unless its presence is betrayed by its being alloyed with Eros. It is in sadism, where the death instinct twists the erotic aim in its own sense and yet at the same time fully satisfies the erotic urge, that we succeed in obtaining the clearest insight into its nature and its relation to Eros. But even where it emerges without any sexual purpose, in the blindest fury of destructiveness, we cannot fail to recognize that the satisfaction of the instinct is accompanied by an extraordinarily high degree of narcissistic enjoyment,

---

[1] A quotation from a poem by Goethe.

owing to its presenting the ego with a fulfillment of the latter's old wishes for omnipotence. The instinct of destruction, moderated and tamed, and, as it were, inhibited in its aim, must, when it is directed towards objects, provide the ego with the satisfaction of its vital needs and with control over nature. Since the assumption of the existence of the instinct is mainly based on theoretical grounds, we must also admit that it is not entirely proof against theoretical objections. But this is how things appear to us now, in the present state of our knowledge; future research and reflection will no doubt bring further light which will decide the matter.

. . . The inclination to aggression is an original, self-subsisting instinctual disposition in man, and . . . it constitutes the greatest impediment to civilization. At one point in the course of this enquiry I was led to the idea that civilization was a special process which mankind undergoes, and I am still under the influence of that idea. I may now add that civilization is a process in the service of Eros, whose purpose is to combine single human individuals, and after that families, then races, peoples and nations, into one great unity, the unity of mankind. Why this has to happen, we do not know; the work of Eros is precisely this. These collections of men are to be libidinally bound to one another. Necessity alone, the advantages of work in common, will not hold them together. But man's natural aggressive instinct, the hostility of each against all and of all against each, opposes this programme of civilization. This aggressive instinct is the derivative and the main representative of the death instinct which we have found alongside of Eros and which shares world-dominion with it. And now, I think, the meaning of the evolution of civilization is no longer obscure to us. It must present the struggle between Eros and Death, between the instinct of life and the instinct of destruction, as it works itself out in the human species. This struggle is what all life essentially consists of, and the evolution of civilization may therefore be simply described as the struggle for life of the human species. And it is this battle of the giants that our nurse-maids try to appease with their lullaby about Heaven.[2]

QUESTIONS

1. According to Freud, what evidence is there for the existence of the death instinct?
2. In what different ways does Eros manifest itself?
3. Compare Freud's notion of the ''social contract'' to Rousseau's.
4. Does Freud's theory of Eros and Thanatos lead to the repudiation of the Enlightenment?
5. In what way are Freud's ideas similar to traditional Judeo-Christian teachings? How are they different?
6. What are your feelings about Freud's observation that ''one can hold God responsible for the existence of the Devil just as well as for the existence of the wickedness which the Devil embodies''?
7. Do you think that Freud's emphasis on sexuality is excessive? Is the libido the underlying reality of existence or merely one facet of it?
8. Do Freud's ideas perpetuate pessimism, despair, and cynicism?
9. Take any aspect of Freud's theories with which you disagree and present your own argument.

---

[2][''Eiapopeia vom Himmel.'' A quotation from Heine's poem *Deutschland*, Caput I.]

32

The Modernist Movement:
Painting, Sculpture,
And Architecture

In the years between 1900 and 1930 there developed a lifestyle that was self-consciously modern. The theories of Freud, often misinterpreted, led to a desire to be "liberated" from the restraints and taboos of proper Victorian society and to greater sexual freedom. Women, having finally gained the vote in England and America, began to demand greater freedoms and more of a place in society for themselves. Young women shocked their elders by wearing their hair and their skirts short and dancing modern dances like the Charleston. Blacks in America, while suffering from Jim Crow laws in the South and limited employment possibilities in the North, nevertheless made substantial contributions to the art and culture of the new age. The most substantial of these was jazz, a totally new art form that we will discuss as music in the next chapter. The modernist age can as well be called the jazz age, for jazz seemed to express the fast, frantic, free way of life that culminated in the Roaring Twenties. Automobiles, airplanes, radio, and technology that made possible the development of another new art form—the motion picture—all contributed to the impression that life was speeding up and changing at an incredible rate and that modern values and styles had to replace old-fashioned ones.

As is often the case, the changes in lifestyle were preceded by changes in the arts. Artists, too, became self-consciously modern, aware that art had to keep pace with, or advance, a rapidly changing society. In addition to jazz, another important new art form, modern dance, was an American creation, but the cradle of modernism in the early twentieth century was really Paris. There young painters, sculptors, writers, musicians, and dancers flocked from all over the world to exchange ideas and to participate in the creation of the new. Many Americans, white and black, fled what they considered to be the culturally backward, repressive atmosphere of the United States to give free rein to their creativity in Paris.

This period of intense modernist activity in Paris, beginning shortly before World War I, is described by Roger Shattuck as "the banquet years." The French accomplishments of the late nineteenth century seemed to offer developing artists a feast on which to nourish themselves. Visual, musical, literary, and theatrical artists were conscious of the interrelationships among their arts as never before. During the first three decades of the twentieth century, there developed an astounding number of literary-artistic-musical schools, all with "-isms" attached to them. Their histories have been made, and we will only mention a few of them here. What we will attempt to grasp through the rich variety of expressions is just what it meant (and means) to be "modern."

Modernist Painting 1900–1930

In the early years of this century two important trends can be distinguished. The first is the continuing transformation of the *figurative* tradition in which the human body and the objects of habitual visual experience form the basis of art. The second is the complete rejection of the visual world for an attempt to communicate through the pure plastic possibilities of the formal elements of painting, sculpture, and graphics. Two prominent figures are associated with the first: a Frenchman, Henri Matisse, and a Spaniard, Pablo Picasso. A Russian, Vasily Kandinsky, and a Dutchman, Piet Mondrian, are representative of the second. We will consider representative works from these trends and look briefly at their influence in the United States. We will then turn on two important modernist developments after World War I: Dada and surrealism.

Henri Matisse (1869–1954)   Matisse emerged as an important artist in an exhibition of his work and that of some colleagues in 1905. Called *Les Fauves* (wild beasts) because of the large areas of strong, simplified colors, slashing brushstrokes, and thick paint that characterized their work, these artists were all clearly inspired by impressionism, Gauguin, and Van Gogh. Matisse's portrait of his wife, *The Green Stripe* (Color Plate XVII), makes use of areas of strong, contrasting colors to create a sense of space and light instead of traditional shading and shadow. Matisse's ability to suggest weight, volume, and space through color juxtaposition was further enhanced by his command of the possibilities of line and contour. In 1905–1906, when Matisse painted *The Joy of Life* (Fig. 32-1), the heavy brushstrokes of his earlier work gave way to flowing contours and colors, spaciously arranged on a light ground. Compared to the canvases of Van Gogh and Gauguin, this work is empty of brooding and is filled with an almost musical lyricism and optimism. This painting truly affirms life and joy, resonating with exploding vigor and sensuality that we will witness in the music and ballet of Stravinsky's *Rite of Spring.*

Pablo Picasso (1881–1973)   Matisse's joyful visions of life were not shared by Picasso. In his early works, done in Paris around the turn of the century, Picasso used as subjects clowns, acrobats, peasants, and the dregs of Parisian night life that had also been used by Manet, Degas, and Toulouse-Lautrec. Filled with melancholy and a brooding sense of alienation, they remain nineteenth-century pictures in spite of Picasso's unconventional use of color, distortion, and space (Fig. 32-2).

Among Matisse's most important predecessors had been Gauguin. Picasso, however, turned to the works of Paul Cézanne, finding in them another way to see and

32-1 Left. Matisse, *The Joy of Life.* (Photograph Copyright 1980 by The Barnes Foundation)

32-2 Below. Picasso, *Family of Saltimbanques.* (National Gallery of Art, Washington, D.C., Chester Dale Collection) experience the world and to realize that experience in a painterly language. Cézanne had reduced objects to a series of visual references arranged in patterns of color and shape that created a sense of volume and space. For example, an orange would be represented as round and orange but with no reference to typical texture, surface formation, or any other transient characteristics of an orange—some are green, others are not orange all over, others have spots. Other objects on the picture surface would be reduced in the same way. A human figure, for example, would not have typical skin color, texture, even gesture. Rather, Cézanne would study the figure until he seemed to find the essence, an essential way for that figure to be represented that was convincing but not dependent upon the painted form being a direct copy of the seen and experienced human form. This process emphasized the nature of painting itself, as a process and of seeing, as a collection of experiences summarized and encapsulated by the mind through human experience. It was this that Picasso built on in his explorations made after the turn of the century.

African Art   Another artistic phenomenon that had a major impact on Picasso and his friends was the art of Africa and the South Pacific. Acquaintance with a completely different formal tradition is usually a very liberating experience to artists. It was so in the nineteenth century when Europeans became acquainted with Japanese prints. When Gauguin and others brought objects to Paris from Africa or the Pacific, interest was stimulated in what had heretofore been considered curiosities brought as memorabilia by colonists, travelers, or ethnographers. This so-called "primitive art" represented, as we saw in the chapter on African art in Volume I, completely different formal traditions. For example, in the mask in Fig. 32-3, the African artist has abstracted from reality those elements that are most important for the meaning and purpose of the mask. These have been exaggerated and combined into a strong, harmonious whole by the purely formal elements of the medium: plane, surface, texture, and shape. The existence of this tradition affirmed the belief of many artists that objects of art could speak in their own right, independent of the need to copy the familiar aspects of the visible world. At first these artists, including Picasso, copied the new forms and

32-3   African Dan mask. (Copyright F. Willett, Glasgow)

shapes, studying them and including them directly in their work. But very rapidly each artist adopted this influence to his particular uses, making the objects almost unrecognizable. Naturally, the majority of the European public did not receive either the African art or the work of artists inspired by it with enthusiasm. An apologist for both, the French poet and art critic Guillaume Apollinaire, argued persuasively for an understanding of African art. The piece that follows (translated by Susan Suleiman) was written in 1918.

Curiosity has found a new field of exploration in the sculptures of Africa and Oceania.

This new branch of curiosity, although born in France, has to this day found more commentators abroad. Since it originated in France, however, we have every reason to believe that it is here that its influence is being most deeply felt. These *fetishes*, which have not been uninfluential in modern art, are all related to the religious passion, which is the source of the purest art.

The interest of these fetishes lies essentially in their plastic form, even though they are sometimes made of precious materials. This form is always powerful, very far removed from our conceptions and yet capable of nourishing the inspiration of artists.

It is not a question of competing with the models of classical antiquity, but of renewing subjects and forms by bringing artistic observation back to the first principles of great art.

In fact, the Greeks learned much more from the African sculptors than has been noted up to now. If it is true that Egypt exerted an appreciable influence on the very human art of Hellas (Greece), one would have to be very unfamiliar with the art of the Egyptians and of the Negro fetishes to deny that the latter provides the key to the hieraticism and the forms characteristic of Egyptian art.

The enthusiasm of today's painters and collectors for the art of fetishes is an enthusiasm for the basic principles of our arts; their taste is renewed through contact with these works. In fact, certain masterpieces of Negro sculpture can compete perfectly well with beautiful works of European sculpture of the greatest periods. I remember an African head in M. Jacques Doucet's collection that can stand up perfectly against some fine pieces of Romanesque sculpture. In any case, no one today would dream of denying these evident truths, except ignorant people who do not want to take the trouble to look at things closely.

Influence of Cézanne and African Art on Picasso   The combined influences of Cézanne and African art help us to better understand *Les Demoiselles d'Avignon*, an unfinished picture that Picasso showed his friends in 1907 (Fig. 32-4). What do we see? A large canvas is filled with female bodies. It is difficult to tell if they are seated, standing, or leaning because the space in which we would expect them to exist has been shattered. Look at the figure on the far left. Does she stand behind, beside, in front of, or in the drapery? Does it bother you that you cannot tell? Look at the center figure. Is she standing or lying down? Why is it confusing? Where are her legs? Can you explain the position of her arms? Which figure seems to be rushing into the space? How can you tell? Which figures seem to have had their faces transformed by masks? Does the seated figure in the lower left face you or sit with her back to you? How does Picasso achieve a three-dimen-

sional effect in the faces of the three figures center and left? How have the bodies been transformed? What does the picture mean? Does it matter if you cannot tell? Why or why not?

Interpretation of this picture is difficult because it is no longer a picture with subject matter that tells a story. What is happening may be clarified by remembering how Picasso and his friends looked at African masks and sculptures. They did not know the meaning or purpose of either, but in spite of that, they could recognize human and animal forms and patterns and colors that rendered an account of everyday objects. Initially, this sense of recognition was important just because it told these Western artists that, indeed, there was more than one way to experience and give form to the world. Just as the medieval or Renaissance artist created conventions to capture experience and transmit knowledge, African artists had created their conventions. Western artists' experience of African art tended to reinforce the new (and very un-African) belief that line, color, and texture, when properly ordered in a work of art, have the power to create a personal response independent of religious or literary meaning. The problem became one of defining and understanding the limits of the power of the formal elements of art. African art, in particular, with its purposeful distortions of space, scale, and location, provided a major impetus for these artists.

Determined to free the picture from its dependence on old formulas, Picasso and his friend Georges Braque (1882–1963) worked together over a period of about four years. Like Cézanne, they considered the act of seeing to be one in which, first, we perceive what we focus on; second, what we perceive is determined by the length of time that we focus; third, we perceive by manipulating objects within our frame of reference; and fourth, we perceive by filling in information based on what we already know. For these two painters, the flat canvas became an imaginary grid with squares of equal size. Thus the canvas that one usually thinks of as having a bottom and top, left, and right sides, and whose characteristics of bottom, top, left, or right side, have an established value (for example, the horizon line is usually between two-thirds and half-way down from the top of the canvas) becomes a surface that can be manipulated in any direction. All directions are of

32-4 Picasso, *Les Demoiselles d'Avignon.* (Collection, The Museum of Modern Art, New York)

equal importance. Like the mapmaker who distills the elaborate, complex, three-dimensional world into an *abstraction* of lines and colors that convey information, the two painters distilled simple, everyday, familiar objects. They eliminated bright colors from their canvases because color itself can be emotionally powerful and evocative. They eliminated the traditional three-dimensional space invented in the Renaissance, and with it all references to fore-, mid-, and background. Objects or fragments of objects could now be placed anywhere in the shallow space. The artist could show us backs and sides of things, arranged at will on the canvas. A face is rendered in profile and full-face; we may see the side of the head and the back of the shoul-

der. References to specific objects are limited or reduced to familiar aspects.

Cubism Examine the picture *Man with a Violin* (Fig. 32-5). What parts of the man do you see? What features of the violin? How does the painter suggest space, light, and the volume and weight of the man's body? Of the violin? Picasso, instead of creating a picture to be perceived in the most habitual, traditional mode gives us a construction, an arrangement of shapes, colors, textures, spaces, and weights that invites us to participate in the process of seeing and knowing. We are not invited completely to "find" the man and his violin but to learn how little we must know in or-

32-5 Picasso, *Man with a Violin.* (Philadelphia Museum of Art: Louise and Walter Arensberg Collection)

der to see and understand. Moreover, we become more and more familiar with the purely formal qualities of the painting like *balance, harmony, contrast* of color, *texture,* and *form* that make up the experience of looking at pictures—an experience that can be enjoyable not because the picture is of "something" but because it "is." These paintings were named "cubist" by a hostile critic who pointed to their most conspicuous aspect—the small facets or planes that intersect and appear somewhat cubelike.

Collages   Neither Picasso nor Braque was content to continue in this style. They began to try other ideas such as adding materials like sand, pasted paper, or rope to the canvas to create the first *collages* (in French, "pasting," "gluing") (Fig. 32-6). The inclusion

of "real" materials in their pictures increased the potential for humor and irony. For example, a head cut out of newspaper is made to stand for a three-dimensional volume, while the lettering on the paper is intrinsically flat. It is a game in which what you see may not necessarily be what you think you see; but, above all, what you see is a *made* object that is important in its own right and not because it is a copy of the familiar, habitual visual world. (See Color Plate XVIII.)

The rational and orderly methodology of early cubism and the simplicity of the early collages were tested by the addition of color and the simplification of the *grid.* To what extent did pictures presenting more recognizable forms still maintain their identity as painted, made things? Picasso's *Three Musicians* (Fig. 32-7) is

32-6 Picasso, *Man with a Hat.* December, 1912. Charcoal, ink, and pasted paper. (Collection, The Museum of Modern Art, New York)

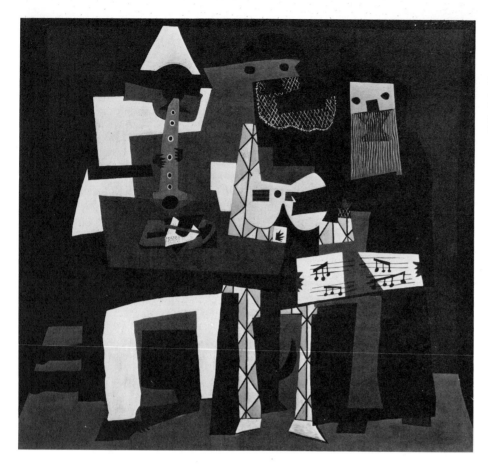

derived from the broken space and complicated, overlapping, superimposed views of *Man with a Violin*. The vivid simple colors, along with the intersecting forms of the musicians and their instruments, create a rhythmic movement that visually echoes the syncopations of jazz.

Guernica   The potential inherent in the language of cubism, however, was nowhere made clearer than in *Guernica* (Fig. 32-8), Picasso's large painting commemorating the total destruction of a Basque village, Guernica, by saturation bombing during the Spanish Civil War. Because the village had given its allegiance to the Republicans in the war, its destruction by the Nationalists was to be a lesson to other opponents.

Consider *Guernica*. What elements from cubism do you discern in this painting? What elements suggest the surreal combination of the expected with the unexpected? What do you think the bull stands for? the suspended light? the broken sword? the running girl? the

mother and child? Does the weeping mother remind you of anyone? Compare the figure of the horse with the one that David painted for Napoleon (Fig. 26-2). What do you think the horse symbolizes? Compare *Guernica* with Goya's *The Shootings of the Third of May, 1808* (Fig. 26-7). How are they alike or different? Is it possible for an artist to transform an event into a generalized, universal statement that can be easily understood? What must the artist do to accomplish this transformation?

In *Guernica*, Picasso did not attempt to depict the bombing of the village itself; instead, he created images that evoke the terror and destruction of war. It is the particular combination of images that induces meaning. To viewers since World War II, the images seem prophetic of the war that was to come and of the possibilities of total destruction. The painting was very controversial in Spain and was on long-term loan to the Museum of Modern Art in New York City. After the elections of 1981 in Spain, Picasso's heirs returned the

32-8 Picasso, *Guernica*. (Prado Museum, Madrid, Spain)

work to Spain, and it is now on permanent exhibit at the cáson del Retiro, an annex of the Prado, the Spanish national museum.

Nonobjective and Expressionist Painting

The belief in the ability of an object to act as a means of communication is nowhere more vividly tested than in the work of the painters Wassily Kandinsky and Piet Mondrian. Here we meet canvases that are completely free of any reference to the habitual, familiar objects and activities of our experience. We are left alone with arrangements of line and color that are, in Kandinsky's words, "a new world," capable of speaking to our conscious as well as our unconscious mind, if we will but permit it, asking not that it be a picture of something but that it just be.

Vasily Kandinsky (1866–1944)   Kandinsky became a painter when he saw one of Monet's *Haystacks* at an exhibition in Moscow. He tells us that he could not distinguish the subject. All that he saw was a veil of shimmering color, producing an emotional sensation like that produced when listening to great music.

Stunned by this experience, Kandinsky traveled all over Europe, painting and absorbing the work of Gauguin, Van Gogh, Monet, and others. Settling in Munich, a place intellectually stimulating like Paris, Kandinsky began to experiment, seeking a method of painting that accomplished his aims. An incident recounted in his *Reminiscences* helps us to understand his concept of the idea of the nonobjective painting:

It was the hour approaching dusk. I returned home with my paint box after making a study, still dreaming and wrapped into the work completed, when suddenly I saw an indescribably beautiful picture, imbibed by an inner glow. First I hesitated, then I quickly approached this mysterious picture, on which I saw nothing but shapes and colors, and the contents of which I could not understand. I immediately found the key to the puzzle; it was a picture painted by me, leaning against the wall, standing on its side. The next day, when there was daylight, I tried to get yesterday's impression of the painting. However, I only succeeded half-ways; on its side too, I constantly recognized the objects and the fine finish of dusk was lacking. I now knew fully well, that the object harms my paintings.

A frightening abyss, a responsible load of all kinds of questions confronted me. And the most important: What should replace the missing object? . . .

Only after many years of patient working, strenuous thinking, numerous careful attempts, constantly developing ability to purely and non-objectively feel artistic forms, to concentrate deeper and deeper into this endless depth, I arrived at the artistic forms, with which I am now working and which, I hope will develop much further.

The process was a long and arduous one. We already know that *line, color,* and *shape* can create sensations of space, movement, weight, and volume. But what of color disassociated from an object? Red, for example, will almost always conjure up images of fire, fire truck, stoplight, or car. Try to imagine a response to "winter"; a response not made of words or images of snow and ice, but of pure shapes, lines, and colors. The process is indeed an arduous one.

Writing as he worked, Kandinsky tried to explain his ideas, particularly in *On the Spiritual in Art,* published in 1912. In this treatise Kandinsky affirms his belief in the power of art to speak to the intellect and intuition of people without benefit of the habitual, familiar objects of the material world. He also advances a philosophical basis for this belief and suggests its social implications. Western man, he felt, had become desensitized by the materialism of his society.

Only by freeing painting from the material could the painter respond to the unconscious, the spiritual, and the immaterial longings of man. Moreover, a response freed from the material world would create a more universally understood language. He warned that his work was only a beginning and that future painters would be able to play on color harmonies as musicians play on the harmonies of the scales. Kandinsky's nonobjective pictures seem to build on Einstein's theories of the relativity of time and space, which were developing at this time. Indeed, Kandinsky embraces the buzzing, booming confusion of Einstein's universe in which all matter is energy. *Painting: Winter,* 1914 (Color Plate XX) appears as an eruption of the energy of the universe. Slashing lines of color race and run, as if to leap from the space of the canvas. Rich in possibilities for fantasy, dream, and daydream, Kandinsky's pictures offered future artists an example of a language of color, line, texture, and shape unfiltered by the material world.

Expressionism   In Munich, Kandinsky formed a group of artists called the Blue Rider. Members of this group and other German artists, writers, and musicians centered in Dresden and Berlin came to be known as expressionists. Expressionism drew on the powerful emotional quality of Van Gogh and on the bold color and line of Gauguin and Matisse. It is essentially, as the name implies, an art of self-expression or subjectivity. Influenced by Freud, expressionist artists (and the writers and musicians associated with them) wished to express the deep, hidden drives of human beings rather than surface "reality." They sensed, along with Marxists, the alienation of the individual in modern society and the dehumanizing effects of bourgeois capitalism. They were dissatisfied with the materialism and complacency of German society and often criticized it harshly in their works. Ernst Kirchner's (1880–1938) painting *Street, Berlin* (1913) is a good example of an expressionist work (Fig. 32-9). What is going on in the

32-9   Ernst Kirchner, *Street, Berlin.* (Collection, The Museum of Modern Art, New York)

32-10 John Sloan, *Sunday Women Drying Their Hair.* (Addison Gallery of American Art, Phillips Academy, Andover, Massachusetts)

picture? What is the artist's attitude toward the way of life portrayed here? How does he express that attitude?

Mondrian and Purism At the opposite pole from expressionism, another group of artists, centered primarily in Holland, celebrated the spirit of progress and man's rational and orderly faculties. The group called De Stilj were dedicated to "the devaluation of tradition, . . . the exposure of the whole swindle of lyricism and sentiment." In their work they stressed the need for abstraction and simplification, for clarity, certainty, and order. One, Piet Mondrian (1872–1944), began as a traditional painter, visited Paris, learned from the cubists, and returned to Holland. He began to remove all references to the familiar visual world from his canvases, concentrating on the "pure" reality of the formal plastic elements of art, which he began to confine to a linear black grid imposed on a white ground. He inserted color, usually red, yellow, or blue (the three primaries) to create contrasts that were resolved in harmonious balance (Color Plate XIX). Compare your experience of this work with *Painting: Winter* by Kan-

dinsky (Color Plate XX). One is fantastic, the other orderly; both grow out of the manipulation of the essential elements of painting.

Modernism in America

The art scene in the United States was very different from that in Europe between 1900 and the beginning of World War II. Many American artists were hostile to the art of Paris, Munich, and Berlin. The painters who comprised the "ashcan school" remained loyal to an essentially realist aesthetic, basing their work on that of Thomas Eakins (see page 292), but their art was more reportorial and concerned with the life and times of the city. (It was in fact this subject matter that gave them their name.) John Sloan (1871–1951), one of the most representative painters of this group, took his subject matter from the daily activities of the ordinary, the poor, the immigrant (Fig. 32-10). The painters in this group were not convinced that European art could make a contribution to the development of a uniquely American art.

However, painters in this group helped to give modern art its first important, large exhibition in the United States. Arranged by an association of American artists, the Armory Show of February 1913, staged at the Armory of the Infantry in New York City, exhibited the work of Cézanne, Van Gogh, Gauguin, Matisse, Kandinsksy, Picasso, and Duchamp, among others. The public was generally shocked and offended, but many American artists were stimulated and attracted by these works, for there already existed a strong stream of innovation. Moreover, these young artists had already found a rallying point and place in the figure of Alfred Stieglitz, a photographer who had studied in Berlin and returned to the United States. Stieglitz opened a gallery at 291 Fifth Avenue, where he exhibited the most advanced work from abroad and attracted artists and critics. Many important American artists were associated with the gallery and with the impact of European ideas on the American scene.

Stuart Davis (1894–1964) For decades an acknowledged leader of American abstraction, Davis evolved his style out of the cubism of Picasso and the ordinary objects of American urban life. Choosing as subject matter cigarette packs, light bulbs, electric fans, rubber gloves, and an eggbeater, Davis subjected these ordinary items to a rigorous process of abstraction (Fig. 32-11). Using very few colors, Davis combined objects that seem caught in an energizing framework. Compare *Egg Beater No. 1 (Abstraction)*, 1927, with Picasso's *Man with a Violin* (Fig. 32-5) and *The Three Musicians* (Fig. 32-7). Which of the two Picassos is more like Davis's work? Why? Is there a particular American quality to Davis's work that you do not find in Picasso's? Can you be specific?

Davis's painting *House and Street* (1931) also gives a powerful portrayal of a typical American scene. The juxtaposition of close-up with distant view and the simplification of forms and colors seem almost cartoon-like, but the energy that the painter gives to the place is hard to ignore. Davis's work demonstrated that abstraction had its place in American painting.

Georgia O'Keeffe (1887–1986) Another important painter in this group, Georgia O'Keeffe married Stieglitz, and was active as a painter until the 1970s.

32-11 Stuart Davis, *Egg Beater No. 1.* (The Philips Collection, Washington, D.C.)

32-12 Stuart Davis, *House and Street,* 1931. (The Whitney Museum of Art, New York)

32-13 Georgia O'Keeffe, *The Radiator Building: Night, New York,* 1927. Oil on canvas, 48 × 30 in. (Carl Van Vechten Gallery of Fine Arts, Fisk University)

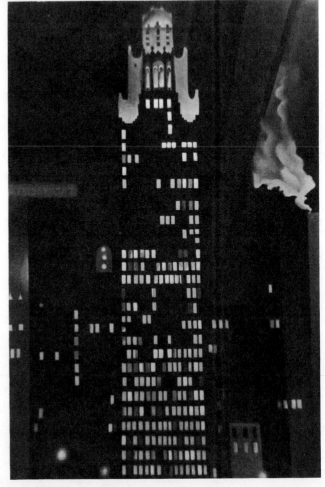

Her work, like that of Davis, seems to be a major bridge between the American desire for a realistic imagery and the idealism implicit in European abstraction. Certainly she created a very modern, personal idiom. She could make works that completely eliminated objects, and she painted the skyscrapers of New York City and the barns of Lake George with a clarity and rectitude comparable to the work of Charles Sheeler and George Demuth, two of her contemporaries (Fig. 32-13).

O'Keeffe is most frequently associated with two kinds of images. The first are scenes of the American Southwest. Her knowledge of the area began in the late "teens," and in the expansive New Mexican arid landscape, she identified feelings and discovered forms in light that seemed to confirm a vision and provide the means of achieving it. Bleached bones and bony mountains, solid adobe walls and cool, shadowed spaces are painted as intensely experienced but universalized in feeling. The juxtaposition of bones with blossoms, the reduction of endless sky to patterns of light were constant subjects of her last thirty-five years (Fig. 32-14).

Second are those in which the object, usually a flower or other plant, occupies the entire picture space (Color Plate XXI). In her clear, painstaking account of the magnified flower, we find a rich ground for symbolic associations. The crisp, smooth, painterly surface, however, presents the object with a cold objectivity that contrasts with our resonating fantasies. This tension between the unavoidable presence of the object and the opportunity for free fantasy seems characteristic of American life; it is a contrast like that between our great dependence on the machine and our fear of its dehumanizing possibilities.

O'Keeffe's paintings, drawings, and watercolors of flowers have always been received with critical ambivalence—great enthusiasm counterbalanced by grave reservations because of her being a woman. Historically, "flower painting" was a "woman's art," and the

complex messages conveyed by her work seemed both to challenge and make fun of the idea that art created by women should be somehow different from that made by men. Further, her artistic reputation had always been colored by her associations with the artists who represented the *avant garde* of American painting. As Stieglitz's wife and model, she appeared as an interesting, "bohemian" figure, not an important painter. A recent major exhibition of her work at the National Gallery of Art takes the position that it is time for serious study because it is her work and not her personality that must withstand critical assessment.

Dada and Surrealism

In 1915 a number of young people from all over Europe converged in Zurich, Switzerland, to create a movement that sought the fantastic and absurd in art, literature, and music. The movement was called Dada, a term whose origin is obscure. The most frequently quoted version is that a French-German dictionary opened at random produced the word *dada*, which means a child's hobby horse or rocking horse. The point is, of course, that life itself is random and uncontrolled: art should reflect the randomness and pessimism that is bred by the recognition of man's inability to control his life. The movement in Zurich was most concerned with poetry and music, producing events that combined the two in a nonsensical manner. Ridiculing the materialism of the middle classes and the optimism of the scientifically oriented progressives, the movement seemed at first merely a destructive one that challenged not only the traditional values of art but also the most recent. Nevertheless, there was a deep seriousness about these people that encouraged the artist to look again at the irrational, the subjective, the unconstructed side of man's psyche as it responded to life in this century.

In painting, the artist who exemplifies Dada is Marcel Duchamp (1887–1968) (one of three brothers who were deeply involved in new movements in Paris), who had already created a masterpiece in his painting *Nude Descending a Staircase, No. 2, 1912* (Fig. 32-15). For us today, familiar with time-lapse photography, films, and the multiple images of advertising, the painting is a

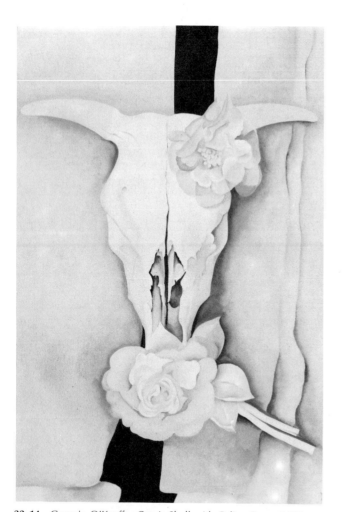

32-14   Georgia O'Keeffe, *Cow's Skull with Calico Roses*, 1931. Oil on canvas, 36 5/16 × 24 1/8 in.

32-15 Marcel Duchamp, *Nude Descending a Staircase, No. 2,* (Philadelphia Museum of Art: Louise and Walter Arensberg Collection)

he had signed a urinal, "R Mutt," and submitted it with the name *Fountain.* It was not shown in the exhibition. These "ready-mades," as Duchamp called them, were offensive to many, but others saw them as the realization and affirmation of the control of the machine and machine-made products in life. In 1915 Duchamp emigrated to New York, where he associated with the group at Stieglitz's 291. There he began a work that came to be considered exemplary of surrealism, the movement in art that emerged from Dada after World War I.

The chief spokesman for the new movement, André Breton, was a writer whose experiences in World War I convinced him of the unlimited depth of the human psyche. Impressed by the ideas of Freud, he identified the unconscious mind as the source for a new synthesis of the sometimes unpleasant concrete world with the world of rich associations created in dream and fantasy. The goal was to free individual creativity

32-16 Marcel Duchamp, *Chocolate Grinder, No. 2.* (Philadelphia Museum of Art: Louise and Walter Arensberg Collection)

remarkably expressive rendering of a figure walking down the stairs. Duchamp, however was not satisfied with painting, he felt that it was a limited process, doomed to end. By attempting a startling variety of approaches, he called into the question all the processes of art. Sometimes he would reduce his subject matter to the components of a fantastic machine; at other times he rendered objects with a scientific accuracy that gave them a superreal and fantastic quality (Fig. 32-16). Then, denying the hand of the artist altogether, he simply chose everyday objects, designating them "art" by the application of his signature. For the Armory Show to respond positively to the conflict between the rational and the irrational, producing a heightened awareness of the vitality of life and the mind that would ameliorate its apparent emptiness. Techniques for achieving this synthesis included collage, automatic drawing, and photographic montage of images. Generally the results were a dreamlike or hallucinatory juxtaposition of images and objects that stimulated personal free association and intense emotional responses.

In this context Marcel Duchamp's work *The Large Glass*, *The Bride Stripped Bare by Her Bachelors, Even* (Fig. 32-17), became a seminal surrealist work. Duchamp had worked on the idea for years, accumulating images that he transferred to a sheet of plate glass where dust, allowed to collect, had been glued in place. Other random elements, the frame, and finally the cracks in the glass itself became part of the work. According to Breton's interpretation, these images reflect the mechanization of persons and of the sexual act. Though such a representation may appear somewhat repulsive, if not inhumane, the artist intended to play on the contrasts of man to machine, the conflict of man with machine, and the perpetual conflicts between the sexes. In so doing, he intended to enlarge our awareness of the unconscious associations that may accompany our lives.

Other artists in various media learned from surrealist techniques how to contradict our familiar and habitual perception of reality. Surrealism has been a source of inspiration not only in painting, sculpture, the graphic arts, and poetry but also in the production of motion pictures.

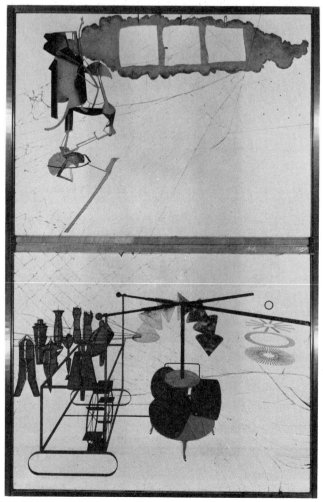

32-17 Marcel Duchamp, *The Bride Stripped Bare by Her Bachelors, Even* (The Large Glass). (Philadelphia Museum of Art: Bequest of Katherine S. Dreier)

Modernism in Sculpture: 1900–1930

Sculpture, like painting and graphics, responded to the same ideas and impulses that had transformed art after 1900. Just as we can distinguish those artists who continue interest in the human form as a means of communication, so we can identify artists who work only in forms, shapes, and colors freed from Renaissance and baroque conventions. Similarly, we can identify cubist sculptors, expressionist sculptors, and sculptors whose work is always associated with Dada and surrealism. We will consider work by two artists, Constantin Brancusi (1876–1957) and Jacques Lipschitz (1891–1973).

Brancusi (1876–1957) was a Rumanian whose work really parallels that of the cubists rather than being directly influenced by it. He was trained in the academic manner; but, after arriving in Paris in 1904, he turned more and more toward the evocation of forms by reducing them to bare essentials. A splendid craftsman with tremendous empathy for the textures and characteris-

32-18 Near right. Brancusi, *Bird in Space*. (Philadelphia Museum of Art: Louise and Walter Arensberg Collection)

32-19 Far right. Lipschitz, *Figure*. (Collection, The Museum of Modern Art, New York. Van Gogh Purchase Fund)

tics of a given material, he described his efforts as a search for the universally expressive essence of forms. *Bird in Space* (Fig. 32-18), made in 1928, can be interpreted as the reduction of a bird's wing, its souring power, its light gracefulness. The beautifully polished surface of the chrome form calls out to our tactile senses, and it is possible to imagine the cool purity of the shape that a caress would produce.

The work of Jacques Lipchitz forms a strong contrast with much of that of Brancusi. Much more directly influenced by the cubist painters, he made low reliefs in stone that can be directly compared to paintings and collages by Braque and Picasso. A free-standing piece like *Figure* (made between 1926 and 1930) is strongly

suggestive of the totemic power of African figures; but the juxtaposition of side with frontal views, which occurs when one moves around the figure in space, is based on the orderly perception of the interrelationship of parts—a characteristic of cubism (Fig. 32-19). Lipchitz modeled figures like these in clay or plasticine for bronze casting; the complex surface, which is rough and extremely tactile, is retained in the casting process. Compare this work with Brancusi's *Bird in Space*. Does *Figure* bear any relationship to other sculpture that has been considered? Why or why not? Does the interpenetration of shapes and spaces bear any relationship to painting that we have seen? Is it possible to imagine such relationships in architecture?

Modernism in Architecture: 1900–1930

While it may seem that Americans had much to learn from Europe in the visual arts, they also had much to contribute. This is nowhere more apparent than in architecture and in a particular genius, Frank Lloyd Wright.

Frank Lloyd Wright (1867–1959) Wright worked with Louis Sullivan, an architect who had made great contributions to the development of the Chicago School. Wright left Sullivan's office in 1893 to work where he lived, in a suburb of Chicago, Oak Park. He had been greatly challenged by Sullivan, but his particular interest in these early years was the single-family dwelling. The typical, two-story wood frame house of the late nineteenth century was, to Wright, a disaster. It was cramped, ugly, dark, and dank. It wasted space, had no relationship to its site, ignored innovations in mechanical systems, and separated man from the land that was his aboriginal home. Wright asked fundamental questions about architecture, beginning with the abstract idea of dwelling, of shelter. He asked what features, forms, and shapes would place man in an harmonious relationship to the earth, giving him the comfort and warmth of the aboriginal cave. He asked what materials should be used, how, and in what forms. He asked questions about the family: how does it function as a small community, and how can the dwelling provide essential privacy for each member within the context of the family? Moreover, he asked how use might be made of growing technology and machine-tooled elements to make the house more livable, comfortable, and responsive, as well as less time-consuming, in terms of its upkeep, to free the family for more personal leisure and growth. The approximately thirty houses that grew up on the prairie of Oak Park were the answers to these questions.

Economical to build, dependent on the direct and simple use of wood, glass, brick, and stucco, the Oak Park houses were made for owners who were neither

32-20 Frank Lloyd Wright, Robie House, Chicago. (Hedrich Blessing, Chicago)

32-21 Floor Plans, Robie House.

1 Garden
2 Porch
3 Billiard Room
4 Children's Playroom
5 Entrance Hall
6 Boiler Room
7 Laundry
8 Lavatory/Bath
9 Garage
10 Auto Court
11 Living Room
12 Dining Room
13 Balcony
14 Guest Room
15 Kitchen
16 Servants
17 Bedrooms

eccentric nor particularly rich. The plans of the houses frequently grew outward from a central core of hearth and services—plumbing, electricity, and heat. Bedrooms were confined to one area, kitchen and servants to another wing; the family-oriented activities were grouped in integrated spaces around the hearth. Overhanging eaves sheltered the long windows and glass doors that opened onto patio, terrace, or balcony. Low walls of stone, brick, or shrubbery separated the houses from the intrusions of the street. The owners loved their homes. Wright's solutions were among the most innovative that this country had seen.

The Robie house in Chicago is a mature expression of Wright's ideas (Figs. 32-20, 32-21). Study the plan. Why does Wright focus the house around the hearth and fireplace? What is the effect of the deep, overhanging eaves, the long continuous lines produced by the roofs and the porches? Where does he use glass? Why does he partially conceal the house from the neighborhood streets? Does the combination of brick and concrete seem a good one? Why not simply use one or the other? The house in the "prairie style," as it came to be known, produced tremendous response in the Europeans who visited Wright in Chicago. His work became exemplary of the possibilities for an architecture that was not "in the styles."

Wright's emphasis on the orderly and rational, coupled with a deep, intuitive feeling for the nature of man and his suitable dwelling, produced a marriage of ideas that struck strong chords in European thought. His emphasis on the use of machined materials—glass, brick, veneers, and, in the Robie house, steel members for the far-reaching eaves—seemed to combine the best of two worlds: technology and the machine, man and his imagination. But, while some of Wright's contributions were influential in Europe, many of his ideas seemed too romantic to the architects and theorists of the school known as the Bauhaus.

The Bauhaus (1919–1933)   Founded at Weimar, then moved to Dessau, Germany, the Bauhaus became the most influential center for architects who shunned the past and wanted to create a rational, functional architecture for the twentieth century. These people wanted to use new materials in a direct way, taking advantage of the machine and machine production not only to create buildings but also to produce the furniture, textiles, light fixtures, and objects appropriate for a purely functional, scientific age. The physical plant for the school (Fig. 32-22) is almost factorylike in its simplicity and directness. In fact, factories and purely commercial design had much influence on the development of these forms. The classroom block is a steel framework enclosed in a curtain of glass. The wall, with which human buildings began, has given way to a thin, light, permeable membrane carrying no weight. It also reminds us of the Crystal Palace, for the ideas created there were admired by the Bauhaus architect.

The program of study at the Bauhaus also reflected the optimism of the new age. Students began with a year-long course in the general principles of design, materials, and color. It was believed that if they could master the principles of design, in various media, then they could use that knowledge to solve any problem. The analogy, of course, is with the scientific method. After learning principles, students applied them by working in the shops of the Bauhaus, learning the various aspects of total design from the ground up, as it were. They could then specialize. The Bauhaus attracted the most advanced thinkers, artists, and designers. Kandinsky taught there, as did Paul Klee, Josef Albers, Walter Gropius, Marcel Breuer, and Miës van der Rohe. Af-

32-22 Walter Gropius, The Bauhaus, 1925–26. Dessau, Germany. (Photograph, Courtesy The Museum of Modern Art, New York)

32-23 Right. Le Corbusier, Villa Savoye, Poissy-sur-Seine, France, 1929–31. (Photograph, Courtesy The Museum of Modern Art, New York)

32-24 Below. Le Corbusier, Villa Savoye. (a) Plan of Ground Floor showing driveway and garage between the columns (pilotis), service areas, and guest quarters. (b) Plan of Second Floor with main living quarters and roof terrace.

GROUND FLOOR

SECOND FLOOR

ter the latter four emigrated to America in the 1930s, their presence had a profound effect on art and architecture in this country.

Le Corbusier (1887–1965) In France Le Corbusier (Charles Édouard Jeanneret) advocated principles like those of the Bauhaus architects, for like Gropius and Miës van der Rohe he had worked with Peter Behrens, the German architect who had laid the groundwork for

the success of the Bauhaus. Beginning as a painter in Paris, Le Corbusier attacked the cubism of that period (ca. 1918) as decorative. With his friend Ozenfant, he advocated an architectural simplicity in painting and the elimination of all subject matter. He sought a kind of pure painting, like that of Mondrian; in this context he also developed his idea of architecture, characterized in this period by a minimalist approach to design. At the same time he coined the phrase that a house should be a "machine for living in." In the years between 1918 and 1930 Le Corbusier pursued the problem of the house. Using reinforced concrete, which is light, strong, and malleable, he combined it with pillars to make the wall independent, free to respond to the open plan, much in the same way that Wright had done. Like Wright, he was concerned with the interpenetration of spaces, but he was more inclined to separate the house from its site, turning the house inward on itself. Compare the Villa Savoye at Poissy (Figs. 32-23, 32-24), 1929–1930, with the Robie house. Notice the difference created by materials. Which house seems more in sympathy with its site? Which house seems the more "rational" and "functional"? Which would you prefer and why?

From Cézanne and Wright to Picasso and Le Corbusier, we have covered the ground of the watershed period of this century in art. We have actually touched down only in a very few places. More is omitted than included. We have tried to outline the predicament of the artist in these years, torn between rational optimism and irrational pessimism; between the desire for an orderly and pure art and architecture and the desire to speak to the anxiety that was given its most awful expression in World War I itself, where the fruits of science produced the gas mask, shell-shock, and the romance of the airplane. On the one hand, all seems pure and promising; on the other, all life seems destined only for suffering and death. The American artist faced the years between the wars in either a self-imposed isolation or a struggle with the implications of European work. When the surrealists arrived in this country in the late 1930s and 1940s, they found a rich and complex milieu in which their ideas, and those of cubism, purism, and expressionism would fuse to produce a great American school that was also truly international.

33

The Modernist Movement: Music, Dance, Photography, and Film

꒱

Stravinsky, the Russian Ballet, and *The Rite of Spring*

Igor Stravinsky, a Russian-born musician whose musical education and taste led him to Paris during the early years of this present century, was part of the artistic revolution that sets the music, art, and literature of the twentieth century apart from all that went before. His musical roots were planted in, and flourished amid, the fertile harmonic gardens of the nineteenth century; but his branches sought light among the complex ideas of the abstract painters, modern dancers, and revolutionary men and women of letters who worked in Europe during the first two decades of our century. Stravinsky became a part, some might say even a causal factor, of a revolution in classical music.

Stravinsky worked closely with a fellow Russian, Sergei Diaghilev, a theatrical impresario who had brought Russian ballet, opera, and painting exhibits to Paris in 1909. The Russian innovations in all these arts, but particularly in ballet, were to have an invigorating effect on Western Europe. In the mid-nineteenth century the world center of ballet had moved from Paris to Saint Petersburg; ballet in the West had become to a great extent reduced to pretty dancing girls executing mechanical movements. The imperial ballet in Russia, however, underwent a "classic revival" that produced the great ballets to the music of Tchaikovsky: *Sleeping Beauty, Swan Lake,* and *Nutcracker.* A young choreographer, Mikhail Fokine, revolted against the somewhat rigid, conventionalized vocabulary of this style of ballet. In a manifesto written in 1904, Fokine called for a greater unity of composition in ballet, more integration with the other arts, and gestures "built on the laws of natural expressiveness" to enable dance to "regain its spiritual forms and qualities." Fokine, whose ideas influenced Diaghilev, became the first choreographer for his Russian Ballet troupe. Fokine's training also produced the troupe's greatest male dancer, Vaslav Nijinsky. The extraordinary innovations of the Diaghilev ballets in Paris sprang from the combined talents of composers such as Stravinsky; dancers and *choreographers;* artists who designed the sets (Picasso among them); and, later on, writers such as Jean Cocteau, all under the masterful direction of Diaghilev.

In Volume I of this text we described in the chapter on the African festival that the unification of dance with the other arts, for the purpose of expressing the basic values or spiritual needs of a community, is typical of African artistic expression. European artists, seeking new ways to combine the arts through dance, were in a sense trying to recover a means of expression that they felt had been lost in their own society. Their search may be viewed as belonging to the "discontents" with "civilization" in the early twentieth century. It was in fact often combined with what is called primitivism, or an attempt to find fresh artistic sources in cultures less intellectualized and less specialized. Painters and sculptors, as we have seen, turned to the arts of Africa and Polynesia. But Stravinsky, with the other Russians in Paris, looked for inspiration to his native land, where folkloric traditions were still rich and "civilization" only recent. Both the primitivist dream and the desire to re-create the unity of the arts were instru-

mental in the conception of Stravinsky's great musical composition *Le Sacre du Printemps (The Rite of Spring)* and its ballet.

Stravinsky himself has described the sources of his inspiration. He remembered the "violent Russian spring" that seemed to begin suddenly and to set the whole earth cracking as the most exciting yearly event of his childhood. The memory of this natural event was no doubt linked to a vision that he had while in the midst of completing *The Firebird,* another ballet score.

> I saw in imagination a solemn pagan rite: sage elders, seated in a circle, watched a young girl dance herself to death. They were sacrificing her to propitiate the god of spring. Such was the theme of the *Sacre du Printemps.* I must confess that this vision made a deep impression on me, and I at once described it to my friend, Nicholas Roerich, he being a painter who had specialized in pagan subjects. He welcomed my inspiration with enthusiasm, and became my collaborator in this creation. In Paris I told Diaghileff [Diaghilev] about it, and he was at once carried away by the idea.[1]

Diaghilev chose the revolutionary Nijinsky to do the choreography; Roerich did the sets, and the entire new production was presented to the Parisian public at the opening of the Théâtre des Champs-Elysées in the spring of 1913.

The subject matter of *The Rite of Spring,* if Russian in inspiration, is in fact universal. In searching for the cultural roots of this piece, we might consider that the prehistoric origins of all modern men hide pagan and barbaric customs that we would now find repulsive and dreadful. Stravinsky's *Rite* is no figment of the imagination. The ritual of human sacrifice to appease angry gods seems to reappear in every mythology, and factual evidence proving the existence of terrifying practices by humans of more recent vintage only serve to remind us that Abraham's intended sacrifice of his son Isaac or the jungle headhunter's devouring of enemies are not entirely fairy tales of another time, place, and people. In early Greece it would appear that the Dionysian festival helped ensure a bountiful harvest in the succeed-

---

[1] Igor Stravinsky, *An Autobiography* (New York: Simon and Schuster, 1936), reprinted (New York: M. & J. Steuer, 1958), p. 31.

ing season by sacrificing the festival king. With the growth of civilization, real sacrifice is replaced by ritual or symbolic sacrifice, but the need to communicate and propitiate one's god or gods seems to remain in some form a part of human nature. It is the desire of man to communicate with elemental forces that challenged Stravinsky's creativity, bringing forth one of the most remarkable musical compositions of the twentieth century.

The scenario, or story line, deals with the veneration of spring by primitive peoples, a process viewed as a mystical rebirth of the earth. The decay of vegetation during the winter was considered to be a weakening of nature's fertility, and the rejuvenation of nature called for a sacrifice in spring, *le sacre du printemps*. A female is chosen, and she pays homage for her people with her life. To show this on the stage, Stravinsky set his music in parts, each section with a self-explanatory title. The music is continuous in each part, and the episodes follow each other without pause.

PART I
Adoration of the Earth

1. Introduction
2. Dance of the Adolescents
3. Dance of Seduction
4. Rounds of Spring
5. Games of the Rival Communities
6. Entrance of the Celebrant
7. Consecration of the Earth
8. Dance of the Earth

PART II
The Sacrifice

1. Introduction
2. Mysterious Circle of the Adolescents
3. Glorification of the Chosen One
4. Evocation of the Ancestors
5. Ritual of the Ancestors
6. Sacrificial Dance of the Chosen One

The Music The music Stravinsky composed to set these ritual dances to had, and still has, a shocking effect on its audiences. Peculiar chords assault the ears.

Not only were the combinations of notes unfamiliar to all but to the most avant-garde listeners of the day; they did not progress through familiar chord patterns that concert patrons had come to expect in music for the ballet. The music was loud, so loud; and it seemed to repeat discord after discord in irregular and jagged rhythms. Worst of all, there were no lovely, singable melodies that a music-loving Frenchman could whistle or hum as he left the theater. In fact, the first audience found this music so distasteful upon hearing it that they literally started a riot. Jean Cocteau describes it thus:

> The public played the role that it had to play. It laughed, spat, hissed, imitated animal cries. They might have eventually tired themselves of that if it had not been for the crowd of esthetes and a few musicians, who, carried by excess of zeal, insulted and even pushed the public of the boxes (the very wealthy in the box seats). The riot degenerated into a fight. Standing in her box, her diadem askew, the old Countess de Pourtales brandished her fan and shouted all red in the face: "It is the first time in sixty years that anyone has dared to make a fool of me!"

What was happening in music in 1913 that could cause such a hostile reaction in Paris? Basically, all the musical values of the past were being questioned and replaced with new, experimental ideas. Stravinsky was not alone in working toward a new tonal idiom, although his solutions differed from those of his important contemporaries—Claude Debussy, Erik Satie, Alexander Scriabin, Arnold Schoenberg, and Anton Webern. But where music to this time had been building on the past—adding to and depending upon tradition—the new music of these composers, Stravinsky included, negated the validity of the past and imposed a new order upon the sounds of music. *Harmony*, in the traditional sense of the word, was discarded; so were the notions of *melody* and *rhythm* that prevailed at the time. New orchestral effects were pried out of the instruments, and new types of heroes, or antiheroes, were sought for the songs and scenarios of the rebellious avant-garde composers.

Stravinsky opens his work with a bassoon solo that is "too high." Traditional composers would never have spotlighted a bassoon in that register because, they thought, it sounds strange. Stravinsky needed a primeval sound, and he found it in the bassoon. He also needed a new harmonic sound, which he found by pitting two chords against each other at the same time, an F-flat chord and an E-flat chord (an E^{b7}).

Needing something to replace *harmonic progression,* he chose to discard progression and substitute repetition. He would take one dissonant cluster of notes, hammering them over and over until he felt that a change was called for aesthetically. Then another cluster of notes would follow; but the choice of pitches for the second set was determined not by the old laws of harmony and chordal resolution, but by the laws of Stravinsky's ear. Like the painter, Picasso, Stravinsky had all the training and technique necessary to create masterpieces in the old style. His was not the frenetic searching of an ignorant musician but the conscious decision of a master. The values of the twentieth century were not the same as those that held sway a few short years before. And the change in values demanded the changes that took place in artistic expression.

Of all the innovative changes that Stravinsky demonstrated in his new composition of 1913, nothing captured the hearts of practicing musicians more emphatically than his use of rhythm. In *The Rite of Spring* we hear irregular series of pulses, changing *meters,* groupings of five and seven where multiples of two and three had been the norm. The effect is a sense of discontinuity and terror: a new style is introduced into twentieth-century music. The rhythm is similar to that of jazz in its energy and very different from the fluctuating pulse-beat of the late romantic composers.

At once both regular and irregular, at once both orderly and chaotic, *The Rite of Spring* communicates in the music basic conflicts between the barbaric and the civilized, the controlled and the ecstatic, the conflict of *id* and *super-ego.* The people of Paris were shocked with what they heard in 1913, but today this work must be called tame in comparison with those of our contemporaries. And as a commentary on how brazen we have become since Stravinsky crashed his orchestra about the ears of his public, we should note that in 1940 Walt Disney used *The Rite of Spring* as background music for a full-length cartoon, *Fantasia,* in

which mesozoic monsters fight and die amid the primordial slime and volcanic dust.

But once one has overcome the effects of the novelty of the sounds themselves, one discovers that order and design are present. Reason prevails, and the artistic laws of unity and variety are still operative. The orchestration is a unifying factor; so is the dance and the story line. Rhythmic elements from earlier sections reappear at later times, sometimes transformed or disguised and sometimes not. The types of melodic units that Stravinsky employs are similar and seem to fit within a discernible style. Contrast is apparent and seems to be used judiciously. Slow sections are interspersed among the fast; heavy orchestration is balanced with solo performance and light accompaniment; chordal writing is matched with linear composition.

For all its newness *The Rite of Spring* does not abandon *tonality,* the basic feature of the harmonic language of the nineteenth century. However, Stravinsky is called upon to use different means to establish a feeling of tonal center for our ears; for, if he cannot use standard chord progressions, cadences, and tonal melodies, what can he employ to lend tonal stability to his composition? Repetition. By repeating a chordal sound over and over, the lowest-sounding pitches assume the functions of chordal roots. They spell out the "key" of the moment. He reinforces this by choosing clusters of tones that can be grouped into familiar chords, sounds that a layman's ear can organize rather quickly. Nor does Stravinsky actually abandon melody. He simply uses lines of notes that do not fit easily into our common practice major-minor tonal system; he chooses intervals that are hard to sing; he sometimes calls upon instruments to play them in manners that are difficult and therefore sound strained; and he does not develop them in the way that a nineteenth-century romantic composer might. Still we can analyze the piece and discern the most important "tunes" or motives of the various sections.

So what are the features that one needs to study before a comprehension of the work is possible? Strangely enough, the answer is probably "none." Stravinsky's *Rite* is music of our time: once the scenario has been digested, the sounds are accepted naturally. We all have the experience of today's television, movie, and radio music to help us, and the common sounds of today are not so different from what was novel in 1913. Stravinsky helped bridge our musical experience to the past or, more properly, connect the past with the music of the present. *The Rite of Spring* is perhaps the single most important composition of the twentieth century for its impact on all the music that followed.

The Ballet   What kind of dance could be created to accompany this music of tones and rhythms unrecognizable to the public of 1913? Certainly the movements on stage were as shocking to the public as the sounds. In *101 Stories of the Great Ballets* George Balanchine, Diaghilev's last choreographer (who later became director of the New York City Ballet), describes the action of the dance and its relationship with the music. The thematic link between dance and death in this ballet recalls that in *Giselle*.

GEORGE BALANCHINE AND FRANCIS MASON

The Rite of Spring

First Tableau—Adoration of the Earth   A musical prelude recalls man's first relations with the world about him. The curtain rises. In a wasteland scene dominated by great masses of stone, young girls and boys sit in separate groups. They do not move, they wait and watch, as if expecting some sign from the stone shafts they revere. The girls rise, as if drawn by the abundance of nature to which the music calls their attention. A wise man stands among the dancers; the girls rush around and around him. Now he moves toward the sacred mound of the enclosure. The girls follow and bow before him. The opening phrase of the ballet—the quiet, plaintive cry of man against all-powerful nature—is repeated.

The strings sound strong, persistent chords that rouse the young men. To the virile beat of the music, they begin to dance, their movements accelerating at its demand, their feet stamping, stamping the earth. The girls join in the dance, the music becomes joyous, and the adolescents abandon themselves to the swift, exuberant rhythms of the orchestra.

This music changes sharply. A new, penetrating melody shrieks warningly and disturbs the young people.

The happiness of the boys and girls shifts abruptly to fierce savagery. They split into different groups; the boys face the girls and move toward them. The boys seem bent on attack, but at the last minute they hesitate; they move back and forth in an almost helpless effort, ignorant of their own true intent. The rhythmic crescendos give place to the soft trilling of flutes. Now the boys break their formation, and each carries a girl away.

Four boys remain on the scene. They choose four girls, lift them up on their backs, and dance slowly, bending low under the weight of their burdens in imitation of the plodding chords of the music. This "Round Dance of Spring" gradually increases in volume, and all the adolescents participate. All the dancers step back as the trilling flutes repeat their love call.

Drums herald the beginning of a contest between two rival tribes. Groups of men from each tribe engage in vigorous games. In the midst of their activity, the wise man, represented in the orchestra by a portentous melody on the tuba, tries to interrupt the games. The stronger theme of the games at first drowns out the wise man's theme, then recedes. The men turn to the wise man. There is a brief, taut silence, then all the men fall to the ground and worship the earth.

The drum rolls loudly, and all rise to dance, as if they had felt the pulse of the earth and been renewed by its power. The dance grows frenzied in its intensity. The curtain falls.

Second Tableau—The Sacrifice   Night is about to fall as this second scene begins; the setting sun has turned the sky scarlet. The girls sit near the wise man at a fire. One of these girls must be chosen by the others to make the sacrifice to the earth: this girl must dance herself to death. The music is calm; the figures on stage are quiet and they are unafraid. The girls regret what they have to do, but they are resigned to it with a kind of physical tiredness that the music reflects. They do not feel that they are victimized by Nature, but rather that they must obey what they believe to be its rules.

Soon the girls rise and move in the patterns of the "Dance of the Mysterious Circles." Their movements are trancelike, as if they themselves were not to make their dreadful decision. Their inspiration arrives, and they rush to the periphery of the scene; the chosen one stands alone in the center of the stage.

Now begins the dance that glorifies the victim. The chosen one remains motionless as the girls and men of the tribe whirl around her. All are transfixed at her power. They invoke the spirit of their ancestors, terrified anew by the force of Nature. Marking the relentless, sharp rhythms of the music with their feet, their dance reaches an ultimate expression of uncontrolled glory in sacrifice.

All the tribe members retire to watch the chosen one. The orchestra sounds strong, militant chords, trumpets blare harshly, cutting the air. The dance of the chosen one begins. The brutal savagery of the demanding music compels her to imitate it. Brief moments of comparative quiet, which seem at first to be periods of rest and release, are in reality more deadly because of the thrashing force that follows them. The girl is now wholly a part of the music, part of the earth. Hypnotized by her movements, the tribe joins in the violent dance. The chosen one begins to lose her strength, but—forced on by the convulsive violence of the music—is endowed with a new, superhuman compulsion. When it seems that Nature can demand no more, the girl is pushed into a fresh frenzy. Then she falls. She is dead.

The men of the tribe catch her up in their arms and hold her high over their heads before the sacred mound. The people of the tribe rush around her, holding up their arms. At the last slapping crescendo of the music, they fall to the earth.

(Dame Marie Rambert, who had been Nijinsky's choreographic assistant, describes the nature of his choreography and the audience reaction.)

"Nijinsky again first of all established the basic position: feet very turned in, knees slightly bent, arms held in reverse of the classical position, a primitive, prehistoric posture. The steps were very simple: walking smoothly or stamping, jumps mostly off both feet, landing heavily. There was only one a little more complicated, the dance for the maidens in the first scene. It was mostly done in groups, and each group has its own precise rhythm to follow. In the dance (if one can call it that) of the Wisest Elder, he walked two steps against every three steps of the ensemble. In the second scene

the dance of the sacrifice of the Chosen Virgin was powerful and deeply moving. I watched Nijinsky again and again teaching it to Maria Piltz. Her reproduction was very pale by comparison with his ecstatic performance, which was the greatest tragic dance I have ever seen.

"The first night of that ballet was the most astonishing event ... at the first sounds of the music, shouts and hissing started in the audience, and it was very difficult for us on the stage to hear the music, the more so as part of the audience began to applaud in an attempt to drown the hissing. We all desperately tried to keep time without being able to hear the rhythm clearly. In the wings Nijinsky counted the bars to guide us. Pierre Monteux conducted undeterred, Diaghilev having told him to continue to play at all costs.

"But after the interlude things became even worse, and during the sacrificial dance real pandemonium broke out. That scene began with Maria Piltz, the Chosen Virgin, standing on the spot trembling for many bars, her folded hands under her right cheek, her feet turned in, a truly prehistoric and beautiful pose. But to the audience of the time it appeared ugly and comical.

"A shout went up in the gallery:

"'Un docteur!'

"Somebody else shouted louder:

"'Un dentiste!'

"Then someone else screamed:

"'Deux dentistes!'

"And so it went on. One elegant lady leaned out of her box and slapped a man who was clapping. But the performance went on to the end.

"And yet now there is no doubt that, musically and choreographically, a masterpiece had been created that night. The only ballet that could compare with it in power was Bronislava Nijinska's *Les Noces*, created in 1923. She, like her brother, produced a truly epic ballet—so far unexcelled anywhere."

Nijinsky's sister Nijinska was in fact a better choreographer than he, though the importance of his innovations are undeniable. Stravinsky was not particularly pleased with Nijinsky's choreography for *The Rite of Spring* and the ballet has been redone many times since. Yet Nijinsky himself, a stunning dancer with great powers of characterization and capable of amazing leaps (Fig. 33-1), has become a legend in our cultural history. He and Anna Pavlova, another Russian who also danced for Diaghilev, are still for many the greatest dancers of the twentieth century. In Nijinsky as in Nietzsche, however, genius bordered on madness. For several years he was confined to an asylum in Switzerland; in 1950 he killed himself in London by leaping out of a window.

Modern Dance

While Mikhail Fokine was working to revitalize ballet in Russia, an American woman from California named Isadora Duncan began an entirely new approach to dance. Duncan, who made a deep impression on Fokine during a visit to Russia in 1905, wanted to free dance entirely from the restrictions of steps, poses, and attitudes. For her, dance meant individual spontaneity and Dionysian contact with nature. She admired classical Greek art for its simplicity and natural forms and believed, like the Greeks, that the human body, without artificial decoration, is the noblest form in art. Yet she was very American in her daring defiance of tradition and reliance on individual feeling. Her dances, she declared, were inspired by her native California; her first dancing masters were "wind and wave and the winged flight of bird and bee." Since every dance she performed was spontaneous and new, she left no school and no choreography behind her. What she did leave was the impression of a soul in movement (Fig. 33-2) on those who watched her, and her re-creation of dance as self-expression left a heritage of complete freedom to those who followed her.

The great innovators in dance in the early twentieth century shared with modernists in the other arts a desire for freedom of expression; an experimental attitude toward the use of elements such as space, texture, and time; and a need to return to primitive and archaic modes of expression. Some of the leaders in the modern dance movement, such as Ruth St. Denis and Louis Horst, sought to recapture both the primitive expressivity of the body and the relationship between dance and religion.

Modern dance differs from ballet in that it abandons not only the traditional steps but also *pointe* (toe-dancing) and the frothy tulle costumes. The portrayal of

33-1   Rodin, *Nijinsky.* (Musée Rodin, Paris/Photo © Bruno Jarret)

woman in most modern dances differs considerably from that in the romantic ballet (as we saw it in *Giselle*) or that in the Russian Neoclassical ballet. The most important innovator in this aspect as in other, more technical ones, is Martha Graham. In her major works from the 1930s through the 1950s, Graham presented woman not as ethereal and ideal, but as earthy, passionate, complex. Her choreography probes the psychic depths of her characters. She reworked classical and biblical myths for dance so that they appeared told

33-2   Isadora Duncan. (Harvard Theatre Collection)

sine) in 1930. A choreographer like Kurt Jooss in Germany composes in an idiom that is partly ballet and partly modern dance. The United States remains the world leader in modern dance and shares the honors in ballet with the Soviet Union and Britain.

Afro-American Dance

Black American dance, although closely allied with the modernist movement, has sought its own directions by exploring its African roots. The black dancer and choreographer could draw on a rich folkloric tradition in black America itself, on European and white American innovations in ballet and modern dance, and on his or her own observations and knowledge of African (as well as Caribbean) dance. The talents that have made use of these elements have created a truly unique idiom in dance.

There is no doubt that American blacks managed to preserve an African style of dance. This developed into social dances like the cake walk and performing dances like the tap dance. Blacks performed in the minstrel shows touring the United States from the 1840s to the beginning of World War I. In spite of the often negative way in which whites took "minstrels," these shows helped to establish blacks as entertainers and influenced the development of the American musical comedy.

The two dancers who did most to establish black dance as an art form were Katherine Dunham and Pearl Primus, both active in the 1930s and 1940s. Pearl Primus, who studied with Martha Graham, established herself as a serious concert dancer although she also performed in night clubs. Becoming interested in African dance, she went to Africa to do research, particularly in the (then) Belgian Congo. She used this knowledge, as well as Afro-American themes, in her choreography. One of her most moving compositions is "The Negro Speaks of Rivers," based on the Langston Hughes poem.

Black dance companies today continue to adapt African and Afro-American styles and themes to modern dance. Alvin Ailey is an exciting, lyrical choreographer and his company one of the best and most successful on the New York scene (Fig. 33-3). His works such as *Revelations*, set to spirituals, and *Roots of the Blues*,

from the woman's viewpoint; for example, she re-created the Oedipus story as the experience of Jocasta. Graham developed a technique built on the principle of contraction and release of the muscles that continues to be taught in schools of dance. The Martha Graham Company is still a major force in the American dance world.

Modern dance and ballet have remained separate art forms, but they have borrowed from each other and influenced each other extensively. Fokine, as we have noted, was influenced by Duncan. Martha Graham danced the leading role in the American premiere of *The Rite of Spring* (with new choreography by Mas-

33-3 *Revelations*, Mari Kajiwara, Melvin Jones, Judith Jamison. (Alvin Ailey American Dance Theater/Photo Fred Fehl)

interpret the Afro-American musical experience in dance. *Cry* is a tribute to black women. The company doing most to bring African dance to the American stage is the young one of Chuck Davis. Davis, who has studied in Africa, presents authentic African dances and his own compositions based on African movements.

Two New Art Forms: Photography and Film

Photography began to evolve into an art form after it was discovered in France in the 1830s. Painters like Courbet, Degas, and Eakins used their own photographs as inspiration for their paintings, and photographers like Nadar and Eugene Atget learned to use the camera to make pictures that were meant to be seen as art and not simply as a copy of the subject represented. Photographs allowed painters and photographers to show viewers objects never before observed by the human eye. By the beginning of the twentieth century

in Europe and America, photography had become an art form and today is fully accepted as such.

It has always been important that photographers not only expose their own film but also develop their own prints, thus controlling the many variables inherent in the process. At first, photographic subject matter was limited to carefully posed compositions such as portraits and staged dramatic scenes. Photographic film or plates were too slow to prevent anything that moved from blurring, and both photographers and their sitters had to be very patient. As the technology improved, so did the ability of photographers to record and respond to life.

Edward Steichen (1879–1973) and Alfred Stieglitz (1864–1946; the husband of Georgia O'Keeffe; see Chapter 32) are the two people most often associated with photography's development as an art form in America in the early twentieth century. Stieglitz showed photography at his New York gallery, 291, along with modern paintings and sculpture by Ameri-

33-4 Alfred Stieglitz, "Winter, Fifth Avenue," 1893 from *Camera Work*, Plate 2, No. 12, 1905. Photogravure, 8⅝" × 6¹/₁₆". (Collection, The Museum of Modern Art, New York)

can and European artists (Fig. 33-4). His magazine, *Camera Work*, reproduced the work of many promising artists. Both Steichen and Steiglitz chose subjects from everyday life, as well as making memorable portraits of friends and notables (Fig. 33-5). Their photographs are studies in lighting and composition, and the portraits are as psychologically revealing and emotionally rich as those done by painters. In the hands of others like Lewis Hine and Jacob Riis, who photographed immigrants struggling to survive in the tenements of New York, photographs became a tool for promoting reform. American life in all its variety was a source for artistic inspiration (Fig. 33-6).

When the Great Depression cloaked the nation, photographers such as Walker Evans, Dorothea Lange, and Russell Lee traveled through the rural South and Mid-

west for the Farm Security Administration, documenting the suffering and displacement caused by the devastated farm economy (Fig. 33-7). Later, Walker Evans's photographs were joined with a text by James Agee, *Let Us Now Praise Famous Men*, that successfully unites words and images to create a work of art.

In the 1920s and 1930s, a group of photographers in California were inspired by Edward Weston (Fig. 33-8). Working primarily with the cumbersome view camera, these artists studied and recorded objects—vegetables, fruit, the human body—as if they were abstract patterns of form, texture, shade, and shadow. They formed a group, F/64 (named after the setting on a view camera that brings the maximum area into sharp focus) and exhibited and published their work. Weston and Ansel Adams, also a member of F/64, emerged as two of the

33-5 Edward Steichen, "Henri Matisse and *The Serpentine*," c. 1910, from *Camera Work*, No. XL 11–XLIII, 1913. Photogravure, 8⅝" × 6¹³/₁₆". Platinum print. (Collection, The Museum of Modern Art, New York. Gift of William A. Grigsby.)

33-6 Jacob Riis, ''Home of an Italian Ragpicker,'' 1888. (The Museum of the City of New York)

33-7 Walker Evans, Hale County, Alabama. 1936. (Collection, Museum of Modern Art)

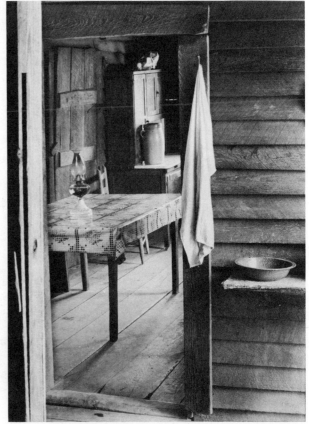

major figures in American photography during this period. Adams's subject, like that of W. H. Jackson and Timothy O'Sullivan before him, was the landscape of the American West (Fig. 33-9).

Photographers like Henri Cartier-Bresson and Eugene Smith showed that small 35mm cameras could be used to work quickly and intuitively, producing images of street scenes and war zones that could stimulate the mind as much as photographs made with larger equipment (Fig. 33-10).

By the mid-1950s, ''art'' photographs would be as widely collected as the work of painters and sculptors. The still photograph, whether black and white or color, has become a particularly appropriate medium for the art of the twentieth century but no more so than its counterpart—also a product of film—the motion picture.

Developed barely six decades after photography, the motion picture—like oral or written literature, painting, sculpture, photography, and the phonograph recording—is a cultural form of recorded memory. With the development of new technology and sound recording, human beings were for the first time able to pre-

33-8 Edward Weston, "Artichoke, Halved," 1930. Gelatin-silver print, 7½" × 9½". (Collection, The Museum of Modern Art, New York. Gift of David H. McAlpin; © 1981 Arizona Board of Regents, Center for Creative Photography)

33-9 Ansel Adams, "Mount Williamson, Storm Clouds," 1945. (Courtesy of the Trustees of The Ansel Adams Publishing Rights Trust. All rights reserved.)

33-10 Henri Cartier-Bresson, "Children Playing in the Ruins, Spain," 1934. (Magnum Photos)

serve not only words and images of their culture but also its actions, sights, and sounds.

Motion pictures were at first limited to short sequences, such as a clown's trick or a locomotive seen head-on, rushing at the audience. But the silent movie, accompanied by captions and live pianists, soon developed into a genuine art form. Perhaps its most memorable figure is Charlie Chaplin (Fig. 33-11), whose portrayal of the "little tramp" baffled by modern civilization made him a true comic hero of the times.

The full-length motion picture that presents an entire drama is obviously analogous to the theater. The mechanics of producing a play, whether on stage or for filming, involve the same elements: actors, script, sets, props, costumes, make-up, lighting, sound effects, director, producer, and marketing (getting the production to audiences). Recording a play on film has both advantages and disadvantages. The principal disadvantage is that the sense of immediacy is lost, and the unspoken communication between performance and audience is missing in the film.

The advantages of cinema include the ability to make a permanent and reproducible record of what happened in front of the camera and the use of *montage*, the ability to edit the performance. Unlike the stage director, the film editor can remove and replace sequences in which an actor forgot his or her lines. He or she can show change in a way that is nearly impossible for a stage director.

In the American film *Citizen Kane* (1941), directed by Orson Welles, there is a sequence introduced in the script by this note:

> The following scenes, which cover a period of nine years, are played in the same set with only changes in lighting, special effects outside the window, and wardrobe.

The scriptwriter could have noted that changes in makeup also occur; the actors seem to become older as the scenes progress. What happens is this: in each of the seven brief scenes, Kane and his wife are shown in the breakfast room. The first scene presents them as newlyweds—happy, in love, and just getting home after being up all night going to six parties. As the

33-11 Charlie Chaplin. (The Museum of Modern Art, New York/Film Stills Archive)

33-12 Scene from *Stagecoach*, 1939. (Culver Pictures, Inc.)

action progresses, the development of their marriage is revealed. Love turns to complacency, then to rancor, and finally to resignation. The last scene is silent—they are reading different newspapers. These scenes unfold rapidly, occupying only a few minutes of film, but they make a point; more importantly, they could not be done as effectively on the stage because of the necessary delays for costume and make-up changes. Naturally, these delays are not shown in the film.

The filmmaker can also move the camera. He or she can show close-ups of an actor, which is impossible for the stage director. He or she can focus attention much more easily than the stage director can, and take the camera out of the theater, easily moving it to many different places.

These differences between plays and films are powerful artistic tools that have been exploited effectively by the greatest filmmakers. Techniques such as flashback, dissolve, and close-up made it possible for avant-garde filmmakers to experiment with layers of time, symbolic images, or portrayal of the unconscious in ways parallel to such presentations in modernist literature and art.

Filmmaking, like photography, has attracted many practitioners. As with all other artistic endeavors, the criteria for success have varied from generation to generation. Following the establishment of the genre in such early masterpieces as *Birth of a Nation* (1915), the Chaplin and Marx Brothers comedies, and Orson Welles's *Citizen Kane* (1941), a host of important directors have created films whose situations, heroes, and heroines have established typical American archetypes: the honest politician in *Mr. Smith Goes to Washington* (1939), the war hero in *Sergeant York* (1941), the gentle giant in *King Kong* (1933), the displaced of the Great Depression in *The Grapes of Wrath* (1940), the cruel mobster in *Scarface* (1932), and the myth of the moviemaking genre itself, the beautiful starlet who achieves great fame in *A Star is Born* (1937). The movies also used the great drama of nineteenth-century American western expansion as the source for the cowboy film, which presented the eternal struggle of good and its success over evil (Fig. 33-12).

Following World War I, a host of movies dealt with the trauma of that experience. With the Great Depression came a series of lavish musicals and hilarious comedies designed to help Americans forget their terrible plight. Fred Astaire and Ginger Rogers appeared in elegantly staged and beautifully choreographed dance numbers that enthralled audiences. After World War II, American and foreign films explored new conventions and new techniques. Cinematographic epics like *The Ten Commandments* (1923), made by Cecil B. DeMille, shared the screen with the intellectually and emotionally complex films from the European, Japanese, and Indian cinema. Each country has developed its own styles and stars. The limits of the media have been stretched considerably from those in force when *Gone with the Wind* was produced in 1938. But the film, gifted with the ability to convey many ideas and images at once, vehicle of popular entertainment as well as serious art form, continues to be a source of controversy.

34

The Modernist Movement: Literature

∋

Closely allied with the various modernist movements in the visual arts, literary artists in the opening decades of the twentieth century showed many of the same formal and thematic concerns. Modernism, however, was and is not simply a movement limited to that era. In literature, as in painting, it became a new way of apprehending the world through art. Every serious artist of the twentieth century has felt the necessity either to react against modernism or to build on its innovations.

A Literature of Exiles Most of the great modernist writers lived, at one time or another, in Paris. Besides the native French writers associated with the Dada, surrealist, and other artistic-literary modernist movements, there were German expressionists, Italian futurists, and other Europeans.

Paris was also the cradle for a dynamic new African literature written in French by intellectuals from the French African colonies, some of whom were involved with the surrealist movement. It is no exaggeration to say that Paris in the early twentieth century was a fermenting center of British and American letters. James Joyce, the Irish novelist and poet who became one of the greatest and most original stylists in the English language, found as his first publisher an American in Paris—Sylvia Beach, who managed the bookstore "Shakespeare and Co." American expatriates such as Gertrude Stein, Ezra Pound, F. Scott Fitzgerald, and Ernest Hemingway also gathered at Miss Beach's bookstore. Gertrude Stein was a close associate and supporter of Picasso and other modern painters, who were highly influential on her style. Stein coined the phrase "the lost generation" to describe these Americans who had fled their country for Europe. Common among them was the feeling that a crass, philistine American public was incapable of understanding or sustaining them and that they needed to turn elsewhere for intellectual and aesthetic nourishment.

The rift between artist and public, first sensed by the romantics and intensified by the Symbolists was, for the modernists, a fact of life. It is not surprising that a literature of expatriates, a literature responsible to no one, is a literature characterized by a sense of exile and by an extreme subjectivity. The lack of contact with a public, except for a small coterie, gives the writer great freedom to experiment but also encourages esotericism. Many of the modernist writers who did not join the expatriates in Paris experienced some sort of exile. The American T. S. Eliot did live briefly in Paris but emigrated to England. Those who were not in physical exile often experienced an inner exile. Franz Kafka, in his own words a "triple exile" as a German-speaking Jew living in Czechoslovakian Prague under the Austro-Hungarian empire, produced the most innovative prose in modern German and some of the most influential modernist images. Kafka's three unfinished novels—*Amerika*, *The Trial*, and *The Castle*—deal with modern man's sense of anguish and alienation in the face of a civilization characterized by a faceless bureaucracy and a cosmos that no longer offers answers to metaphysical questions. Perhaps his best-known work is the long story *Metamorphosis*, which deals with an ordinary

salesman who awakens one morning to find himself transformed into a giant beetle. Unlike many modernists, Kafka writes in an apparently logical order, with clear sentences and close attention to external details. It is only after reading for a while that we realize that we are in a grotesque world in which our ordinary values and logic do not apply, a world that conveys the nightmarish quality of everyday life. Like the expressionist painters, Kafka presents distorted, shocking images that represent some of our deepest unconscious fears. The hunger artist, in the story by that title reprinted here, is such an image. The story may also be interpreted as a treatment of the modernist theme of the public's failure to comprehend the artist and the artist's suffering.

Exploration of the Unconscious and Technical Experimentation   In spite of their sense of exile and their feeling of being misunderstood, the modernists on the whole maintained a strong belief in the saving power of art, a continuation of the late nineteenth century's adherence to the religion of art. In a declining, empty civilization, art appeared as a refuge, a form of salvation. Many of the new ideas and concerns of the twentieth century seemed to writers, as well as to artists, to necessitate a radical breakup of traditional forms. Einstein's theories and the general sense of a breach in continuity after the first World War surely had their impact, but perhaps the greatest influence was Freud's discovery of the unconscious. Surrealist poets in France, some of whom were also surrealist painters, experimented with rendering the raw state of the unconscious through "automatic writing," that is, abandoning all conventional syntax and logic and simply letting words flow out through the pen. The most important experiments in rendering psychological states, however, were done by novelists. The Frenchman Marcel Proust, in his monumental *Remembrance of Things Past*, found a new language for the expression of his characters' most subtle feelings and an inner, as opposed to a chronological, sense of time. The inner sense of time was also explored by the German Thomas Mann in his *Magic Mountain*. The Englishwoman Virginia Woolf experimented with language and time to convey inner reality in novels such as *To the Lighthouse* and *Mrs. Dalloway*; the American William Faulkner used extremely long, "ungrammatical" sentences to express a world below the surface of appearance. The most radical experiments in this vein were done by the Irishman James Joyce. The unconscious or semiconscious part of the mind, as Freud showed, functions outside the logical order and time frame established by reason. It works rather by association, by summoning images that merge past, present, and future. To convey this state, Joyce used the device of the "interior monologue" or "stream of consciousness," abandoning rules of grammar and syntax, even inventing new words. The effect is similar to the abandonment of perspective and the juxtaposition of planes and of images in modernist painting. Joyce's *Ulysses*, written in 1922, although a long novel, takes place in the course of one day in Dublin. Because of the interior monologue technique, however, the novel can actually span all of the time within the characters' memory. In addition, the day in Dublin loosely parallels the events in Homer's *Odyssey* (hence the title), thus opening up a mythic dimension. The central character of the book is Leopold Bloom; the selection reprinted below is part of a half-dreaming monologue of Bloom's wife, Molly. Molly's erotic fantasies and Joyce's use of "dirty" words caused *Ulysses* to be banned in the United States until 1933. Molly has been unfaithful to her husband, but in these final pages of the novel she recalls their early love together and ends the novel with a life-affirming "Yes!"

Visual Aspects of Literature   Other experimental modernist writers, especially poets, became interested in attempting to do with words something comparable to what modernist painters were doing in their medium. Rendering startling, concrete images as opposed to vague, loose, "romantic" sentiments in poetry became a preoccupation of Ezra Pound, another American exile and founder of the "imagist" school of poetry. Pound studied Chinese and Japanese, as well as medieval French and Italian poets, in a search for "visual" poetry on which to model his own work. Gertrude Stein, through a kind of word painting, attempted to bring cubism into literature. The American poet E. E. Cummings, who signed his name e e cummings, was a painter as well as a poet. He broke up the traditional typographical appearance of the poem on the page while experimenting with sound effects that this

break-up could enhance. Cummings, like most modernists, is sharply critical of the society around him, yet his view of life is refreshingly affirmative, at times conventionally lyrical.

Poetry of the City and the Theme of Spiritual Emptiness   A certain world-weariness invades much of modernist writing. The devastations of World War I seemed to confirm already-present philosophical assumptions about the futility and fragility of man's existence. With traditional religion and other sustaining myths dead, the individual was often left only with questions. Politics, to most moderns, did not offer a substitute for religion; even love, or any form of real communication between individuals, seemed to many extremely problematic in the modern world. One of the best chroniclers of this state of emotional vacuum is T. S. Eliot. Eliot's most ambitious poem on this theme, "The Waste Land," portrays the spiritual desolation of a modern city, London, through references to ancient literature and oriental mythology, among others. He footnotes the lines "Unreal City / Under the brown fog of a winter dawn" with a reference to the first two lines of Baudelaire's "The Seven Old Men" (see p. 326) The influence of Baudelaire and of other French symbolist poets was in fact a decisive one for Eliot. It enabled him to throw off conventionally poetic language and imagery and to depict modern reality in all its sordidness through a language that is both dense and everyday and through images that reflect the dinginess and the futility of modern city life. Eliot sought to eliminate abstract language and explanations of feelings from his poetry and instead to convey emotion through images evoked from the external world—what he called the "objective correlative."

The first of the two poems printed here was written around 1910, when Eliot was still a student at Harvard University, and published in 1917 with *Prufrock and Other Poems*. The city it depicts is probably Boston, but the details recall as well Baudelaire's Paris, and the monotonous rhythms of urban life that are its subject matter could be found in any big city. By the time he wrote "The Love Song of J. Alfred Prufrock," Eliot, who was born in St. Louis, Missouri, had moved to London. While the dingy city portrayed in the first two stanzas is reminiscent of "Preludes" (and the "yellow fog" again quotes Baudelaire's "The Seven Old Men"), the setting of the rest of the poem moves to London interiors inhabited by upper-class English society. Prufrock is a typically "modern" man, unable to make decisions, to act, or even to feel—an overcivilized human being in an overcivilized society. The irony with which Eliot depicts his character has become a stable feature of much other twentieth-century literature. It may be of interest to note that Eliot is also the author of *The Book of Practical Cats*, the basis of the book for Andrew Lloyd Webber's musical *Cats*, and that "Preludes," as well as some of Eliot's other early poems, are quoted in the song "Memory."

Eliot eventually solved his personal problems with meaninglessness and emptiness by converting to the Anglican church and becoming a loyal British subject. Still, for many, the spiritual anguish at the core of modernism has remained a central fact of twentieth-century existence. The great Irish poet W. B. Yeats (though not addressing this issue) seems to sum up this state: "Things fall apart, the centre cannot hold. . . ."

FRANZ KAFKA (1883–1924)

A Hunger Artist

(*translated by Willa and Edwin Muir*)

During these last decades the interest in professional fasting has markedly diminished. It used to pay very well to stage such great performances under one's own management, but today that is quite impossible. We live in a different world now. At one time the whole town took a lively interest in the hunger artist; from day to day of his fast the excitement mounted; everybody wanted to see him at least once a day; there were people who bought season tickets for the last few days and sat from morning till night in front of his small barred cage; even in the nighttime there were visiting hours, when the whole effect was heightened by torch flares; on fine days the cage was set out in the open air, and then it was the children's special treat to see the hunger artist; for their elders he was often just a joke that happened to be in fashion, but the children stood open-mouthed, holding each other's hands for greater security, marveling at him as he sat there pallid in black tights, with his ribs sticking out so prominently, not even on a seat but down among straw on the ground, sometimes giving a courteous nod, answering questions with a constrained smile, or perhaps stretching an arm through the bars so that one might feel how thin it was, and then again withdrawing deep into himself, paying no attention to anyone or anything, not even to the all-important striking of the clock that was the only piece of furniture in his cage, but merely staring into vacancy with half-shut eyes, now and then taking a sip from a tiny glass of water to moisten his lips.

Besides casual onlookers there were also relays of permanent watchers selected by the public, usually butchers, strangely enough, and it was their task to watch the hunger artist day and night, three of them at a time, in case he should have some secret recourse to nourishment. This was nothing but a formality, instituted to reassure the masses, for the initiates knew well enough that during his fast the artist would never in any circumstances, not even under forcible compulsion, swallow the smallest morsel of food; the honor of his profession forbade it. Not every watcher, of course, was capable of understanding this, there were often groups of night watchers who were very lax in carrying out their duties and deliberately huddled together in a retired corner to play cards with great absorption, obviously intending to give the hunger artist the chance of a little refreshment, which they supposed he could draw from some private hoard. Nothing annoyed the artist more than such watchers; they made him miserable; they made his fast seem unendurable; sometimes he mastered his feebleness sufficiently to sing during their watch for as long as he could keep going, to show them how unjust their suspicions were. But that was of little use; they only wondered at his cleverness in being able to fill his mouth even while singing. Much more to his taste were the watchers who sat close up to the bars, who were not content with the dim night lighting of the hall but focused him in the full glare of the electric pocket torch given them by the impresario. The harsh light did not trouble him at all, in any case he could never sleep properly, and he could always drowse a little, whatever the light, at any hour, even when the hall was thronged with noisy onlookers. He was quite happy at the prospect of spending a sleepless night with such watchers; he was ready to exchange jokes with them, to tell them stories out of his nomadic life, anything at all to keep them awake and demonstrate to them again that he had no eatables in his cage and that he was fasting as not one of them could fast. But his happiest moment was when the morning came and an enormous breakfast was brought them, at his expense, on which they flung themselves with the keen appetite of healthy men after a weary night of wakefulness. Of course there were people who argued that this breakfast was an unfair attempt to bribe the watchers, but that was going rather too far, and when they were invited to take on a night's vigil without a breakfast, merely for the sake of the cause, they made themselves scarce, although they stuck stubbornly to their suspicions.

Such suspicions, anyhow, were a necessary accompaniment to the profession of fasting. No one could possibly watch the hunger artist continuously, day and night, and so no one could produce first-hand evidence that the fast had really been rigorous and continuous; only the artist himself could know that, he was therefore bound to be the sole completely satisfied spectator of his own fast. Yet for other reasons he was never satisfied; it was not perhaps mere fasting that had brought him to such skeleton thinness that many people had regretfully to keep away from his exhibitions, because the sight of him was too much for them, perhaps it was dissatisfaction with himself that had worn him down. For he alone knew, what no other initiate knew, how easy it was to fast. It was the easiest thing in the world. He made no secret of this, yet people did not believe him, at the best they set him down as modest, most of them, however, thought he was out for publicity or else was some kind of cheat who found it easy to fast because he had discovered a way of making it easy, and then had the impudence to admit the fact, more or less. He had to put up with all that, and in the course of time had got used to it, but his inner dissatisfaction always rankled, and never yet, after any term of fasting—this must be granted to his credit—had he left the cage of his own free will. The longest period of fasting was fixed by his impresario at forty days, beyond that term he was not allowed to go, not even in great cities, and there was good reason for it, too. Experience had proved that for about forty days the interest of the public could be stimulated by a steadily increasing pressure of advertisement, but after that the town began to lose interest, sympathetic support began notably to fall off;

there were of course local variations as between one town and another or one country and another, but as a general rule forty days marked the limit. So on the fortieth day the flower-bedecked cage was opened, enthusiastic spectators filled the hall, a military band played, two doctors entered the cage to measure the results of the fast, which were announced through a megaphone, and finally two young ladies appeared, blissful at having been selected for the honor, to help the hunger artist down the few steps leading to a small table on which was spread a carefully chosen invalid repast. And at this very moment the artist always turned stubborn. True, he would entrust his bony arms to the outstretched helping hands of the ladies bending over him, but stand up he would not. Why stop fasting at this particular moment, after forty days of it? He had held out for a long time, an illimitably long time; why stop now, when he was in his best fasting form, or rather, not yet quite in his best fasting form? Why should he be cheated of the fame he would get for fasting longer, for being not only the record hunger artist of all time, which presumably he was already, but for beating his own record by a performance beyond human imagination, since he felt that there were no limits to his capacity for fasting? His public pretended to admire him so much, why should it have so little patience with him; if he could endure fasting longer, why shouldn't the public endure it? Besides, he was tired, he was comfortable sitting in the straw, and now he was supposed to lift himself to his full height and go down to a meal the very thought of which gave him a nausea that only the presence of the ladies kept him from betraying, and even that with an effort. And he looked up into the eyes of the ladies who were apparently so friendly and in reality so cruel, and shook his head, which felt too heavy on its strengthless neck. But then there happened yet again what always happened. The impresario came forward, without a word—for the band made speech impossible—lifted his arms in the air above the artist, as if inviting Heaven to look down upon its creature here in the straw, this suffering martyr, which indeed he was, although in quite another sense; grasped him round the emaciated waist, with exaggerated caution, so that the frail condition he was in might be appreciated; and committed him to the care of the blenching ladies, not without secretly giving him a shaking so that his legs and body tottered and swayed. The artist now submitted completely; his head lolled on his breast as if it had landed there by chance; his body was hollowed out; his legs in a spasm of self-preservation clung close to each other at the knees, yet scraped on the ground as if it were not really solid ground, as if they were only trying to find solid ground; and the whole weight of his body, a featherweight after all, relapsed onto one of the ladies, who, looking round for help and panting a little—this post of honor was not at all what she had expected it to be—first stretched her neck as far as she could to keep her face at least free from contact with the artist, then finding this impossible, and her more fortunate companion not coming to her aid but merely holding extended on her own trembling hand the little bunch of knucklebones that was the artist's, to the great delight of the spectators burst into tears and had to be replaced by an attendant who had long been stationed in readiness. Then came the food, a little of which the impresario managed to get between the artist's lips, while he sat in a kind of half-fainting trance, to the accompaniment of cheerful patter designed to distract the public's attention from the artist's condition; after that, a toast was drunk to the public, supposedly prompted by a whisper from the artist in the impresario's ear; the band confirmed it with a mighty flourish, the spectators melted away, and no one had any cause to be dissatisfied with the proceedings, no one except the hunger artist himself, he only, as always.

So he lived for many years, with small regular intervals of recuperation, in visible glory, honored by the world, yet in spite of that troubled in spirit, and all the more troubled because no one would take his trouble seriously. What comfort could he possibly need? What more could he possibly wish for? And if some good-natured person, feeling sorry for him, tried to console him by pointing out that his melancholy was probably caused by fasting, it could happen, especially when he had been fasting for some time, that he reacted with an outburst of fury and to the general alarm began to shake the bars of his cage like a wild animal. Yet the impresario had a way of punishing these outbreaks which he rather enjoyed putting into operation. He would apologize publicly for the artist's behavior, which was only to be excused, he admitted, because of

the irritability caused by fasting; a condition hardly to be understood by well-fed people; then by natural transition he went on to mention the artist's equally incomprehensible boast that he could fast for much longer than he was doing; he praised the high ambition, the good will, the great self-denial undoubtedly implicit in such a statement; and then quite simply countered it by bringing out photographs, which were also on sale to the public, showing the artist on the fortieth day of a fast lying in bed almost dead from exhaustion. This perversion of the truth, familiar to the artist though it was, always unnerved him afresh and proved too much for him. What was a consequence of the premature ending of his fast was here presented as the cause of it! To fight against this lack of understanding, against a whole world of non-understanding, was impossible. Time and again in good faith he stood by the bars listening to the impresario, but as soon as the photographs appeared he always let go and sank with a groan back on to his straw, and the reassured public could once more come close and gaze at him.

A few years later when the witnesses of such scenes called them to mind, they often failed to understand themselves at all. For meanwhile the aforementioned change in public interest had set in; it seemed to happen almost overnight; there may have been profound causes for it, but who was going to bother about that; at any rate the pampered hunger artist suddenly found himself deserted one fine day by the amusement seekers, who went streaming past him to other more favored attractions. For the last time the impresario hurried him over half Europe to discover whether the old interest might still survive here and there; all in vain; everywhere, as if by secret agreement, a positive revulsion from professional fasting was in evidence. Of course it could not really have sprung up so suddenly as all that, and many premonitory symptoms which had not been sufficiently remarked or suppressed during the rush and glitter of success now came retrospectively to mind, but it was now too late to take any countermeasures. Fasting would surely come into fashion again at some future date, yet that was no comfort for those living in the present. What, then, was the hunger artist to do? He had been applauded by thousands in his time and could hardly come down to showing himself in a street booth at village fairs, and as for adopting another profession, he was not only too old for that but too fanatically devoted to fasting. So he took leave of the impresario, his partner in an unparalleled career, and hired himself to a large circus; in order to spare his own feelings he avoided reading the conditions of his contract.

A large circus with its enormous traffic in replacing and recruiting men, animals and apparatus can always find a use for people at any time, even for a hunger artist, provided of course that he does not ask too much, and in this particular case anyhow it was not only the artist who was taken on but his famous and long-known name as well, indeed considering the peculiar nature of his performance, which was not impaired by advancing age, it could not be objected that here was an artist past his prime, no longer at the height of his professional skill, seeking a refuge in some quiet corner of a circus, on the contrary, the hunger artist averred that he could fast as well as ever, which was entirely credible, he even alleged that if he were allowed to fast as he liked, and this was at once promised him without more ado, he could astound the world by establishing a record never yet achieved, a statement which certainly provoked a smile among the other professionals, since it left out of account the change in public opinion, which the hunger artist in his zeal conveniently forgot.

He had not, however, actually lost his sense of the real situation and took it as a matter of course that he and his cage should be stationed, not in the middle of the ring as a main attraction, but outside, near the animal cages, on a site that was after all easily accessible. Large and gaily painted placards made a frame for the cage and announced what was to be seen inside it. When the public came thronging out in the intervals to see the animals, they could hardly avoid passing the hunger artist's cage and stopping there for a moment, perhaps they might even have stayed longer had not those pressing behind them in the narrow gangway, who did not understand why they should be held up on their way towards the excitements of the menagerie, made it impossible for anyone to stand gazing quietly for any length of time. And that was the reason why the hunger artist, who had of course been looking forward to these visiting hours as the main achievement of his life, began instead to shrink from them. At

first he could hardly wait for the intervals; it was exhilarating to watch the crowds come streaming his way, until only too soon—not even the most obstinate self-deception, clung to almost consciously, could hold out against the fact—the conviction was borne in upon him that these people, most of them, to judge from their actions, again and again, without exception, were all on their way to the menagerie. And the first sight of them from the distance remained the best. For when they reached his cage he was at once deafened by the storm of shouting and abuse that arose from the two contending factions, which renewed themselves continuously, of those who wanted to stop and stare at him—he soon began to dislike them more than the others—not out of real interest but only out of obstinate self-assertiveness, and those who wanted to go straight on to the animals. When the first great rush was past, the stragglers came along, and these, whom nothing could have prevented from stopping to look at him as long as they had breath, raced past with long strides, hardly even glancing at him, in their haste to get to the menagerie in time. And all too rarely did it happen that he had a stroke of luck, when some father of a family fetched up before him with his children, pointed a finger at the hunger artist and explained at length what the phenomenon meant, telling stories of earlier years when he himself had watched similar but much more thrilling performances, and the children, still rather uncomprehending, since neither inside nor outside school had they been sufficiently prepared for this lesson—what did they care about fasting?—yet showed by the brightness of their intent eyes that new and better times might be coming. Perhaps, said the hunger artist to himself many a time, things would be a little better if his cage were set not quite so near the menagerie. That made it too easy for people to make their choice, to say nothing of what he suffered from the stench of the menagerie, the animals' restlessness by night, the carrying past of raw lumps of flesh for the beasts of prey, the roaring at feeding times, which depressed him continually. But he did not dare to lodge a complaint with the management; after all, he had the animals to thank for the troops of people who passed his cage, among whom there might always be one here and there to take an interest in him, and who could tell where they might seclude him if he called attention to his existence and thereby to the fact that, strictly speaking, he was only an impediment on the way to the menagerie.

A small impediment, to be sure, one that grew steadily less. People grew familiar with the strange idea that they could be expected, in times like these, to take an interest in a hunger artist, and with this familiarity the verdict went out against him. He might fast as much as he could, and he did so; but nothing could save him now, people passed him by. Just try to explain to anyone the art of fasting! Anyone who has no feeling for it cannot be made to understand it. The fine placards grew dirty and illegible, they were torn down; the little notice board telling the number of fast days achieved, which at first was changed carefully every day, had long stayed at the same figure, for after the first few weeks even this small task seemed pointless to the staff; and so the artist simply fasted on and on, as he had once dreamed of doing, and it was no trouble to him, just as he had always foretold, but no one counted the days, no one, not even the artist himself, knew what records he was already breaking, and his heart grew heavy. And when once in a time some leisurely passer-by stopped, made merry over the old figure on the board and spoke of swindling, that was in its way the stupidest lie ever invented by indifference and inborn malice, since it was not the hunger artist who was cheating, he was working honestly, but the world was cheating him of his reward.

Many more days went by, however, and that too came to an end. An overseer's eye fell on the cage one day and he asked the attendants why this perfectly good cage should be left standing there unused with dirty straw inside it; nobody knew, until one man, helped out by the notice board, remembered about the hunger artist. They poked into the straw with sticks and found him in it. "Are you still fasting?" asked the overseer, "when on earth do you mean to stop?" "Forgive me, everybody," whispered the hunger artist; only the overseer, who had his ear to the bars, understood him. "Of course," said the overseer, and tapped his forehead with a finger to let the attendants know what state the man was in, "we forgive you." "I always wanted you to admire my fasting," said the hunger artist. "We do admire it," said the overseer, affably. "But you shouldn't admire it," said the hunger artist. "Well

then we don't admire it," said the overseer, "but why shouldn't we admire it?" "Because I have to fast, I can't help it," said the hunger artist. "What a fellow you are," said the overseer, "and why can't you help it?" "Because," said the hunger artist, lifting his head a little and speaking, with his lips pursed, as if for a kiss, right into the overseer's ear, so that no syllable might be lost, "because I couldn't find the food I liked. If I had found it, believe me, I should have made no fuss and stuffed myself like you or anyone else." These were his last words, but in his dimming eyes remained the firm though no longer proud persuasion that he was still continuing to fast.

"Well, clear this out now!" said the overseer, and they buried the hunger artist, straw and all. Into the cage they put a young panther. Even the most insensitive felt it refreshing to see this wild creature leaping around the cage that had so long been dreary. The panther was all right. The food he liked was brought him without hesitation by the attendants; he seemed not even to miss his freedom; his noble body, furnished almost to the bursting point with all that it needed, seemed to carry freedom around with it too; somewhere in his jaws it seemed to lurk; and the joy of life streamed with such ardent passion from his throat that for the onlookers it was not easy to stand the shock of it. But they braced themselves, crowded round the cage, and did not want ever to move away.

COMMENTS AND QUESTIONS

1. Kafka's style is in some ways a realistic one. In what sense is this story realistic and in what sense is it not?
2. Is the image of the hunger artist "expressionistic"? If so, what emotions or ideas does it express? Can you compare the portrayal of the hunger artist to the lonely man in Van Gogh's *Night Café* or the people in Kirchner's *Street*? (pp. 319, 352)
3. The hunger artist has been seen as an expression of the alienation of the artist in society or the isolation of the spiritual man from the sensual man. Support or criticize these interpretations.
4. How do you interpret the dying artist's revelation that he could never find the food that pleased him?

Plate XVI Cézanne, *Mont-Sainte-Victoire.*
(The Phillips Collection, Washington, D. C.)

Plate XVII Matisse, *Portrait of Mme. Matisse (The Green Stripe).*
(Royal Museum of Fine Arts, J. Rump Collection,
Copenhagen/© S.P.A.D.E.M., 1980)

Plate XVIII Georges Braque, *Musical Forms*, 1918. (Philadelphia Museum of Art, The Louise and Walter Arensberg Collection)

Plate XIX Mondrian, *Composition with Red, Blue, and Yellow*, 1921. (Collection Haags Gemeentemuseum, The Hague)

Plate XX Vasily Kandinsky, *Painting No. 201*, 1914. Oil on canvas, 64¼″ × 48¼″. (Collection, Museum of Modern Art, New York. Nelson A. Rockefeller Fund.)

Plate XXI Georgia O'Keeffe, *Sky Above Clouds IV*. Oil on canvas, 243.8 cm × 731.5 cm.
(Paul and Gabriella Rosenbaum Foundation Restricted Gift, and gift of Georgia O'Keeffe, 1983)

Plate XXII Jacob Lawrence, *Forward*, 1967. (North Carolina Museum of Art, Raleigh)

Plate XXV Andy Warhol, *Campbell's Soup*, 1965. Oil silk-screened on canvas, 36¹/₈″ × 24″. (Collection, The Museum of Modern Art, New York. Philip Johnson Fund.)

Plate XXIV Andy Warhol, *Gold Marilyn Monroe*, 1962. Synthetic polymer paint, silkcreeened, and oil on canvas, 6′ 11¼″ × 57″. (Collection, The Museum of Modern Art, New York. Gift of Philip Johnson.)

Plate XXIII Judy Chicago, Mary Wollstonecraft plate and runner from *The Dinner Party*. (© 1979 Judy Chicago/Photograph by Donald Woodman)

JAMES JOYCE (1880-1941)

From Ulysses

. . . a quarter after what an unearthly hour I suppose theyre just getting up in China now combing out their pigtails for the day well soon have the nuns ringing the angelus theyve nobody coming in to spoil their sleep except an odd priest or two for his night office the alarmclock next door at cockshout clattering the brains out of itself let me see if I can doze off 1 2 3 4 5 what kind of flowers are those they invented like the stars the wallpaper in Lombard Street was much nicer the apron he gave me was like that something only I only wore it twice better lower this lamp and try again so as I can get up early Ill go to Lambes there beside Findlaters and get them to send us some flowers to put about the place in case he brings him home tomorrow today I mean no no Fridays an unlucky day first I want to do the place up someway the dust grows in it I think while Im asleep then we can have music and cigarettes I can accompany him first I must clean the keys of the piano with milk whatll I wear shall I wear a white rose or those fairy cakes in Liptons I love the smell of a rich big shop at 7½d. a lb or the other ones with the cherries in them and the pinky sugar 11d. a couple of lbs of course a nice plant for the middle of the table Id get that cheaper in wait wheres this I saw them not long ago I love flowers Id love to have the whole place swimming in roses God of heaven theres nothing like nature the wild mountains then the sea and the waves rushing then the beautiful country with fields of oats and all kinds of things and all the fine cattle going about that would do your heart good to see rivers and lakes and flowers all sorts of shapes and smells and colours springing up even out of the ditches primroses and violets nature it is as for them saying theres no God I wouldnt give a snap of my two fingers for all their learning why dont they go and create something I often asked him atheists or whatever they call themselves go and wash the cobbles off themselves first then go howling for the priest and they dying and why why because theyre afraid of hell on account of their bad conscience ah yes I know them well who was the first person in the universe before there was anybody that made it all who ah that they dont know neither do I so there you are they might as well try to stop the sun from rising tomorrow the sun shines for you he said the day we were lying among the rhododendrons on Howth head in the grey tweed suit and his straw hat the day I got him to propose to me yes first [I gave him the bit of seedcake out of my mouth and it was leapyear like now yes 16 years ago my God after that long kiss I near lost my breath yes he said I was a flower of the mountain yes so we are flowers all a womans body yes that was one true thing he said in his life and the sun shines for you today yes that was why I liked him because I saw he understood or felt what a woman is and I knew I could always get round him and I gave him all the pleasure I could leading him on till he asked me to say yes] and I wouldnt answer first only looked out over the sea and the sky I was thinking of so many things he didn't know of Mulvey and Mr Stanhope and Hester and father and old captain Groves and the sailors playing all birds fly and I say stoop and washing up dishes they called it on the pier and the sentry in front of the governors house with the thing round his white helmet poor devil half roasted and the Spanish girls laughing in their shawls and their tall combs and the auctions in the morning the Greeks and the jews and the Arabs and the devil knows who else from all the ends of Europe and Duke street and the fowl market all clucking outside Larby Sharons and the poor donkeys slipping half asleep and the vague fellows in the cloaks asleep in the shade on the steps and the big wheels of the carts of the bulls and the old castle thousands of years old yes and those handsome Moors all in white and turbans like kings asking you to sit down in their little bit of a shop and Ronda with the old windows of the posadas glancing eyes a lattice hid for her lover to kiss the iron and the wineshops half open at night and the castanets and the night we missed the boat at Algeciras the watchman going about serene with his lamp and O that awful deepdown torrent O and the sea the sea crimson sometimes like fire and the glorious sunsets and the figtrees in the Alameda gardens yes and all the queer little streets and pink and blue and yellow houses and the rosegardens and the jessamine and geraniums and cactuses and Gibraltar as a girl where I was a Flower of the mountain yes when I put the rose in my hair like the Andalusian girls used or shall I wear a red yes and how he kissed me under the Moorish wall and I thought well as well him as another and then I asked him with my eyes to

ask again yes and then he asked me would I yes to say
yes my mountain flower and first I put my arms
around him yes and drew him down to me so he could
feel my breasts all perfume yes and his heart was going
like mad and yes I said yes I will Yes.

QUESTIONS

1. How long does it take you, as a reader, to "get in" to
   this text and discover what is going on? How do you
   react to it initially?
2. Does Joyce's technique effectively represent a state
   of semiconsciousness? Why or why not?
3. Show from the text how time is "flattened out"
   here; that is, how past, present, and future are superimposed. In what sense is this representation of psychic reality more "real" than a realistic text?
4. Trace the *motif* of the flower in this text. How does
   it function?

EZRA POUND (1885–1972)

The River-Merchant's Wife: A Letter

(*after Rihaku*[1])

While my hair was still cut straight across my forehead
I played about the front gate, pulling flowers.
You came by on bamboo stilts, playing horse,
You walked about my seat, playing with blue plums.
And we went on living in the village of Chokan:
Two small people, without dislike or suspicion.

At fourteen I married My Lord you.
I never laughed, being bashful.
Lowering my head, I looked at the wall.
Called to, a thousand times, I never looked back.

At fifteen I stopped scowling,
I desired my dust to be mingled with yours
For ever and for ever and for ever.
Why should I climb the look out'

At sixteen you departed,
You went into far Ku-to-yen, by the river of swirling
    eddies,
And you have been gone five months.
The monkeys make sorrowful noise overhead.

You dragged your feet when you went out.
By the gate now, the moss is grown, the different
    mosses,
Too deep to clear them away!

The leaves fall early this autumn, in wind.
The paired butterflies are already yellow with August
Over the grass in the West garden;
They hurt me. I grow older.
If you are coming down through the narrows of the
    river Kiang,
Please let me know beforehand,
And I will come out to meet you
    As far as Cho-fu-Sa.

In a Station of the Metro[1]

The apparition of these faces in the crowd;
Petals on a wet, black bough.

QUESTIONS

1. Do you find "In a Station of the Metro" effective as
   poetry? Can you compare the technique used to a
   technique in modern painting?
2. How does "The River-Merchant's Wife" render visual images in poetry?
3. Can you compare the influence of the Orient on
   European painting (see page 314) to its influence on
   poetry?

---

[1] Japanese name for an eighth-century Chinese poet, Li Po.

[1] Of this poem Pound writes in *Gaudier-Brzeska: A Memoir* (1916):
"Three years ago in Paris I got out of a 'metro' train at La Concorde,
and saw suddenly a beautiful face, and then another and another,
and then a beautiful child's face, and then another beautiful
woman, and I tried all that day to find words for what this had
meant to me, and I could not find any words that seemed to me
worthy, or as lovely as that sudden emotion. And that evening . . . I
was still trying and I found, suddenly, the expression. I do not mean
that I found words, but there came an equation . . . not in speech,
but in little splotches of colour. . . . The 'one-image poem' is a form
of super-position, that is to say, it is one idea set on top of another. I
found it useful in getting out of the impasse in which I had been
left by my metro emotion. I wrote a thirty-line poem, and destroyed it. . . . Six months later I made a poem half that length; a
year later I made the following *hokku*-like sentence."

E. E. CUMMINGS (1894–1962)

[(ponder,darling,these busted statues]

(ponder,darling,these busted statues
of yon motheaten forum be aware
notice what hath remained
—the stone cringes
clinging to the stone,how obsolete

lips utter their extant smile . . . .
remark

a few deleted of texture
or meaning monuments and dolls

resist Them Greediest Paws of careful
time all of which is extremely
unimportant)whereas Life

matters if or

when the your- and my-
idle vertical worthless
self unite in a peculiarly
momentary

partnership(to instigate
constructive
                Horizontal
business . . . . even so,let us make haste
—consider well this ruined aqueduct

lady,
which used to lead something into somewhere)

[space being(don't forget to remember)Curved]

Space being(don't forget to remember)Curved
(and that reminds me who said o yes Frost
Something there is which isn't fond of walls)

an electromagnetic(now I've lost
the)Einstein expanded Newton's law preserved
conTinuum(but we read that beFore)

of Course life being just a Reflex you
know since Everything is Relative or

to sum it All Up god being Dead(not to

mention inTerred)
                LONG LIVE that Upwardlooking
Serene Illustrious and Beatific
Lord of Creation,MAN:
                at a least crooking
of Whose compassionate digit,earth's most terrific

quadruped swoons into billiardBalls!

QUESTIONS

1. Compare "ponder, darling . . ." with John Donne's poem "The Flea" in Chapter 20. How has Cummings used both tradition and the modernist aesthetic in his poem?
2. What implications does Cummings draw from Einstein's law of relativity? How does he express them poetically?

T. S. ELIOT (1888–1965)

Preludes

I

The winter evening settles down
With smell of steaks in passageways.
Six o'clock.
The burnt-out ends of smoky days.
And now a gusty shower wraps
The grimy scraps
Of withered leaves above your feet
And newspapers from vacant lots;
The showers beat
On broken blinds and chimney-pots,
And at the corner of the street
A lonely cab-horse steams and stamps.
And then the lighting of the lamps.

II

The morning comes to consciousness
Of faint stale smells of beer
From the sawdust-trampled street

With all its muddy feet that press
To early coffee-stands.
With the other masquerades
That time resumes,
One thinks of all the hands
That are raising dingy shades
In a thousand furnished rooms.

III

You tossed a blanket from the bed,
You lay upon your back, and waited;
You dozed, and watched the night revealing
The thousand sordid images
Of which your soul was constituted;
They flickered against the ceiling.
And when all the world came back
And the light crept up between the shutters
And you heard the sparrows in the gutters,
You had such a vision of the street
As the street hardly understands;
Sitting along the bed's edge, where
You curled the papers from your hair,
Or clasped the yellow soles of feet
In the palms of both soiled hands.

IV

His soul stretched tight across the skies
That fade behind a city block,
Or trampled by insistent feet
At four and five and six o'clock;
And short square fingers stuffing pipes,
And evening newspapers, and eyes
Assured of certain certainties,
The conscience of a blackened street
Impatient to assume the world.

I am moved by fancies that are curled
Around these images, and cling:
The notion of some infinitely gentle
Infinitely suffering thing.

Wipe your hand across your mouth, and laugh;
The worlds revolve like ancient women
Gathering fuel in vacant lots.

QUESTIONS

1. What sights and sounds of the city has Eliot included in his poem? What is their effect?
2. In what respects is this poem consciously "modern," in contrast to, for example, a Romantic poem?
3. Identify the tone and the main sentiment of the poem.

T. S. ELIOT (1888-1965)

The Love Song of J. Alfred Prufrock

> S'io credessi che mia risposta fosse
> a persona che mai tornasse al mondo,
> questa fiamma staria senza più scosse.
> Ma per ciò che giammai di questo fondo
> non tornò vivo alcun, s'i'odo il vero,
> senza tema d'infamia ti rispondo.[1]

Let us go then, you and I,[2]
When the evening is spread out against the sky
Like a patient etherised upon a table;
Let us go, through certain half-deserted streets,
The muttering retreats
Of restless nights in one-night cheap hotels
And sawdust restaurants with oyster-shells:
Streets that follow like a tedious argument
Of insidious intent
To lead you to an overwhelming question . . .
Oh, do not ask, "What is it?"
Let us go and make our visit.

In the room the women come and go
Talking of Michelangelo.

The yellow fog that rubs its back upon the window-
    panes,
The yellow smoke that rubs its muzzle on the window-
    panes,

---

[1] Epigraph from Dante's *Inferno*, Canto 27, "If I thought that my anwer was to someone who would ever return to the world, this flame would shake no more. But since no one has ever returned alive from this place (hell), if I hear rightly, without fear of infamy I will answer you."

[2] Prufrock and a companion (or his own alter ego?) are going to make a visit to a woman.

Licked its tongue into the corners of the evening,
Lingered upon the pools that stand in drains,
Let fall upon its back the soot that falls from chimneys,
Slipped by the terrace, made a sudden leap,
And seeing that it was a soft October night,
Curled once about the house, and fell asleep.[3]

And indeed there will be time
For the yellow smoke that slides along the street
Rubbing its back upon the window-panes;
There will be time, there will be time
To prepare a face to meet the faces that you meet;
There will be time to murder and create,
And time for all the works and days of hands
That lift and drop a question on your plate;
Time for you and time for me,
And time yet for a hundred indecisions,
And for a hundred visions and revisions,
Before the taking of a toast and tea.

In the room the women come and go
Talking of Michelangelo.

And indeed there will be time
To wonder, "Do I dare?" and, "Do I dare?"
Time to turn back and descend the stair,
With a bald spot in the middle of my hair—
(They will say: "How his hair is growing thin!")
My morning coat, my collar mounting firmly to the
    chin,
My necktie rich and modest, but asserted by a simple
    pin—
(They will say: "But how his arms and legs are thin!")
Do I dare
Disturb the universe?
In a minute there is time
For decisions and revisions which a minute will
    reverse.

For I have known them all already, known them all—
Have known the evenings, mornings, afternoons,

I have measured out my life with coffee spoons;
I know the voices dying with a dying fall
Beneath the music from a farther room.
    So how should I presume?

And I have known the eyes already, known them all—
The eyes that fix you in a formulated phrase,
And when I am formulated, sprawling on a pin,
When I am pinned and wriggling on the wall,
Then how should I begin
To spit out all the butt-ends of my days and ways?
    And how should I presume?

And I have known the arms already, known them all—
Arms that are braceleted and white and bare
(But in the lamplight, downed with light brown hair!)
Is it perfume from a dress
That makes me so digress?
Arms that lie along a table, or wrap about a shawl.
    And should I then presume?
    And how should I begin?
                .   .   .   .   .

Shall I say, I have gone at dusk through narrow streets
And watched the smoke that rises from the pipes
Of lonely men in shirt-sleeves, leaning out of
    windows? . . .

I should have been a pair of ragged claws
Scuttling across the floors of silent seas.
                .   .   .   .   .

And the afternoon, the evening, sleeps so peacefully!
Smoothed by long fingers,
Asleep . . . tired . . . or it malingers,
Stretched on the floor, here beside you and me.
Should I, after tea and cakes and ices,
Have the strength to force the moment to its crisis?
But though I have wept and fasted, wept and prayed,
Though I have seen my head (grown slightly bald)
    brought in upon a platter,[4]
I am no prophet—and here's no great matter;

---

[3] Note that Eliot has taken the image of the yellow fog from Baudelaire's "The Seven Old Men" and expanded it here. He also incorporated "anthill of a city" (fourmillante cité) from the same poem into "The Waste Land."

[4] Refers to the head of John the Baptist, brought to Queen Herodias.

I have seen the moment of my greatness flicker,
And I have seen the eternal Footman hold my coat,
    and snicker,
And in short, I was afraid.

And would it have been worth it, after all,[5]
After the cups, the marmalade, the tea,
Among the porcelain, among some talk of you and me,
Would it have been worth while,
To have bitten off the matter with a smile,
To have squeezed the universe into a ball
To roll it toward some overwhelming question,
To say: "I am Lazarus, come from the dead,
Come back to tell you all, I shall tell you all"—
If one,[6] settling a pillow by her head,
    Should say: "That is not what I meant at all.
    That is not it, at all."

And would it have been worth it, after all,
Would it have been worth while,
After the sunsets and the dooryards and the sprinkled
    streets,
After the novels, after the teacups, after the skirts that
    trail along the floor—
And this, and so much more?—
It is impossible to say just what I mean!
But as if a magic lantern threw the nerves in patterns
    on a screen:
Would it have been worth while
If one, settling a pillow or throwing off a shawl,
And turning toward the window, should say:
    "That is not it at all,
    That is not what I meant, at all."

      .   .   .   .   .   .

No! I am not Prince Hamlet, nor was meant to be;
Am an attendant lord, one that will do
To swell a progress,[7] start a scene or two,
Advise the prince; no doubt, an easy tool,
Deferential, glad to be of use,
Politic, cautious, and meticulous;
Full of high sentence, but a bit obtuse;

At times, indeed, almost ridiculous—
Almost, at times, the Fool.

I grow old . . . I grow old . . .
I shall wear the bottoms of my trousers rolled.[8]

Shall I part my hair behind? Do I dare to eat a peach?
I shall wear white flannel trousers, and walk upon the
    beach.
I have heard the mermaids singing, each to each.

I do not think that they will sing to me.

I have seen them riding seaward on the waves
Combing the white hair of the waves blown back
When the wind blows the water white and black.
We have lingered in the chambers of the sea
By sea-girls wreathed with seaweed red and brown
Till human voices wake us, and we drown.

QUESTIONS

1. This poem presents itself as a *narrative,* but the action that occurs is very slight. Tell what it is.
2. Describe the character of Prufrock. What images does Eliot use to tell us about him?
3. Does Prufrock's problem seem to you a particularly modern one? Why?
4. In what sense, if any, is this a "love song"?
5. Is there any justification for the quotation from Dante's *Inferno?*

Virginia Woolf (1882–1941) and Modern Feminism Along with her work as a novelist, Virginia Woolf was profoundly interested in the feminist movement that had flourished in England since the days of John Stuart Mill and had assumed renewed importance in the 1920s. Women in England received full voting rights in 1928, the year in which Woolf composed her most widely read feminist work, *A Room of One's Own.* The book grew out of a series of lectures that she gave on "women and fiction." It eventually became a

---

[5] The use of the past tense here suggests that the moment for Prufrock to speak has passed.
[6] Prufrock's woman friend.
[7] A royal journey.

[8] The latest fashion.

mixture of an essay and a first-person fiction with a narrator called Mary Seton. It begins with the narrator's account of her visit to "Oxbridge," a college for men, and to "Fernham," a recently established college for women. At the first she was served an abundant luncheon of sole and partridge, at the second a meager dinner of boiled beef, prunes, and custard. The two scenes evoke the wealth of the male establishment and the fundamental poverty and dependence of women.

Woolf contends that economic independence and equal opportunity for education and experience are even more important than the vote to the feminist cause. As to the question of women and fiction, she says that, in order to write, "a woman must have money and a room of her own." Few women have created great works of art, because they have been denied opportunities to develop their talents. After examining the question historically and critically, Woolf makes a plea for an "androgynous" literature. The greatest creations will come through a fusing of male and female elements without sacrificing one to the other.

A Room of One's Own takes up other matters besides the feminist question. In the first selection printed here, the narrator's view of a Manx cat from a window during the "Oxbridge" luncheon occasions a meditation on the whole question of modernism—that is, the profound changes in society and in art that the Great War brought about. The second selection, which reads like a complete story in itself, might be called "Shakespeare's sister." Here, the memory of a remark by an old bishop, that "it was impossible for any woman—past, present, or to come—to have the genius of Shakespeare," leads Woolf (or the narrator) to a kind of historical musing on what might have happened to a talented woman of Shakespeare's era who wanted to write for the theater.

VIRGINIA WOOLF

A Room of One's Own

I

If by good luck there had been an ash-tray handy, if one had not knocked the ash out of the window in default, if things had been a little different from what they were, one would not have seen, presumably, a cat without a tail. The sight of that abrupt and truncated animal padding softly across the quadrangle changed by some fluke of the subconscious intelligence the emotional light for me. It was as if some one had let fall a shade. Perhaps the excellent hock was relinquishing its hold. Certainly, as I watched the Manx cat pause in the middle of the lawn as if it too questioned the universe, something seemed lacking, something seemed different. But what was lacking, what was different, I asked myself, listening to the talk. And to answer that question I had to think myself out of the room, back into the past, before the war indeed, and to set before my eyes the model of another luncheon party held in rooms not very far distant from these; but different. Everything was different. Meanwhile the talk went on among the guests, who were many and young, some of this sex, some of that; it went on swimmingly, it went on agreeably, freely, amusingly. And as it went on I set it against the background of that other talk, and as I matched the two together I had no doubt that one was the descendant, the legitimate heir of the other. Nothing was changed; nothing was different save only—here I listened with all my ears not entirely to what was being said, but to the murmur or current behind it. Yes, that was it—the change was there. Before the war at a luncheon party like this people would have said precisely the same things but they would have sounded different, because in those days they were accompanied by a sort of humming noise, not articulate, but musical, exciting, which changed the value of the words themselves. Could one set that humming noise to words? Perhaps with the help of the poets one could. A book lay beside me and, opening it, I turned casually enough to Tennyson. And here I found Tennyson was singing:

There has fallen a splendid tear
  From the passion-flower at the gate.
She is coming, my dove, my dear;
  She is coming, my life, my fate;
The red rose cries, "She is near, she is near";
  And the white rose weeps, "She is late";
The larkspur listens, "I hear, I hear";
  And the lily whispers, "I wait."

Was that what men hummed at luncheon parties before the war? And the women?

My heart is like a singing bird
  Whose nest is in a water'd shoot;
My heart is like an apple tree
  Whose boughs are bent with thick-set fruit;
My heart is like a rainbow shell
  That paddles in a halcyon sea;
My heart is gladder than all these
  Because my love is come to me.

Was that what women hummed at luncheon parties before the war?

There was something so ludicrous in thinking of people humming such things even under their breath at luncheon parties before the war that I burst out laughing, and had to explain my laughter by pointing at the Manx cat, who did look a little absurd, poor beast, without a tail, in the middle of the lawn. Was he really born so, or had he lost his tail in an accident? The tailless cat, though some are said to exist in the Isle of Man, is rarer than one thinks. It is a queer animal, quaint rather than beautiful. It is strange what a difference a tail makes—you know the sort of things one says as a lunch party breaks up and people are finding their coats and hats.

This one, thanks to the hospitality of the host, had lasted far into the afternoon. The beautiful October day was fading and the leaves were falling from the trees in the avenue as I walked through it. Gate after gate seemed to close with gentle finality behind me. Innumerable beadles were fitting innumerable keys into well-oiled locks; the treasure-house was being made secure for another night. After the avenue one comes out upon a road—I forget its name—which leads you, if you take the right turning, along to Fernham. But there was plenty of time. Dinner was not till half-past seven. One could almost do without dinner after such a luncheon. It is strange how a scrap of poetry works in the mind and makes the legs move in time to it along the road. Those words—

There has fallen a splendid tear
  From the passion-flower at the gate.
She is coming, my dove, my dear—

sang in my blood as I stepped quickly along towards Headingley. And then, switching off into the other measure, I sang, where the waters are churned up by the weir:

My heart is like a singing bird
  Whose nest is in a water'd shoot;
My heart is like an apple tree . . .

What poets, I cried aloud, as one does in the dusk, what poets they were!

In a sort of jealousy, I suppose, for our own age, silly and absurd though these comparisons are, I went on to wonder if honestly one could name two living poets now as great as Tennyson and Christina Rossetti were then. Obviously it is impossible, I thought, looking into those foaming waters, to compare them. The very reason why the poetry excites one to such abandonment, such rapture, is that it celebrates some feeling that one used to have (at luncheon parties before the war perhaps), so that one responds easily, familiarly, without troubling to check the feeling, or to compare it with any that one has now. But the living poets express a feeling that is actually being made and torn out of us at the moment. One does not recognize it in the first place; often for some reason one fears it; one watches it with keenness and compares it jealously and suspiciously with the old feeling that one knew. Hence the difficulty of modern poetry; and it is because of this difficulty that one cannot remember more than two consecutive lines of any good modern poet. For this reason—that my memory failed me—the argument flagged for want of material. But why, I continued, moving on towards Headingley, have we stopped humming under our breath at luncheon parties? Why has Alfred ceased to sing

She is coming, my dove, my dear?

Why has Christina ceased to respond

My heart is gladder than all these
Because my love is come to me?

Shall we lay the blame on the war? When the guns fired in August 1914, did the faces of men and women show so plain in each other's eyes that romance was killed? Certainly it was a shock (to women in particular with their illusions about education, and so on) to see the faces of our rulers in the light of the shell-fire. So ugly they looked—German, English, French—so stupid. But lay the blame where one will, on whom one will, the illusion which inspired Tennyson and Christina Rossetti to sing so passionately about the coming of their loves is far rarer now than then. One has only to read, to look, to listen, to remember. But why say "blame"? Why, if it was an illusion, not praise the catastrophe, whatever it was, that destroyed illusion and put truth in its place? For truth . . . those dots mark the spot where, in search of truth, I missed the turning up to Fernham. . . .

II

. . . I could not help thinking, as I looked at the works of Shakespeare on the shelf, that the bishop was right at least in this; it would have been impossible, completely and entirely, for any woman to have written the plays of Shakespeare in the age of Shakespeare. Let me imagine, since facts are so hard to come by, what would have happened had Shakespeare had a wonderfully gifted sister, called Judith, let us say. Shakespeare himself went, very probably—his mother was an heiress—to the grammar school, where he may have learnt Latin—Ovid, Virgil and Horace—and the elements of grammar and logic. He was, it is well known, a wild boy who poached rabbits, perhaps shot a deer, and had, rather sooner than he should have done, to marry a woman in the neighbourhood, who bore him a child rather quicker than was right. That escapade sent him to seek his fortune in London. He had, it seemed, a taste for the theatre; he began by holding horses at the stage door. Very soon he got work in the theatre, became a successful actor, and lived at the hub of the universe, meeting everybody, knowing everybody, practising his art on the boards, exercising his wits in the streets, and even getting access to the palace of the queen. Meanwhile his extraordinarily gifted sister, let us suppose, remained at home. She was as adventurous, as imaginative, as agog to see the world as he was. But she was not sent to school. She had no chance of learning grammar and logic, let alone of reading Horace and Virgil. She picked up a book now and then, one of her brother's perhaps, and read a few pages. But then her parents came in and told her to mend the stockings or mind the stew and not moon about with books and papers. They would have spoken sharply but kindly, for they were substantial people who knew the conditions of life for a woman and loved their daughter—indeed, more likely than not she was the apple of her father's eye. Perhaps she scribbled some pages up in an apple loft on the sly, but was careful to hide them or set fire to them. Soon, however, before she was out of her teens, she was to be betrothed to the son of a neighbouring wool-stapler. She cried out that marriage was hateful to her, and for that she was severely beaten by her father. Then he ceased to scold her. He begged her instead not to hurt him, not to shame him in this matter of her marriage. He would give her a chain of beads or a fine petticoat, he said; and there were tears in his eyes. How could she disobey him? How could she break his heart? The force of her own gift alone drove her to it. She made up a small parcel of her belongings, let herself down by a rope one summer's night and took the road to London. She was not seventeen. The birds that sang in the hedge were not more musical than she was. She had the quickest fancy, a gift like her brother's, for the tune of words. Like him, she had a taste for the theatre. She stood at the stage door; she wanted to act, she said. Men laughed in her face. The manager—a fat, loose-lipped man—guffawed. He bellowed something about poodles dancing and women acting—no woman, he said, could possibly be an actress. He hinted—you can imagine what. She could get no training in her craft. Could she even seek her dinner in a tavern or roam the streets at midnight? Yet her genius was for fiction and lusted to feed abundantly upon the lives of men and women and the study of their ways. At last—for she was very young, oddly like Shakespeare the poet in her face, with the same grey eyes and rounded brows—at last Nick Greene the actor-manager took pity on her; she found herself with child by that gentleman and so—who shall measure the heat and violence of the poet's heart when caught and tangled in a woman's body?—killed herself one winter's night and lies buried at some cross-roads where the omnibuses now stop outside the Elephant and Castle.

That, more or less, is how the story would run, I think, if a woman in Shakespeare's day had had Shakespeare's genius. But for my part, I agree with the deceased bishop, if such he was—it is unthinkable that any woman in Shakespeare's day should have had Shakespeare's genius. For genius like Shakespeare's is not born among labouring, uneducated, servile people. It was not born in England among the Saxons and the Britons. It is not born today among the working classes.

How, then, could it have been born among women whose work began, according to Professor Trevelyan, almost before they were out of the nursery, who were forced to it by their parents and held to it by all the power of law and custom? Yet genius of a sort must have existed among women as it must have existed among the working classes. Now and again an Emily Brontë or a Robert Burns blazes out and proves its presence. But certainly it never got itself on to paper. When, however, one reads of a witch being ducked, of a woman possessed by devils, of a wise woman selling herbs, or even of a very remarkable man who had a mother, then I think we are on the track of a lost novelist, a suppressed poet, of some mute and inglorious Jane Austen, some Emily Brontë who dashed her brains out on the moor or mopped and mowed about the highways crazed with the torture that her gift had put her to. Indeed, I would venture to guess that Anon, who wrote so many poems without signing them, was often a woman. It was a woman Edward Fitzgerald, I think, suggested who made the ballads and the folk-songs, crooning them to her children, beguiling her spinning with them, or the length of the winter's night.

This may be true or it may be false—who can say?—but what is true in it, so it seemed to me, reviewing the story of Shakespeare's sister as I had made it, is that any woman born with a great gift in the sixteenth century would certainly have gone crazed, shot herself, or ended her days in some lonely cottage outside the village, half witch, half wizard, feared and mocked at. For it needs little skill in psychology to be sure that a highly gifted girl who had tried to use her gift for poetry would have been so thwarted and hindered by other people, so tortured and pulled asunder by her own contrary instincts, that she must have lost her health and sanity to a certainty. No girl could have walked to London and stood at a stage door and forced her way into the presence of actor-managers without doing herself a violence and suffering an anguish which may have been irrational—for chastity may be a fetish invented by certain societies for unknown reasons—but were none the less inevitable. Chastity had then, it has even now, a religious importance in a woman's life, and has so wrapped itself round with nerves and instincts that to cut it free and bring it to the light of day demands courage of the rarest. To have lived a free life in London in the sixteenth century would have meant for a woman who was poet and playwright a nervous stress and dilemma which might well have killed her. Had she survived, whatever she had written would have been twisted and deformed, issuing from a strained and morbid imagination. And undoubtedly, I thought, looking at the shelf where there are no plays by women, her work would have gone unsigned. That refuge she would have sought certainly. It was the relic of the sense of chastity that dictated anonymity to women even so late as the nineteenth century. Currer Bell, George Eliot, George Sand, all the victims of inner strife as their writings prove, sought ineffectively to veil themselves by using the name of a man. Thus they did homage to the convention, which if not implanted by the other sex was liberally encouraged by them (the chief glory of a woman is not to be talked of, said Pericles, himself a much-talked-of man), that publicity in women is detestable. Anonymity runs in their blood. The desire to be veiled still possesses them. They are not even now as concerned about the health of their fame as men are, and, speaking generally, will pass a tombstone or a signpost without feeling an irresistible desire to cut their names on it, as Alf, Bert or Chas. must do in obedience to their instinct, which murmurs if it sees a fine woman go by, or even a dog, Ce chien est à moi. And, of course, it may not be a dog, I thought, remembering Parliament Square, the Sieges Allee and other avenues; it may be a piece of land or a man with curly black hair. It is one of the great advantages of being a woman that one can pass even a very fine negress without wishing to make an Englishwoman of her.

That woman, then, who was born with a gift of poetry in the sixteenth century, was an unhappy woman, a woman at strife against herself. All the conditions of her life, all her own instincts, were hostile to the state of mind which is needed to set free whatever is in the brain. But what is the state of mind that is most propitious to the act of creation, I asked. Can one come by any notion of the state that furthers and makes possible that strange activity? Here I opened the volume containing the Tragedies of Shakespeare. What was Shakespeare's state of mind, for instance, when he wrote *Lear* and *Antony and Cleopatra*? It was certainly the state of mind most favourable to poetry that there has ever existed. But Shakespeare himself said nothing about it. We only know casually and by chance that he "never blotted a line." Nothing indeed was ever said by the artist himself about his state of mind until the eighteenth century perhaps. Rousseau perhaps began it. At any rate, by the nineteenth century self-consciousness had developed so far that it was the habit for men of letters to describe their minds in confessions and autobiographies. Their lives also were written, and their letters were printed after their deaths. Thus, though we do not know what Shakespeare went through when he wrote *Lear*, we do know what Carlyle went through when he wrote the *French Revolution*; what Flaubert went through when he wrote *Madame Bovary*; what Keats was going through when he tried to write poetry against the coming of death and the indifference of the world.

And one gathers from this enormous modern literature of confession and self-analysis that to write a work of genius is almost always a feat of prodigious difficulty. Everything is against the likelihood that it will come from the writer's mind whole and entire. Generally material circumstances are against it. Dogs will bark; people will interrupt; money must be made; health will break down. Further, accentuating all these difficulties and making them harder to bear is the world's notorious indifference. It does not ask people to write poems and novels and histories; it does not need them. It does not care whether Flaubert finds the right word or whether Carlyle scrupulously verifies this or that fact. Naturally, it will not pay for what it does not want. And so the writer, Keats, Flaubert, Carlyle, suffers, especially in the creative years of youth, every form of distraction and discouragement. A curse, a cry of agony, rises from those books of analysis and confession. "Mighty poets in their misery dead"—that is the burden of their song. If anything comes through in spite of all of this, it is a miracle, and probably no book is born entire and uncrippled as it was conceived.

But for women, I thought, looking at the empty shelves, these difficulties were infinitely more formidable. In the first place, to have a room of her own, let alone a quiet room or a sound-proof room, was out of the question, unless her parents were exceptionally rich or very noble, even up to the beginning of the nineteenth century. Since her pin money, which depended on the good will of her father, was only enough to keep her clothed, she was debarred from such alleviations as came even to Keats or Tennyson or Carlyle, all poor men, from a walking tour, a little journey to France, from the separate lodging which, even if it were miserable enough, sheltered them from the claims and tyrannies of their families. Such material difficulties were formidable; but much worse were the immaterial. The indifference of the world which Keats and Flaubert and other men of genius have found so hard to bear was in her case not indifference but hostility. The world did not say to her as it said to them, Write if you choose; it makes no difference to me. The world said with a guffaw, Write? What's the good of your writing? Here the psychologists of Newnham and Girton might come to our help, I thought, looking again at the blank spaces on the shelves. For surely it is time that the effect of discouragement upon the mind of the artist should be measured, as I have seen a dairy company measure the effect of ordinary milk and Grade A milk upon the body of the rat. They set two rats in cages side by side, and of the two one was furtive, timid and small, and the other was glossy, bold and big. Now what food do we feed women as artists upon? I asked, remembering, I suppose, that dinner of prunes and custard.

COMMENTS AND QUESTIONS

1. The first passage in many ways typifies Woolf's style and artistic interests. She is primarily interested in subtle, interior, subconscious events. The sight of the Manx cat, for example, "changed by some fluke of the subconscious intelligence the emotional light for me." What might the Manx cat represent and how does it change the narrator's emotional state?

2. Woolf contrasts the poetry of two famous Victorian poets, Alfred Lord Tennyson and Christina Rossetti, with the work of modernist poets. A comparison of the expression of love in the two poems cited with that in Eliot's "Prufrock" would make the same point. What are the differences, both in style and content? How does Woolf explain the difficulty of modern poetry?

3. Does Woolf's observation that the same exterior events (for example, parties before and after the war) may be totally different because of an imperceptible inner "humming" seem plausible to you? What has the war changed?

4. Is the story of "Shakespeare's sister" convincing? What does it say about women and creativity?

5. What is the point of the account of the scientific experiment at the end of the passage?

6. To what extent have conditions for the intellectual or creative woman changed since 1928?

35

New Americans on the World Cultural Scene: The Rise of Afro-American and Latin American Cultures

As the aftermath of World War I contributed to a certain skepticism toward traditional Western humanistic values along with a revived interest in non-Western and so-called primitive cultures on the part of Europeans and Euro-Americans, cultural traditions that had previously appeared peripheral in global terms began to attract attention and to flourish on their own. Participation in the war effort was in large part responsible for a new self-awareness displayed by black U.S. citizens during the years between the wars. The Mexican revolutionary era (1910–1916) stimulated a growth of cultural awareness not only on the part of Mexicans but of all Latin Americans. Afro-American and Latin American artists and writers of the interwar years were, in varying degrees, influenced both by the innovations of European modernism and by their rediscovery and reevaluation of their own cultural traditions.

The Rise of Afro-American Culture

Although consciousness of emancipation from racial and racist stereotypes, such as the minstrel clown, into what was called the "New Negro" had its origin in the prewar years, changes in American society after World War I intensified the process. Economic opportunities produced by the war brought blacks to Northern cities in great numbers. The war dislodged blacks not only from the South but also from other countries throughout the world, as blacks from the French and British West Indies and Africa all gathered in Northern cities, New York in particular. But while many blacks developed their racial consciousness in New York and articulated it there, others from Martinique, Haiti, and Senegal delivered radical racial manifestoes from Paris and London. The result was that Pan-Africanism, the quest for black unity throughout the world, became a dominant attitude and ideology.

In addition to making Afro-Americans conscious of the international dimension of their racial struggle, the war stimulated their eagerness to produce racial peace and equality in the United States. If they could march and fight alongside white Americans to make the world "safe for democracy," then the same, they reasoned, could be done for racial harmony in the United States. As the shift in black leadership changed from the accommodationist policy of Booker T. Washington to the radical protest of the intellectual W. E. B. Du Bois, Afro-Americans became more racially conscious and self-assertive, proclaiming themselves to be human beings worthy of respect. Du Bois states the case in *The Souls of Black Folks*:

The history of the American Negro is the history of this strife,—this longing to attain self-conscious manhood, to merge his double self into a better and truer self. In this merging he wishes neither of the older selves to be lost. He would not Africanize America, for America has too much to teach the world and Africa. He would not bleach his Negro soul in a flood of white Americanism, for he knows that Negro blood has a message for the world. He simply wishes to make it possible for a man to be both a Negro and an American, without being cursed and spit upon by his fellows, without having the doors of Opportunity closed roughly in his face.

This determined quest for racial equality and America's insistence on racial segregation produced the "bloody summer" of 1919, when race riots erupted in more than twenty-five U.S. cities. In reaction to this outburst of violence, the poet Claude McKay, born in Jamaica and later part of the Harlem Renaissance, wrote his now well-known poem "If We Must Die."

CLAUDE McKAY (1890–1948)

If We Must Die

If we must die, let it not be like hogs
Hunted and penned in an inglorious spot,
While round us bark the mad and hungry dogs,
Making their mock at our accursed lot.
If we must die, O let us nobly die,
So that our precious blood may not be shed
In vain; then even the monsters we defy
Shall be constrained to honor us though dead!
O kinsmen! we must meet the common foe!
Though far outnumbered let us show us brave,
And for their thousand blows deal one deathblow!
What though before us lies the open grave?
Like men we'll face the murderous, cowardly pack,
Pressed to the wall, dying but fighting back!

The inability to produce rapid racial equality caused many blacks to become disillusioned with life in America altogether. One such person, Marcus Aurelius Garvey, also from the Caribbean island of Jamaica, attempted to alleviate this problem by initiating a "back to Africa" movement. Many middle-class Afro-Americans fought Garvey's idea. Some genuinely felt that Afro-Americans should work out their destiny in America, not Africa. For others, the term *Afro-American* was itself a source of shame. The hyphen represented for them not a source of pride but rather bondage to a dark, backward country and brutal past they wanted to forget. Garvey was thus shunned by the bourgeoisie and laughed at by the intellectuals for his antics. Even so, he was an important influence on the image that Afro-Americans shaped for themselves after World War I. He is reported to have had a following of anywhere between half a million and 6 million. The black masses apparently loved him.

The essence of Garvey's "back to Africa" message was that black was superior to white and that the destiny of Afro-Americans lay in Africa, not America. Garvey's efforts, however, were not confined to getting blacks back to Africa, a place Garvey himself was never to see. He also attempted to produce Afro-American pride and self-help through a program of black capitalistic enterprise that anticipated the work and ideas of Elijah Muhammad and his Nation of Islam. The Universal African Legion, Black Cross Nurses, the Universal African Motor Corps, the Black Eagle Flying Corps, and the Black Star Line represent only a few of his efforts. Although these programs and organizations were largely a failure, Garvey was most instrumental in strengthening the Afro-American's sense of racial pride and in encouraging him to think about his heritage, roots, or racial past.

The Harlem Renaissance   The Harlem Renaissance, a florescence of creative activity in art, music, poetry, drama, and fiction, was a logical extension of the Afro-American's new racial, cultural, and political thinking. The movement started around 1919, reached its peak in the years 1925 to 1928, and tapered off in 1932. As an artistic, cultural, and social journey of self-discovery, it was an important time for all Afro-Americans. As Alain Locke, one of the movement's cultural mentors, expressed it in 1925:

> The pulse of the Negro world has begun to beat in Harlem. . . . hope rests in the revaluation by white and black alike of the Negro in terms of his artistic endowments and cultural contributions, not only in his folk-art, music especially, which has always found appreciation, but in larger, though humbler and less acknowledged ways. . . . A second crop of the Negro's gifts promises still more largely. He now becomes a conscious contributor and lays aside the status of a beneficiary and ward for that of a collaborator and participant in American civilization. The great social gain in this is the releasing of our talented group from the arid fields of controversy and debate to the productive fields of creative expression.

Locke, who often compared the Afro-American's cultural reawakening to the national movements of folk expression that were taking place in Ireland, Czechoslovakia, Yugoslavia, India, China, Egypt, Russia, Palestine, and Mexico, later edited an anthology called *The New Negro*. Designed specifically to register the inner life of the Afro-American and to document him culturally and socially, *The New Negro* reflected the idealism and optimism of most American progressive reformers, black and white. For Locke, DuBois, James Weldon Johnson, Charles S. Johnson, Carl Van Vechten, and other Harlem Renaissance leaders and participants, the creative expressions of Afro-Americans were viewed as a means toward racial peace and as adequate proof of their ability to participate in American life.

Although such hopes were not immediately realized, the Harlem Renaissance did witness an unprecedented amount of interracial activities and cooperation. By 1920 the "coon" shows had given way to the talented performances of such black actors and musicians as Josephine Baker, Charles Gilpin, Paul Robeson, Frank Wilson, Noble Sissle, and Eubie Blake. In both Europe and America interest in the New Negro was focused around jazz, African art, and the cult of the primitive. The Afro-American was in vogue, as his lifestyle had become a fad.

Jazz   The writer F. Scott Fitzgerald justly labeled the decades of the 1920s and 1930s "The Jazz Age." Indeed, the end of World War I marks the emergence of jazz music as a national rage. Spawned in the urban poverty of Black America, and born of the mingling of sacred and secular, African, European classical, and American folk music sources, this all-American art form spread from New Orleans to Kansas City, Chicago, and New York with lightning speed and ultimately found enthusiastic adherents and vociferous critics all across the land and in Europe as well. Jazz came of age at the same time the radio and recording industries did, and the networks were soon bringing the new sounds of the 20s into nearly every home in America.

Jazz is an improvisatory art. Every great performer transforms the basic materials, recreates them. In a very real sense, every jazz performance is a new work, and through live performance, recordings and radio, musicians everywhere learned from each other. The amateurs and hacks borrowed what they could imitate; the great talents assimilated what they heard only to move forward in an evolving art form. As early as January of 1917, musicians from New Orleans, the Original Dixieland Jazz Band, were playing in New York, and it was not long before they were in the recording studios. The hot music from New Orleans was soon heard in parlors from Maine to California. It might be said that the history of the jazz age is etched in the grooves of ten-inch, three-minute-play, shellac discs.

Jazz is a performance art. Its giants have been first and foremost virtuoso performers, whether vocalists or instrumentalists. The most successful of them knew how to combine a constantly high level of musical inventiveness with crowd-pleasing showmanship. One man exemplifies all the traits of the great jazz artist. Born into the abject povery of black, uptown New Orleans on the Fourth of July, 1900, Louis "Satchmo" Armstrong apprenticed in local bands for several years, emulating his idol, Joe "King" Oliver. When the call came in 1922 to join "King" Oliver's Creole Jazz Band in Chicago, Louis was not only ready but soon became the star. Throughout those years he developed a brilliant trumpet technique that not only made him the leading jazz virtuoso of the day, but allowed him to turn new musical ideas into sound in some of the most creative jazz solos ever known.

Before long, as leader of his own groups, he began to temper the "hot" New Orleans style with elements of the New York ensemble sound of Fletcher Henderson and even a little of the "sweet" dance sounds of Guy Lombardo's Royal Canadians. The new synthesis can be heard on his recordings of "Cakewalking Babies" or the later "Struttin' with Some Barbeque." Louis's recordings with his Hot Five and Hot Seven are classics, outstanding accomplishments even compared to the great flurry of jazz activity of the time. (See note on p. 459.)

Throughout his career, Louis Armstrong suffered, like all black musicians, from the racism and segregation of his native country, even as his extraordinary improvisatory skills and his ebullient personality as an entertainer brought him worldwide recognition and honor. In the later years, when his highly acclaimed European tours had won him the official title of America's Ambassador of Jazz, his style still combined virtuoso trumpet playing and the "scat-singing" that had become his trademark (that is, vocal performances that are instrumentally conceived and vocalized on nonsense syllables) with large doses of "cornball" showmanship. Most would agree that the black man was pro-

tecting his ego with humor, but for a time this great man even had to suffer the rejection of many of his own people who interpreted such antics as selling out, playing Uncle Tom. Louis Armstrong carried his burden well, but he knew the meaning of "Black and Blue."

Many first-class musicians were associated over the years with Louis Armstrong, and one of the most important was Earl "Fatha" Hines. Their association, beginning in 1927, produced a major change in Louis' style as well as in the role the piano was to take in jazz ensembles. Some of the most extraordinary virtuoso pieces of the day were recorded when these two men collaborated. "Weather Bird," a duet for trumpet and piano, is unmatched as a combination whose sum is greater than the parts. It is a perfect example of how the working jazz musician draws upon a finite set of musical phrases and then reworks, reshapes, and develops them under the impetus of the creative moment and the muses. During the performance he seeks a new sound, a clever turn of phrase, or an exciting rhythmic innovation. Through this process of reshaping a limited number of musical ideas within the solo, improvisational composition comes about. Structural unity and invention are developed partially through conscious thought, but a stronger determinant is the subconscious interplay of stored mental structures and habitual, reflexive lip and finger patterns. "Satch" and "Fatha" put it all together.

Duke Ellington (1899–1974) The economic gloom that resulted from the stock market crash of 1929 created a taste for dreamy, sentimental, and blindly optimistic popular songs. Hot jazz began to lose its audience, and a number of new substyles began to develop. Also, for purely musical reasons, the emergence of the big-band concept brought a shift in jazz styles. Throughout the decade of the 1930s, a new jazz orchestra sound was taking over, a smooth, swinging music featuring mellow moods and a new sense of ensemble, interspersed with improvised solos, some hot and others not. One of the giants of the new swing music was Edward Kennedy "Duke" Ellington. Starting out as a pianist and bandleader in the late 1920s, "Duke" soon began to explore the possibilities of the new musical territory in his own compositions. One of his notable accomplishments was the introduction of his own brand of chromatic harmonic thinking into jazz; another was his exploration of a broader timbral palette; and a third was the concept of writing and orchestrating music for particular jazz soloists, the members of his orchestra. Through his piano explorations he broke out of the traditional mold of simple triadic harmony to an expanded harmonic vocabulary. An excellent example is his composition, "Sophisticated Lady," with its sliding, chromatic chords. His ear for sound per se (timbre) led him to score for muted brass, slides and growls, percussion effects, and winds from low baritone sax to high clarinet. Almost every recording of Ellington's orchestra illustrates a range of tonal color. The blend of composed music and swinging jazz, of arrangement and solo performance, give the music of Duke Ellington its special appeal. "East St. Louis Toodle-Oo" or "Harlem Airshaft" or "Mood Indigo" are both jazz compositions and jazz performances, pieces of music and social commentary. As the titles reflect the world of Duke Ellington, so does the music. Duke and his orchestra also became examples and models for black America as well. They were successful, even in poverty. They were men of accomplishment and respect, even though their personal fortunes were, to a large extent, dependent upon the health of the larger society and frustrated by their race. But in spite of difficulty and hostility, the Ellington orchestra rode out the storm.

Langston Hughes (1902–1967) Of the many writers who began to flourish in Harlem during the 1930s, Langston Hughes was undoubtedly the best known. "The Weary Blues," which epitomizes "jazz" or "blues" poetry, displays most of the qualities that dominated Hughes' poetry throughout his career: it is loose in form, songful, and idiomatic in vocabulary.

LANGSTON HUGHES

The Weary Blues

Droning a drowsy syncopated tune,
Rocking back and forth to a mellow croon,
   I heard a Negro play.
Down on Lenox Avenue the other night

By the pale dull pallor of an old gas light
   He did a lazy sway. . . .
   He did a lazy sway. . . .
To the tune o' those Weary Blues.
With his ebony hands on each ivory key
He made that poor piano moan with melody.
   O Blues!
Swaying to and fro on his rickety stool
He played that sad raggy tune like a musical fool.
   Sweet Blues!
Coming from a black man's soul.
   O Blues!
In a deep song voice with a melancholy tone
I heard that Negro sing, that old piano moan—
   "Ain't got nobody in all this world,
   Ain't got nobody but ma self.
   I's gwine to quit ma frownin'
   And put ma troubles on de shelf."
Thump, thump, thump, went his foot on the floor.
He played a few chords then he sang some more—
   "I got de Weary Blues
   And I can't be satisfied.
   Got de Weary Blues
   And can't be satisfied—
   I ain't happy no mo'
   And I wish that I had died."
And far into the night he crooned that tune.
The stars went out and so did the moon.
The singer stopped playing and went to bed.
While the Weary Blues echoed through his head
He slept like a rock or a man that's dead.

The few lines beginning with "Thump" best illustrate Hughes' jazz rhythms. Poetry for Hughes was a distillation, in rhythm, of what he took to be the distinct black medley of life, and few could match his ability to capture, in language, the moods and emotions of the common black.

Two basic impulses sustaining Hughes' drive to write about the common black folk were his genuine love for his race and his attachment to his town, Harlem. The Simple stories (with the folk commentator, Jessie B. Simple) and "The Negro Speaks of Rivers" make clear Hughes' recognition of the unity between all blacks and the vital spark of African life and culture.

LANGSTON HUGHES

The Negro Speaks of Rivers

I've known rivers!
I've known rivers ancient as the world and older than
    the flow of human blood in human veins.
My soul has grown deep like the rivers.

I bathed in the Euphrates when dawns were young,
I built my hut near the Congo and it lulled me to sleep,
I looked upon the Nile and raised the pyramids above
    it.

I heard the singing of the Mississippi when Abe
    Lincoln went down to New Orleans,
And I've seen its muddy bosom turn all golden in the
    sunset.

I've known rivers:
Ancient, dusky rivers,
My soul has grown deep like the rivers.

Jean Toomer (1894–1967) A lesser-known but highly interesting writer of the Harlem Renaissance was Jean Toomer, a man of mixed race who described himself as "French, Dutch, Welsh, Negro, German, Jewish, and Indian . . . inevitably an American." Spiritually, however, Toomer considered himself to be black, for his need for artistic expression pulled him "deeper and deeper into the Negro group." Although Toomer wrote prolifically during his lifetime, he published only one book, entitled *Cane*. Published in 1923, *Cane* is a collection of poems and prose sketches, many in highly original, experimental styles. The following piece shows Toomer's ability to adapt modernist techniques to evoke the black experience.

JEAN TOOMER

Karintha

    Her skin is like dusk on the eastern horizon,
    O cant you see it, O cant you see it,
    Her skin is like dusk on the eastern horizon
    . . . When the sun goes down.

Men always wanted her, this Karintha, even as a child, Karintha carrying beauty, perfect as dusk when the sun goes down. Old men rode her hobby-horse upon their knees. Young men danced with her at frolics when they should have been dancing with their grown-up girls. God grant us youth, secretly prayed the old men. The young fellows counted the time to pass before she would be old enough to mate with them. This interest of the male, who wishes to ripen a growing thing too soon, could mean no good to her.

Karintha, at twelve, was a wild flash that told the other folks just what it was to live. At sunset, where there was no wind, and the pine-smoke from over by the sawmill hugged the earth, and you couldnt see more than a few feet in front, her sudden darting past you was a bit of vivid color, like a black bird that flashes in light. With the other children one could hear, some distance off, their feet flopping in the two-inch dust. Karintha's running was a whir. It had the sound of the red dust that sometimes makes a spiral in the road. At dusk, during the hush just after the saw-mill had closed down, and before any of the women had started their supper-getting-ready songs, her voice, high-pitched, shrill, would put one's ears to itching. But no one ever thought to make her stop because of it. She stoned the cows, and beat her dog, and fought the other children. . . . Even the preacher, who caught her at mischief, told himself that she was as innocently lovely as a November cotton flower. Already, rumors were out about her. Homes in Georgia are most often built on the two-room plan. In one, you cook and eat, in the other you sleep, and there love goes on. Karintha had seen or heard, perhaps she had felt her parents loving. One could but imitate one's parents, for to follow them was the way of God. She played "home" with a small boy who was not afraid to do her bidding. That started the whole thing. Old men could no longer ride her hobby-horse upon their knees. But young men counted faster.

    Her skin is like dusk,
    O cant you see it,
    Her skin is like dusk,
    When the sun goes down.

Karintha is a woman. She who carries beauty, perfect as dusk when the sun goes down. She has been married many times. Old men remind her that a few years back they rode her hobby-horse upon their knees. Karintha smiles, and indulges them when she is in the mood for it. She has contempt for them. Karintha is a woman. Young men run stills to make her money. Young men go to the big cities and run on the road. Young men go away to college. They all want to bring her money. These are the young men who thought that all they had to do was to count time. But Karintha is a woman, and she has had a child. A child fell out of her womb onto a bed of pine-needles in the forest. Pine-needles are smooth and sweet. They are elastic to the feet of rabbits . . . A sawmill was nearby. Its pyramidal sawdust pile smouldered. It is a year before one completely burns. Meanwhile, the smoke curls up and hangs in odd wraiths about the trees, curls up, and spreads itself out over the valley . . . Weeks after Karintha returned home the smoke was so heavy you tasted it in water. Some one made a song:

> Smoke is on the hills. Rise up.
> Smoke is on the hills, O rise
> And take my soul to Jesus.

Karintha is a woman. Men do not know that the soul of her was a growing thing ripened too soon. They will bring their money; they will die not having found it out . . . Karintha at twenty, carrying beauty, perfect as dusk when the sun goes down. Karintha . . .

> Her skin is like dusk on the eastern horizon,
> O cant you see it, O cant you see it,
> Her skin is like dusk on the eastern horizon
> . . . When the sun goes down.

Goes down . . .

QUESTIONS

1. Through what specific linguistic effects does Toomer create this portrait of a black woman?
2. Compare the techniques used in this word portrait with those in the portrait of Molly Bloom by Joyce.

Assessments of the accomplishments of the Harlem Renaissance differ markedly. Most historians and literary critics agree, however, that its major significance lies in its contribution to the Afro-American's consciousness of his blackness and his black heritage, his search for black values, and his quest for a new beginning in America.

Afro-American Art

The period following World War I marked the emergence of Afro-American art on the national and international levels just as it did for Afro-American writing. The art of Afro-America had been a varied conglomeration of many interests, schools of thought, and modes of expression. The works of early Afro-American artists such as Edward M. Bannister, Edmonia Lewis (the first black female sculptor), R. S. Duncanson, and Henry O. Tanner were for the most part academic in treatment, cosmopolitan in theme, and lacking in race consciousness. These artists viewed themselves primarily as artists and only incidentally as black. As a result of this attitude, they were considered pretentious by both blacks and whites, since the fine arts were generally associated with security, leisure, wealth, and "high culture."

Picasso and the other artists who discovered African art in Paris helped to stimulate interest in it in the United States. While some black artists in America rejected identification with African art, as they did with Africa itself, others spoke of the need to develop an Afro-American art idiom based on African forms. Thus the decades of the 1920s and 1930s witnessed racially conscious Afro-American artists who dealt with many of the themes that were articulated in the New Negro movement: the celebration of the beauty of black people, the illumination of the history of the Afro-American experience, and the search for identity and roots.

Horace Pippin (1888–1946) Pippin was one of the black artists discovered in this period who achieved considerable fame and financial success. When the United States entered World War I, he enlisted and was sent to France with an all-black regiment. He fought in the trenches and was wounded, losing the use of his right arm. Pippin returned to his family, married, and lived quietly as a disabled person for about ten years. He then decided he had to make pictures and taught himself to draw holding his limp right arm in his left hand. The first image he created was burned by a hot poker on a board. Then followed a series of powerful images dealing with war—ravaged landscapes, falling bombs, mud, cold, broken forms and everywhere the presence of death. These terrible visions seemed to free Pippin and there emerged rich, complex images of life as he had experienced it. Sometimes these pictures dealt directly with the black past, like the series on John Brown. *John Brown Going to His Hanging* (Fig. 35-1) is filled with tension and anxiety. The small black woman in the foreground who faces the viewer is probably Pippin's grandmother. Other paintings are evocative of home and hearth and a pleasant life among poor rural families. *Domino Players* (Fig. 35-2) is filled with ease, comfort, and life. Like the painting of Van Gogh, the German Expressionists, or Matisse, Pippin's work is significant, not because it is an attempt to precisely recreate the seen world, but because he gives visual form to his internal world of ideas and emotions. These forms—the paintings—are a powerful, successful means of communication. The viewer experiences the horrors of war or the comfort of life in a plain rural setting.

Aaron Douglas (1898–1979) Pippin's work, when compared with that of Aaron Douglas, one of the most successful artists to emerge from the Harlem Renaissance, seems eons away, almost archaic in contrast to Douglas's geometric forms and stylized figures. Douglas is rightly regarded as the pioneer of African style among Afro-American painters. Two of his well-known murals in the Countee Cullen Branch of the New York Public Library are reproduced here (Figs. 35-3, 35-4). The murals, entitled *Aspects of Negro Life*, depict the cultural and historical background of Afro-Americans. Thus it is only visually and stylistically that Pippin and Douglas differ; they share their subject matter.

Jacob Lawrence (b. 1927) Another important Afro-American painter whose work has been associated with arousing consciousness of black history and experience is Jacob Lawrence, who was among the many young artists supported by the WPA Artists Relief Program. American scene painting, and American responses to European modernism, combine with his experience as a black to form his art. Lawrence has always dealt with American themes, particularly work and the urban experience. He also painted several important series that narrate major events in Afro-American history. The best-known, perhaps is the series on the life of Harriet Tubman, a black woman who helped slaves gain access to freedom on the underground railway. The painting illustrated here, *Forward* (Color Plate XXII), is executed in Lawrence's typical manner. The surface is very flat and matte, like a Renaissance wall mural. The abstracted figures are carefully arranged in a compressed space and the narrative is described through strong bodily gestures. The colors are also strong, flat, and limited to a few hues. This kind of work may be compared with the work of a number of other American artists, such as Milton Avery, who were also active in this period. Lawrence, like some other black artists who were deeply influenced by European modernism, experienced hostility not only toward his race but also toward his manner of painting. However, this did not deter him from creating a remarkable body of work, which can be associated not only with the black American past but also with the shared and universal themes of freedom and repression, human life, and work.

Afro-American Sculpture It was in sculpture that a consciously African Afro-American style was most clearly expressed. The works of Richmond Barthé and Sargent Johnson offer the best examples of such sculpture. Sargent Johnson's bust *Chester* (Fig. 35-5) and Barthé's *African Dancer* (Fig. 35-6) are both particularly striking for their African qualities. Using your knowledge from the section on African art in Volume I, what African qualities can you identify?

The works of Barthé and Johnson, like those of Douglas and Pippin, differ from each other and from African art. The forces that motivated artists in America in the 1930s and 1940s cannot be the same as those that motivated the artist of the Benin head or the Dogon votive figure. Yet the search for roots, as surely as the presence of successful artists, exerted a profound influence on the black artists in America who reached maturity after the Second World War. The recognition that the past, as well as the present, is profoundly different and tremendously rich, is liberating.

35-1 Horace Pippin, *John Brown Going to His Hanging.* 1942. (Pennsylvania Academy of the Fine Arts)

35-2 Horace Pippin, *Domino Players.* Oil on composition board, 1943. (The Phillips Collection)

Modernism and the Rise of Latin American Culture

While blacks in the United States were rediscovering their African heritage and attempting to integrate it with their American experience, Americans in the heterogeneous cultural and geographic area south of the Rio Grande and in the Caribbean islands were rediscovering the importance of their native American, African, and European heritages. When the thirty-five-year-old Diaz dictatorship was overthrown in 1910 in Mexico, not only the social fabric but eventually the entire cultural orientation of the country underwent a profound alteration. This upheaval, combined with the general disillusionment among the intellectuals caused by World War I, shifted the emphasis from a slavish imitation of European, essentially French, patterns to a renaissance of the Mayan, Aztec, and Olmec heritages of the country. These and other indigenous cultures, so long considered inferior by many of the elite, became by the 1920s a fertile source of serious study and artistic inspiration. José Vasconcelos, then minister of education, stimulated art and literature in immediate and direct ways. He commissioned a group of young artists to paint murals on new and old public buildings. Orozco, Siqueiros, Rivera, and others created paintings representing and interpreting Mexico's rich Indian and

35-3, 35-4 Aaron Douglas, *Aspects of Negro Life*. (New York Public Library)

35-5 Left. Sargent Johnson, *Chester*. (San Francisco Museum of Modern Art, Albert M. Bender Collection)

35-6 Below, Richmond Barthé, *African Dancer* (Collection of the Whitney Museum of American Art, New York)

colonial past and, in allegories, its revolutionary present and future. José Clemente Orozco's *Cortés y La Malinche* (Figure 35-7) illustrates the origin of Mexico's mixed racial heritage by its depiction of Cortés the conqueror and La Malinche, his Indian mistress, as a kind of Mexican Adam and Eve, but one must not fail to note the dead or dying figure at their feet. *Tenochtitlan* (Figure 35-8) depicts Rivera's idealized vision of the Indian past before the arrival of the Spanish invaders. Mural paintings were meant to instruct a public largely illiterate and ignorant of the social and cultural forces of the nation's past. Then, in order to combat this illiteracy more directly, Vasconcelos undertook a campaign to teach everyone to read and write, and, as a logical ancillary, he established a government printing press in order to make available inexpensive editions of world classics and works by Mexico's own writers. In one sense he created a public and a general interest for national writers. Mariano Azuela, one of the first and most important chroniclers of the chaos of the Mexican revolution, saw his masterpiece, *Los de abajo (The Underdogs)*, republished in 1925.

35-7 José Clemente Orozco, *Cortés y La Malinche*. (Museum of Modern Art of Latin America/OAS)

Vasconcelos also encouraged the formation of a national symphony orchestra under the genial leadership of Jorge Chávez, who introduced significant indigenous elements into classical musical forms. Chávez, in such works as *"Sinfonia India"* (*Indian Symphony*) successfully proved that Indian and folk music and instruments constituted a worthy base for serious symphonic music. Eventually the world-famous *Ballet folklórico de México* evolved from his efforts.

Many writers, musicians, artists, and architects from other nations in Latin America and even from Europe came to Mexico to observe, learn, and participate during the 1920s and 1930s. Mexico's success was contagious, and indigenous movements soon flourished throughout Latin America. In the Caribbean and Brazil, the large black populations provided a rich source of vital, genuine innovation. In Brazil, for example, Gilberto Freyre's sociological studies of the significance of the black slave in Brazil's history inspired writers and poets to distill their own direct experiences into literature. In addition to the past as artistic stimulus, there also coexisted the "futurity" of what Latin America could or would become.

Latin America as a land of the future, coupled with the gathering clouds of the Spanish Civil War (1936–1939) and of World War II, brought many Europeans to rediscover America. In 1936 under the influence of Le Corbusier, Lúcio Costa and Oscar Niemeyer designed and built the now historically significant Ministry of Education Building in Rio. The building represented a unique and stunning adaptation to local climatic needs. The great Brazilian painter Cándido Portinari, like his fellow muralists in Mexico, contributed a series of murals for the building's interior depicting the agricultural and mineral wealth of Brazil and glorifying the anonymous men and women who labor in these pursuits. He also created an impressive abstract mural executed in ceramic tiles for the building's exterior. This same painter, again like his Mexican colleagues, evidenced a strong social commitment in both his easel and mural painting. The dramatic and poignant *Os retirantes (The Migrants)* (Fig. 35-9) portrays the plight of the landless, rural poor who flee the drought-plagued Brazilian Northeast in order to seek the chimera of a better life in the burgeoning urban areas.

In a very real sense, the past, present, and future fused together in Latin America. Stone-age Indians coexisted with *bauhaus*, the primitive with the cosmopolitan. Time mixes created magical, surrealistic conditions. The magical, which had been absent from the European tradition since the Middle Ages thrived here. America, in the Hispanic sense of the word, represented a vital, authentic superreality. This startling blend of cultures, along with the ever-present impact of the great artistic experiments of European and North American modernism, gave birth to the movement known as *la vanguardia*, the *avant-garde* or "vanguard." The Spanish term *modernismo* had been used to define an earlier movement more akin to French symbolism. In Spanish America, *la vanguardia* sur-

35-8 Diego Rivera, *Tenochtitlán*. (Museum of Modern Art of Latin America/OAS)

faced in art, music, and literature during the first years of the 1920s. In Portuguese-speaking Brazil, the new modernism boldly manifested itself in *"a semana de arte moderna,"* an important "modern" art exhibit held in São Paulo in April 1922.

In the literature of what we might call the Latin American modernist period, some of which was not "discovered" by the first world until much later, three types of writers flourished: those who sought only inspiration and aesthetic values in indigenous themes expressed in realist-naturalist modes; those who pursued cosmopolitan and universal themes adapting the avant-garde and European "-isms" to their literary re-

quirements; and those who combined the search for the truly autochthonous with avant-garde techniques.

Among the writers of the first group are Mariano Azuela, Ciro Alegria, the Peruvian novelist who dealt with the life of the Andean Indians and the *mestizos*, and José Lins do Rego, who recreated the life of the Brazilian plantation societies of the Northeast. None of these writers rooted in the traditions of the past and the present made stylistic innovations a priority. They wrote simply and straightforwardly of what they had known and lived. Their writings are often infused with a marked moral or social concern for their disinherited compatriots. In the second group of writers and poets,

35-9 Candido Portinari, *Os retirantes*. (Museu de Arte de São Paulo, Brazil/photo by Luiz Hossaka)

an interest or desire to join with the rest of the world is evident. Jorge Luis Borges of Buenos Aires, "vast suburb of the world," Julio Cortázar, also of Argentina, and Clarice Lispector of Brazil are representative. In the third group, Miguel Angel Asturias of Guatemala and Pablo Neruda of Chile (both Nobel laureates) attempted to reconcile indigenous themes with vanguard techniques. They sought to give an American voice to the American reality. We have here reprinted prose and poetry by representatives of each group: Azuela, Borges, Asturias, and Neruda.

Mariano Azuela (1873–1952)—Mexico Chronologically the first to deal with the Mexican revolution, Mariano Azuela's vision is, nevertheless, unrevolutionary. In *Los de abajo* and subsequent novels, he undertook to criticize those who corrupted the goals of the revolution and took advantage of its chaos to enrich themselves or gain power. In this selection from the concluding chapter of Part I, two major, allegorical characters—Luis Cervantes, the urban, middle-class

opportunist, and Alberto Solís, the disaffected revolutionary—meet. While observing the devastated town below, Solis and Cervantes discuss the nature of the revolution and its impact on its people.

MARIANO AZUELA

From *Los de abajo*

(translated by E. Munguía, Jr.)

The firing lessened, then slowly died out. Luis Cervantes, who had been hiding amid a heap of ruins at the fortification on the crest of the hill, made bold to show his face. How he had managed to hang on, he did not know. Nor did he know when Demetrio and his men had disappeared. Suddenly he had found himself alone; then, hurled back by an avalanche of infantry, he fell from his saddle; a host of men trampled over him until he rose from the ground and a man on horseback hoisted him up behind him. After a few moments, horse and riders fell. Left without rifle, revolver, or arms of any kind, Cervantes found himself lost in the midst of white smoke and whistling bullets. A hole amid a debris of crumbling stone offered a refuge of safety.

"Hello, partner!"

"Luis, how are you!"

"The horse threw me. They fell upon me. Then they took my gun away. You see, they thought I was dead. There was nothing I could do!" Luis Cervantes explained apologetically. Then:

"Nobody threw me down," Solís said. "I'm here because I like to play safe."

The irony in Solís' voice brought a blush to Cervantes' cheek.

"By God, that chief of yours is a man!" Solís said. "What daring, what assurance! He left me gasping—and a hell of a lot of other men with more experience than me, too!"

Luis Cervantes vouchsafed no answer.

"What! Weren't you there? Oh, I see! You found a nice place for yourself at the right time. Come here, Luis, I'll explain; let's go behind that rock. From this meadow to the foot of the hill, there's no road save this path below. To the right, the incline is too sharp; you can't do anything there. And it's worse to the left; the ascent is so dangerous that a second's hesitation means a fall down those rocks and a broken neck at the end of it. All right! A number of men from Moya's brigade who went down to the meadow decided to attack the enemy's trenches the first chance they got. The bullets whizzed about us, the battle raged on all sides. For a time they stopped firing, so we thought they were being attacked from behind. We stormed their trenches— look, partner, look at that meadow! It's thick with corpses! Their machine guns did that for us. They mowed us down like wheat; only a handful escaped. Those Goddamned officers went white as a sheet; even though we had reinforcements they were afraid to order a new charge. That was when Demetrio Macías plunged in. Did he wait for orders? Not he! He just shouted:

"'Come on, boys! Let's go for them!'

"'Damn fool!' I thought, 'What the hell does he think he's doing!'

"The officers, surprised, said nothing. Demetrio's horse seemed to wear eagle's claws instead of hoofs, it soared so swiftly over the rocks. 'Come on! Come on!' his men shouted, following him like wild deer, horses and men welded into a mad stampede. Only one young fellow stepped wild and fell headlong into the pit. In a few seconds the others appeared at the top of the hill, storming the trenches and killing the Federals by the thousand. With his rope, Demetrio lassoed the machine guns and carried them off, like a bull herd throwing a steer. Yet his success could not last much longer, for the Federals were far stronger in numbers and could easily have destroyed Demetrio and his men. But we took advantage of their confusion, we rushed upon them and they soon cleared out of their position. That chief of yours is a wonderful soldier!"

Standing on the crest of the hill, they could easily sight one side of the Bufa peak. Its highest crag spread out like the feathered head of a proud Aztec king. The three-hundred-foot slope was literally covered with dead, their hair matted, their clothes clotted with grime and blood. A host of ragged women, vultures of prey, ranged over the tepid bodies of the dead, stripping one man bare, despoiling another, robbing from a third his dearest possessions.

Amid clouds of white rifle smoke and the dense black vapors of flaming buildings, houses with wide doors and windows bolted shone in the sunlight. The streets seemed to be piled upon one another, or wound picturesquely about fantastic corners, or set to scale the hills nearby. Above the graceful cluster of houses, rose the lithe columns of a warehouse and the towers and cupola of the church.

"How beautiful the revolution! Even in its most barbarous aspect it is beautiful," Solís said with deep feeling. Then a vague melancholy seized him, and speaking low:

"A pity what remains to do won't be as beautiful! We must wait a while, until there are no men left to fight on either side, until no sound of shot rings through the air save from the mob as carrion-like it falls upon the booty; we must wait until the psychology of our race, condensed into two words, shines clear and luminous as a drop of water: *Robbery! Murder!* What a colossal failure we would make of it, friend, if we, who offer our enthusiasm and lives to crush a wretched tyrant, became the builders of a monstrous edifice holding one hundred or two hundred thousand monsters of exactly the same sort. People without ideals! A tyrant folk! Vain bloodshed!"

Large groups of Federals pushed up the hill, fleeing from the "high hats." A bullet whistled past them, singing as it sped. After his speech, Alberto Solís stood lost in thought, his arms crossed. Suddenly, he took fright.

"I'll be damned if I like these plaguey mosquitoes!" he said. "Let's get away from here!"

So scornfully Luis Cervantes smiled that Solís sat down on a rock quite calm, bewildered. He smiled. His gaze roved as he watched the spirals of smoke from the rifles, the dust of roofs crumbling from houses as they fell before the artillery. He believed he discerned the symbol of the revolution in these clouds of dust and smoke that climbed upward together, met at the crest of the hill and, a moment after, were lost. . . .

"By heaven, now I see what it all means!"

He sketched a vast gesture, pointing to the station. Locomotives belched huge clouds of black dense smoke rising in columns; the trains were overloaded with fugitives who had barely managed to escape from the captured town.

Suddenly he felt a sharp blow in the stomach. As though his legs were putty, he rolled off the rock. His ears buzzed. . . . Then darkness . . . silence . . . eternity. . . .

QUESTIONS

1. Why and how did the two find themselves on the hilltop?
2. What specific criticisms does Solís make? On what are they based?
3. In what kinds of words and images is the revolution described?
4. What tone pervades these final pages, and how does it apply to the author's message?

Jorge Luis Borges (1899–1986)—Argentina Borges may prove to be this century's most important and influential writer. The dissemination of his works worldwide since the late 1950s and their impact on readers and other writers have virtually canonized him. His name has become adjectivized: "Borgesian," like Proustian or Joycean denotes a content and writing style that is unique but for which modernist precedents such as Kafka were important. Most of his major "fictions" were written and published before 1952, but it was only with his "discovery" in French translation in the late 1950s and early 1960s that he became internationally acclaimed. Although initially an excellent poet and essayist, his reputation rests on a hybrid somewhere between the essay and the short story. Metaphysical ruminations about time, reality, philosophies, religions, and man's place in the universe provide the stimulus and basis for his work. "Death and the Compass," a classic detective mystery first published in the magazine *Sur* in 1942, provides the framework for an examination of the patterns of time, space, and man. As Borges has written in an English commentary to the story, "A triangle is suggested but the solution is really based on a rhombus. . . . The killer and the slain, whose minds work in the same way, may be the same man."

JORGE LUIS BORGES
Death and the Compass
(translated by Donald A. Yates)

Of the many problems which exercised the reckless discernment of Lönnrot, none was so strange—so rigorously strange, shall we say—as the periodic series of bloody events which culminated at the villa of Triste-le-Roy, amid the ceaseless aroma of the eucalypti. It is true that Erik Lönnrot failed to prevent the last murder, but that he foresaw it is indisputable. Neither did he guess the identity of Yarmolinsky's luckless assassin, but he did succeed in divining the secret morphology behind the fiendish series as well as the participation of Red Scharlach, whose other nickname is Scharlach the Dandy. That criminal (as countless others) had sworn on his honor to kill Lönnrot, but the latter could never be intimidated. Lönnrot believed himself a pure reasoner, an Auguste Dupin, but there was something of the adventurer in him, and even a little of the gambler.

The first murder occurred in the Hôtel du Nord—that tall prism which dominates the estuary whose waters are the color of the desert. To that tower (which quite glaringly unites the hateful whiteness of a hospital, the numbered divisibility of a jail, and the general appearance of a bordello) there came on the third day of December the delegate from Podolsk to the Third Talmudic Congress, Doctor Marcel Yarmolinsky, a gray-bearded man with gray eyes. We shall never know whether the Hôtel du Nord pleased him; he accepted it with the ancient resignation which had allowed him to endure three years of war in the Carpathians and three thousand years of oppression and pogroms. He was given a room on Floor R, across from the suite which was occupied—not without splendor—by the Tetrarch of Galilee. Yarmolinsky supped, postponed until the following day an inspection of the unknown city, arranged in a *placard* his many books and few personal possessions, and before midnight extinguished his light. (Thus declared the Tetrarch's chauffeur who slept in the adjoining room.) On the fourth, at 11:03 A.M., the editor of the *Yidische Zaitung* put in a call to him; Doctor Yarmolinsky did not answer. He was found in his room, his face already a little dark, nearly nude beneath a large anachronistic cape. He was lying not far from the door which opened on the hall; a deep knife wound had split his breast. A few hours later, in the same room amid journalists, photographers and policemen, Inspector Treviranus and Lönnrot were calmly discussing the problem.

"No need to look for a three-legged cat here,"

Treviranus was saying as he brandished an imperious cigar. "We all know that the Tetrarch of Galilee owns the finest sapphires in the world. Someone, intending to steal them, must have broken in here by mistake. Yarmolinsky got up; the robber had to kill him. How does it sound to you?"

"Possible, but not interesting," Lönnrot answered. "You'll reply that reality hasn't the least obligation to be interesting. And I'll answer you that reality may avoid that obligation but that hypotheses may not. In the hypothesis that you propose, chance intervenes copiously. Here we have a dead rabbi; I would prefer a purely rabbinical explanation, not the imaginary mischances of an imaginary robber."

Treviranus replied ill-humoredly:

"I'm not interested in rabbinical explanations. I am interested in capturing the man who stabbed this unknown person."

"Not so unknown," corrected Lönnrot. "Here are his complete works." He indicated in the wall-cupboard a row of tall books: a *Vindication of the Cabala*; *An Examination of the Philosophy of Robert Fludd*; a literal translation of the *Sepher Yezirah*; a *Biography of the Baal Shem*; a *History of the Hasidic Sect*; a monograph (in German) on the Tetragrammaton; another, on the divine nomenclature of the Pentateuch. The inspector regarded them with dread, almost with repulsion. Then he began to laugh.

"I'm a poor Christian," he said. "Carry off those musty volumes if you want; I don't have any time to waste on Jewish superstitions."

"Maybe the crime belongs to the history of Jewish superstitions," murmured Lönnrot.

"Like Christianity," the editor of the *Yidische Zaitung* ventured to add. He was myopic, an atheist and very shy.

No one answered him. One of the agents had found in the small typewriter a piece of paper on which was written the following unfinished sentence:

The first letter of the Name has been uttered

Lönnot abstained from smiling. Suddenly become a bibliophile or Hebraist, he ordered a package made of the dead man's books and carried them off to his apartment. Indifferent to the police investigation, he dedicated himself to studying them. One large octavo volume revealed to him the teachings of Israel Baal Shem Tobh, founder of the sect of the Pious; another, the virtues and terrors of the Tetragrammaton, which is the unutterable name of God; another, the thesis that God has a secret name, in which is epitomized (as in the crystal sphere which the Persians ascribe to Alexander of Macedonia) his ninth attribute, eternity—that is to say, the immediate knowledge of all things that will be, which are and which have been in the universe. Tradition numbers ninety-nine names of God; the Hebraists attribute that imperfect number to magical fear of even numbers; the Hasidim reason that that hiatus indicates a hundredth name—the Absolute Name.

From this erudition Lönnrot was distracted, a few days later, by the appearance of the editor of the *Yidische Zaitung*. The latter wanted to talk about the murder; Lönnrot preferred to discuss the diverse names of God; the journalist declared, in three columns, that the investigator, Erik Lönnrot, had dedicated himself to studying the names of God in order to come across the name of the murderer. Lönnrot, accustomed to the simplifications of journalism, did not become indignant. One of those enterprising shopkeepers who have discovered that any given man is resigned to buying any given book published a popular edition of the *History of the Hasidic Sect*.

The second murder occurred on the evening of the third of January, in the most deserted and empty corner of the capital's western suburbs. Towards dawn, one of the gendarmes who patrol those solitudes on horseback saw a man in a poncho, lying prone in the shadow of an old paint shop. The harsh features seemed to be masked in blood; a deep knife wound had split his breast. On the wall, across the yellow and red diamonds, were some words written in chalk. The gendarme spelled them out . . . That afternoon, Treviranus and Lönnrot headed for the remote scene of the crime. To the left and right of the automobile the city disintegrated; the firmament grew and houses were of less importance than a brick kiln or a polar tree. They arrived at their miserable destination: an alley's end, with rose-colored walls which somehow seemed to reflect the extravagant sunset. The dead man had already been identified. He was Daniel Simon Azevedo, an individual of some fame in the old northern suburbs, who had risen from wagon driver to political tough, then degenerated to a thief and even an informer. (The singular style of his death seemed appropriate to them: Azevedo was the last representative of a generation of bandits who knew how to manipulate a dagger, but not a revolver.) The words in chalk were the following:

The second letter of the Name has been uttered

The third murder occurred on the night of the third of February. A little before one o'clock, the telephone in Inspector Treviranus' office rang. In avid secretiveness, a man with a guttural voice spoke; he said his name was Ginzberg (or Ginsburg) and that he was prepared to communicate, for reasonable remuneration, the events surrounding the two sacrifices of Azevedo and Yarmolinsky. A discordant sound of whistles and horns drowned out the informer's voice. Then, the connection was broken off. Without yet rejecting the possibility of a hoax (after all, it was carnival time), Treviranus found out that he had been called from the Liverpool House, a tavern on the rue de Toulon, that dingy street where side by side exist the cosmorama and the coffee shop, the bawdy house and the bible sellers. Treviranus spoke with the owner. The latter (Black Finnegan, an old Irish criminal who was immersed in, almost overcome by, respectability) told him that the last person to use the phone was a lodger, a certain Gryphius, who had just left with some friends. Treviranus went immediately to Liverpool House. The owner related the following. Eight days ago Gryphius had rented a room above the tavern. He was a sharp-featured man with a nebulous gray beard, and was shabbily dressed in black; Finnegan (who used the room for a purpose which Treviranus guessed) demanded a rent which was undoubtedly excessive; Gryphius paid the stipulated sum without hesitation. He almost never went out; he dined and lunched in his room; his face was scarcely known in the bar. On the night in question, he came downstairs to make a phone call from Finnegan's office. A closed cab stopped in front of the tavern. The driver didn't move from his seat; several patrons recalled that he was wearing a bear's mask. Two harlequins got out of the cab; they were of short stature and no one failed to observe that they were very drunk. With a tooting of horns, they burst into Finnegan's office; they embraced Gryphius,

who appeared to recognize them but responded coldly; they exchanged a few words in Yiddish—he in a low, guttural voice, they in high-pitched, false voices—and then went up to the room. Within a quarter hour the three descended, very happy. Gryphius, staggering, seemed as drunk as the others. He walked—tall and dizzy—in the middle, between the masked harlequins. (One of the women at the bar remembered the yellow, red and green diamonds.) Twice he stumbled; twice he was caught and held by the harlequins. Moving off toward the inner harbor which enclosed a rectangular body of water, the three got into a cab and disappeared. From the footboard of the cab, the last of the harlequins scrawled an obscene figure and a sentence on one of the slates of the pier shed.

Treviranus saw the sentence. It was virtually predictable. It said:

The last of the letters of the Name has been uttered

Afterwards, he examined the small room of Gryphius-Ginzberg. On the floor there was a brusque star of blood, in the corners, traces of cigarettes of a Hungarian brand; in a cabinet, a book in Latin—the *Philologus Hebraeo-Graecus* (1739) of Leusden—with several manuscript notes. Treviranus looked it over with indignation and had Lönnrot located. The latter, without removing his hat, began to read while the inspector was interrogating the contradictory witnesses to the possible kidnapping. At four o'clock they left. Out on the twisted rue de Toulon, as they were treading on the dead serpentines of the dawn, Treviranus said:

"And what if all this business tonight were just a mock rehearsal?"

Erik Lönnrot smiled and, with all gravity, read a passage (which was underlined) from the thirty-third dissertation of the *Philologus: Dies Judacorum incipit ad solis occasu usque ad solis occasum diei sequentis.*

"This means," he added, "'The Hebrew day begins at sundown and lasts until the following sundown.'"

The inspector attempted an irony.

"Is that fact the most valuable one you've come across tonight?"

"No. Even more valuable was a word that Ginzberg used."

The afternoon papers did not overlook the periodic

disappearances. *La Cruz de la Espada* contrasted them with the admirable discipline and order of the last Hermetical Congress; Ernst Palast, in *El Mártir*, criticized "the intolerable delays in this clandestine and frugal pogrom, which has taken three months to murder three Jews"; the *Yidische Zaitung* rejected the horrible hypothesis of an anti-Semitic plot, "even though many penetrating intellects admit no other solution to the triple mystery"; the most illustrious gunman of the south, Dandy Red Scharlach, swore that in his district similar crimes could never occur, and he accused Inspector Franz Treviranus of culpable negligence.

On the night of March first, the inspector received an impressive-looking sealed envelope. He opened it; the envelope contained a letter signed "Baruch Spinoza"and a detailed plan of the city, obviously torn from a Baedeker. The letter prophesied that on the third of March there would not be a fourth murder, since the paint shop in the west, the tavern on the rue de Toulon and the Hôtel du Nord were "the perfect vertices of a mystic equilateral triangle"; the map demonstrated in red ink the regularity of the triangle. Treviranus read the *more geometrico* argument with resignation, and sent the letter and the map to Lönnrot—who, unquestionably, was deserving of such madnesses.

Erik Lönnrot studied them. The three locations were in fact equidistant. Symmetry in time (the third of December, the third of January, the third of February); symmetry in space as well . . . Suddenly, he felt as if he were on the point of solving the mystery. A set of calipers and a compass completed his quick intuition. He smiled, pronounced the word Tetragrammaton (of recent acquisition) and phoned the inspector. He said:

"Thank you for the equilateral triangle you sent me last night. It has enabled me to solve the problem. This Friday the criminals will be in jail, we may rest assured."

"Then they're not planning a fourth murder?"

"Precisely because they *are* planning a fourth murder we can rest assured."

Lönnrot hung up. One hour later he was traveling on one of the Southern Railway's trains, in the direction of the abandoned villa of Triste-le-Roy. To the south of the city of our story, flows a blind little river of muddy water, defamed by refuse and garbage. On the far side is an industrial suburb where, under the protection of a political boss from Barcelona, gunmen thrive. Lönnrot smiled at the thought that the most celebrated gunman of all—Red Scharlach—would have given a great deal to know of his clandestine visit. Azevedo had been an associate of Scharlach; Lönnrot considered the remote possibility that the fourth victim might be Scharlach himself. Then he rejected the idea . . . He had very nearly deciphered the problem; mere circumstances, reality (names, prison records, faces, judicial and penal proceedings) hardly interested him now. He wanted to travel a bit, he wanted to rest from three months of sedentary investigation. He reflected that the explanation of the murders was in an anonymous triangle and a dusty Greek word. The mystery appeared almost crystalline to him now; he was mortified to have dedicated a hundred days to it.

The train stopped at a silent loading station. Lönnrot got off. It was one of those deserted afternoons that seem like dawns. The air of the turbid, puddled plain was damp and cold. Lönnrot began walking along the countryside. He saw dogs, he saw a car on a siding, he saw the horizon, he saw a silver-colored horse drinking the crapulous water of a puddle. It was growing dark when he saw the rectangular belvedere of the villa of Triste-le-Roy, almost as tall as the black eucalypti which surrounded it. He thought that scarcely one dawning and one nightfall (an ancient splendor in the east and another in the west) separated him from the moment long desired by the seekers of the Name.

A rusty wrought-iron fence defined the irregular perimeter of the villa. The main gate was closed. Lönnrot, without much hope of getting in, circled the area. Once again before the insurmountable gate, he placed his hand between the bars almost mechanically and encountered the bolt. The creaking of the iron surprised him. With a laborious passivity the whole gate swung back.

Lönnrot advanced among the eucalypti treading on confused generations of rigid, broken leaves. Viewed from anear, the house of the villa of Triste-le-Roy abounded in pointless symmetries and in maniacal repetitions: to one Diana in a murky niche corresponded a second Diana in another niche; one balcony was reflected in another balcony; double stairways led to double balustrades. A two-faced Hermes projected a monstrous shadow. Lönnrot circled the house as he had the villa. He examined everything; beneath the level of the terrace he saw a narrow Venetian blind.

He pushed it; a few marble steps descended to a vault. Lönnrot, who had now perceived the architect's preferences, guessed that at the opposite wall there would be another stairway. He found it, ascended, raised his hands and opened the trap door.

A brilliant light led him to a window. He opened it: a yellow, rounded moon defined two silent fountains in the melancholy garden. Lönnrot explored the house. Through anterooms and galleries he passed to duplicate patios, and time after time to the same patio. He ascended the dusty stairs to circular antechambers; he was multiplied infinitely in opposing mirrors; he grew tired of opening or half-opening windows which revealed outside the same desolate garden from various heights and various angles; inside, only pieces of furniture wrapped in yellow dust sheets and chandeliers bound up in tarlatan. A bedroom detained him; in that bedroom, one single flower in a porcelain vase; at the first touch the ancient petals fell apart. On the second floor, on the top floor, the house seemed infinite and expanding. *The house is not this large*, he thought. *Other things are making it seem larger: the dim light, the symmetry, the mirrors, so many years, my unfamiliarity, the loneliness.*

By way of a spiral staircase he arrived at the oriel. The early evening moon shone through the diamonds of the window; they were yellow, red and green. An astonishing, dizzying recollection struck him.

Two men of short stature, robust and ferocious, threw themselves on him and disarmed him; another, very tall, saluted him gravely and said:

"You are very kind. You have saved us a night and a day."

It was Red Scharlach. The men handcuffed Lönnrot. The latter at length recovered his voice.

"Scharlach, are you looking for the Secret Name?"

Scharlach remained standing, indifferent. He had not participated in the brief struggle, and he scarcely extended his hand to receive Lönnrot's revolver. He spoke; Lönnrot noted in his voice a fatigued triumph, a hatred the size of the universe, a sadness not less than that hatred.

"No," said Scharlach. "I am seeking something more ephemeral and perishable, I am seeking Erik Lönnrot. Three years ago, in a gambling house on the rue de Toulon, you arrested my brother and had him sent to jail. My men slipped me away in a coupé from the gun battle with a policeman's bullet in my stomach. Nine days and nine nights I lay in agony in this desolate, symmetrical villa; fever was demolishing me, and the odious two-faced Janus who watches the twilights and the dawns lent horror to my dreams and to my waking. I came to abominate my body, I came to sense that two eyes, two hands, two lungs are as monstrous as two faces. An Irishman tried to convert me to the faith of Jesus; he repeated to me the phrase of the *goyim*: All roads lead to Rome. At night my delirium nurtured itself on that metaphor; I felt that the world was a labyrinth, from which it was impossible to flee, for all roads, though they pretend to lead to the north or south, actually lead to Rome, which was also the quadrilateral jail where my brother was dying and the villa of Triste-le-Roy. On those nights I swore by the God who sees with two faces and by all the gods of fever and of the mirrors to weave a labyrinth around the man who had imprisoned my brother. I have woven it and it is firm: the ingredients are a dead heresiologist, a compass, an eighteenth-century sect, a Greek word, a dagger, the diamonds of a paint shop.

"The first term of the sequence was given to me by chance. I had planned with a few colleagues—among them Daniel Azevedo—the robbery of the Tetrarch's sapphires. Azevedo betrayed us: he got drunk with the money that we had advanced him and he undertook the job a day early. He got lost in the vastness of the hotel; around two in the morning he stumbled into Yarmolinsky's room. The latter, harassed by insomnia, had started to write. He was working on some notes, apparently, for an article on the Name of God; he had already written the words: *The first letter of the Name has been uttered.* Azevedo warned him to be silent; Yarmolinsky reached out his hand for the bell which would awaken the hotel's forces; Azevedo countered with a single stab in the chest. It was almost a reflex action; half a century of violence had taught him that the easiest and surest thing is to kill . . . Ten days later I learned through the *Yidische Zaitung* that you were seeking in Yarmolinsky's writings the key to his death. I read the *History of the Hasidic Sect*; I learned that the reverent fear of uttering the Name of God had given rise to the doctrine that that Name is all powerful and recondite. I discovered that some Hasidim, in search of that secret Name, had gone so far as to perform human sacrifices . . . I knew that you would make the conjecture that the Hasidim had sacrificed the rabbi; I set myself the task of justifying that conjecture.

"Marcel Yarmolinsky died on the night of December third; for the second 'sacrifice' I selected the night of January third. He died in the north; for the second 'sacrifice' a place in the west was suitable. Daniel Azevedo was the necessary victim. He deserved death; he was impulsive, a traitor; his apprehension could destroy the entire plan. One of us stabbed him; in order to link his corpse to the other one I wrote on the paint shop diamonds: *The second letter of the Name has been uttered.*

"The third murder was produced on the third of February. It was, as Treviranus guessed, a mere sham. I am Gryphius-Ginzberg-Ginsburg; I endured an interminable week (supplemented by a tenuous fake beard) in the perverse cubicle on the rue de Toulon, until my friends abducted me. From the footboard of the cab, one of them wrote on a post: *The last of the letters of the Name has been uttered.* That sentence revealed that the series of murders was *triple.* Thus the public understood it; I, nevertheless, interspersed repeated signs that would allow you, Erik Lönnrot, the reasoner, to understand that the series was quadruple. A portent in the north, others in the east and west, demand a fourth portent in the south; the Tetragrammaton—the name of God, JHVH—is made up of *four* letters; the harlequins and the paint shop sign suggested *four* points. In the manual of Leusden I underlined a certain passage: that passage manifests that Hebrews compute the day from sunset to sunset; that passage makes known that the deaths occurred on the *fourth* of each month. I sent the equilateral triangle to Treviranus. I foresaw that you would add the missing point. The point which would form a perfect rhomb, the point which fixes in advance where a punctual death awaits you. I have premeditated everything, Erik Lönnrot, in order to attract you to the solitudes of Triste-le-Roy."

Lönnrot avoided Scharlach's eyes. He looked at the trees and the sky subdivided into diamonds of turbid yellow, green and red. He felt faintly cold, and he felt, too, an impersonal—almost anonymous—sadness. It was already night; from the dusty garden came the futile cry of a bird. For the last time, Lönnrot considered the problem of the symmetrical and periodic deaths.

"In your labyrinth there are three lines too many," he said at last. "I know of one Greek labyrinth which is a single straight line. Along that line so many philosophers have lost themselves that a mere detective might well do so, too. Scharlach, when in some other incarnation you hunt me, pretend to commit (or do commit) a crime at A, then a second crime at B, eight kilometers from A, then a third crime at C, four kilometers from A and B, half-way between the two. Wait for me afterwards at D, two kilometers from A and C, again half-way between both. Kill me at D, as you are now going to kill me at Triste-le-Roy."

"The next time I kill you," replied Scharlach, "I promise you that labyrinth, consisting of a single line which is invisible and unceasing."

He moved back a few steps. Then, very carefully, he fired.

QUESTIONS

1. In the text, there is an almost constant juxtaposition of things associated with the numbers three and four. What are these, and how do they pertain to the story?
2. Borges likes to play with words, preferring the denotation, or the strictly literal meaning of a word, to the connotation, or the affective and sometimes equivocal, ambiguous meaning of the word. For example, he describes the first murder scene as occurring in "that tall prism," the Hôtel du Nord. What is the precise definition of the word *prism*, and how does this fit into the story?
3. What kinds of time are evident in the story?
4. The characters' names are important to the structure of the story, as well as to the erasure of their individuality. What associations exist among red, Scharlach, Lönnrot, and Erik? Are there any others?

5. At the conclusion of the story, Lönnrot ironically proposes a single-line labyrinth for the final murder in some future cycle of time. This "labyrinth" is based on Zeno's paradox (the Eleatic paradoxes). What is this paradox, and how does it apply to "Death and the Compass"?

Miguel Angel Asturias (1899–1974)—Guatemala

In 1967 Asturias was awarded the Nobel Prize in Literature. For most of his adult life, he had fought the repressive dictatorships of his country, distilling his experiences into such masterworks as *El Señor Presidente* and *Week-end-en Guatemala*. The selection here is from *Leyendas de Guatemala*, written while a student in Paris and published in 1930. These "legends," a blend of dream, story, myth, and poetry, represented his first efforts at recreating the rich Maya-Quiché[1] world he knew so profoundly. In "Tatuana's Tale," a magical, mythical world is portrayed.

MIGUEL ÁNGEL ASTURIAS

Tatuana's Tale

(translated by Patricia Emigh and Frank MacShane)

Father Almond Tree, with his pale pink beard, was one of the priests who were so richly dressed that the white men touched them to see if they were made of gold. He knew the secret of medicinal plants, the language of the gods that spoke through translucent obsidian, and he could read the hieroglyphics of the stars.

One day he appeared in the forest, without being planted, as though brought there by spirits. He was so tall he prodded the clouds, he measured the years by the moons he saw, and was already old when he came from the Garden of Tulan.

On the full moon of Owl-Fish (one of the twenty months of the four-hundred-day year), Father Almond Tree divided his soul among the four roads. These led to the four quarters of the sky: the black quarter, the Sorcerer Night; the green quarter, Spring Storm; the red quarter, Tropical Ecstasy; the white quarter, Promise of New Lands.

---

[1] The Quiché Maya are an ancient Mayan people who originated in Guatemala and eventually expanded into Mexico.

"O Road! Little Road!" said a dove to White Road, but White Road did not listen. The dove wanted Father Almond Tree's soul so that it would cure its dreams. Doves and children both suffer from dreams.

"O Road! Little Road!" said a heart to Red Road, but Red Road did not listen. The heart wanted to distract Red Road so it would forget Father Almond Tree's soul. Hearts, like thieves, don't return what others leave behind.

"O Road! Little Road!" said a vine trellis to Green Road, but Green Road did not listen. It wanted the Father's soul to get back some of the leaves and shade it had squandered.

How many moons have the roads been traveling?'

The fastest, Black Road, whom no one spoke to along the way, entered the city, crossed the plaza and went to the merchants' quarter, where it gave Father Almond Tree's soul to the Merchant of Priceless Jewels in exchange for a little rest.

It was the hour of white cats. They prowled back and forth through the streets. Wonder of rosebushes! The clouds looked like laundry strung across the sky.

When Father Almond Tree found out what Black Road had done, he once again took on human form, shedding his tree-like shape in a small stream that appeared like an almond blossom beneath the crimson moon. Then he left for the city.

He reached the valley after a day's travel, just at evening time when the flocks are driven home. The shepherds were dumbfounded by this man in a green cloak and pale pink beard. They thought he was an apparition and answered his questions in monosyllables.

Once in the city, he made his way to the western part of town. Men and women were standing around the public fountains. The water made a kissing sound as it filled their pitchers. Following the shadows to the merchants' quarter, he found that part of his soul Black Road had sold. The Merchant of Priceless Jewels kept it in a crystal box with gold locks. He went up to the Merchant, who was smoking in a corner, and offered him two thousand pounds of pearls for the piece of soul.

The Merchant smiled at the Father's absurd suggestion. Two thousand pounds of pearls? No, his jewels were priceless.

Father Almond Tree increased his offer. He would

give him emeralds, big as kernels of corn, fifty acres of them, enough to make a lake.

The Merchant smiled again. A lake of emeralds? No, his jewels were priceless.

He would give him amulets, deer's eyes that bring rain, feathers to keep storms away, marijuana to mix with his tobacco.

The Merchant refused.

He would give him enough precious stones to build a fairy-tale palace in the middle of the emerald lake!

The Merchant still refused. His jewels were priceless—why go on talking about it? Besides, he planned to exchange this piece of soul for the most beautiful slave in the slave market.

It was useless for Father Almond Tree to keep on making offers and show how much he wanted to get his soul back. Merchants have no hearts.

A thread of tobacco smoke separated reality from dream, black cats from white cats, the Merchant from his strange customer. As he left, Father Almond Tree banged his sandals against the doorway to rid himself of the cursed dust of the house.

After a year of four hundred days, the Merchant was returning across the mountains with the slave he had bought with Father Almond Tree's soul. He was accompanied by a flower bird who turned honey into hyacinths, and by a retinue of thirty servants on horseback.

The slave was naked. Her long black hair, wrapped in a single braid like a snake, fell across her breasts and down to her legs. The Merchant was dressed in gold and his shoulders were covered with a cape woven from goat hair. His thirty servants on horseback stretched out behind like figures in a dream.

"You've no idea," said the Merchant to the slave, reining in his horse alongside hers, "what your life will be like in the city! Your house will be a palace, and all my servants will be at your call, including me, if you like." His face was half lit by the sun. "There," he continued, "everything will be yours. Do you know I refused a lake of emeralds for the piece of soul I exchanged for you? We'll lie all day in a hammock and have nothing to do but listen to a wise old woman tell stories. She knows my fate and says that it rests in a gigantic hand. She'll tell your fortune as well, if you ask her."

The slave turned to look at the countryside. It was a landscape of muted blues, growing dimmer in the distance. The trees on either side formed so fanciful a design it might have appeared on a woman's shawl. The sky was calm, and the birds seemed to be flying asleep, winglessly. In the granite silence, the panting of the horses as they went uphill sounded human.

Suddenly, huge solitary raindrops began to spatter on the road. On the slopes below, shepherds shouted as they gathered their frightened flocks. The horses stepped up their pace to find shelter, but there wasn't enough time. The wind rose, lashing the clouds, and ripping through the forest until it reached the valley, which vanished from sight under blankets of mist, while the first lightning bolts lit up the countryside like the flashes of a mad photographer.

As the horses stampeded, fleeing in fear, reins broken, legs flying, manes tangled in the wind and ears pressed back, the Merchant's horse stumbled and threw the man to the foot of a tree which at that instant, split by lightning, wrapped its roots about him like a hand snatching up a stone and hurled him into the ravine.

Meanwhile Father Almond Tree, who had remained in the city, wandered the streets like a madman, frightening children, going through garbage, talking to donkeys, oxen and stray dogs, which, like men, are all sad-eyed animals.

"How many moons have the roads been traveling?" he asked from door to door, but the people were dumfounded by this man in a green cloak and pale pink beard, and they slammed them shut without answering as though they'd seen a specter.

At length Father Almond Tree stopped at the door of the Merchant of Priceless Jewels and spoke to the slave, who alone had survived the storm.

"How many moons have the roads been traveling?"

The answer which began to form froze on her lips. Father Almond Tree was silent. It was the full moon of Owl-Fish. In silence their eyes caressed each other's faces like two lovers who have met after a long separation.

They were interrupted by raucous shouts. They were arrested in the name of God and the King, he as a warlock and she as his accomplice. Surrounded by crosses and swords, they were taken to prison, Father Almond

Tree with his pale pink beard and green cloak, the slave displaying flesh so firm it seemed to be made of gold.

Seven months later, they were condemned to be burned alive in the Plaza Mayor. On the eve of the execution, Father Almond Tree tattooed a little boat on the slave's arm with his fingernail.

"Tatuana, by means of this tattoo," he said, "you will be able to flee whenever you are in danger. I want you to be as free as my spirit. Trace this little boat on a wall, on the ground, in the air, wherever you wish. Then close your eyes, climb aboard and go . . .

"Go, my spirit is stronger than a clay idol.

"My spirit is sweeter than the honey gathered by bees sipping from the honeysuckle.

"As my spirit, you'll become invisible."

At once, Tatuana did what Father Almond Tree said: she drew a little boat, closed her eyes, and, as she got in, the boat began to move. So she escaped from prison and death.

On the following morning, day of the execution, the guards found in the cell only a withered tree, whose few almond blossoms still retained their pale pink color.

QUESTIONS

1. When do you think "Tatuana's Tale" occurs? On what do you base your answer?
2. How do Mayan elements manifest themselves, and for what purpose?
3. What meanings or interpretations does the legend have?
4. Do you see any points of comparison between this retelling of a Mayan legend and the African legends in Volume I?

Pablo Neruda (1904–1973)—Chile   The poetry of Neruda, another Nobel laureate, evolved from symbolism into some of the richest, most innovative free verse and imagery of this century. Man, and those things touched, made, or affecting him, are his subjects. Neruda is the poet of *cosalismo* ("thing-ism"), which transforms some of the most humble plants, minerals, and animals into subjects of beautiful poems. His poetry ranges from the profound, hermetic, and complex works of *Residencia en la tierra I, II* (Res-

idence on Earth, Parts I and II) and *Canto general* (General Song), in which appears his renowned "Heights of Macchu Picchu", to the simple and touching odes to a variety of subjects. The selection here is from *Navegaciones y regresos* (Voyages and Homecomings), first published in 1959, and is representative of his *cosalismo* and humanism.

PABLO NERUDA

Ode to Broken Things
(translated by Malcolm J. Parr)

Things keep breaking
in the home
as though impelled
by an unseen and willful brute:
not my hands,
not yours,
not the girls
with the hard nails
and starry feet:
it wasn't anything or anyone,
it wasn't the wind,
it wasn't the orange noon,
or the earth's shadows,
it wasn't a nose, an elbow,
a curving hip,
an ankle
or the air:
the plate split, the lamp slipped
and all the flowerpots toppled
one by one,
in the middle of October,
crimson-heaped,
weighed down with violets,
and one other pot, empty,
spinning, spinning, spinning,
through the winter
until all that was left
was powder,
a shattered memory, a glowing dust.

And the clock
from which the sound
was
our life's voice,
the hidden
thread
of the weeks,
joining
so many hours
one by one
to honey and silence,
to so many births and
even that clock
fell and among
the broken pieces of gl.
its delicate blue entrail
throbbed
and its long heart
spun out.

Life goes on grinding
glasses, wearing out clothes,
destroying,
pulverizing
patterns,
and what time lets last is as it were
an island or a ship at sea,
passing,
locked in by brittle dangers,
and the menaces of relentless waters.

Let's put everything at once,
clocks, plates, wineglasses carved in ice,
in one sack and carry
our treasures down to the sea:
and all our possessions
will be lost

smashing and roaring
like a river bursting its banks;
and may the sea
in its toiling tides
bring back for us
all those useless things
that nobody breaks
but were broken nevertheless.

QUESTIONS

1. What is an "ode"? Why does Neruda employ this form?
2. What structural and lexical devices are used to make this poetry?
3. What is the ode's theme, and how is it developed?

THE EARLY TWENTIETH CENTURY: DISCONTINUITIES AND NEW TRADITIONS

Western Cultural Doubt There is no doubt that the early twentieth century marked a deep cleft in the Western humanistic tradition. The expectations for an increasingly civilized world based largely on immense accomplishments in the material realm were dashed by World War I. Not only did the war starkly reveal the well of irrationality and violence present in human nature, but technological progress allowed these forces to express themselves with lethal effect. For many thinkers, artists, and writers, the Greco-Roman reliance on reason, the Judeo-Christian hope in God, and, more immediately, the nineteenth century's optimistic materialism no longer seemed valid cultural centers. The titles of two important early twentieth-century books sum up the state of affairs: Freud's *Civilization and Its Discontents* and Spengler's *The Decline of the West.*

The peace treaty of 1919 finally brought hostilities to a halt, but for the next two decades, Western culture was haunted by the fear of another war. The Great Depression of the early 1930s further exacerbated the situation. For many, Marxism offered an attractive alternative to traditional capitalism. That the next war would be one of classes rather than nations became a real possibility. In Germany and Italy, leaders arose—embodiments of an irrational nationalism—who promised to squelch class conflict by violent measures. The Western democracies felt trapped between the extremism of both left and right. Given such instability, it is surprising that the next war did not finally erupt until 1939.

Influence of Africa The weariness with their own cultural roots led artists of the early twentieth century to look elsewhere for inspiration. It is at this point that the African cultural root really makes its entry into the Western humanities. European and American painters and sculptors experimenting with abstraction found that African artists, who had long been creating in this style, had much to teach them. African writers who had been educated in the Western tradition turned toward their native cultures for fresh subject matter and stylistic innovation. Dancers and choreographers saw in the African union of dance with religious rites and other forms of cultural expression an art form more meaningful than the stylized, artificial ballet. African rhythms and tonalities entered into Western music in the form of jazz and profoundly altered its course. Finally, Afro-American writers, thinkers, artists, musicians, and dancers began to turn back toward their African heritage, seeking ways of combining it with their American experience and in the process creating an important new voice on the world cultural scene.

Influence and Emergence of Other Cultures Africa was not the only culture to which discontented Westerners turned. Some were attracted to what they viewed as the spirituality of the orient as opposed to the materialism of the occident. Writers like Ezra Pound found the brilliant imagery in Chinese and Japanese poetry a source for experimentation. Other artists and writers turned to the arts of southeast Asia, Polynesia, or to whatever seemed primitive or at least not overcivilized. Igor Stravinsky found in the rites of his native Russia energizing sources for creating new musical sounds. Choreographers and dancers like Nijinsky and Duncan tried to express a new "primitive" wholeness in their dance. Frank Lloyd Wright looked even further away toward the aboriginal cave for a basis for his innovations in architecture. In Latin America, artists and intellectuals looked to the heritage of pre-

Columbian as well as European civilizations, fusing cultural roots in new forms and creations. Writers such as Borges would rise to world prominence as inheritors of European modernism.

Break-Up in the Arts   The sense of break with tradition and contact with new traditions gave the artist in this period an exhilarating sense of freedom; so did new discoveries in the sciences, such as Freud's unconscious and Einstein's relativity. The name *modernism* covers a variety of experimental movements in the arts, only a few of which we have mentioned in this chapter. The breaking apart of traditional forms—of traditional ways of perceiving space, time, and reality—and the synthesizing of elements in new ways are perhaps the essential characteristics of modernism. In literature this included Joyce's abandonment of syntax, mixture of time frames, and portrayal of the unconscious; E. E. Cummings' free colloquial poetry; and Franz Kafka's stark, fantastic realism. Painting shows Picasso's experiments with abstractions of the human figure and Kandinsky's total abandonment of subject matter for the portrayal of an inner world of form and color. The music of Stravinsky demonstrates a reorganization of the elements of rhythm, harmony, and melody. Dance does away with the "classical" steps of ballet to create new forms. The new arts of photography and film reorganize traditional ways of viewing time and space.

Feminism   The new sense of freedom and of break with tradition, particularly after the first World War, affected customs, manners, and ways of life, as well as the arts. One of the most important legacies of this new vision was the growing concern over equality for women, culminating in the women's rights and suffragette movements and, ultimately, the vote, in England and the United States. Virginia Woolf's *A Room of One's Own* is one of the most eloquent statements on the needs and rights of the modern creative women. Contemporary feminism owes a great deal to its precursors in the modernist era.

Connections with Cultural Roots   We should perhaps stress at this point that, although modernism makes a radical break with tradition, it does not make a total break. Its innovations would not be possible without a cultural tradition to react against and, in some sense, to continue. Joyce's radically experimental novel is based on one of the oldest narratives in the Greco-Roman tradition, Homer's *Odyssey*. Distortion in art for expression of the unseen was a characteristic of medieval art and part of the inheritance of the modernists. Modern poetry, modern cinema, and modern dance are incomprehensible without the prior forms of lyric, drama, and ballet. Modernism, in the form of ongoing experimentation, is very much still with us. In the late twentieth century, we will witness a proliferation of cultural plurality.

PART NINE

Cultural Plurality: The Middle and Late Twentieth Century

36

Absurdity and Alienation: The Second World War and the Postwar Period

~

World War II World War II, beginning in 1939, only twenty years after the Treaty of Versailles, seemed like a continuation of World War I. Great Britain and France, two of the victors in World War I, wearily faced the prospect of having to do battle again with their old enemy Germany, now allied with Italy. Encouraged by fascist successes in the Spanish Civil War, Germany and Italy were eager to demonstrate their military prowess on a large scale. Unprepared for war, the two democracies had tried appeasement the year before at Munich. In September 1938 they delivered up the German-speaking part of Czechoslovakia to Hitler, who claimed to be contented with this settlement. In March 1939, however, he incorporated most of what was left of Czechoslovakia into Germany. Now France and England would not back down, and, when in September Hitler invaded Poland, they went to war.

World War II was to last four years and involve fighting on every continent of the globe. Having already gobbled up half of China, Japan joined the Axis in 1941 in the hope of being able to annex some of the colonial possessions of the Western democracies in Asia. Both Russia and the United States entered the war in 1941 on the side of Great Britain; by this time France was under German domination. In the early stages of the war the Axis powers had the initiative, but by late 1942 the Allies were slowly moving to the offensive. The Allies gradually took over the whole of North Africa from the Italians and Germans and in the spring of 1943 invaded Sicily. At the same time the Russians, despite a terrible loss of life, outlasted the Germans at Stalingrad, their farthest point of penetration in Russia, and began pushing the Germans back toward the west. In the Pacific the Americans initiated their campaign of island hopping, defeating one Japanese garrison after the other until by early 1945 they were within three hundred miles of Japan itself. In 1944, while the Russians continued their advance all along the eastern front, the Allied armies invaded France; by the spring of 1945 Germany was invaded from both east and west. On May 8, 1945, Germany surrendered unconditionally. The dropping of the atomic bomb on two Japanese cities in August terrified the Japanese into surrendering officially on September 2, 1945.

In contrast with World War I civilians suffered more casualties than did the military. The systematic extermination of populations by the Germans and the intensive bombing of cities by both sides explain the large losses. The introduction of the atomic bomb at the very end of the war dramatically illustrated what would occur in the event of a third world war. The apprehension was only increased by the introduction of an arms race in nuclear weapons, which began with the Soviet development of its own atomic bomb in 1946.

The Postwar Period

After the Second World War, the center of power moved out of Western Europe, and the United States became potentially the most powerful country in the world. However, the power configuration was a bipolar one, with the United States and the Soviet Union attempting to attract the other powers into their respective spheres of influence. The dissolution of the colonial empires of the European powers, either with or without the latter's consent, produced scores of new nations and furnished a fertile field for propaganda activities on both sides.

The hope of the Allies during the war had been for an international peace-keeping institution after the war; in 1945 at San Francisco the United Nations was created for that purpose. Like the League of Nations, however, the United Nations was crippled from the start by the reluctance of nations to give up any of their sovereignty. Although it provided a means for direct communication between the world powers, the organization could not prevent the reinstitution of hostile alliance systems. The United States sought its security in a number of European and Asian alliances with democratic and right-wing governments, whereas the Soviet Union fortified its position by a tight alliance with communist satellite countries in Eastern Europe and active support for sympathetic political factions elsewhere. The communist conquest of China in 1949 seemed especially alarming to the West, and in the United States itself a fear of subversion inspired a series of investigations to ferret out spies and communist sympathizers. By the early 1950s, moreover, the United States was waging war in Korea, endeavoring to stop the spread of communism in that area. Many feared that the hostility between the two superpowers, known as the Cold War, would soon reach a point of open conflict.

It did not. The closest the United States and the Soviet Union came to direct confrontation in the years immediately following the termination of the Korean War in 1953 came in 1962. In that year President Kennedy, declaring that Soviet shipments of missiles to Cuba constituted a threat to American security, placed a naval blockade around the island. At almost the last hour before contact between Soviet freighters and American warships, Soviet premier Khrushchev backed down and agreed to remove the missiles on the island. Clearly the stakes were too high, and neither people would risk a war by interfering directly in the sphere of influence of the other.

World War II and its aftermath left the humanities in a crisis situation. The attempted genocide of the Jews, the large-scale death camps, and finally the use of the atomic bomb raised terrifying questions about the extreme possibilities of man's inhumanity to man. The role of the humanities as a humanizing force, the ideal of traditional humanism, had to be put seriously in doubt. Were there not S.S. men who listened to their Bach or read their Goethe after a day's work at the gas chambers? The possibility of instant extermination through nuclear war continues to make many of the traditional forms and values seem obsolete.

Literature and the Holocaust: Primo Levi (1919–1987) Because of the unprecedented cruelty experienced in the nightmarish world of the Nazi concentration camps, many intellectuals, both Jews and non-Jews, declared that this was a subject unfit for "literature" or for "art" because the horror of it was inexpressible in artistic terms and that either silence or direct, nonartistic testimony was the only possible reaction. In spite of this opinion, a flood of novels, poems, films, and other documents dealing with the experience of Jewish, gypsy, and other "racial" concentration camp inmates, as well as with that of those interned or deported for political reasons, has seen and continues to see publication. Many of the accounts emphasize the unspeakable horrors perpetrated by the Nazis, apparently with the goal of forcing the prisoners to abandon their humanity. Reduced through deprivation to elementary feelings of hunger, thirst, cold, and fear, presented with a constant image of themselves as objects, it is hardly surprising that some prisoners abandoned themselves to a subhuman existence. There are numerous stories of inmates stealing bread from weaker fellow prisoners, of trafficking in gold teeth or in prostitution with the Nazis, even of cannibalism. Other renderings of the experience, however, stress that inmates reduced through suffering to the barest state humanly possible either abandon their humanity or accede to a higher spiritual life. On the part of deeply religious Jews and Christians and even of fervently committed Marxists, this is perhaps not surprising. But this type of spiritual experience was possible even for those whose faith was more humanistic than religious.

Perhaps the most sensitive writer to have succeeded in communicating the experience to those who did not undergo it was Primo Levi, an Italian Jew who survived a year in the most infamous of all the Nazi camps, Auschwitz. Levi's *Se Questo è un uomo*, published in 1958 and translated into English as *If This Is a Man* in 1979, is a horrifying and yet extremely sober and artistic account of the literal hell of the camp. One of the

discoveries that Levi makes in Auschwitz is the strangely vital, fundamental value of his profound knowledge of the humanities. There is irony but real edification in the fact that Levi, a nonreligious Jew, rediscovers what it is to be human through his memory of Dante's *Divine Comedy*, the supreme poem of Roman Catholicism but also the great cultural monument for all Italians. In the chapter of *If This Is a Man* printed here, Levi attempts to teach Italian and Dante to a French fellow-prisoner by reciting what he remembers of Canto 26 of the *Inferno*, the canto of Ulysses. In the context, the words of the poet take on a new meaning. In order to appreciate this passage fully, the reader is advised to reread Canto 26 of the *Inferno* in Volume I, Chapter 8.

PRIMO LEVI

If This Is a Man

Chapter 11

THE CANTO OF ULYSSES
(translated by Stuart Woolf)

There were six of us, scraping and cleaning the inside of an underground petrol tank; the daylight only reached us through a small manhole. It was a luxury job because no one supervised us; but it was cold and damp. The powder of the rust burnt under our eyelids and coated our throats and mouths with a taste almost like blood.

The rope-ladder hanging from the manhole began to sway: someone was coming. Deutsch extinguished his cigarette, Goldner woke Sivadjan; we all began to vigorously scrape the resonant steelplate wall.

It was not the *Vorarbeiter*,[1] it was only Jean, the Pikolo of our Kommando.[2] Jean was an Alsatian student; although he was already twenty-four, he was the youngest Häftling of the Chemical Kommando. So that he was given the post of Pikolo, which meant the messenger-clerk, responsible for the cleaning of the hut, for the distribution of tools, for the washing of bowls and for keeping record of the working hours of the Kommando.

---

[1]*Vorarbeiter:* the foreman, a prisoner.
[2]*Kommando:* a unit of workers within the camp.

Jean spoke French and German fluently: as soon as we recognized his shoes on the top step of the ladder we all stopped scraping.

"Also, Pikolo, was gibt es Neues!"[3]

"Qu'est ce qu'il-y-a comme soupe aujourd'hui!"[4]

. . . in what mood was the Kapo? And the affair of the twenty-five lashes given to Stern? What was the weather like outside? Had he read the newspaper? What smell was coming from the civilian kitchen? What was the time?

Jean was liked a great deal by the Kommando. One must realize that the post of Pikolo represented a quite high rank in the hierarchy of the Prominents: the Pikolo (who is usually no more than seventeen years old) does no manual work, has an absolute right to the remainder of the daily ration to be found on the bottom of the vat and can stay all day near the stove. He "therefore" has the right to a supplementary half-ration and has a good chance of becoming the friend and confidant of the Kapo, from whom he officially receives discarded clothes and shoes. Now Jean was an exceptional Pikolo. He was shrewd and physically robust, and at the same time gentle and friendly: although he continued his secret individual struggle against death, he did not neglect his human relationships with less privileged comrades; at the same time he had been so able and persevering that he had managed to establish himself in the confidence of Alex, the Kapo.

Alex had kept all his promises. He had shown himself a violent and unreliable rogue, with an armour of solid and compact ignorance and stupidity, always excepting his intuition and consummate technique as convict-keeper. He never let slip an opportunity of proclaiming his pride in his pure blood and his green triangle, and displayed a lofty contempt for his ragged and starving chemists: *"Ihr Doktoren! Ihr Intelligenten!"*[5] he sneered every day, watching them crowd around with their bowls held out for the distribution of the ration. He was extremely compliant and servile before the civilian *Meister* and with the SS he kept up ties of cordial friendship.

He was clearly intimidated by the register of the Kommando and by the daily report of work, and this had been the path that Pikolo had chosen to make himself indispensable. It had been a long, cautious and subtle task which the entire Kommando had followed for a month with bated breath; but at the end the porcupine's defence was penetrated, and Pikolo confirmed in his office to the satisfaction of all concerned.

Although Jean had never abused his position, we had already been able to verify that a single word of his, said in the right tone of voice and at the right moment, had great power; many times already it had saved one of us from a whipping or from being denounced to the SS. We had been friends for a week: we discovered each other during the unusual occasion of an air-raid alarm, but then, swept by the fierce rhythm of the Lager, we had only been able to greet each other fleetingly, at the latrines, in the washroom.

Hanging with one hand on the swaying ladder, he pointed to me: *"Aujourd'hui c'est Primo qui viendra avec moi chercher la soupe."*[6]

Until yesterday it had been Stern, the squinting Transylvanian; now he had fallen into disgrace for some story of brooms stolen from the store, and Pikolo had managed to support my candidature as assistant to the *"Essenholen,"* the daily corvée of the ration.

He climbed out and I followed him, blinking in the brightness of the day. It was warmish outside, the sun drew a faint smell of paint and tar from the greasy earth, which made me think of a holiday beach of my infancy. Pikolo gave me one of the two wooden poles, and we walked along under a clear June sky.

I began to thank him, but he stopped me: it was not necessary. One could see the Carpathians covered in snow. I breathed in the fresh air, I felt unusually light-hearted.

"Tu es four de marcher si vite. On a le temps, tu sais."[7] The ration was collected half a mile away; one had to return with the pot weighing over a hundred pounds supported on the two poles. It was quite a tiring task, but it meant a pleasant walk there without a load, and the ever-welcome chance of going near the kitchens.

We slowed down. Pikolo was expert. He had chosen the path cleverly so that we would have to make a long

---

[3]"What's new, little one?"
[4]"What kind of soup is there today?"
[5]"You doctors, you intellectuals."

---

[6]"Today it's Primo who will come with me for the soup."
[7]"You're crazy to walk so fast. We have time, you know.

detour, walking at least for an hour, without arousing suspicion. We spoke of our houses, of Strasbourg and Turin, of the books we had read, of what we had studied, of our mothers: how all mothers resemble each other! His mother too had scolded him for never knowing how much money he had in his pocket; his mother too would have been amazed if she had known that he had found his feet, that day by day he was finding his feet.

An SS man passed on a bicycle. It is Rudi, the *Blockführer*. Halt! Attention! Take off your beret! *"Sale brute, celui-là. Ein ganz gemeiner Hund."*[8] Can he speak French and German with equal facility? Yes, he thinks indifferently in both languages. He spent a month in Liguria, he likes Italy, he would like to learn Italian. I would be pleased to teach him Italian: why not try? We can do it. Why not immediately, one thing is as good as another, the important thing is not to lose time, not to waste this hour.

Limentani from Rome walks by, dragging his feet, with a bowl hidden under his jacket. Pikolo listens carefully, picks up a few words of our conversation and repeats them smiling: *"Zup-pa, cam-po, acqua."*[9]

Frenkl the spy passes. Quicken our pace, one never knows, he does evil for evil's sake.

. . . The canto of Ulysses. Who knows how or why it comes into my mind. But we have no time to change, this hour is already less than an hour. If Jean is intelligent he will understand. He *will* understand—today I feel capable of so much.

. . . Who is Dante? What is the Comedy? That curious sensation of novelty which one feels if one tries to explain briefly what is the Divine Comedy. How the Inferno is divided up, what are its punishments. Virgil is Reason, Beatrice is Theology.

Jean pays great attention, and I begin slowly and accurately:

"Then of that age-old fire the loftier horn
Began to mutter and move, as a wavering flame
Wrestles against the wind and is over-worn;
And, like a speaking tongue vibrant to frame
Language, the tip of it flickering to and fro
Threw out a voice and answered: 'When I came. . .'"

Here I stop and try to translate. Disastrous—poor Dante and poor French! All the same, the experience seems to promise well: Jean admires the bizzare simile of the tongue and suggests the appropriate word to translate "age-old."

And after "When I came?" Nothing. A hole in my memory. "Before Aeneas ever named it so." Another hole. A fragment floats into my mind, not relevant: ". . . nor piety To my old father, not the wedded love That should have comforted Penelope. . . ," is it correct?

". . . So on the open sea I set forth."

Of this I am certain, I am sure, I can explain it to Pikolo, I can point out why "I set forth"[10] is not *"je me mis,"* it is much stronger and more audacious, it is a chain which has been broken, it is throwing oneself on the other side of a barrier, we know the impulse well. The open sea: Pikolo has travelled by sea, and knows what it means: it is when the horizon closes in on itself, free, straight ahead and simple, and there is nothing but the smell of the sea; sweet things, ferociously far away.

We have arrived at Kraftwerk, where the cable-laying Kommando works. Engineer Levi must be here. Here he is, one can only see his head above the trench. He waves to me, he is a brave man, I have never seen his morale low, he never speaks of eating.

"Open sea," "open sea," I know it rhymes with "left me": ". . . and that small band of comrades that had never left me," but I cannot remember if it comes before or after. And the journey as well, the foolhardy journey beyond the Pillars of Hercules, how sad, I have to tell it in prose—a sacrilege. I have only rescued two lines, but they are worth stopping for:

". . . that none should prove so hardly
To venture the uncharted distances . ."

"to venture":[11] I had to come to the Lager to realize that it is the same expression as before: "I set forth." But I say nothing to Jean, I am not sure that it is an important observation. How many things there are to say, and the sun is already high, midday is near. I am in a hurry, a terrible hurry.

---

[8]"Dirty beast, that one. A common dog."
[9]Soup, field, water.

[10]'misi me' [translator's note].
[11]'si metta' [translator's note].

Here, listen Pikolo, open your ears and your mind, you have to understand, for my sake:

"Think of your breed; for brutish ignorance
Your mettle was not made; you were made men,
To follow after knowledge and excellence."

As if I also was hearing it for the first time: like the blast of a trumpet, like the voice of God. For a moment I forget who I am and where I am.

Pikolo begs me to repeat it. How good Pikolo is, he is aware that it is doing me good. Or perhaps it is something more: perhaps, despite the wan translation and the pedestrian, rushed commentary, he has received the message, he has felt that it has to do with him, that it has to do with all men who toil, and with us in particular; and that it has to do with us two, who dare to reason of these things with the poles for the soup on our shoulders.

"My little speech made every one so keen . . ."

. . . and I try, but in vain, to explain how many things this "keen" means. There is another lacuna here, this time irreparable. ". . . the light kindles and grows Beneath the moon" or something like it; but before it? . . . Not an idea, "keine Ahnung" as they say here. Forgive me, Pikolo, I have forgotten at least four triplets.

"Ca ne fait rien, vas-y tout de même."[12]
". . . When at last hove up a mountain, grey
With distance, and so lofty and so steep,
I never had seen the like on any day."

Yes, yes, "so lofty and so steep," not "very steep,"[13] a consecutive proposition. And the mountains when one sees them in the distance . . . mountains . . . oh, Pikolo, Pikolo, say something, speak, do not let me think of my mountains which used to show up against the dusk of evening as I returned by train from Milan to Turin!

Enough, one must go on, these are things that one thinks but does not say. Pikolo waits and looks at me.

I would give today's soup to know how to connect "the like on any day" to the last lines. I try to reconstruct it through the rhymes, I close my eyes, I bite my fingers—but it is no use, the rest is silence. Other verses dance in my head: ". . . The sodden ground belched wind . . . ," no, it is something else. It is late, it is late, we have reached the kitchen, I must finish:

"And three times round she went in roaring smother
With all the waters; at the fourth the poop
Rose, and the prow went down, as pleased Another."

I keep Pikolo back, it is vitally necessary and urgent that he listen, that he understand this "as pleased Another" before it is too late; tomorrow he or I might be dead, or we might never see each other again, I must tell him, I must explain to him about the Middle Ages, about the so human and so necessary and yet unexpected anachronism, but still more, something gigantic that I myself have only just seen, in a flash of intuition, perhaps the reason for our fate, for our being here today . . .

We are now in the soup queue, among the sordid, ragged crowd of soup-carriers from other Kommandos. Those just arrived press against our backs. "Kraut unde Rüben! Kraut und Rüben." The official announcement is made that the soup today is of cabbages and turnips: "Choux et navets. Kaposzta és répak."

"And over our heads the hollow seas closed up."

QUESTIONS

1. Why does Levi choose the Ulysses canto to teach to his friend?
2. What new meanings do the lines recited take on in this context? How do they differ from those intended by Dante in the context of the *Divine Comedy?*
3. What does this brief passage convey to you about the concentration camp experience?

Sartre and Existentialism   The most influential philosophical and literary movement to grow out of the war years became known as existentialism. As a philosophy, existentialism had actually been developed much earlier, through the influence of Nietzsche, and the work of Martin Heidegger and Karl Jaspers in Germany. It was, however, the French intellectual Jean-Paul Sartre (1905–1980), who did most to bring existentialism into the arts and into a search for an authen-

---

[12] "It doesn't matter, go ahead anyway."
[13] "alta tanto," not "molto alta" [translator's note].

tic way of life on the part of many of the disaffected youth of Europe and America. Sartre's seminal philosophical work, *Being and Nothingness* (1943), was born not only of his readings in German philosophy but through his experiences in the war years as well. As a soldier, Sartre experienced combat as well as confinement in a German prisoner-of-war camp where he wrote his first play. Back in Paris, he lived through the years of the German occupation of France, a humiliating and often nightmarish experience of defeat and captivity that lasted from 1940 until the liberation of Paris in 1944. It seemed to Sartre and to other French intellectuals at that time that the choice before the French was clear: collaborate with the enemy (and doing nothing was in itself a form of collaboration) or resist the enemy by participating in the resistance movement. Resistance could take many forms: joining the *maquis* (underground military groups) to blow up bridges or trains used by the Nazis; hiding Jews or helping them to escape; writing for the underground press; helping to recruit and organize for the movement. Being captured by the Gestapo and identified as a member of the Resistance often met imprisonment, torture, deportation, or execution. The extremity of the situation and the tests to which it put human choice were crucial to Sartre's development as an artist and a thinker.

At the heart of Sartrean existentialism is a sense of limitless and therefore anxiety-producing human freedom. Life for each human being is a series of situations requiring choices and acts; the acts that one chooses determine what one *is*. According to Sartre, man is not given *being*, but only *existence*. There is no God; there are no absolute standards of morality or of truth. Each person must forge his own morality, his own truth, must indeed create his own being out of his existence. First, however, people must be aware of the dreadful state of freedom that is their true state of existence. Something like a Nietzschean "re-valuation of all values" is needed, but there is no superman to give guidance, only the individual. Sartre's words "life begins on the other side of despair" express the necessity for recognition of one's freedom. His "man is the sum of his acts" indicates that one's self is to be created through the use of this freedom.

Sartre found philosophy too limiting a vehicle with which to express the fundamental concerns of human beings. In a novel, *Nausea*, written before the war, he had already treated the theme of the absurdity (or, as he called it, the "contingency") of life and the outmoded hollowness of moralities such as traditional humanism. The main character of the novel, an intellectual named Roquentin, experiences an "existential crisis" as he confronts the meaninglessness of his existence. Yet *Nausea* ends on a note of hope as Roquentin listens to a record of the American jazz song "Some of these Days," with the feeling that he, like the composer of the song, may be able to transform his feeling into a work of art.

Sartre also wrote three volumes of a novel, *Roads to Freedom*, dealing with the Occupation and War years in France, but he never finished the fourth volume. During the war he turned to the theater, which was better adapted to illustrating his theory that each situation in human life is like a trap. One works one's way out of the trap by exercising one's freedom, making a choice, and acting on it. One of Sartre's best plays, the one-act *No Exit*, portrays three dead characters trapped in a hell that they themselves created because they were unable to exercise their freedom during their lifetime. In his adaptation of the Greek myth of Orestes in *The Flies*, Sartre portrays a character who does choose freedom by revolting against the gods and the authorities that hold his city in subjection. When Orestes proclaimed "I am my liberty!" the French Resistance sympathizers, seizing the play's relationship to their occupied city, applauded wildly. It took the Nazi censors somewhat longer to recognize the significance of the play.

In the essay that follows, written shortly after the liberation of France, Sartre looks back on the hard years of occupation and resistance with a certain nostalgia. The paradoxical first sentence jolts the reader into a consideration of the peculiar meaning of Sartrean liberty. For Sartre, the awareness of being in a situation limited by death and the necessity to choose a course of action from within that situation made life under the Occupation the essence of the human condition as seen by existentialism with a clarity that the complexities of postwar life obscured. In this short text, Sartre not only gives a sense of the experience of an occupied people but also some of the fundamental tenets of his philosophy. The translation is by Alastair Hamilton.

JEAN-PAUL SARTRE

The Republic of Silence

We have never been so free as under German occupation. We had lost every right, and above all the right of speech: we were insulted every day and we had to remain silent; we were deported as laborers, as Jews, as political prisoners; everywhere, on the walls, in the newspapers, and on the screen, we saw the foul and listless face which our oppressors wanted to give us. Because of all this we were free. Since the Nazi venom penetrated our very thoughts, every true thought was a victory. Since an all-powerful police tried to force us to be silent, each word became as precious as a declaration of principle. Since we were hounded, every one of our movements had the importance of commitment. The often atrocious circumstances of our struggle had at last put us in a position to live our life without pretenses—to live in this torn, unbearable condition which we call the human condition. Exile, captivity, and above all death, which is ably disguised in periods of happiness, became the perpetual object of our concern; we discovered that they were not evitable accidents or even constant but external threats: they had become our *lot*, our destiny, the source of our reality as men. Each second we fully realized the meaning of the trite little phrase "All men are mortal." And the choice which each man made on his own was genuine, since he made it in the presence of death, since he would always have been able to express it in terms of "better death than . . ." And I'm not talking of the elite formed by the true resistants, but of every Frenchman who, at every hour of the day and night, for four years, said no. The cruelty of the enemy pushed us to the extremes of our condition by forcing us to ask these questions which we avoid in peacetime: each of us—and what Frenchman did not at one point find himself in this position?—who knew certain details concerning the Resistance wondered anxiously: "If I were tortured, would I hold out?" Thus the question of liberty was raised and we were on the brink of the deepest knowledge that man can have of himself. Because man's secret is not his Oedipus complex or his inferiority complex, it is the limit of his freedom, it is his power to resist torture and death. To those who were active in the underground, the circumstances of this struggle were a new experience: they did not fight in the open, like soldiers; they were hunted in solitude, arrested in solitude, and it was all alone that they resisted torture: alone and naked before well-shaved, well-fed, well-dressed executioners who laughed at their wretched flesh, who with clean consciences and unlimited power, looked as though they were in the right. And yet at the depths of this solitude it was the others, all the others, all the comrades of the Resistance whom they defended. One word was enough to cause ten, a hundred arrests. Is not total responsibility in total solitude the revelation of our liberty? The need, the solitude, the enormous risk were the same for everybody, for the leaders and the men. For those who carried messages and did not know what they contained as for those who organized the whole Resistance, there was only one sentence: imprisonment, deportation, death. There is no army in the world with such equal risks for the soldiers and the general. And that is why the Resistance was a real democracy: for the soldier and for the leader there was the same danger, the same responsibility, the same absolute liberty in discipline. Thus, in darkness and in blood, the strongest republic was formed. Each of its citizens knew that he owed himself to everyone and could only count on himself; each one performed his historic part in total solitude. Each one, in defiance of the oppressor, undertook to be himself; irremediably and by freely choosing himself, he chose freedom for everybody. This republic without institutions, without army or police, had to be conquered by each Frenchman and established at every moment against Nazism. We are now on the brink of another Republic:[1] can't we preserve by day the austere virtues of the Republic of Silence and Night?

QUESTIONS

1. How does Sartre see the situation of the Occupation as a microcosm of the human condition?
2. In what way does individual liberty entail responsibility for Sartre?

---

[1]The Fourth Republic; France's new government after the liberation.

Camus   The war and postwar literature of existentialism must include not only the fiction and theater of Sartre but also that of Albert Camus (1913–1960) who, nonetheless, refused to call himself an existentialist. In his novel *The Stranger*, written on the eve of the war and published in 1942, as well as in his essay *The Myth of Sisyphus*, Camus demonstrates his concept of the "absurd"—the fundamental meaninglessness of human life and traditional beliefs. Camus's concept of the absurd is perhaps clearest in the following quotation from *The Myth of Sisyphus*:

> A world that can be explained by reasoning, however faulty, is a familiar world. But in a universe that is suddenly deprived of illusions and of light, man feels a stranger. His is an irremediable exile, because he is deprived of memories of a lost homeland as much as he lacks the hope of a promised land to come. This divorce between man and his life, the actor and his setting, truly constitutes the feeling of Absurdity.

Thus the human mind demands reason, logic, order, and an explanation for the way things are, but the world offers none. The individual must then create his own morality, his own way of resisting the "absurd."

Yet for Camus there was always "another side of the coin." His native continent being North Africa rather than Europe, he retained a belief in the regenerative value of nature—sea and sun—that is absent from Sartre's work. His postwar novel, *The Plague* (1948) is about the effects of an imaginary plague on the Algerian city of Oran, but it is often read as an allegory of the German occupation of Paris. Camus, like Sartre, portrays human beings making choices in the face of an extreme situation. But Camus's values are finally closer to those of traditional humanism than Sartre's are. His heroes choose, in the face of death, in the face of absurdity, simply to do what they can, to help each other, to fight the plague. Friendship and love are in the end more important than political commitment. The revolt against the absurd becomes a way of reaffirming one's humanity. *The Plague* and Camus's philosophical work *The Rebel* precipitated a break between the two men who had become intellectual leaders in Western culture. The reasons were complex, but basically Sartre was critical of what he felt was Camus's compromise with humanism and liberalism.

Sartre himself later moved toward a radically Marxist position, modifying considerably his view of human beings as totally free. Camus, who died in an "absurd" automobile accident in 1960, had retained his faith in the individual rebel, shunning all forms of totalitarian belief systems.

If the philosophical essay *The Myth of Sisyphus* constitutes Camus's most developed statement of "the absurd," Sisyphus himself is not mentioned until the very end. In the passage that follows, Camus portrays his "absurd hero," a figure from Greek mythology taken to represent the condition of modern man. Rewritings of ancient Greek myths (such as Sartre's *The Flies*) were in fact common in French literature around the time of World War II. It seemed that those who lived through tragic situations could seek truth or at least guidance through a reevaluation of a fundamental root of Western culture. Camus's Sisyphus braves his superiors, the gods, states by his choice the value he places on earthly life, and, paradoxically, through his very consciousness of the meaninglessness of his condition, forges his own liberty and happiness.

ALBERT CAMUS

From *The Myth of Sisyphus*

The gods had condemned Sisyphus to ceaselessly rolling a rock to the top of a mountain, whence the stone would fall back of its own weight. They had thought with some reason that there is no more dreadful punishment than futile and hopeless labor.

If one believes Homer, Sisyphus was the wisest and most prudent of mortals. According to another tradition, however, he was disposed to practice the profession of highwayman. I see no contradiction in this. Opinions differ as to the reasons why he became the futile laborer of the underworld. To begin with, he is accused of a certain levity in regard to the gods. He stole their secrets. Aegina, the daughter of Aesopus, was carried off by Jupiter. The father was shocked by that disappearance and complained to Sisyphus. He, who knew of the abduction, offered to tell about it on condition that Aesopus would give water to the citadel of Corinth. To the celestial thunderbolts he preferred the benediction of water. He was punished for this in the underworld. Homer tells us also that Sisyphus had put Death in chains. Pluto could not endure the sight of his deserted, silent empire. He dispatched the god of war, who liberated Death from the hands of her conqueror.

It is said also that Sisyphus, being near to death, rashly wanted to test his wife's love. He ordered her to cast his unburied body into the middle of the public square. Sisyphus woke up in the underworld. And there, annoyed by an obedience so contrary to human love, he obtained from Pluto permission to return to earth in order to chastise his wife. But when he had seen again the face of this world, enjoyed water and sun, warm stones and the sea, he no longer wanted to go back to the infernal darkness. Recalls, signs of anger, warnings were of no avail. Many years more he lived facing the curve of the gulf, the sparkling sea, and the smiles of earth. A decree of the gods was necessary. Mercury came and seized the impudent man by the collar and, snatching him from his joys, led him forcibly back to the underworld, where his rock was ready for him.

You have already grasped that Sisyphus is the absurd hero. He *is*, as much through his passions as through his torture. His scorn of the gods, his hatred of death, and his passion for life won him that unspeakable penalty in which the whole being is exerted toward accomplishing nothing. This is the price that must be paid for the passions of this earth. Nothing is told us about Sisyphus in the underworld. Myths are made for the imagination to breathe life into them. As for this myth, one sees merely the whole effort of a body straining to raise the huge stone, to roll it and push it up a slope a hundred times over; one sees the face screwed up, the cheek tight against the stone, the shoulder bracing the clay-covered mass, the foot wedging it, the fresh start with arms outstretched, the wholly human security of two earth-clotted hands. At the very end of his long effort measured by skyless space and time without depth, the purpose is achieved. Then Sisyphus watches the stone rush down in a few moments toward that lower world whence he will have to push it up again toward the summit. He goes back down to the plain.

It is during that return, that pause, that Sisyphus interests me. A face that toils so close to stones is already stone itself! I see that man going back down with a heavy yet measured step toward the torment of which he will never know the end. That hour like a breathing-space which returns as surely as his suffering, that is the hour of consciousness. At each of those moments when he leaves the heights and gradually sinks toward the lairs of the gods, he is superior to his fate. He is stronger than his rock.

If this myth is tragic, that is because its hero is conscious. Where would his torture be, indeed, if at every step the hope of succeeding upheld him? The workman of today works every day in his life at the same tasks, and this fate is no less absurd. But it is tragic only at the rare moments when it becomes conscious. Sisyphus, proletarian of the gods, powerless and rebellious, knows the whole extent of his wretched condition: it is what he thinks of during his descent. The lucidity that was to constitute his torture at the same time crowns his victory. There is no fate that cannot be surmounted by scorn.

If the descent is thus sometimes performed in sorrow, it can also take place in joy. This word is not too much. Again I fancy Sisyphus returning toward his rock, and the sorrow was in the beginning. When the images of earth cling too tightly to memory, when the call of happiness becomes too insistent, it happens that melancholy rises in man's heart: this is the rock's victory, this is the rock itself. The boundless grief is too heavy to bear. These are our nights of Gethsemane. But crushing truths perish from being acknowledged. Thus, Oedipus at the outset obeys fate without knowing it. But from the moment he knows, his tragedy begins. Yet at the same moment, blind and desperate, he realizes that the only bond linking him to the world is the cool hand of a girl. Then a tremendous remark rings out: "Despite so many ordeals, my advanced age and the nobility of my soul make me conclude that all is well." Sophocles' Oedipus, like Dostoevsky's Kirilov, thus gives the recipe for the absurd victory. Ancient wisdom confirms modern heroism.

One does not discover the absurd without being tempted to write a manual of happiness. "What! by such narrow ways—?" There is but one world, however. Happiness and the absurd are two sons of the same earth. They are inseparable. It would be a mistake to say that happiness necessarily springs from the absurd discovery. It happens as well that the feeling of the absurd springs from happiness. "I conclude that all is well," says Oedipus, and that remark is sacred. It echoes in the wild and limited universe of man. It teaches that all is not, has not been, exhausted. It drives out of this world a god who had come into it with dissatisfaction and a preference for futile sufferings. It makes of fate a human matter, which must be settled among men.

All Sisyphus' silent joy is contained therein. His fate belongs to him. His rock is his thing. Likewise, the absurd man, when he contemplates his torment, silences all the idols. In the universe suddenly restored to its silence, the myriad wondering little voices of the earth rise up. Unconscious, secret calls, invitations from all the faces they are the necessary reverse and price of victory. There is no sun without shadow, and it is essential to know the night. The absurd man says yes and his effort will henceforth be unceasing. If there is a personal fate, there is no higher destiny, or at least there is but one which he concludes is inevitable and despicable. For the rest, he knows himself to be the master of his days. At that subtle moment when man glances backward over his life, Sisyphus returning toward his rock, in that slight pivoting he contemplates that series of unrelated actions which becomes his fate, created by him, combined under his memory's eye and soon sealed by his death. Thus, convinced of the wholly human origin of all that is human, a blind man eager to see who knows that the night has no end, he is still on the go. The rock is still rolling.

I leave Sisyphus at the foot of the mountain! One always finds one's burden again. But Sisyphus teaches the higher fidelity that negates the gods and raises rocks. He too concludes that all is well. This universe henceforth without a master seems to him neither sterile nor futile. Each atom of that stone, each mineral flake of that nightfilled mountain, in itself forms a world. The struggle itself toward the heights is enough to fill a man's heart. One must imagine Sisyphus happy.

QUESTIONS

1. What, exactly, is Sisyphus' condition, and how, in Camus's vision, is it representative of modern man?

2. What seems to be the relationship between tragedy and happiness for Camus?

3. How does Camus's style differ from Sartre's? How does this style reflect Camus's view of the human condition?

4. Can you relate the myth of Sisyphus to the experiences of the concentration camp and the Occupation?

Influences of Existentialism   Existentialism as a lifestyle in Europe and America in the postwar years produced a group of young people who rebelled against the traditional values of their parents and sought to assert their freedom in a meaningless world. In France they gathered in cafés for discussions with Sartre and his friends, to hear the "existentialist" songs of Juliette Greco, or to listen to American jazz. In the United States, somewhat later, they went "on the road" or "dropped out," running away from what they perceived to be meaningless and false in American life. "Beatniks" and "hippies" were, indirectly at least, influenced by popularized existentialism.

The French existentialists' consciousness of the absurdity of human life was balanced by the pressing need for social and political commitment. In exercising one's freedom by choosing to resist Nazi control, anguish and despair could, in some limited way at least, end in triumph. In the years following the war, however, such extreme situations, or clear opportunities for commitment, did not often present themselves. One could, of course, commit onself to a Marxist revolution, but the rise of Stalin in the Soviet Union made that solution seem much less attractive. The terrible knowledge of the concentration camps and the nuclear bomb made life seem precarious and individual human efforts vain. The sense of despair, gloom, and absurdity in existentialism seemed more relevant than its more heroic side.

Postwar Literature

Much of the literature of the 1940s and 1950s, in the United States as well as in Europe, shows a direct or indirect influence of existentialism. Jack Kerouac's runaways and bums, Norman Mailer's heroes, and even many of Hemingway's lonely figures in his later works struggle with their existence in a world devoid of meaning. As in the "lost generation" of the twenties, many American writers went to live in Europe, especially in France, during this period. Europe seemed particularly attractive to black intellectuals, discouraged with the continuing segregation and racism in the United States.

James Baldwin (1924–1987)   One important American writer who left the United States to live in France was James Baldwin. Born illegitimate and later oppressed by a tyrannical stepfather who was a laborer and storefront preacher, Baldwin spent his childhood in Harlem. Teachers in his high school soon recognized his literary gifts, and after graduation he moved to Greenwich Village in the hopes of living as a writer. He felt estranged, however, both from the black world in which he had grown up and from the white artist-intellectual establishment. In the winter of 1944–45 he met Richard Wright, his "idol since childhood," who obtained some grant money for him, and, like Wright, went to live in Paris. His stay in France involved an intense struggle with Wright as a new father figure and a search for his own identity. On his return to the United States in the 1960s, Baldwin was to become an articulate spokesman for the civil rights movement. His later essays, such as *The Fire Next Time*, predict "the shape of the wrath to come" if the vestiges of American racism are not eradicated.

"Sonny's Blues" is perhaps Baldwin's best piece of short fiction. Published in 1957, it may be viewed as an account of an existentialist dilemma within the context of the black community. Just as Sartre's Roquentin, in his anguished search for a meaningful existence, perceives the possibility of meaning in a jazz record, so Sonny, in his quest for identity, breaks through with his music. Sonny has revolted against the middle-class norms represented by his brother, the narrator of the story. The brother's inability to understand Sonny's choice of Charlie Parker as a model for his musical aspirations shows his removal from the post-war bebop subculture that Sonny's friends represent. Sonny's search for freedom is both individual and collective. In renouncing what seem to be the empty values of a white-ruled society which his brother has adopted, Sonny makes the existential choice of his own life's direction within the context of the black community. It is their

sorrow, joy, and energy, as well as his own, that he will communicate through his music.

JAMES BALDWIN

Sonny's Blues

I read about it in the paper, in the subway, on my way to work. I read it, and I couldn't believe it, and I read it again. Then perhaps I just stared at it, at the newsprint spelling out his name, spelling out the story. I stared at it in the swinging lights of the subway car, and in the faces and bodies of the people, and in my own face, trapped in the darkness which roared outside.

It was not to be believed and I kept telling myself that as I walked from the subway station to the high school. And at the same time I couldn't doubt it. I was scared, scared for Sonny. He became real to me again. A great block of ice got settled in my belly and kept melting there slowly all day long, while I taught my classes algebra. It was a special kind of ice. It kept melting, sending trickles of ice water all up and down my veins, but it never got less. Sometimes it hardened and seemed to expand until I felt my guts were going to come spilling out or that I was going to choke or scream. This would always be at a moment when I was remembering some specific thing Sonny had once said or done.

When he was about as old as the boys in my classes his face had been bright and open, there was a lot of copper in it; and he'd had wonderfully direct brown eyes, and great gentleness and privacy. I wondered what he looked like now. He had been picked up, the evening before, in a raid on an apartment downtown, for peddling and using heroin.

I couldn't believe it: but what I mean by that is that I couldn't find any room for it anywhere inside me. I had kept it outside me for a long time. I hadn't wanted to know. I had had suspicions, but I didn't name them, I kept putting them away. I told myself that Sonny was wild, but he wasn't crazy. And he'd always been a good boy, he hadn't ever turned hard or evil or disrespectful, the way kids can, so quick, so quick, especially in Harlem. I didn't want to believe that I'd ever see my brother going down, coming to nothing, all that light in his face gone out, in the condition I'd already seen so many others. Yet it had happened and here I was, talking about algebra to a lot of boys who might, every one of them for all I knew, be popping off needles every time they went to the head. Maybe it did more for them than algebra could.

I was sure that the first time Sonny had ever had horse, he couldn't have been much older than these boys were now. These boys, now, were living as we'd been living then, they were growing up with a rush and their heads bumped abruptly against the low ceiling of their actual possibilities. They were filled with rage. All they really knew were two darknesses, the darkness of their lives, which was now closing in on them, and the darkness of the movies, which had blinded them to that other darkness, and in which they now, vindictively, dreamed, at once more together than they were at any other time, and more alone.

When the last bell rang, the last class ended, I let out my breath. It seemed I'd been holding it for all that time. My clothes were wet—I may have looked as though I'd been sitting in a steam bath, all dressed up, all afternoon. I sat alone in the classroom a long time. I listened to the boys outside, downstairs, shouting and cursing and laughing. Their laughter struck me for perhaps the first time. It was not the joyous laughter which—God knows why—one associates with children. It was mocking and insular, its intent was to denigrate. It was disenchanted, and in this, also, lay the authority of their curses. Perhaps I was listening to them because I was thinking about my brother and in them I heard my brother. And myself.

One boy was whistling a tune, at once very complicated and very simple, it seemed to be pouring out of him as though he were a bird, and it sounded very cool and moving through all that harsh, bright air, only just holding its own through all those other sounds.

I stood up and walked over to the window and looked down into the courtyard. It was the beginning of the spring and the sap was rising in the boys. A teacher passed through them every now and again, quickly, as though he or she couldn't wait to get out of that courtyard, to get those boys out of their sight and off their minds. I started collecting my stuff. I thought I'd better get home and talk to Isabel.

The courtyard was almost deserted by the time I got downstairs. I saw this boy standing in the shadow of a doorway, looking just like Sonny. I almost called his name. Then I saw that it wasn't Sonny, but somebody we used to know, a boy from around our block. He'd been Sonny's friend. He'd never been mine, having been too young for me, and, anyway, I'd never liked him. And now, even though he was a grown-up man, he still hung around that block, still spent hours on the street corner, was always high and raggy. I used to run into him from time to time and he'd often work around to asking me for a quarter or fifty cents. He always had some real good excuse, too, and I always gave it to him, I don't know why.

But now, abruptly, I hated him. I couldn't stand the way he looked at me, partly like a dog, partly like a cunning child. I wanted to ask him what the hell he was doing in the school courtyard.

He sort of shuffled over to me, and he said, "I see you got the papers. So you already know about it."

"You mean about Sonny? Yes, I already know about it. How come they didn't get you?"

He grinned. It made him repulsive and it also brought to mind what he'd looked like as a kid. "I wasn't there. I stay away from them people."

"Good for you." I offered him a cigarette and I watched him through the smoke. "You come all the way down here just to tell me about Sonny?"

"That's right." He was sort of shaking his head and his eyes looked strange, as though they were about to cross. The bright sun deadened his damp dark brown skin and it made his eyes look yellow and showed up the dirt in his conked hair. He smelled funky. I moved a little away from him and I said, "Well, thanks. But I already know about it and I got to get home."

"I'll walk you a little ways," he said. We started walking. There were a couple of kids still loitering in the courtyard and one of them said good night to me and looked strangely at the boy beside me.

"What're you going to do?" he asked me. "I mean, about Sonny?"

"Look. I haven't seen Sonny for over a year, I'm not sure I'm going to do anything. Anyway, what the hell *can* I do?"

"That's right," he said quickly, "ain't nothing you can do. Can't much help old Sonny no more, I guess."

It was what I was thinking and so it seemed to me he had no right to say it.

"I'm surprised at Sonny, though," he went on—he had a funny way of talking, he looked straight ahead as though he were talking to himself—"I thought Sonny was a smart boy, I thought he was too smart to get hung."

"I guess he thought so too," I said sharply, "and that's how he got hung. And how about you? You're pretty goddamn smart, I bet."

Then he looked directly at me, just for a minute. "I ain't smart," he said. "If I was smart, I'd have reached for a pistol a long time ago."

"Look. Don't tell *me* your sad story, if it was up to me, I'd give you one." Then I felt guilty—guilty, probably, for never having supposed that the poor bastard *had* a story of his own, much less a sad one, and I asked, quickly, "What's going to happen to him now?"

He didn't answer this. He was off by himself some place. "Funny thing," he said, and from his tone we might have been discussing the quickest way to get to Brooklyn, "when I saw the papers this morning, the first thing I asked myself was if I had anything to do with it. I felt sort of responsible."

I began to listen more carefully. The subway station was on the corner, just before us, and I stopped. He stopped, too. We were in front of a bar and he ducked slightly, peering in, but whoever he was looking for didn't seem to be there. The juke box was blasting away with something black and bouncy and I half watched the barmaid as she danced her way from the juke box to her place behind the bar. And I watched her face as she laughingly responded to something someone said to her, still keeping time to the music. When she smiled one saw the little girl, one sensed the doomed, still-struggling woman beneath the battered face of the semi-whore.

"I never *give* Sonny nothing," the boy said finally, "but a long time ago I come to school high and Sonny asked me how it felt." He paused, I couldn't bear to watch him, I watched the barmaid, and I listened to the music which seemed to be causing the pavement to shake. "I told him it felt great." The music stopped, the barmaid paused and watched the juke box until the music began again. "It did."

All this was carrying me some place I didn't want to go. I certainly didn't want to know how it felt. It filled everything, the people, the houses, the music, the dark, quicksilver barmaid, with menace; and this menace was their reality.

"What's going to happen to him now?" I asked again.

"They'll send him away some place and they'll try to cure him." He shook his head. "Maybe he'll even think he's kicked the habit. Then they'll let him loose"—he gestured, throwing his cigarette into the gutter. "That's all."

"What do you mean, that's *all*?"

But I knew what he meant.

"I *mean*, that's all." He turned his head and looked at me, pulling down the corners of his mouth. "Don't you know what I mean?" he asked softly.

"How the hell *would* I know what you mean?" I almost whispered it, I don't know why.

"That's right," he said to the air, "how would *he* know what I mean?" He turned toward me again, patient and calm, and yet I somehow felt him shaking, shaking as though he were going to fall apart. I felt that ice in my guts again, the dread I'd felt all afternoon; and again I watched the barmaid, moving about the bar, washing glasses, and singing. "Listen. They'll let him out and then it'll just start all over again. That's what I mean."

"You mean—they'll let him out. And then he'll just start working his way back in again. You mean he'll never kick the habit. Is that what you mean?"

"That's right," he said, cheerfully. "*You* see what I mean."

"Tell me," I said at last, "why does he want to die? He must want to die, he's killing himself, why does he want to die?"

He looked at me in surprise. He licked his lips. "He don't want to die. He wants to live. Don't nobody want to die, ever."

Then I wanted to ask him—too many things. He could not have answered, or if he had, I could not have borne the answers. I started walking. "Well, I guess it's none of my business."

"It's going to be rough on old Sonny," he said. We reached the subway station. "This is your station?" he asked. I nodded. I took one step down. "Damn!" he said, suddenly. I looked up at him. He grinned again. "Damn if I didn't leave all my money home. You ain't got a dollar on you, have you? Just for a couple of days, is all."

All at once something inside gave and threatened to come pouring out of me. I didn't hate him any more. I felt that in another moment I'd start crying like a child.

"Sure," I said. "Don't sweat." I looked in my wallet and didn't have a dollar, I only had a five. "Here," I said. "That hold you?"

He didn't look at it—he didn't want to look at it. A terrible, closed look came over his face, as though he were keeping the number on the bill a secret from him and me. "Thanks," he said, and now he was dying to see me go. "Don't worry about Sonny. Maybe I'll write him or something."

"Sure," I said. "You do that. So long."

"Be seeing you," he said. I went on down the steps.

And I didn't write Sonny or send him anything for a long time. When I finally did, it was just after my little girl died, he wrote me back a letter which made me feel like a bastard.

Here's what he said:

DEAR BROTHER,

You don't know how much I needed to hear from you. I wanted to write you many a time but I dug how much I must have hurt you and so I didn't write. But now I feel like a man who's been trying to climb up out of some deep, real deep and funky hole and just saw the sun up there, outside. I got to get outside.

I can't tell you much about how I got here. I mean I don't know how to tell you. I guess I was afraid of something or I was trying to escape from something and you know I have never been very strong in the head (smile). I'm glad Mama and Daddy are dead and can't see what's happened to their son and I swear if I'd known what I was doing I would never have hurt you so, you and a lot of other fine people who were nice to me and who believed in me.

I don't want you to think it had anything to do with me being a musician. It's more than that. Or maybe less than that. I can't get anything straight in my head down here and I try not to think about what's going to happen to me when I get outside again. Sometime I think I'm going to flip and *never* get outside and sometime I think I'll come straight back. I tell you one thing, though, I'd rather blow my brains out than go through this again. But that's what they all say, so they tell me. If I tell you when I'm coming

to New York and if you could meet me, I sure would appreciate it. Give my love to Isabel and the kids and I was sorry to hear about little Gracie. I wish I could be like Mama and say the Lord's will be done, but I don't know it seems to me that trouble is the one thing that never does get stopped and I don't know what good it does to blame it on the Lord. But maybe it does some good if you believe it.

Your brother,
SONNY

Then I kept in constant touch with him and I sent him whatever I could and I went to meet him when he came back to New York. When I saw him many things I thought I had forgotten came flooding back to me. This was because I had begun, finally, to wonder about Sonny, about the life that Sonny lived inside. This life, whatever it was, had made him older and thinner and it had deepened the distant stillness in which he had always moved. He looked very unlike my baby brother. Yet, when he smiled, when we shook hands, the baby brother I'd never known looked out from the depths of his private life, like an animal waiting to be coaxed into the light.

"How you been keeping?" he asked me.

"All right. And you?"

"Just fine." He was smiling all over his face. "It's good to see you again."

"It's good to see you."

The seven years' difference in our ages lay between us like a chasm: I wondered if these years would ever operate between us as a bridge. I was remembering, and it made it hard to catch my breath, that I had been there when he was born; and I had heard the first words he had ever spoken. When he started to walk, he walked from our mother straight to me. I caught him just before he fell when he took the first steps he ever took in this world.

"How's Isabel?"

"Just fine. She's dying to see you."

"And the boys?"

"They're fine, too. They're anxious to see their uncle."

"Oh, come on. You know they don't remember me."

"Are you kidding? Of course they remember you."

He grinned again. We got into a taxi. We had a lot to say to each other, far too much to know how to begin.

As the taxi began to move, I asked, "You still want to go to India?"

He laughed. "You still remember that. Hell, no. This place is Indian enough for me."

"It used to belong to them," I said.

And he laughed again. "They damn sure knew what they were doing when they got rid of it."

Years ago, when he was around fourteen, he'd been all hipped on the idea of going to India. He read books about people sitting on rocks, naked, in all kinds of weather, but mostly bad, naturally, and walking barefoot through hot coals and arriving at wisdom. I used to say that it sounded to me as though they were getting away from wisdom as fast as they could. I think he sort of looked down on me for that.

"Do you mind," he asked, "if we have the driver drive alongside the park? On the west side—I haven't seen the city in so long."

"Of course not," I said. I was afraid that I might sound as though I were humoring him, but I hoped he wouldn't take it that way.

So we drove along, between the green of the park and the stony, lifeless elegance of hotels and apartment buildings, toward the vivid, killing streets of our childhood. These streets hadn't changed, though housing projects jutted up out of them now like rocks in the middle of a boiling sea. Most of the houses in which we had grown up had vanished, as had the stores from which we had stolen, the basements in which we had first tried sex, the rooftops from which we had hurled tin cans and bricks. But houses exactly like the houses of our past yet dominated the landscape, boys exactly like the boys we once had been found themselves smothering in these houses, came down into the streets for light and air and found themselves encircled by disaster. Some escaped the trap, most didn't. Those who got out always left something of themselves behind, as some animals amputate a leg and leave it in the trap. It might be said, perhaps, that I had escaped, after all, I was a school teacher; or that Sonny had, he hadn't lived in Harlem for years. Yet, as the cab moved uptown through streets which seemed, with a rush, to darken with dark people, and as I covertly studied Sonny's face, it came to me that what we both were seeking through our separate cab windows was that part of ourselves which had been left behind. It's al-

ways at the hour of trouble and confrontation that the missing member aches.

We hit 110th Street and started rolling up Lenox Avenue. And I'd known this avenue all my life, but it seemed to me again, as it had seemed on the day I'd first heard about Sonny's trouble, filled with a hidden menace which was its very breath of life.

"We almost there," said Sonny.

"Almost." We were both too nervous to say anything more.

We live in a housing project. It hasn't been up long. A few days after it was up it seemed uninhabitably new, now, of course, it's already run-down. It looks like a parody of the good, clean, faceless life—God knows the people who live in it do their best to make it a parody. The beat-looking grass lying around isn't enough to make their lives green, the hedges will never hold out the streets, and they know it. The big windows fool no one, they aren't big enough to make space out of no space. They don't bother with the windows, they watch the TV screen instead. The playground is most popular with the children who don't play at jacks, or skip rope, or roller skate, or swing, and they can be found in it after dark. We moved in partly because it's not too far from where I teach, and partly for the kids; but it's really just like the houses in which Sonny and I grew up. The same things happen, they'll have the same things to remember. The moment Sonny and I started into the house I had the feeling that I was simply bringing him back into the danger he had almost died trying to escape.

Sonny has never been talkative. So I don't know why I was sure he'd be dying to talk to me when supper was over the first night. Everything went fine, the oldest boy remembered him, and the youngest boy liked him, and Sonny had remembered to bring something for each of them; and Isabel, who is really much nicer than I am, more open and giving, had gone to a lot of trouble about dinner and was genuinely glad to see him. And she's always been able to tease Sonny in a way that I haven't. It was nice to see her face so vivid again and to hear her laugh and watch her make Sonny laugh. She wasn't, or, anyway, she didn't seem to be, at all uneasy or embarrassed. She chatted as though there were no subject which had to be avoided and she got Sonny past his first, faint stiffness. And thank God she was there, for I was filled with that icy dread again. Everything I did seemed awkward to me, and everything I said sounded freighted with hidden meaning. I was trying to remember everything I'd heard about dope addiction and I couldn't help watching Sonny for signs. I wasn't doing it out of malice. I was trying to find out something about my brother. I was dying to hear him tell me he was safe.

"Safe!" my father grunted, whenever Mama suggested trying to move to a neighborhood which might be safer for children. "Safe, hell! Ain't no place safe for kids, nor nobody."

He always went on like this, but he wasn't, ever, really as bad as he sounded, not even on weekends, when he got drunk. As a matter of fact, he was always on the lookout for "something a little better," but he died before he found it. He died suddenly, during a drunken weekend in the middle of the war, when Sonny was fifteen. He and Sonny hadn't ever got on too well. And this was partly because Sonny was the apple of his father's eye. It was because he loved Sonny so much and was frightened for him, that he was always fighting with him. It doesn't do any good to fight with Sonny. Sonny just moves back, inside himself, where he can't be reached. But the principal reason that they never hit it off is that they were so much alike. Daddy was big and rough and loud-talking, just the opposite of Sonny, but they both had—that same privacy.

Mama tried to tell me something about this, just after Daddy died. I was home on leave from the army.

This was the last time I ever saw my mother alive. Just the same, this picture gets all mixed up in my mind with pictures I had of her when she was younger. The way I always see her is the way she used to be on a Sunday afternoon, say, when the old folks were talking after the big Sunday dinner. I always see her wearing pale blue. She'd be sitting on the sofa. And my father would be sitting in the easy chair, not far from her. And the living room would be full of church folks and relatives. There they sit, in chairs all around the living room, and the night is creeping up outside, but nobody knows it yet. You can see the darkness growing against the window-panes and you hear the street noises every now and again, or maybe the jangling beat of a tambourine from one of the churches close by, but it's real quiet in the room. For a moment nobody's talking, but every face looks darkening, like the sky outside. And my mother rocks a little from the waist, and my father's eyes are closed. Everyone is looking at something a child can't see. For a minute they've forgotten the children. Maybe a kid is lying on the rug half asleep. Maybe somebody's got a kid on his lap and is absent-mindedly stroking the kid's head. Maybe there's a kid, quiet and big-eyed, curled up in a big chair in the corner. The silence, the darkness coming, and the darkness in the faces frightens the child obscurely. He hopes that the hand which strokes his forehead will never stop—will never die. He hopes that there will never come a time when the old folks won't be sitting around the living room, talking about where they've come from, and what they've seen, and what's happened to them and their kinfolk.

But something deep and watchful in the child knows that this is bound to end, is already ending. In a moment someone will get up and turn on the light. Then the old folks will remember the children and they won't talk any more that day. And when light fills the room, the child is filled with darkness. He knows that every time this happens he's moved just a little closer to that darkness outside. The darkness outside is what the old folks have been talking about. It's what they've come from. It's what they endure. The child knows that they won't talk any more because if he knows too much about what's happened to *them*, he'll know too much too soon, about what's going to happen to *him*.

The last time I talked to my mother, I remember I was restless. I wanted to get out and see Isabel. We weren't married then and we had a lot to straighten out between us.

There Mama sat, in black, by the window. She was humming an old church song, *Lord, you brought me from a long ways off.* Sonny was out somewhere. Mama kept watching the streets.

"I don't know," she said, "if I'll ever see you again, after you go off from here. But I hope you'll remember the things I tried to teach you."

"Don't talk like that," I said, and smiled. "You'll be here a long time yet."

She smiled, too, but she said nothing. She was quiet for a long time. And I said, "Mama, don't you worry about nothing. I'll be writing all the time, and you be getting the checks. . . ."

"I want to talk to you about your brother," she said, suddenly. "If anything happens to me he ain't going to have nobody to look out for him."

"Mama," I said, "ain't nothing going to happen to you *or* Sonny. Sonny's all right. He's a good boy and he's got good sense."

"It ain't a question of his being a good boy," Mama said, "nor of his having good sense. It ain't only the bad ones, nor yet the dumb ones that gets sucked under." She stopped, looking at me. "Your Daddy once had a brother," she said, and she smiled in a way that made me feel she was in pain. "You didn't never know that, did you?"

"No," I said, "I never knew that," and I watched her face.

"Oh, yes," she said, "your Daddy had a brother." She looked out of the window again. "I know you never saw your Daddy cry. But *I* did—many a time, through all these years."

I asked her, "What happened to his brother? How come nobody's ever talked about him?"

This was the first time I ever saw my mother look old.

"His brother got killed," she said, "when he was just a little younger than you are now. I knew him. He was a fine boy. He was maybe a little full of the devil, but he didn't mean nobody no harm."

Then she stopped and the room was silent, exactly as it had sometimes been on those Sunday afternoons. Mama kept looking out into the streets.

"He used to have a job in the mill," she said, "and, like all young folks, he just liked to perform on Saturday nights. Saturday nights, him and your father would drift around to different places, go to dances and things like that, or just sit around with people they knew, and your father's brother would sing, he had a fine voice, and play along with himself on his guitar. Well, this particular Saturday night, him and your father was coming home from some place, and they were both a little drunk and there was a moon that night, it was bright like day. Your father's brother was feeling kind of good, and he was whistling to himself, and he had his guitar slung over his shoulder. They was coming down a hill and beneath them was a road that turned off from the highway. Well, your father's brother, being always kind of frisky, decided to run down this hill, and he did, with that guitar banging and clanging behind him, and he ran across the road, and he was making water behind a tree. And your father was sort of amused at him and he was still coming down the hill, kind of slow. Then he heard a car motor and that same minute his brother stepped from behind the tree, into the road, in the moonlight. And he started to cross the road. And your father started to run down the hill, he says he don't know why. This car was full of white men. They was all drunk, and when they seen your father's brother they let out a great whoop and holler and they aimed the car straight at him. They was having fun, they just wanted to scare him, the way they do sometimes, you know. But they was drunk. And I guess the boy, being drunk, too, and scared, kind of lost his head. By the time he jumped it was too late. Your father says he heard his brother scream when the car rolled over him, and he heard the wood of that guitar when it give, and he heard them strings go flying, and he heard them white men shouting, and the car kept on a-going and it ain't stopped till this day. And, time your father got down the hill, his brother weren't nothing but blood and pulp."

Tears were gleaming on my mother's face. There wasn't anything I could say.

"He never mentioned it," she said, "because I never let him mention it before you children. Your Daddy was like a crazy man that night and for many a night thereafter. He says he never in his life seen anything as dark as that road after the lights of that car had gone away. Weren't nothing, weren't nobody on that road, just your Daddy and his brother and that busted guitar. Oh, yes. Your Daddy never did really get right again. Till the day he died he weren't sure but that every white man he saw was the man that killed his brother."

She stopped and took out her handkerchief and dried her eyes and looked at me.

"I ain't telling you all this," she said, "to make you scared or bitter or to make you hate nobody. I'm telling you this because you got a brother. And the world ain't changed."

I guess I didn't want to believe this. I guess she saw this in my face. She turned away from me, toward the window again, searching those streets.

"But I praise my Redeemer," she said at last, "that He called your Daddy home before me. I ain't saying it to throw no flowers at myself, but, I declare, it keeps me from feeling too cast down to know I helped your father get safely through this world. Your father always acted like he was the roughest, strongest man on earth. And everybody took him to be like that. But if he hadn't had *me* there—to see his tears!"

She was crying again. Still, I couldn't move. I said, "Lord, Lord, Mama, I didn't know it was like that."

"Oh, honey," she said, "there's a lot that you don't know. But you are going to find it out." She stood up from the window and came over to me. "You got to hold on to your brother," she said, "and don't let him fall, no matter what it looks like is happening to him and no matter how evil you gets with him. You going to be evil with him many a time. But don't you forget what I told you, you hear?"

"I won't forget," I said. "Don't you worry, I won't forget. I won't let nothing happen to Sonny."

My mother smiled as though she were amused at something she saw in my face. Then, "You may not be able to stop nothing from happening. But you got to let him know you's *there*."

Two days later I was married, and then I was gone. And I had a lot of things on my mind and I pretty well forgot my promise to Mama until I got shipped home on a special furlough for her funeral.

And, after the funeral, with just Sonny and me alone in the empty kitchen, I tried to find out something about him.

"What do you want to do?" I asked him.

"I'm going to me a musician," he said.

For he had graduated, in the time I had been away, from dancing to the juke box to finding out who was playing what, and what they were doing with it, and he had bought himself a set of drums.

"You mean, you want to be a drummer?" I somehow had the feeling that being a drummer might be all right for other people but not for my brother Sonny.

"I don't think," he said, looking at me very gravely, "that I'll ever be a good drummer. But I think I can play a piano."

I frowned. I'd never played the role of the older brother quite so seriously before, had scarcely ever, in fact, *asked* Sonny a damn thing. I sensed myself in the presence of something I didn't really know how to handle, didn't understand. So I made my frown a little deeper as I asked: "What kind of musician do you want to be?"

He grinned. "How many kinds do you think there are?"

"Be *serious*," I said.

He laughed, throwing his head back, and then looked at me. "I *am* serious."

"Well, then, for Christ's sake, stop kidding around and answer a serious question. I mean, do you want to be a concert pianist, you want to play classical music and all that, or—or what?" Long before I finished he was laughing again. "For Christ's *sake*, Sonny!"

He sobered, but with difficulty. "I'm sorry. But you sound so—*scared!*" and he was off again.

"Well, you may think it's funny now, baby, but it's not going to be so funny when you have to make your living at it, let me tell you *that*." I was furious because I knew he was laughing at me and I didn't know why.

"No," he said, very sober now, and afraid, perhaps, that he'd hurt me, "I don't want to be a classical pianist. That isn't what interests me. I mean"—he paused, looking hard at me, as though his eyes would help me to understand, and then gestured helplessly, as though perhaps his hand would help—"I mean, I'll have a lot of studying to do, and I'll have to study *everything*, but I mean, I want to play *with*—jazz musicians." He stopped. "I want to play jazz," he said.

Well, the word had never before sounded as heavy, as real, as it sounded that afternoon in Sonny's mouth. I just looked at him and I was probably frowning a real frown by this time. I simply couldn't see why on earth he'd want to spend his time hanging around night clubs, clowning around on bandstands, while people pushed each other around a dance floor. It seemed—beneath him, somehow. I had never thought about it before, had never been forced to, but I suppose I had always put jazz musicians in a class with what Daddy called "good-time people."

"Are you *serious*?"

"Hell, *yes*, I'm serious."

He looked more helpless than ever, and annoyed, and deeply hurt.

I suggested, helpfully: "You mean—like Louis Armstrong?"

His face closed as though I'd struck him. "No. I'm not talking about none of that old-time, down home crap."

"Well, look, Sonny, I'm sorry, don't get mad. I just don't altogether get it, that's all. Name somebody—you know, a jazz musician you admire."

"Bird."

"Who?"

"Bird! Charlie Parker! Don't they teach you nothing in the goddamn army?"

I lit a cigarette. I was surprised and then a little amused to discover that I was trembling. "I've been out of touch," I said. "You'll have to be patient with me. Now. Who's this Parker character?"

"He's just one of the greatest jazz musicians alive," said Sonny, sullenly, his hands in his pockets, his back to me. "Maybe *the* greatest," he added, bitterly, "that's probably why *you* never heard of him."

"All right," I said, "I'm ignorant. I'm sorry. I'll go out and buy all the cat's records right away, all right?"

"It don't," said Sonny, with dignity, "make any difference to me. I don't care what you listen to. Don't do me no favors."

I was beginning to realize that I'd never seen him so upset before. With another part of my mind I was thinking that this would probably turn out to be one of those things kids go through and that I shouldn't make it seem important by pushing it too hard. Still, I didn't think it would do any harm to ask: "Doesn't all this take a lot of time? Can you make a living at it?"

He turned back to me and half leaned, half sat, on the kitchen table. "Everything takes time," he said, "and—well, yes, sure, I can make a living at it. But what I don't seem to be able to make you understand is that it's the only thing I want to do."

"Well Sonny," I said, gently, "you know people can't always do exactly what they *want* to do—"

"*No*, I don't know that," said Sonny, surprising me. "I think people *ought* to do what they want to do, what else are they alive for?"

"You getting to be a big boy," I said desperately, "it's time you started thinking about your future."

"I'm thinking about my future," said Sonny, grimly. "I think about it all the time."

I gave up. I decided, if he didn't change his mind, that we could always talk about it later. "In the meantime," I said, "you got to finish school." We had already decided that he'd have to move in with Isabel and her folks. I knew this wasn't the ideal arrangement because Isabel's folks are inclined to be dicty and they hadn't especially wanted Isabel to marry me. But I didn't know what else to do. "And we have to get you fixed up at Isabel's."

There was a long silence. He moved from the kitchen table to the window. "That's a terrible idea. You know it yourself."

"Do you have a *better* idea?"

He just walked up and down the kitchen for a minute. He was as tall as I was. He had started to shave. I suddenly had the feeling that I didn't know him at all.

He stopped at the kitchen table and picked up my cigarettes. Looking at me with a kind of mocking, amused defiance, he put one between his lips. "You mind?"

"You smoking already?"

He lit the cigarette and nodded, watching me through the smoke. "I just wanted to see if I'd have the courage to smoke in front of you." He grinned and blew a great cloud of smoke to the ceiling. "It was easy." He looked at my face. "Come on, now. I bet you was smoking at my age, tell the truth."

I didn't say anything but the truth was on my face, and he laughed. But now there was something very strained in his laugh. "Sure. And I bet that ain't all you was doing."

He was frightening me a little. "Cut the crap," I said. "We already decided that you was going to go and live at Isabel's. Now what's got into you all of a sudden?"

"*You* decided it," he pointed out. "I didn't decide nothing." He stopped in front of me, leaning against the stove, arms loosely folded. "Look, brother. I don't want to stay in Harlem no more, I really don't." He was very earnest. He looked at me, then over toward the kitchen window. There was something in his eyes I'd never seen before, some thoughtfulness, some worry all his own. He rubbed the muscle of one arm. "It's time I was getting out of here."

"Where do you want to *go*, Sonny?"

"I want to join the army. Or the navy, I don't care. If I say I'm old enough they'll believe me."

Then I got mad. It was because I was so scared. "You must be crazy. You goddamn fool, what the hell do you want to go and join the *army* for?"

"I just told you. To get out of Harlem."

"Sonny, you haven't even finished *school*. And if you really want to be a musician, how do you expect to study if you're in the *army?*"

He looked at me, trapped, and in anguish. "There's ways. I might be able to work out some kind of deal. Anyway, I'll have the G.I. Bill when I come out."

"*If* you come out." We stared at each other. "Sonny, please. Be reasonable. I know the setup is far from perfect. But we got to do the best we can."

"I ain't learning nothing in school," he said. "Even when I go." He turned away from me and opened the window and threw his cigarette out into the narrow alley. I watched his back. "At least, I ain't learning nothing you'd want me to learn." He slammed the window so hard I thought the glass would fly out, and turned back to me. "And I'm sick of the stink of these garbage cans!"

"Sonny," I said, "I know how you feel. But if you don't finish school now, you're going to be sorry later that you didn't." I grabbed him by the shoulders. "And you only got another year. It ain't so bad. And I'll come back and I swear I'll help you do *whatever* you want to do. Just try to put up with it till I come back. Will you please do that? For me?"

He didn't answer and he wouldn't look at me.

"Sonny. You hear me?"

He pulled away. "I hear you. But you never hear anything *I* say."

I didn't know what to say to that. He looked out of the window and then back at me. "OK," he said, and sighed. "I'll try."

Then I said, trying to cheer him up a little, "They got a piano at Isabel's. You can practice on it."

And as a matter of fact, it did cheer him up for a minute. "That's right," he said to himself. "I forgot that." His face relaxed a little. But the worry, the thoughtfulness, played on it still, the way shadows play on a face which is staring into the fire.

But I thought I'd never hear the end of that piano. At first, Isabel would write me, saying how nice it was that Sonny was so serious about his music and how, as soon

as he came in from school, or wherever he had been when he was supposed to be at school, he went straight to that piano and stayed there until suppertime. And, after supper, he went back to that piano and stayed there until everybody went to bed. He was at the piano all day Saturday and all day Sunday. Then he bought a record player and started playing records. He'd play one record over and over again, all day long sometimes, and he'd improvise along with it on the piano. Or he'd play one section of the record, one chord, one change, one progression, then he'd do it on the piano. Then back to the record. Then back to the piano.

Well, I really don't know how they stood it. Isabel finally confessed that it wasn't like living with a person at all, it was like living with sound. And the sound didn't make any sense to her, didn't make any sense to any of them—naturally. They began, in a way, to be afflicted by this presence that was living in their home. It was as though Sonny were some sort of god, or monster. He moved in an atmosphere which wasn't like theirs at all. They fed him and he ate, he washed himself, he walked in and out of their door; he certainly wasn't nasty or unpleasant or rude, Sonny isn't any of those things; but it was as though he were all wrapped up in some cloud, some fire, some vision all his own; and there wasn't any way to reach him.

At the same time, he wasn't really a man yet, he was still a child, and they had to watch out for him in all kinds of ways. They certainly couldn't throw him out. Neither did they dare to make a great scene about that piano because even they dimly sensed, as I sensed, from so many thousands of miles away, that Sonny was at that piano playing for his life.

But he hadn't been going to school. One day a letter came from the school board and Isabel's mother got it—there had, apparently, been other letters but Sonny had torn them up. This day, when Sonny came in, Isabel's mother showed him the letter and asked where he'd been spending his time. And she finally got it out of him that he'd been down in Greenwich Village, with musicians and other characters, in a white girl's apartment. And this scared her and she started to scream at him and what came up, once she began—though she denies it to this day—was what sacrifices they were making to give Sonny a decent home and how little he appreciated it.

Sonny didn't play the piano that day. By evening, Isabel's mother had calmed down but then there was the old man to deal with, and Isabel herself. Isabel says she did her best to be calm but she broke down and started crying. She says she just watched Sonny's face. She could tell, by watching him, what was happening with him. And what was happening was that they penetrated his cloud, they had reached him. Even if their fingers had been a thousand times more gentle than human fingers ever are, he could hardly help feeling that they had stripped him naked and were spitting on that nakedness. For he also had to see that his presence, that music, which was life or death to him, had been torture for them and that they had endured it, not at all for his sake, but only for mine. And Sonny couldn't take that. He can take it a little better today than he could then but he's still not very good at it and, frankly, I don't know anybody who is.

The silence of the next few days must have been louder than the sound of all the music ever played since time began. One morning, before she went to work, Isabel was in his room for something and she suddenly realized that all of his records were gone. And she knew for certain that he was gone. And he was. He went as far as the navy would carry him. He finally sent me a postcard from some place in Greece and that was the first I knew that Sonny was still alive. I didn't see him any more until we were both back in New York and the war had long been over.

He was a man by then, of course, but I wasn't willing to see it. He came by the house from time to time, but we fought almost every time we met. I didn't like the way he carried himself, loose and dreamlike all the time, and I didn't like his friends, and his music seemed to be merely an excuse for the life he led. It sounded just that weird and disordered.

Then we had a fight, a pretty awful fight, and I didn't see him for months. By and by I looked him up, where he was living, in a furnished room in the Village, and I tried to make it up. But there were lots of other people in the room and Sonny just lay on his bed, and he wouldn't come downstairs with me, and he treated these other people as though they were his family and I weren't. So I got mad and then he got mad, and then I told him that he might just as well be dead as live the way he was living. Then he stood up and he told me not to worry about him any more in life, that he *was*

dead as far as I was concerned. Then he pushed me to the door and the other people looked on as though nothing were happening, and he slammed the door behind me. I stood in the hallway, staring at the door. I heard somebody laugh in the room and then the tears came to my eyes. I started down the steps, whistling to keep from crying, I kept whistling to myself, *You going to need me, baby, one of these cold, rainy days.*

I read about Sonny's trouble in the spring. Little Grace died in the fall. She was a beautiful little girl. But she only lived a little over two years. She died of polio and she suffered. She had a slight fever for a couple of days, but it didn't seem like anything and we just kept her in bed. And we would certainly have called the doctor, but the fever dropped, she seemed to be all right. So we thought it had just been a cold. Then, one day, she was up, playing, Isabel was in the kitchen fixing lunch for the two boys when they'd come in from school, and she heard Grace fall down in the living room. When you have a lot of children you don't always start running when one of them falls, unless they start screaming or something. And, this time, Grace was quiet. Yet, Isabel says that when she heard that *thump* and then that silence, something happened in her to make her afraid. And she ran to the living room and there was little Grace on the floor, all twisted up and the reason she hadn't screamed was that she couldn't get her breath. And when she did scream, it was the worst sound, Isabel says, that she'd ever heard in all her life, and she still hears it sometimes in her dreams. Isabel will sometimes wake me up with a low, moaning, strangled sound and I have to be quick to awaken her and hold her to me and where Isabel is weeping against me seems a mortal wound.

I think I may have written Sonny the very day that little Grace was buried. I was sitting in the living room in the dark, by myself, and I suddenly thought of Sonny. My trouble made his real.

One Saturday afternoon, when Sonny had been living with us, or, anyway, been in our house, for nearly two weeks, I found myself wandering aimlessly about the living room, drinking from a can of beer, and trying to work up the courage to search Sonny's room. He was out, he was usually out whenever I was home, and Isabel had taken the children to see their grandparents.

Suddenly I was standing still in front of the living room window, watching Seventh Avenue. The idea of searching Sonny's room made me still. I scarcely dared to admit to myself what I'd be searching for. I didn't know what I'd do if I found it. Or if I didn't.

On the sidewalk across from me, near the entrance to a barbecue joint, some people were holding an old-fashioned revival meeting. The barbecue cook, wearing a dirty white apron, his conked hair reddish and metallic in the pale sun, and a cigarette between his lips, stood in the doorway, watching them. Kids and older people paused in their errands and stood there, along with some older men and a couple of very tough-looking women who watched everything that happened on the avenue, as though they owned it, or were maybe owned by it. Well, they were watching this, too. The revival was being carried on by three sisters in black, and a brother. All they had were their voices and their Bibles and a tambourine. The brother was testifying and while he testified two of the sisters stood together, seeming to say, Amen, and the third sister walked around with the tambourine outstretched and a couple of people dropped coins into it. Then the brother's testimony ended and the sister who had been taking up the collection dumped the coins into her palm and transferred them to the pocket of her long black robe. Then she raised both hands, striking the tambourine against the air, and then against one hand, and she started to sing. And the two other sisters and the brother joined in.

It was strange, suddenly, to watch, though I had been seeing these street meetings all my life. So, of course, had everybody else down there. Yet, they paused and watched and listened and I stood still at the window. *"Tis the old ship of Zion,"* they sang, and the sister with the tambourine kept a steady, jangling beat, *"It has rescued many a thousand!"* Not a soul under the sound of their voices was hearing this song for the first time, not one of them had been rescued. Nor had they seen much in the way of rescue work being done around them. Neither did they especially believe in the holiness of the three sisters and the brother, they knew too much about them, knew where they lived, and how. The woman with the tambourine, whose voice dominated the air, whose face was bright with joy, was divided by very little from the woman who stood watching her, a cigarette between her heavy, chapped lips, her hair a cuckoo's nest, her face scarred and swollen from many beatings, and her black eyes glittering like coal. Perhaps they both knew this, which was why, when, as rarely, they addressed each other, they addressed each other as Sister. As the singing filled the air the watching, listening faces underwent a change, the eyes focusing on something within; the music seemed to soothe a poison out of them; and time seemed, nearly, to fall away from the sullen, belligerent, battered faces, as though they were fleeing back to their first condition, while dreaming of their last. The barbecue cook half shook his head and smiled, and dropped his cigarette and disappeared into his joint. A man fumbled in his pockets for change and stood holding it in his hand impatiently, as though he had just remembered a pressing appointment further up the avenue. He looked furious. Then I saw Sonny, standing on the edge of the crowd. He was carrying a wide, flat notebook with a green cover, and it made him look, from where I was standing, almost like a schoolboy. The coppery sun brought out the copper in his skin, he was very faintly smiling, standing very still. Then the singing stopped, the tambourine turned into a collection plate again. The furious man dropped in his coins and vanished, so did a couple of the women, and Sonny dropped some change in the plate, looking directly at the woman with a little smile. He started across the avenue, toward the house. He has a slow, loping walk, something like the way Harlem hipsters walk, only he's imposed on this his own halfbeat. I had never really noticed it before.

I stayed at the window, both relieved and apprehensive. As Sonny disappeared from my sight, they began singing again. And they were still singing when his key turned in the lock.

"Hey," he said.

"Hey, yourself. You want some beer?"

"No. Well, maybe." But he came up the window and stood beside me, looking out. "What a warm voice," he said.

They were singing *If I could only hear my mother pray again!*

"Yes," I said, "and she can sure beat that tambourine."

"But what a terrible song," he said, and laughed. He dropped his notebook on the sofa and disappeared into the kitchen. "Where's Isabel and the kids?"

"I think they went to see their grandparents. You hungry?"

"No." He came back into the living room with his can of beer. "You want to come some place with me tonight?"

I sensed, I don't know how, that I couldn't possibly say No. "Sure. Where?"

He sat down on the sofa and picked up his notebook and started leafing through it. "I'm going to sit in with some fellows in a joint in the Village."

"You mean, you're going to play, tonight?"

"That's right." He took a swallow of his beer and moved back to the window. He gave me a sidelong look. "If you can stand it."

"I'll try," I said.

He smiled to himself and we both watched as the meeting across the way broke up. The three sisters and the brother, heads bowed, were singing *God be with you till we meet again.* The faces around them were very quiet. Then the song ended. The small crowd dispersed. We watched the three women and the lone man walk slowly up the avenue.

"When she was singing before," said Sonny, abruptly, "her voice reminded me for a minute of what heroin feels like sometimes—when it's in your veins. It makes you feel sort of warm and cool at the same time. And distant. And—and sure." He sipped his beer, very deliberately not looking at me. I watched his face. "It makes you feel—in control. Sometimes you've got to have that feeling."

"Do you?" I sat down slowly in the easy chair.

"Sometimes." He went to the sofa and picked up his notebook again. "Some people do."

"In order," I asked, "to play?" And my voice was very ugly, full of contempt and anger.

"Well"—he looked at me with great, troubled eyes, as though, in fact, he hoped his eyes would tell me things he could never otherwise say—"they *think* so. And *if* they think so—!"

"And what do *you* think?" I asked.

He sat on the sofa and put his can of beer on the floor. "I don't know," he said, and I couldn't be sure if he were answering my question or pursuing his thoughts. His face didn't tell me. "It's not so much to *play.* It's to *stand* it, to be able to make it at all. On any level." He frowned and smiled: "In order to keep from shaking to pieces."

"But these friends of yours," I said, "they seem to shake themselves to pieces pretty goddamn fast."

"Maybe." He played with the notebook. And something told me that I should curb my tongue, that Sonny was doing his best to talk, that I should listen. "But of course you only know the ones that've gone to pieces. Some don't—or at least they haven't *yet* and that's just about all *any* of us can say." He paused. "And then there are some who just live, really, in hell, and they know it and they see what's happening and they go right on. I don't know." He sighed, dropped the notebook, folded his arms. "Some guys, you can tell from the way they play, they on something *all* the time. And you can see that, well, it makes something real for them. But of course," he picked up his beer from the floor and sipped it and put the can down again, "they *want* to, too, you've got to see that. Even some of them that say they don't—*some,* not all."

"And what about you?" I asked—I couldn't help it. "What about you? Do *you* want to?"

He stood up and walked to the window and remained silent for a long time. Then he sighed. "Me," he said. Then: "While I was downstairs before, on my way here, listening to that woman sing, it struck me all of a sudden how much suffering she must have had to go through—to sing like that. It's *repulsive* to think you have to suffer that much."

I said: "But there's no way not to suffer—is there, Sonny?"

"I believe not," he said, and smiled, "but that's never stopped anyone from trying." He looked at me. "Has it?" I realized, with this mocking look, that there stood between us, forever, beyond the power of time or forgiveness, the fact that I had held silence—so long!—when he had needed human speech to help him. He turned back to the window. "No, there's no way not to suffer. But you try all kinds of ways to keep from drowning in it, to keep on top of it, and to make it seem—well, like *you.* Like you did something, all right, and now you're suffering for it. You know?" I said nothing. "Well you know," he said, impatiently, "why *do* people suffer? Maybe it's better to do something to give it a reason, *any* reason."

"But we just agreed," I said, "that there's no way not to suffer. Isn't it better, then, just to—take it?"

"But nobody just takes it," Sonny cried, "that's what I'm telling you! *Everybody* tries not to. You're just hung up on the *way* some people try—it's not *your* way!"

The hair on my face began to itch, my face felt wet. "That's not true," I said, "that's not true. I don't give a damn what other people do, I don't even care how they suffer. I just care how *you* suffer." And he looked at me. "Please believe me," I said, "I don't want to see you—die—trying not to suffer."

"I won't," he said, flatly, "die trying not to suffer. At least, not any faster than anybody else."

"But there's no need," I said, trying to laugh, "is there? in killing yourself."

I wanted to say more, but I couldn't. I wanted to talk about will power and how life could be—well, beautiful. I wanted to say that it was all within; but was it? or, rather, wasn't that exactly the trouble? And I wanted to promise that I would never fail him again. But it would all have sounded—empty words and lies.

So I made the promise to myself and prayed that I would keep it.

"It's terrible sometimes, inside," he said, "that's what's the trouble. You walk these streets, black and funky and cold, and there's not really a living ass to talk to, and there's nothing shaking, and there's no way of getting it out—that storm inside. You can't talk it and you can't make love with it, and when you finally try to get with it and play it, you realize *nobody's* listening. So *you've* got to listen. You got to find a way to listen."

And then he walked away from the window and sat on the sofa again, as though all the wind had suddenly been knocked out of him. "Sometimes you'll do *anything* to play, even cut your mother's throat." He laughed and looked at me. "Or your brother's." Then he sobered. "Or your own." Then: "Don't worry. I'm all right now and I think I'll *be* all right. But I can't forget—where I've been. I don't mean just the physical place I've been, I mean where I've *been*. And *what* I've been."

"What have you been, Sonny?" I asked.

He smiled—but sat sideways on the sofa, his elbow resting on the back, his fingers playing with his mouth and chin, not looking at me. "I've been something I didn't recognize, didn't know I could be. Didn't know anybody could be." He stopped, looking inward, looking helplessly young, looking old. "I'm not talking about it now because I feel *guilty* or anything like that—maybe it would be better if I did, I don't know.

Anyway, I can't really talk about it. Not to you, not to anybody," and now he turned and faced me. "Sometimes, you know, and it was actually when I was most *out* of the world, I felt that I was in it, and that I was *with* it, really, and I could play or I didn't really have to *play*, it just came out of me, it was there. And I don't know how I played, thinking about it now, but I know I did awful things, those times, sometimes, to people. Or it wasn't that I *did* anything to them—it was that they weren't real." He picked up the beer can; it was empty; he rolled it between his palms: "And other times—well, I needed a fix, I needed to find a place to lean, I needed to clear a space to *listen*—and I couldn't find it, and I—went crazy, I did terrible things to *me*, I was terrible *for* me." He began pressing the beer can between his hands, I watched the metal begin to give. It glittered, as he played with it, like a knife, and I was afraid he would cut himself, but I said nothing. "Oh well. I can never tell you. I was all by myself at the bottom of something, stinking and sweating and crying and shaking, and I smelled it, you know? *my* stink, and I thought I'd die if I couldn't get away from it and yet, all the same, I knew that everything I was doing was just locking me in with it. And I didn't know," he paused, still flattening the beer can, "I didn't know, I still *don't* know, something kept telling me that maybe it was good to smell your own stink, but I didn't think that *that* was what I'd been trying to do—and—who can stand it?" and he abruptly dropped the ruined beer can, looking at me with a small, still smile, and then rose, walking to the window as though it were the lodestone rock. I watched his face, he watched the avenue. "I couldn't tell you when Mama died—but the reason I wanted to leave Harlem so bad was to get away from drugs. And then, when I ran away, that's what I was running from—really. When I came back, nothing had changed, *I* hadn't changed, I was just—older." And he stopped, drumming with his fingers on the windowpane. The sun had vanished, soon darkness would fall. I watched his face. "It can come again," he said, almost as though speaking to himself. Then he turned to me. "It can come again," he repeated. "I just want you to know that."

"All right," I said, at last. "So it can come again. All right."

He smiled, but the smile was sorrowful. "I had to try to tell you," he said.

"Yes," I said. "I understand that."

"You're my brother," he said, looking straight at me, and not smiling at all.

"Yes," I repeated, "yes. I understand that."

He turned back to the window, looking out. "All that hatred down there," he said, "all that hatred and misery and love. It's a wonder it doesn't blow the avenue apart."

We went to the only night club on a short, dark street, downtown. We squeezed through the narrow, chattering, jam-packed bar to the entrance of the big room, where the bandstand was. And we stood there for a moment, for the lights were very dim in this room and we couldn't see. Then, "Hello, boy," said a voice and an enormous black man, much older than Sonny or myself, erupted out of all that atmospheric lighting and put an arm around Sonny's shoulder. "I been sitting right here," he said, "waiting for you."

He had a big voice, too, and heads in the darkness turned toward us.

Sonny grinned and pulled a little away, and said, "Creole, this is my brother. I told you about him."

Creole shook my hand. "I'm glad to meet you, son," he said, and it was clear that he was glad to meet me *there*, for Sonny's sake. And he smiled, "You got a real musician in *your* family," and he took his arm from Sonny's shoulder and slapped him, lightly, affectionately, with the back of his hand.

"Well. Now I've heard it all," said a voice behind us. This was another musician, and a friend of Sonny's, a coal-black, cheerful-looking man, built close to the ground. He immediately began confiding to me, at the top of his lungs, the most terrible things about Sonny, his teeth gleaming like a lighthouse and his laugh coming up out of him like the beginning of an earthquake. And it turned out that everyone at the bar knew Sonny, or almost everyone; some were musicians, working there, or nearby, or not working, some were simply hangers-on, and some were there to hear Sonny play. I was introduced to all of them and they were all very polite to me. Yet, it was clear that, for them, I was only Sonny's brother. Here, I was in Sonny's world. Or, rather: his kingdom. Here, it was not even a question that his veins bore royal blood.

They were going to play soon and Creole installed me, by myself, at a table in a dark corner. Then I watched them, Creole, and the little black man, and Sonny, and the others, while they horsed around, standing just below the bandstand. The light from the bandstand spilled just a little short of them and, watching them laughing and gesturing and moving about, I had the feeling that they, nevertheless, were being most careful not to step into that circle of light too suddenly: that if they moved into the light too suddenly, without thinking, they would perish in flame. Then, while I watched, one of them, the small, black man, moved into the light and crossed the bandstand and started fooling around with his drums. Then—being funny and being, also, extremely ceremonious—Creole took Sonny by the arm and led him to the piano. A woman's voice called Sonny's name and a few hands started clapping. And Sonny, also being funny and being ceremonious, and so touched, I think, that he could have cried, but neither hiding it nor showing it, riding it like a man, grinned, and put both hands to his heart and bowed from the waist.

Creole then went to the bass fiddle and a lean, very bright-skinned brown man jumped up on the bandstand and picked up his horn. So there they were, and the atmosphere on the bandstand and in the room began to change and tighten. Someone stepped up to the microphone and announced them. Then there were all kinds of murmurs. Some people at the bar shushed others. The waitress ran around, frantically getting in the last orders, guys and chicks got closer to each other, and the lights on the bandstand, on the quartet, turned to a kind of indigo. Then they all looked different there. Creole looked about him for the last time, as though he were making certain that all his chickens were in the coop, and then he—jumped and struck the fiddle. And there they were.

All I know about music is that not many people ever really hear it. And even then, on the rare occasions when something opens within, and the music enters, what we mainly hear, or hear corroborated, are personal private, vanishing evocations. But the man who creates the music is hearing something else, is dealing with the roar rising from the void and imposing order on it as it hits the air. What is evoked in him, then, is of another order, more terrible because it has no words, and triumphant, too, for that same reason. And his triumph, when he triumphs, is ours. I just watched Sonny's face. His face was troubled, he was working hard, but he wasn't with it. And I had the feeling that, in a way, everyone on the bandstand was waiting for him, both waiting for him and pushing him along. But as I began to watch Creole, I realized that it was Creole who held them all back. He had them on a short rein. Up there, keeping the beat with his whole body, wailing on the fiddle, with his eyes half closed, he was listening to everything, but he was listening to Sonny. He was having a dialogue with Sonny. He wanted Sonny to leave the shore line and strike out for the deep water. He was Sonny's witness that deep water and drowning were not the same thing—he had been there, and he knew. And he wanted Sonny to know. He was waiting for Sonny to do the things on the keys which would let Creole know that Sonny was in the water.

And, while Creole listened, Sonny moved, deep within, exactly like someone in torment. I had never before thought of how awful the relationship must be between the musician and his instrument. He has to fill it, this instrument, with the breath of life, his own. He has to make it do what he wants it to do. And a piano is just a piano. It's made out of so much wood and wires and little hammers and big ones, and ivory. While there's only so much you can do with it, the only way to find this out is to try and make it do everything.

And Sonny hadn't been near a piano for over a year. And he wasn't on much better terms with his life, not the life that stretched before him now. He and the piano stammered, started one way, got scared, stopped; started another way, panicked, marked time, started again; then seemed to have found a direction, panicked again, got stuck. And the face I saw on Sonny I'd never seen before. Everything had been burned out of it, and, at the same time, things usually hidden were being burned in, by the fire and fury of the battle which was occurring in him up there.

Yet, watching Creole's face as they neared the end of the first set, I had the feeling that something had happened, something I hadn't heard. Then they finished, there was scattered applause, and then, without an instant's warning, Creole started into something else, it was almost sardonic, it was *Am I Blue*. And, as though he commanded, Sonny began to play. Something began

to happen. And Creole let out the reins. The dry, low, black man said something awful on the drums, Creole answered, and the drums talked back. Then the horn insisted, sweet and high, slightly detached perhaps, and Creole listened, commenting now and then, dry, and driving, beautiful and calm and old. Then they all came together again, and Sonny was part of the family again. I could tell this from his face. He seemed to have found, right there beneath his fingers, a damn brand-new piano. It seemed that he couldn't get over it. Then, for awhile, just being happy with Sonny, they seemed to be agreeing with him that brand-new pianos certainly were a gas.

Then Creole stepped forward to remind them that what they were playing was the blues. He hit something in all of them, he hit something in me, myself, and the music tightened and deepened, apprehension began to beat the air. Creole began to tell us what the blues were all about. They were not about anything very new. He and his boys up there were keeping it new, at the risk of ruin, destruction, madness, and death, in order to find new ways to make us listen. For, while the tale of how we suffer, and how we are delighted, and how we may triumph is never new, it always must be heard. There isn't any other tale to tell, it's the only light we've got in all this darkness.

And this tale, according to that face, that body, those strong hands on those strings, has another aspect in every country, and a new depth in every generation. Listen, Creole seemed to be saying, listen. Now these are Sonny's blues. He made the little black man on the drums know it, and the bright, brown man on the horn. Creole wasn't trying any longer to get Sonny in the water. He was wishing him Godspeed. Then he stepped back, very slowly, filling the air with the immense suggestion that Sonny speak for himself.

Then they all gathered around Sonny and Sonny played. Every now and again one of them seemed to say, Amen. Sonny's fingers filled the air with life, his life. But that life contained so many others. And Sonny went all the way back, he really began with the spare, flat statement of the opening phrase of the song. Then he began to make it his. It was very beautiful because it wasn't hurried and it was no longer a lament. I seemed to hear with what burning he had made it his, with what burning we had yet to make it ours, how we could cease lamenting. Freedom lurked around us and I understood, at last, that he could help us to be free if we would listen, that he would never be free until we did. Yet, there was no battle in his face now. I heard what he had gone through, and would continue to go through until he came to rest in earth. He had made it his: that long line, of which we knew only Mama and Daddy. And he was giving it back, as everything must be given back, so that, passing through death, it can live forever. I saw my mother's face again, and felt, for the first time, how the stones of the road she had walked on must have bruised her feet. I saw the moonlit road where my father's brother died. And it brought something else back to me, and carried me past it, I saw my little girl again and felt Isabel's tears again, and I felt my own tears begin to rise. And I was yet aware that this was only a moment, that the world waited outside, as hungry as a tiger, and that trouble stretched above us, longer than the sky.

Then it was over. Creole and Sonny let out their breath, both soaking wet, and grinning. There was a lot of applause and some of it was real. In the dark, the girl came by and I asked her to take drinks to the bandstand. There was a long pause, while they talked up there in the indigo light and after awhile I saw the girl put a Scotch and milk on top of the piano for Sonny. He didn't seem to notice it, but just before they started playing again, he sipped from it and looked toward me, and nodded. Then he put it back on top of the piano. For me, then, as they began to play again, it glowed and shook above my brother's head like the very cup of trembling.

QUESTIONS

1. What relationship does Baldwin see between art and religion?
2. What views of life and its meaning are in conflict in this story? Which one, if any, appears to triumph?
3. What does the "privacy" of Sonny's character come from, and what are its results?
4. Interpret the following passage and relate it to the theme of the story: "For, while the tale of how we suffer, and how we are delighted, and how we may triumph is never new, it always must be heard."
5. Can Sonny's and the narrator's dilemmas be called "existentialist"? In what sense?

6. What is the significance of the music of Charlie Parker ("Bird") in the story? (See the next section.)

Postwar Music

What was the effect of World War II on music in America? In general, it served as a watershed that separated the traditions of the past from the new music of the day, a barrier that both protected the old traditions on one side and sped the waters of the *avant-garde* down the other. The advanced technology of the war effort gave classical music the computers, tape recorders, and electronic equipment developed for military purposes as new instruments for composition and performance. Popular music was likewise affected, and jazz was popular music. The Special Services units of the armed forces employed thousands of young musicians full time to entertain the troops. Soldiers on duty listened to recorded jazz, and soldiers on leave frequented nightclubs in which live jazz was the rule. The music of the Swing Era remained popular, but a new style of jazz was also created, partially in reaction to the musical restrictions of Swing, and partially as a result of the emerging freedoms and greater equality of black Americans.

Charlie Parker (1920–1955) The veneration of Sonny and his friends for Charlie Parker is representative of the feelings of many black and white musicians, as well as other young rebels of the postwar era. "Yardbird" or "Bird" was in a sense the embodiment of all the pent-up frustrations of black America after the war, a man who represented the crowning achievement of Afro-American genius but was rejected and ignored by society at large. Wasted by drugs, alcohol and a self-abusive life, he died at 35. Yet his music continued to speak—the walls of Harlem, the underpasses of Chicago, and the blackboards of Los Angeles read "Bird lives!" The style he created, bebop, or bop, as it became known, broke with the tradition that had kept jazz tied to dance music and to popular songs. Jazz continued to evolve as the country emerged from World War II, and the higher technical competence of the swing soloists had created a breed of virtuoso who could improvise at break-neck speed. Bebop introduced continually shifting accents, new, rude sounds, unexpected harmonies—and its adepts improvised at speeds that set them apart from, and above, other jazzmen. The bop musicians, or "hipsters," developed their own private language, their own style of dress, and even an antisocial performance style (turning their backs on audiences, walking off stage when they had finished their solos) that set them apart. More importantly, they also developed a free way of treating the standard harmonic and melodic materials that allowed them to transform popular ballads into totally new jazz compositions. In his recording of "Koko," for example, Bird imposes a new tune over the changes (the pattern of harmonies) of the popular and innocuous song "Cherokee (Indian Love Song)."

Another good example of Bird's style is in "Parker's Mood."[1] It is a music of freedom unfettered by the rules of popular music. The melodies are not regular, they are asymmetric. A fanfare-like flourish that opens and closes it demands attention. A laid-back phrase or two followed by a torrent of cascading sounds makes the listener struggle to follow the old, familiar blues pattern. It is a song without words, it is defiant, it is self-assured and fragile at the same time. In 1940, Charlie Parker was unknown; in 1948, when he recorded "Parker's Mood," he was famous; and in 1955, he was dead. So much energy, suffering, and vision became focused and supercharged in this one man, and only through his horn was he able to speak to and for a people. Through his music he would show the way to a freedom he himself never had. His voice and presence in the 1940s and 1950s, was a penetrating cry for the social awakening that America experienced in the 1960s. In a way he, too, was a martyr for his people, but it takes the wisdom and skill of a James Baldwin to help us understand that "Sonny's Blues" and "Parker's Mood" are our music.

Painting and Sculpture after World War II

The sense of the absurd, the feeling of alienation from society, and the emphasis on individual self-

expression that were manifest in writing and in jazz music appeared also in the visual arts. In painting, the ferment that fed the Armory Show of 1913 continued, and by the late 1940s a large number of painters reached maturity. Stuart Davis, for example, had followed the lines of development suggested by the abstraction process of cubism and, influenced by jazz, made larger canvases filled with vaguely familiar objects, rhythmically charged with energy derived from distortion and intense color. "Owh! In San Pao" (Fig. 36-1), painted in 1951, is a careful arrangement of interlocking, overlapping forms that create a busy swirl of front, back, beside, and behind kaleidoscopic patterns held against the vibrant yellow surface by words, letters, and dots. Davis's signature is an active part of the design and punctuates the space as sharply as the bright sounds of the jazz musician fill the air. Georgia O'Keefe moved to the Southwest where she created haunting visions

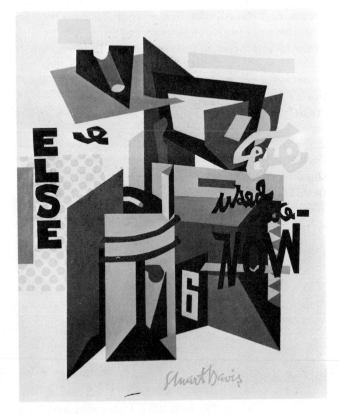

36-1 Stuart Davis, *Owh! In San Pao*. 1951. (Collection of the Whitney Museum of American Art, New York)

---

[1] Charlie Parker recorded over 175 blues performances, and the availability of specific recorded performances is difficult to predict. "Parker's Mood" was recorded in New York in September of 1948 and is available on Savoy MGV-12009. It has been reissued many times, and most college libraries will have it in the *Smithsonian Collection of Classic Jazz* (P6 11891), record side 8, cut number 3 (available from W. W. Norton & Co., 500 Fifth Avenue, New York, NY 10110).

based on the desert. These and other American artists provided the strong background against which a new style appeared in the years following World War II.

This style, called abstract expressionism, or action painting, was the product of many factors—America, the emigration of many artists from Europe during the war years, and the confluence of an almost obsessive individualism with the desire to make original and deeply serious paintings. In retrospect, the painters whose work is commonly described by the term seem to be a most heterogeneous group of individuals, and lumping them together superficial and presumptuous. Nevertheless, it is possible to discern enough similarities to explain the name. Consider this canvas by Jackson Pollock (Fig. 36-2). First, it is a very large painting, wall-sized in fact. Second, it reminds us of a work by Kandinsky in that it has no identifiable subject matter except the formal one that is the product of the combination of shapes, forms, and colors on the surface. It seems to be derived in part from the cubist notion, also supported by Kandinsky, that a painting is good because it *is*, not because it represents something. But we also know from Kandinsky, the cubists, and the surrealists

(as well as from Van Gogh and Gauguin) that lines, colors, and shapes are capable of communicating directly with the viewer, through the unconscious and the intuitive. By appealing to these faculties rather than the rational, intellectualizing ones, the artist involves the spectator in a dialogue with the pure elements of the painting.

We also know, particularly from Kandinsky, how very difficult it is to create a picture outside of the habitual and familiar, so we might ask how Pollock has created such seemingly random patterns on the canvas. Pollock created his paintings by dripping, pouring, and splashing paint on a canvas laid out on the floor. It was his belief that in this uninhibited way of working, he surrendered control of his rational processes; the work produced would be a reflection of interior, personal drives and motivations. He also believed that in this way his paintings would speak directly to the unconscious, therefore allowing the viewer to apprehend a shared universality existing beyond the habitual and familiar. In this painting we seem to have the unification of a number of ideas that had already emerged in the early twentieth century. The large scale of this

36-2 Jackson Pollock, *Blue Poles, 1952.* (Australian National Gallery, Canberra)

work, however, gives it unrelieved energy and an over-whelming appeal to the emotional and subjective, capable of creating an environment that is one with the viewer.

Not all the painters who were a part of the abstract expressionism school made paintings that had no recognizable objects. But all the painters involved gave primacy to the unconscious and to the physical act, the gesture of making the work. The two aims are, in a way, almost mutually exclusive. If the painter is to be uninhibited and have his gestures as free from conscious motivation as possible, then from the moment that the first bit of paint is laid down, the painter becomes involved in an emotionally charged situation.

You can demonstrate this for yourself. Take a piece of paper. Put down a random line. Now you must decide, will the first line determine the placement of the second, or will you attempt to let the second line be as random as the first? Once two lines are down you are forced, almost unconsciously, to make some kind of decision about the placement of a third line, or form. Imagine how complicated this would become if you were working not only with a black line but with colored lines. The factors that are unconsciously forcing you into a decision-making situation are first, the sheet of paper, which acts as a kind of frame; second, there is your natural orientation to the world: top, bottom, left, right, front, back, beside, behind. Then there is an unconscious need to make the arrangement "look right," to produce a sense of balance and rhythm, order and harmony. Whether these needs are inborn or the product of culture does not matter in this instance. What is clear is the need to make "sense" of the thing; to find a personal structure and to impose it on the experience. Thus, on the one hand, the struggle is for a decisive subjective statement; on the other, it is a struggle with the powerful forces generated by the familiar knowledge of seeing, knowing, and experiencing both the painterly world and the habitual world.

It is this ambiguity between ends and means that makes abstract expressionist paintings so strong, enduring, and powerful. Drawn into the dialogue that the painter carries on with his canvas and paint, the viewer experiences the emotionally charged event of which the canvas is a record. At the same time it was this ambiguity that made this kind of painting a diffi-cult act to sustain. Like Monet, who sought more and more transient effects in the landscape, these painters were forced to greater and greater personal and emotional extremes to sustain creative energy; otherwise, their gestures ran the risk of becoming hollow and repetitive. According to one abstract expressionist painter, the need for simplicity, clarity, order, and objectivity becomes overwhelming in the face of spending so much emotional energy.

Sculptors could not by the very nature of their work participate in this drive for the spontaneous; they could, however, derive their visions from similar processes. Thus, David Smith (1906–1965) combined familiar and unfamiliar shapes to produce pieces that seem inspired by nightmares, dreams, and visions of chaos. Alexander Calder (1898–1976) could, by combining forms, create sculpture that was shaped in response to the environment in which it was placed. His mobiles have a fascinating energy that involves the viewer as they revolve and move up and down in the atmosphere.

Perhaps the most significant idea with regard to understanding the work of all these artists is the realization that what goes on between the object and the viewer is personal, private, and only as rich and complex as the viewer is willing to make it. On the one hand, this is the expression of a profound belief in the importance of the individual and a deep confidence that viewers want to be involved in profound and moving experiences. But when the art that is produced is as confusing and disturbing as it is challenging and invigorating, the artist cannot assume that the viewer will eagerly engage in a kind of existentialist dialogue about what is, in fact, occurring in the conscious mind and out of the depths of immediate experience. These artists have called attention to the interior world of the viewer, and what many of them have showed is an irrational, alienated human being whose individuality is as much a burden as a gift. The Swiss-Italian sculptor, Alberto Giacometti (1901–1966), who lived in Paris and was a friend of Sartre's, created a memorable figure-type that seemed to epitomize the human condition as viewed by the existentialist. Whether male or female, adult or child, this attenuated, gouged and stretched form stalks the plaza, the hall, the playground or the street, creating, as Sartre said, its own space around it.

The architecture of the postwar period presents a

very different picture and will be discussed in the next chapter in conjunction with more recent developments.

The Theater of the Absurd

The 1950s saw an important revival of writing for the theater, a new type of drama that the British critic Martin Esslin baptized "the theatre of the absurd." Although they have never formed a school and are in many respects highly different one from the other, the "absurdist" playwrights, most of whom are still writing, do share a radically new vision of the theatrical medium. Several of them came to Paris from other countries but adopted French as their language of expression. These include the Irishman Samuel Beckett, the Rumanian Eugène Ionesco, the Spaniard Fernando Arrabal. The French ex-convict Jean Genet (1910–1985), brought to prominence by Sartre, was in a sense an exile in his own country. Esslin also grouped the English playwright Harold Pinter and the American Edward Albee among the practitioners of theater of the absurd. In a sense, these playwrights have developed Camus's philosophy of the "absurd" into a literary form. Their theatrical world is one in which traditional elements like plot and character are almost abandoned, and language is freed from its everyday, logical restraints. Their experimentation grows out of both modernism and existentialism, but they tend to lack both the modernist belief in the redemptive value of art and the existentialist credo that man can create his own meaning in a meaningless world.

Arrabal   Fernando Arrabal (b. 1932), whose work shows many of the "absurdist" tendencies, began his career alone and independent of any movement. Born in Spain at the beginning of the civil war, he grew up in the repressive atmosphere of the Franco dictatorship. By his early twenties, when he moved to France, he had already written several plays, including the one here, although he knew very little about the work of other "absurdist" writers. The institutions which supported the Franco dictatorship—the army, the police and the Church—appear in a grotesque form in all of Arrabal's plays. His characters, those who are not allied with the forces of repression, are childlike, spontaneous people, alienated from but often crushed by society. Arrabal's

plays often present tragic situations with a comic treatment. Theater, for him, should be seen more in its ancient function as a ceremony than as a realistic portrayal of life. Totally opposed to the classical aesthetic of unity of tone and *verisimilitude*, Arrabal is closer to the baroque in his claim that a theatrical performance can and should mix tragedy with farce and sublime poetry with sordid vulgarity.

Picnic on the Battlefield, Arrabal's most often performed play, is clearly centered on the theme of the total absurdity of war. The situation, and particularly the ending, are potentially tragic, but Arrabal's puppet-like characters and their preposterous actions make the effect on the spectator a comic one. Written in 1952, the play was perhaps directly inspired by the Korean war, but its impact extends to the phenomenon of war in general. To appreciate the distance between a literature of the thirties and forties exhorting social commitment and a postwar literature of alienation and absurdity, one need only compare El Cojo, who gives meaning to his life by joining in battle with his comrades, with the two soldiers Zapo and Zépo in the following play. The translation is by Barbara Wright.

FERNANDO ARRABAL

Picnic on the Battlefield

CHARACTERS

ZAPO, *a soldier*
MONSIEUR TÉPAN, *the soldier's father*
MADAME TÉPAN, *the soldier's mother*
ZÉPO, *an enemy soldier*
FIRST CORPSMAN
SECOND CORPSMAN

THE SCENE.   *A battlefield. Barbed wire stretches from one end of the stage to the other, with sandbags piled against it. Battle is in full swing. We hear bombs bursting, rifle shots and machine-gun fire.*
Alone on stage, hidden flat on his belly among the sandbags, ZAPO *is very frightened.*
The fighting stops. Silence.
From a knitting-bag, ZAPO *takes out a ball of wool, knitting needles, and starts knitting a sweater that is already quite well along. The field telephone beside him suddenly rings.*

ZAPO   Hello . . . hello . . . yes, sir, Captain. . . . Yes, this is the sentry in Section 47. . . . Nothing new, Captain.

. . . Excuse me, Captain, when are we going to start fighting again? . . . and what am I supposed to do with the grenades? Should I send them on up front or to the rear? . . . Don't get annoyed, I didn't say that to upset you. . . . And, Captain, I'm really feeling pretty lonesome. Couldn't you send me a companion out here? . . . Even the goat. (*Evidently the Captain gives him a good dressing down.*) Yes sir, Captain, yes sir! (ZAPO *hangs up. We hear him grumbling to himself. Silence.*)

(*Enter* MONSIEUR *and* MADAME TÉPAN, *carrying baskets as though they are off on a picnic. Their son, who is sitting with his back turned, does not see them arriving.*)

M. TÉPAN (*ceremoniously*)   My boy, get up and kiss your mother on the forehead.

(*Taken by surprise,* ZAPO *gets up and, with a great deal of respect, gives his mother a kiss on the forehead. He is about to speak, but his father beats him to it.*)

Now give *me* a kiss.

ZAPO   My dear sweet parents, how did you ever dare come all the way out to a dangerous spot like this? You must leave here right away.

M. TÉPAN   Are you trying to tell your father what war and danger are all about? For me, all this is only a game. How many times do you think I've jumped off the subway while it was still moving?

MME TÉPAN   We thought you were probably bored, so we came to pay you a little visit. After all, this war business must get pretty tiresome.

ZAPO   It all depends.

M. TÉPAN   I know perfectly well what goes on. In the beginning it's all new and exciting. You enjoy the killing and throwing grenades and wearing a helmet; it's quite the thing, but you end up bored as hell. In my day, you'd have really seen something. Wars were a lot livelier, much more colorful. And then best of all, there were horses, lots of horses. It was real pleasure: If the Captain said "Attack!" before you could shake a stick we were all assembled on horseback in our red uniforms. That was something to see. And then we'd go galloping forward, sword in hand, and suddenly find ourselves hard against the enemy. And they'd be at their finest too, with their horses—there were always loads and loads of beautifully round-bottomed horses and their polished boots, and their green uniforms.

MME TÉPAN   No, the enemy uniform wasn't green. It was blue. I remember perfectly well it was blue.

M. TÉPAN   And I say it was green.

MME TÉPAN   When I was little I went out on the balcony any number of times to watch the battle, and I'd say to the little boy next door, "I'll bet you a gumdrop the Blues win." And the Blues were our enemies.

M. TÉPAN   All right, so you win.

MME TÉPAN   I always loved battles. When I was little, I always said that when I grew up I wanted to be a Colonel in the Dragoons. But Mama didn't want me to. You know what a stickler she is.

M. TÉPAN   Your mother's a real nincompoop.

ZAPO   Forgive me, but you've got to leave. You can't go walking into a war when you're not a soldier.

M. TÉPAN   I don't give a damn. We're here to have a picnic with you in the country and spend a nice Sunday.

MME TÉPAN   I even made a lovely meal. Sausage, hard-boiled eggs, I know how much you like them! Ham sandwiches, red wine, some salad and some little cakes.

ZAPO   O.K., we'll do whatever you say. But if the Captain comes along he'll throw a fit. Plus the fact that he doesn't go for the idea of visiting the battlefront. He keeps telling us: "War calls for discipline and grenades, but no visits."

M. TÉPAN   Don't you worry about it, I'll have a few words with your Captain.

ZAPO   And what if we have to start fighting again?

M. TÉPAN   You think that scares me, I've seen worse. Now if it was only cavalry battles! Times have changed, that's something you don't understand. (*A pause.*) We came on motorcycle. Nobody said anything.

ZAPO   They probably thought you were arbitrators.

M. TÉPAN   We did have some trouble getting through, though. With all those jeeps and tanks.

MME TÉPAN   And the very minute we arrived, you remember that bottleneck because of the cannon?

M. TÉPAN   During wartime, you've got to be prepared for anything. Everybody knows that.

MME TÉPAN   Well now, we're ready to start eating.

M. TÉPAN   Right you are, I could eat a horse. It's the smell of gunpowder that does it.

MME TÉPAN   We'll eat sitting down on the blanket.

ZAPO   All right to eat with my rifle?

MME TÉPAN   Let your rifle alone. It's bad manners to bring your rifle to the table. (*A pause.*) Why, child, you're filthy as a little pig. How did you manage to get in such a mess? Let's see your hands.

ZAPO (*Ashamed, he shows them.*)   I had to crawl along the ground during maneuvers.

MME TÉPAN   How about your ears?

ZAPO   I washed them this morning.

MME TÉPAN   That should do then. Now how about your teeth? (*He shows them.*) Very good. Now who's going to give his little boy a great big kiss for brushing his teeth so nicely? (*To her husband.*) Well, give your son a kiss for brushing his teeth so nicely. (M. TÉPAN *gives his son a kiss.*) Because, you know, one thing I just won't allow is not washing, and blaming it on the war.

ZAPO   Yes, Mama.

(*They eat.*)

M. TÉPAN   Well, my boy, have you been keeping up a good shooting score?

ZAPO   When?

M. TÉPAN   Why, the last few days.

ZAPO   Where?

M. TÉPAN   Right here and now. After all, you *are* fighting a war.

ZAPO   No, no great shakes. I haven't kept up a very good score. Practically no bull's-eyes.

M. TÉPAN   Well, what have you been scoring best with in your shooting, enemy horses or soldiers?

ZAPO   No, no horses. There aren't any horses any more.

M. TÉPAN   Well, soldiers then?

ZAPO   Could be.

M. TÉPAN   Could be? Aren't you sure?

ZAPO   It's just that I . . . I fire without taking aim (*a pause*) and when I fire I say an *Our Father* for the guy I shot.

M. TÉPAN   You've got to show more courage. Like your father.

MME TÉPAN   I'm going to put a record on the phonograph. (*She puts on a record: a Spanish*

pasodoble. Sitting on the ground, they all three listen.)

M. TÉPAN   Now that's real music. Yes, ma'am. I tell you. *Olé!*

(*As the music continues, an enemy soldier,* ZÉPO, *enters. He is dressed like* ZAPO. *Only the color of his uniform is different.* ZÉPO *wears green;* ZAPO *wears gray. Standing unseen behind the family, his mouth agape,* ZÉPO *listens to the music. The record comes to an end.* ZAPO, *getting up, spots* ZÉPO. *Both raise their hands in the air, while* M. *and* MME TÉPAN *look at them startled.*)

M. TÉPAN   What's going on?

(ZAPO *seems about to act, but hesitates. Then, very decisively, he points his rifle at* ZÉPO.)

ZAPO   Hands up!

(ZÉPO, *more terrified than ever, raises his hands still higher.* ZAPO *doesn't know what to do. All of a sudden, he hurriedly runs toward* ZÉPO *and taps him gently on the shoulder, saying*)

ZAPO   You're it! (*Pleased as punch, to his father.*) There you are! A prisoner!

M. TÉPAN   That's fine. Now what are you going to do with him?

ZAPO   I don't know. But could be they'll make me a corporal.

M. TÉPAN   In the meantime, tie him up.

ZAPO   Tie him up? What for?

M. TÉPAN   That's what you do with prisoners, you tie 'em up!

ZAPO   How?

M. TÉPAN   By his hands.

MME TÉPAN   Oh yes, you've definitely got to tie his hands. That's the way I've always seen it done.

ZAPO   All right. (*To the prisoner.*) Please put your hands together.

ZÉPO   Don't do it too hard.

ZAPO   Oh, no.

ZÉPO   Ouch! You're hurting me.

M. TÉPAN   Come on now, don't mistreat your prisoner.

MME TÉPAN   Is that the way I brought you up? Haven't I told you over and over again that you've got to be considerate of your fellow man?

ZAPO   I didn't do it on purpose. (*To* ZÉPO.) Does it hurt the way it is now?

ZÉPO   No, like this it doesn't hurt.

M. TÉPAN   Speak right up and tell him if it does. Just pretend we're not here.

ZÉPO   This way it's O.K.

M. TÉPAN   Now his feet.

ZAPO   His feet too? How long does this go on?

M. TÉPAN   Didn't they teach you the rules?

ZAPO   Sure.

M. TÉPAN   Well?

ZAPO   (to ZÉPO, very politely)   Would you kindly be good enough to please sit down on the ground?

ZÉPO   All right, but don't hurt me.

MME TÉPAN   See! Now he's taking a dislike to you.

ZAPO   No. No he's not. I'm not hurting you, am I?

ZÉPO   No, this is fine.

ZAPO   (out of nowhere)   Papa, suppose you took a snapshot with the prisoner down there on the ground and me standing with my foot on his stomach?

M. TÉPAN   Say, yes! That'll look classy.

ZÉPO   Oh, no you don't. Not that!

MME TÉPAN   Let him. Don't be so stubborn.

ZÉPO   No. I said no and mean no.

MME TÉPAN   Just a little old snip of a snapshot. What difference could that possibly make to you? Then we could put it in the dining room right next to the Lifesaving Certificate my husband got thirteen years ago.

ZÉPO   No, you'll never talk me into it.

ZAPO   But why should you refuse?

ZÉPO   I've got a fiancée. And if she ever sees the snapshot, she'll say I don't know how to fight a war.

ZAPO   No, all you have to do is tell her it isn't you at all, it's a panther.

MME TÉPAN   C'mon, say yes.

ZÉPO   All right, but I'm only doing it to please you.

ZAPO   Stretch all the way out.

(ZÉPO stretches all the way out. ZAPO puts one foot on his stomach and grabs his rifle with a military air.)

MME TÉPAN   Throw your chest out more.

ZAPO   Like this?

MME TÉPAN   Yes, that's it. Don't breathe.

M. TÉPAN   Make like a hero.

ZAPO   How do you mean a hero, like this?

M. TÉPAN   It's a cinch. Make like the butcher when he was telling us what a lady-killer he is.

ZAPO   Like so?

M. TÉPAN   Yes, that's it.

MME TÉPAN   Just be sure your chest is puffed way out, and don't breathe.

ZÉPO   Are you about finished?

M. TÉPAN   Have a little patience. One . . . two . . . three.

ZAPO   I hope I'll come out all right.

MME TÉPAN   Oh yes, you looked very military.

M. TÉPAN   You were fine.

MME TÉPAN   That makes me want to have my picture taken, too.

M. TÉPAN   Now there's a good idea.

ZAPO   All right. I'll take it if you want me to.

MME TÉPAN   Give me your helmet so I'll look like a soldier.

ZÉPO   I don't want any more pictures. Even one was too much.

ZAPO   Don't feel that way. Come right down to it, what difference could it make?

ZÉPO   That's my final say.

M. TÉPAN   (to his wife)   Don't push him. Prisoners are always very touchy. If we keep it up, he'll get mad and spoil all our fun.

ZAPO   Well now, what are we going to do with him?

MME TÉPAN   We could ask him to eat with us. What do you think?

M. TÉPAN   I don't see any reason why not.

ZAPO   (to ZÉPO)   All right then, how'd you like to eat with us?

ZÉPO   Uh . . .

M. TÉPAN   We brought along a nice bottle of wine.

ZÉPO   Well, in that case O.K.

MME TÉPAN   Make yourself right at home. Don't be afraid to ask for things.

ZÉPO   Fine.

M. TÉPAN   Well now, how about you, have you been keeping up a good shooting score?

ZÉPO   When?

M. TÉPAN   Why, the last few days.

ZÉPO   Where?

M. TÉPAN   Right here and now. After all, you *are* fighting a war.

ZÉPO   No, no great shakes. I haven't kept up a very good score. Practically no bull's-eyes.

M. TÉPAN   Well, what have you been scoring best with in your shooting, enemy horses or soldiers?

ZÉPO   No, no horses. There aren't any horses any more.

M. TÉPAN   Well, soldiers then?

ZÉPO   Could be.

M. TÉPAN   Could be? Aren't you sure?

ZÉPO   It's just that I . . . I fire without taking aim (a pause) and when I fire I say a *Hail Mary* for the guy I shot.

ZAPO   A *Hail Mary?* I'd have thought you'd say an *Our Father.*

M. TÉPAN   Come, my boy, you have to be courageous.

ZÉPO   No. Always a *Hail Mary.* (A pause.) It's shorter.

MME TÉPAN (to ZÉPO)   If you like, we can untie you.

ZÉPO   No, leave me this way. It doesn't matter.

M. TÉPAN   You're not going to start putting on airs with us? If you want us to untie you, just say the word.

MME TÉPAN   Please feel free.

ZÉPO   Well, if you really mean it, untie my feet. But it's just to please you people.

M. TÉPAN   Zapo, untie him.

(ZAPO *unties him.*)

MME TÉPAN   Well now, feel better?

ZÉPO   Sure do. But listen, maybe I'm causing you too much trouble.

M. TÉPAN   Not at all. Make yourself right at home. And if you want us to undo your hands, just say so.

ZÉPO   No, not my hands, too. I don't want to overdo it.

M. TÉPAN   Not at all, my boy, not at all. I tell you, you don't disturb us one bit.

ZÉPO   All right, go ahead and untie my hands then. But just while we eat, huh? I don't want you to think when you give me an inch I'm going to take a mile.

M. TÉPAN   Untie his hands, sonny.

MME TÉPAN   Well, since our honorable prisoner is so nice, we're going to have a lovely day here in the country.

ZÉPO   Don't call me "honorable" prisoner. Just say "prisoner" plain and simple.

MME TÉPAN   You're sure that won't make you feel bad?

ZÉPO   No, not at all.

M. TÉPAN   Well, you're certainly unpretentious, anyway.

(*Sound of airplanes.*)

ZAPO   Airplanes. They're going to bomb us for sure.

(ZAPO *and* ZÉPO *dive for the sandbags and hide.*)

ZAPO (to his parents)   Run for cover! The bombs are going to land right on you.

(*The sound of the planes drowns out everything. Immediately bombs start falling. Shells explode nearby. Deafening racket.* ZAPO *and* ZÉPO *are crouching among the sandbags.* M. TÉPAN *goes on calmly talking to his wife, who answers him with equal calm. Because of the bombardment we cannot hear their conversation.* MME TÉPAN *heads for one of the picnic baskets, from which she takes an umbrella. She opens it. The* TÉPANS *take shelter under the umbrella as though it were raining. Standing there, they shift from one foot to the other, in rhythm, all the while discussing personal matters. The bombardment continues. At last, the airplanes take off. Silence.* M. TÉPAN *stretches one arm out from under the umbrella to make certain there is no longer anything coming down from the sky.*)

M. TÉPAN   You can close your umbrella now.

(MME TÉPAN *closes it. Together they go over to their son and prod him on the behind a couple of times with the umbrella.*)

M. TÉPAN   All right, come on out. The bombing's over.

(ZAPO *and* ZÉPO *come out of their hiding place.*)

ZAPO   They didn't get you?

M. TÉPAN   You don't expect anything to happen to your father, do you? (Proudly.) Little bombs like that? Don't make me laugh.

(*From the left, a pair of Red Cross* CORPSMEN *enter, carrying a stretcher.*)

FIRST CORPSMAN   Any bodies?

ZAPO   No, none here.

FIRST CORPSMAN   You're sure you took a good look?

ZAPO   Absolutely.

FIRST CORPSMAN   And there's not one single body?

ZAPO   Didn't I just say so?

FIRST CORPSMAN   Not even someone wounded?

The Second World War and the Postwar Period 467

ZAPO   Not even.

SECOND CORPSMAN   Well, we're really up the creek! (*To* ZAPO, *persuasively.*) Take a good look all around here, see if you don't turn up a stiff someplace.

FIRST CORPSMAN   Don't press the issue. They told you once and for all there aren't any.

SECOND CORPSMAN   What a lousy deal!

ZAPO   I'm really very sorry. I swear I didn't plan it that way.

SECOND CORPSMAN   That's what they all say. That there aren't any corpses, and that they didn't plan it that way.

FIRST CORPSMAN   So let the man alone!

M. TÉPAN (*obligingly*)   If we can help you at all, we'd be delighted to. At your service.

SECOND CORPSMAN   Well, I don't know. If we keep on like this, I really don't know what the Captain's going to say to us.

M. TÉPAN   What seems to be the trouble?

SECOND CORPSMAN   Just that the others are all getting sore wrists carrying out the dead and wounded, while we still haven't come up with anything? And it's not because we haven't been looking.

M. TÉPAN   I see. That really is a bore. (*To* ZAPO.) You're quite sure there are no corpses?

ZAPO   Obviously, Papa.

M. TÉPAN   You looked under the sandbags?

ZAPO   Yes, Papa.

M. TÉPAN (*angrily*)   Why don't you come right out and say you don't want to have any part in helping these good gentlemen?

FIRST CORPSMAN   Don't jump on him like that. Leave him alone. We'll just hope we have better luck in some other trench where maybe everybody'll be dead.

M. TÉPAN   I'd be delighted for you.

MME TÉPAN   So would I. Nothing pleases me more than to see people who take their work seriously.

M. TÉPAN (*indignantly, to anyone within hearing*) Well, isn't anyone going to do anything for these gentlemen?

ZAPO   If it was up to me, it'd be good as done.

ZÉPO   Same here.

M. TÉPAN   Look here now, isn't one of you at least wounded?

ZAPO (*ashamed*)   No, not me.

M. TÉPAN (*to* ZÉPO)   What about you?

ZÉPO (*ashamed*)   Me either. I never was lucky.

MME TÉPAN (*delighted*)   I just remembered! This morning, while I was peeling onions, I cut my finger. How's that?

M. TÉPAN   Why of course! (*Really in the swing of things.*) They'll put you on the stretcher and carry you right off!

FIRST CORPSMAN   Sorry, it's no good. Women don't count.

M. TÉPAN   Well, that didn't get us anywhere.

FIRST CORPSMAN   It doesn't matter.

SECOND CORPSMAN   Maybe we can get our fill in the other trenches. (*They start to go off.*)

M. TÉPAN   Don't you worry, if we find a corpse we'll hang onto it for you. There's not a chance we'd give it to anybody but you.

SECOND CORPSMAN   Thank you very much, sir.

M. TÉPAN   It's nothing, my boy. It's the very least I could do.

(*The* CORPSMEN *make their goodbyes. All four of the others reply in kind. The* CORPSMEN *exit.*)

MME TÉPAN   That's what's so pleasant about spending Sunday out in the battlefield. You always run into such nice folks. (*A pause.*) Come to think of it, why is it you're enemies?

ZÉPO   I don't know. I'm not too well educated.

MME TÉPAN   I mean is it from birth, or did you become enemies after?

ZÉPO   I don't know. I don't know a thing about it.

M. TÉPAN   Well then, how did you come to go to war?

ZÉPO   One day I was home fixing my mother's iron and a man came by and said to me: "Are you Zépo?" . . . "Yes." . . . "Good, you've got to go to war." So I asked him, "What war?" And he said to me: "Don't you read the newspapers? You are a hick!" So I told him yes I did, but not all that war stuff . . .

ZAPO   That's just what happened to me; exactly what happened to me.

M. TÉPAN   Sure, they came after you, too.

MME TÉPAN   No, it's not the same. You weren't fixing the iron that day, you were repairing the car.

M. TÉPAN   I was talking about the rest of it. (*To* ZÉPO.) Go on. Then what happened?

ZÉPO   Well, then I told him that I had a fiancée, and if I didn't take her to the movies on Sunday, she wouldn't know what to do with herself. He said that that didn't matter.

ZAPO   Same as me. Exactly the same as me.

ZÉPO   Well, then my father came down and he said I couldn't go to war because I didn't have a horse.

ZAPO   Like my father said.

ZÉPO   The man said they didn't use horses any more, and I asked him if I could take along my fiancée. He said no. Then I asked him could I take along my aunt to make me custard every Thursday. I like custard.

MME TÉPAN   (realizing that she has forgotten something)   Oh! The custard!

ZÉPO   Again he said no.

ZAPO   The way he did to me.

ZÉPO   And ever since then, here I am, nearly always all alone in the trench here.

MME TÉPAN   As long as you're so much alike, and both so bored, I think you and your honorable prisoner might play together this afternoon.

ZAPO   Oh no, Mama! I'm too scared. He's an enemy.

M. TÉPAN   Oh come on now, don't be scared.

ZAPO   If you knew what the general told us about the enemy.

MME TÉPAN   What did he tell you?

ZAPO   He said the enemy soldiers are very mean. When they take prisoners, they put pebbles in their socks so it hurts when they walk.

MME TÉPAN   How horrible! What savages!

M. TÉPAN   (indignantly, to ZÉPO)   Aren't you ashamed to be part of an army of criminals?

ZÉPO   I didn't do anything. I'm not mad at anybody.

MME TÉPAN   He's trying to put one over on us, acting like a little saint.

M. TÉPAN   We should never have untied him. Probably all we have to do is have our backs turned for him to go putting pebbles in our socks.

ZÉPO   Don't be so mean to me.

M. TÉPAN   How do you expect us to be? I'm shocked. I know just what I'm going to do. I'm going to find the Captain and ask him to let me go into battle.

ZAPO   He won't let you. You're too old.

M. TÉPAN   Well then I'll go buy a horse and a saber and I'll go to war on my own.

ZÉPO   Please, madame, don't treat me like this. Besides, I was just going to tell you, *our* general said the same thing about you people.

MME TÉPAN   How could he dare tell such a lie?

ZAPO   The very same thing, honest?

ZÉPO   Yes, the very same thing.

M. TÉPAN   Maybe it's the same one who talked to both of you.

MME TÉPAN   Well, if it is the same general, the least he could do is use a different speech. Imagine telling everybody the same thing.

M. TÉPAN   (to ZÉPO, changing his tone)   Can I fill your glass again?

MME TÉPAN   I hope you enjoyed our little lunch.

M. TÉPAN   It was better than Sunday, anyway.

ZÉPO   What happened then?

M. TÉPAN   Well, we went out to the country and laid all our chow out on the blanket. While we had our backs turned, a cow came along and ate the whole lunch, including the napkins.

ZÉPO   What a glutton, that cow!

M. TÉPAN   Yes, but then to get even, we ate the cow.

(*They laugh.*)

ZAPO   (to ZÉPO)   I bet they weren't hungry after that.

M. TÉPAN   To your health!

(*They all drink.*)

MME TÉPAN   (to ZÉPO)   Tell me something, what do you do for amusement in the trenches?

ZÉPO   Just to pass the time and keep myself amused, I take odds and ends of rags and make little flowers out of them. See, I get bored a lot.

MME TÉPAN   And what do you do with these rag flowers?

ZÉPO   At first I used to send them to my fiancée, but one day she told me that the cellar and the greenhouse were already filled with them, that she didn't know what to do with them any more, and would I mind sending her something else for a change?

MME TÉPAN   And what did you do?

ZÉPO   I tried learning something else, but I couldn't do it. So, to pass the time, I just go on making my rag flowers.

MME TÉPAN   And then do you throw them away?

ZÉPO   No, now I've found a way to make use of them:
I furnish one flower for each of my buddies who
dies. That way, I know that even if I make a whole
lot, there'll never be enough.

M. TÉPAN   You found a good way out.

ZÉPO (*timidly*)   Yes.

ZAPO   Well, you know what I do so's not to get bored
is knit.

MME TÉPAN   But tell me, do all the soldiers get bored
the way you two do?

ZÉPO   That depends on what they do for relaxation.

ZAPO   Same thing over on our side.

M. TÉPAN   Well then, let's stop the war.

ZÉPO   But how?

M. TÉPAN   Very easy. You tell your buddies that the
enemy doesn't want to fight, and you tell the same
thing to your comrades. And everybody goes home.

ZAPO   Terrific.

MME TÉPAN   That way you can finish fixing the iron.

ZAPO   How come nobody ever thought of that before?

MME TÉPAN   It takes your father to come up with
ideas like that. Don't forget he's a Normal School
graduate, and a philatelist, too.

ZÉPO   But what will all the field-marshals and the
corporals do?

M. TÉPAN   We'll give 'em guitars and castanets to keep
'em quiet.

ZÉPO   Excellent idea.

M. TÉPAN   See how easy it is? It's all settled.

ZÉPO   We'll wow 'em.

ZAPO   Boy, will my buddies be glad!

MME TÉPAN   What do you say we celebrate and put on
that pasodoble we were listening to before?

ZÉPO   Wonderful!

ZAPO   Yes, put on the record, Mama.

(MME TÉPAN *puts on the record. She winds the phonograph and waits. Not a sound is heard.*)

M. TÉPAN   You can't hear anything.

MME TÉPAN (*going to the phonograph*)   Oh! . . . I
made a boo-boo! Instead of putting on a record, I put
on a beret.

(*She puts the record on. A lively pasodoble is heard.* ZAPO
dances with ZÉPO; MME TÉPAN *with her husband.*
The field telephone rings. None of the group hears it.
They go on dancing in a lively manner.
*The phone rings again. The dancing continues. Battle
breaks out once more with a great din of bombs, rifle fire,
and the crackle of machine-guns. Having noticed nothing, the two couples keep on dancing gaily.*
*A sudden machine-gun blast mows them all down. They
fall to the ground, stone dead. One bullet seems to have
nicked the phonograph: the music keeps repeating the
same strain over and over, like a record with a scratch in
it. We hear this repeated strain for the remainder of the
play.*
From the left, the two CORPSMEN *enter, carrying the
empty stretcher.*)

FAST CURTAIN

QUESTIONS

1. Describe the characters in the play. How developed
   are they? To what extent are you as reader/spectator
   involved with them?
2. How are the similarities between Zapo and Zépo
   brought out? What is the effect of this?
3. How does Mr. Tépan's "idea" come about?
4. Is the comic tone maintained throughout or does
   the play ever become serious?
5. What is your opinion of the ending?
6. Does "theater of the absurd" seem an apt description of this play? Why or why not?

37

Toward a Postmodern Culture

To define trends while they are still occurring is a particularly risky enterprise, especially when one is trying to characterize the direction in which a whole society is moving. Nonetheless, the consistency with which contemporary thinkers tend to compare the last thirty years with the previous period gives some assurance that they are on the right track. These thinkers commonly speak of our age as one of postindustrialism, postmodernism, posthumanism, and the like—language suggesting an awareness that a significant period of historical times has ended but that no label for the present age as yet seems adequate. The *age of the computer*, the *electronic age*, the *television age*, and the *nuclear age* have been suggested, but none of these seems comprehensive enough. This final chapter endeavors to give some outline to the shape of the new age.

From the 1960s Through the 1980s

America's large-scale involvement in Vietnam, beginning in 1964 and lasting until the recalling of troops in 1972, marked a watershed in the political life of the United States. In a sense fought daily on the evening-news television screen, the Vietnam War was for the United States government as much a battle for citizens' support as it was a struggle against the Viet Cong and the North Vietnamese. Secret invasions, exaggerated body counts, claims of winning belied repeatedly by striking enemy victories, and beneath the phenomena the burning issue of whether American troops ought to be engaged in such a war at all—all this evoked a degree of protest unknown in American history since the Civil War. With the protests came the countercharges regarding the motives of the protestors and the effect of demonstrations on the course of the war. Many feared that the United States was losing the basic consensus needed to keep a political body alive. Protests directed against the war in many cases developed into a critique of the entire fabric of American society. The "counter-culture" attracted more and more of the disaffected young.

> The '60s became the age of the underground. Underground films. . . . Underground political activity. . . . Underground publications. . . . Underground religious movements and underground education. . . .
>
> The '60s was . . . the age of permissiveness. . . . It was a time of the Free Speech Movement, of draft card burning, of nudity on stage and screen, of Women's Lib and Gay Lib, of Black Power, of long hair, of the miniskirt and the see-through blouse, of the virtual disappearance of censorship of movies, stage productions, books, and magazines, of topless and bottomless dancers and waitresses, of SDS and Young Americans for Freedom, of Hippies and Yippies, of marijuana and LSD, of wiretapping, mass arrests, mace, and assassination. The breakdown of faith in American institutions and the suspicion that the state, church, schools, and family were failing to guide people to meaningful lives persuaded more and more persons—not all of them young—to, in the classic phrase of the 1960s, "do their own thing.[1]

---

[1] Charles Hamm, "Changing Patterns in Society and Music: The U. S. Since World War II," in Charles Hamm, Bruno Nettl, and Ronald Byrnside, *Contemporary Music and Music Cultures* (Englewood Cliffs, N.J.: Prentice-Hall, 1975), p. 62f.

The humiliation of the president who had become closely associated with the war in 1973 served perhaps to help America close the book on one of the most politically disruptive periods in its history, but the shock of the great oil shortage in the winter of 1973–74 made Americans painfully aware again that they could no longer control the world and that a group of Middle Eastern powers could, if they wished, bring the country to economic ruin. As a whole, the decade of the 1970s was a period of renewed talk of "the decline of the West" and of skepticism about the ability of political leaders to make more than superficial improvements in society. The 1970s were also the decade that Tom Wolfe characterized as that of the "me generation," with the attentions of the young and the not-so-young turned less toward revolutionizing society than toward self-fulfillment by means of encounter groups, yoga, charismatic and other nonmainstream religions, or by free-wheeling life-styles, drugs, and sexual liberation. The considerable expansion of the women's movement and the gay-liberation movement, however, brought out the links between the personal and the political.

American optimism reasserted itself in the 1980s, choosing to overlook a rapidly increasing national debt, an enormous trade imbalance, and the onslaught of foreign investors eager to buy up American assets. Until the last part of the decade, moreover, the effects of these factors on the daily life of most Americans were almost imperceptible. On the other hand, the Reagan administration's policy of low taxes, a minimal inflation rate, and a buoyant stock market created something of a capitalistic idyll. The counterparts of the 1980s to the hippies of the 1960s were the yuppies—young men and women whose goals in life consisted of a pursuit of financial well-being and the latest physical comforts. Nevertheless, the drastic fall in the stock market in October 1987 chastened investor optimism while the country increasingly confirmed its status as the world's biggest debtor nation. Although still the richest, most powerful people on the planet, Americans had to face some tough challenges if they were to retain their preeminence. At the same time, they had to govern their responses by the knowledge that a misguided policy could mean the ruin of the global economy.

The 1980s witnessed a return of conservatism on

many fronts and radical changes in others. Mainstream religions saw a rise in membership, but so did the "electronic church," at least until the discovery that some of its prominent leaders had been involved in sexual scandals. The sudden and dramatic spread of the killer disease AIDS caused a serious reevaluation of the sexual revolution and the drug culture. Although we have not "gone back" to the fifties—domestic arrangements now on the whole recognize more autonomy and equality for women—there has been a noticeable return to matrimony, monogamy, and family values. At the same time, continuing developments in reproductive technologies, such as "test-tube babies" and surrogate motherhood, constantly force us to rethink the nature of the family and the ethical questions posed by these new technologies. The nature of community, until only recently primarily defined in terms of neighborhood and family, must also be constantly redefined. With a plethora of information from all parts of the world more and more readily available through the electronic media of computers and televisions, our participation in what Marshall McLuhan twenty years ago called the "global village" has greatly expanded.

The Third World and Changes in American Society

By the 1970s both the United States and the Soviet Union came to realize that new, independent nations in Africa and developing countries in Asia and Latin America no longer accepted unquestioningly the lead of either superpower. These nations are now a force to be reckoned with in the United Nations forum, because the Third World easily outnumbers the populations of the United States, the Soviet Union, and their close allies. Whereas the First and Second worlds still attempt to retain their spheres of influence, Third World countries increasingly assert the will to steer their own course. After years of intervention, the Soviet Union in 1988 finally began to withdraw its troops from Afghanistan. Although at this writing, the United States continues to give some form of support to the *contras* in Nicaragua and other Latin American political groups perceived to be pro-Western, there has been large-scale popular opposition to such intervention (particularly after the Iran-*contra* affair), and the fear of "another Vietnam" still looms large.

While the Third World continues to grow in population and in political importance, it is clear that a significant number of its inhabitants continue to choose to live in North America. The aftermath of the Vietnam War brought about an exodus of Southeast Asians, the "boat people,"and in a reaffirmation of its greatest traditions, the United States opened its doors to hundreds of thousands of these refugees. So extensive was the influx that the racial balance in a number of America's cities was radically altered. As in the past, American society was prepared to absorb the costs of educating these new citizens in the expectation that they would add their talents to the common pool. More recently, the number of immigrants, both legal and illegal, from Mexico, Central and South America, and the Caribbean has also dramatically increased. Spanish is now the main language in several U.S. communities, and the question of the desirability of bilingual education (with Spanish and oriental languages the "second language") continues to be hotly debated. It is clear that American society is becoming more and more culturally pluralistic. With the rise in diverse ethnic groups has come an increased demand for social and economic justice and for recognition of cultural identity. Groups demanding some form of "liberation" include Native Americans, blacks, Chicanos (Spanish-speaking Americans), and oriental Americans.

Black Liberation   The most longstanding and perhaps most representative of these liberation movements is the black-liberation movement. It can be dated back to the slave revolts and the Civil War, but it has become an established, if diversified, force primarily in the years since World War II. In 1954, however, the decision of the Supreme Court in *Brown* v. *Board of Education of Topeka* that compulsory segregation in the public schools denied equal protection under the law marked the real beginning of an all-out struggle for equality in American society. Almost immediately, blacks, impatient with the slow-moving court system, took matters into their own hands. In 1955, blacks in Montgomery, Alabama, under the leadership of Martin Luther King, boycotted a local bus line when a black woman, Rosa Parks, was arrested for refusing to give her seat to a white passenger. The ultimate success of the boycott showed the power that united action could produce, and succeeding years witnessed the organization of "sit-ins" and "freedom rides" throughout the South as well as protests in the North against the more subtle kind of segregation prevalent there. This phase of the civil rights movement was crowned with success by the passage of the Civil Rights Act of 1964, which had among its more important provisions the prohibition against segregation in public places and discrimination in employment. With this accomplished, Martin Luther King, Jr., by now the leading national figure in the movement, struck out at discrimination in voting rights, an effort that led up to the Voting Rights Act of 1965.

The middle years of the 1960s marked the rise of more militant black groups, led by men such as Stokely Carmichael and Floyd McKissick. Their slogan was "Black Power," which meant the creation of separate economic and social institutions as power bases for black communities. At the same time, these leaders expressed a willingness to meet the traditional violence the white community inflicted on blacks with violence of their own. More conservative leaders like King and Leroy Wilkins could not accept this militant stance and the civil rights movement clearly became divided.

Through the years, the movement has had its martyrs, such as Medgar Evers, the NAACP field secretary killed in Mississippi in 1963, or Viola Liuzzo, a white civil rights worker killed in Alabama in 1965. But the most stunning loss came in 1968 when Martin Luther King was assassinated in Memphis, Tennessee. His last effort was focused on economic disparity between blacks and whites, a problem of inequality far more difficult to resolve politically than those of segregation and voting rights.

The Black Aesthetic   For many blacks, the black liberation movement meant a growing consciousness of the African roots of their culture. Influenced by the idea of *négritude*, a cultural movement begun by French-speaking African and West Indian writers during the 1930s, American blacks in the 1960s began to affirm their identity with blacks around the world. First coined as a concept in Aimé Césaire's poem "Cahier d'un retour au pays natal" (*Return to My Native Land*), *négritude* is essentially a revolt against colonialism and an effort toward self-definition and self-

appraisal. It emphasizes traditional African beliefs, their survival throughout the diaspora, the African's "sense of the divine," and his ability to perceive the supernatural within the natural, in order to create and define a Pan-African cultural universe.

The writings of the Algerian Frantz Fanon served as major revolutionary statements for Third World thinking during the 1960s. In *Les Damnés de la terre* (*The Wretched of the Earth*) Fanon examined the psychological consequences of colonialism, and in *Black Skin, White Masks*, he examined what he called the "master-slave" relationship between the black colonized and the white colonizer. Although politics was an explicit part of the *négritude* movement for writers like Fanon, for others the movement remained primarily cultural and intellectual. Léopold Sédar Senghor of Senegal, West Africa, defined *négritude* as the "sum total of African values." He spoke of a special spiritual endowment of the African, of a "Negro soul," that was shared by blacks of African descent throughout the world. The African approach to the world was said to constitute "intuitive reason," as opposed to the Greek (thus Western) approach of "logical reason." Whereas logical reason involves a confrontation of subject and object, intuitive reason involves a kind of participation and communion, in which subject and object become one. In Senghor's words, "Emotion is African, as Reason is Hellenic."

Although the movement was popular among French-speaking black intellectuals, many African and Afro-American writers looked upon it with skepticism and suspicion. English-speaking Africans, such as Ezekiel Mphalele, James Ngugi, and Nobel Prize winner Wole Soyinka criticized *négritude* because of its "romantization" of Africa and celebration of the past. Black writing, according to Soyinka and others, should serve a more critical function by dealing with social problems and other realities. Among Afro-American writers, many, including Ralph Ellison and James Baldwin, insisted that the culture of the Afro-American was as much American as it was African. Others, however, saw *négritude* as the way toward a worldwide spiritual unity of blacks and a polemic against the dominant values and ideals of Western civilization. Malcolm X, Ron Karenga, LeRoi Jones (Amiri Baraka), and other black nationalists were instrumental in convincing many

Afro-Americans that in the time of revolutionary struggle, traditional Western ideals are irrelevant and therefore must be abolished. As a result, one of the central missions of the black aesthetic movement (also known as the black arts movement) became what the literary critic Addison Gayle, Jr., called the de-Americanization of black people.

This de-Americanization of black people, along with the hostility and protest literature that often accompanied it, constituted only one phase of the movement's development. Its members soon came to the conclusion that protest literature and other modes of speaking to an unsympathetic American society were all futile. Consequently, they began to address themselves to other blacks by investing their work with the distinctive styles, rhythms, and colors of the ghetto as found, for instance, in the music of Aretha Franklin, Otis Redding, Nina Simone, and James Brown. Thus, as an artistic style, the black aesthetic may be viewed as an attempt to develop an idiom, symbolism, imagery, mythology, and iconology that reflect the uniqueness of the Afro-American experience. The following list of seven Black Aesthetic categories offered by Don L. Lee is a good example of this effort:

1. polyrhythmic, uneven, short, and explosive lines
2. intensity; depth, yet simplicity; spirituality, yet flexibility
3. irony; humor; signifying
4. sarcasm—a new comedy
5. direction; positive movement; teaching, nation building
6. subject matter—concrete; reflects a collective and personal lifestyle
7. music: the unique use of vowels and consonants with the developed rap demands that the poetry be read, and read out loud.

Implicit in these categories is the notion that the rules of grammatical form may be suspended and that poetry needs to be taken away from the academic level and written according to the realities of the black masses— to express their joys, sorrows, and concerns.

The three poems that follow represent different expressions of the black aesthetic movement. In a style and structure typical of the movement, Amiri Baraka gives a brief lesson in history as he reflects on the so-

cial, ideological, and political dimensions of the black struggle. In moving images and rhythmic explosions, Sonia Sanchez surveys the sorrows and joys, burdens and triumphs of the black female and her maternal instincts. Gwendolyn Brooks, a precursor of the movement and later participant, explores in "The Life of Lincoln West" the question of black identity and black pride in the context of Western notions of beauty.

AMIRI BARAKA (LEROI JONES) (1934–   )

Leadbelly Gives an Autograph

Pat your foot
and turn
         the corner. Nat Turner, dying wood
of the church. Our lot
is vacant. Bring the twisted myth
of speech. The boards brown and falling
away. The metal bannisters cheap
and rattly. Clean new Sundays. We thought
it possible to enter
the way of the strongest.

But it is rite that the world's ills
erupt as our own. Right that we take
our own specific look into the shapely
blood of the heart.
         Looking thru trees
the wicker statues blowing softly against
the dusk.
Looking thru dusk
thru dark-
ness. A clearing of stars
and half-soft mud.

The possibilities of music. First
that it does exist. And that we do,
in that scripture of rhythms. The earth,
I mean the soil, as melody. The fit you need,
the throes. To pick it up and cut
away what does not singularly express.

Need.
Motive.
The delay of language.

A strength to be handled by giants.

The possibilities of statement. I am saying, now,
what my father could not remember
to say. What my grandfather
was killed
for believing.

            Pay me off, savages.
            Build me an equitable human assertion.

One that looks like a jungle, or one that looks like the
    cities
of the West.   But I provide the stock. The beasts
and myths.
            The City's Rise!
               (And what is history, then? An old deaf
                  lady
                  burned to death
                  in South Carolina.)

QUESTIONS

1. Why does Baraka personify history as "an old deaf lady burned to death in South Carolina"?
2. The black aesthetic movement was accompanied by a theology of black liberation. Discuss Baraka's reference to religion, the ministry, and the church. What roles have they played historically in the Afro-American's quest for freedom and equality? What roles are they currently playing?
3. Explain the significance of music and speech in the culture of Afro-American and other "marginal" ethnic groups. What does Baraka mean by the expression "delay of language"?
4. Identify allusions to the African diaspora. Who are the "savages" and "beasts," and where are the "jungles" and "cities"?

SONIA SANCHEZ (1934–)

present

this women vomiten her
  hunger over the world
this melancholy woman forgotten
before memory came

this yellow movement bursten forth like
Coltrane's melodies all mouth
  buttocks moven like palm trees,
this honeycoatedalabamianwoman
raining rhythms of blue / blk / smiles
this yellow woman carryen beneath her breasts
  pleasures without tongues
  this woman whose body weaves
  desert patterns,
this woman, wet with wanderen,
reviven the beauty of forests and winds
is tellen u secrets
gather up yo odors and listen
as she sings the mold from memory

            there is no place
for a soft / blk / woman
there is no smile green enough or
summertime words warm enough to allow my
    growth
and in my head
i see my history
standen like a shy child
and i chant lullabies
as i ride my past on horseback
tasten the thirst of yesterday tribes
hearen the ancient / blk / woman
me singen hay-hay
        hay-hay-hay-ya-ya-ya
        hay-hay-hay
        hay-hay-ya-ya-ya
                like a slow scent
beneath the sun
        and i dance my
creation and my grandmothers gatheren
from my bones like great wooden birds
spread their wings
while their long / legged / laughter /
stretches the night.
            and i taste the
seasons of my birth. mangoes. papayas
drink my woman / coconut / milks
stalk the ancient grandfathers
sippen on proud afternoons
walk with a song round my waist
tremble like a new / born / child troubled

with new breaths
                    and my singen
becomes the only sound of a
blue / blk / magical / woman. walken.
womb ripe. walken. loud with mornings. walken
maken pilgrimage to herself. walken.

QUESTIONS

1. Black aesthetic poetry is noted for its bold images and figures of speech. Identify some of them, and explain how they relate to the poem's overall theme.
2. How effective is Sanchez's decision to ignore the standard rules of grammatical form? What ideological statement is she making?
3. What, for Sanchez, gives the black woman a privileged place in Afro-American history?
4. Is there a "maternal instinct"? Discuss the claim that black women are more maternal than white women.

GWENDOLYN BROOKS (1917–   )

The Life of Lincoln West

Ugliest little boy
that everyone ever saw.
That is what everyone said.

Even to his mother it was apparent—
when the blue-aproned nurse came into the
northeast end of the maternity ward
bearing his squeals and plump bottom
looped up in a scant receiving blanket,
bending, to pass the bundle carefully
into the waiting mother-hands—that this
was no cute little ugliness, no sly baby waywardness
that was going to inch away
as would baby fat, baby curl, and
baby spot-rash. The pendulous lip, the
branching ears, the eyes so wide and wild,
the vague unvibrant brown of the skin,
and, most disturbing, the great head.
These components of That Look bespoke
the sure fibre. The deep grain.

His father could not bear the sight of him.
His mother high-piled her pretty dyed hair and
put him among her hairpins and sweethearts,
dance slippers, torn paper roses.
He was not less than these,
he was not more.

As the little Lincoln grew,
uglily upward and out, he began
to understand that something was
wrong. His little ways of trying
to please his father, the bringing
of matches, the jumping aside at
warning sound of oh-so-large and
rushing stride, the smile that gave
and gave and gave—Unsuccessful!
Even Christmases and Easters were spoiled.
He would be sitting at the
family feasting table, really
delighting in the displays of mashed potatoes
and the rich golden
fat-crust of the ham or the festive
fowl, when he would look up and find
somebody feeling indignant about him.

What a pity what a pity. No love
for one so loving. The little Lincoln
loved Everybody. Ants. The changing
caterpillar. His much-missing mother.
His kindergarten teacher.

His kindergarten teacher—whose
concern for him was composed of one
part sympathy and two parts repulsion.
The others ran up with their little drawings.
He ran up with his.
She
tried to be as pleasant with him as
with others, but it was difficult.
For she was all pretty! all daintiness,
all tiny vanilla, with blue eyes and fluffy
sun-hair. One afternoon she
saw him in the hall looking bleak against
the wall. It was strange because the
bell had long since rung and no other
child was in sight. Pity flooded her.

She buttoned her gloves and suggested
cheerfully that she walk him home. She
started out bravely, holding him by the
hand. But she had not walked far before
she regretted it. The little monkey.
Must everyone look? And clutching her
hand like that . . . Literally pinching
it . . .

At seven, the little Lincoln loved
the brother and sister who
moved next door. Handsome. Well-
dressed. Charitable, often, to him. They
enjoyed him because he was
resourceful, made up
games, told stories. But when
their More Acceptable friends came they turned
their handsome backs on him. He
hated himself for his feeling
of well-being when with them despite—
Everything.

He spent much time looking at himself
in mirrors. What could be done?
But there was no
shrinking his head. There was no
binding his ears.

"Don't touch me!" cried the little
fairy-like being in the playground.

Her name was Nerissa. The many
children were playing tag, but when
he caught her, she recoiled, jerked free
and ran. It was like all the
rainbow that ever was, going off
forever, all, all the sparklings in
the sunset west.

One day, while he was yet seven,
a thing happened. In the down-town movies
with his mother a white
man in the seat beside him whispered
loudly to a companion, and pointed at
the little Linc.
"THERE! That's the kind I've been wanting

to show you! One of the best
examples of the specie. Not like
those diluted Negroes you see so much of on
the streets these days, but the
real thing.

Black, ugly, and odd. You
can see the savagery. The blunt
blankness. That is the real
thing."

His mother—her hair had never looked so
red around the dark brown
velvet of her face—jumped up,
shrieked "Go to—" She did not finish.
She yanked to his feet the little
Lincoln, who was sitting there
staring in fascination at his assessor. At the author of
      his new idea.

All the way home he was happy. Of course,
he had not liked the word
"ugly."
But, after, should he not
be used to that by now? What had
struck him, among words and meanings
he could little understand, was the phrase
"the real thing."
He didn't know quite why,
but he liked that.
He liked that very much.

When he was hurt, too much
stared at—
too much
left alone—he
thought about that. He told himself
"After all, I'm
the real thing."

It comforted him.

QUESTIONS

1. Read Brooks's description of Lincoln in the second
   stanza. Does it suggest ugliness? What constitutes

physical repulsiveness? What constitutes physical beauty?

2. Who or what does the kindergarten teacher represent? What are her strengths and weaknesses?

3. Who are the ''diluted Negroes'' in the poem? In what sense can it be said that Lincoln's parents are diluted?

4. The expression ''real thing'' has numerous connotations. Discuss its meanings for the white man in the movies, for Lincoln's mother, and for Lincoln himself.

Black Aesthetic Art   Black aesthetic art was, like the literature and music of the movement, considered functional, collective, and didactic. While the dominant trend of art before the 1960s was to illustrate the frustration, oppression, and domination of Afro-Americans, the new art centered on positive and determined cultural enrichment. Like Mexican and other Latin American artists before them, black artists of the 1960s chose outdoor murals for their high visibility to every-

one in the black neighborhoods. In these murals, the artists sought to give form and color to everyday black life, to create new images and heroes, and to provide positive teachings. In the mural *Knowledge Is Power, Stay in School* (Fig. 37-1), Dana Chandler instructs his viewers in the value of knowledge and education. Erect and sturdy black men and women are depicted freeing both children and adults from the egg (visibly white) of oppression and racism. The dominant colors of the black revolution movement—red, black and green— stand for blood, skin color (or Africa), and renewed life, respectfully.

Jazz of the Sixties: Ornette Coleman (1930–)

The career of one leading jazz musician exemplifies the cultural and social upheavals that took place in America beginning in the 1960s. The changes in his music and in his public image reflect transformations taking place in American society among all races and socioeconomic groups. In many ways, jazz saxophonist Or-

37-1   Dana Chandler, *Knowledge is Power, Stay in School*. Street Mural, Roxbury, Mass. © 1988 Mark Diamond)

nette Coleman is and was as much a social leader as he is a musical artist of the first rank, and his struggles with both music and society tell us much about ourselves and our country.

The significance of Coleman's contribution can be measured accurately only against a broad spectrum of music history. Jazz has many great figures—men and women of extraordinary musical talent, artistic acumen, and virtuosic technique, whose legacy of refined creation is loved, respected, replayed, recreated, imitated, and built upon. In this regard, jazz is like all other serious art musics of the world. But Coleman's contribution to jazz was unlike the achievements of Oscar Peterson, Duke Ellington, Louis Armstrong, or Mary Lou Williams; even those of Charlie Parker, Thelonious Monk, and Miles Davis were essentially different, in that each built upon the tradition handed to them by their musical predecessors. Ornette Coleman changed the nature of the language itself.

How many times in the history of Western music have there been changes in conception so pronounced that the musicians themselves, at the time the first events occurred, actually noticed a radical shift and designated a new style? In the last thousand years in the West, one can count these events on the fingers of both hands. This rarity is in itself a measure of the attainment, as well as the daring and fortitude, of the jazz artist Ornette Coleman. By way of comparison, one might look to the beginning of the fourteenth century when Philippe de Vitry declared that the then-new music with duple rhythms, new notation, and pervasive secular interests constituted in *Ars nova* (new art).

Around 1960, Ornette Coleman revolted against the restraints of jazz harmonies and traditional rhythm sections and replaced the standard monodic and harmonic style of jazz with a complicated tapestry of atonal polyphony. In so doing, he incorporated into jazz the *free form* concept that is pivotal to his thinking and the new style.

Surely the environment surrounding Coleman in the late 1950s did not lack jazz explorers paddling furiously against the current of the mainstream. Saxophonist Sonny Rollins experimented with time signatures uncommon in jazz and recorded "Valse Hot" and "Blue Seven"; Teo Macero incorporated electronic sounds and electronically distorted sounds into his music and

recorded his "Sounds of May"; the exciting John Coltrane moved quickly toward "sheets of sound" and rapid harmonic changes with his "Giant Steps" album; and Miles Davis ushered in "modal" jazz when he recorded "Kind of Blue."

These examples alone represent experiments in rhythm, form, timbre, instrumental technique, harmonic progression, and modal improvisation, but they all fit within the mainstream techniques of jazz of the 1950s. This is the backdrop that set the stage for the dramatic entrance of Ornette Coleman.

Born in Texas in 1930, Ornette Coleman had little formal musical training, but by 1944, at the age of fourteen, he was playing with rhythm-and-blues bands in the Fort Worth area. In the 1940s, the black community of America lacked the cohesion and unity of purpose that it developed in the 1960s. Just after World War II, the United States was not an integrated society, especially in the South. Hostility between races was prevalent, and even within the black community racial tension and unrest was rife. Coleman, although only one among many admirable black leaders, was an important and noteworthy catalyst in the process that first cemented the black community and later demanded and won recognition, respect, and equality for an oppressed minority. But it required of him a personal struggle that was both conscious and painful.

To illustrate, in 1949 when Coleman was nineteen, he visited a musician in New Orleans, the cornetist Melvin Lastie, and accompanied his friend to a job in nearby Baton Rouge. Ornette's personal manner, even then, was free rather than conventional; he wore long, straightened hair and a beard at a time when polite male blacks were clean shaven and wore a "razor cut." Both his playing and his appearance were put on the line. Coleman relates:

> And I was sittin' there listening to the band and all of a sudden a guy came in and said some musicians wanted to meet me outside. So I went outside and there were these really big guys, six or seven of them. I said, "How you doin'?" And one of them said, "Where you from?" And I said, "Oh, I'm from Fort Worth." And they were all black guys. . . . They started using "nigger" and all this, and "You're not from Texas with your beard like that and your long hair. You must be one of those Yankee kind of niggers!" And all of a sudden a guy kicked

me in my stomach and then he kicked me in the ass and I had my horn cradled in my arms and I blacked out 'cause blood was everywhere. . . . They were just beating me to death. One guy took my tenor and threw it down the street. Then Melvin and the band came out and discovered I was beat up and they took me to the police department. The cops said, "What you doing with that long hair?" And they started calling me nigger and they told me that if them other niggers didn't finish me, *they were gonna.*

So I went back to Melvin's house, and I was thinking just like my mother had told me, that the tenor was bad luck. David had an alto, and he said, "I'll let you borrow my alto."[1]

From this anecdote we gain insight into the society in which Coleman matured, the society that would undergo a social revolution in the succeeding years, especially the period following the appearance of the record album *Free Jazz.* Coleman's role in this societal change was not direct, but the music that sprang from the horns of Ornette's followers in the 1960s—men like Archie Shepp, Sun Ra, John Coltrane, and groups like the Art Ensemble of Chicago—became the music of black Americans on the rise. It became a significant voice of dissent, drawing to itself the symbolism of individual and minority rights, people power, nonconformity, and freedom of expression. To say that this music answered this need innocently and by chance would be to ignore the statements and lives of its musicians, their choices of titles for the compositions, the venue of its performance, the mode of its expression, the emotion and content of its words, and the blackness of its performers.

The essence of free jazz is its liberation from tradition, the environment that restricts expression and inhibits change. *Tomorrow Is the Question, Change of a Century,* and *Free Jazz*[2] are all prophetic statements, especially when one considers that they were published in 1959 and 1960. But Ornette Coleman did not overtly seek social change. What transpired on a national and international level, and the role he and his music played in that development, resulted from releasing the frustrations of an entire race. He played his part by expressing his individuality in his music and letting his music exert its power on others. He did not say that music should underpin or accompany a revolt. He was and is first and foremost a musician who is primarily concerned with *The Shape of Jazz to Come.*

Society changed, in a somewhat free-form movement, to the sound of his jazz. Shortly after the incident in Louisiana, Colemen was working in California and developing his style. It was there that he met Donald Cherry, a trumpeter of like mind and extraordinary technique. In 1959, Coleman attended the Lenox School of Jazz in Massachusetts, where he interacted with John Lewis, Gunther Schuller, and other musicians thoroughly grounded in the European classical traditions, both ancient and modern. At the same time, he was reevaluating his own life and declared, along with the literary followers of the black aesthetic, "Black is beautiful." *Change of the Century,* recorded in 1959, foreshadows the revolution that is about to erupt. Long solo lines, enormous bursts of notes, and semi-unisons that gather the form together at oddly spaced points are some of the noteworthy characteristics. One might say that this work exemplifies and marks the end of Coleman's first period—the years of learning, growth, development, and change.

Free Jazz (1960) is the masterpiece that broke with tradition, set the standard, influenced other musicians, and truly moved jazz in a new direction. Here one finds improvisation on a grand scale and a unique sound never employed in jazz before. This effort represents a true penetration into a new frontier. One will look in vain for harmonies, recognizable melodies, rhythms to tap one's foot to. The ensemble is different—a double quartet—and the sound is harsh, strident, penetrating, and loud. Where traditional jazz dealt with well-shaped melodic units (often singable) and well-ordered harmonic progressions, this jazz employs the near total freedom of action and reaction among musicians of like mind. The importance of the soloist is lessened as the total blend of the entire ensemble is attenuated. Instrumental virtuosity, in the old sense of the word, holds little value here, where fast notes and slow notes vie equally for the listener's attention. The production

---

[1] Interview with Ornette Coleman by Jonathan Foose, November 6, 1981, quoted in Jason Berry et al., *Up from the Cradle: New Orleans Music since World War II* (Athens: University of Georgia Press, 1986), pp. 43ff.
[2] Contemporary S7569, Atlantic 1327, and Atlantic 1364, respectively.

of the music becomes a communal action, very much an African characteristic. The blending of ancient and modern, traditional and experimental, into an artistic cluster is a signal accomplishment.

Surrounded by creative musicians, Ornette Coleman continued to search not only for the sound of the future but also for clues to the past. For a while, he returned to the tenor sax, an instrument of his youth, which, in his quest for roots, he hoped might provide him with a "real" black voice. He also experimented with additional sounds from his instruments and even with the syntactical value of silence in a time art. This can be heard in "Silence" (1965), which he recorded in Europe because of the lack of enthusiasm for his music at home.[3]

Soon after, he began to compose works for classical ensembles, as he still does, but his writing is stiff. He relies too much on repetition and repetitive ideas. All of the composed works are interesting pieces stemming from great talent, but Coleman lacks the training and discipline of those other composers—Gunther Schuller, Elliott Carter, Pierre Boulez, and Leon Kirchner—with whom he is competing. The spontaneity of the experienced improvising performer is not apparent in his composed works.

On the other hand, another of his experiments, for which he has received much criticism, has merit. He began performing on both trumpet and violin as well as the saxophone. One can hear Ornette on violin in "Sound Gravitation"[4] Although criticized at the time for his performance abilities on this instrument, Coleman is bringing new textures and timbres to jazz with his approach to violin performance.

Coleman is still searching for new frontiers. "Harmolodic Bebop" from the *Caravan of Dreams*[5] album was recorded in 1985 by his group Prime Time. This work shows Coleman's new interest in electronic instruments and his continuing mastery of his free jazz style. "Song X"[6] with Pat Metheny was also recorded in 1985. This is exciting music by two masters at home in a natural surrounding.

Today, *Free Jazz* is over a quarter of a century old, and in retrospect, we might ask: "How significant was the change?" "What effect has it had on other jazz musicians and their music?" "Has it played a role in influencing the composition and performance of music beyond the world of jazz?" and "Has this music affected society at large, and in what way?"

Ornette Coleman's music led other jazz musicians to question their values and sent many of these musicians on musical and spiritual quests of their own. He is a significant artist, and we can observe his influence on the music of John Coltrane, Muhal Richard Abrams and the Association for the Advancement of Creative Musicians, the Art Ensemble of Chicago, Archie Shepp, Anthony Braxton, Cecil Taylor, and even Miles Davis. *Free Jazz* is a classic, a classic of jazz dating from the 1960s.

Women's Liberation

Feminism, or "the woman question" as it used to be called, seems to come to the forefront and then subside at various times throughout Western history. We have seen various feminist questions addressed in Mary Wollstonecraft's *Vindication of the Rights of Women*, in John Stuart Mill's *On the Subjection of Women*, in the women's suffrage movement, and in Virginia Woolf's *A Room of One's Own*. In the decades following the suffrage movement of the 1920s, once women had obtained the vote in England and America, feminist issues gave way to the more immediately urgent problems posed by the depression and the War. And yet, the movement was launched. Women who took over men's jobs while the men were fighting in the war learned that they could do "men's work." In 1948, just three years after the end of the war and after women obtained the vote in France, a ground-breaking work of feminist theory appeared: Simone de Beauvoir's *The Second Sex*.

De Beauvoir, author of many works of fiction and philosophical essays, was an important figure in the French existentialist movement. The lifelong companion of Jean-Paul Sartre—both of them eschewed marriage as a repressive institution—she developed her own

[3]"Silence," from *The Great London Concert* (Arista 1900).
[4]"Sound Gravitation" from *The Empty Foxhole* (Blue Note 84246).
[5]"Harmolodic Bebop" from *Opening the Caravan of Dreams* (Caravan of Dreams 85001).
[6]"Song X" from *Song X* (Geffen 24096-2)

brand of existentialism, most importantly applying existentialist ideas to feminism. *The Second Sex* is a long and ambitious treatise that views the phenomenon of woman from historical, biological, psychological, sociological, and philosophical points of view. One of de Beauvoir's major points is that woman has always been treated as "the Other," "the second sex," something less than a full human being. Growing up in a patriarchal and repressive society, women have always encountered barriers to the assertion of their individuality and freedom. Like Virginia Woolf, de Beauvoir sees woman's economic dependence on men as a major obstacle. At the end of her book, she calls for a "liberation" of women, including equal opportunity in the work force.

The first reaction to *The Second Sex* was hostility, especially in France, de Beauvoir's native country. French men and women alike did not like the attack they perceived on woman's traditional role as wife, homemaker, and mother. The book was more enthusiastically received in the United States, but even there by only a handful of people. The decade of the 1950s, on both sides of the Atlantic, in fact saw a return, on the part of the majority of women, to the traditional roles and the ideal of the "nurturer" of husband and children. To be "feminine" was to stay in one's place, not to be assertive. It is this conception of femininity that Betty Friedan was to attack in another groundbreaking work, *The Feminine Mystique* (1963).

In the radicalized atmosphere of the 1960s, many young women did step out of the traditional bounds of "femininity," but even there they were often treated as auxiliaries—the ones to make coffee and sandwiches while the men discussed radical politics. It was not until the 1970s that the women's movement really mushroomed, profoundly affecting the lives of women of all ages and social classes. "Consciousness-raising" groups were formed to help women clarify what oppressed them and to liberate themselves, women's studies programs were organized at universities, the National Organization for Women with Betty Friedan as president was founded, and other women's groups on all sides of the political spectrum sprang up. Legal and political battles against various types of discrimination and for passage of the Equal Rights Amendment continue. A great many works of feminist theory, too numerous and too diverse to be discussed here, have appeared since that time.

It is almost impossible to find a single text that represents contemporary feminism. The movement has been accused by some as being too white and middle class in orientation, yet black, Chicano, and Native American women have made important contributions. Feminism has had and continues to have significant repercussions in all of the arts, as well as in theory and in politics. One important black feminist is the writer Alice Walker, author of the Pulitzer Prize–winning novel *The Color Purple*. In the short story below, taken from her collection entitled *In Love and Trouble*, Walker deals with modern woman's preoccupation with beauty, rebellion against male authority, and struggle for personal freedom. The poems by Adrienne Rich, a long-time activist in the woman's movement, as well as one of the foremost contemporary American poets, exemplify the use of feminist themes in poetry. The selection from a 1978 speech Rich gave on the theme of motherhood brings out a theme that relates to a specifically feminist and controversial artist, Judy Chicago.

ALICE WALKER (1944–)

"Really, *Doesn't* Crime Pay?"

(*Myrna*)

September, 1961

page 118

I sit here by the window in a house with a thirty-year mortgage, writing in this notebook, looking down at my Helena Rubenstein hands . . . and why not? Since I am not a serious writer my nails need not be bitten off, my cuticles need not have jagged edges. I can indulge myself—my hands—in Herbessence nailsoak, polish, lotions, and creams. The result is a truly beautiful pair of hands: sweet-smelling, small, and soft. . . .

I lift them from the page where I have written the line "Really, *Doesn't* Crime Pay?" and send them seeking up my shirt front (it is a white and frilly shirt) and smoothly up the column of my throat, where gardenia scent floats beneath my hairline. If I should spread my arms and legs or whirl, just for an instant, the sweet smell of my body would be more than I could bear. But I fit into my new surroundings perfectly; like a jar of cold cream melting on a mirrored vanity shelf.

page 119

"I have a surprise for you," Ruel said, the first time he brought me here. And you know how sick he makes me now when he grins.

"What is it?" I asked, not caring in the least.

And that is how we drove up to the house. Four bedrooms and two toilets and a half.

"Isn't it a beauty?" he said, not touching me, but urging me out of the car with the phony enthusiasm of his voice.

"Yes," I said. It is "a beauty." Like new Southern houses everywhere. The bricks resemble cubes of raw meat; the roof presses down, a field hat made of iron. The windows are narrow, beady eyes; the aluminum glints. The yard is a long undressed wound, the few trees as bereft of foliage as hairpins stuck in a mud cake.

"Yes," I say, "it sure is a beauty." He beams, in his chill and reassured way. I am startled that he doesn't still wear some kind of military uniform. But no. He came home from Korea a hero, and a glutton for sweet smells.

"Here we can forget the past," he says.

page 120

We have moved in and bought new furniture. The place reeks of newness, the green walls turn me bilious. He stands behind me, his hands touching the edges of my hair. I pick up my hairbrush and brush his hands away. I have sweetened my body to such an extent that even he (especially he) may no longer touch it.

I do not want to forget the past; but I say "Yes," like a parrot. "We can forget the past here."

The past of course is Mordecai Rich, the man who, Ruel claims, caused my breakdown. The past is the night I tried to murder Ruel with one of his chain saws.

May, 1958

page 2

Mordecai Rich

Mordecai does not believe Ruel Johnson is my husband. "*That* old man," he says, in a mocking, cruel way.

"Ruel is not old," I say. "Looking old is just his way." Just as, I thought, looking young is your way, although you're probably not much younger than Ruel.

Maybe it is just that Mordecai is a vagabond, scribbling down impressions of the South, from no solid place, going to none . . . and Ruel has never left Hancock County, except once, when he gallantly went off to war. He claims travel broadened him, especially his two months of European leave. He married me because although my skin is brown he thinks I look like a Frenchwoman. Sometimes he tells me I look Oriental: Korean or Japanese. I console myself with this thought: My family tends to darken and darken as we get older. One day he may wake up in bed with a complete stranger.

"He works in the store," I say. "He also raises a hundred acres of peanuts." Which is surely success.

"That many," muses Mordecai.

It is not pride that makes me tell him what my husband does, is. It is a way I can tell him about myself.

page 4

Today Mordecai is back. He tells a funny/sad story about a man in town who could not move his wife. "He huffed and puffed," laughed Mordecai, "to no avail." Then one night as he was sneaking up to her bedroom he heard joyous cries. Rushing in he found his wife in the arms of another woman! The wife calmly dressed and began to pack her bags. The husband begged and pleaded. "Anything you want," he promised. "What *do* you want?" he pleaded. The wife began to chuckle and, laughing, left the house with her friend.

Now the husband gets drunk every day and wants an ordinance passed. He cannot say what the ordinance will be against, but that is what he buttonholes people to say: "I want a goddam ordinance passed!" People who know the story make jokes about him. They pity him and give him enough money to keep him drunk.

page 5

I think Mordecai Rich has about as much heart as a dirt-eating toad. Even when he makes me laugh I know that nobody ought to look on other people's confusion with that cold an eye.

"But that's what I am," he says, flipping through the pages of his scribble pad. "A cold eye. An eye looking for Beauty. An eye looking for Truth."

"Why don't you look for other things?" I want to know. "Like neither Truth nor Beauty, but places in people's lives where things have just slipped a good bit off the track."

"That's too vague," said Mordecai, frowning.

"So is Truth," I said. "Not to mention Beauty."

page 10

Ruel wants to know why "the skinny black tramp"— as he calls Mordecai—keeps hanging around. I made the mistake of telling him Mordecai is thinking of using our house as the setting for one of his Southern country stories.

"Mordecai is from the North," I said. "He never saw a wooden house with a toilet in the yard."

"Well maybe he better go back where he from," said Ruel, "and shit the way he's used to."

It's Ruel's pride that is hurt. He's ashamed of this house that seems perfectly adequate to me. One day we'll have a new house, he says, of brick, with a Japanese bath. How should I know why?

page 11

When I told Mordecai what Ruel said he smiled in that snake-eyed way he has and said, "Do *you* mind me hanging around?"

I didn't know what to say. I stammered something. Not because of his question but because he put his hand point-blank on my left nipple. He settled his other hand deep in my hair.

"I am married more thoroughly than a young boy like you could guess," I told him. But I don't expect that to stop him. Especially since the day he found out I wanted to be a writer myself.

It happened this way: I was writing in the grape arbor, on the ledge by the creek that is hidden from the house by trees. He was right in front of me before I could put my notebook away. He snatched it from me and began to read. What is worse, he read aloud. I was embarrassed to death.

"No wife of mine is going to embarrass me with a lot of foolish, vulgar stuff," Mordecai read. (This is Ruel's opinion of my writing.) *Every time he tells me how peculiar I am for wanting to write stories he brings up having a baby or going shopping, as if these things are the same. Just something to occupy my time.*

"If you have time on your hands," he said today,

"why don't you go shopping in that new store in town."

I went. I bought six kinds of face cream, two eyebrow pencils, five nightgowns and a longhaired wig. Two contour sticks and a pot of gloss for my lips.

And all the while I was grieving over my last story. Outlined—which is as far as I take stories now—but dead in embryo. My hand stilled by cowardice, my heart the heart of a slave.

page 14

Of course Mordecai wanted to see the story. What did I have to lose?

"Flip over a few pages," I said. "It is the very skeleton of a story, but one that maybe someday I will write."

"The One-Legged Woman," Mordecai began to read aloud, then continued silently.

The characters are poor dairy farmers. One morning the husband is too hung over to do the milking. His wife does it and when she has finished the cows are frightened by thunder and stampede, trampling her. She is also hooked severely in one leg. Her husband is asleep and does not hear her cry out. Finally she drags herself home and wakes him up. He washes her wounds and begs her to forgive him. He does not go for a doctor because he is afraid the doctor will accuse him of being lazy and a drunk, underserving of his good wife. He wants the doctor to respect him. The wife, understanding, goes along with this.

However, gangrene sets in and the doctor comes. He lectures the husband and amputates the leg of the wife. The wife lives and tries to forgive her husband for his weakness.

While she is ill the husband tries to show he loves her, but cannot look at the missing leg. When she is well he finds he can no longer make love to her. The wife, sensing his revulsion, understands her sacrifice was for nothing. She drags herself to the barn and hangs herself.

The husband, ashamed that anyone should know he was married to a one-legged woman, buries her himself and later tells everyone that she is visiting her mother.

While Mordecai was reading the story I looked out over the fields. If he says one good thing about what I've written, I promised myself, I will go to bed with him. (How else could I repay him? All I owned in any supply were my jars of cold cream!) As if he read my mind he sank down on the seat beside me and looked at me strangely.

"*You* think about things like this?" he asked.

He took me in his arms, right there in the grape arbor. "You sure do have a lot of heavy, sexy hair," he said, placing me gently on the ground. After that, a miracle happened. Under Mordecai's fingers my body opened like a flower and carefully bloomed. And it was strange as well as wonderful. For I don't think love had anything to do with this at all.

page 17

After that, Mordecai praised me for my intelligence, my sensitivity, the depth of the work he had seen—and naturally I showed him everything I had: old journals from high school, notebooks I kept hidden under tarpaulin in the barn, stories written on paper bags, on table napkins, even on shelf paper from over the sink. I am amazed—even more amazed than Mordecai—by the amount of stuff I have written. It is over twenty years' worth, and would fill, easily, a small shed.

"You must give these to me," Mordecai said finally, holding three notebooks he selected from the rather messy pile. "I will see if something can't be done with them. You could be another Zora Hurston[1]—" he smiled—"another Simone de Beauvoir!"[2]

Of course I am flattered. "Take it! Take it!" I cry. Already I see myself as he sees me. A famous authoress, miles away from Ruel, miles away from anybody. I am dressed in dungarees, my hands are a mess. I smell of sweat. I glow with happiness.

"How could such pretty brown fingers write such ugly deep stuff?" Modecai asks, kissing them.

page 20

For a week we deny each other nothing. If Ruel knows (how could he not know? His sheets are never fresh), he says nothing. I realize now that he never considered Mordecai a threat. Because Mordecai seems to have nothing to offer but his skinny self and his funny talk. I gloat over this knowledge. Now Ruel will find that I am not a womb without a brain that can be bought with Japanese bathtubs and shopping sprees. The moment of my deliverance is at hand!

page 24

Mordecai did not come today. I sit in the arbor writing down those words and my throat begins to close up. I am nearly strangled by my fear.

page 56

I have not noticed anything for weeks. Not Ruel, not the house. Everything whispers to me that Mordecai has forgotten me. Yesterday Ruel told me not to go into town and I said I wouldn't, for I have been hunting Mordecai up and down the streets. People look at me strangely, their glances slide off me in a peculiar way. It is as if they see something on my face that embarrasses them. Does everyone know about Mordecai and me? Does good loving show so soon? . . . But it is not soon. He has been gone already longer than I have known him.

page 61

Ruel tells me I act like my mind's asleep. It is asleep, of course. Nothing will wake it but a letter from Mordecai telling me to pack my bags and fly to New York.

page 65

If I could have read Mordecai's scribble pad I would know exactly what he thought of me. But now I realize he never once offered to show it to me, though he had a chance to read every serious thought I ever had. I'm afraid to know what he thought. I feel crippled, deformed. But if he ever wrote it down, that would make it true.

page 66

Today Ruel brought me in from the grape arbor, out of the rain. I didn't know it was raining. "Old folks like us might catch rheumatism if we don't be careful," he joked. I don't know what he means. I am thirty-two. He is forty. I never felt old before this month.

page 79

Ruel came up to bed last night and actually cried in my arms! He would give anything for a child, he says.

"Do you think we could have one?" he said.

"Sure," I said. "Why not?"

He began to kiss me and carry on about my goodness.

---

[1]Afro-American novelist (1891–1960).
[2]French feminist writer (1980–1986).

I began to laugh. He became very angry, but finished what he started. He really does intend to have a child.

page 80

I must really think of something better to do than kill myself.

page 81

Ruel wants me to see a doctor about speeding up conception of the child.

"Will you go, honey?" he asks, like a beggar.

"Sure," I say. "Why not?"

page 82

Today at the doctor's offic the magazine I was reading fell open at a story about a one-legged woman. They had a picture of her, drawn by someone who painted the cows orange and green, and painted the woman white like a white cracker, with little slit-blue eyes. Not black and heavy like she was in the story I had in mind. But it is still my story, filled out and switched about as things are. The author is said to be Mordecai Rich. They show a little picture of him on a back page. He looks severe and has grown a beard. And underneath his picture there is that same statement he made to me about going around looking for Truth.

They say his next book will be called "The Black Woman's Resistance to Creativity in the Arts."

page 86

Last night while Ruel snored on his side of the bed I washed the prints of his hands off my body. Then I plugged in one of his chain saws and tried to slice off his head. This failed because of the noise. Ruel woke up right in the nick of time.

page 95

The days pass in a haze that is not unpleasant. The doctors and nurses do not take me seriously. They fill me full of drugs and never even bother to lock the door. When I think of Ruel I think of the song the British sing: "Ruel Britannia"! I can even whistle it, or drum it with my fingers.

September, 1961

page 218

People tell my husband all the time that I do not look crazy. I have been out for almost a year and he is begin-

ning to believe them. Nights, he climbs on me with his slobber and his hope, cursing Mordecai Rich for messing up his life. I wonder if he feels our wills clashing in the dark. Sometimes I see the sparks fly inside my head. It is amazing how normal everything is.

page 223

The house still does not awaken to the pitter-patter of sweet little feet, because I religiously use the Pill. It is the only spot of humor in my entire day, when I am gulping that little yellow tablet and washing it down with soda pop or tea. Ruel spends long hours at the store and in the peanut field. He comes in sweaty, dirty, tired, and I wait for him smelling of Arpège, My Sin, Wind Song, and Jungle Gardenia. The women of the community feel sorry for him, to be married to such a fluff of nothing.

I wait, beautiful and perfect in every limb, cooking supper as if my life depended on it. Lying unresisting on his bed like a drowned body washed to shore. But he is not happy. For he knows now that I intend to do nothing but say yes until he is completely exhausted.

I go to the new shopping mall twice a day now; once in the morning and once in the afternoon, or at night. I buy hats I would not dream of wearing, or even owning. Dresses that are already on their way to Goodwill. Shoes that will go to mold and mildew in the cellar. And I keep the bottles of perfume, the skin softeners, the pots of gloss and eye shadow. I amuse myself painting my own face.

When he is quite, quite tired of me I will tell him how long I've relied on the security of the Pill. When I am quite, quite tired of the sweet, sweet smell of my body and the softness of these Helena Rubenstein hands I will leave him and this house. Leave them forever without once looking back.

QUESTIONS

1. In "Really, *Doesn't* Crime Pay?" Walker employs the tale-within-a-tale technique. In what way does the theme of the inner story, "The One-Legged Woman," enlarge or mirror the narrator's predicament?

2. What is the narrator's attitude toward her body? Do

you think that such an attitude points to a significant flaw in the modern woman?
3. What does the narrator mean when she says, "I fit
into my new surroundings perfectly; like a jar of
cold cream melting on a mirrored vanity shelf"?
4. Why does the narrator continue to live with her husband, Ruel Johnson? Why does she try to slice off his
head with a chain saw?
5. Discuss the similarities and differences between
Mordecai Rich and Ruel Johnson. Which, if either,
of the two is more tolerable as a male companion?
6. What techniques of rebellion or resistance to male
domination are employed by the narrator?

ADRIENNE RICH (1929–)

Trying to Talk with a Man

Out in this desert we are testing bombs,

that's why we came here.

Sometimes I feel an underground river
forcing its way between deformed cliffs
an acute angle of understanding
moving itself like a locus of the sun
into this condemned scenery.

What we've had to give up to get here—
whole LP collections, films we starred in
playing in the neighborhoods, bakery windows
full of dry, chocolate-filled Jewish cookies,
the language of love-letters, of suicide notes,
afternoons on the riverbank
pretending to be children

Coming out to this desert
we meant to change the face of
driving among dull green succulents
walking at noon in the ghost town
surrounded by a silence

that sounds like the silence of the place
except that it came with us
and is familiar
and everything we were saying until now

was an effort to blot it out—
coming out here we are up against it

Out here I feel more helpless
with you than without you

You mention the danger
and list the equipment
we talk of people caring for each other
in emergencies—laceration, thirst—
but you look at me like an emergency

Your dry heat feels like power
your eyes are stars of a different magnitude
they reflect lights that spell out: EXIT
when you get up and pace the floor

talking of the danger
as if it were not ourselves
as if we were testing anything else

Translations

You show me the poems of some woman
my age, or younger
translated from your language

Certain words occur: enemy, oven, sorrow
enough to let me know
she's a woman of my time

obsessed

with Love, our subject:
we've trained it like ivy to our walls
baked it like bread in our ovens
worn it like lead on our ankles
watched it through binoculars as if
it were a helicopter
bringing food to our famine
or the satellite
of a hostile power

I begin to see that woman doing things: stirring rice
ironing a skirt
typing a manuscript till dawn

trying to make a call
from a phonebooth

The phone rings unanswered
in a man's bedroom
she hears him telling someone else
Never mind. She'll get tired—
hears him telling her story to her sister

who becomes her enemy
and will in her own time
light her own way to sorrow

ignorant of the fact this way of grief
is shared, unnecessary
and political

The Ninth Symphony of Beethoven Understood at Last as a Sexual Message

A man in terror of impotence
or infertility, not knowing the difference
a man trying to tell something
howling from the climacteric
music of the entirely
isolated soul
yelling at Joy from the tunnel of the ego
music without the ghost
of another person in it, music
trying to tell something the man
does not want out, would keep if he could
gagged and bound and flogged with chords of Joy
where everything is silence and the
beating of a bloody fist upon
a splintered table

QUESTIONS

1. Define the connection between the personal relationship and the bomb testing site in "Trying to Talk with a Man." How does the poet establish this relationship?
2. Define the concept of love in "Translations." What is the effect of the *similes* in the stanza beginning "with Love . . ."?
3. What is the meaning of "political" in "Translations?" Why do you think that the poem ends with this word?
4. Describe the rhythm in "The Ninth Symphony . . ." Do you see any relationship to Beethoven's music?
5. What is the "sexual message"?
6. What kind of dialogue is established here between a contemporary poet and a major monument of Western culture?

Motherhood: The Contemporary Emergency and the Quantum Leap

One of the most powerful social and political catalysts of the past decade has been the speaking of women with other women, the telling of our secrets, the comparing of wounds and the sharing of words. This hearing and saying of women has been able to break many a silence and taboo; literally to transform forever the way we see. Let this be a time, then, for hearing and speaking together, for breaking silences, not only within yourselves but among all our selves: the daughter and the mother; the black woman and the white; the lesbian mother and the married housewife; the woman who has chosen single or communal motherhood and the woman who has chosen to use her life in ways which do not include the raising of children; the woman who has given up custody of her children and the woman who is fighting to keep hers; the stepdaughter, the foster-mother, the pregnant woman; the daughter who has never known her mother, the mother who has no daughters. What we all, collectively, have lived, as the daughters of women, as the mothers of children, is a tale far greater than any three or four of us can encompass: a tale only beginning to be told. I hope that here, speaking to and hearing one another, we can begin to fling cables of recognition and attention across the conditions that have divided us. And so I begin . . . by urging each of you to take responsibility for the voicing of her experience, to take seriously the work of listening to each other and the work of speaking, whether in private dialogue or in larger groups. In order to change what is, we need to give speech to what *has been*, to imagine together what *might be*.

I have seen massive sculpturelike weavings, of jute, hemp, and wool, in which many varicolored strands are quickly visible like vines or striations; but when you come closer and try to touch this or that strand, your hand enters a dense, bristling mesh, thick with knotted and twisted filaments, some harsh and rough to the fingers, others surprisingly silky and strong. In writing *Of Woman Born*, and in thinking about motherhood ever since, I have felt a similar sensation, of elemental exploration and of complex discovery. Let us try then to do justice to the complexity of this immense weaving, even as we single out particular strands or finger particular knots that seem to account for the whole. For motherhood is the great mesh in which all human relations are entangled, in which lurk our most elemental assumptions about love and power.

If we speak of motherhood at all, we are inevitably speaking of something far more than the relationship of a woman with her children. And even this relationship has been shaped long before the first child's birth. All women are daughters of women—is this an obvious, a simple-minded statement? or does it reach through the layers of the weaving to inner chambers only now beginning to be explored by women? It has been suggested by Margaret Mead that possibly a deep chemical affinity exists, of which we as yet know nothing, between the body of the mother and her still unborn female child. It has been affirmed by Nancy Chodorow, that through the intense mother-daughter relationship women come into a deep and richer inner life than men, and, even when heterosexual, tend to be more deeply attached to women than to men, and more capable than men of relationship.[1] Both Chodorow and Dorothy Dinnerstein feel strongly that the solution to sexual inequality would be a radical change in the system of parenting, that is, that parenting must be shared equally between women and men. I wish here to suggest other forces which sit in wait in the birth-chamber as a woman completes her first nine months of mothering.

Historically, cross-culturally, a woman's status as childbearer has been the test of her womanhood. Through motherhood, every woman has been defined from outside herself: mother, matriarch, matron, spinster, barren, old maid—listen to the history of emotional timbre that hangs about each of these words. Even by default motherhood has been an enforced identity for women, while the phrases "childless man" and "nonfather" sound absurd and irrelevant to us.

And so this woman in labor is on the one hand, even perhaps in terror and pain, doing what history has told her it was her duty and destiny to do; while at the same time doing what her mother did, reenacting a scene, which both separates her from her own mother (for now she is, supposedly, herself a woman and no longer a child) and creates her more intensely in her mother's image. . . .

Motherhood, the family, are still too often relegated to the realm of the "private and personal." "For love," women are assumed to provide unflagging emotional care, not only to children but to men; while in terms of the physical work we do, our enormous, unpaid contribution to every economy is everywhere dismissed as only the natural service of women to men and children. We would rightly be skeptical of a feminism which denied the value and dignity of traditional women's work in the home. But in fact it is not feminists who have belittled and devalued the work of the housewife and mother: It is the statisticians, the political scientists, the economists, the image-makers of television and other advertising, the professionals, who depict the woman at home as "not working," as invisible, as an empty-headed consumer. Listen to the idiotic baby-voices allotted to women in canned radio commercials, look at the grimacing smiles of housewives and mothers as depicted on television, observe the obscene patronizing of women on game shows, read the childrais-

[1] *The Reproduction of Mothering* (Berkeley: University of California, 1978), p. 198.

[2] For a detailed documentation and analysis of the creation of "the woman problem" by postindustrial science, especially medicine, see B. Ehrenreich and D. English, *For Her Own Good: 150 Years of the Experts' Advice to Women* (New York: Doubleday/Anchor, 1978), a brilliant study marred only by its failure to deal with heterosexuality itself as a primary mandate to women.

ing and sex manuals, equally patronizing, written by the male doctor experts.[2] The feminist movement has from the first demanded choice as each women's right, respect for each woman's being; feminist artists, historians, anthropologists have been the first to show concern and respect for the crafts of the midwives and grandmothers, the anonymous work of women's hands, the oral culture of women sitting in kitchens, the traditional arts and remedies passed on from mother to daughter, the female culture never granted the reverence accorded to "high art." A recognition of women's unquenchable creativity—contained so often within domestic limits, yet astounding in its diversity—has been one of the deep perceptions of a feminism which looks with fresh eyes on all that has been trivialized, devalued, forbidden, or silenced in female history. And so we can both take pride in all that women have done for "love"—including the resourceful, heroic coping of ordinary women everywhere—and also ask: "Why should women, and women only, work for love only? And what kind of love is this, which means always to be for others, never for ourselves?"

Judy Chicago: The Dinner Party As the excerpt from Rich's speech indicates, feminists in the late 1970s and 1980s began to go beyond demands for equality with men to seek out and assert value in traditional women's work devalued by a male-oriented society. The artist Judy Chicago set out to celebrate both the traditional achievements of women and women's creativity in the "minor arts" in her monumental work *The Dinner Party*. In the spring of 1979 *The Dinner Party* went on exhibit at the San Francisco Museum of Modern Art. The work took five years to complete and involved about four hundred people. It is supposed to symbolize the history of women in Western civilization but might also be understood as a symbol of the controversies that surround the feminist movement in art (Fig. 37-2).

On a large table shaped like an equilateral triangle are arranged thirty-nine place settings (thirteen to a side) of porcelain plate, goblet, and cutlery on elaborate embroidered and appliqued runners whose decorations identify the individual mythical or historical figure symbolized by the plate. The predominant motif of most of the plates is the female genitalia, abstracted and represented in lustrous forms and colors in the technique of modern hand-painted china.

The table is placed on a ceramic floor whose tiles are covered with the names of another 999 women from past to present. The first wing of the table, "Pre-History to Rome," includes a primordial goddess (the earth mother, the matriarchical society), Sophia (wisdom), Hatshepsut (queen of Egypt), Sappho (the Greek Lesbian poet) and Boadecea, the Briton warrior queen who fought the Roman invaders. The second wing, "From the Beginning of Christianity to the Reformation," has settings for St. Bridget, Theodora (wife of Jus-

37-2 Judy Chicago, *The Dinner Party*. (Photo © Michael Alexander, Through the Flower Corp.)

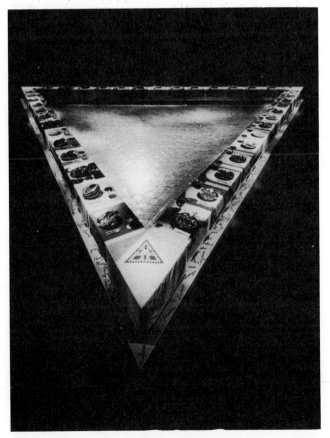

tinian and empress of Byzantium), Eleanor of Aquitaine, Christine de Pisan (the poet), Elizabeth I, and the Italian painter Artemsia Gentileschi. The third wing, "From the American Revolution to the women's revolution," seats Anne Hutchinson, Sacajawea, Caroline Herschel, Mary Wollstonecraft, Sojourner Truth, Susan B. Anthony, Elizabeth Blackwell, Emily Dickinson, Ethel Smyth, Margaret Sanger, Natalie Barney, Virginia Woolf, and Georgia O'Keeffe (see Color Plate XXIII).

Controversy has arisen regarding the choice of dinner guests, but much more was provoked by Chicago's focus on the female genitalia as the major representative motif for the dinner plates. Some critics have called her work insulting, others simplistic (is that the *only* symbol of woman?), and still other critics have not questioned the motif but noted that the plates are simply not good art but rather are uninspired and banal. Almost unanimous approval, however, has been given to the needlework of the thirty-nine runners and the white linen tablecloths. This work elevates and inspires because it is of such high quality and because it recalls the exquisite needlework that has adorned the rich, powerful, and priestly in Western society for millennia. Both china painting and needlework, minor arts always associated with women, were treated as high or fine arts by Chicago. This idea in itself is an important one. *The Dinner Party* also attracted many audiences and stimulated much thinking.

Art, propaganda, or both? *The Dinner Party,* like other feminist enterprises—the new Museum of Woman's Art in Washington, D.C., for example, or the masked, anonymous Gorilla Girls, whose advertisements in art magazines have tried to prove that a white male establishment controls art exhibitions and juries in the major museums, and thus access to galleries, patrons, power, and profit—have raised both the ire and the consciousness of many people. *The Dinner Party* attracted large crowds in Houston, Boston, Atlanta, San Francisco, and New York City. Many people were deeply moved, other scoffed, and still others have decried the deliberate separation of women from men. But none would deny that the feminist movement has brought a new energy and self-confidence to artists who are also women while contributing to the growing pluralism of art in general, in which no particular school or movement holds sway.

Postindustrialism

At least some of the talk current in the 1970s of "the decline of the West" was the product of a partial vision of social and economic change. The depressed state of the American automobile and steel industries, and the growing number of workers who, once laid off, would probably never return to full-time employment, were only symptomatic of the passing away of America's industrial age and the beginning of postindustrialism. It is difficult to provide a chronology for the development, but by the early seventies white-collar workers outnumbered blue-collared workers in the country by five to one.[1] By this time a majority of the American working population was engaged, not in agriculture and industry, but in some kind of service work—that is, in areas like health, education, government, transportation, utilities, and finance. Among the white-collar workers, moreover, the fastest-growing segments were professionals and technicians, especially scientists and engineers.

The rapid increase in these latter occupations provides evidence of the centrality, in a postindustrial society, of theoretical knowledge and its transformation into abstract systems of symbols designed to control innovation and make social planning possible. Advancement in technological areas no longer lies with the tinkerers like Henry Ford or Thomas A. Edison but rather with the masters of highly intricate bodies of theoretical knowledge. Through the use of computers, society has the capacity to organize and utilize vast quantities of data, which allows for informed investigation of major problems, such as cleaning up the environment and defense strategy. These new statistical and logical techniques, focused on defining rational action and the means to achieve it, are replacing the intuitive judgments founded on immediate cause-and-effect relationships, which are often deceptive.

---

[1] Daniel Bell, *The Coming of Post-Industrial Society: A Venture in Social Forecasting* (New York: Basic Books, 1973), p. 17. The above account is based on Bell's analysis.

The new heroes in this age are the scientists and engineers, and the creative centers of intellectual technology are the universities and research laboratories of government and industry. The massive interest of today's students in acquiring computer literacy and technological and scientific training represents a response to the fact that the world has changed and that for many, such knowledge is a guarantee of places in the forefront of the future society. If American industry is bound to suffer in the new age, American leadership of research and development in the post-industrial age will more than balance the loss. Nonetheless, the adjustment will be painful in human terms.

Postmodernism in Culture and the Arts

Three important aspects of postindustrial society seem to affect everyone in some way:

1. the dominant role of the mass media, especially television, in politics, in advertising and in our general awareness of the world
2. the control exercised by the information networks and the increasing dependence on computer technology
3. a pervasive consumerism which encourages the acquisition of more and more goods and services.

All of these have helped to create a new popular culture, worldwide rather than local or regional, and based on the consumption of images rather than on contact with people, events, and live performance. Yet previous cultural modes continue to survive along side and within the new. If we look at the incredible array of artifacts and information easily available—fat romantic narratives lining shelves at the airport, piped music juxtaposing Renaissance dances with the Talking Heads, plotless dramas on off-off Broadway and seemingly infinite plots stretching out the days of *General Hospital*, instant cultural heroes or villains in personae such as Oliver North or Jim and Tammy Bakker, a screen ethic of instant sexual gratification and a church ethic of neopuritanism, people from all parts of the world and all different backgrounds eagerly awaiting the next episode of "Dallas," the continuing proliferation of books and newspapers and the growing types and amounts of information available from computers—we might well believe ourselves to be living in several temporal and spatial dimensions at once. This is precisely what we might call the *postmodern scene.*

Where does this situation leave the artist and the arts? We have seen that, since the Romantic period, there has developed a gradually widening cleavage between popular or mass culture on one hand and "high" or élitist culture on the other. The cleavage was recognized as an inescapable fact of life during the heyday of modernism. Six hundred people, according to Ezra Pound, are all that it takes to make a culture. Taking their art very seriously, exploring new frontiers in the use of language, sound, and visual forms, the modernist artists knew that they were creating only for the few who had the leisure and the sophistication to understand their works. Modernism in the arts is far from dead, and for many, the notion of the artist as an individual struggling to express his or her highly individual view of the world still obtains. Yet new currents have entered the cultural stream.

Critics in the 1960s, sensing a turning away from the tenets of modernism, began to speak of "postmodern" architecture and art, dance, music, and literature. Since then, the term has caught on and been extended to characterize culture in general. Initially, the term was used in a negative sense. Some literary critics, for example, felt that the legacy of the great modernists such as Eliot, Joyce, and Kafka, with their intense devotion to high art and their essentially humanistic faith in human intelligence and human language, was being abandoned. Others welcomed the turning away from a type of art that seemed out of touch with the realities of mass, electronic culture. A critic like Leslie Fiedler embraced the art that he saw emerging from the antiintellectual, antiestablishment trends in the counterculture. The "postmodern" sensibility was, he claimed, apocalyptic, antirational, and joyous, capable of absorbing "pop" culture.

Another critic, Ihab Hassan, who has written extensively about postmodernism, characterizes it as an "art of silence." The artists and writers he chooses to represent postmodernism are not necessarily less difficult or obscure than the modernists, but they lack the modernist faith in the saving power of the work of art and

Modernism	Postmodernism
• urbanism, city as cosmos	• destruction of the city; the world as "global village" or as "spaceship earth."
• "alienation" from industrialism and technology	• use of media and of computer as extension of consciousness
• individualism, expression of self	• fragmentation of the individual; impersonality, "cool"
• emphasis on form, purpose, design	• antiform or open form; play, chance
• art object/finished work	• process/performance/happening
• use of material (outpouring of words, paint, sound)	• fascination with reproduction of images and surfaces; use of silence
• emphasis on craft, technique, seriousness of art.	• irony toward "work of art," anti-"deep meaning," playful
• consciousness of historic evolution of styles.	• mixing of different styles and genres, pastiche

therefore produce an art that tends to be playful and to mock itself. The list of contrasts above, taken primarily from Hassan's book *The Dismemberment of Orpheus*, identifies some of the essential contrasts between the modernist and postmodernist sensibilities.

In a 1986 essay entitled "Pluralism in Postmodern Perspective,"[1] Ihab Hassan updated his reflections on postmodernism with a list of eleven more characteristics, or "definiens" as he called them. For our purposes, the most interesting of these are indeterminacy, fragmentation, and decanonization. The "ultimate opprobrium" of the postmodernist is said to be totalization. Thus the clear and fixed idea, the synthesis, the work of art as a whole or in itself, and indeed the very notions of masterwork, of great author or artist, of pure style, and of an unchanging, commonly accepted cultural tradition are all put into question. Such a shift in mentality could have profound consequences for the humanities. One result that has already begun to take place has been the "opening up" of the canon of works and texts taught in schools to include genres, writing, and art previously excluded or relegated to the domain of minor. Hassan's remarks on postmodernism led him to the following conclusions:

(a) critical pluralism is deeply implicated in the cultural field of postmodernism; and (b) a limited critical pluralism is in some measure a reaction against the radical relativism, the ironic indetermanences, of the postmodern condition; it is an attempt to contain them.

Postmodern Music and Dance

Not everyone, by any means, accepts the label "postmodern" as a valid description of, or even a tendency in, contemporary culture. Yet if used with an awareness of the difficulties of describing one's own era, it may be a helpful guide. A few brief examples from music and dance may serve as illustrations before we go on to study some examples from architecture, painting, and literature.

John Cage, a composer considered by many a kind of apostle of the postmodern, published in 1961 a work called *Silence*. His idea was to have the audience listen to the random sounds around them, to consider these as art. He told them:

nothing is accomplished by writing a piece of music
nothing is accomplished by hearing a piece of music
nothing is accomplished by playing a piece of music
our ears are now in excellent condition

Cage has continued to experiment with random sound and silence. In quite another vein, the music of com-

[1]Ihab Hassan, "Pluralism in Postmodern Perspective," in *The Postmodern Turn: Essays in Postmodern Theory and Culture* (Athens: Ohio University Press, 1987), pp. 167–187.

posers like Miles Davis and Ornette Coleman who mix jazz, popular rock, "serious" electronic music, and African music, may also be considered postmodern. In dance, the choreographer Merce Cunningham, who collaborated extensively with Cage, is generally considered the progenitor of postmodernism. Cunningham broke away from the modern dance of Martha Graham, with its symbolism and psychological exploration, to create a dance of pure movement, with the dancers often dancing to silence. Younger contemporary choreographers have tended to do away with dance as "art," having untrained performers sweep the floor, lay still, or deliver a monologue, calling everything "dance." Others, like Laura Dean, use repetitious geometric patterns—for example, whirling in continuous circles. Twyla Tharp, in one postmodern vein, incorporates social dances from the 1920s through the 1950s into her choreography, as well as experimenting with ordinary "nondance" movements and nonstage environments.

Architecture from the International Style to Postmodernism

The term *postmodern* has been used more consistently in architecture than in any other art form. In order to approach it, we will first have to review developments in architecture since the onset of modernism.

Although the abstract principles of the style could be applied to any architectural problem, probably the one that seemed to cry out most for a new kind of realization was the skyscraper. The Lever Building (Fig. 37-3) the first important skyscraper in the International Style, was designed by Skidmore, Owings, and Merrill for Lever Brothers' headquarters site on Park Avenue in New York City. The glass-curtain wall of the tower, the tower separated from the ground and from the entrance floor, the courtyard with green trees and open space create an image of the best of technology and progress. The only decoration is that provided by the materials, by reflections, and by the spaces themselves. The tall office building is elegant and crisp, and makes a very powerful corporate image. Buildings like these began to proliferate.

When the Seagram Building, designed by Mies, was erected on Park Avenue, it seemed to be the final state-

37-3   The Lever Building, New York. (Ezra Stoller/Esto)

ment about the potentialities of the International Style. Constructed of bronze-anodized steel and dark glass, isolated on the edge of its impersonal plaza, outfitted with sumptuous interiors of wood veneers, bronze, and marble, the Seagram Building was the epitome of corporate wealth and success, and of the unabated technological and economic progress, indeed, hegemony of America in the early 1960s.

The International Style was the "progressive" style. Apartment complexes, colleges, private housing, grocery stores, fire and police stations, hotels, motels, hospitals—whatever was to appear new, modern, and up-to-date—was built in this mode. The box might be of splendid marble, bronze, and dark glass, or of plain stucco and concrete, or of brick with plate-glass windows, but the sameness began to suggest that perhaps this formal language, this style, had limitations, and that there might be other forms for building and more appropriate sources of inspiration for the contemporary age.

In 1967 the Museum of Modern Art again published a book perhaps as important in the history of architecture as *The International Style. Complexities and Contradictions in Architecture* was written by Robert Venturi, a young graduate of the Yale School of Architecture. The book summed up an evolutionary process that had already begun and would continue for decades. *Complexities and Contradictions* said exactly what some architects had already demonstrated and what would prove challenging to many more: architecture need not be confined to the cool, rational box of the International Style. Architecture should be humorous, contextual, traditional, personal, and emotional. Venturi's book constituted a statement of the failure of confidence that many in the architectural profession had in the forms, ideas, and logic of the International Style.

The late work of some of the great masters of the International Style in the 1960s reflects the beginnings of such a change in taste. In his only building built in America, the Carpenter Center at Harvard University (Fig. 37-4), completed in 1963, Le Corbusier turned away from the pure geometry of his early work to use concrete and steel-reinforced concrete as a malleable sculptural medium. Frank Lloyd Wright's Guggenheim Museum (Fig. 37-5) at 81st Street and Park Avenue in New York, built in 1959, is a highly personal, controversial building, both for a city and as an art museum. Centrifugal and vertiginous, at times the building seems to be better for people than for art. Eero Saarinen worked in a variety of forms and materials, attempting to give symbolic expression and imagery to building. The Dulles Airport outside Washington, D.C. (Fig. 37-6), shows his use of reinforced concrete and steel with a glass curtain to create a building expressive of the idea of flight, movement, and energy.

The disenchantment with the International Style encouraged journalists and architectural critics to seek out a deliberately "postmodern" non–International Style building that would establish, if not the vocabulary at least the ideas, that would form the inspiration for a truly postmodern architecture. This building has usually been identified as the 1978 design for the AT&T headquarters building in New York City by Philip Johnson, once a chief practitioner and propagator of the International Style. The building, with its crowning parapet—a swan-necked, broken-pedimented top similar to that of an eighteenth-century Chippendale highboy (as it is sometimes derisively described)—makes a stunning addition to the New York skyline (Fig. 37-7). At street-entry level, a barrel vault cuts into a columnar screen, and the entry portico looks like a Roman triumphal arch moved to the building base. Smooth, butt-jointed granite slabs face walls with almost negligible windows. The contrast with Mies Seagram's glass box building is stark and deliberate.

The historical allusions of Johnson's building are also deliberate and are the consequence not only of dissatisfaction with the International Style but also renewed interest in historical architecture for its own sake. Academic interest in the architecture of the past received validation from exhibitions like *The Architecture of the Ecole des Beaux-Arts* (October 1975–January 1976) at the Museum of Modern Art (Fig. 37-8), which revealed a great deal about the difference in ideals, training, and understanding that created the scorned neoclassical architecture of the past.

Of almost equal importance to this changed attitude has been the growth of the historic preservation movement, which began as an elite movement to save buildings associated with great men and great deeds and broadened at the grass-roots level in towns and cities across America as urban renewal and road building threatened the historic fabric of many places. In response to public pressure, the federal government, through the Department of the Interior, established the National Register of Historic Places. This project established standards for the listing, care, and restoration of historic structures and sites and encouraged local and state governments to survey, identify, photograph, research, and preserve sites of local, regional, or national significance. The existing fabric of many residential, commercial, and industrial neighborhoods has been saved because their presence records important moments and events in American history. Today many of these buildings are being preserved because it is realized that they are part of the total complex that characterized Big City or Small Town, USA (Fig. 37-9).

This movement was joined by architects who for

37-4 Le Corbusier, Carpenter Center, Cambridge, Massachusetts. (Harvard University News Office)

37-5 Frank Lloyd Wright, Guggenheim Museum, New York City.
(Courtesy of the Guggenheim Museum)

37-6 Eero Saarinen, Dulles Airport. 1962. (© Dandelet)

37-7 Philip Johnson and John Burgee, AT & T Headquarters Building, New York City, 1980. (© 1988 Peter Mauss/Esto)

many years had insisted that good design should be based on the context, with ideas drawn from the existing fabric and built with local materials and in concert with local traditions. So strident and successful had been the popularizers of the International Style that many important architects in America were overlooked for years while they quietly and successfully practiced architecture sympathetic to their regions in California, or the MidWest, or the South. Now teachers, critics, and practitioners consider this architecture truly "American," because it relates directly to the place where it is built rather than being based on an abstract canon of rules.

Certainly the new corporate and institutional architecture of the past twenty years has been more complex, varied, controversial, and contradictory in appearance than that of the International Style. Three examples of recent work that have attracted attention are Louis Kahn's Mellon Center for British Studies at Yale University, Charles Moore's Piazza d'Italia in New Orleans, and Richard Meier's Hartford Seminary (Fig. 37-10). Each building represents a different approach to design.

Louis Kahn's Mellon Center, which combines an art museum and library, derives its forms from the func-

37-8 McKim, Mead, and White, Pennsylvania Station, New York City, 1906–1910. Demolished, 1964. This building, an example of neo-classicism, uses the language of Greek and Roman architecture to create a monumental public transportation palace. (The Bettmann Archive)

37-9 South Street Seaport, New York City. The top photo was taken before restoration work began, the bottom one after it was finished. As in other historic preservation and rehabilitation efforts, an attempt has been made to recreate the original atmosphere of the area. Note the original or authentically reproduced building facades, cobblestone paving, lampposts, and signs. (Top: © 1984 Peter Aaron/Esto. Bottom: Photo courtesy of Benjamin Thompson & Associates, Architects, Cambridge, Mass.)

tion of the building and from its location in a complex urban neighborhood. The building itself seems somewhat self-effacing. The exterior is fairly plain and fits into the low-rise collection of small commercial buildings in which it sits. The interior, however, is a rich, complex space that serves the user and the art displayed inside.

In contrast, Charles Moore's Piazza d'Italia derives its forms from classicism and the world of neon and advertising. Challenged to provide a lively focus for this part of New Orleans, Moore has taken the architectural vocabulary that one would find in the streets of an Italian city. Columns, architraves, and arches were built using a lightweight construction technique

37-10 Richard Meier, Hartford Seminary, Hartford, Connecticut. (Ezra Stoller © Esto)

employing neon decoration that contributes to the liveliness and movement of the fountains. The Piazza inspires a feeling of gaiety and fun.

Richard Meier's Hartford Seminary is a late-twentieth-century reinterpretation of the vocabulary of Le Corbusier with high-tech materials. The stunning bright, white building sits in a much older neighborhood, but it does not seem out of place. Its scale and the elegance of the design make it welcoming and friendly.

Thus, each building represents a way of designing that accounts for the past and gives consideration to its site and to the uses for which it is designed. Each architect has interpreted the demands of the problem with different results. This variety may be much more significant than any style name because these buildings may indicate that in architecture, as in art, pluralism is good for design.

Postmodern Painting and Sculpture

Abstract expressionism was predicated on the romantic belief that the imagination is the sure and ready source of artistic originality. This belief built on the ideas of the European surrealists who emphasized the primacy of the subconscious and the dream as the source of creativity. These ideas produced the action, the painterly gesture of the abstract expressionists. This emphasis could, however, be the source of hollow rhetoric and shrill emotionalism, producing art far in quality from that of Pollock and others in the group. Thus the vitality that brought action painting into being also caused its methods to be seriously questioned. Just as architects began to sense change in the air in the early 1960s, so those in the other visual arts began to produce a variety of work rather than that of a single school. Among this variety was so-called "Pop" art, a style built on assessing, assimilating, and reusing the images of popular culture. Using real things, images from daily life, as an inspiration for art was not a new idea. Stuart Davis had painted match boxes, light bulbs, and antiseptic bottles and the cubists had used newspapers, pipes, and wine bottles. But Andy Warhol's presentation of popular figures like Marilyn Monroe (Color Plate XXIV) or Jack Kennedy was different. Silk-screening added color to the images derived from familiar photographs, and a repeated image or one made on a heroic scale gave them a new dimension. The Campbell's soup can, a successful advertising and marketing image, when reproduced at 3 × 4 feet in green and red (Color Plate XXV), triggered a new awareness of the relationships between art and advertising and the potential irony and humor of the relationship. Warhol also used the same techniques to present less pleasant objects for the viewer's contemplation. An electric chair in vivid color or repetition, such as an oversized sheet of stamps, could communicate other ideas about modern popular culture.

Op(optical) art appeared at about the same time. These artists were concerned with the complexity of manipulating the emotional or intellectual response to a visually stimulated experience (see Fig. 37-11). Other isms—conceptualism, minimalism, superrealism, photorealism—piled one upon the other as the art scene changed, both in America and abroad. But in spite of this apparent confusion, certain themes and ideas appeared again and again. The use of images from advertising, films, television, and marketing; the reappearance of the human figure; the production of paintings

with the appearance of photographs; the use of images drawn from painting itself—brushes, tubes of paint, other, older paintings; historical allusions and humorous punning on words and images; the creation of work using means drawn from other media or imitating other media: all these appeared in the work of many different artists. Roy Lichtenstein, for example, produced paintings of paint brushes, antique temples, and cartoons, all by imitating the dot-screen technique of color comic-strip reproduction but produced by hand or mechanically, on a scale never intended by the original process (Fig. 37-12). Lichtenstein also made paintings in the manner of and as a kind of homage to Cezanne, Picasso, Monet, and in the style of several recent periods of art. Malcolm Morley, an Englishman, began as an abstract expressionist, then in the mid-1960s began to produce paintings that imitated photographic images—picture postcards of cruise boats, French chateaux, the covers of magazines. These enlarged and intensified images are extremely powerful and Morley has been able to use them to comment on society, as in a copied travel poster of South Africa with a bloody "X" painted over it, or to comment on art, as in the huge painting of a reproduction of Vermeer's painting, *Artist in the Studio*. Morley's paintings are memorable because they do

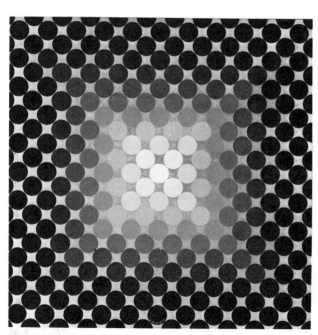

37-11 Victor Vasarely, "CTA-104-E." 1965. (Collection, The Museum of Modern Art, New York. Given in memory of G. David Thompson by his New York friends)

37-12 Roy Lichtenstein, "Little Big Painting." Oil, 1965. (Gift of the Friends of the Whitney Museum of American Art)

not permit the viewer the luxury of ignoring the work but the viewer may choose to concentrate only on the surface and not on the ideas behind the representation. But involvement is always required, and that is the *raison d'être* of this art, as of previous styles—to stimulate the viewer into interaction with the work.

The visual arts have shown a growing interest in the total environment as susceptible to manipulation in ways that recall the complex architectural, sculptural, and painterly arrangements of the seventeenth century. The earthworks that the sculptor Michael Heizer constructed in southern Nevada (Fig. 37-13), the curtain that Christo hung in Rifle Gorge, Colorado (Fig. 37-14), the beams of Corten steel that Richard Serra planted in the earth—all make fun of art in an ironic way while calling attention to the natural environment, attempting to make a kind of peace with it through imaginative uses of technology, and engaging the viewer in an active relationship with the situation. Environmental pieces, whether created for a museum or installed in urban, institutional, or natural sites, are capable of altering the viewer's understanding of both the site and the object, giving new life and interest to both, and to the viewer as well.

Postmodern Literature and Theory

As postmodern architecture plunders the whole repertoire of past styles, and postmodern painting makes pastiches of traditional painting while calling into question the very notion of "art," so do certain postmodern writers comment ironically on the literary canon of the past while questioning the possibility of still writing "literature." The traditional genres that we have observed throughout this book—lyric poetry, tragic drama, prose fiction—tend to become blurred, mixed, or done away with entirely in postmodern writing. Street theater and happenings did away with the stage; new journalists such as Tom Wolfe and the later writings of Norman Mailer mixed subjective impressions with straight reporting; lyric poetry, as we saw in the texts of Adrienne Rich, does not hesitate to comment on political and social questions; short story and diary intermingle, as in the case of Alice Walker; science fiction and journalistic commentaries intermingle in Kurt Vonnegut's work; and pop culture appears alongside

high culture in poems such as the one by Robert Hollander reprinted here. Along with this blurring of genres has come a newfound eminence for what used to be called literary criticism and is now referred to simply as "theory."

The field of theory is far too complex and vast to summarize here, but one point, however simplified, needs to be made: the importance of the nature of language in understanding literature and other cultural phenomena. For a critic and theorist such as Roland Barthes (1915–1980), language is in the last analysis about itself: that is, a text is self-referential, and we should not confuse it with some hypothetical "outside reality." Michel Foucault (1926–1984), who called himself an "archeologist of knowledge," spoke about language in the following terms:

> Having become a dense and consistent historical reality, language forms the locus of tradition, of the unspoken habits of thought, of what lies hidden in a people's mind. . . . Expressing their thoughts in words of which they are not the masters, enclosing them in verbal forms whose historical dimension they are unaware of, men believe that their speech is their servant and do not realize that they are submitting themselves to its demands.

And so we are caught in the prison house of language. There is no sovereign subject, no great author who meant to say something; there are only texts made of words on which we can write commentaries of commentaries. What Foucault proclaims is nothing less than the death of classical humanism. We have gone from a God-centered world to a human-centered world, to a world without center, a world as text.

This view of language is also reflected in a literature that appears to be about itself or about the infinite possibilities of language. Although we discussed the Argentinian Jorge Luis Borges in the section on modernism, where he belongs in many ways, his stories that consist of commentaries on commentaries on texts may be considered postmodern. Postmodern in their concern with language as well as in their use of media are the works of two other Argentinians: Julio Cortazar, who experimented with the limits and limitations of the short story and novel in *Hopscotch* and in *Blowup and Other Short Stories*, and Manuel Puig, who in works such as *Betrayed by Rita Hayworth* and *The Kiss of the Spider Woman* portrays the increasing

37-13 Michael Heizer, "Double Negative," 1969-70. Size 1500 × 50 × 30 feet; 240,000 tons of rhyolite and sandstone displaced. Virgin River Mesa, Nevada. (Collection: Virginia Dwan. Photo courtesy Xavier Fourcade, Inc., New York)

37-14 Christo, "Valley Curtain," 1970-72. Width: 1250–1368 feet. Height:185–365 feet. 200,000 square feet of nylon polyamide; 110,000 pounds of steel cable; 800 tons of concrete. Grand Hogback, Rifle, Colorado. (Photo by Harry Shunk)

incursions of the fictional world of the mass media, particularly of Hollywood films, into the "real" world. The Cuban fiction writer Guillermo Cabrera Infante, and the Nicaraguan poet Ernesto Cardenal, both of whom are discussed here, exemplify other aspects of postmodernism. While Latin American literature since the period in the late 1960s called *el boom* has been one of the major forces in postmodernism, many North American and European writers are often grouped under the rubric "postmodern" as well. Among them are the German Peter Handke, the Italian Italo Calvino, the Irish-French writer Samuel Beckett, and the North Americans Donald Barthelme, Ronald Sukenick, Ishmael Reed, and John Barth, one of whose short-short stories is reprinted here.

Some Examples of Postmodern Writing

JOHN BARTH (1930–)

Autobiography: A Self-Recorded Fiction

You who listen give me life in a manner of speaking.

I won't hold you responsible.

My first words weren't my first words. I wish I'd begun differently.

Among other things I haven't a proper name. The one I bear's misleading, if not false. I didn't choose it either.

I don't recall asking to be conceived! Neither did my parents come to think of it. Even so. Score to be settled. Children are vengeance.

I seem to've known myself from the beginning without knowing I knew; no news is good news; perhaps I'm mistaken.

Now that I reflect I'm not enjoying this life: my link with the world.

My situation appears to me as follows: I speak in a curious, detached manner, and don't necessarily hear myself. I'm grateful for small mercies. Whether anyone follows me I can't tell.

Are you there? If so I'm blind and deaf to you, or you are me, or both're both. One may be imaginary; I've had stranger ideas. I hope I'm a fiction without real hope. Where there's a voice there's a speaker.

ROBERT HOLLANDER (1933–)

You Too? Me Too—Why Not? Soda Pop

I am
look
ing at
the Co
caCola
bottle
which is
green wi
th ridges
just like

c   c   c
o   o   o
l   l   l
u   u   u
m   m   m
n   n   n
s   s   s

and on itself it says
COCA-COLA
reg.u.s.pat.off.

exactly like an art pop statue of that kind of bottle but not so green that the juice inside gives other than the co lor it has when I pour it out in a clear glass glass on this table top (It's making me thirsty all this winking and beading of Hippocrene[1] please let me pause drinking the fluid in) ah! it is enticing how each color is the same brown in green bottle brown in uplifted glass making each utensil on the table laid a brown fork in a brown shade making me long to watch them harvesting the crop which makes the deep-aged rich brown wine of America that is to say which makes soda   pop

---

[1]Note the reference to Keats' "Ode to a Nightingale" (see p. 234).

I see I see myself as a halt narrative: first person, tiresome. Pronoun sans ante or precedent, warrant or respite. Surrogate for the substantive; contentless form, interestless principle; blind eye blinking at nothing. Who am I. A little *crise d'identité*[1] for you.

I must compose myself.

Look, I'm writing. No, listen, I'm nothing but talk; I won't last long. The odds against my conception were splendid; against my birth excellent; against my continuance favorable. Are yet. On the other hand, if my sort are permitted a certain age and growth, God help us, our life expectancy's been known to increase at an obscene rate instead of petering out. Let me squeak on long enough, I just might live forever: a word to the wise.

My beginning was comparatively interesting, believe it or not. Exposition. I was spawned not long since in an American state and born in no better. Grew in no worse. Persist in a representative. Prohibition, Depression, Radicalism, Decadence, and what have you. An eye sir for an eye. It's alleged, now, that Mother was a mere passing fancy who didn't pass quickly enough; there's evidence also that she was a mere novel device, just in style, soon to become a commonplace, to which Dad resorted one day when he found himself by himself with pointless pen. In either case she was mere, Mom; at any event Dad dallied. He has me to explain. Bear in mind, I suppose he told her. A child is not its parents, but sum of their conjoined shames. A figure of speech. Their manner of speaking. No wonder I'm heterodoxical.

Nothing lasts longer than a mood. Dad's infatuation passed; I remained. He understood, about time, that anything conceived in so unnatural and fugitive a fashion was apt to be freakish, even monstrous—and an advertisement of his folly. His second thought therefore was to destroy me before I spoke a word. He knew how these things work; he went by the book. To expose ourselves publicly is frowned upon; therefore we do it to one another in private. He me, I him; one was bound to be the case. What fathers can't forgive is that their offspring receive and sow broadcast their shortcomings. From my conception to the present moment

Dad's tried to turn me off; not ardently, not consistently, not successfully so far; but persistently, persistently, with at least half a heart. How do I know? I'm his bloody mirror!

Which is to say, upon reflection I reverse and distort him. For I suspect that my true father's sentiments are the contrary of murderous. That one only imagines he begot me; mightn't he be deceived and deadly jealous? In his heart of hearts he wonders whether I mayn't after all be the get of a nobler spirit, taken by beauty past his grasp. Or else, what comes to the same thing, to me, I've a pair of dads, to match my pair of moms. How account for my contradictions except as the vices of their versus? Beneath self-contempt, I particularly scorn my fondness for paradox. I despite pessimism, narcissism, solipsism,[2] truculence, word-play, and pusillanimity, my chiefer inclinations; loathe self-loathers *ergo me*;[3] have no pity for self-pity and so am free of that sweet baseness. I doubt I am. Being me's no joke.

I continued the tale of my forebears. Thus my exposure; thus my escape. This cursed me, turned me out; that, curse him, save me; right hand slipped me through left's fingers. Unless on a third hand I somehow preserved myself. Unless unless: the mercy-killing was successful. Buzzards let us say made brunch of me betimes but couldn't stomach my voice, which persists like the Nauseous Danaid.[4] We . . . monstrosities are easilier achieved than got rid of.

In sum I'm not what either parent or I had in mind. One hoped I'd be astonishing, forceful, triumphant—heroical in other words. One dead. I myself conventional. I turn out I. Not every kid thrown to the wolves ends a hero: for each survivor, a mountain of beast-baits; for every Oedipus, a city of feebs.[5]

---

[2]Narcissism is the love of oneself; solipsism is the philosophical position that nothing exists but the contents of one's own mind.
[3]*Ergo me* is Latin for "therefore me."
[4]A Danaid is one of the mythical fifty daughters of Danaus, ruler of Argus, who ordered his daughters to murder their husbands on their wedding night.
[5]Oedipus, the mythical ruler of Thebes (rhymes with "feebs") unknowingly killed his father and married his mother. Oedipus was left out on a hillside (exposed) when born because his father, Laïos, wished to avoid the prophecy that he would be slain by his son. Oedipus was saved by shepherds, who raised him. See Sophocles' tragedy *Oedipus Rex* in Vol. I.

---

[1]A *crise d'identité* is French for "identity crisis."

So much for my dramatic exposition: seems not to've worked. Here I am, Dad: Your creature! Your caricature!

Unhappily, things get clearer as we go along. I perceive that I have no body. What's less, I've been speaking of myself without delight or alternative as self-consciousness pure and sour; I declare now that even that isn't true. I'm not aware of myself at all, as far as I know. I don't think . . . I know what I'm talking about.

Well, well, being well into my life as it's been called I see well how it'll end, unless in some meaningless surprise. If anything dramatic were going to happen to make me successfuller . . . agreeabler . . . endurabler . . . it should've happened by now, we will agree. A change for the better still isn't unthinkable; miracles can be cited. But the odds against a wireless *deus ex machina*[6] aren't encouraging.

Here, a confession: Early on I too aspired to immortality. Assumed I'd be beautiful, powerful, loving, loved. At least commonplace. Anyhow human. Even the revelation of my several defects—absence of presence to name one—didn't fetch me right to despair: crippledness affords its own heroisms, does it not; heroes are typically gimpish, are they not. But your crippled hero's one thing, a bloody hero after all; your heroic cripple another, etcetcetcetcet. Being an ideal's warped image, my fancy's own twist figure, is what undoes me.

I wonder if I repeat myself. One-track minds may lead to their origins. Perhaps I'm still in utero,[7] hung up in my delivery; my exposition and the rest merely foreshadow what's to come, the argument for an interrupted pregnancy.

Womb, coffin, can—in any case, from my viewless viewpoint I see no point in going further. Since Dad among his other failings failed to end me when he should've, I'll turn myself off if I can this instant.

Can't. *Then if anyone hears me, speaking from here inside like a sunk submariner, and has the means to my end, I pray him do us both a kindness.*

Didn't. Very well, my ace in the hole: *Father, have mercy, I dare you! Wretched old fabricator, where's your shame! Put an end to this, for pity's sake! Now! Now!*

So. My last trump, and I blew it. Not much in the way of a climax; more a climacteric. I'm not the dramatic sort. May the end come quietly, then, without my knowing it. In the course of any breath. In the heart of any word. This one. This one.

Perhaps I'll have a posthumous cautionary value, like gibbeted corpses,[8] pickled freaks. Self-preservation, it seems, may smell of formaldehyde.[9]

A proper ending wouldn't spin out so.

I suppose I might have managed things to better effect, in spite of the old boy. Too late now.

Basket case. Waste.

Shake up some memorable last words at least. There seems to be time.

Nonsense, I'll mutter to the end, one word after another, string the rascals out, mad or not, heard or not, my last words will be my last words.

QUESTIONS

1. Who is the speaker of this story?
2. Who is the speaker's father?
3. How does the speaker call attention to the structure of the story?
4. In what ways is the relationship between a protagonist and its author an example of narcissism, of solipsism?
5. How is the Oedipus story a model of the relationship between an author and his protagonist?
6. How are the puns appropriate to this story?

Ernesto Cardenal (1925–), Nicaragua This poet priest, as so many other Latin Americans before him, has lived under the harsh oppression of a long-term dictatorship. He combines Christian and Biblical

---

[6]*Deus ex machina* literally means "god from a machine," a stage device used in Greek drama that would lower an actor, dressed up as a god, to unravel complicated plots and bring about a happy ending.
[7]*In utero* is a medical term for "in the womb."

---

[8]Gibbeted corpses were dead persons left hanging on the gallows.
[9]Formaldehyde is a chemical used for preserving dead bodies.

forms with themes of social protest and revolution. His is the voice of the voiceless. An echo of liberation theology can be heard in much of his profoundly religious poetry. Since the overthrow of the Somozas he has become an active participant in the formation of a new Nicaragua. Poetic works such as *Hora cero (Zero Hour)*, *Epigramas*, and *Oracion por Marilyn Monroe (A Prayer for Marilyn Monroe)* reflect both postmodern themes and a pervasive tone of imminent social upheaval.

ERNESTO CARDENAL

Epigrama 18 •

De pronto suena en la noche una sirena
de alarma, larga, larga,
el aullido lúgubre de la sirena
de incendio o de la ambulancia blanca de la muerte
como el grito de la cegua en la noche,
que se acerca y se acerca sobre las calles
y las casas y sube, sube, y baja
y crece, crece, baja y se aleja
creciendo y bajando. No es incendio ni muerte:
            Es Somoza* que pasa.

———

*Dictator of Nicaragua from 1967 to 1984.

Epigram 18 •

(translated by Thomas Merton)

Suddenly in the night the sirens
sound their long, long, long alarm,
the siren's miserable howl
of fire, or death's white ambulance
like a ghost wailing in the night,
coming closer and closer above the streets
and the houses, it rises, rises, and falls,
and it grows, grows, falls and goes away
growing and dying. It's neither a fire nor a death:
            Just the Dictator flashing by.

Salmo 5 •

Escucha mis palabras oh Señor
            Oye mis gemidos
Escucha mi protesta
Porque no eres tú un Dios amigo de los dictadores
ni partidario de su política
ni te influencia la propaganda
ni estás en sociedad con el gángsters

No existe sinceridad en sus discursos
ni en sus declaraciones de prensa

Hablan de paz en sus discursos
mientras aumentan su producción de guerra

Hablan de paz en las Conferencias de Paz
y en secreto se preparan para la guerra

            Sus radios mentirosos rugen toda la noche

Psalm 5 •

(translated by John R. Kelly)

Listen to my words oh Lord
            Hear my cries
Listen to my protest
Because you are not a God friendly to dictators
nor party to their politics
nor does their propaganda influence you
nor are you in league with the gangster

No sincerity exists in their speeches
nor in their press releases

They talk of peace in their speeches
While they increase their war production

They talk of peace at Peace Conferences
and secretly they prepare for war

            Their lying radios roar all night

Sus escritorios están llenos de planes criminales
                  y expedientes siniestros
Pero tú me salvarás de sus planes

Hablan con la boca de las ametralladoras
Sus lenguas relucientes
                  son las bayonetas. . .

Castígalos oh Dios
                  malogra su política
confunde sus memorándums
                  impide sus programas

A la horna de la Sirena de Alarma
tú estarás conmigo
tú serás mi refugio el día de la Bomba

Al que no cree en la mentira de sus anuncios
comerciales
ni en sus campañas publicitarias ni en sus campañas
politicas
                  tú lo bendices
Lo rodeas con tu amor
                  como con tanques blindados

Their desks are full of criminal plans
                  and sinister files
But you will save me from their plans

They speak with the mouth of machine guns
Their glistening tongues
                  are the bayonets. . .

Punish them oh God
                  wreck their politics
Confuse their memoranda
                  hinder their programs

At the hour of the Alarm Siren
You will be with me
You will be my refuge on the day of the Bomb

He who does not believe in the lie of their
commercials
nor their advertising campaigns nor in their political
campaigns
                  You bless him
You surround him with your love
                  like an armored tank

Prayer for Marilyn Monroe
(translated by Robert Pring-Mill)

Lord
accept this girl called Marilyn Monroe throughout
    the world
though that was not her name
(but You know her real name, that of the orphan
    raped at nine,
the shopgirl who tried to kill herself aged just
    sixteen)
who now goes into Your presence without make-up
without her Press Agent
without her photographs or signing autographs
lonely as an astronaut facing the darkness of outer
    space.
When she was a child, she dreamed she was naked
    in a church
                  (according to *Time*)
standing in front of a prostrate multitude, heads to
    the ground, and had to walk on tiptoe to avoid
    the heads.
You know our dreams better than the psychiatrists.
Church, house, or cave all represent the safety of the
    womb
but also something more. . . .
The heads are admirers, so much is clear (that
mass of heads in the darkness below the beam to
    the screen).
But the temple isn't the studio of 20th-Century Fox.
The temple, of gold and marble, is the temple of her
    body
in which the Son of Man stands whip in hand
driving out the money-changers of 20th-Century Fox
who made Your house of prayer a den of thieves.

Lord,
in this world defiled by radioactivity and sin,
surely You will not blame a shopgirl
who (like any other shopgirl) dreamed of being a
    star.
And her dream became "reality" (Technicolor
    reality).
All she did was follow the script we gave her,
that of our own lives, but it was meaningless.
Forgive her Lord and forgive all of us
for this our 20th Century
and the Mammoth Super-Production in whose
    making we all shared.

She was hungry for love and we offered her
    tranquilizers.
For the sadness of our not being saints
    they recommended Psychoanalysis.
Remember Lord her increasing terror of the camera
and hatred of make-up (yet her insistence on fresh
    make-up
for each scene) and how the terror grew
and how her unpunctuality at the studios grew.

Like any other shopgirl
she dreamed of being a star.
And her life was as unreal as a dream an analyst
    reads and files.

Her romances were kisses with closed eyes
which when the eyes are opened
are seen to have been played out beneath the
    spotlights and the spotlights are switched off

and the two walls of the room (it was a set) are
    taken down
while the Director moves away notebook in hand,
    the scene being safely canned.
Or like a cruise on a yacht, a kiss in Singapore, a
    dance in Rio,
a reception in the mansion of the Duke and Duchess
    of Windsor viewed in the sad tawdriness of a
    cheap apartment.

The film ended without the final kiss.
They found her dead in bed, hand on the phone.

And the detectives never learned who she was going
    to call.
It was as
though someone had dialed the only friendly voice
and heard a prerecorded tape just saying "WRONG
    NUMBER";
or like someone wounded by gansters, who
reaches out toward a disconnected phone.

Lord, whoever
it may have been that she was going to call
but did not (and perhaps it was no one at all
or Someone not in the Los Angeles telephone book),
    Lord, You pick up that phone.

QUESTIONS

1. For what reasons does Cardenal employ such traditional modes as the epigram, prayer, and psalm?
2. What relationship does Cardenal's "Psalm 5" have to the Old Testament's Psalm 5? Why has he used this form and what is its theme?
3. What post-Modernist themes appear in "Prayer for Marilyn Monroe"? Why has the poet employed a prayer as his vehicle here?
4. Compare the image of Marilyn Monroe in this poem to that used by Andy Warhol in his silk-screen (Color Plate XXIV)

Guillermo Cabrera Infante (1929–   ), Cuba
This "boomer" published his first book of short stories, entitled *Ast en la paz como en la guerra* (In peace as in war), in 1957; it was followed in 1964 by his *Tres Tristes Tigres* (Three Trapped Tigers), one of the most resonant explosions of the "boom". In 1973 he wrote his own English translation of "Un nido de gorriones en el toldo" (A Sparrow's Nest in the Awning), but as is evident from the literal translation of the Spanish, his "Nest, Door, Neighbors" presented here goes beyond mere translation in order to become essentially a complete new story. In 1986 Cabrera Infante published his latest work, *Holy Smoke*, a novel entirely dedicated to that legendary Cuban "institution" the cigar. *The Times'* critic John Gross wrote in 1986 that "he weaves his way from one theme to another, as though in a to-

bacco trance, turning aside to follow an idiosyncratic fancy, gliding back to his starting point. Everything reminds him of something else, and everything else reminds him of a cigar." Many of the techniques characteristic of Cabrera Infante and postmodernism are to be found in "Nest, Door, Neighbors." Parody, puns, the interplay between Spanish and English, the vitality of the spoken word captured in print, allusions to mass media creatures and creations, and ellipses provide the structure to this story.

GUILLERMO CABRERA INFANTE

Nest, Door, Neighbors

An odd old couple—Americans residing in Havana circa 1957—lived next door then. They were a very small and extremely quiet pair whom we never met socially. Though we shared with them the same terrace—actually a long and narrow balcony constantly aspiring to the condition of terrace—divided by a low concrete partition, I don't think I ever said hello to them. In fact, I don't recall meeting either of them even once in the communal corridor and they rarely came out onto the terrace—except to warm themselves in the sun on the two or three days in winter when it's cold in Cuba. On these rare occasions they always kept themselves to themselves and so did we.

I remember they had a green awning over their side of the terrace. I *remember*! It is as if Damocles said he remembered there was some sort of sword hanging over him. Remember, hell! To remember you have first to forget—and how could I ever forget?

Long before the event I'm going to tell you about, the Americans' godawful awning became my wife's pet obsession.

—As they never lower it—she used to say,—the awning's always rolled up—which is a good gag line as (unconscious) gag lines go. But then she had to follow her tag line (or her tagmeme) with trying tirades against awnings, waste, Americans, wasted Americans awnings, the English language, onions, *awnings*, awnings and awnings.

—That awning might as well not be up there at all—she habitually concluded.—It's all such a waste!

One evening I was sitting comfortably in a canvas chair on the terrace, my head in a book, when my wife came to tell me that two sparrows had made a nest in the crookedly folded awning. *Hay un nido de gorriones en el toldo*, she told me, speaking in that language which is Spanish when it is written but becomes Cuban when read.

—That sparrow over there—she said (pointing) though I've often wondered if she actually said *gorrión*, sparrow, or *gorrón*, Cuban for lazy bum—, it stays inside all the time while the other one has to go out to find straws.

—An ideal arrangement—I commented.

—How come?

—*Es el macho*. The one flying around is the female.

—How do you know?—she asked suspiciously.

—Because she's duller.

—*Caramba!*—she said and glared at me but didn't say anything else. Oh well, *those* were the days...!

Snugly tucked in the pocket of the awning the fat little cock-sparrow was curiously but unconcernedly watching its smaller, drabber mate trying to get into the fold with its beak full of dried grass.

I suggested that we—meaning she—ought to tell the people next door, least they pull the awning down and the eggs fall out and smash. My wife looked at me as if I were a rare breed: *el hombre tierno*. The original tender-hearted man.

—They might have hatched by then—she added maternally,—and they would fall out and crash before they could fly. Such a waste of lives!

—Naturally—I said absentmindedly, about to go back to my book.

—You speak English, why don't you go and tell them?

The connection between my English and their awning was a faulty one, so I said *Algun día*, which can be translated from suave, vague Spanish into rough but still imprecise English as—someday.

It was as if I had said next century. Her face changed and she said sourly but softly:

—Then you should go do it today.

—I can't go now my love. I have to finish this book.

Her former admiration died as admirations die generally—with their boos on.

—So it's more important to finish a book than to save the lives of those poor little birds?—she said sadly. Even more so, as you don't know how sad *pobres pajaritos* sounds, unless of course you read it aloud in the evening.

—But darling, they haven't even *finished* building their nest!

—And you have to wait till you see the poor little dead creatures smashed flat on the ground before you go and tell them? Is that it?

—But—

—*No es así?*

—Look dear, I have to write a paper on the living dead languages for—a dead-bird look from her. She's won.—All right, all right! I'll go as soon as I've finished this page. See?—showing page.—It's the smallest one in the book.

staggering; in most cases a translator has no choice but to duplicate as nearly as possible the cognitive content of the original, sacrificing the pun as such, or to render a pun in the second—the second?—language, not departing any further than necessary from the cognitive meaning of the utterance as a whale. An example often cited to show boat problem and triumphant compromise is a translation into French of the two-line gag: "Is life worth living?" "It depends on the liver!" The French reply to *"La vie, vaut-elle la peine?"* (an "idiomatic" dead ringer for "Is life worth living?") is "Question de *foie*," where foie is the name of the organ we call liver, though the pun lies in its homonymy with *foi* ("faith").

(Vale la vida la pena? Eso depende del pene. Where *pena* is the Spanish dead ringer for "worth" and also a synonym of "sorrow," but looks exactly like the feminine gender of *pene*, the organ we call penis, a live ringer.)

But since a *Hamlet* or a *Faust* or an *Iliad* or a *Don Quixote* no less than a facile witticism depends for its effect on the selection and arrangement of its parts, down to the smallest LINGUISTIC OVERTONES 139

But when I got up to go she had already changed her mind.

—Look, leave it till tomorrow. It's rather late now and anyhow they've never lowered the awning before, have they?

—Right you are!—I said. If you think you are, I thought.—Tomorrow it is. I'll go and tell them when I come from school.

—Good-she said.—But don't make tomorrow *mañana*, I stared at her, then I returned to my book.

detail, every choice made by a translator is crucial to the meaning of the whale *whole! whole!* He must constantly choose among synonyms, and often chance the word order within the sentence because of the structural difference between two languages. He may have to decide whether to clarify, in the translation, an expression that is ambiguous in the original, or whether to substitute a different metaphorical reference for one that would convey the intended meaning to readers of the *target?* language. He may have to supply for slang or *tobba—taboo* diction in the original, some informal phrasing that will sound natural to the readers of the translation—though not necessarily with the exact flavor or naturalness that the original carries to its readers

His decision may have to begin even with the title
UN NIDO DE GORRIONES EN UN TOLDO

Next day when I got back from work I decided to go and tell the old couple about the nest. It was a little after five in the evening. The building where I live (eternal edifice! I still live there on the page, though the building itself and its surroundings have since 1965 disappeared forever) is a big block of flats made of stucco and erected around a patio with a tall thin areca palm standing stiff above an undergrowth of crotons, cacti and amapolas.

As a brazen breeze made the evening fresh, I felt more like taking my time. It was the beginning of spring and the setting sun was a rosy spout and everything—including the aloof areca—was soaking pink. (Even my pen was dipped in pink and I was about to write that the stucco looked like a meringue shell when I, the writer, hurried him, the character, indoors.)

But the door next-door was its stolid, solid mahogany self.

After ringing the bell twice a blonde girl came to the door. How old was she? Wearing as she was a loose red and yellow striped gown, a bright yellow ribbon tied at the waist, sandals on her feet, gorgeous golden hair falling long and wavy across the pleasant dome of an unwrinkled forehead, I wondered if she was yet sixteen. She was not beautiful but had the All-American girl's naive appeal, freckles and all. She nervously twirled one long end of her cordon belt and for a moment it became a yellow baton.

But I never pictured her as a majorette. Then I thought she looked like a vintage Doris Day. Today I'd rather say she was a young version of Lee Remick, Carol Lynley in her prime, Tuesday Weld *avant l'image.* In eight words—she didn't look at all like a maid. Thelma Ritter could be a maid in my ideal cast but not Doris Day—and the aupair girl had· yet to come.

—*Están los de la casa?*

—Sorry—un-Doris-Day-like, tight-lipped shy smile— No Spanish.

No Spanish spoken here and my English was as broken then as it is baroque now.

—The old ones, are they at home?—I asked her and I knew González-González was a ventriloquist who was using me as his dummy.

—You mean grandpa and granny?—she said.—No, they've gone out. Won't be back till suppertime.

But it wasn't only I who had a ventriloquist hidden somewhere. Her voice didn't seem to belong either to her or to the Doris Day image. As a matter of fact it became Thelma Ritter better. She spoke rapidly, swallowing her final words and I could barely catch them— *captar* being the exact verb.

—Well . . . it's about their sparrows . . . they have a net—*nest.*

Did she chuckle or merely gasp?

—That's news to me! Didn't know my grandparents bred sparrows.

Well, I hadn't thought her capable of teasing me or of cracking jokes. But then you can't call *that* a joke, even if she meant it as one. When I realized she *was* kidding me, I began to be flustered, and decided to tell her all about the next, nest and the awning to extricate myself and then take leave. I told her, as best I could, how concerned *I* was that they shouldn't destroy the nest unwittingly. I found that unconsciously or not I had left my wife out of the story completely. I did not even mention that I lived next door.

She smiled more graciously than shyly, seemed to reflect mildly on my story for a moment, shook her head in mock-blonde disbelief and then said:

—Won't you come in, please? I'd like you to show me where the nest is. I'll surely tell my grandparents about the sparrows when they come back.

I went in. The apartment was less luxuriously furnished than I had imagined. (I have this habit of always imagining better homes than other people actually live in.) The kitchen was arranged differently and the living-room looked bigger—probably because it had less furniture. But it was very much like our apartment, though instead of Cuban Kitsch it was decorated American Atrocious—with some redundant rugs scattered around for warm comfort.

When we went out—she straight ahead, I hesitantly— through a bedroom onto the terrace, the sun was dabbing, dubbing night purple on the *façade* of the neighboring buildings. The French blinds over the doorway to our balcony were down. Looking blindly at the shuttered doors I remembered it was Friday—the day of my wife's French lesson.

In the awning, the sparrows seemed busy finishing their nest before sunset—or rather before summer. Sootier than ever, one of them was bringing back a long curved Pascalian *palito* that refused to get through such a small opening. The bird fluttered, tried to hold its claws on the selvage and pushed at the reluctant reed, which bent still further but definitely did not want to go into the untidy nest. Something was wrong somewhere and the bird was puzzled but couldn't tell why.

The very moment I recognized as the *male* the toiling, troubled sparrow struggling with the stubborn straw, the female put her tiny head out of the entrance as if trying to get out—just when her husband was trying to get in. Naturally, she found her exit blocked by the unusually industrious male. But she tried, tried and tried again to leave the nest as the male did all he could to get in. (She's tried, he's tired.) In the end the male grew bored with the strenuous job and let go of the straw. Next the sparrow dove into the nest and darted out again—or was it the female this time, finally being able to come out? Whichever it was, it flew swiftly away to disappear among the distant trees.

—That's cute—said the girl and immediately corrected herself:—or stupid. Or both!

Then she giggled and then she laughed. She had a frank or freak laugh which scarcely stirred her body further. It was like a laughing voice—or laughter *parlando.*

It was beginning to get chilly. The tropical breeze

was becoming a persistent norther cooling the terrace and the evening. The sun, a rosy wreck, had already sunk in the deep blue sea. We went back in.

—Won't you sit down?

I accepted her invitation a bit too eagerly and sat down on a stool backed against the window-frame. She was already going into the living room but, having half-seen me already sitting there, she smiled in profile and turned back from the doorway into the bedroom. She sat on the bed—the only other piece of furniture in the room. I realized my *faux pas* only when she tried to dismiss it so graciously. (Her sitting down on the bed reminds me of the story about the king and his peasant guest who drank the lemon water from the wash-bowl, and how the king soothed the court's *Schadenfreude* by drinking the concoction himself with gusto, having added a dash of sugar to invent lemonade.) But I dared neither laugh off nor repair my uncool, uncouth error. That was my first mistake. My second one was that I did what almost all courteous and timid people do these days—shy—then-Freudian. Namely, to lay another egg.

—Hwat is jour name—I asked her in my implacable accent.

She smiled again and for a moment I had the impression she was thinking of something other than her name.

—Jill. And yours?

—*Silvestre.*

—That's a pretty name.

I must have shaken my head in disapproval. I hated my name.

—I mean I like it—she said.—I don't think I should ever be able to pronounce it though. But I like it the way you say it.

—Of course you can pronounce it.

(Positive teaching—I am a teacher but I don't teach languages—I teach language.)

—No, I couldn't.

—Try. You only have to say all the e's alike, like in better.

(What did I tell you?)

—I never could.

—Try just once.

—I'll never be able to, believe me.

—Try.

She tried. She did her best to pronounce this hideous

name of mine but said something that sounded rather like—

—No, not silver tray. I am not a tray and definitely not made of silver, as you can see—almost turning around—for yourself.

I was about to coin a counterfeit on my being brass not Silver Latin—but it was not necessary. She was already laughing again. I didn't mind her laugh so much now that we were both laughing.

—You see. I'll never manage it. But I like the way you say it. Say it again.

—Silvestre.

—Say it.

—Silvestre.

—Say it.

—Silvestre.

—Go on. Sayitsayit*say*it!

She threw herself back on the bed, laughing. (I liked her laugh less than boringly repeating over and over my name, a senseless repetition that acted on me like speech therapy—my name is now a dumb appendix I've learned to live with ever since. And yet to this very day and hour I find myself disliking her laugh intensely whenever I hear it in my memory.) Laughing, I could see her bare crooked teeth with a wire brace to straighten them. I think her laugh needed a brace too.

When she stopped laughing some two days later she lay back, her face to the ceiling. Her gown had risen a lot above her knees and I could almost see where her thighs began or ended.

—Journeym is—

That was me trying to avoid the silence with a void voice.

— . . . nice all so.

I shut up my merciless mouth.

Then she spoke, very slowly at the start.

—There's nothing nice about me.

She almost sniggered.

—Not even my name.

She pursed her lips.

—Not my name especially. It's stupid or cute or both and it doesn't suit me at all. At all! It's not nice. I'm not nice, nothing is nice around me—she embraced the room, Havana, the world with her vertical arms.—Nothing is nice, nothing's nice! Nothingsnice!

The fresh silence lasted longer then the last but I

filled it up with my worries. I knew that if she said another word it would be something outlandish. But it would be worse if I said something first—I would certainly lay yet another egg.

She sat up again. She was serious, deadly so. She remained silent and for a moment I thought that she would utter the next word and it would be a four-letter word. Would I understand it?

(I knew then almost all the English swear-words used by men but not even one foul word used by women. I was convinced that there should be in English a different set of four-letter words strictly for feminine use, as happens in Spanish. But then again most swear-words in English become something else when translated into Spanish. For instance, the word hell could be literally rendered as *infierno*, which is not a particularly strong term—a *terno*—in Spain and even less in Cuba, perhaps because we are closer to it. Furthermore, our hell has never enjoyed the prestige of taboo its English counterpart had in films and elsewhere. On the other hand, the Spanish idiomatic dead ringer for hell is *carajo*—which exactly means prick in at least two of the meanings of the word in English. I must confess that this subject was as confusing linguistically to me in the past as it was humanly perplexing to have this girl in front of me in the present.)

In the present that had by now become a pretense— it was all a false predicament because she just looked at me and I noticed that her eyes were not angry. The anger, if there was any, lay only in her twisted mouth— and that could be the force of gravity or even her wire brace's fault—I don't know, I'm no dentist. But, though her eyes were not angry, there was something odd about her pupils, an awkward movement or perhaps some strange fixedness—I don't know, I'm no optician, either. Though I can safely say that the effect was uncanny.

—I must live.

That was my voice—or rather, my accent.

—*What?*

—I have to go now.

—Oh, I see. You mean *leave.*

—Jess.

Did she smile? At least her words died in her distending lips smiling vertically at the ceiling.

—Don't go yet.

I was concerned about her grandparents—or my wife—suddenly coming in.

—I most too.

Yes, she was smiling, then she was sneakingly snickering, then she stood up suddenly, and deftly untied the plaited cloth cord. Her dress became loose and I noticed that it was one of those convertible gowns that change shape with a belt.

—I love your accent. Don't ever lose it.

I never did lose my accent but she was ever loosing her gown. That kind of dress was all the rage at the time and for some unfathomable, albeit shallow, reason I found it stunningly sexy. Until then my mind had reasons which my eyes knew nothing of—from that moment on, my eyes could have their reasons too. Her dress fell over more loose until it went down to her feet. She kicked the shapeless gown away with the technique of habit. (There is plenty of opportunities here for word-play, puns and wisecracks—she was kicking the habit, see?—but I didn't care for them at that time, as I was concentrated on watching her dress and her undressing.) The airborne garment flew across the room to crash against a wall and it fell in a heap to the floor. From where I was it looked to me like a dead dress.

She was standing there, naked except for the black lingerie. She was barefoot to boot. I could see she had strong legs, (pink) feet firmly planted in the (motley) Moorish mosaic. For the first time I stopped wondering how old she was.

—I like your hair too—she said.

Was she going to tell me not to lose it either?

—I've always liked very black hair.

I said precisely nothing.

—I like black. Black night, black hair, black—

Undergarments? Forests? People?

— . . . boards.

She came over to me and ran her hand through my hair. Abruptly she stooped to kiss me. Her kiss was harsh and I could feel the brace pressing against my lips—then against my teeth, then against my gums, then against my tongue. I looked at her eyes. I was wrong, they were not odd but longing. Mine were probably squinting.

I took her firmly by the waist with one arm and caressed her thighs, her back, her lingeried, lingering breasts.

Then I tried to undo her black bra.

—Don't! Please don't! *Please!*

She spoke into my mouth, her words soothing my bruised lips with her placating plosives, her everlasting liquids, her sinuous sibilants. There was no annoyance in her voice, only rigidness—then, without pausing for breath, she went on kissing me. *Kissing kissing kissing kissing kissing kissing kissing* I couldn't think of relatives nor of birds *kissing her.*

Then we stopped kissing—she stopped kissing me to straighten herself up. But she stood facing me—her navel looking vacantly at me like a blind Cyclops.

I tasted blood in my mouth. But before I could discover whether she had cut into my lips or not—searching for blood on my lips with the tip of my finger, inspecting my probing forefinger—I felt a stinging blow on my face and my head went hot all over. She had slapped me three or four times before I knew what was hitting me. Both my cheeks were burning red and a tear started from my right eye. (Or was it from my left eye?)

—That's what it is, isn't it?—she shouted.

She left the room in a twitching rage. The last I saw of her were her legs. She's got legs like a ball player, I thought.

I remained on the stool, uncertain whether to get up or to stay on or vanish. I thought of nothing. No, I was thinking about my sitting on the stool all the time, like a concert pianist. Playing by boxed ear.

I heard sobs and tried to locate where they came from—someone was crying in the next room—or perhaps in the apartment next door. I got up and as I didn't dare to go out onto the terrace I went into the living-room—where I found Jill collapsed across the table, her head in her arms, her shoulders quivering. I was sorry for her and forgot the strip and the teasing and the slapsting. Did I forget it all because I truly felt sorry for her or because I expected more kisses and perhaps something extra? Or was I merely slaphappy?

When I touched one of her bare shoulders she stopped trembling.

—Leave me alone—she said. Her ventriloquist wasn't Ritter but Garbo.

—Please don't cry.

From the table rose a sound between a stifled sob and a guffaw.

—What makes *you* think I was crying?

She lifted her head and released such a guttural laugh that it sounded almost like a belch.

—Did you think *I* was crying? Why, that's the funniest thing I've heard today. And I've heard some funny things today, believe me!

(I did not know then what she meant but now I'm inclined to think she alluded to my accent.)

She got up and put her face close to mine so that I could see she wasn't crying. She was not crying but she squinted.

—Me? Crying?

She laughed nastily.

—Jerk!

She moved towards the door and put her hand on the knob. But instead of opening the door she rested her head against the top panel. Now she really was crying, she was really crying, she was crying. She was just crying quietly softly sweetly but all the same I was afraid that the whole neighborhood would hear through the thick-panelled solid mahogany Spanish-American door.

—You fool! Fool fool fool!—she muttered to the door. Then I felt she obviously didn't mean me, and I wondered whom she meant as I went over to her and put my hand on her head. (Her hair looked soft and silky but it wasn't. It didn't need a shampoo but it surely needed something—I don't know what, I'm no hair stylist.) She stopped crying but did not look at me again. She turned the knob and opened the door. I tried to close it but she resisted it. I insisted. She persisted. I desisted.

She pulled the door gently, firmly open.

—Will I ever see you again?—was my silly question.

She gave me a brave girl look. No more tears. She shook her hair—probably as she tried hard not to give me a silly answer.

—They're sending me back home tomorrow morning.

—I see.

I did not see. I understand now what she meant but then I thought she had to start packing in a hurry when she added—

—He's packed me off today.

She opened the door wide and I went out. I gave her a long last look and saw that there would eventually be more tears. But not even her good-by look was meant for me. It was then that I noticed that her underwear needed mending.

—Good-by, Jill.

—By, Silver Try.

Two or three days later I was reading a different book on the same subject—or maybe just the opposite—anyway, I had tried to forget it all and noticed that it was easier trying to forget than trying to remember—though perhaps remembering was a lot easier than forgetting—well, what the hell!, I thought, !que carajo!, after all I'm no psychologist—I'm only a fool who's probably a week older and not any wiser for that—but when the heavy door closed darkly on me yesterday—I stood for a while facing it, staring back at its black, blind stare—I noticed that there was a white speck on it—a square spot—a blank blemish—it was a card with a name—or rather two—on it: Mr. & Mrs. Clemmons—and I tried to ring again immediately after she closed the door this morning, not because I wanted to see her again but to convince myself that the thing—whatever it was—had not happened, that I had imagined it all just as I was about to ring for the first time—which is just now—which in fact I didn't—or which indeed I did—but no one came to the door—no one would come because there was nobody there—it all actually came from a quotation in Hawthorne on the noiseless steps of things that almost happen—that the house, Havana, the world, was as empty as the apartment, which was uninhabited or inhabited possibly by Miss Havisham's ghost—in a minute—that it all came from Poe, from James—or perhaps from within myself—nothing—nice or not nice—nothing has happened!—she like an event, has not occurred—or as She she was invented: a figurine of speech and the story a filum of my imagination Jill never existed. My name was never Silvestre. She wasn't she. I, Latin ni tal I. It was all untrue.

—Silvestre?

It was my wife's voice speaking from behind me. I could only see her hand (grabbing the doorframe) with half an eye. She was poised vaguely somewhere on the threshold of my consciousness. Extreme of.

—What horrible people!

—Yes dear?

—Qué gente horrible pero qué, qué gente!

—People? What people dear?

—Our next-door neighbors, that's who! They're horrible!

On the last exclamation mark I raised my face from the book and looked at the twin terrace. (From abstract written language to the concrete balcony.) One of the old people, the woman (at first I thought it was the man), was lowering the awning and the chirping sparrows were fluttering around the rapidly distending canvas.

—That old couple! !Esos viejos! They're lowering their awning!

—So I see my love.

Two little eggs had fallen on the floor but a third one had just broken against the edge of the divider, making a yellow liquid viscous obscene stain on the bright brown brick. The old woman seemed as astonished as the bird and as my wife—and twice as helpless as she ran inside, trembling, calling in a voice—as we say in Spanish—soft but altered:—Walter! Walter!

The two sparrows went on chirping distressedly (or gaily) and fluttering wildly (or methodically or even ritually) around the broken eggs. The garrulous female alighted beside the formless mess and pecked it and ate from the coloidal yolk a little. Then she lifted a damp straw and flew up to where the nest had been. Then she tried to find the nest but there was only a void. Then she dove onto the canvas and scrabbled on the faded cloth, skidding on the once green awning in her quest for her nest. She seemed more bewildered or birdbrained than ever and the straw fell from her oblique beak. Both she and the male sparrow flew away when the old lady returned with the old man. I couldn't see his face nor his demeanour, for my wife—indignation let loose—intruded. However, I think I saw an air-mail envelope in the old man's hands.

My wife went to the end of our balcony and glared at our neighbors futilely, blindly but invisibly challenging the distraught old couple—obviously oblivious of her. Then she came over to the narrator, venting her fury on him and his totally innocent book in a compact single indictment in the form of a question:

—Soyoudidntellthemaboutitafterall?

Then I looked at my wife that is no longer my wife as I look now at her word-sentence and I see myself saying nothing on my behalf. Not even that oft-repeated four-letter Spanish word. *Nada.* My defence was my diffidence.

But today, many years and a few translations later, I often wonder what that Jill did. What did *she*—not "surely" but exactly—tell her grandparents about the sparrows, about their present, *past*, nest and future lives now destroyed, about our finally common awning?

QUESTIONS

1. How does the author use the spoken language to create or define his characters? Is this successful?

2. Why do you think Jill is leaving Havana?

3. What kind of narrator is Silvestre?

4. Cabrera Infante provides certain limited information to and about his characters which allows his readers to participate in the creation or completion of his story. What possible explanations does the story have based upon what the narrator and other characters say or do? What possible significance does the air-mail letter in the old man's hands have?

THE HUMANITIES: CONTINUITIES?

The human creations of the present day exhibit a discontinuity with tradition in appearance even more radical than did those of the early twentieth century. The great systems of the past that once served as intellectual frameworks "fell apart," as we have seen, at that time. As yet, no dominant system of belief has arisen to restore to Western culture its lost unity. Our own time is rather one of searching, of experimentation, and of multiplicity in morality and ideology as well as in the arts. The artistic freedom for which the great modernist innovators struggled has been achieved, or overachieved. Whereas the artists who made the first break with the representation of the real world shocked their public by challenging its cultural assumptions and traditions, contemporary artists confront a public that is virtually shockproof. The necessity to innovate seems constant; indeed styles, trends, and schools appear and disappear within periods of a few years. The fact that they also coexist makes the contemporary scene one characterized by a bewildering but exhilarating plurality of forms.

The explanation of this state of affairs lies not only in the evolution of the humanities themselves but also in the economic, political, and social environment in which the changes have taken place. In contrast to ancient Greece or to traditional Africa, support for arts and letters in the West has been until recently in the keeping of a well educated, relatively small class of individuals, who had both leisure and wealth to devote to such pursuits. During the past century, with the beginnings of redistribution of income and the rise in the standards of living and literacy in the lower classes, this cultural hegemony has gradually diminished. Mass communications, too, have increased the facility and speed with which cultural products can be distributed. But mass communications also change the nature of these products. A play seen on television or a symphony heard on compact disc offers a different experience from those seen and heard in a theater or concert hall. As more and more cultural material is communicated to us electronically, the question of whether the forms we call "literature," "art," and "music" will survive as such is a legitimate one.

Mass communication has also vastly increased our awareness of the cultures outside the one in which we live and has given us, in Marshall McLuhan's phrase, the impression of living in a "global village." This in turn has tended to make our sense of cultural relativity deeper and more pervasive than it was in the days of Montaigne or Voltaire. The shifting balance of the West's position in international politics has also had its effect here. Western culture, which has imposed its values on the rest of the planet, at least since the seventeenth century, is no longer an unquestioned leader. Political power is bringing the Third World countries cultural power as well. The "boom" in Latin American culture and the importance of writers from south of the Rio Grande on the postmodern literary scene may be symptomatic. More remote cultures become constantly more accessible. In the course of a day, we may watch a program on tribal life in the South Pacific, attend the performance of a touring company doing Chinese dances, hear a lecture on Islam and the problems of the Middle East, listen to Japanese music or to medieval European music on authentic instruments reproduced by Japanese technology, and look through a newly published novel by an African writer. In addition, many people from the educated classes of the Third World are attempting to adapt Western styles and values to the traditions of their own cultures, and some Europeans and Americans, sensing a spiritual vacuum in the West, have turned toward Eastern philosophies and religions such as Zen Buddhism or yogic meditation.

The feeling of being able to exist in several temporal, spatial, and cultural zones at once is, as we have seen, characteristic of the "postmodern" era. Expressing this sense of pluralism, postmodern architects, for example, play with elements of various styles. In the humanities in general, the new pluralism has led to a movement toward opening up the canon, or the "sacred texts," of the tradition. Feminists have called attention to the neglect of the study of creative works by women and also propose fresh approaches to the reading of old texts. Blacks and other minorities have succeeded in legitimizing their formerly neglected contributions.

In the "postmodern" arts, popular and high culture, less distinct than formerly, blend and exchange forms. Contemporary serious composers learn from and incorporate pop, rock, and jazz; painters and advertisers share some of the same visual language; films and television programs speak to cultured and uncultured alike. Still, it is possible to make at least one basic distinction between the true artist and the producer of mass entertainment. The former demands from his or her public an *active* participation—an involvement of the mind, spirit, and senses—very much, as we have seen, within the humanistic spirit. The latter, in accord with many other aspects of modern life, encourages passive consumption.

Rather than luring or spellbinding their audiences with a smooth, finished product, many artists today like to show the wheels in their machines. People in the theater are constantly reminded that they are witnessing a play, an artifice, and not a window on the world. The actors may even enter into a dialogue with the audience. Similarly, novelists, poets, and filmmakers tend to say, in effect, "I am writing a novel," "I am trying to create a poem," "I am making a film." Visual artists, taking their work out of the museum and into the environment, emphasize both the differences between their creations and the natural world, and the dialogue that must take place between them. Architects are not afraid to expose such things as wiring and plumbing. Musicians make compositions of *sounds*, not pure music, using tape recorders and electronic synthesizers. A composer like John Cage wants his audience to be aware of the silences in his compositions and of the sounds in the environment heard during those silences.

Our acceptance of an art without bounds is closely related to the growing tendency to integrate the arts into society. The elitist quality, characteristic of Western art since the Renaissance, might in a sense be viewed as a deviation from the history of the humanities not only in other areas of the world but even in Europe itself. Our present vision of art as a form of relating to the world and to other human beings seems to echo John Donne's words, "No man is an island." Although modern Americans lack the cohesive, unitary vision of the ancient Greeks or the traditional Africans, they, too, are coming to treat the humanities as playing a vital role in the life of the community and to see the artist as making a social contribution.

While in some ways postmodern expressions are more accessible and more in tune with popular culture than were their modernist counterparts, in other ways they are more remote. Although they may use electronics, advertising images, and other modes, postmodern artists may nonetheless be making a violent critique of bland, passive mass culture. The whole domain of "theory" is certainly difficult for the average reader and even for many highly educated readers to access. Yet in their demonstrations of our dependence on images, our imprisonment in "textuality" or systems of language, and the collapse of traditional Western notions of reality, the theorists have formulated some of the important underpinnings of contemporary culture.

Everyone is aware of the fact that our world today is characterized by increased bureaucracy and regimentation. Data banks, computers, and officials intervene constantly in daily life. This regimentation is in large part motivated by the belief that fairness to everyone requires governmental order and supervision, but it often has the effect of making individuals feel that they are being reduced to automatons. This phenomenon, certainly a threat to humanistic values from many points of view, seems, however, to have led to a widespread awareness of the need for creative expression, and for the humanities generally, in modern life. One of the most important tasks before those dedicated to the humanities today is to help prevent the vital, creative being from being replaced by a passive, docile consumer.

Naturally, if the humanities are to be relevant to contemporary problems, they must keep pace with the rapid changes in contemporary life. What is called for are forms and thoughts oriented toward the future, not a self-satisfied idealization of the past. Yet, paradoxically, the humanist who would be future-oriented must be well versed in the past. Human beings are not islands in time, just as they are not islands in space—their modes of feeling and thinking, as well as their material way of life, are to a great extent shaped by what took place before they existed. It is only through awareness of cultural roots, as we have tried to emphasize throughout this book, that men and women can be equipped to understand and to shape the humanities of the future. Of course, every generation will conceive of its roots in slightly different ways and will find that certain works or periods from the past speak to it more urgently than do others. We are only beginning, for example, to understand the African contribution to our cultural heritage and to be aware of what other non-Western cultures have to contribute to our present needs. The Western humanities, with their roots in the Greco-Roman and Judeo-Christian cultures, are still present in all our forms of expression. Even if artists see Beethoven's Ninth Symphony as a sexual message or the *Mona Lisa* as a computer printout, if they work with laser beams rather than gold paint, if they decry the cultural hegemony of the monuments of the Western world, they affirm a certain kind of continuity by the very force of their reaction. In the midst of change and diversity, we can be fairly certain that if we manage not to destroy our planet, people centuries from now will still be reading Dostoevsky, visiting Versailles, and listening to Beethoven. They will react to these works with their intelligence and sensibility, absorbing them as part of their individual and collective cultures. North Americans and Europeans will also, with increasing frequency, integrate aspects of African, Asian, Latin American, and other artistic and philosophical creations into their culture. It is possible that we will eventually witness the evolution of a world culture with forms of artistic communication accessible to everyone. The ways in which the tradition of the humanities will be carried forward into the future will be determined by its present students.

Glossary

Italics are used within the definitions to indicate terms that are themselves defined elsewhere in the glossary and, in a few cases, to distinguish titles of works or foreign words.

ABA Form   MUSIC: A particular organization of parts used in a musical *composition* in which there are three units, the first and third of which are the same. See *Da capo aria.*

Absolutism   The theory that all political power in a society is derived from one authority, normally a monarch.

Abstract   VISUAL ARTS: Not representational or *illusionistic.* Describes painting or sculpture that simplifies or distills figures from the material world into *forms,* lines, *colors.*

Affect   MUSIC: The production of emotional reactions in the listener by certain musical sounds, according to a theory from the baroque period. For example, sorrow should be characterized by slow-moving music, hatred by very repulsive harmonies.

Allegory   LITERATURE, VISUAL ARTS: The technique of making concrete things, animals, or persons represent abstract ideas or morals. A literary allegory usually takes the form of a *narrative* which may be read on at least two levels; for example, Dante's *Divine Comedy.* Medieval sculptures often have allegorical significance.

Anaphora (ah-na'for-ah)   LITERATURE: A rhetorical figure which uses the repetition of the same word or phrase to introduce two or more clauses or lines of verse.

Antithesis   LITERATURE: The balance of parallel word groups conveying opposing ideas.

Apse (aap'ss)   ARCHITECTURE: A large semicircular or polygonal *niche, domed* or *vaulted.* In a Roman basilica the apse was placed at one or both ends or sides of the building. In a Christian church it is usually placed at the east end of the *nave* beyond the *choir.*

Arcade   ARCHITECTURE: A covered walk made of *arches* on *piers* or *columns,* rather than *lintels.*

Arch   ARCHITECTURE: 1. Commonly, any curved structural member that is used to span an opening. 2. Specifically, restricted to the spanning members of a curved opening that are constructed of wedge-shaped stones called *voussoirs.* Arches may be of many shapes, basically round or pointed.

Aria (ah'ree-ah)   MUSIC: An elaborate *composition* for solo voice with instrumental accompaniment.

Aristocracy   Form of government from Greek word meaning "rule by the few for the common good."

Arpeggiated   MUSIC: Describes a rippling effect produced by playing the notes of a chord one after another instead of simultaneously. See *Chord.*

Atmospheric Perspective   See *Perspective.*

Atonal   MUSIC: Describes music written with an intentional disregard for a central keynote (or tonal center). This style of composition was developed after World War I by Arnold Schoenberg and his followers.

Axis   VISUAL ARTS: The imaginary line that can be passed through a building or a figure, around which the principal parts revolve. See *Balance.*

Balance   VISUAL ARTS: The creation of an apparent equilibrium or *harmony* between all the parts of a *composition,* be it a building, painting, or sculpture.

Balustrade   ARCHITECTURE: A rail or handrail along the top edge of a roof or balcony, made up of a top horizontal rail, a bottom rail, and short *columns* between.

Baroque   Term first applied to the visual arts and later to the music and literature of the 17th and 18th centuries to designate a style characterized by energy, movement, realism, and violent contrasts. The baroque style is often set in opposition to the orderly and formal "classical" style of the High Renaissance.

Cadence   MUSIC: A formula or cliché that indicates a point of repose. The cadence is one of several possible melodic, rhythmic, or harmonic combinations that signal a slowing down or stopping of the forward motion.

Cantilever ARCHITECTURE: 1. A horizontally projecting member, sometimes called a bracket, used to carry the cornice or eaves of a building. 2. A beam or slab, projecting beyond the wall or supporting column, whose outward thrust or span is held down at one end only. See Robie House (Ch. 32).

Chord MUSIC: The simultaneous sounding of three or more usually harmonious tones.

Chordal MUSIC: Characterized by the employment of *chords* in a logical progression of harmonies.

Choreographer DANCE: Person responsible for the *choreography* of a dance.

Choreography DANCE: The design and arrangement of the movements of a ballet or modern dance.

Chromatic MUSIC: Describes a scale progressing by halftones instead of the normal degrees of the scale; e.g., in C major: c-c#-d-d#-e instead of c-d-e. VISUAL ARTS: Refers to the visual spectrum of hues. See *Color*.

Classic, Classical ALL ARTS: Recognized generally to be excellent, time-tested. LITERATURE AND VISUAL ARTS: 1. From ancient Greece or Rome. 2. From "classical" (fifth century B.C.) Greece or having properties such as *harmony, balance,* moderation, and magnitude characteristic of art of that period. See also *Neoclassicism*. MUSIC: The musical *style* of the late 18th century. Leading composers in the classical style are Haydn, Mozart, and the early Beethoven.

Coda MUSIC: A passage of music added to the end of a piece to confirm an impression of finality.

Collage (kohl-lahzh') VISUAL ARTS: From the French, *coller,* "to glue." A technique for creating *compositions* by pasting or in some way attaching a variety of materials or objects to a flat surface or canvas.

Color VISUAL ARTS: A quality perceived in objects by the human eye that derives from the length of the light waves reflected by individual surfaces. The visible spectrum is divided into six basic hues: red, orange, yellow, green, blue, and violet. Red, yellow and blue are called the *primary colors;* the others, which result from mixing adjacent primary colors, are called *secondary colors.* White, black, and grays result from mixing these six hues and are not *chromatic;* they cannot be distinguished by hue, only by value. Value is the property of a color that distinguishes it as light or dark. Colors that are "high" in value are light colors; those that are "low" in value are dark colors. Adding white to a color will raise its value to make a *tint;* adding black to a color will lower its value to make a *shade.* Saturation is the property of a color by which its vividness or purity is distinguished. See also *Complementary Colors, Cool Colors, Warm Colors*.

Comedy LITERATURE: A drama that ends happily, intended to provoke laughter from its audience. Comedy often includes *satire* on types of characters or societies.

Complementary Colors Hues that form a neutral grey when mixed but, when juxtaposed, form a sharp contrast. The complementary of any *primary color* (red, yellow, or blue) is made by mixing the other two primaries. Example: The complementary of red is green, obtained by mixing yellow with blue.

Composition VISUAL ARTS: The arrangements of elements within the work in order to create a certain effect based on a variety of principles and conventions: e.g., *balance, color, contour, focal point,* proportion, scale, *symmetry, volume.* MUSIC: The putting together of elements such as *melody, harmony, rhythm,* and orchestration into a musical *form.* The term may be used similarly to denote a putting together of elements in a dance or film. LITERATURE: The act of composing an oral or written work.

Concerto (con-chair'toe) MUSIC: A composition for one or more solo instruments and an orchestra, each competing with the other on an equal basis.

Content ALL ARTS: What the *form* contains and means. Content may include subject matter and theme. The quality of a work of art is often judged by the appropriateness, or apparent inseparability, of form and content.

Continuo MUSIC: In the scores of baroque composers (Bach, Handel) the bass part, performed by the harpsichord or organ, together with a viola da gamba or cello. The continuo, during the baroque era, provided the harmonic structure of the pieces being performed.

Contour PAINTING, DRAWING: The visible edge or outline of an object, *form* or shape, used especially to suggest volume or mass by means of the distinctness, thickness, or color of the edge or line.

Contrapuntal (con-tra-pun'tal) MUSIC: In a *style* that employs *counterpoint*.

Cool Colors VISUAL ARTS: Blues, greens, and associated hues. Cool colors will appear to recede from the viewer in a picture, while *warm colors* will tend to project.

Cornice ARCHITECTURE: 1. The horizontal projection that finishes the top of a *wall.* 2. In classical architecture, the third or uppermost horizontal section of an *entablature.* See *Orders.*

Counterpoint MUSIC: Music consisting of two or more *melodies* played simultaneously. The term is practically synonymous with *polyphony.*

Da Capo Aria (dah cah'poh ahr'ee-ah)   MUSIC: A particular type of *aria* that developed in the baroque period (17th and 18th centuries). It consists of two sections, the first of which is repeated after the second. The result is the *ABA form*. See *Aria, ABA Form*.

Deduction   PHILOSOPHY: Reasoning from a general principle to a specific fact or case, or from a premise to a logical conclusion.

Democracy   From the Greek word meaning "rule by the people." A form of government in which the electorate is coincident with the adult population (sometimes only the adult males) of a community.

Despotism   Government by a ruler with unlimited powers.

Dialectic   PHILOSOPHY: 1. Platonic—A method of logical explanation of beliefs, proceeding by question and answer. 2. Hegelian and Marxian—A logical method that proceeds by the contradiction of opposites (thesis, antithesis) to their resolution in a synthesis.

Dome   ARCHITECTURE: A curved or hemispherical roof structure spanning a space and resting on a curved, circular, or polygonal base. Theoretically, a dome is an *arch* rotated 360 degrees around a central *axis*.

Dynamics   MUSIC: Words or signs that indicate the varying degrees of loudness in the music. For instance, *forte* (loud), *piano* (soft, quiet), *diminuendo* (decrease volume gradually).

Ego   In Freudian theory, one of the three parts of the mind. The ego is the conscious, controlling, self-directed part.

Empiricism   PHILOSOPHY: The theory that knowledge is derived from observation of nature and by experiment.

Entablature   ARCHITECTURE: The upper section of a classical *order* resting on the capitals of the columns and including architrave, frieze, *cornice*, and pediment.

Eros   1. In Greek mythology, son of Aphrodite and god of sexual love, called "Cupid" by the Romans. 2. For Freud, the vital, life-giving human force, originating in but not limited to sexual desire.

Ethics   PHILOSOPHY: The branch of philosophy dealing with problems of good and bad, right and wrong, in human conduct.

Facade (fa-sahd')   ARCHITECTURE: A face of a building.

Fetish   Statue or other object believed to embody supernatural power.

Figurative   VISUAL ARTS: Describes painting or sculpture in which the human body and the objects of habitual visual experience are clearly recognizable in the work.

Focal Point   VISUAL ARTS: The place of major or dominant interest on which the eyes repeatedly focus in a painting, drawing, or architectural arrangement.

Foreshortening   PAINTING: The method of representing objects or parts of objects as if seen from an angle so that the object seems to recede into space instead of being seen in a frontal or profile view. The technique is based on the principle of continuous diminution in size along the length of the object or figure. See *Perspective* and *Vanishing Point*.

Form   ALL ARTS: The arrangement or organization of the elements of a work of art in space (visual arts) or time (literary, musical, performing arts). A form may be conventional or imposed by tradition (the Greek temple, the sonnet, the sonata, the five-act play) or original with the artist. In the latter case, form is said to follow from, or adapt itself to, *content*.

Free Verse   LITERATURE: Poetic lines with no conventional meter or rhyme.

Fresco   PAINTING: The technique of making a painting on new, wet plaster. Fresco painting was particularly favored it Italy from Roman times until the eighteenth century.

Fugal   MUSIC: Characteristic of the *fugue*.

Fugue (fewg)   MUSIC: A *composition* based on a *theme* (known as the *subject*) that is stated at the beginning in one voice part alone and is then restated by the other voice parts in succession. The theme reappears at various places throughout the composition in one voice part or another in combination with forms of itself.

Gable   ARCHITECTURE: The triangular space at the end of a building formed by the slopes of a pitched roof, extending from the *cornice* or eaves to the ridge. In classical architecture the gable is called a pediment.

Gallery   ARCHITECTURE: A long, covered area, usually elevated, that acts as a passageway on the inside or exterior of a building.

Genre (john'ruh)   LITERATURE: A literary type or form. Genres include *tragedy, comedy,* epic, *lyric, novel,* short story, essay.

Grid   VISUAL ARTS: A pattern of vertical and horizontal lines forming squares of uniform size on a chart, map, drawing, etc.

Groin Vault   See *Vault*.

Groundplan   ARCHITECTURE: A drawing of a horizontal *section* of a building that shows the arrangement of the *walls*, windows, supports, and other elements. A groundplan is used to produce blueprints.

Ground Plane   PAINTING: In a picture, the surface, apparently receding into the distance, on which the figures seem to stand. It is sometimes thought of as comparable to a kind of stage space.

Harmonic Modulation MUSIC: The change of key within a composition. Modulations are accomplished by means of a *chord* (or chords) common to the old key as well as the new one.

Harmony MUSIC: The chordal structure of music familiar to most Western listeners in popular music accompanied by guitars, in Romantic orchestral music, etc.

Homophonic (hawm-o-fon'ic) Characteristic of *homophony*.

Homophony (hoh-maw'foh-nee) MUSIC: A single *melody* line supported by its accompanying *chords* and/or voice parts. See *Monophony, Polyphony, Chord,* and *Texture.*

Hue See Color.

Hyperbole (high-purr'boh-lee) LITERATURE: A figure of speech that uses obvious exaggeration.

Iamb (eye'amb) LITERATURE: A metrical "foot" consisting of one short (or unaccented) syllable and one long (or accented) syllable. Example: hĕllō.

Iambic Pentameter (eye-am'bic pen-tam'eh-ter) LITERATURE: The most common metrical line in English verse, consisting of five *iambs.* Example, from Shakespeare: "Shăll Ī cŏmpāre thĕe tō ă sūmmĕr's dāy?"

Id In Freudian theory, one of the three parts of the mind. The id is the instinctive, non-controlled part.

Illusionism VISUAL ARTS: The attempt by artists to create the illusion of reality in their work. Illusionism may also be called *realism.* It is important to remember that illusionism is not the motivating intention of all works of art.

Image ALL ARTS: The representation of sense impressions to the imagination. Images are a fundamental part of the language of art. They differ from the abstract terminology of science and philosophy in that they are a means whereby complex emotional experience is communicated. Images may be tactile, auditory, olfactory, etc., but the word is ordinarily used for visual impressions.

Impasto (em-pah'stoh) PAINTING: Paint that has the consistency of thick paste, used for bright highlights or to suggest *texture.* Examples: Rembrandt and Van Gogh.

Improvisation MUSIC: The art of performing spontaneously rather than recreating written music.

Induction PHILOSOPHY: Reasoning from particular facts or cases to a general conclusion.

Inflection MUSIC: The shaping or changing of a musical passage in a way that is unique to the individual performer of the music.

Inquisition A former tribunal in the Roman Catholic Church directed at the suppression of heresy.

Irony LITERATURE: A manner of speaking by which the author says the opposite of what he means, characteristically using words of praise to imply scorn. Dramatic or tragic irony means that the audience is aware of truths which the character speaking does not understand.

Lantern ARCHITECTURE: The windowed turret or tower-like form that crowns a *dome* or roof.

Libretto (lih-bret'toe) MUSIC: The text of an opera, *oratorio,* or other dramatic musical work.

Linear Perspective See *Perspective.*

Lyric LITERATURE: A short poem characterized by personal feeling and intense emotional expression. Originally, in Greece, lyrics were accompanied by the music of a lyre. Today they may often be set to music.

Medium (pl. media) ALL ARTS: 1. The material or materials with which the artist works. Examples from VISUAL ARTS: paint, stone, wood, bronze, plaster, concrete. MUSIC: sound. LITERATURE: language. CINEMA: film. DANCE: human body. DRAMA: language, costume, lighting, actors, sound, etc. 2. Modern means of communication (television, radio, newspapers). 3. PAINTING: A substance such as oil, egg, or water with which *pigment* is mixed.

Melodic Elaboration MUSIC: The ornamentation of *melody* by one or more of a number of possible musical devices, such as added notes, interval changes, etc.

Melody MUSIC: A succession of musical *tones.* Often the melody is known as the "tune," and is not to be confused with the other accompanying parts of a song. See *Homophony.*

Metaphor LITERATURE: A figure of speech that states or implies an analogy between two objects or between an object and a mental or emotional state. Example: "My days are in the yellow leaf;/The flowers and fruits of love are gone" (Byron) makes an analogy between the poet's life and the seasonal changes of a tree.

Metaphorical Describing statements or representations to be taken as analogy, not to be taken literally.

Meter POETRY: A regularly recurring rhythmic pattern. Meter in English is most commonly measured by accents, or stresses, and syllables. The most common metric "foot" in English is the *iamb.* The most common verse line is the *iambic pentameter* (five iambs). MUSIC: A pattern of fixed temporal units. For example, ¾ meter means one beat to a quarter note and three beats to a measure. In a musical *composition* meter is the basic grouping of notes in time.

Modeling VISUAL ARTS: 1. The creation of a three-dimensional *form* in clay or other responsive material, such as wax, soap, soft bone, ivory, etc. 2. By analogy, in painting and drawing, the process of suggesting a three-dimensional *form* by the creation of *shade* and shadow.

Modernism   Generic name given to a variety of movements in all the arts, beginning in the early 20th century. Promotes a subjective or inner view of reality and uses diverse experimental techniques.

Molding   ARCHITECTURE: A member used in construction or decoration that produces a variety in edges or contours by virtue of its curved surface.

Monophonic (mo-no-fohn'ic)   Characteristic of *monophony*.

Monophony (mo-nof'o-nee)   MUSIC: A simple *melody* without additional parts or accompaniment, such as the music of a flute playing alone or of a woman singing by herself. See *Homophony, Polyphony, Texture.*

Motif (moh-teef'), **Motive** (moh-teev')   LITERATURE: A basic element which recurs, and may serve as a kind of foundation, in a long poem, fiction, or drama. A young woman awakened by love is the motif of many tales, such as *Sleeping Beauty.* VISUAL ARTS: An element of design repeated and developed in a painting, sculpture or building. MUSIC: A recurring melodic phrase, sometimes used as a basis for variation.

Mural   PAINTING: Large painting in oil, fresco, or other *medium* made for a particular *wall*, ceiling, or similar large surface.

Narrative   LITERATURE: 1. (noun) Any *form* that tells a story or recounts a sequence of events (*novel, tale,* essay, article, film). 2. (adj.) In story form, recounting.

Narthex   ARCHITECTURE: The entrance hall or porch that stands before the *nave* of a church.

Naturalism   LITERATURE, VISUAL ARTS: 1. Faithful adherence to the appearance of nature or outer reality. 2. A late-nineteenth-century literary movement that developed in France but had great impact in the United States. The naturalists wished to apply scientific laws to literature and to show in particular how human beings are the creations of their environment.

Nave   ARCHITECTURE: In Roman architecture, the central space of a basilica; in Christian architecture, the central longitudinal or circular space in the church, bounded by aisles.

Nave Arcade   ARCHITECTURE: The open passageway or screen between the central space and the *side aisles* in a church.

Neoclassicism   ALL ARTS: A movement that flourished in Europe and America in the late seventeenth and eighteenth centuries, heavily influenced by the classical style of Greece and Rome. Neoclassical art and literature is characterized by sobriety, balance, logic, and re-

straint. The corresponding musical style (18th century) is usually called *classical.*

Nonobjective   VISUAL ARTS: Not representing objects in the material world.

Novel   LITERATURE: A lengthy prose narrative, traditionally spanning a broad period of time, containing a plot and developing characters. The modern European novel took form in the eighteenth century.

Oil Painting   The practice of painting by using *pigments* suspended in oil (walnut, linseed, etc.).

Oratorio   MUSIC: An extended musical setting for solo voices, chorus, and orchestra, of a religious or contemplative nature. An oratorio is performed in a concert hall or church, without scenery, costumes, or physical action. One of the greatest examples is Handel's *Messiah.*

Orchestration   MUSIC: Orchestration is the art of writing music for the instruments of the orchestra that will bring out desired effects of the various instruments. Indeed, it is the art of "blending" the voices of the orchestra so that a pleasing sound is the end result.

Orders   ARCHITECTURE: Types of columns with *entablatures* developed in classical Greece. The orders are basically three: Doric, Ionic, and Corinthian. They determine not only the scale and therefore dimensions of a temple but also the experience generated by the building, or its *style.*

Oxymoron (ock-see-mohr'on)   LITERATURE: A figure of speech that brings together two contradictory terms, such as "sweet sorrow."

Palazzo (pa-laht'so)   ARCHITECTURE: Italian for palace, or large, impressive building.

Palladian   ARCHITECTURE: Designating the Renaissance architectural style of Andrea Palladio.

Parapet   ARCHITECTURE: In an exterior *wall*, the part entirely above the roof. The term may also describe a low wall that acts as a guard at a sudden edge or drop, as on the edge of a roof, battlement, or wall.

Parody   LITERATURE: A work that exaggerates or burlesques another, serious one. Often a parody pokes fun at an author and his style. The parody may be compared to a visual caricature or cartoon.

Pathos (pay'thaws)   ALL ARTS: A quality that sets off deep feeling or compassion in the spectator or reader.

Pentatonic Scale   MUSIC: Five-note scale that occurs in the music of nearly all ancient cultures. It is common in West African music and is found in jazz.

Perspective   VISUAL ARTS: Generally, the representation of three-dimensional objects in space on a two-dimensional surface. There are a variety of means to achieve this. The most familiar is that of "linear perspective" developed in the fifteenth century and codified by Brunelleschi, in which all parallel lines and edges of surfaces recede at the same angle and are drawn, on the picture plane, to converge at a single *vanishing point.* The process of diminution in size of objects with respect to location is very regular and precise. Other techniques, often used in combination with linear perspective, include: (a) vertical perspective—objects further from the observer are shown higher up on the picture, (b) diagonal perspective—objects are not only higher but aligned along an oblique *axis* producing the sensation of continuous recession, (c) overlapping, (d) *foreshortening,* (e) *modeling,* (f) *shadows,* and (g) atmospheric perspective, the use of conventions such as blurring of outlines, alternation of hue toward blue, and decrease of *color* saturation.

Philosophe (fee-low-soph') Eighteenth-century French intellectual and writer; not usually a systematic philosopher.

Phrase   MUSIC: A natural division of the *melody;* in a manner of speaking, a musical "sentence."

Picture Plane   PAINTING: The surface on which the picture is painted.

Picture Space   PAINTING: The space that extends behind or beyond the picture plane; created by devices such as *linear perspective.* Picture space is usually described by foreground, middleground, and background.

Pigment   PAINTING: The grains or powder that give a *medium* its *color.* Can be derived from a variety of sources: clays, stones, metals, shells, animal and vegetable matter.

Pitch   MUSIC: A technical term identifying a single musical sound, taking into consideration the frequency of its fundamental vibrations. Some songs, or instruments, are pitched high and others are pitched low.

Plan   See *Groundplan.*

Plane   A flat surface.

Plasticity   VISUAL ARTS: The quality of roundness, palpability, solidity, or three-dimensionality of a *form.*

Podium   ARCHITECTURE: The high platform or base of a Roman temple or any elevated platform.

Polis (poh'liss)   The ancient Greek city-state.

Polyphonic (paul-ee-fon'ick)   Characteristic of *polyphony.*

Polyphony (paul-if'o-nee)   MUSIC: Describes *compositions* or *improvisations* in which more than one *melody* sounds simultaneously, that is, two or more tunes at the same time. Polyphony is characterized by the combining of a number of individual melodies into a harmonizing and agreeable whole. See *Homophony, Monophony,* and *Texture.*

Portico   ARCHITECTURE: Porch or covered walk consisting of a roof supported by columns.

Primary Colors   Red, Yellow, Blue—the three primary hues of the spectrum. See *Color.*

Prose   LITERATURE: Generally, may mean any kind of discourse, written or spoken, which cannot be classified as poetry. More specifically, prose refers to written expression characterized by logical, grammatical order, *style,* and even *rhythm* (but not *meter*).

Rationalism   PHILOSOPHY: The theory that general principles are essentially deductive; i.e., deducible from an examination of human reason. Reason, not the senses, is the ultimate source of basic truths.

Realism   LITERATURE, VISUAL ARTS: A movement which began in the mid-nineteenth century and which holds that art should be a faithful reproduction of reality and that artists should deal with contemporary people and their everyday experience.

Recitative (reh-see-tah-teev')   MUSIC: A vocal style used to introduce ideas and persons in the musical *composition,* or to relate a given amount of information within a short period of time. The recitative has practically no melodic value. This device is employed extensively in Handel's *Messiah.*

Republic   A form of government in which ultimate power resides in the hands of a fairly large number of people but not necessarily the entire community. This power is exercized through representatives. The word derives from Latin meaning "public thing."

Response   MUSIC: A solo-chorus relationship in which the soloist alternates performance with the chorus.

Responsorial   MUSIC: Describing the performance of a chant in alternation between a soloist and a chorus. (It is unlike antiphonal music, where alternating choruses sing.)

Rhythm   ALL ARTS: An overall sense of systematic movement. In music, poetry, and dance this movement may be literally felt; in the visual arts it refers to the regular repetition of a *form,* conveying a sense of movement by the contrast between a form and its interval.

Ridge   ARCHITECTURE: The line defined by the meeting of the two sides of a sloping roof.

Romanticism   A movement in all of the arts as well as in philosophy, religion, and politics that spread throughout Europe and America in the early nineteenth century. The romantics revolted against the Neoclassical emphasis on order and reason and substituted an inclination for nature and imagination. See Chs. 26 & 27.

Satire   A mode of expression that criticizes social institutions or human foibles humorously. The Romans invented the verse satire, but satire may appear in any literary *genre*, in visual art, in film, mime, and dance.

Secondary Colors   See *Color.*

Section   ARCHITECTURE: The drawing that represents a vertical slide through the interior or exterior of a building, showing the relation of floor to floor.

Shade   PAINTING: A *color* mixed with black. Mixing a color with white produces a *tint.*

Shading   VISUAL ARTS: The process of indicating by graphics or paint the change in *color* of an object when light falls on its surface revealing its three-dimensional qualities. Shading can be produced not only by a change of color, but also by the addition of black, brown, or gray, or by drawing techniques.

Shadow   VISUAL ARTS: The *form* cast by an object in response to the direction of light.

Side Aisle   ARCHITECTURE: The aisles on either side of, and therefore parallel to, the *nave* in a Christian church or Roman basilica.

Simile   (sim'eh-lee) LITERATURE: A type of *metaphor* which makes an explicit comparison. Example: "My love is like a red, red rose."

Sonata   MUSIC: An important form of instrumental music in use from the baroque era to the present. It is a *composition* usually with three or four movements, each movement adhering to a pattern of contrasting tempos. Example: Allegro, Adagio, Scherzo, Allegro.

Sonnet   LITERATURE: A *lyric* poem of fourteen lines, following one of several conventions. The two main types of sonnet are the Italian (Petrarchan) which divides the poem into octave (eight lines) and sestet (six lines) and the English (Shakespearean) which divides the poem into three quatrains of four lines each and a final rhyming couplet.

Stretto   MUSIC: The repetition of a *theme (subject)* that has been collapsed by diminishing the time values of the notes. As a result, the listener is literally propelled to the dramatic end or climactic conclusion of the music. Handel used this *fugal* device effectively in the last chorus of his *Messiah.*

Structure   ALL ARTS: The relationship of the parts to the whole in a work of art. A structure may be mechanical (division of a play into acts, a symphony into movements) or may be more concealed and based on such things as the inter-relationships of *images, themes, motifs, colors,* shapes. In a *narrative* the structure usually refers to the arrangement of the sequence of events. In architecture structure may refer either to the actual system of building or to the relationships between the elements of the system of building.

Style   ALL ARTS: Characteristics of *form* and technique that enable us to identify a particular work with a certain historical period, place, group, or individual. The *impressionist* painters in France at the end of the nineteenth century used light and *color* in a particular way: a painting in which this technique is followed has an impressionistic style. But the use of certain *forms, colors,* design and *composition* enables us to distinguish within this group the style of Renoir from that of Monet. Afro-European *rhythms* and *improvisation* distinguish a jazz style, but within that general category are many schools of jazz or even different styles of one individual, such as Duke Ellington. Literary style is determined by choices of words, sentence *structure* and syntax *rhythm,* figurative language, rhetorical devices, etc. One may speak of an ornate, simple, formal, or colloquial style; of a period style such as *Neoclassical, romantic, realist;* or of an individual's style. Style is sometimes contrasted with *content.*

Subject   ALL ARTS: What the work is about. The subject of the painting "Mont Ste Victoire" is that particular mountain; the subject of Richard Wright's *Native Son* is a young black man in Chicago. MUSIC: The *melody* used as the basis of a *contrapuntal composition* (e.g., the subject of a *fugue*).

Suite   MUSIC: An important instrumental form of baroque music, consisting of a grouping of several dance-like movements, all in the same key.

Superego   In Freudian theory, one of the three parts of the mind. The superego is the censuring faculty, replacing parents or other authorities.

Symbol   VISUAL ARTS, LITERATURE: An *image* that suggests an idea, a spiritual or religious concept, or an emotion beyond itself. It differs from *metaphor* in that the term of comparison is not explicitly stated. Symbols may be conventional; i.e., have a culturally defined meaning such as the Christian cross or the Jewish star of David. Since the nineteenth century, symbols have tended to denote a variety or an ambiguity of meanings.

Symbolism   1. The use of symbol in any art. 2. A literary school which began in France in the late nineteenth century, characterized by the use of obscure or ambiguous *symbols.*

Symmetry   VISUAL ARTS: The balance of proportions achieved by the repetition of parts on either side of a central *axis.* The two sides may be identical, in which case we can speak of bilateral symmetry.

Syncopation   MUSIC: A rhythmic device characterized as

a deliberate disturbance of a regularly recurring pulse. Accented offbeats or irregular *meter* changes are two means of achieving syncopation.

Tactile   VISUAL ARTS, LITERATURE: Refers to the sense of touch. In the visual arts, tactile values are created by techniques and conventions that specifically stimulate the sense of touch in order to enhance suggestions of weight, volume (roundness), visual approximation, and therefore three-dimensionality. Writers may also create tactile effects, as in the description of cloth, or skin.

Tale   LITERATURE: A simple *narrative*, whose subject matter may be real or imaginary, and whose purpose is primarily to entertain. Tales may also make use of "morals" to instruct.

Tempera (tehm'per-ah)   PAINTING: Technique in which the *pigment* is suspended in egg, glue, or similar soluble *medium*, like water. Tempera paint dries very quickly and does not blend easily, producing a matte (flat, non-reflective) surface, because, unlike *oil paint*, it is essentially an opaque medium.

Texture   VISUAL ARTS: Surface quality (rough, smooth, grainy, etc.) LITERATURE: Elements such as *imagery*, sound patterns, etc. apart from the *subject* and *structure* of the work. MUSIC: The working relationship between the *melody* line and the other accompanying parts, or the characteristic "weaving" of a musical *composition*. There are three basic musical textures: *Monophonic* (a single line), *Homophonic* (a melody supported by *chords*), and *Polyphonic* (multiple melodic lines).

Thanatos   Greek word for death. For Freud, the death-wish or death-force, opposed to Eros, the life force.

Theme   VISUAL ARTS: A *color* or pattern taken as a subject for repetition and modification. Example: a piece of sculpture may have a cubical theme. MUSIC: A *melody* which constitutes the basis of variation and development. Example: "The Ode to Joy" song in the last movement of Beethoven's *Ninth Symphony*. LITERATURE AND PERFORMING ARTS: An emotion or idea that receives major attention in the work. A novel or film may contain several themes, such as love, war, death. A dance may be composed on the theme of struggle, joy, etc. Theme is sometimes used in this sense for visual arts and music as well.

Thrust   ARCHITECTURE: The downward and outward pressure exerted by a *vault* or *dome* on the *walls* supporting it.

Timbre (taam'bruh)   MUSIC: The quality or "color" of a particular musical *tone* produced by the various instruments. For instance, the very "nasal" sound of the oboe

is markedly different from the very "pure" sound of the flute.

Tint   VISUAL ARTS: The *color* achieved by adding white to a hue to raise its *value*, in contrast to a *shade*, which is a hue mixed with black to lower its value.

Tonal   MUSIC: Organized around a pitch center. A tonal *composition* is one in which the *pitches* of all the various *chords* and *melodies* relate well to one another. Tonal music has a recognizable beginning, middle, and end. See *Chord, Melody, Pitch*.

Tonality   MUSIC: The specific *tonal* organization of a composition.

Tone   ALL ARTS: The creation of a mood or an emotional state. In painting, tone may refer specifically to the prevailing effect of a *color*. Thus, a painting may be said to have a silvery, bluish, light, or dark tone as well as a wistful, melancholy, or joyful tone. The term may also refer to *value* or *shade* (see *Color*). In literature, tone usually describes the prevailing attitude of an author toward his material, audience, or both. Thus a tone may be cynical, sentimental, satirical, etc. In music, "tone color" may be used as a synonym for *timbre*. Tone in music also means a sound of definite *pitch* and duration (as distinct from noise), the true building material of music. The notes on a written page of music are merely symbols that represent the tones that actually make the music.

Tragedy   LITERATURE: A serious drama that recounts the events in the life of a great person which bring him or her from fortune to misfortune. Tragedies usually meditate on the relation between human beings and their destiny. Tragedies first developed in ancient Greece; other great periods of tragedy include Elizabethan England and France under Louis XIV. The word may be used to describe a novel or story.

Transept   ARCHITECTURE: The transverse portion of a church that crosses the central *axis* of the *nave* at right angles between the nave and *apse* to form a cross-shaped (cruciform) planned building.

Value   See *Color*.

Vanishing Point   PAINTING: The point of convergence for all lines forming an angle to the *picture plane* in pictures constructed according to the principles of linear *perspective*.

Vault   ARCHITECTURE: The covering or spanning of a space employing the principle of the *arch* and using masonry, brick, plaster, or similar malleable materials. The extension of an arch infinitely in one plane creates a barrel or tunnel vault. The intersection of two barrel vaults at right angles to each other produces a cross or groin vault. Ribs are sometimes placed along the intersections of a groin vault to produce a ribbed vault.

Veneer   VISUAL ARTS: A thin layer of precious or valuable material glued or otherwise attached to the surface of another, less expensive, or less beautiful material. The Romans, for example, applied thin layers of marble to the concrete and rubble fill surfaces of their buildings to produce a more splendid effect. In this century, valuable woods like walnut or mahogany are applied as veneers to the surfaces of plywood.

Verisimilitude   Literally, "true-seeming." LITERATURE: A doctrine prevalent in the *Neoclassical* period, which hold that elements in a story must be so arranged that they seem to be true or that they could actually occur.

VISUAL ARTS: The effect of near-perfect emulation or reproduction of objects in the visual world. Not to be confused with *realism*.

Wall   ARCHITECTURE: A broad, substantial upright slab that acts as an enclosing *form* capable of supporting its own weight and the weight of beams or *arches* to span and enclose space.

Warm Colors   VISUAL ARTS: The hues commonly associated with warmth—yellow, red, and orange. In *compositions* the warm colors tend to advance, in contrast to the *cool colors*, which tend to recede from the viewer.

Watercolor   PAINTING: Technique using water as the *medium* for very fine *pigment*. Watercolor dries very fast and can be extremely transparent.

Index

Index references are to page numbers throughout. See also the Table of Contents, Chronicle of Events, List of Maps, List of Color Plates, and Glossary.